Justice Blind?

IDEALS AND REALITIES

OF AMERICAN CRIMINAL JUSTICE

Matthew B. Robinson

Appalachian State University

Prentice
Hall

Upper Saddle River, New Jersey 07458

Library of Congress Cataloging-in-Publication Data

Robinson, Matthew B.
    Justice blind? : ideals and realities of American criminal justice / by Matthew B. Robinson.
      p.   cm.
    Includes bibliographical references and index.
    ISBN 0-13-033444-8
      1. Criminal justice, Administration of—United States.   2. Social justice—United States.
  I. Title.

HV9950 R635 2002
364.973—dc21   2001021859

Publisher: Jeff Johnston
Executive Assistant and Supervisor: Brenda Rock
Senior Acquisitions Editor: Kim Davies
Assistant Editor: Cheryl Adam
Managing Editor: Mary Carnis
Production Management: Stratford Publishing Services
Production Editor: Judy Ashkenaz, Stratford Publishing Services
Interior Design: Stratford Publishing Services
Production Liaison: Adele M. Kupchik
Director of Manufacturing and Production: Bruce Johnson
Manufacturing Buyer: Cathleen Petersen
Cover Design Coordinator: Miguel Ortiz
Formatting: Stratford Publishing Services
Electronic Art Creation: Stratford Publishing Services
Editorial Assistant: Sarah Holle
Director of Marketing Communication and New Media: Frank Mortimer, Jr.
Marketing Manager: Ramona Sherman
Marketing Assistant: Barbara Rosenberg
Marketing Coordinator: Adam Kloza
Printer/Binder: R.R. Donnelley and Sons, Inc.
Copy Editor: Judy Ashkenaz
Proofreader: Marsha Kunin
Cover Design: Joe Sengotta
Cover Illustration: Bill Burrows, SIS.Images.com
Cover Printer: Phoenix Color Printers

Prentice-Hall International (UK) Limited, *London*
Prentice-Hall of Australia Pty. Limited, *Sydney*
Prentice-Hall Canada Inc., *Toronto*
Prentice-Hall Hispanoamericana, S.A., *Mexico*
Prentice-Hall of India Private Limited, *New Delhi*
Prentice-Hall of Japan, Inc., *Tokyo*
Prentice-Hall Singapore Pte. Ltd.
Editora Prentice-Hall do Brasil, Ltda., *Rio de Janeiro*

10 9 8 7 6 5 4 3 2 1

ISBN 0-13-033444-8

Justice starts at home.

Thanks to Ran-Ma for instilling such a strong sense of justice
and compassion in her son.

Thanks to Brandt for helping to develop the fight in your little brother.

And thanks to Holly for being my partner in the fight against injustice.
I love you.

CONTENTS

CHAPTER ELEVEN
The Ultimate Sanction: Death As Justice? 327

CHAPTER TWELVE
Summary, Conclusions, and Recommendations for the Future 361

LIST OF FIGURES AND TABLES

FIGURES

TABLES

PREFACE

Injustice anywhere is a threat to justice everywhere.

— MARTIN LUTHER KING, "A Letter from the Birmingham Jail"

As eloquently written by Dr. Martin Luther King, Jr., in his letter from a jail cell in Birmingham, Alabama, when an injustice occurs anywhere, justice everywhere is threatened. King wrote this letter on April 16, 1963, after being jailed for "civil disobedience," a peaceful, nonviolent form of resistance. The letter was his response to criticisms that, as an "outsider" from Atlanta, he had no business in Birmingham.

King countered: "I cannot sit idly by in Atlanta and not be concerned about what happens in Birmingham. . . . We are caught in an inescapable network of mutuality, tied in a single garment of destiny. Whatever affects one directly, affects all indirectly. Never again can we afford to live with the narrow, provincial 'outside agitator' idea. Anyone who lives inside the United States can never be considered an outsider anywhere within its bounds."

So, injustice anywhere in America is a threat to all persons living in the United States. And injustice in America is every American's business. The injustices of American criminal justice are the motivation for this book.

As children, we grow up reciting Francis Bellamy's Pledge of Allegiance, written in 1892. It originally stated: "I pledge allegiance to the flag of the United States of America, and to the Republic for which it stands, one nation (under God), indivisible, with liberty and justice for all."

"With liberty and justice for all"—this is the ideal we all pledge to assure. But what are "liberty" and "justice"? And does "for all" really include all of us?

When I began my college experience as a criminology and criminal justice major, I had some ideas in my head about what the U.S. criminal justice system was supposed to achieve. I thought that the criminal justice system was supposed to protect us from harmful acts committed intentionally by other people. In my first semester, however, I learned that the system of justice in the United States is focused on only a small portion of all harmful acts. Many other behaviors that are committed intentionally, acts that kill and injure people and result in loss of property, nevertheless are not "crimes" or are not vigorously pursued by agencies of social control.

Later, in graduate school, I learned about the massive criminal justice expansion of the last thirty years of the twentieth century, an expansion driven not by facts about crime or increasing crime rates but by politics, fear, and the desire to be punitive (and at times downright hateful) toward certain segments of the population. To me, this incongruence between the ideals of American criminal justice and the realities of the U.S. criminal justice system didn't seem right.

How can the United States spend so much money and direct so much effort toward punishing a relatively small portion of harmful behaviors while virtually ignoring so many others? Why would we disinvest in the nation's future by overrelying on methods of crime control that we know are ineffective, while failing even to try methods that seem more promising? None of this seems "just" to me.

If justice really meant what I had always thought it meant, how could a system of criminal *justice* in the United States, of all places, be so unjust? This is the question addressed in this book. *Justice Blind? Ideals and Realities of American Criminal Justice* attempts to demonstrate how and why the U.S. system of criminal justice fails to live up to its ideals, and thus is unjust.

This book grew out of my experiences with teaching an introductory criminal justice course more than thirty times. Through my teaching, I realized that no introductory criminal justice text on the market exposed readers to the realities of criminal justice in the United States. This book strives to do that.

THE MAIN ASSERTION OF *JUSTICE BLIND?*

The book proceeds from the following assertions:

- Myths and stereotypes about crime, criminals, and criminal justice are created when acts are defined as crimes by the criminal law.
- These myths and stereotypes are reinforced as the mass media broadcast stories about crime, criminals, and criminal justice.
- These myths and stereotypes are also reinforced as police, courts, and corrections enforce the criminal law.
- Because U.S. criminal law is inherently biased against certain groups (e.g., the poor, people of color, and women), the activities of police, courts, and corrections are also biased.

This does not suggest that the U.S. media, police, courts, and corrections are intentionally biased. Rather, by focusing on those acts that come to be defined as "serious" in the criminal law, each of these institutions becomes biased in an "innocent" way. The figure on page xv illustrates how this "innocent" bias is created in the United States. The arrows suggest that each step of the process affects all other stages—that is, that myths and stereotypes about crime, criminals, and criminal justice created by the criminal law are strengthened as the criminal justice system and the media operate. Throughout this book, I elaborate on this process and provide evidence for the main assertions listed here.

Chapter One introduces the American criminal justice system and outlines its ideal goals: doing justice and reducing crime. The chapter demonstrates two conflicting views of justice, one based on assuring fairness and equality as required by the United States Constitution (due process), the other based on holding the guilty accountable for the harms they inflict on others (crime control). I argue that, since about 1970, American criminal justice has taken a path more

The Process of Innocent Bias

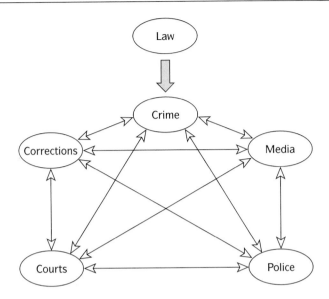

consistent with a crime control model than with a due process model. The result has been an erosion of U.S. Constitutional protections, with little crime reduction in return. In fact, American criminal justice now devotes a larger proportion of its resources to police and corrections than to courts, providing more evidence that we are following a crime control model of criminal justice. Using a critical interpretation, I suggest that the criminal justice system in the United States is in fact pursuing some alternative goals, including serving limited political interests and controlling certain segments of the population. By examining how crime has increasingly become a political issue, the reader learns how the U.S. system of criminal justice may be serving functions other than those it ideally should serve.

Chapter One identifies the ideals of criminal justice in the United States and introduces several important issues that students need to understand to gain a complete understanding of the reality of criminal justice in America. Once these have been established, I turn to the process of innocent bias outlined in the figure at the top of this page. Because the process begins with the passage of laws, Chapter Two examines what the law is, where the law comes from, and the different types of law in the United States. This critical examination of who makes the law illustrates how the criminal law creates innocent bias.

The passage of criminal laws leads to the establishment of some behaviors as crimes. Chapter Three begins by defining the term *crime* and goes on to show that the label "crime" is not appropriately used to characterize the most harmful acts against individuals and society. Harms caused by street crimes are compared with those caused by white-collar deviance, which includes harmful acts not considered "serious" by the government. Chapter Three also discusses how crime is measured in the United States and introduces the topics of U.S. crime rates and crime trends.

Chapter Four discusses how crime is portrayed in the American mass media: what the media cover and what they ignore. I demonstrate that the mass media tend to overemphasize street crime while underemphasizing white-collar deviance. Why does this occur? This chapter introduces and discusses various explanations of media inaccuracy about crime and criminal justice. Throughout the chapter, I explain how media inaccuracy contributes to innocent biases in American criminal justice.

Given the biases of U.S. criminal law, which focuses on street crimes while virtually ignoring the most harmful acts against people and property, and given the biases of media coverage, Chapter Five examines whether the criminal justice system as a whole is biased against particular groups of people in the United States. Following a detailed discussion of whether the "war on crime" is really a war on poor people and people of color, the chapter concludes with a discussion of the role of gender in criminal justice.

In Chapter Six, I provide one example of a war on crime (the "war on drugs") that is clearly aimed at these relatively powerless groups. Historically, the U.S. criminal justice system has focused on those drugs perceived to be used by poor people and people of color, while the most harmful drugs, tobacco and alcohol, have most often been legal, even though they cause far more damage than all illegal drugs combined. I critically assess the logic of the American drug war and conclude that decriminalization of drugs is a viable alternative.

The remaining chapters follow the other stages of the model shown in the figure on page xv. In Chapter Seven, I explain why the organization of policing in the United States creates biases against poor people and people of color. I argue that it is not that police officers are biased but, rather, that American policing is organized in a way that creates innocent bias in the criminal justice system.

Chapter Eight concerns pretrial procedures and trials, and Chapter Nine deals with issues related to sentencing. In these chapters, I point out major sources of criminal justice bias in the courts. Chapters Ten and Eleven, respectively, concern incarceration and the death penalty, two of the most destructive penalties available within American criminal justice. These chapters question the logic of these crime reduction policies, particularly given that each is demonstrably biased in its application.

Finally, Chapter Twelve summarizes the main points of the earlier chapters and then offers a number of specific proposals for overcoming significant biases in American criminal justice. I believe that nothing less than justice itself depends on accepting those recommendations.

FEATURES

Justice Blind? contains several useful features for students of criminology, criminal justice, sociology, social problems, political science, and related disciplines. Each chapter contains an "Issue in Depth" section that explores one issue raised in the chapter. Throughout the book, highlighted "main points" appear, which summarize important points to remember. Finally, each chapter concludes with a series of Discussion Questions that deal with the important material discussed.

TO THE READER

Unlike many introductory criminal justice texts, *Justice Blind?* contains a careful analysis of the role that race, class, and gender play in crime and criminal justice. The critical approach of *Justice Blind?* is also unique. Most introductory criminal justice texts start with the perspective that the U.S. criminal justice system meets its ideal goals. They introduce and discuss main concepts and terms without offering critical assessments. I want you, the reader, to learn not only about the ideals of criminal justice in America, but also about the realities. Whereas other texts emphasize the way things are *supposed to* operate, this book places greater emphasis on the way the criminal justice system *really* operates.

This book focuses on injustice in the justice system, an important topic for students and citizens alike to understand. Of course, people who study criminal justice and who work in the criminal justice system need to gain an understanding of basic, introductory-level concepts and issues in order to become more knowledgeable and to become better employees. Many fine texts are on the market to meet this need. But this book takes a different approach: it begins with injustice as a problem.

In fact, I suggest that injustice is a social problem that plagues the United States. Lauer and Lauer (2000), in their book *Troubled Times*, write that social problems begin "as a sense of something wrong in society—of suffering and deprivation growing out of a situation of injustice." I hope this book convinces you that something is very wrong with criminal justice in America. I hope that, because of this work, injustice within the U.S. criminal justice system will be viewed as a significant social problem. This is why several of the topics addressed in this book (e.g., drug use, as well as race, class, and gender) also may be appropriate for social problems classes.

As you read this book, I challenge you to keep an open mind. Do not allow your deeply entrenched beliefs about crime, criminal justice, or politics interfere with your understanding of the main argument of the book. If this reading has been assigned to you, remember that you do not have to agree with the arguments I put forth in this book, but you do need to understand them. In fact, I challenge you to read the book from a critical perspective, not automatically believing everything you read. Read the book from a perspective that will allow you to discover your own truth. Your own truth, after all, is the only truth that will matter to you.

ACKNOWLEDGMENTS

This book is the product of many years of thought and study, both formal and informal. I would like to thank the faculty and staff of the Florida State University School of Criminology and Criminal Justice for the wonderful education I received there. Much of what I learned there inspired this book. Also, I want to thank my colleagues and friends at Appalachian State University who made the transition to faculty life much easier, and who have given me tremendous opportunities for personal and professional growth.

I want to thank each of the reviewers for your hard work. I especially appreciate the feedback I got from David Friedrichs, Sarah Eschholz, and Ronald Iacovetta, three reviewers who went above and beyond the call of duty. Thanks also to Derek Paulsen for reviewing my chapter on the media. I offer my sincere thanks to my research assistants, Anna Sheely and Dickie Lee Brown, who helped me compile the extensive bibliographies. I also want to thank Kim Davies, my senior acquisitions editor with Prentice Hall, who saw promise in the project, and Cheryl Adam and Judy Ashkenaz, who worked very hard making the final product come together. Finally, thanks so much to my students, especially those who took my special topics class (Injustice in America) at Appalachian State University, which led directly to this book. I appreciate all of you.

CHAPTER ONE

WHAT IS THE PURPOSE OF
THE CRIMINAL JUSTICE SYSTEM?
IDEALS AND REALITIES

KEY CONCEPTS

- **What is the criminal justice system?**
- **Ideal goals of the criminal justice system**
- **What is justice?**
- **Alternative goals of the criminal justice system**
- **Functions versus purposes of criminal justice**
- **The role of politics and power in criminal justice**
- **Issue in Depth: Justitia—The Lady Justice**

INTRODUCTION

What is the criminal justice system? Why do we have it? Does it achieve its goals? Are we winning the war on crime? If not, why not? This chapter introduces the ideal goals of the criminal justice system, including doing justice and reducing crime. Although *justice* is difficult to define, at least two conflicting conceptions of justice emerge, consistent with two competing ideal models of justice known as the *crime control* and *due process* models. This chapter demonstrates how criminal justice policy in the United States has shifted toward a crime control model of criminal justice over the past three decades, at the expense of individual Constitutional protections and due process. I suggest that failures of the U.S. criminal justice system are explained by this shift, and I demonstrate that the system achieves other outcomes, beneficial mostly to powerful politicians, the wealthy, and the limited interests of criminal justice professionals.

WHAT IS THE CRIMINAL JUSTICE SYSTEM?

When people talk about the "criminal justice system," they are talking about its interdependent components—the police, courts, and correctional facilities within the federal government's criminal justice system, as well as the criminal justice systems of each of the fifty states. Walker (1998: 26) thus claims that the United States actually has 51 criminal justice systems. Additionally, each state has scores of municipalities, each with its own law enforcement agencies and, in some cases, its own forms of courts and correctional facilities.

> *The* criminal justice system includes the interdependent components of the police, courts, and correctional facilities within the federal government's criminal justice system and the criminal justice systems of each of the fifty states.

You can think of the criminal justice system as a whole, made up of these three interdependent components, something like a pie with three pieces. Each of these components has its own functions and personnel (Cole and Smith, 2000; Schmalleger, 2001).

The primary responsibilities of each component of criminal justice include the following:

- *Police:* Investigating alleged criminal offenses, apprehending suspected criminal offenders, assisting the prosecution with obtaining criminal convictions at trial, keeping the peace in the community, preventing crime, providing social services, upholding Constitutional protections.
- *Courts:* Determining guilt or innocence of suspected offenders at trial (adjudication), sentencing the legally guilty to some form(s) of punishment, interpreting laws made by legislative bodies, setting legal precedents, upholding Constitutional protections.
- *Corrections:* Carrying out the sentences of the courts by administering punishment, providing care and custody for accused and convicted criminals.

Although each of these agencies of criminal justice has its own goals, *ideally* they will also share the goals of the larger criminal justice system. This means personnel of each part of the system should refrain from behaving in ways that may threaten these ideal goals. One goal I will discuss later in this chapter is "doing justice," which means holding the guilty accountable for their criminal acts while ensuring that the criminal justice process is fair and impartial.

When police investigate criminal offenses and make arrests, their desire to reduce crime should not interfere with ensuring that the right person is caught. Additionally, their own personal prejudices and animosities should not affect their behaviors when interacting with citizens. Furthermore, members of the courtroom workgroup, including the prosecutor and defense attorney, should always remember that they are, first and foremost, officers of the court, and therefore are not entitled to allow their desire to win cases to interfere with their commitment to the ethics of their profession. Judges also should be fair in administering sentences so that justice is achieved and should ensure that prosecutors and defense attorneys follow the law. Finally, correctional facilities must not permit offenders to be assaulted or unduly humiliated for the sake of the enjoyment or empowerment of their employees. Punishment should be administered humanely and fairly. As you will see throughout this book, this logic has been lost on U.S. politicians, who have made criminal justice more and more punitive over the past thirty years.

> *M*any people do not view the criminal justice system as a system because, with three main components acting at three levels of government, the fight against crime is not an efficient, smoothly running process.

It's easy to see why some are reluctant to refer to criminal justice in the United States as a "system." With three main components, each acting at three levels of government, the fight against crime is not an efficient, smoothly running process. Some view the three criminal justice components as a system, but many do not. As you will learn in this book, the criminal justice system is not an "integrated system with a single, coordinated set of objectives and programs" (Gottfredson, 1999: 8). Unlike most other systems, it is not organized, orderly, or efficient. And each part of the system has developed separately from the others. Each has "developed within different governmental structures, each has different sources of support and different budgets, and each has different objectives. Each has developed its own requirements for staffing, drawing on different resource pools for personnel and requiring different programs of training and education." As explained by the National Criminal Justice Commission, "the decisions made at each level of the system can severely impact other elements. Yet there is no systematic process used in making decisions. Rather, each component is left to its own, often fighting for resources against other parts of the system" (Donziger, 1996: 181). As noted by Arrigo (1999: 1): "The conditions under which the criminal justice system maintains an effective administration of law enforcement, criminal courts, and correctional practices can and does get bogged down in a number of competing, sometimes even conflicting, circumstances." These are some of the reasons that many criminal justice scholars do not view the criminal justice system as a system and why some instead call it a "network" (e.g., Cox and Wade, 1998).

Yet, all of the agencies of criminal justice are expected to work together to achieve the goals of the criminal justice system as a whole, and each component of criminal justice is affected by the actions of the others. For these reasons, in this book I will refer to our criminal justice system as a *system.* Walker (1998: 29) says it this way: "The systems model focuses attention on the flow of cases between agencies, the interrelationships (or 'components'), and the pervasiveness of discretionary decision making in controlling the flow of cases." No one component can operate without the others. Police must solve crime by making arrests of suspects; otherwise, courts have no need to hold trials. Similarly, if courts do not convict people, then correctional facilities such as prisons have no one to punish. Finally, if correctional facilities do not effectively administer punishment in communities, then police will surely be overrun by crime. If we are to achieve our overall criminal justice goals, the three components must work together efficiently. The fact that they do not currently work this way in *reality* does not mean they should not *ideally* work this way.

> *A*ll of the agencies of criminal justice are expected to work together to achieve the goals of the criminal justice system as a whole.

The three parts of the system are not equal in size, as law enforcement has historically employed the most personnel and has had the largest operating budget (see Figure 1.1). The rationale for this will be discussed in more depth later in this chapter. For now, keep in mind that all criminal justice cases must come into the system through police contact, so to some degree it

FIGURE 1.1

Components of the Criminal Justice System

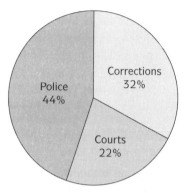

Percentages reflect amount
of criminal justice spending.

SOURCE: Bureau of Justice Statistics (1996 data).

is logical for police to be the largest part of the system. That is, police are the source of input for the criminal justice process.

The following box lists and briefly discusses each step of the typical criminal justice process. It is at each of the stages where potential biases can affect the outcome of justice in America. In subsequent chapters, I will identify how these stages are plagued with biases against particular groups in society.

The typical criminal justice process

The criminal justice system operates through numerous steps in a specified sequential order. This does not necessarily mean that the criminal justice system operates like an assembly line. There may be long delays between one stage and the next. For example, a crime may go unreported to the police for a long period of time, as happens when a victim does not discover

> *The* criminal justice system operates through numerous steps in a specified sequential order.

his or her victimization immediately, or when a murder goes unsolved for some period of time. Because murder cases have no statute of limitations, they can go to trial at any time in the future as long as a suspect has been identified and arrested. Additionally, accused offenders may sit in jail in preventive detention, awaiting trial, for more than a year.

When cases move quickly through the criminal justice process, the process can be accurately described as an assembly line. The criminal justice system moves more expeditiously for some types of cases and for some types of defendants than for others. Whether this is fair and therefore just will be discussed in Chapter Nine. Typically, poor people are processed through the system quickly while wealthy citizens (who rarely are processed by the system at all) can afford to tie the process up if it is to their benefit to do so.

At each stage of the criminal justice process, many cases do not pass on to the next stage because of a process called *filtering,* which allows some cases to be screened out of the criminal justice system. Cases are filtered out of the system for dozens of reasons. Examples are provided in this section as we move through each stage of the process.

Crime

Obviously, the criminal justice process begins with the commission of a crime. The issue of what is crime will be discussed in Chapter Three. A short definition of a crime is "an act in violation of the criminal law." For example, theft occurs when a person takes property from its owner with the intent to deprive the owner of the property permanently. Normally, when a crime is committed, it is not immediately detected by the police (Wrobleski and Hess, 2000). Rather, it is typically reported to the police either by the victim or by another citizen who discovers the crime. Therefore, any law or criminal justice policy that discourages citizens from getting involved in the process will be detrimental to the operation of the criminal justice system.

> *The* first stage of the criminal justice process is the commission of a crime. A crime is an act in violation of the criminal law.

Criminal offenses reported to the police by citizens are not automatically assumed to be crimes. That may sound strange, but citizens may think they have been victimized by crimes when, in fact, the act that was committed against them did not violate the criminal law. Whether reported acts violate the criminal law is determined by police when they conduct an investigation. Even when crimes have actually been committed, police do not necessarily conduct a thorough investigation; they use their discretion in deciding whether to act or not. Discretion is the ability of an agent to act according to his or her own professional judgment rather than some preset rules of procedures (Cole and Smith, 2000; Schmalleger, 2001). Using their discretion, police may determine that the crime committed is so minor that it does not warrant the expenditure of police resources, or that the likelihood of solving the crime or recovering stolen property is too remote.

Think about the disadvantage the police already face when a crime has been committed. The suspect is typically long gone before the police arrive. It is estimated that 75% of all crimes are "cold crimes," crimes in which a suspect is not caught at the scene of the crime (Wrobleski and Hess, 2000). Given that policing in the United States is largely reactive and dependent on citizen reports, it is very difficult to do a good job of clearing cases by making arrests. Thus, the majority of crimes that are committed do not lead to an arrest.

Of course, the likelihood of "clearing a case by arrest" is a function of the type of crime committed. Murders are the most likely type of street crime to lead to an arrest, for several reasons. First, murder victims are almost always discovered by police. Second, the crime is heinous in nature, so police take this offense very seriously. Third, in at least half of murders in the United States, the victim is killed by an acquaintance or relative. This makes it easier to locate the offender. Other crimes, such as theft, are less likely to be cleared by arrest. Thefts are not always discovered by the victims. Even when they are, they may be considered minor or not worthy of calling the police for some other reason. Also, thefts are more likely to be committed by strangers than by people known to the victim, so that locating suspects is much more difficult for the police.

The bottom line is that police do not even know about most crimes, even those committed on the street. Estimates suggest that police discover somewhere between 30% and 50% of all street crimes in any given year (Schmalleger, 2001; Walker, 1998). The remaining 50% to 70% of street crimes never even enter the system because they are not discovered. The main reason this "dark figure of crime" remains hidden to the police and thus to the criminal justice system is that many crimes are simply not reported to the police by victims or witnesses. For reasons that are not the fault of police, law enforcement is highly ineffective at apprehending suspects and therefore at reducing crime and doing justice.

---

*E*stimates suggest that police discover somewhere between 30% and 50% of all street crimes in any given year.

Furthermore, for every 1,000 persons in the United States, there are only 2.7 police officers on the street (Maguire and Pastore, 1999). If only 5% of these 1,000 persons are serious, repetitive criminals, this would mean that, on average, there are only 2.7 police officers on the street for every 50 career criminals (e.g., see Wolfgang, Figlio, and Sellin, 1972). And this figure only includes street crimes; it does not include those who commit white-collar crimes and deviance, which are discussed in Chapter Three. Imagine 2.7 police officers in your community trying to keep up with the criminal acts of 50 career criminals, plus the occasional acts of the rest of you who violate the law.

Investigation

Police investigation, the second stage in the criminal justice process, begins when the patrol officer responds to the scene of the alleged crime. If police determine that the act was not illegal, then the case gets filtered out of the criminal justice system and thus does not lead to the next stage, arrest. If the responding officers determine that a crime was in fact committed, their primary job is to "solve the crime," which in law enforcement terms equates to making an arrest. Ideally, a criminal investigation leads the police to answer the question, "Who done it?" Patrol officers conduct a "preliminary investigation" at the crime scene; later, when the scene has been secured, trained detectives conduct a "secondary investigation." The primary goal of the preliminary investigation is to secure the crime scene to protect the integrity of the evidence and to identify, locate, and question potential witnesses and/or victims. The secondary or follow-up investigation will lead to a more thorough collection, preservation, and presentation of evidence (Wrobleski and Hess, 2000).

---

*I*deally, a criminal investigation leads the police to answer the question, "Who done it?"

Arrest

Once police identify a suspect by collecting enough high-quality evidence, their goal is to remove the alleged offender from the street. This is usually accomplished through an arrest. An arrest occurs when the police take a suspect into custody so that prosecution of the suspect may begin. Generally, arrests must be based on probable cause—a reasonable belief that a particular person has committed a crime. For serious crimes such as felonies, police officers "must have knowledge of sufficient facts and circumstances that would allow a person of reasonable caution to believe that a crime has been committed" (Gottfredson, 1999: 31).

An arrest occurs when the police take a suspect into custody so that a prosecution of the suspect may begin.

At this point in the process, some cases are filtered out before the next stage, booking. For example, juveniles may be sent directly to the juvenile justice system. If police discover they arrested the wrong person, the suspect may be immediately released.

At the point of arrest, police are required to read a suspect his or her *Miranda* rights, so named because of the 1966 Supreme Court case *Miranda v. Arizona.* Since this ruling, police have been required to read suspects their Constitutional protections when an arrest occurs or is imminent. The *Miranda* warning reads:

> You have the right to remain silent. If you choose to give up this right, anything you do say can and will be used against you in a court of law. You have the right to an attorney. If you cannot afford one, one will be appointed to you.

Suspects are then asked if they understand these rights and, if so, whether they want to give up their rights and make statements or answer questions. Many claim that this requirement places an undue burden on the police and makes it harder for the criminal justice system to obtain convictions because it encourages criminals to withhold vital information from the police.

As a result of such concerns, numerous exceptions to this rule have been established through case law (see Chapter Seven). Should *Miranda* warnings be required? Are they important for assuring justice? Is a suspect's Fifth Amendment right to refrain from self-incrimination more important than the community's right to convict guilty criminals?

Booking

After arrest, booking occurs. At this point, an administrative record is made of the suspect. Typically, his or her photograph and fingerprints are taken, and he or she may be questioned further by the police and/or placed in a lineup for witness or victim identification.

After booking, the suspect may be charged with specific criminal offenses, if the prosecutor thinks there is a sufficient quality and quantity of evidence indicating that the suspect is indeed guilty of the offenses charged. A person can always be released and later rearrested if further evidence of the suspect's guilt is discovered. Release is another form of filtering.

Booking occurs when an administrative record is made of the suspect.

Initial Appearance

After being formally charged with a crime or crimes by the prosecution, the suspect makes an initial appearance before a judge. At this stage, the suspect is notified of the charges against him or her, is advised of his or her rights, and may either post bail to be released from criminal justice system supervision, or be held in preventive detention in cases where the judge determines there is either a flight risk or some danger to the community (see Chapter Eight). If the judge determines that there is not enough evidence to warrant the charges, the case may be dismissed by the judge and hence filtered out of the system.

> *A*t the initial court appearance the suspect is notified of the charges, is advised of his or her rights, and either may post bail to be released from criminal justice system supervision, or may be held in preventive detention if the judge determines there is either a risk of flight or a danger to the community.

Preliminary Hearing / Grand Jury

Assuming a case is not dismissed, the next stage in the criminal justice process is either a preliminary hearing or a grand jury, depending on the jurisdiction in which the case is being heard. Both of these mechanisms are ideally intended to ensure that innocent persons are not hastily, maliciously, or arbitrarily prosecuted. In reality, these processes are typically one-sided and almost always result in a finding that there is probable cause to warrant a person being detained until trial (Walker, 1998). This can be a major impediment to fairness in the criminal justice process, because findings of preliminary hearings and grand juries are routinely published in local media, perhaps creating assumptions among the public that named defendants are already guilty of crimes, even though in fact they have not yet been convicted of anything.

In about half of the states, a preliminary hearing is held to determine if there is enough evidence to hold the case over for trial. If the judge does not find probable cause that the named person(s) committed the named offense(s), the case may be dismissed and filtered out of the system. In cases where the judge finds probable cause, the accused is held for trial on the basis of an *information,* which is a formal charging document against the accused.

> *I*n about half of the states, a preliminary hearing is held to determine if there is enough evidence to hold the case over for trial. In federal cases and in some states, a grand jury is empaneled to determine if there is enough evidence to file an "indictment" that charges the suspect with the named crime(s).

In federal cases and in other states, a grand jury is empaneled to determine if there is enough evidence to file an *indictment* charging the suspect with the named crime(s). If the grand jury, made up of a panel of civilians, finds that there is sufficient evidence to warrant a trial, it issues a *true bill;* if not, it issues a *no bill* and the suspect is filtered out of the system. Again, most cases heard by a grand jury—as many as 99.5% (Sullivan and Nachman, 1984)— lead to an indictment. This has led some to call the grand jury process a "rubber stamp" for the prosecution (Walker, 1998).

Arraignment

At arraignment, the next step in the process, the accused is read the information or indictment by the judge. The suspect then has the right to enter a plea of guilty, not guilty, or *nolo contendere* (no contest). Upon a plea of guilty or no contest, sentencing may take place immediately because a trial is not necessary to determine guilt. Pleas of guilty are not to be accepted by the judge unless several assurances from the accused are received. As will be discussed in Chapter Eight, the reality is that plea bargaining occurs in more than 90% of all cases before U.S. courts, and the suspect is presumed guilty by virtually all involved, including the suspect's own attorney.

---

*A*rraignment is when the accused is read the information or indictment by the judge. The suspect then has the right to enter a plea of guilty, not guilty, or nolo contendere (no contest).

Trial

Although the right to trial is mentioned in the Declaration of Independence, three amendments to the U.S. Constitution, and numerous Supreme Court decisions, very few U.S. citizens have a reasonable expectation of a criminal trial when charged with a crime. As noted, more than 90% of defendants plead guilty to the charge(s) and thus do not need a trial. When a trial does occur, it becomes a contest between the government (prosecution) and the accused

---

*A*lthough the Declaration of Independence, three amendments to the U.S. Constitution, and numerous Supreme Court decisions all mention the right to trial, very few citizens in the United States have a reasonable expectation of a criminal trial when charged with a crime. More than 90% of defendants plead guilty to the charges, thereby avoiding a trial.

(defense) to win and secure their own interests. Ideally, our system of justice is *adversarial*, because it is supposed to feature two adversaries fighting it out for the truth. But the ideal is very different from the reality. Gaines, Kaune, and Miller (2000: 286) state it this way: "Television dramas often depict the courtroom as a battlefield, with prosecutors and defense attorneys spitting fire at each other over the loud and insistent protestations of a frustrated judge. Consequently, many people are somewhat disappointed when they witness a real courtroom at work." Even when trials do occur, they commonly produce cooperation rather than battle.

The typical trial process is discussed in Chapter Eight. Ideally, the truth of a suspect's guilt will emerge at trial, where guilt must be established "beyond a reasonable doubt" by the prosecution. In plea bargaining, by contrast, guilt or innocence is not determined. Instead, guilt is assumed and sentencing is the only issue to be resolved.

Trials are most likely to occur in cases where suspects are charged with serious offenses, particularly violent offenses such as murder (Cole and Smith, 2000; Schmalleger, 2001). Criminal trials are very expensive; for minor offenses, plea bargains are less time-consuming and therefore a much more cost-effective use of government resources to carry out justice. Criminal trials are rare precisely because, in most cases, all parties involved assume the guilt of the suspect simply because *some* evidence suggests the suspect is guilty. Many ask, "If they weren't guilty, why would we be arresting them in the first place?" The answer is that the standard of evidence needed to make an arrest ("probable cause") is much lower than that needed to sustain a criminal conviction ("beyond a reasonable doubt"). Yet, even the typical defense attorney in the United States (a public defender assigned to a poor client) has little financial incentive and limited resources to determine whether due process was followed or whether his or her client is actually innocent of the charges. So, although the ideal of American justice is the trial, in reality, trials are the exception to the rule of plea bargaining. According to Langbein (2000: 25):

We are accustomed to viewing the Bill of Rights as a success story. With it, the American constitution-makers opened a new epoch in the centuries-old struggle to place effective limits on the abuse of state power. Not all of the Bill of Rights is a success story, however . . . we would do well to take note of that chapter of the Bill of Rights that has been a spectacular failure: The Framers' effort to embed jury trial as the exclusive mode of proceeding in cases of serious crime.

Think of the Sixth Amendment to the U.S. Constitution, which states: "In all criminal prosecutions, the accused shall enjoy the right to a speedy and public trial, by an impartial jury of the State and district wherein the crime shall have been committed. . . ." Langbein writes: "'All' is not a word that constitution-makers use lightly. The drafters of the Sixth Amendment used it and meant it." Article III of the Constitution says the same thing: "The Trial of all Crimes, except in Cases of Impeachment, shall be by Jury. . . ." Today in the United States, Langbein writes, "In place of 'all,' a more accurate term to describe the use of jury trial in the discharge of our criminal caseload would be 'virtually none.'" Thus, "our guarantee of routine criminal trial is a fraud" (Langbein, 2000: 26).

Sentencing

When defendants are found guilty by a jury of their peers or by a *bench trial* (where a judge determines guilt or innocence), the next step in the process is sentencing. When suspects are found not guilty or *acquitted*, they are filtered out of the system and cannot be retried for the same offense because of the Fifth Amendment protection of freedom from double jeopardy. Sentencing addresses the question: "What do we do with the legally guilty? What punishment

> *S*entencing addresses the question of what punishment should be administered to the legally guilty.

should be administered? Judges typically bear the responsibility for passing sentences, which are recommended by juries. As will be discussed in Chapter Nine, judges have discretion within certain guidelines in *indeterminate* sentences (which specify a range of possible sanctions) but have less discretion in *determinate* sentences (which are specific to the type of crime committed), and no discretion in *mandatory* sentences.

Appeal

Those convicted of criminal offenses, particularly serious crimes, have the right to appeal their convictions to *appellate courts*, or courts of appeals. Those convicted through plea bargains give up this right, along with many others. Convicted offenders can appeal on the basis of any matter of law—for example, that the trial court somehow failed to follow proper procedures or that Constitutional rights were violated at some point in the process. Perhaps unlawfully obtained evidence was admitted into trial, or maybe a defendant's evidence was wrongfully excluded from trial. In these cases, appeals may be allowed, yet in more than 80% of cases, appeals are denied (Meeker, 1984; Williams, 1991). Because appeals are made on matters of law rather than fact, a convicted criminal cannot simply argue that he or she is "really innocent!" Calls to review jury decisions often fall on deaf ears.

> $\mathscr{C}$onvicted offenders can appeal on the basis of any matter of law—for example, that proper procedures were not observed by the trial court or that Constitutional rights were violated.

Some claim that such appeals are based on "legal technicalities" and should be limited so that the criminal justice system can operate more efficiently and effectively. Others point out that procedural errors may lead to mistakes in adjudication, meaning that innocent persons may be wrongfully convicted; therefore, Constitutional protections should not be equated with legal technicalities.

Corrections

Once a sentence is passed, correctional services such as probation, jails, prisons, and numerous other agencies administer the sanctions imposed by the court. Probation, a form of pun-

> $\mathscr{C}$orrectional services administer criminal sanctions imposed by the court.

ishment that allows the offender to live in the community under certain rules, is the most widely used form of the criminal justice sanction in the United States (see Chapter Nine). Probation, the cheapest sanction available, is intended for less serious offenders. Jails and prisons are forms of incarceration, where offenders are deprived of their freedom and locked away from the rest of society. The destructive nature of incarceration is discussed in Chapter Ten. Jails are intended for persons sentenced to less than one year of incarceration, prisons for those sentenced to more than one year of incarceration (Clear and Cole, 1994).

Release

Once a sentence has been fully served, a person is released from the criminal justice system in what is supposed to be the final stage of the process. Offenders are also commonly released early from incarceration through the process of parole, which allows the offender to be released back into the community prior to serving his or her full sentence, as long as he or she agrees to live under certain rules. In the current "get tough" environment in the United States, parole has been abolished at the federal level and in many states.

> $\mathscr{O}$nce a sentence has been served, a person is released from the criminal justice system in what is supposed to be the process's final stage.

Although release is supposed to be the final stage of the criminal justice process, the reality of release is that offenders are routinely harassed by police and/or their parole officers after being released from the system (Evans, 1997). When crimes are committed nearby, especially when they fit the *modus operandi* (M.O.) of a known offender out on parole, he or she is automatically considered a likely suspect. So much for "paying your debt to society"! Police and parole officers also may seek cooperation in developing leads for crimes committed by known associates of the offender.

As you will see later in this chapter, local and state criminal justice agencies are much larger than the federal system of criminal justice, both in terms of the number of persons they employ and in terms of their overall operating budgets. Policing (law enforcement) is primarily a local government responsibility in the United States, while judicial processes (courts) and corrections are handled primarily at the state level. The implications of these facts for justice in the United States will be discussed later in this chapter.

From this brief introduction, you can conclude that one thing the U.S. criminal justice system is aimed at doing is reacting to crime—catching, convicting, and punishing criminals. But is that all? Is this the only reason we have police, courts, and corrections—to deal with the nation's crime problem? Or is there something else that the criminal justice system is supposed to do?

IDEAL GOALS OF THE CRIMINAL JUSTICE SYSTEM

Believe it or not, there is no "official" source one can consult in order to find out what the U.S. criminal justice system is intended to do. You might find this curious: How can we possibly know how well the system is *really* doing if we do not know what it is *intended* to do? The closest we can come to a government statement of intended criminal justice outcomes is the 1967 President's Commission on Law Enforcement and Administration of Justice report, *The Challenge of Crime in a Free Society.* The authors wrote that the justice system was intended to "enforce the standards of conduct necessary to protect individuals and the community."

> *A*ccording to the 1967 President's Commission on Law Enforcement and Administration of Justice report, *The Challenge of Crime in a Free Society,* the justice system is intended to "enforce the standards of conduct necessary to protect individuals and the community."

This seems straightforward enough, but exactly whose standards of conduct should be enforced? And what is meant by "to protect individuals and the community"? Does this mean only that the criminal justice system should protect individuals and communities from criminals? If so, how? Does it also mean that suspected criminals should be protected from the government? Does protecting the community from crime mean eroding Constitutional protections of all Americans? Answers to these questions are not clear.

This is partly due to the fact that the last national report on crime was published over thirty years ago by the Eisenhower Commission. In fact, the last time specific recommendations for criminal justice reform were formally reported was by the 1967 President's Commission. Since this time, no president of the United States has appointed a group to analyze crime or criminal justice policy.

> *T*he last national report on crime was published over thirty years ago by the Eisenhower Commission. The last time specific recommendations for criminal justice reform were formally reported was by the 1967 President's Commission, a group appointed to analyze crime and criminal justice policy.

In the 1990s, a group called the National Criminal Justice Commission initiated an investigation of the U.S. criminal justice system (Donziger, 1996). The findings of their scathing indictment, published under the title *The Real War on Crime,* will be discussed at various points in this book.

One thing we can cull from this source, and most basic introductory criminal justice texts, is that the criminal justice system is aimed at least two goals:

- Doing justice
- Reducing crime

Doing Justice

First and foremost, the basis of the criminal justice system is doing justice. There are two somewhat conflicting conceptions of justice, one concerned with holding the guilty accountable for

> *The* basis of the criminal justice system is doing justice.

their crimes and the other with ensuring that the criminal justice process is fair and impartial. "Doing justice" implies both that guilty people will be punished for their wrongful acts and that innocent persons will not wrongly be subjected to the criminal justice process. Which is the most important conception of justice? If you had to choose to emphasize one conception of justice over the other, which would you choose? I return to these issues in a more detailed discussion of "justice" in this chapter.

> *Doing* justice implies both that guilty people will be punished for their actions and that innocent persons will not wrongly be subjected to the criminal justice process.

Reducing Crime

The second goal of the criminal justice system is reducing crime, which can be achieved through *reactive* means (after the crime occurs) or *proactive* means (before the crime occurs). The former type of crime fighting is generally called *crime control,* whereas the latter is often referred to as *crime prevention* (Rosenbaum, Lurigio, and Davis, 1998). Amazingly, the U.S. Constitution does not list "crime control" as a responsibility of the U.S. government. Therefore, the U.S.

> *The* criminal justice system's other objective is reducing crime, through either reactive means (crime control) or proactive means (crime prevention).

Congress was not explicitly empowered with this authority. The Constitution does state, however, that our government must "establish Justice, [and] insure domestic tranquility," and this makes crime control an implied power of government (Marion, 1995: 6). Because crime control activities are *not* specifically granted to the federal government, and because they are *not* specifically denied to the states, crime control has historically been the responsibility of state governments. Since the 1960s, however, crime control has become increasingly a national issue as a consequence of the politicization of crime in elections, discussed later in this chapter, and media coverage of crime (see Chapter Four).

In the United States, crime reduction is mostly reactive in nature. For example, American policing has historically been aimed at reacting to calls for service from crime victims (after the crimes occur). Our system of justice tries to apprehend, prosecute, convict, and punish offenders *after* a crime is discovered by or reported to the police. It is important to point out here that reactive criminal justice operations are not likely to reduce crime because they do not eliminate the root causes of crime. This is why the National Criminal Justice Commission claims: "We cannot expect the criminal justice system to create strong families, deliver jobs, or provide hope to young people" because it is not charged with doing so (Donziger, 1996: 61). In fact, because the criminal justice system does little to address the major sources of criminal behavior, crime prevention through the U.S. criminal justice system is not likely (Sherman et al., 1997).

> *In* the United States, crime reduction is mostly reactive in nature.

Crime prevention includes any means to eliminate the causes of crime so that crime does not occur and does not need to be dealt with by criminal justice agencies (Robinson, 1999). Although some American criminal justice activity is aimed at crime prevention, the great bulk of it can be described as crime control. There is some evidence that crime prevention can be effective, if appropriately designed, implemented, and supported (Sherman et al., 1997). In Chapter Nine, I discuss some crime prevention efforts that have proved either effective or promising.

Reducing crime is obviously a desirable goal. But the most important point to remember while reading this book is that doing justice is *ideally* the primary goal of our criminal justice system. That is, although reducing crime is an important goal, it is of secondary importance to doing justice (Cole and Smith, 2000).

WHAT IS JUSTICE?

Arrigo (1999: 2) writes that the meaning of justice "is by no means easy to interpret or simple to discern." As mentioned earlier, there are at least two conflicting conceptions of justice, depending on who is asked. To crime victims, justice may simply mean getting even with the offenders who harmed them. For example, a rape victim may define justice for the attacker as imprisonment, or even castration or death, and might perceive anything less as unjust. When people are intentionally victimized and the guilty are not held accountable for their actions, justice clearly has *not* been obtained. This is because the offender has unfairly gained an advantage over the victim; the mythical scales of justice shown in Figure 1.2 have wrongfully been tilted in favor of the offender. The scales of justice depicted in the figure are in balance only when the harms inflicted on crime victims are righted by administering punishment to their offenders.

FIGURE 1.2
The Mythical Scales of Justice

Retribution, a main reason for administering criminal sanctions to offenders (see Chapter Nine), implies that the harm inflicted by the criminal upon the victim will in some way be returned by the government to the offender. In the United States, when a criminal hurts someone, he or she is viewed as deserving of punishment: "An eye for an eye, a tooth for a tooth," so to speak. Victims now regularly view punishment of their offenders as one of their rights (Beckett and Sasson, 2000). This is one conception of justice.

Justice has an alternative meaning, as well. In some ways, this definition is related to the one above, for it is concerned with assuring that the scales of justice are not imbalanced. This conception of justice is based on fairness and impartiality. It assumes that all persons will be treated equally in the eyes of the law—that justice will be blind. Justice thus would not be present when any group is somehow left out or singled out for differential treatment by the law.

This conception of justice is represented by the figure of "a blindfolded woman with a scale in one hand and a sword in the other" (see the Issue in Depth at the end of this chapter for a discussion of "Lady Justitia," whose image adorns this book). It is also what is meant by "With liberty and justice for all" in the U.S. Constitution—that the government will treat its citizens with "fairness, equity" and in a manner that is right (Kappeler, Blumberg, and Potter, 2000: 215).

From the title of this book—*Justice Blind?*—you may guess that I am at least not sure whether our system of justice achieves this measure of justice. In fact, I will provide evidence that American criminal justice is unjust in many ways. Justice must be blind or it is not just at all. I will demonstrate in this book that the U.S. system of criminal justice is biased against the poor and against people of color, and that it discriminates to a lesser degree on the basis of gender (see Chapter Five).

This depiction of justice is also reflected in the American Declaration of Independence. American settlers criticized their "British brethren" for being "deaf to the voice of justice" (Gottfredson, 1999: 50). Ideally, this was one reason that people came to found this country in the interests of justice apart from the interests of the British monarchy. Of course, history testifies to a different reality. Early Americans wiped out numerous indigenous peoples and enslaved other groups in the name of Manifest Destiny, a nineteenth-century doctrine based on the premise that the Americans had the God-given right—indeed, the duty—to expand their territory and cultural influence throughout North America (e.g., see Koning, 1993). Still, early Americans envisioned a country where all "men" could live and thrive and further their own interests without the burdens imposed by the British monarchy.

Conflicting Views of Justice

Each conception of justice is important when it comes to studying and understanding the criminal justice system. Americans will not support a criminal justice system that fails to punish those who deserve it. Ideally, they will not support a system that wrongfully convicts the innocent or is biased against any group. Pound (1912) wrote long ago that justice requires that serious offenders be convicted and punished and that the innocent and unfortunate not be wrongly oppressed. Similarly, Harrigan (2000: 315) notes that "Justice is served neither if a guilty person is let go nor if an innocent person is punished."

These two conceptions of justice—punishing the guilty but ensuring fairness and impartiality—often conflict. The law places restrictions on the actions of criminal justice actors so that Constitutional rights of individuals are not violated. With unlimited powers, law enforcement agencies probably could do a much better job at fighting crime, but numerous liberties that we currently enjoy (such as the right to privacy) would have to be sacrificed. Imagine how much more effectively police could detect crimes if they could enter your home, peek into your windows, tap your phones, and monitor your e-mail without first having to establish probable cause!

Given the limits within which the criminal justice system must operate, it is difficult to catch, convict, and punish criminal offenders. For example, the exclusionary rule states that illegally

> *G*iven the current limits of the criminal justice system, it is difficult to catch, convict, and punish criminal offenders.

seized evidence cannot be used to establish legal guilt against a defendant. The Supreme Court held in *Mapp v. Ohio* (1961) that the rule had to be applied universally to all criminal proceedings, including those by state governments against individual citizens. This requirement may make it less likely that a *factually guilty* criminal will be found *legally guilty* in a court of law. Alternatively, our current efforts to fight crime at almost any cost have led to the establishment of measures intended to protect "victims' rights . . . [that] have lowered evidentiary requirements, eliminated the insanity defense, and weakened exclusionary rules designed to block the introduction of illegally obtained evidence" (Beckett and Sasson, 2000: 163).

Walker (1998: 176) argues that many so-called victims' rights initiatives are really efforts to get "tough on crime." He writes that the President's Task Force on Victims of Crime, for example, "recommended legislation 'to abolish the exclusionary rule,' 'to abolish parole,' to permit hearsay evidence at preliminary hearings, and to authorize preventive detention." Part of the frustration that victims feel when they suffer harm at the hands of criminals stems from the fact that, technically, the only "victim" of crime is the government. This means that victims are not entitled to get justice for themselves; rather, the state is authorized to conduct crime control efforts in the interest of community safety.

Yet, the U.S. justice system must strive to achieve a balance between fighting crime (to do justice for its victims) and being fair and impartial (to do justice for the accused). Justice for the community requires both. Thus, throughout our history, the priorities of the American justice system have shifted back and forth, much like a pendulum. During some periods, emphasis has been placed on apprehending and punishing criminals over ensuring fairness in the criminal justice process. At other times, crime fighting has taken a back seat to ensuring that the system operates impartially. Additionally, what we do to fight crime in the United States depends on our view of what causes crime (Lilly, Cullen, and Ball, 1995). For example, when criminality is viewed as a function of bad people making bad choices, we are more likely to be punitive in our response, whereas when crime is viewed as a product of bad environments affecting innocent persons, we are more likely to engage in rehabilitative efforts (Beckett, 1997). Given the actions we are taking to reduce crime at the turn of the twenty-first century, what do you think politicians believe are the causes of crime?

Due Process versus Crime Control

There has always been tension between those who believe in "due process" and those who believe in "crime control." These terms represent two models of justice put forth by Herbert Packer (1968), in his book *The Limits of the Criminal Sanction.* Although neither of the two models actually exists or ever can in reality, Packer attempted to describe two polar extremes—one model most concerned with preserving individual liberties and the other with maintaining order in the community and fighting crime.

Figure 1.3 depicts these models at opposite ends of a continuum. The due process model is aimed at ensuring that individual liberties are protected at all costs, even if guilty people sometimes go free. In other words, the due process model values individual freedom, and the way to

> *The* due process model is aimed at assuring that individual liberties are protected at all costs, even if guilty people sometimes go free. The due process model values individual freedom, and the best way to safeguard individual freedom is to uphold Constitutional protections.

protect individual freedom is to uphold Constitutional protections. It places a high value on the adversarial nature of justice, whereby a prosecutor and defense attorney battle it out in court to find the truth and make sure that justice is achieved. *Reliability* is the most important value of the due process model, for it is imperative that the right person be convicted of the crime of which he

FIGURE 1.3

Due Process and Crime Control Models of Criminal Justice

	Crime Control	Due Process
Most Important Goal	Reduce crime	Protect rights
Cherished Value	Efficiency	Reliability
In Practice	Increase powers of police, prosecutors	Limit discretion of police, prosecutors

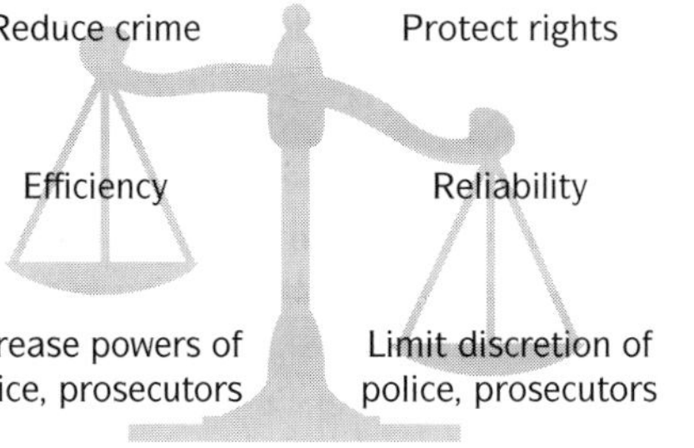

or she is accused. Packer's metaphor for this model was an "obstacle course" because, in order to ensure that no innocent persons were wrongfully convicted, the prosecution would have to overcome numerous obstacles in order to convict anyone.

The crime control model is aimed at protecting the community by lowering crime rates, even if, on occasion, innocent persons are mistakenly convicted. The crime control model also values individual freedom but suggests that the way to protect individual freedom is to protect people

---

The crime control model's goal is to protect the community by lowering crime rates, even if innocent persons are sometimes mistakenly convicted. The crime control model also values individual freedom, but it suggests that the way to protect individual freedom is to protect people from criminals.

---

from criminals. It places a high value on informal processes such as plea bargaining (when a prosecutor and defense attorney agree out of court to an appropriate sentence for an accused criminal) to expedite criminal justice operations. In this model, very few criminal trials are held, because they are expensive and unnecessary for establishing legal guilt. *Efficiency* is the most important value of the crime control model, for it is imperative that the system operate as quickly as possible in order to keep up with the large numbers of criminal cases that enter the system each day. Packer's metaphor for this model was an "assembly line" because individual defendants would be quickly processed through the justice system outside of the courtroom through plea bargaining. Plea bargaining is discussed more fully in Chapter Eight.

Note that *justice* is an important value in both models. Yet, proponents of each model view justice differently. Figure 1.4 illustrates how justice can be viewed either as an outcome or as a process. People who view justice as an *outcome,* usually supporters of the crime control model, think that justice means giving people what they deserve: guilty people deserve punishment, whereas

FIGURE 1.4
Justice As an Outcome and a Process

Justice as . . .	would mean . . .	Example	Term
an outcome	giving everyone what he or she is due	Convicting the guilty, acquitting the innocent	Corrective
a process	treating everyone fairly, equally	Not discriminating on the basis of race, class, or gender	Procedural

innocent people do not. I call this version of justice *corrective justice.* Others, typically proponents of the due process model, see justice as a *process.* People who value what I call *procedural justice* are more concerned with ensuring that everyone is treated fairly and equally while being processed through the criminal justice system. This means not allowing discrimination on the basis of factors such as race, class, or gender.

> *J*ustice can be viewed either as an outcome or as a process. Justice as an outcome means giving people what they deserve—guilty people deserve punishment, innocent people do not. Others, typically proponents of the due process model, see justice as a process, one charged with ensuring that everyone is treated fairly and equally while being processed through the criminal justice system, not allowing discrimination on the basis of race, class, gender, or other factors.

Each of these conceptions of justice is important to many Americans, but criminal justice activity over the past few decades reflects an emphasis on corrective justice at the expense of procedural justice. In other words, U.S. policymakers are more concerned with holding the guilty accountable for their crimes than with ensuring fairness and equity in the system, even in the face of overwhelming evidence that innocent people have been convicted of crimes they did not commit (for evidence of wrongful convictions, see the Issue in Depth at the end of Chapter Nine). This is unfortunate, because of the inherent infallibility associated with all human activity (Gaines et al., 2000: 21).

Democrats tend to support the due process model, whereas Republicans tend to support crime control efforts. Traditionally, Democrats have been more "liberal" and have placed greater value on individual rights than on community protection, whereas Republicans have been more "conservative" and thus more supportive of government efforts to fight crime (Baker and Meyer, 1980; Biskupic, 1991; Van Horn, Baumer, and Gormley, 1992). Because the crime control and due process models are ideals, and because of the competing values of reducing crime and doing justice, the history of criminal justice in the United States can be characterized as a pendulum swinging back and forth between the two ideals, much as the political affiliation of voters shifts over time. For example, the Warren Supreme Court (1953–1969) can be considered a "due process" court because its rulings were more consistent with upholding individual rights. The Burger Supreme Court (1969–1986) is more accurately characterized as a "crime control" court because it was less protective of individual rights and made decisions that limited *Miranda* protections (for more, see Marion, 1995; O'Brien, 1993; Steel and Steger, 1988). Beckett and Sasson (2000: 59) go as far as to characterize Burger Court activity as an "assault on defendants' rights." The Rehnquist Supreme Court (1986–present) is also generally in line with the "crime control" model, as it has made it easier to convict the "factually guilty" and to avoid losing cases as a result of legal technicalities that previously made it easier for the guilty to go free. The Rehnquist Court has "given greater flexibility to the police and corrections personnel, making changes in the death penalty, unreasonable searches and seizures, and the exclusionary rule" (Marion, 1995: 51). Some of its rulings, however, such as *U.S. v. Dickerson* (2000), which upheld the requirement that police read suspects the *Miranda* warning prior to interrogation, have been more consistent with the due process model.

In April 2000, the U.S. Supreme Court heard arguments that reading the *Miranda* warning should no longer be required because it interferes with police officers' efforts to gain evidence necessary for criminal conviction of the guilty. The following box focuses on the Supreme Court's ruling.

The recent *Miranda* decision

In the case of *U.S. v. Dickerson* (2000), the Supreme Court upheld the *Miranda* requirements by a vote of 7–2. At issue was a 1968 federal law that allowed voluntary confessions by suspects to be admitted into court even if the defendant had not been read his or her rights. This law conflicted with the Supreme Court's decision in *Miranda v. Arizona* (1966).

Chief Justice William Rehnquist wrote the majority opinion of the Court, in which he stated: "We hold that Miranda, being a constitutional decision of this Court, may not be . . . overruled by an Act of Congress, and we decline to overrule Miranda ourselves. We therefore hold that Miranda and its progeny in this Court govern the admissibility of statements made during custodial interrogation in both state and federal courts."

Rehnquist added that because the "advent of modern custodial police interrogation brought with it an increased concern about confessions obtained by coercion," *Miranda* requirements were considered more important than ever by the Court. Rehnquist wrote, for example, that being questioned by the police places a "heavy toll on individual liberty and trades on the weakness of individuals."

Ironically, the appeal of the original 1966 *Miranda* decision did not come from a law enforcement agency. In fact, most police administrators have always believed that *Miranda* provides an important protection for all Americans. They recognize that reading *Miranda* warnings to suspects is part of their professional responsibility of upholding the Constitutional right of suspects not to incriminate themselves. Because police have always been able to use strategies to convince suspects to waive their right not to incriminate themselves (e.g., see Leo, 1996), Miranda is not and never has been a major impediment to effective policing. Uchida and Bynum (1991) claim that very little evidence is ever excluded because of *Miranda* violations.

Edward Lazarus (2000), author of "How Miranda Really Works and Why It Really Matters," wrote (about three weeks before the recent decision came down):

> As matters currently stand, when police officers fail to observe Miranda, judges almost always limit themselves . . . to finding "technical" violations of Miranda, thereby allowing prosecutors to use evidence derived from challenged confessions and to keep defendants from testifying in their own defense. Judges almost never take the extra step of finding a confession to be actually involuntary—which would deprive the prosecution of any evidence obtained as a resulted of the tainted confession.
>
> Indeed, in practice, and wholly apart from the much-debated issue of whether Miranda inhibits police from obtaining confessions, the ruling has become largely symbolic. It allows judges to scold police for misbehavior and pay lip service to the right against self-incrimination, while minimizing the actual effect on police and prosecutors.

The Court ruled that *Miranda* warnings have become intertwined with the fabric of American society. That is, *Miranda* protects a right that is crucial to being free from unwarranted government interference into our lives, a right that is so cherished by Americans that it cannot be eliminated by Court order.

Which model do you most support? Whether you would support a due process model or a crime control model may depend on which you feel is more important, protecting your individual Constitutional rights or protecting the community from crime. This may not be an easy choice, because both are worthy pursuits. Before you decide, remember that your rights as an American are the major difference between living in a democracy such as the United States or an authoritarian, police state such as China or the former Soviet Union.

---

*S*ometimes, ensuring that all individuals' rights are protected means that guilty people will go free. Alternatively, getting all the "bad guys" will mean that some "good guys" may get caught up in the criminal justice system, too.

Sometimes, ensuring that all individuals' rights are protected means that guilty people will go free. Alternatively, getting all the "bad guys" means that some "good guys" may get caught up in the criminal justice system, too. Ask yourself, which would be worse—being confronted by a criminal who was wrongly freed, or being wrongfully accused of a crime by your own government? In which situation would you be more likely to win?

How you answer such questions may determine whether you are a proponent of a due process system of justice or a crime control system of justice. Whatever the case, you must remember that the U.S. criminal justice system will never be 100% representative of either the due process or the crime control model. Rather, our system of justice attempts to stay in balance, by upholding individual Constitutional protections while effectively fighting crime. Gottfredson (1999: 27) writes: "Because we value freedom, we react strongly to violations or threats of violation of our persons or property. We resist any threat to our liberty by agencies of our government. [But] [b]ecause we value safety, we expect the criminal justice system to protect us. We want both protection for ourselves and for our own liberty."

The most important lesson to be learned from Packer's discussion is that there is an inherent conflict between protecting individuals' Constitutional rights and fighting crime. It is difficult to do one well without being somewhat of a failure at the other.

Justice Today

Where are we today? And what are the implications for justice in America? The following box illustrates that most criminal justice resources go to police and corrections, with courts receiving the fewest resources. What does this suggest about whether we are following a crime control or due process model of justice?

Resources devoted to criminal justice in the United States

A system that places a higher value on crime fighting than on due process might allocate a larger percentage of its resources to police, because they are responsible for making arrests of suspected offenders, and/or to corrections, because its agencies have sole authority over punishing offenders. A system that places a greater value on due process might allocate a larger share of resources to courts, because the judicial process determines the guilt or innocence of criminal justice clients. The primary protection innocent persons have from government over-zealousness is high-quality defense attorneys and neutral, objective judges. If we value due process, these actors ought to be well equipped to do their jobs.

The following discussion is organized around these issues:

- Which component of criminal justice has the most employees?
- Which component of criminal justice is allocated the most financial resources?

Employees of criminal justice

In 1995, the U.S. criminal justice system employed nearly two million people, including over 900,000 working in law enforcement, over 400,000 working in courts, and over 650,000 working in corrections. So, of the three components of justice, the fewest people work in U.S.

> *M*ost criminal justice resources go to police and corrections, with courts receiving the fewest resources. This is more consistent with a crime control model of justice.

courts. This is more consistent with a crime control model of criminal justice than a due process model.

There are nearly 19,000 law enforcement agencies in the United States, employing a total of over 730,000 sworn officers. Nearly 14,000 of these agencies are city police departments, employing over 410,000 officers. The next largest type of agency is the county sheriff's office, with just over 3,000 departments and 150,000 deputies. Special police departments total over 1,300 agencies and 43,000 officers, and there are over 700 Texas constable agencies employing nearly 2,000 officers. Compare these numbers with the 49 primary state police agencies, which employ over 54,000 officers, and the very small number of federal agencies (with more than 100 agents), which employ nearly 75,000 officers. Clearly, law enforcement in the United States is a local phenomenon, as most police officers work for local (city and county) agencies.

Courts employ far fewer employees than police departments. Given that prosecution is a state-level phenomenon (because most crimes are acts against the state government), I'll limit my discussion to state courts. There are just over 2,300 state court prosecutors' offices, staffed by a total of 71,000 attorneys, investigators, and support staff. In 1996, these employees were responsible for convicting nearly one million adults. Were these people convicted "beyond a reasonable doubt" by a "jury of their peers"? Given the imbalance in criminal justice employees, it would be hard to imagine having trials for all of these defendants. In fact, almost all of these convictions by state courts were achieved through the process of plea bargaining. Half of the prosecutors' offices in the United States employed no more than nine people.

Given that the largest share of defendants charged with felonies in state courts are indigent clients who cannot afford their own attorneys, an examination of defense systems for these indigent clients will help us learn about the state of defense attorneys generally in the United States. In 1992, almost 80% of defendants who were charged with felonies in the nation's largest counties were assigned public counsel. The poor traditionally receive legal representation from assigned counsel systems and public defenders' offices. In 1992, 64% of state prosecutors' offices in the United States reported a public defender program in their jurisdiction, followed by 58% that reported an assigned counsel system. Additionally, 25% indicated that their district entered into contract with law firms, private attorneys, or local bar associations to provide legal representation for the poor. Whether publicly provided counsel provides defense of a lower quality than private attorneys is a matter of interesting debate (see Chapter Nine), but the facts may speak for themselves. For example, nearly 75% of inmates in state prisons and about 50% of those in federal prisons were represented by publicly provided attorneys.

Private attorneys may not be any more likely than public defenders to gain acquittals for their clients or to achieve less severe sentences for them, but recall that justice is a process as much as it is an outcome. Clearly, publicly assigned defense attorneys (who are paid a flat salary no matter what the outcome or how well they prepare their cases) have less financial incentive than private attorneys (who may be paid by the hour or per motion filed) to assure fair and Constitutional proceedings for their clients. Given that the average public defender has over 5 cases per day, 7 days per week, 52 weeks per year (assuming they work weekends, holidays, and vacation time), it is hard to fathom holding trials for all of these clients (Cole and Smith, 2000).

It should not be hard to imagine that, with more than one million felony criminal convictions in any given year, correctional facilities must employ a large number of employees. Recall that in 1995, more than 650,000 people were employed in corrections. At the end of 1996, 5.5 million people were under some form of criminal justice supervision, including probation, parole, and incarceration in jail or prison. At the end of 1998, state and federal prisons housed nearly 1.9 million inmates. How much does all of this cost? You must be wondering, especially given that criminal justice is funded by taxpayer dollars. That's your money, after all. That is the next issue addressed.

Financial resources for criminal justice

American governments at the federal, state, and local levels spent over $112 billion in 1995 for criminal and civil justice. This is almost twice the amount spent in 1985, when justice spending was approximately $65 billion. In Chapter Three, I will review what happened with crime rates during this same time period. One might expect to have seen huge decreases in crime rates during this time period, but this is not what happened.

Most justice spending (85%) is incurred by state and local governments. The largest share of justice spending went to law enforcement ($48.6 billion). Almost as much was spent on corrections, including jails, prisons, probation, and parole ($39.8 billion). The smallest share of resources was spent on prosecution and other legal services ($24.5 billion). In 1990, we spent only $1.3 billion on defending the nation's poor through publicly provided defense attorneys.

Let us assume that only 10% of law enforcement time and money is spent actually providing law enforcement–related activities (see Chapter Seven). This would mean that 10% of the $48.6 billion (or $4.86 billion) went to fight street crime. If law enforcement activity resulted in 80% of those arrested being poor, this would mean that police spend about $3.7 billion just catching poor criminals, and several billion more prosecuting them. Compare this figure with the $1.3 billion spent defending them. See where our priorities are?

In American criminal justice, government agencies allocate much more funding for police to apprehend suspected criminals and for correctional facilities to punish convicted criminals. Overburdened courts receive relatively little funding, despite the fact that it is the role of the courts to ensure that justice is served— that is, that the innocent are not wrongfully convicted and that the guilty do not go free. Implications for justice in the United States are hard to understand fully, but the bottom line appears to be that we are less concerned with spending resources to determine that we get the "right" people than we are at just getting any people and punishing them. This may be an alarming realization for Americans who believe in justice.

From the discussion in the box on resources devoted to criminal justice, it appears that we as a nation have embraced crime control values. President Bill Clinton stated in 1994:

> The American people have been very clear. . . . The most important job is to keep the streets and the neighborhoods of America safe. The first responsibility of Government is law and order. Without it, people can never really pursue the American dream. And without it, we're not really free. (Quoted in Gaines et al., 2000: 11)

Does this statement sound more in line with a crime control or a due process model?

Other chapters of this book will provide evidence that U.S. policymakers have chosen a crime control model at the expense of individual Constitutional protections. The result is that many of our civil liberties are being or have been eroded. As Beckett (1997: 67) writes: "Law and order politics lead to a disregard for civil rights and due process." This is particularly sad, not just because we are less free from potential government interference in our lives, but also because the criminal justice system is so ineffective at reducing crime. Perhaps if crime were eliminated, we could accept and appreciate less justice. In fact, crime rates in the United States are still high. They have consistently declined since the early 1970s, but these declines are not likely due to anything the criminal justice system has done. In essence, we have been forced to give up some of our Constitutional protections for very little in return (see Chapter Three for a discussion of falling crime rates). This is a frightening thought.

In the past three decades, the United States has witnessed a rapid expansion of American criminal justice, an expansion driven not by facts about crime or increasing crime rates but, instead, by politics, fear, and an increasingly punitive attitude about crime and criminals (Beckett and Sas-

> *In* the past three decades, the United States has witnessed a rapid expansion of the criminal justice system, one driven not by facts about crime or growing crime rates but instead by politics, fear, and an increasingly punitive attitude about crime and criminals.

son, 2000: 8; Donziger, 1996: 63). For example, state spending from 1976 to 1989 increased dramatically for correctional budgets (up 95%) but fell for non-Medicare welfare (down 41%), highways (down 23%), and higher education (down 6%) (Gold, 1990: 16). We now spend more than $100 billion annually fighting crime (Maguire and Pastore, 1997). This led Jerome Miller (1994: 479), affiliated with the National Center on Institutions and Alternatives, to write:

> During the 1980s and 1990s, in the midst of two decades of social neglect, America's white majority presented its inner cities with an expensive gift—a new and improved criminal justice system. This new and improved system would, the government promised, bring domestic tranquility—with particular relevance to African Americans. No expense was spared in crafting and delivering it inside city gates. It was, in fact, a Trojan Horse . . . [because] . . . [a]s governmen-

tal investment in social and employment programs in the inner city held stable or decreased, the criminal justice system was ratcheted up to fill the void. With it came a divisive philosophy, destructive strategies, and particularly vicious tactics that would exacerbate violence and social disorganization.

Miller utilized investments in criminal justice activity over the past several decades, coupled with simultaneous disinvestments in social programs, to argue that the United States has shifted its efforts to solve social problems from a "social safety net" approach to a "dragnet" approach. This means U.S. policymakers seem more willing to spend taxpayer money catching criminals (after they commit crime) than preventing crime (before it happens) by helping people deal with the life-shattering effects of poverty.

In fact, corrections spending at the national level increased three times as fast as military spending in the 1980s and 1990s (Donziger, 1996: 48). So, when you talk about the nation's "enemy," you are much more likely to be talking about an American than at any previous time in our history. As a further illustration, the National Criminal Justice Commission examines the war on drugs and writes: "The enemy in this war is *our own people* (Donziger, 1996: 218; emphasis in original).

Do not be fooled into thinking that this increasingly punitive approach is attributable to citizen demand. Public opinion polls do show some support for many current criminal justice approaches

> *The* United States' increasingly punitive approach is not attributable to citizen demand.

(Roberts and Stalans, 2000), but many claim that public support for "get tough" criminal justice approaches comes from public misconceptions about who is subject to these policies. That is, when citizens answer questions about their degree of support for a particular type of punishment, they are typically thinking about violent criminals. In fact, most offenders are nonviolent and actually produce little harm to society. When given more information about less punitive sentencing alternatives, Americans are far less punitive than politicians seem to believe (Donziger, 1996: 60–61).

How has the U.S. government sold crime control to its own citizens? Goode and Ben-Yehuda (1994b: 31) claim that images of crime suggest that "society has become morally lax" and thus "a revival of traditional values may be necessary; if innocent people are victimized by crime, a crackdown on offenders will do the trick." This involves "more laws, longer sentences, more police, more arrests, and more prison cells." Because many of the premises on which our crime control efforts are based are false claims, some government "criminal justice-speak" amounts to propaganda: "Propaganda is a technique for influencing social action based on intentional distortions and manipulation of communications. . . . While not all media and government presentation, or even a majority of it, is a conscious attempt at propaganda, many crime myths are the product of propaganda techniques" (Kappeler et al., 2000: 22).

Criminal justice expansion—including placing 100,000 more police officers on the streets and constructing more than 1,000 new prisons and jails (Schlosser, 1998), which are overpopulated by

> *U.*S. criminal justice expansion has disproportionately affected poor people and people of color.

as much as 25%—has disproportionately affected poor people and people of color. And recently, the rate of female incarceration has increased faster than the rate of male incarceration. Not only are the poor and minorities more likely to be incarcerated and subjected to other forms of punishment, their families and communities are also thus more likely to suffer the consequences (see Chapter Five). These consequences, ironically, include increased exposure to criminogenic conditions. This has led many in the criminal justice community to conclude that we now have "good reason to worry about" the implications of criminal justice expansion "for social justice and democracy" (Beckett and Sasson, 2000: 5).

One threat of increased criminal justice expansion is to individual freedoms of Americans, as established in the U.S. Constitution. Remember that much of the law was set up to protect individuals from their own government. Historical accounts of the purpose of the U.S. criminal justice system suggest that it was originally created to protect innocent citizens from an arbitrary and overzealous government. The founders of the U.S. government set up our government so that government practices, including criminal justice practices, would be limited by law. In Chapter Two, you will see how your Constitutional rights allow you to enjoy certain protections from unwarranted government interference in your life.

---

*O*ne threat of increased criminal justice expansion is to Americans' individual freedoms, as established in the U.S. Constitution.

ALTERNATIVE GOALS OF THE CRIMINAL JUSTICE SYSTEM

Is the criminal justice system really intended to do what criminal justice scholars claim it is intended to do? Some question the stated goals of the criminal justice system and posit that the system is really intended to do something else entirely. For example, Jeffrey Reiman (1998), as might be guessed from the title of his book, *The Rich Get Richer and the Poor Get Prison*, suggests that the criminal justice system is really intended to fail at achieving justice and reducing crime. Although this may seem silly at first, Reiman's argument is that some failures amount to success, depending on what is really sought.

Serving Interests and Controlling the Population

Reiman posits the "pyrrhic defeat theory," which suggests that "the failure of the criminal justice system yields such benefits to those in positions of power that it amounts to a success" (p. 5). His main argument is that interests of those in power are served when we focus almost exclusively on street crimes rather than other types of harmful behaviors. At the same time, those people whom

---

*J*effrey Reiman (1998: 5) argues that "the failure of the criminal justice system yields such benefits to those in positions of power that it amounts to a success." He asserts that the interests of those in power are served when we focus almost exclusively on street crimes, overlooking other types of harmful behaviors. Those we fear most (e.g., young minority males) are routinely sent off to some form of government-controlled institution or community alternative. This amounts to a form of population control.

---

we fear most (e.g., young, minority males) are routinely rounded up by the police and sent off to some form of government-controlled institution or community alternative. This amounts to a form of population control, so that the enemies in the war on crime can never win, can never achieve the types of success that can be enjoyed by those with the power to achieve. The following box discusses examples of how control of criminals serves limited interests.

How does population control serve interests?

Think about all of the people in American prisons and jails. Currently, just over two million people are incarcerated in the United States. Guess what? Even though they are not free people working outside in the labor force, they are not counted as part of the unemployment rate. One estimate in the mid-1990s suggested that the U.S. unemployment rate would increase at least 1.5% if we counted all the men in our nation's prisons, many of whom are not employable because of a lack of education and/or legitimate work skills (Reiman, 1998). When the president of the United States stands up in front of the American people and speaks about unemployment, he does not have to count incarcerated people as part of the unemployment rate, even though they really are. This serves his political interests, as well as those of his party.

Additionally, some criminologists have equated crime control with industry. Without any doubt, crime pays tremendous dividends for business interests. Businesses now compete for contracts to provide products and services to American jails and prisons. In fact, companies such as the Corrections Corporation of America now run their own correctional facilities for profit. Once businesses have vested interests in making profits on crime control, it is logical that business-friendly government will do whatever it takes to ensure a steady supply of offenders, so that the criminal justice system can continue to pay off (Christie, 1994). Perhaps this is why correctional officer hiring and training has become the "fastest-growing function" of government (Lilly and Knepper, 1993: 155).

It is ironic, if you stop and think about it, how many people benefit from our "wars" against crime and drugs. Kappeler et al. (2000: 45) write that enormous sums of money and millions of jobs are created by criminal justice, including about $65 billion spent on private security alone. If politicians in the 1970s, 1980s, and 1990s had not chosen to pursue crime with such vigor, leading to staggering increases in criminal justice spending and tremendous disparities in the criminal justice system based on race, class, and gender, would I have written this book? In essence, even I benefit from criminal justice–sponsored population control (but at least I seek a resolution to injustice in the United States).

Among other things, Reiman argues that the label of "crime" (particularly "serious crime") is not used for the most harmful and frequently occurring acts that threaten us. He claims that the criminal law distorts the image of crime so that the most dangerous threats are seen as coming from below us (i.e., from the lower class) when they really come from above us (i.e., from the upper class). In later chapters, I provide evidence that this is true by discussing how the law is biased against certain segments of the population (Chapter Two), and by showing which types of crime are actually the most dangerous (Chapter Three), and how the media portray crime (Chapter Four). Additionally, the war on crime may in effect be a war against particular segments of the U.S. population (Chapter Five), and our efforts to curb drug use in the United States may be aimed primarily at what are perceived to be poor people's drugs (Chapter Six).

The segments of the population being controlled by America's crime control efforts are poor minorities. Several criminologists have noted that the criminal justice system is, in effect, the primary mechanism in the United States responsible for controlling the "poor masses" (Rusche and Kirchheimer, 1939), who are the nation's "surplus population" (Quinney, 1977). According to this line of reasoning, the criminal justice system is supposed to punish the "problem populations" (Spitzer, 1975) and the "dangerous classes" (Melosi, 1989). Such hypotheses have been supported by evidence showing that poor, unemployed members of racial minority groups are likely to receive harsher sentences than employed minority group members and Caucasians (e.g., see Chiricos and Bales, 1991; Chiricos and Delone, 1992; Nobling, Spohn, and Delone, 1998).

Consistent with this evidence, Morris (1988: 113) writes that "the whole law and order movement that we have heard so much about is, in operation though not in intent, anti-black and anti-underclass—not in plan, not in desire, not in intent, but in operation." It is hard to imagine a system of criminal justice in the United States aimed at serving limited interests and controlling certain segments of the population. Before you dismiss this possibility, however, consider these two important points:

- Our criminal justice system may achieve certain functions without actually intending to achieve them.
- The American criminal justice process is first and foremost a political process.

Each of these points is discussed in the next section.

FUNCTIONS VERSUS PURPOSES OF CRIMINAL JUSTICE

Criminal justice in the United States may achieve certain functions without actually intending to achieve them. This is an important distinction to understand. As Reiman (1998) points out, politi-

---

*C*riminal justice in the United States may achieve certain unintended functions.

---

cal processes can achieve certain outcomes without being purposeful. He argues that criminal justice system failure was not set in place by some vast conspiracy of old, rich, white men who wanted to protect their limited interests. Instead, Reiman argues, criminal justice evolved over time into a system that is unjust and that protects limited interests. Those who benefit from this obviously have no reason to change the system, and those harmed by the inherent biases of the system do not have the intellectual or financial means to change it.

Herbert Gans (1995) makes a similar argument in his book *The War against the Poor.* I will return to the thrust of this argument in Chapter Five, but essentially Gans argues that American government has always been engaged in a war against poor people (including criminals), particularly the "undeserving underclass." Gans writes that "labeling the poor as undeserving . . . has some uses, or positive functions, or beneficial consequences, for more fortunate Americans . . . resulting in material and immaterial benefits, even though they are not immediately apparent, particularly to the people who benefit from them" (p. 91). Gans goes on to explain that functions are not the same as purposes:

> They are not what people intend to do, but are the consequences of what they actually do, whatever their initial purposes. Consequently, functions are usually neither intended nor recognized when they first emerge, and some are unintended but unavoidable because they follow from the demands of politically important groups. Whatever their origin, however, once these functions exist and produce benefits, their beneficiaries may develop an interest in them and even establish interest groups to defend them.

Figure 1.5 shows spending by the U.S. government on state welfare and criminal justice. Notice how cash assistance to the poor has declined while criminal justice spending has increased. Given that the poor are disproportionately likely to be minorities, this means government funding has decreased for poor minorities. Welfare reform laws and welfare-to-work programs are also aimed primarily at minorities, even though most people on welfare are not minority group members (Tonry, 1995). Tonry claims that such welfare reform laws are not likely to be effective in communities where African American males are absent (p. 6). And, as I will show in Chapter Five, criminal justice efforts disproportionately affect minority males and their communities. Tonry writes: "Poor minority communities cannot prosper when so many of their

FIGURE 1.5

Spending by the U.S. Government on State Welfare and Criminal Justice

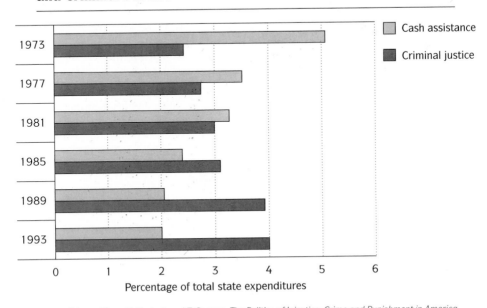

SOURCE: Adapted from K. Beckett and T. Sasson, *The Politics of Injustice: Crime and Punishment in America* (Thousand Oaks, CA: Pine Forge Press, 2000), p. 63.

> *O*ver the past couple of decades, cash assistance to the poor has declined while criminal justice spending has increased.

young men are prevented from settling into long-term personal relationships, getting or keeping jobs, and living conventional lives" (p. vii). Ironically, criminal justice policy has created these outcomes. And government policies of the 1980s "openly and successfully fought to reduce federal funding for social, educational, and housing programs and for aid to cities . . . promoted a strategy of federal disinvestment in the inner cities, which accelerated their deterioration and diminished the scope and quality of urban public services" (p. 40).

Is it possible that the criminal justice system serves functions vital to preserving the status quo in the United States, even though these functions are not intended? And if this is so, why don't those with relatively less power rise up and demand change? Reiman explains that they simply do not have the power or the will to do so. Another reason may be that criminal justice is less a system of justice than it is a system of politics.

THE ROLE OF POLITICS AND POWER IN CRIMINAL JUSTICE

What Is Politics?

Politics is about who gets what economic benefits in society, when they get them, and how they get them (Lasswell, 1936). It is concerned with deciding who gets to keep most of the income generated in the United States, and how that income will be used (Harrigan, 2000). Politics is also about allocating society's values (Easton, 1953), at least for those who have the ability to have their values enacted into law. Then, resources are allocated for purposes of legitimating these values through government authority. One mechanism to achieve this is criminal justice.

> *P*olitics is about who gets what economic benefits in society, when they get them, and how they get them. Politics dictates who gets to keep most of the income generated in the United States, and how that income will be used. It is also about allocating society's values.

How Are Politics and Criminal Justice Related?

Politics and criminal justice are intimately linked and inseparable. Because of the close tie between politics and criminal justice, it may be easier to understand how some interests get served while others are ignored or even harmed. For example, those with political power, or "the ability of individuals or groups to influence government as it allocates a society's resources" (Harrigan, 2000: 25), are more likely to have their interests served at the expense of others.

Although criminal justice policy development is affected by groups other than lawmakers, including the media, voters, lobbying groups, and other special interests (see Chapter Two), politicians play the largest role in setting the crime control agenda. This is because of their power. Power comes in various forms (e.g., political, economic, moral), and is "the ability to have a say, or to have influence, in what the government's policies are going to be" (Marion, 1995: 4, citing Lowi and Ginsberg, 1990). Because politicians create policies of criminal justice, they have power to determine the path of our nation's efforts to control and prevent crime. The U.S. Congress, for example, has the power to define crimes, create criminal justice agencies, provide or withhold funding from criminal justice programs (Steel and Steger, 1988), and act as a public forum for public debate (Marion, 1995:15).

> $\mathcal{P}$olitics is involved in criminal justice in numerous ways—most significantly, in deciding which behaviors should be considered "crimes." Crime is defined through a political process by a very small group of people in the United States (lawmakers or legislators).

Politics is involved in criminal justice in numerous ways. The most significant way is in deciding which behaviors should and should not be considered "crime." Crime is defined through a political process by a very small group of people in the United States (lawmakers or legislators) who, ideally, are representatives of the people. Richard Quinney's (1970) concept of the "social reality of crime" demonstrates that crime is imaginary rather than real; that is, it is invented by human beings with the power to do so (see Chapter Three). Therefore, all criminal justice policies that emanate from the criminal law are "merely definitions developed by people (authorities) who possess the power to shape, enforce, and administer such policies" (Arrigo, 1999: 6). Crime and criminal justice practices are thus efforts by the powerful to control others and maintain power.

Kappeler et al. (2000), in *The Mythology of Crime and Criminal Justice*, argue that since crime is defined in a political process, crime issues and criminal justice policy decisions will be affected by the same factors that influence all political issues. These factors include partisanship (e.g., Democrats fighting Republicans), symbolic crusading (e.g., by moral entrepreneurs, claims-makers, the media, and others with vested interests in bringing crime problems to the public's attention). What may get lost in the shuffle are key truths about crime and criminal justice.

A recent example of criminal justice policy illustrates how politics affects criminal justice processes. In September 1994, President Bill Clinton signed a $30 billion crime bill (the Violent Crime Control and Law Enforcement Act). Its stated purpose was "to prevent crime, punish criminals, and restore a sense of safety and security to the American people" (as quoted in Gaines et al., 2000: 25). This law allowed for the hiring of 100,000 new police for the streets and the construction of thousands of new prison cells, changes that would supposedly make it easier to catch suspected criminals and provide living spaces for those who were ultimately convicted of criminal offenses. Additionally, the death penalty was expanded to cover dozens of additional murders, and some styles of assault weapons were banned. Numerous provisions were established that made it easier to convict defendants more quickly and to carry out their punishment in a less costly manner (Beckett and Sasson, 2000: 72). Finally, limited funding was generated for crime prevention programs (Masci, 1994a, 1994b), but this was ultimately cut by 1996 legislation (Beckett and Sasson, 2000: 73).

Were any of the components of this new crime bill going to actually reduce crime rates in the United States? Reiman (1998: 2) writes: "No one can deny that if you lock enough people up, and allow the police greater and greater power to interfere with the liberty and privacy of citizens, you will eventually prevent some crime that might otherwise have taken place." Yet, it was highly unlikely that such criminal justice policy would produce large declines in crime, given that crime rates are driven by factors beyond the control of the criminal justice system, such as employment rates, poverty rates, and the age of the population (see Chapter Three).

Here's one example of how ineffective this crime bill will likely be: Imagine the promise of 100,000 new police on the street. Assuming that we ever achieve this goal, keep in mind that there will never actually be 100,000 more police on the streets *at one time*. It takes at least five additional officers to provide one additional officer on the street around the clock because of varied shifts, vacations, illnesses, and so forth (Bayley, 1993). This means that if an additional 100,000 new police officers were hired, only 20,000 additional officers around the clock would be on the streets. If these officers were hired equally to police the 50 states, each state would gain only 400 additional officers. How many would this mean for your town or city? It is pretty clear that 20,000 additional "around the clock" officers will not prevent much crime. Further, evidence suggests that much of the federal money allocated to police departments through block grants has really been used to increase technological capabilities of police departments instead of hiring new officers.

So what was this legislation really intended to do? As noted by Marion (1995:1): this "legislation was merely a symbolic gesture to increase politicians' popularity in the months before the upcoming mid-term elections." Politicians did not want to be seen by the public or portrayed by their opponents as "soft on crime." Since the 1960s, being "tough on crime" has been a necessary criterion for being a politician (Rosch, 1985). Whether this approach is effective is not discussed because in politics it is not relevant. How this approach interferes with your individual rights is virtually ignored.

The following box contains statements made by politicians of the 1990s. These comments are not casual, off-the-cuff remarks. Instead, they reflect behind-the-scenes, carefully planned strategies (especially the advertisements) by some politicians to grab power and hold it, something that is not highly informed by, or beneficial to, the electorate.

Recent comments by politicians about crime

- Texas Senator Phil Gramm said on television that he wanted a "real crime bill" that "grabs violent criminals by the throat, puts them in prison, and that stops building prisons like Holiday Inns."
- North Carolina congressional candidate Frederick Heineman proposed that the North American Free Trade Agreement (NAFTA) be used to send U.S. criminals to Mexico so that they could be "warehoused more cheaply" (in Beckett and Sasson, 2000: 72).
- President George W. Bush, who was formerly governor of Texas, attacked the previous Texas governor, Ann Richards, for being soft on crime, even though she supported the death penalty, increased state incarcerations, and reduced early release of violent offenders. Bush ran a political advertisement that was staged to look like footage of a real criminal attack of a man abducting a woman at gunpoint ("the people in the ad were the sound man and makeup artist of a production company") (Donziger, 1996: 7). Then a police officer was shown covering a dead body with a blanket. The point of the ad was to criticize Richards for releasing 7,700 offenders before their scheduled release dates.

- Florida governor Jeb Bush (brother of President George W. Bush), while campaigning for office, ran a political ad on television showing a woman who blamed his opponent, Governor Lawton Chiles, for failing to execute the killer of her daughter. The woman is shown speaking to the camera, saying: "Her killer is still on death row, and we're still waiting for justice. We don't get it from Lawton Chiles because he's too liberal on crime." The truth is that Chiles could not put the man to death because legal issues were still being heard in court. Chiles also had executed as many criminals as his Republican predecessor, who was supposedly tougher on crime (in Donziger, 1996: 80–81).
- Bill McCullom, U.S. representative from Florida, talking to a radio reporter about juvenile delinquents, said: "They're not children anymore. They're the most violent criminals on the face of the earth" (in Krajicek, 1998: 205).
- Ernest Fletcher, candidate for a Kentucky legislative seat, ran a television ad featuring a young, blond woman named Jessica, who said:

> It was the worst day of my life. My attacker was convicted and got six months in jail. Ernesto Scorscone [Fletcher's political opponent] was his lawyer. He must have thought six months was too harsh. Because twice Scorscone appealed just to get the case thrown out or the sentences reduced. Now Scorscone's telling us he's tough on crime. But he's not being honest with you. Everyone deserves a defense. But to me, Scorscone is more concerned with criminals' rights than victims' rights.

The words "Raped," "Shot Twice," and "Left for Dead" appeared on the television screen while Jessica was speaking because Jessica had been abducted, raped, and shot by her attacker. What Fletcher did not tell viewers was that the case had happened two decades before the election, that Scorscone was a public defender who had been appointed to the case by the court, that the law at the time only allowed a maximum sentence of four years given that the accused was a juvenile, and that the appeals were filed because of evidence suggesting that the accused might in fact be innocent (in Kappeler et al., 2000: 46–47).

The authors of the National Criminal Justice Commission's report, *The Real War on Crime*, describe such efforts by U.S. politicians to deal with crime as a "hoax": "Politicians at every level—federal, state, and local—have measured our obsession, capitalized on our fears, campaigned on 'get tough' platforms, and won" (Donziger, 1996: 2). The gist of the argument by the National Criminal Justice Commission is that the war on crime, though a victory for politicians and other limited interests, has mostly been a failure for Americans.

How Did Criminal Justice Become So Political?

If this is true, how did we as a nation get to such a point? Numerous scholars have illustrated how crime originally became a significant political issue in the United States (e.g., see Cronin, Cronin, and Milakovich, 1981; Marion, 1995; Scheingold, 1984; Wilson, 1975). Most attribute the politicization of crime at the national level to charges made by Republican senator Barry Goldwater, who ran for president in 1964 against Democratic president Lyndon Johnson. Goldwater blamed Johnson for rising crime rates and characterized the president as "soft on crime" (Rosch, 1985). One statement by Goldwater illustrates his beliefs clearly:

> History shows us that nothing prepares the way for tyranny more than the failure of public officials to keep the streets safe from bullies and marauders. We Republicans seek a government that attends to its fiscal climate, encourage a free and a competitive economy and enforcing law and order. (Quoted in Beckett, 1997: 31)

Goldwater also attacked public assistance programs by linking them to crime:

> If it is entirely proper for the government to take away from some to give to others, then won't some be led to believe that they can rightfully take from anyone who has more than they? No wonder law and order has broken down, mob violence has engulfed great American cities, and our wives feel unsafe in the streets. (Quoted in Beckett, 1997: 35)

This type of "tough" stance on crime was typical in the 1964 campaign.

Other events of the 1960s helped to make crime and criminal justice national concerns. For example, Beckett (1997: 28) claims that "the discourse of law and order was initially mobilized by southern officials in their effort to discredit the civil rights movement." Clearly, southern agencies of criminal justice, in particular law enforcement agencies, characterized and fought civil rights activities as acts of crime rather than as struggles for civil rights. Peaceful protests, sit-ins, marches, and similar methods of civil disobedience were characterized as evidence of a disrespect for law and order rather than as struggles for basic human rights. This characterization permitted and even mandated government intervention against civil rights leaders and led to the characterization of Martin Luther King, Jr., as the most dangerous man in America. A statement from former Republican vice president Richard Nixon claimed that "the deterioration of respect for the rule of law can be traced directly to the spread of the corrosive doctrine that every citizen possesses an inherent right to decide for himself which laws to obey and when to disobey them" (in Beckett and Sasson, 2000: 50). Some claim that, even today, *crime* is a code word for race, because it refers "indirectly to racial themes but do[es] not directly challenge popular democratic or egalitarian ideals" (Omi, 1987: 120; also see Edsall and Edsall, 1991).

Since the 1960s, crime has been a national issue that has been used for political gain (and loss) in each presidential election and also in hundreds of elections at other levels of government (for

---

*S*ince the 1960s, crime has been a national issue exploited for political gain (and loss) in each presidential election and also in hundreds of elections at other levels of government.

---

an excellent summary of crime in presidential campaigns, see Marion, 1995). The National Criminal Justice Commission claims: "Since 1968, six major anti-crime bills have passed Congress and been signed into law by presidents. In one way or another, all of these bills have been used by elected officials to convince the public that Washington was getting 'tough' on crime by increasing sentences for certain types of offenses" (Donziger, 1996: 13). The 1994 crime bill described earlier is no exception.

The federal government seems perfectly willing to continue controlling criminal justice policy. It ensures its control over state efforts to reduce crime by promising billions of dollars to states that follow its lead—for example, by allocating prison funds to states that require offenders to serve at least 85% of their sentences and by encouraging states to try juveniles as adults (Donziger, 1996). States agree to engage in such criminal justice practices so that they will not lose resources from the federal government. Hence, criminal justice policy at the state level flows less from its potential efficacy than from the states' financial concerns. The politicization of crime at the national level has created this paradox.

Crime and Politics Today

However crime first became such a political issue, it is clear that in today's heated political environment, even local, city-level elections sometimes deteriorate into political rhetoric about being "tough on crime." For example, in a mayoral election in Tallahassee, Florida, the incumbent charged his opponent with being soft on crime because he advocated replacing DARE (Drug Abuse Resistance Education) in schools with alternative strategies. Even though the opponent provided evidence of DARE's ineffectiveness (e.g., see Rosenbaum and Hanson, 1998) and had the support of the local police chief on the issue, the incumbent was successfully reelected as a man of "good common sense."

The most notable use of a crime as a political issue was seen in the "Willie Horton" charges made against Democratic presidential hopeful Michael Dukakis by future Republican president George Bush in 1988. As governor of Massachusetts, Dukakis had supported early release programs from prison as a means to reduce prison overcrowding and as a low-risk way to reintegrate offenders into the community through meaningful employment. An inmate from Massachusetts named Willie Horton, on his ninth furlough from prison, committed a brutal rape and assault. This incident led Bush to attack Dukakis as "soft on crime"; Bush assured citizens that if he was elected president, he would continue to expand criminal justice powers to fight crime. Even though the "Horton case was atypical and exaggerated," it worked: Bush was successfully elected president of the United States (Merlo and Benekos, 2000: 14). Merlo and Benekos claim that the Willie Horton incident taught all politicians some important lessons about winning and losing:

- Don't be portrayed as being "soft on crime";
- Portray your opponent as "soft on crime";
- Simplify the crime issue; and
- Reinforce messages with emotional context. (pp. 14–16)

In each election since then, it has been hard to tell Republicans apart from Democrats on crime control issues, because both have supported more police, more power for prosecutors, more prisons, more money for the war on drugs, more executions, limiting appeals for death row inmates, and so forth.

In the 1980s, Republican presidents Ronald Reagan and George Bush wanted a faster-moving, tougher criminal justice system and helped shift the perception of the causes of crime from society to the individual. A Reagan statement illustrates his party's stance on crime control: "Government's function is to protect society from the criminal, not the other way around" (in

Beckett, 1997: 48). Under Democratic president Bill Clinton in the 1990s, the focus was much the same, including more police on the streets and tougher sentences for convicted criminals. Clinton's 1994 crime bill, discussed earlier, allocated $8.8 billion for hiring more police and $7.9 billion in state prison grants. In the 1980s and 1990s, significant increases occurred in incarceration rates, and now both parties sell being "tough" on crime to the masses (Merlo and Benekos, 2000),

Kappeler et al. (1996: 49) argue:

> Exaggerating and distorting the amount and shape of the crime threat is standard fare for politicians. Democrats and Republicans compete to see who can spend the most money and appear the most punitive in putting together crime control legislation. . . . It is not scientific proof which persuades, it is appeal to fear about serial killers, stalkers, drive-by-shootings, carjackings, and violent predators. Supporting such measures will no doubt curry favor with the voting public; telling the truth could lead to premature retirement.

Nevertheless, proposing shortsighted and simplistic criminal justice policies not only is misleading to consumers and voters, it tends to "conceal what is really at stake" with crime-related issues (Marion, 1995: 94, citing Scheingold, 1984).

The complex causes of criminal behavior are almost never discussed by politicians, at least in public. Citizens and voters allow this because they have little accurate understanding of the nature of crime and crime trends and because they place their trust in legislators to study such issues carefully. As a result, criminal justice policies that may not work and even those that have been proved ineffective are virtually never criticized from within the system.

CONCLUSION

The U.S. criminal justice system, made up of police, courts, and corrections, ideally aims to do justice and reduce crime. There are at least two conflicting meanings of justice, one concerned mostly with holding the guilty accountable for their crimes and the other with ensuring fairness in the criminal justice process. American criminal justice has, over the past few decades, prioritized its crime control concerns over its due process concerns. The result has been an erosion of U.S. Constitutional protections, with little benefit in terms of crime reduction. Instead of doing justice, the U.S. criminal justice system may serve other functions, including serving limited interests and controlling certain segments of the population. It is clear that criminal justice does not exist or occur in a vacuum. Our efforts to do justice and to reduce crime are driven by political factors even more than by actual crime rates, evidence of criminal justice failure, or concerns over eroding Constitutional protections. This in itself may be perceived as unjust by U.S. citizens and taxpayers, who should be able to expect more from their leaders than playing politics about crime and criminal justice, especially when so much is at stake.

ISSUE IN DEPTH
Justitia—The Lady Justice

The lady justice who appears on the cover of this book, peeking out from beneath a blindfold, has a name. This figure, named "Justitia" after the Roman goddess of justice, may have its origins in the Greek mythological goddess Themis, who is considered the goddess of divine justice (Hansen, 1999). Justitia has also appeared in Christian imagery "as a personification of the ancient virtue" of justice (Curtis and Resnick, 1987: 1729).

Justitia has outlasted symbols of every other virtue of humankind. As Curtis and Resnick (1987: 1733) write, "show us a hulking woman with scales, blindfold, and sword, and the association is immediate: Justice."

What is the significance of the symbol of lady justice?

The most common understanding of this symbol today is that the figure of "a blindfolded woman with a scale in one hand and a sword in the other" demonstrates that we are dedicated to treating all Americans with "fairness, equity" and in a manner that is right (Kappeler et al., 2000: 215). Such a figure implies that the imposition of justice will not be affected by demographic characteristics such as race, social class, or gender.

In essence, according to the myth of Justitia, everyone deserves equal justice: "Justitia is blindfolded so that she may be impartial" (Curtis and Resnick, 1987: 1727). Hansen (1999: 1) explains that she is a symbol of "the fair and equal administration of the law, without corruption, avarice, prejudice, or favor."

What follows is a summary of six main points about the lady justice made by Dennis Curtis and Judith Resnick (1987), published in the *Yale Law Journal*. Consider these points when deciding for yourself what "justice blind" is supposed to mean.

- Justitia is not always depicted as blind.

At many times in history, Justitia wears no blindfold but simply stares forward. In other depictions, her eyes can be seen beneath or through wide spaces in a blindfold, or she is depicted peeking out, as she does in the image on the book cover. It is claimed that the appearance of Justitia's blindfold "coincided with the establishment of professional, independent judges, who stood apart from the sovereign and were not simply acting at its behest" (p. 1757). Thus, the blindfold signified that justice was to be carried out neither in the interests of the powerful nor in fear of the powerful. An alternative conception of the blindfold is discussed later.

- Justitia typically carries scales.

The meaning of her scales may be traced back to the Egyptian Book of the Dead (c. 1400 B.C.), the Old Testament (Job 31:6), and to weighing as a symbol of judgment in the Koran. Clearly, scales imply some type of weighing, although there is disagreement about what is to be weighed. The most commonly accepted meaning of the scales is that "each man receives that which is due him, no more and no less" (p. 1749).

- Justitia also is commonly depicted holding a sword.

The significance of the sword, like that of the blindfold, is not clear. Most agree, however, that the sword is a symbol of the power of Justitia to condemn or punish those who "fail in their public duties" (p. 1744). It "represents the rigor of justice, which does not hesitate to punish" (p. 1749).

- Justitia has been depicted with other ambiguous items, including a cornucopia, a fasces (bundle of rods), a scepter, books, a human skull, an ostrich or a crane, and a dog and snake.

The meaning of these symbols is not clear. Some claim that they have positive meanings while others suggest negative meanings. For example, is the ostrich a symbol of gluttony (an ostrich will eat anything before it) or of valor and endurance (its diet might even include metal)? An ostrich puts its head in the sand. Is this an indication of forgetfulness or of stupidity? Or is the ostrich another symbol of impartiality, because its feathers are so evenly distributed across its body? (p. 1742). Most illustrations of Justitia do not contain such items, but when they are included, no one can be certain of their significance.

- Justitia may create a false impression of what justice is.

The more negative images of Justitia have been relegated to archives, while the more common images—Justitia in white robes, with the blindfold, scales, and sword—adorn courthouses and other government buildings in the United States. Many of us have never become aware of some of the more grotesque images of Justitia, or they have disappeared from our consciousness. For example, Justitia has been depicted without hands, which may suggest that she will avoid accepting bribes or punishing the guilty too brutally (p. 1754). Other images of Justitia surrounded by severed human heads are also generally unrecognizable. It is possible that our current conception of justice is thus sanitized so that only positive images come to mind in the presence of Justitia.

An alternative view of Justitia is possible: "Sword and scales need not only remind us that Justice can be powerful and correct; they can also be interpreted as indications of Justice as harsh, unsympathetic, and unyielding." The blindfold may be interpreted as an indication that justice is blind—to abuses that occur right under her nose. It may thus suggest "a failure to see the truth" (p. 1756). Perhaps the blindfold symbolizes Justitia's limitations or is even a censure for past faults. Or "is she blindfolded not to see the many injuries imposed in her name?" (p. 1757).

For these reasons, Gottfredson (1999: 21) argues that the blindfold should be removed from figures showing Justitia. He writes: "Much of the criticism of the criminal justice system concerns a perceived lack of fairness and evenhanded-ness in decisions about accused and convicted offenders. The blindfold makes a good point, but it should be removed." Gottfredson suggests that, with "eyes open," Justitia will be able to ensure that American justice will be fair, ethically sound, and more effective.

- Justitia is a symbol used by the powerful to justify their actions in the name of "justice."

For example, when a person is convicted of a crime by a jury of his or her peers, the government is granted the right to punish the person: "The imposition of judgment, with its requisite violence, is an essential, inevitable aspect of gover-nance. How convenient, how distancing from human subjectivity and fallibility, if such decisions go forth in the name of Justice" (Curtis and Resnick, 1987: 1748).

No other cardinal or theological virtue is essential to the acts of lawmakers and law enforcers in exacting justice: "All sovereigns claim (notwithstanding evidence to the contrary) that their violence goes forth in the name of Justice." Clearly, humankind is fallible—we make mistakes. In the name of justice and its implied partiality, governments have used and will continue to use force against their citizens, to restrict their citizens' liberty, and even to execute their citizens (p. 1734). The "conscious use of justice imagery by governments" may be an effort by them to "legitimate their exercises of power by associating them-selves with the concept of justice" (p. 1743). In some ways, Justitia is "propa-ganda" to reassure Americans that actions of the government are in line with a "higher right" (p. 1746).

Images of justice may "teach, inspire, pacify, or otherwise influence viewers" (p. 1743). In the United States, Justitia suggests to young people that this is a fair country. It inspires us as a symbol of dedication against vices and injustices. It can pacify us, as well, for in the presence of Justitia, we may assume that our government is just even in the face of evidence suggesting that it is not. We may tend to ignore conspicuous injustices, perhaps because we are forced to accept the judgments of powerful people in the name of justice (p. 1767).

Whatever Justitia is really intended to mean, I concur with Dennis Curtis and Judith Resnick (1987: 1764) when they write, "our hopes that justice . . . simultaneously be attuned to individual nuances and be evenhanded; that objectivity and subjectivity both be present; that justice know all that is needed but not know that which might corrupt or unfairly influence; that justice be rig-orous in its equality yet 'now and then' relax in compassion."

This book assumes that American criminal justice should be blind to factors such as race, gen-der, and social class; thus, the cover of the book is adorned by a blindfolded lady justice. She is peeking out, suggesting that perhaps American justice is not blind. Throughout the book, I exam-ine how well the U.S. criminal justice system achieves its goals of doing justice and reducing crime. The main concern is, "how *just* is American criminal justice?" That is, "Is justice really blind?"

Discussion Questions

- What is the "criminal justice system"?
- What are the three main components or parts of the criminal justice system?
- List some of the reasons that some claim that *system* is not an accurate term for the operations of the criminal justice system.
- Outline the main stages of the criminal justice system; that is, explain how a case proceeds from commission of a crime all the way to release from corrections.
- What are the ideal goals of the American criminal justice system?
- What is "justice"? Compare *corrective justice* (justice as an outcome) and *procedural justice* (justice as a process).
- Compare the ideal models of justice described by Herbert Packer: the due process and crime control models.
- Which ideal model of criminal justice does American criminal justice more closely resemble? Why?
- What are the differences between crime control and crime prevention?
- What types of activities of police, courts, and corrections are aimed at preventing crime?
- Which component of the criminal justice system has the most resources? Why?
- Which component of the criminal justice system employs the most people? Why?
- Identify the two alternative goals of the criminal justice system discussed in the chapter. Do you think that the criminal justice system intentionally sets out to achieve these goals? Why or why not?
- Discuss how the criminal justice system serves functions beneficial to limited interests in the United States.
- Explain the ways in which politics plays a role in criminal justice operations.
- What does the symbol of the Lady Justice mean?

CHAPTER TWO

THE LAW: PROVIDING EQUAL PROTECTION OR CREATING BIAS?

KEY CONCEPTS

- What is the law?
- Where does the law come from?
- Types of law
- What is the purpose of the criminal law?
- Who makes the law?
- Issue in Depth: American Business—Downsizing for Profit

INTRODUCTION

This chapter begins with a definition of law and a discussion of where the law comes from. Distinctions are made between natural law, or law dictated by a higher source, and positive law, or law made by sovereign human beings. Different types of positive law are discussed, including Constitutional law, statutory law, case law, and administrative law. I also demonstrate the primary differences between the criminal law, which defines acts as crimes against the government, and civil law, which regulates torts or acts against individuals. This chapter also outlines the purposes of the criminal law. A vital part of this chapter is a detailed exploration of who makes the law. To illustrate that the criminal law may not represent all Americans, I examine demographic characteristics of lawmakers and voters and illustrate how rare voting is in the United States. I show how special interests shape the criminal law through lobbying and financial donations to campaigns and elections. From this investigation, it seems likely that the U.S. criminal justice system is biased in the favor of the wealthy and powerful.

WHAT IS THE LAW?

Have you ever wondered how certain acts became criminal? For example, how did killing another person become the crime of murder? Has killing always been illegal? The answer is no. Even today, there are several ways of killing someone that still would not be considered crimes. These include killing someone in self-defense, killing someone in the line of duty as a police officer or military soldier, and execution of someone by the state through the administration of the death penalty. Each of these means of killing is legal.

Why is it that some forms of killing are legal while other forms of killing are called "crimes"? Apparently, some forms of killing do not warrant the status of "crime." A behavior becomes a crime only when it is labeled a crime through the passage of a law. It is as simple as that. Rush (2000: 193) defines the law as "A general rule for the conduct of members of the community, either emanating from the governing authority by positive demand or approved by it, and habitually enforced by some public authority by the imposition of sanctions of penalties for its violation." Gilmer (1986: 194) defines the law as "a method for the resolution of disputes; A rule or action to which people obligate themselves to conform, via their elected representatives and other officials." From these two definitions, you can see that if lawmakers do not view an act as wrong, immoral, unethical, or harmful, the behavior will not be called a crime.

> $\mathcal{A}$ behavior becomes a crime only when it is labeled a crime through the passage of a law.

Thus, crimes are created when elected representatives decide to codify, or write down, behaviors as wrong, immoral, unethical, or harmful (Schmalleger, 1999). As you will see in Chapter Three, a crime occurs when a person either acts, fails to act, attempts to act, or agrees to act *in a way that is in violation of the criminal law,* without defense or justification. Because the law is what makes an act a crime, two important deductions can be made with regard to crime:

> $\mathcal{C}$rimes are created when elected representatives decide to codify behaviors as wrong, immoral, unethical, or harmful.

- No behavior is automatically a crime unless it is defined by the government as a crime.
- Any behavior can be made a crime.

With regard to the first point, many criminal justice scholars claim a distinction between *mala in se* crimes, those acts that are inherently evil or bad, and *mala prohibita* crimes, those acts that are evil or bad only because the government has labeled them criminal (Schmalleger, 1999). This is really an artificial distinction, because no behavior is inherently wrong. It only becomes wrong when the government says that it is wrong. This is why there is *no behavior* that has been considered wrong in every society at all times in history. In numerous places, in fact, rape is *still* not illegal despite its atrocious nature. Some states in the United States still do not consider it rape when a man is forced into sex. Others still do not call it rape when a husband forces his wife into unwanted sexual activity.

> *No* behavior is automatically a crime unless it is defined by the government as a crime, and any behavior can be made a crime.

Sheryl Lindsell-Roberts (1994) demonstrates the second point in her amusing book, *Loony Laws and Silly Statutes*. In my state, North Carolina, for example, it is a crime for a man to talk to a woman who is attending an all-women's college while she is on campus. It is also a crime in North Carolina to take a deer swimming in water above its knees! In Florida, where I was born, it is against the law to take a bath with your clothes off. All that time, I was breaking the law! It is also a crime in Florida to doze off under a hair dryer. These types of criminal laws can be found in every state.

Lindsell-Roberts's book provides examples of laws in every state that are unbelievable! The following box contains some examples from her book.

Examples of loony laws and silly statutes

- In Tennessee, it is against the law to drive while sleeping.
- In California, it is a crime for a woman to drive her car in a housecoat.
- In Alabama, it is against the law to drive while barefoot or in bedroom slippers.
- In Florida, it is a crime to transport livestock aboard school buses.
- In Vermont, it is against the law to jump from a plane unless it is a true emergency.
- In Maine, it is a crime to walk down the sidewalk with your shoelaces untied.
- In Canada, it is against the law to board a plane after it has already taken off.
- In Florida, it is a crime to go underneath a sidewalk.
- In Washington, it is against the law to pretend that your parents are rich.
- In Kentucky, it's a crime to use a reptile as part of a religious service.
- In Massachusetts, it is against the law to eat peanuts while in church.
- In New Jersey, it is a crime to slurp soup.
- In Indiana, it is against the law to shoot open a can of soup.
- In Rhode Island, it is a crime to throw pickle juice on a trolley.
- In Tennessee, it is against the law to throw a banana peel on the sidewalk.
- In Ohio, it is a crime to hunt or shoot on Sundays.
- In Wyoming, it is against the law to obstruct the view of fellow spectators by wearing a hat in a public theater.
- In Kansas, it is a crime to eat rattlesnake meat in public.
- In Minnesota, it is against the law to dance in public places.
- In Kentucky, it is a crime to remarry the same man four times.
- In Colorado, it is against the law to throw shoes at a wedding.
- In Missouri, it is a crime to carry a bear down the highway unless it is caged.
- In Washington, it is against the law to punch a bull in the nose.
- In Texas, it is against the law to milk someone else's cow.

- In Ohio, it is a crime to fish with explosives.
- In Indiana, it is against the law to take a bath during the winter.
- In Connecticut, it is a crime to chew tobacco without a doctor's permission.
- In Louisiana, it is against the law to gargle while in public.
- In Oregon, it is a crime to force a dead person to serve on a jury.

You may be wondering how such acts can be crimes. It is likely that at some time in history, these acts were considered problematic, probably because some people actually engaged in these acts and some type of harm resulted. Every state has such loony laws and silly statutes on the books, even though they are not likely being enforced widely (if at all). When these laws are not enforced, do they need to be removed from the books?

Source: Adapted from Sheryl Lindsell-Roberts, *Loony Laws and Silly Statutes* (New York: Sterling, 1994).

WHERE DOES THE LAW COME FROM?

Acts are defined as crimes by human beings. Specifically, crimes are created by the U.S. Congress at the federal level, by legislatures at the state level, and by courts at every level of government when they interpret the law and set precedents through case law (Schmalleger, 1999). The Congress at the federal level and all state legislatures have the power to define behaviors as crimes. For example, at both levels of government, it is against the law to steal a car forcibly from another person; this is often called "carjacking." Rush (2000: 44) defines *carjacking* as "The unauthorized seizure of a vehicle by the use of force, threats, or coercion." According to Rush, federal law mandates a 15-year sentence for carjacking and a life sentence if a person is killed during the offense. In Louisiana, it is currently legal for a person to use lethal force against another if the person believes he or she is being carjacked.

> *C*rimes are created by the U.S. Congress at the federal level, by legislatures at the state level, and by courts at each level of government when they interpret the law and set precedents through case law.

Courts interpret the meaning of the written law and, in so doing, actually clarify what the written law means. For example, if a man forced a driver out of his or her car so that he could take his pregnant wife to the hospital during labor, would that be considered carjacking? A court would likely have to decide this issue, and in essence, would be making law by setting a precedent that all other courts in the same jurisdiction would be required to follow (see Chapter Eight). If a court heard a case in which a man was charged with carjacking under these circumstances and decided that such an act did *not* meet the definition of the crime in the statute (because the man did not intend to steal the car and thus did not intend to commit a carjacking), it would not be considered carjacking for human beings to engage in this behavior.

But where do we human beings get our law? Where did we get the notion that laws needed to be written down? The criminal law sets forth boundaries for acceptable behavior to ensure that we know what behaviors are wrong and what can happen to us if we commit wrongful acts. But where did the notions of right and wrong come from? An examination of different types of American law might answer these questions.

TYPES OF LAW

There are many types of law in the United States. Figure 2.1 depicts the main types of law and illustrates the relationships between them.

Natural Law

One type of law, known as natural law, is law from a higher source. If you are religious, this might be God's law—for example, the Ten Commandments delivered to Moses as explained in the Holy Bible. Natural law could also be considered "laws of the gods" (in polytheistic cultures). But natural law also exists for nonreligious people. Natural law might be the laws of "the force," for example, or laws of human nature. Natural law, whatever your beliefs about religion, is a recognition that there are wrong behaviors that are simply bad in themselves—often referred to as *mala in se* offenses. Other acts are inherently right, good, or just. Natural law in essence is greater than humankind—it was here before we got here and will be here after we depart. Schmalleger (1999: 16) defines natural law as those laws that "are fundamental to human nature and discoverable by human reason, intuition, or inspiration, without the need for reference to man-made laws."

> *N*atural law is a recognition that there are wrong behaviors that are simply bad in themselves, often referred to as *mala in se* offenses.

The main problem with natural law is that no one can possibly know what it is. If there are universal truths, behaviors that are inherently good and bad, how can we know what they are? For example, if God has his or her own idea about what is right and wrong, how can we know unless

FIGURE 2.1
Types of Law

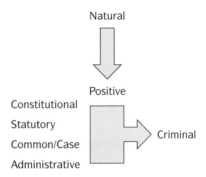

he or she comes down from Heaven and tells us? Since we cannot experience God directly with our empirical senses—that is, we cannot see, hear, or touch God—it is logically impossible to know God's laws.

Even if we rely on the Holy Bible to learn about natural law, which version do we use? How would we know which version is the correct one? Since religion is a matter of faith rather than evidence, you either believe it or you don't (Bohm, 2001). This makes natural law useless as a source of law for the purpose of informing us about right and wrong and for judging individuals' behaviors as right or wrong. So Americans end up disagreeing about rights and wrongs (even though we all do agree that there are rights and wrongs).

Positive Law

How do we decide whether some behavior should be considered right or wrong? How do we decide which behaviors are so wrong that they should be called crimes? We do this by electing people to make the law for us. Laws made by us—human beings—are referred to as positive law. Positive law consists of laws made by sovereign human beings. Those with the authority to make laws write them, and the rest of us have to abide by them in the face of potential sanctions for violating the law. The relationship between positive law and natural law is that natural law informs positive law. That is, positive law is based on or rooted in natural law. Legislators, on the basis of their conceptions of right and wrong and those of their constituents (natural law), define some acts as wrong by labeling them "crimes" or "torts." A *crime* is an act in violation of the criminal law (see Chapter Three). A *tort* is an act that is harmful against an individual; it is handled in a

---

*P*ositive law consists of laws made by sovereign human beings. Those with the authority to make laws write them, and the rest of us have to abide by them in the face of potential sanctions for law violations.

---

civil court rather than a criminal court. I'll return to the differences between criminal law and civil law later in this chapter. For now, think of this example: ex–football star O. J. Simpson was accused, but found not guilty at trial, of murdering his wife and her male friend. Murder is a behavior that leads to a trial in a criminal court. Later, O. J. Simpson was tried and found liable for the wrongful deaths of Nicole Brown and Ronald Goldman. He was not convicted for the murders of two people (a crime) in criminal court, but he was found responsible or liable for their wrongful deaths (a tort) in civil court.

The advantage of positive law is that it makes the law predictable. Because the law is written down by human beings, other human beings can consult the law and know what types of behaviors are permitted and which are prohibited. This is why "ignorance of the law is no excuse" for breaking it. We also can easily find out what the possible sanctions are for violating the law. If you want to know what is illegal in your state and what can happen to you if you break a particular law, just consult the criminal statute books in any law library in your state, or find the laws of your state on the Internet at www.findlaw.com.

Positive law comes to us from many sources. Positive law includes Constitutional law, statutory law, case law, and administrative law, all of which have been informed by common law (Cole and

Smith, 2000; Schmalleger, 1999). Constitutional law comes to us from the U.S. Constitution and from the constitutions of each of the 50 states. The following box discusses the U.S. Constitution. Constitutional law establishes individual rights for people in the United States, and thus sets forth limitations on government power. Statutory law comes to us from legislatures of the federal government (the U.S. Congress) and each of the 50 states. Statutory law defines crimes and sets forth potential punishments for violations of the written law. Case law is made by courts at the state and federal level when judges interpret statutes and make rulings on individual cases. Case law helps governments and citizens understand what statutes and constitutions mean. Rush (2000: 93) defines administrative law as "Statutes, regulations, and orders that govern public agencies . . . rules governing the administrative operations of the government."

---

*P*ositive law includes Constitutional law, statutory law, case law, and administrative law; all are informed by common law.

The U.S. Constitution

The Constitution of the United States granted numerous rights to individual citizens. For example, the Bill of Rights guarantees individual citizens protection from acts of the federal government, including the following rights:

- Freedom from unreasonable searches and seizures (Fourth Amendment)
- Freedom from arrest or search without probable cause (Fourth Amendment)
- Freedom from self-incrimination (Fifth Amendment)
- Freedom from double jeopardy (Fifth Amendment)
- Freedom from being deprived of life, liberty, or property without due process of law (Fifth Amendment)
- Freedom from cruel and unusual punishment (Eighth Amendment)
- Freedom from excessive bail or fines (Eighth Amendment)
- Right to speedy, public, and fair trial by jury (Sixth Amendment)
- Right to an impartial jury (Sixth Amendment)
- Right to counsel (Sixth Amendment)

The Equal Protection Clause and the Due Process Clause of the Fourteenth Amendment extended these rights to protect citizens from acts of their state government, as well. In essence, no level of American government can deprive its citizens of these rights.

These constitutional protections demonstrate that America's founders wanted to ensure, for all time, that its citizens would enjoy certain individual rights and would be free from such forms of government oppression. Some common sayings of criminal justice reinforce this ideal. Ever hear these?

- "All suspects are innocent until proven guilty."
- "It's better to let guilty men go free than to wrongfully punish innocent ones."

These sayings reflect an inherent belief that rules of criminal procedure are important to Americans. These rules of criminal procedure are referred to as *due process,* also defined as "ensuring that laws are reasonable and that they are applied in a fair and equal manner" (Rush, 2000: 120). No American is to be deprived of his or her life, freedom, or property without due process, because due process is required by the U.S. Constitution. Thus, when any American is subjected to some part of the criminal justice process (e.g., arrest, conviction, punishment) without due process, nothing less important than the U.S. Constitution is threatened.

The primary purpose of the U.S. Supreme Court is to interpret the meaning of individual cases for the Constitution. According to Walker, Spohn, and Delone (2000: 289):

> The Supreme Court consistently has affirmed the importance of protecting criminal suspects' rights. The Court has ruled, for example, that searches without warrants are generally unconstitutional, that confessions cannot be coerced, that suspects must be advised of their rights and provided with attorneys to assist them in their defense, that jurors must be chosen from a representative cross-section of the population, and that the death penalty cannot be administered in an arbitrary and capricious manner.

You might be surprised as you read this book that despite these *ideal* protections, many of these protections are not *really* enjoyed by many Americans.

What was the purpose of the Constitution?

A more critical and perhaps even cynical interpretation of the Constitution suggests that the Constitution was and is biased against certain groups in society. Kappeler, Blumberg, and Potter (2000: 217) write: "The framers of the Constitution may have been engaged in unselfish efforts to construct an impartial rule of law, but women could not vote, and slavery was legal—constraints of the worldview at that time."

Charles Beard, in *An Economic Interpretation of the Constitution of the United States* (1913), discusses how the construction of the Constitution was a process biased against the poor. For example, of the five economic groups that existed in 1787, when the document was drafted in Philadelphia, "the four poorest groups had no representatives at the convention: women, slaves, indentured servants, and propertyless white men" (Harrigan, 2000: 45). Every delegate involved in drafting the Constitution was a white male who owned enough property to be allowed to vote. According to Beard, of the 55 delegates, 38 owned government bonds, 24 earned their living through banking or some other financial investment, 15 owned slaves, and 14 had investments in western lands. Given the makeup of the delegates, was the Constitution drafted at least partly to protect their limited interests?

The construction of the Constitution was a process biased against the poor. For example, of the five economic groups of people in 1787 when the document was drafted in Philadelphia, "the four poorest groups had no representatives at the convention: women, slaves, indentured servants, and propertyless white men" (Harrigan, 2000: 45).

Harrigan (2000: 47) suggests that three different types of provisions were written into the Constitution to protect the limited financial interests of wealthy, white male delegates:

- Those that protected their private property rights
- Those that insulated the national government from popular rule

- Those that minimized the influence of the lower-status population in the ratification process

The protections of private property rights included provisions that benefited businesses engaged in trade and economy, bankers and creditors, slave holders, and holders of securities under the Articles of Confederation. Popular rule was not set up in the Constitution because people did not directly vote for the president, the Court, or the Senate. Only House members were originally elected by the people, and people could vote only if their congressional districts had at least 30,000 people. This benefited the wealthy. Barriers to voting (such as property ownership requirements) were constructed to discourage a large percentage of people from voting. Because of this, Harrigan concludes:

> The lower-status population did indeed have nothing to say about the drafting of the Constitution and (whether by choice or coercion) had little to say about ratifying it. Important provisions in the Constitution protected economic interests that were more valuable to the upper-status population than to the lower-status population (p. 53).

Given such an apparent built-in bias in favor of the wealthy, it may not be hard to imagine that some biases would still be around today. Perhaps they would even have multiplied, expanded into areas such as tax codes and legal codes. If so, we would expect that a mechanism would need to be in place to support and maintain these biases in favor of the wealthy. Is it possible that the criminal justice system is this mechanism?

There is evidence that the American criminal justice system fails to achieve its goals of doing justice and reducing crime. In essence, our system is biased against certain groups in the United States and also fails to appreciably reduce crime. The National Criminal Justice Commission concurs. They demonstrate that the criminal justice system offers little return for the massive investments we have made. For example, although from 1980 to 1993 probation increased 154%, jail admissions increased by 177%, prison admissions increased by 188%, and the number of people on parole increased by 205%, reported Index Crimes did not decline but actually increased by 5%. The more valid National Crime Victimization Survey (NCVS) showed a reduction of only 16% for criminal victimizations during this same time period (Donziger, 1996: 37). That hardly can be called a success.

How can it be that the world's most powerful nation, capable of traveling to other worlds in space and of curing scores of illnesses, remains so blind to our criminal justice failures? One possible, though radical, rationale for our allegiance to failing methods of crime fighting is that our criminal justice system is intended to achieve goals other than doing justice and reducing crime. How likely do you think it is that the criminal justice system actually is intended to control certain segments of the population and to serve limited interests, as suggested in Chapter One?

Common Law

Common law is a term used to describe the legal traditions of England before America was founded (Schmalleger, 1999). Common law consists of the traditions and customs of British judges that were passed down from judge to judge over time. Common law was not written down as strict legal rules but, rather, included "general principles to guide judges" (Gottfredson, 1999: 49). As noted, common law informs each of the types of positive law because American positive law grew out of the traditions and customs of England. Gottfredson explains that English common law informed American law by establishing these principles:

- The supremacy of the law
- The inviolability of person and property
- The local nature of criminal jurisdiction
- Due process of law
- The rule that no one should be compelled in any criminal prosecution to be a witness against himself or herself
- The right to a trial by jury

From these sources of positive law, we get the criminal law, which can be divided into two distinct types: substantive criminal law and procedural criminal law. Substantive law is the "substance" of the law, as it defines which behaviors are illegal and what punishments can follow as a result of breaking the written law (Schmalleger, 1999). The following box provides examples of substantive criminal law in my state, North Carolina.

---

*S*ubstantive law is the "substance" of the law, as it defines which behaviors are illegal and what punishments can follow as a result of breaking the written law.

Some interesting North Carolina laws

All of the following acts are Class 2 or 3 misdemeanors, punishable by maximum punishment of more than 30 days but not more than six months imprisonment for Class 2 misdemeanors, and maximum punishment of 30 days or less imprisonment (or only a fine) for Class 3 misdemeanors:

- § *14-72.3. Stealing a shopping cart:* It is unlawful to remove a shopping cart from the premises of a store without the consent, given at the time of the removal, of the store owner, manager, agent or employee, where "shopping cart" means the type of push cart commonly provided by grocery stores, drugstores, and other retail stores for customers to transport commodities within the store and from the store to their motor vehicles outside the store and "premises" includes the motor vehicle parking area set aside for customers of the store.
- § *14-400. Tattooing; body piercing:* It is unlawful to tattoo the arm, limb, or any part of the body of any other person under 18 years of age.
- § *14-401.17. Unlawfully removing or destroying electronic dog collars:* It is unlawful to intentionally remove or destroy an electronic collar or other electronic device placed on a dog by its owner to maintain control of the dog.
- § *14-113. Obtaining money by false representation of physical defect:* It is unlawful to falsely represent yourself in any manner whatsoever as blind, deaf, dumb, or crippled or otherwise physically defective for the purpose of obtaining money or other thing of value or of making sales of any character of personal property. Any person so falsely representing

himself or herself as blind, deaf, dumb, crippled or otherwise physically defective, and securing aid or assistance on account of such representation, shall be deemed guilty.

- § *14-131. Trespassing on land under option by the federal government:* It is unlawful to, on lands under option which have formally or informally been offered to and accepted by the North Carolina Department of Environment and Natural Resources by the acquiring federal agency and tentatively accepted by said Department for administration as State forests, State parks, State game refuges or for other public purposes, cut, dig, break, injure or remove any timber, lumber, firewood, trees, shrubs or other plants; or any fence, house, barn or other structure; or to pursue, trap, hunt or kill any bird or other wild animals or take fish from streams or lakes within the boundaries of such areas without the written consent of the local official of the United States having charge of the acquisition of such lands.
- § *14-460. Riding on train unlawfully:* It is unlawful to, with the intention of being transported free in violation of law, ride or attempt to ride on top of any car, coach, engine, or tender, on any railroad in this State, or on the drawheads between cars, or under cars, on truss rods, or trucks, or in any freight car, or on a platform of any baggage car, express car, or mail car on any train.

These acts must have been problematic in the state of North Carolina, or they would not likely be considered crimes. Your state has similar laws based on unique problems that its citizens experience. Remember, *any behavior* can be made criminal at any time.

Procedural criminal law puts forth the "procedures" that governments must follow when carrying out the law (Cole and Smith, 2000; Schmalleger, 1999). Procedural criminal law thus establishes limits on the government's power when attempting to apprehend and prosecute suspected criminals. An example of procedural criminal law is found in the Bill of Rights of the U.S. Constitution. Recall that the Bill of Rights lays out protections that all people ideally enjoy if and when they are subjected to criminal justice processes. Ideally, if these rights are somehow violated by police, the courts, or correctional facilities, consequences can include dismissal of charges, the overturning of criminal convictions, and even financial reimbursement to the victim (Peoples, 2000; Stuckey, Robertson, and Wallace, 2001).

> *P*rocedural criminal law puts forth the "procedures" that governments must follow when carrying out the law.

Criminal Law and Civil Law

The criminal law and the civil law are very different. Table 2.1 illustrates these differences. For example, the criminal law is concerned with harmful acts committed against the government. All crimes are technically viewed as acts against the government rather than against individuals. Civil

TABLE 2.1

Criminal versus Civil Law

	CRIMINAL	CIVIL
Participants	State versus individual	Individual versus individual
Possible outcome	Conviction	Liability
	Punishment of offender	Financially compensate victim
Intent required?	Yes	No
Standard of proof	Beyond reasonable doubt	Preponderance of evidence
Rules of evidence	Very stringent	Less stringent

law, however, is concerned with harmful acts committed against individuals. The criminal law leads to trials involving the state or government against an individual—for example, the *State of California v. O. J. Simpson.* The civil law leads to trials where one individual faces another. When you think of the civil law, you may think of popular television shows like *Judge Judy, The People's Court,* or *Judge Joe Brown.* Criminal trials can lead to either a criminal conviction or an acquittal (a finding of not guilty). When an offender is found guilty, he or she can be punished by any of a whole range of potential sanctions (see Chapter Nine). For someone to be convicted, it must be demonstrated beyond reasonable doubt that the offender committed the named act(s) and did so intentionally (on purpose). Civil trials, however, lead to a finding of either liability or no liability. That is, the accused is either held responsible for the act or not. If found to be liable, the accused usually will be required to compensate the victim financially for the harm(s) inflicted. Intent is not required in civil court, and the standard of proof is much lower. In a civil court, the burden of proof is a preponderance of evidence, meaning that a simple majority of the evidence must suggest that the accused is responsible.

---

*C*rimes are technically viewed as acts against the government rather than against individuals. Civil law, however, is concerned with harmful acts committed against individuals.

One final difference between the criminal law and the civil law is that the rules of evidence are much more stringent in the criminal law, meaning that is easier to get evidence admitted into a civil court than a criminal court. You might wonder how it is that a person can be tried twice for the same offense, given the Constitutional right to freedom from double jeopardy. Because the criminal and civil courts have different jurisdictions and are intended for different purposes, being tried in each court does not constitute double jeopardy.

WHAT IS THE PURPOSE OF THE CRIMINAL LAW?

Early political theorists such as Hobbes, Locke, and Rousseau argued that when individuals form a society, they must enter into a "social contract" to surrender some of their individual rights in return for the protection of their personal safety and property. The social contract is codified by making law. In modern Western societies such as the United States, "crimes" are acts against the government rather than against individuals. This definition of *crime* gives the state the right to prosecute wrongdoers and to administer punishment in the name of the actual crime victims. At the same time, individual citizens are forbidden from engaging in "vengeance" or "vigilantism."

For this type of system to work, the government must assure its citizens that their sacrifices are worth it. It does this primarily by providing protection, peace, and order. In other words, the government is responsible for enforcing laws, catching and punishing criminals, and protecting the community from harm (Marion, 1995). These efforts are aimed at crime control, a goal of the criminal justice system discussed in Chapter One. But recall the inherent struggle between achieving the system's goals of crime control and ensuring due process. The law must be "both an engine of government and a brake which restrains government" (Gottfredson, 1999: 47). This means the government can use force to make sure the criminal law is not violated, but not so much force that it interferes with the rights of individual citizens. As I discuss each of the three components of the criminal justice system later in the book, you will see how each attempts to carry out the criminal law without violating individual Constitutional protections.

For the purposes of this chapter, I will focus on the function of the criminal law that is concerned with defining behaviors that are illegal. There are at least two competing interpretations of whose interests are represented when behaviors are defined as illegal. Those who believe in the *consensus* view believe that the law reflects societal interests and that "crimes" therefore are acts that a majority of the population view as immoral, wrong, and harmful. Crimes are thus deviations from the norm. This model is based on the belief that the "law reflects common consciousness and interests of society" (Marion, 1995: 21). According to its proponents, the criminal law "serves as a banner to announce the values of society. It tells us where the boundaries of acceptable behavior lie and links those who violate the boundaries—criminals—with evil, pain, incarceration, and disgrace" (Kappeler et al., 2000: 216).

> *The* consensus view of the law suggests that the law reflects societal interests and that "crimes" therefore are acts that are viewed by a majority of the population as immoral, wrong, and harmful.

Several studies have shown a remarkable level of agreement among citizens about which crimes should be considered most serious. These studies typically reveal a higher level of perceived seriousness for the violent street crimes included in the Uniform Crime Reports (e.g., see Carlson and Williams, 1993; Cohen, 1991; Cullen, Link, and Travis, 1985; Epperlein and Nienstedt, 1989; Gebotys and Dasgupta, 1987; Gebotys, Roberts, and Dasgupta, 1988; Meier and Short, 1985; Miethe, 1982; O'Connell and Whelan, 1996; Parton, Hansel, and Stratton, 1991; Rauma, 1991; Sebba, 1984; Warr, 1991). Some would claim that this is evidence that the criminal law clearly serves the interests of the public. But which came first—public support for the law or the law itself? Isn't it possible that people perceive harmful acts as more or less serious based on their status in the criminal law?

I advocate a different approach to determining crime serious, consistent with scholars such as Friedrichs (1999). This approach would pronounce acts as more or less serious on the basis of the degree of harm the acts cause. That is, more harmful acts would be considered more serious, and less harmful acts would be called less serious. The criminal law does reflect this approach in some ways—for example, murder is more serious than theft. Yet, in many ways, the criminal law does not define the most harmful acts as more serious, providing evidence for proponents of the *conflict* model of the law.

Proponents of the conflict model of the law believe that the law reflects the limited interests of powerful members of society. Thus, "crimes" are not necessarily the most harmful acts; instead, they are acts committed by relatively powerless people (e.g., the poor) (Vold, 1958). Those with political or economic power, and special-interest groups, are likely to have their beliefs reflected in the law, according to those who believe in the conflict model. As Goode and Ben-Yuhuda (1994b: 78) write: "Definitions of right and wrong do not drop from the skies, nor do they simply ineluctably percolate from society's mainstream opinion; they are the result of disagreement, negotiation, conflict, and struggle. The passage of laws raises the issue of who will criminalize whom." Similarly, Akers (1996: 142) writes: "The dominant groups can see to it that their particular definitions of normality or deviance will become enacted as law, ensconced in public policy, and protected by the operation of the criminal justice system."

---

*P*roponents of the conflict model of the law believe that the law reflects limited interests of the powerful members of society, and thus "crimes" are not necessarily the most harmful acts. Instead they are acts committed by relatively powerless people (e.g., the poor).

In the United States, poor people are labeled as troublemakers more than any other group (Gans, 1995: 18-21). Gans writes that the process begins with the *label-makers* (in the case of crime, they are legislators). Legislators define certain acts committed by the poor as crimes and then rely on *alarmists* to spread the word about the dangers of the acts (in the case of crime, they are the media) and on *counters* to supply numbers indicating that the problem is serious or widespread (in the case of crime, they are the police and politicians). So, is the law biased against the poor? If you believe that the government should pass laws to protect us from harms, then you might feel that the law is biased if it only attempts to protect us from harms committed by poor people.

Hobbes argued that government's "sole purpose" was to give citizens the ability to "pursue their natural rights, including the rights to life, to liberty, and to enjoy personal property"—that is, to "provide safety for the citizens" (Marion, 1995: 4–5). To the degree the government does not do this, the government is failing to do its job. I will illustrate in Chapter Three that our government ignores many harmful acts, such as white-collar crime and deviance. To the degree that they ignore these harms, our government is failing to provide us with justice and to protect us from things that kill us, injure us, and take our property. A violation of the law—a crime—is clearly a potential threat to the social order. Many crimes, because of the harms they cause to society, are considered serious and thus warrant criminal justice intervention. However, other crimes are not severe enough to warrant criminal justice intervention (see Chapter Six for the example of drug crimes in the United States).

Failure to define intentional or other forms of culpable harms as "crimes" can also pose a threat to social order, because citizens may perceive that their government is failing to protect them. Reiman (1998: 59) states it this way: "The point of prohibiting an act by the criminal law is to protect society from an injurious act. . . . The label [of crime] is applied appropriately when it is used to identify all, or at least the worst of, the acts that are harmful to society. The label is applied inappropriately when it is attached to any harmless act or when it is not attached to seriously harmful acts." You will see in Chapter Three that the label of crime, especially "serious crime," is not reserved for the acts that actually threaten us the most. Instead, it is a label for harmful acts that we perceive to be crimes of the poor—that is, for street crime.

In order to gain a clear understanding of why this is so, it is crucial that I critically explore the legislative process in the United States, including who makes the law, who votes for the law, and how special interests shape the law.

WHO MAKES THE LAW?

The criminalization process, like all criminal justice activity, starts with the lawmaking stage. By defining crimes (substantive criminal law) and setting forth the rules that criminal justice actors must follow (procedural criminal law), the criminal law dictates what police, courts, and corrections do. That is, the criminal law sets forth what is considered a crime and what sanctions can follow from illegal behaviors. Therefore, the activities of police, courts, and corrections personnel all directly stem from the law. As introduced in Chapter One, once the law is in place, police enforce the criminal law by responding to calls for service, investigating alleged crimes, and apprehending suspects. Courts determine the guilt of suspects and impose criminal sanctions on the legally guilty. Correctional facilities and programs carry out the sanctions of the courts and administer punishment to sentenced offenders. These institutions of criminal justice thereby reinforce the validity of the law and of all stereotypes created by that law.

> *B*y defining crimes (substantive criminal law) and by setting forth the rules that criminal justice actors must follow (procedural criminal law), the criminal law dictates what police, courts, and corrections do.

This section examines who makes the law by illustrating key demographics of lawmakers. I will then turn to voting behavior in order to illustrate who votes for the law and who does not. Then, the effects of special interests and lobbying on the law are explored. Taken together, these analyses suggest that the criminal law may be biased in favor of the wealthy and powerful.

Demographics of Lawmakers

To the degree that lawmakers are representative of all of society, it is likely that laws will represent all people in society. Table 2.2 compares demographic characteristics of state and federal legislators with those of the general U.S. population. At the federal level (106th Congress, 1999–2001), the U.S. House contains 39 African Americans (9%) and 63 minority group members overall (14%). The U.S. Senate contains no African Americans (0%) and 3 members of minority groups overall (3%). Therefore, the majority of legislators at the federal level are Caucasian, including 86% of House members and 97% of senators. In terms of gender, there are 58 women in the U.S. House (13%) and 9 women in the U.S. Senate (9%). Therefore, the majority of federal legislators are men, including 87% of House members and 91% of senators. The average age of federal legislators in the House is 53 years, 58 years in the Senate, and 54 years old overall (*Congressional Quarterly*, 1999). At the state level, there are 388 African American state representatives (7%) and 123 African American state senators (6%). Therefore, the majority of legislators at the state level are Caucasian (approximately 90%). In terms of gender, 22% of state legislators are women; the majority are men. The average age of state legislators is approximately

TABLE 2.2
Demographic Characteristics of State and Federal Legislators

	U.S. Population[a]	U.S. Congress[b]	State Legislators
Median age	34.6 years	54.0 years	49.4 years[c]
Percentage women	51.1%	12.5%	22.0%[d]
Percentage Caucasian	82.8%	87.7%	90.0%[e]
Percentage African American	12.7%	7.3%	6.9%[f]

SOURCES:
[a]U.S. Census, July 1, 1996, estimate.
[b]*Congressional Quarterly,* January 9, 1999.
[c]Based on an estimate from a study of 900 state lawmakers from 16 states (Woo, 1994).
[d]National Conference on State Legislators, 1999.
[e]Based on an estimate from the National Conference of State Legislatures, (Gold, 1990).
[f]*Black Elected Officials: A National Roster* (Joint Center for Political and Economic Studies, 1993).

49.4 years, compared with 34.6 years in the U.S. general population, meaning legislators at both federal and state levels are older on average than the general population. Approximately 51% of U.S. citizens are women, meaning women are underrepresented as lawmakers. Approximately 83% of U.S. citizens are Caucasian and almost 13% are African American, meaning Caucasians are overrepresented as lawmakers while African Americans are underrepresented (U.S. Census, 1996).

---

*L*awmakers are not representative of the general population in terms of demographic characteristics such as race and gender.

It can be concluded that lawmakers are not representative of the general population in terms of demographic characteristics such as race and gender. In fact, when one considers all elected officials, at federal, state, and local levels of government, African Americans hold less than 2% of elected offices, despite accounting for about 13% of the general population (Joint Center for Political and Economic Studies, 1993).

Voting Behavior

Elected "representatives" may still represent the voter, but most people do not vote. For example, 63% of people 18 years old or older are registered to vote, and only 45% voted in the 1996 elections (U.S. Census, 1999). Harrigan (2000: 178–179) explains that in an indirect, representative democracy such as the United States, "Without meaningful elections, there is no meaningful democracy."

Before I move on to whether voters are representative of the population generally, think about this: If people do not vote, how do representatives know what normal citizens think? The law cannot represent the masses, and the collective conscience of society cannot be incorporated into the criminal law, if people do not vote.

Voters are not representative of the general population demographically, either. The majority of voters are Caucasian (82%), and only 10% of voters are African Americans. The highest percentage of voters come from certain subgroups in society. For example, in 1996, 58% of voters were over age 45. Voting is highest among the most educated as well, as 64% of people with four or more years of college voted in 1996. Voting in 1996 was highest for government employees at 64%. Voting is lowest in the South (41%), where poverty and minority residence are very high (U.S. Census, 1999). According to Harrigan (2000), lower rates of voting by the poor should be attributed to the fact that poor people have been systematically shut out of the electoral process, not that they are bad citizens. Economic stress threatens good citizenship. Harrigan also argues that voters can have tremendous power to the degree that politicians fear voters will be antagonized. Yet, he also discusses how very powerful interest groups have their will enacted into law. An example of the tobacco industry is discussed later.

---

*V*oters are not representative of the general population demographically.

Special Interests/Lobbying

Harrigan (2000: 188) notes that the *average* winner of a House of Representatives seat in 1996 spent $673,000 on his or her campaign, whereas the *average* winner of a Senate seat spent $4.7 million. National party organizations in 1996 spent a total of $2 billion in all federal races. Where does this money come from? Although "members of Congress come largely from the upper strata," legislators are allowed to raise money from outside sources in order to be elected (p. 215).

One example of how money shapes the law is soft money. Simon and Hagan (1999) claim that soft money contributions total about $200 million each year. "Soft money"—money that can be used to build support for political parties—is not subject to campaign finance rules, and candidates can also use an unlimited amount of their own money when running for election. As explained by Harrigan (2000: 194); "soft money is a rich person's game, and soft money contributions and issue ad expenditures by interest groups also reflect a bias" against the poor. Donation of goods and services also is unlimited. Many corporations give more than $100,000 each to the major political parties because Federal Election Commission rules allow unlimited donations by corporations of goods and services, which are not counted as money.

"*S*oft money"—money that can be used to build support for political parties—is not subject to campaign finance rules, and candidates also can use an unlimited amount of their own money when running for election.

Groups other than powerful elites are involved in the codification of criminal law (Castellano and McGarrell, 1991). For example, the general public makes demands, and events such as media reporting and some forty thousand lobbying actions among more than a dozen interest groups affect legislation (Brunk and Wilson, 1991; also see Hagan, 1989; McGarrell, 1993; Walker, Spohn, and Delone, 1996; Wright, 1993). Interest groups are collectives of individuals with a common interest or goal who seek to influence public policy (Berry, 1984). Most of the forty thousand lobbying groups in the United States represent corporations from the United States and abroad (Simon and Hagan, 1999: 47). Interest groups are the "core of democracy, because they represent channels through which people can band together to counteract the advantages that the economic elite have in a political system" (Harrigan, 2000: 165). But given that the poor are the least likely to belong to interest groups (Davis and Smith, 1996), and that the richest one-third of U.S. citizens are nearly twice as likely as the poorest one-third to belong to such a group, interest group activity is biased in favor of the wealthy. Here's one example: less than 5% of the U.S. population gives any serious contribution to politicians at all levels of government. Additionally, only one-quarter of one percent (0.25%) gives $200 or more to politicians. This accounts for 80% of all monies donated to political campaigns in the United States (Domhoff, 1998: 218). Simon and Hagan (1999: 13) thus claim that "the richest 1 to 5 percent of the population pays for political campaigns. The resultant system is something of a corrupt gravy train that only the rich and powerful may board."

---

*L*ess than 5% of the U.S. population gives any serious contribution to politicians at all levels of government. Only 0.25% give $200 or more to politicians.

Political action committees (PACs) may also give up to $10,000 to any politician. According to Simon and Hagan (1999: 15), "4,016 PACs registered in Washington, DC, gave a staggering $391,760,117 in 1994 to candidates at all levels of government." This included $131 million from corporate PACs. According to Harrigan (2000: 191), in 1996, 4,500 PACs spent nearly $500 million on federal elections alone. The voter is left with the realization that his or her vote, letter, phone call, fax, e-mail, or personal visit carries relatively little weight in a political process driven by money.

National political parties raised over $193 million in soft money for 1997–1998, more than twice as much as in 1993–1994. A leading donor to political parties is "big tobacco": between 1991 and 1997, the tobacco industry gave almost $14 million in soft money contributions to national parties, including $11.3 million to Republicans. Not surprisingly, in June 1998, Senate Republicans defeated legislation that would have raised over $500 billion over 25 years through a $1.10 tax increase on a pack of cigarettes (Common Cause, 1999; Salant, 1999).

Most significant is that both sides of the aisle regularly accept money from the same lobbying groups. For example, in 1997–1998 alone, 20 tobacco donors gave nearly $1.9 million to Democrats ($900,000 from Philip Morris) and 29 donors gave almost $9.7 million to Republicans ($4.3 million from Philip Morris) (Common Cause, 1999; Salant, 1999). Meanwhile, the public, 75% of whom are not smokers, suffers tremendous harms as a result of tobacco use. Given the harmfulness of this drug, its legal status does not make sense (Robinson, 1998). Tobacco executives have avoided criminal convictions for their negligent and reckless behaviors in part because of the tobacco lobby's historical stranglehold on Congress (which has recently tightened even in the wake of increased realization of industry deception). At the same time, people continue to smoke and die because of big tobacco's seemingly bottomless advertising budget and willingness to target even children to ensure the sale of its products.

One major interest group that attempts to influence criminal justice policy is the National Rifle Association (NRA). Butterfield (1995) claims that the NRA has the largest political action committee in the nation. Even outside the realm of gun control legislation, the NRA has had an influence on criminal justice policy. For example, the National Criminal Justice Commission writes:

> On the eve of the vote on the 1994 federal crime bill, the NRA bought full-page advertisements in major newspapers urging Congress to increase its allocation for new prison construction from $13 billion to $21 billion and to eliminate crime prevention programs. The ads were part of a

public relations initiative called *CrimeStrike*, whose stated purpose was to create a "citizen's movement" to "put real justice back in our criminal justice system" and to "keep violent criminals off our streets." The NRA bankrolled the first "three strikes" initiative in Washington, helped fund a similar, successful ballot initiative in California, and financed a successful campaign to convince the Texas legislature to spend $1 billion on new prisons. (Donziger, 1996: 82)

What is most troubling about interest groups such as the NRA is that often their claims undergo little or no careful analysis. The National Criminal Justice Commission demonstrates how some NRA campaigns have been based on misleading claims and have inaccurately presented data to support their arguments.

> The media are also not doing their part. Bernard Kalb stated in 1995 at a media forum: If you believe, as we all do, that the media is [*sic*] the sentinel of democracy, then the sentinel, for the most part, is [*sic*] AWOL. . . . A public that is misinformed, under informed, ill informed is not a country whose citizens are using democracy. If you're prepared to entrust democracy to politicians, then you can live with the kind of programs that you're getting today. But if you believe that democracy requires nourishment, requires real journalistic vitamins rather than a lot of empty calories, then the emptiness, to a large extent, of television news, the preoccupation, the tilt toward "blah-blah" rather than substance, has in my view, very, very, very dangerous consequences. (In Krajicek, 1995: 180–181)

I will return to the media's failure to focus on important issues in Chapter Four.

Given that the law is made by people who are very different from the typical U.S. citizen, that most people do not inform the law through voting, and that lobbying and special interests influence the law so greatly, is it possible that the law does not really provide protection from the harms that most threaten us? Morgan-Sharp (1999: 383) explains that because the law is made "mainly by rich white men and persons who share their interests" but is sold as defining behaviors that are unacceptable to the majority of Americans, we may mistakenly believe that the law protects us.

Read the Issue in Depth at the end of this chapter for one example of a behavior (corporate downsizing) that can have significant detrimental effects on individuals, families, communities, and society generally. Yet, not only is corporate downsizing permitted, but it is actually encouraged for the limited benefits of a select few. Karmen (1999: 74) writes that the

> current trend toward a high-tech service economy coupled with deindustrialization (the decline of American manufacturing) is bringing about pervasive long-term structural unemployment for those lacking the requisite skills . . . [which] will further polarize the population into a prospering upper class, struggling middle class, and a growing "surplus population" (what some call the underclass or outclass of marginalized, excluded, demoralized, crushed, defeated, self-destructive, and ineffectively rebellious jobless, homeless, and hungry people). Contained within run-down inner-city neighborhoods and scattered pockets of poverty in outlying districts, these victims of economic dislocations will be viciously preyed upon by more desperate people who live among them.

In essence, downsizing and similar business initiatives promote crime (Hagan, 1994). In his book *Crime and Disrepute*, Hagan argues that "crime is a cost of social inequality, which grows in proportion to America's capital disinvestment policies" (quoted in Blomberg, 1996: 383). Specifically, "capital disinvestment stimulates the interconnected processes of residential segregation, racial inequality, and geographic concentration of poverty that in turn indirectly encourage subcultural adaptations" such as crime. Yet, when downsizing is considered by businesses and promoted by governments, its likely effects on crime are not discussed. Do you think this is logical? Is it right? The issue is discussed further in the Issue in Depth at the end of this chapter.

CONCLUSION

The law, which defines the behaviors that will be pursued by agencies of criminal justice and those that will be broadcast by the media, is created by human beings through a legislative process that is heavily skewed in favor of the wealthy and powerful. (Perhaps this is why some have said that there are two things you just do not want to see being made: sausage and the law.) Because legislators are predominantly Caucasian, male, and wealthy, because voters are also predominantly Caucasian, well off, and well educated, and because monied interests have greater access to legislators than other citizens do, the law is heavily biased against powerless groups in society. The first result of this is that the label of "crime" may not be used to identify those acts that are really the most dangerous to society.

ISSUE IN DEPTH
American Business—Downsizing for Profit

What Is Downsizing?

In the late 1980s and the 1990s, the United States began to experience unprecedented job losses due to a phenomenon known as *downsizing*, as corporations laid off employees in large, ever-increasing numbers in order to reduce operating costs and increase profits (Gordon, 1996). U.S. businesses have been reluctant to use the term *downsizing* because of its negative implications. Instead, they may talk about *reengineering*—a term that evokes images of impersonal organizational or bureaucratic change. When one hears that a corporation is in the process of reengineering, one might think that it is being altered in some technical way that is relevant only to the structure of the corporation. But the meaning of the term is actually much broader, and the implications of corporate reengineering extend well beyond corporate structure.

Reengineering is a process that may result in large numbers of employees being given a permanent, irrevocable good-bye, either all at once or over an extended period of time. Corporate managers have developed numerous euphemisms for reengineering: employees are either downsized, laid off, separated, severed, or unassigned (*New York Times*, 1997). The process of organizing and reorganizing workers is also commonly referred to as "rightsizing," "process innovation," "horizontal organization structure," and "turning the organization on its side."

Downsizing, however, is probably the best term for this process, which occurs when a corporation fires employees in an effort to become smaller, more efficient, and more profitable. Although the word *downsize* appeared in the

English language in the 1970s, it was not applied specifically to humans or included in the college edition of the *American Heritage* dictionary until 1982; before that time, *downsizing* referred solely to the shrinking size of cars (*New York Times*, 1997).

Although many of the terms listed here suggest a sterile, unemotional process, corporate downsizing is in fact generally viewed negatively by citizens both inside and outside of the corporate structure. Light has been shed on the "ugly truth" of "corporate executions," whereby individual workers lose their jobs because of "corporate greed" (Downs, 1995). Downsizing results in a simultaneous triumph of capital and betrayal of work, which must be understood in the context of the "Judas economy" of American capitalism (Golden, 1997). Downsizing allows corporations to get fat and mean while workers are squeezed (Gordon, 1996). Corporate downsizing is a highly political issue, supported by both Republicans and Democrats in the United States (Moore, 1996). In part because of the negative outcomes of corporate downsizing, there has been rebellion against capitalism generally in Europe (Edmondson, 1997), although downsizing has occurred in some European countries as well as in the United States.

Downsizing quickly became a popular topic in both the mainstream and the academic literature. In addition to studies documenting the benefits and harms associated with corporate downsizing, many have cashed in on downsizing's existence. For example, the *New York Times* 1997 special report on corporate downsizing described the creation of merger offices within numerous major corporations for the main purpose of assisting in downsizing efforts. Corporations hire so-called corporate headhunters to help them decide whom to fire. Others have written books as a result of downsizing, including survival guides for managers who are charged with leading their corporations through the downsizing process and long-range plans for corporations that want to plan their downsizing efforts carefully (Chairs-Sims, 1991). Such books are not written exclusively for the benefit of corporations; some suggest guidelines that individuals, organizations, and communities can use to respond to mass layoffs (Leana and Feldman, 1992). Individuals who have been downsized have written about their experiences (Snyder, 1997). Some writers, recognizing the harms associated with corporate downsizing, have made efforts to encourage corporations not to participate in the process. For example, some have set out to demonstrate that it is possible for a corporation to grow and to break the cycle of downsizing that has been so pervasive in the United States (von Brachel, 1994). Even these individuals are cashing in to some degree on the widespread downsizing that has occurred in the United States.

How Widespread Is Downsizing?

Corporate downsizing is not a new phenomenon, except perhaps in its targets (Dentzer, 1996). It apparently started in the late 1970s but was not heavily practiced in the United States until the 1980s and 1990s (*New York Times*,

1997), when it spread to large corporations, small partnerships, government agencies, universities and public school systems, and nonprofit organizations (Downs, 1995). Downsizing in the 1990s, as compared with the massive layoffs of the 1980s, has affected even the college educated—the very people who gained the skills and knowledge that ideally would protect them from being fired (Dentzer, 1996). A study conducted by the American Management Association in 1994 found that two-thirds of all workers who were laid off were college-educated, salaried employees. Downsizing in the 1990s has had greater effects in the manufacturing sector, whereas in the 1980s the greatest effects were felt in white-collar and service industries, and has had greater effects on older, female, Hispanic, and white employees than the layoffs of the 1980s. Additionally, downsizing in the 1990s has most commonly occurred in the Northeast and West, rather than the Midwest as in the 1980s. The affected downsized populations of the 1990s have also been described as office rather than factory employees (Gardner, 1995).

Downsizing is very common in corporate business in the United States. In fact, there are 50% more victims of downsizing in the United States every year than there are victims of violent crime. Downsizing is so common in the United States that the U.S. Bureau of Labor Statistics publishes quarterly statistical reports on "mass layoffs." More than 43 million jobs have been lost to downsizing since 1979 (*New York Times*, 1997). Furthermore, 75% of households have had a close encounter with downsizing since 1980, and 33% of people have actually lost a job because of downsizing. Another 40% know someone who has lost a job through downsizing. Despite these alarming figures, since 1979 there has actually been a net gain of over 27 million jobs in the United States.

Unfortunately, the majority of people who have been downsized (65%) report earning lower salaries in their new jobs than they earned in the jobs they lost; that is, only slightly more than one-third earn equivalent or higher wages in their next jobs. Not surprisingly, one in ten adults who have been downsized report that downsizing led to a major crisis in their lives (*New York Times*, 1997). These statistics, when put in the overall context of the U.S. economy, become more troubling. For example, the ratio of earnings for chief executive officers (CEOs) to workers is twice as high in the United States as the average ratio for other countries (Wolman and Calamosca, 1997). Major corporations that have recently laid off between 10,000 and 85,000 employees are headed by CEOs with salaries that range from $1.1 million to $25.3 million (Downs, 1995). At the same time, income disparity, the gap between the haves and the have-nots, is drastically up in the United States. For example, the top 5% of earners in the United States witnessed increases in real income of approximately 16% between 1990 and 1994; almost every other group saw real income decline by as much as 7% (*New York Times*, 1997). Class divisions appear to be strengthened by downsizing, particularly when it is driven by technological advances (Kreyche, 1996). Overall household income actually rose 10% during this period of downsizing, but almost all of this gain (97%) has been enjoyed by the richest 20%. Median wages, adjusted for inflation, were actually less in 1994 than they were in 1979 (*New York Times*, 1997).

The Rationale Behind Downsizing

The practice of corporate downsizing is justified in many ways. One common argument used to vindicate corporate downsizing is that it has not affected the overall growth of employment (Arnst, 1994), as discussed earlier. This may be true, but this fact does not speak to the harmful effects of downsizing on individuals, families, communities, and society in general, which will be identified and discussed in this section.

Corporate downsizing is based on the assumption that the failures of corporations (e.g., losses or low profits) result from inadequacies of employees and their managers (Wolman and Calamosca, 1997). As a result, corporations look within to find solutions and often conclude that some employees are unnecessary or are to blame for corporate failures, and therefore are expendable. A common myth associated with downsizing is that it has most affected middle-level managers of corporations who are simply not needed. In fact, managers as a percentage of all nonfarm employees actually increased approximately 14% from 1991 to 1995, during a period of intense downsizing. Between 15% to 20% of employees of private corporations are managers or supervisors even after downsizing; their combined salaries and benefits total approximately $1.3 trillion, roughly equal to one-fifth of the U.S. gross domestic product (GDP) (Gordon, 1996). This has led some to conclude that even after downsizing, corporations remain "fat," top-heavy, and "mean," despite the layoffs of lower-paid employees.

The rationale behind corporate downsizing is complex. Part of what allows downsizing to continue in the United States is that workers and labor generally are demonized in the mass media, whereas corporations are relatively protected in part because of their ownership of media outlets (Douglas, 1996). A thorough discussion of why corporations should downsize is contained in the book *Reengineering the Corporation* (Hammer and Champy, 1994). These authors claim that the payoffs for downsizing include reduced business-related costs, increased quality in employee performance, and increased customer satisfaction. Downsizing also grants immediate reductions in operating costs and gives corporations opportunities to get free publicity via the news media, to fire workers with poor performance records, and to appear decisive in the face of uncertain economic conditions (Downs, 1995). Further, it gives corporations increased control of their employees (Wolman and Calamosca, 1997).

Downsizing also gives corporations psychological advantages over their employees. Employees report purposely seeking new job skills in hopes that they will become indispensable to their employers, an effort that undeniably benefits the corporation (Capelli, 1997). Of course, if employees gain new skills as a result of the threat of downsizing, this may actually benefit the employees by making them more mobile (Arnst, 1994). A more subtle justification of downsizing is that it provides more work for psychologists (Noer, 1993).

In essence, the perception is that downsizing is good for the economy (Edmondson, 1997). For example, downsizing is perceived to be good for investment values, and actual increases in stock prices have followed announcements of mass layoffs by particular corporations. These companies, which laid off between 10,500 and 60,000 employees, saw increases in stock prices between 3% and 31%. The bottom line is: downsizing creates short-term profits for corporations (Downs, 1995) because it provides a mechanism for suppressing wage costs. This has led some corporations to call corporate downsizing "unavoidable" and even "healthy" (Wolman and Calamosca, 1997).

In some cases, corporations claim that mass layoffs are driven by factors beyond their control. For example, job loss may be blamed on technological advances, with the claim that machines are simply more efficient and cost-effective than people, or on more efficient competitors (Kreyche, 1996). Corporations sometimes claim that downsizing allows workers to be shifted into areas where they are more needed (Dentzer, 1996).

Conclusion: The Downside of Downsizing

Despite the supposed need for downsizing, it also has a "flip side" (Wolman and Calamosca, 1997). Research indicates that corporations that engage in downsizing rarely realize their stated goals (Zweig, 1995). In a survey of 1,005 corporations conducted by Wyatt and Company, only one-third of the corporations indicated that profits increased after layoffs as great as they had expected; less than one-half indicated that the layoffs resulted in reductions in expenses as great as had been expected; and four out of five corporations ended up refilling positions vacated by downsizing. A follow-up study of 531 corporations showed that more than three-quarters reported laying off employees, that the vast majority of these (85%) did so to increase profits, but that in fact less than half (46%) saw any measurable increases in profits. Thirty-four percent of the corporations reported slight increases in worker productivity after layoffs, but 58% had reportedly sought this. Only 31% achieved increased customer service, although 61% had sought it. Within only one year, most of the companies had hired employees to fill the positions vacated by the job cuts (Downs, 1995).

The most obvious downside to downsizing is the negative effects experienced by those who suddenly lose their jobs (Good, 1995; Wilson, 1995). As reported here, the majority of those who are downsized earn lower salaries and/or end up in part-time or temporary positions (*New York Times*, 1997). In effect, corporate downsizing serves as a form of "career derailment" because careers are at least seriously interrupted, if not destroyed (Stratton, 1996). Those who are laid off also tend to have more negative views toward politics generally and toward government and the capitalist economic system in particular, and tend to be more pessimistic about the economy and the direction that the country is heading. Laid-off employees are also angrier than those unaffected by downsizing (*New York Times*, 1997).

There also appears to be a positive relationship between losing a job to downsizing and experiencing stress and all the health problems associated with it, including divorce and marital separation. A negative relationship exists between job loss and one's level of civic activities in the community, and episodes of domestic violence, too, may result from corporate downsizing. There is a positive relationship between incarceration rates and the percentage of administrative and managerial employment in 10 advanced countries; countries with the highest percentage of administrative and managerial employees also have the highest incarceration rates (Gordon, 1996). Whether this is because increased crime rates result from downsizing is unclear; it may simply be that countries that are most willing to downsize are also most likely to respond to crime by locking people up. It's also possible, although not confirmed, that crime rates may increase in countries that lay off workers because downsizing can lead to increases in urban growth, which may be a factor in increases in street crime (Buckley and Barovick, 1994).

Despite the inherent logic that underlies laying off a relatively small number to save the majority, engaging in corporate downsizing may be an example of "cutting off your nose to spite your face," because the negative effects of downsizing may extend to many or all employees within the corporation (Zweig, 1995). Such effects are experienced by workers who are not laid off, because the practice of downsizing produces low morale and productivity in employees in general (Dentzer, 1996). When some employees within the corporation are laid off, those who are kept on may experience job insecurity, stress, and negative attitudes. Further consequences can be role ambiguity and role overload (Forst, 1996)—perceptions by employees that they do not know their proper role in the corporation or that they have too many roles to fill. Employees who work for corporations that are downsizing tend to report feeling less loyal to their company and feeling that their corporation is less loyal to them. They also report sensing increased competition between individual employees within the corporation, which prompts them to work more hours in order to keep their jobs (*New York Times*, 1997).

Corporate downsizing also may lead to concern in other citizens, whether or not they work for large corporations. For example, in a recent study, health and safety professionals indicated high concerns about corporate downsizing (Scannell, 1996). An additional unfortunate consequence of downsizing in U.S. society is that it provides a rationale for scapegoating: groups "below" (e.g., the poor, minorities, immigrants, illegal aliens) are blamed for lost jobs when the real cause lies in the decision making of powerful groups "above" (*New York Times*, 1997).

Downsizing by corporations thus serves as one example of how wealthy persons who run businesses get wealthy. The worker, who is relatively less wealthy and powerful than the CEO, ends up paying for this in the ways discussed in this section.

Discussion Questions

- Define the law.
- Explain the difference between so-called *mala in se* and *mala prohibita* crimes. Provide examples of each. Do you think this distinction is an important one? Why or why not?
- Make a list of different types of law, and define each.
- What is the difference between *natural law* and *positive law*?
- Try to think of some behaviors that you think violate natural law but not positive law. Also, are there behaviors that violate positive law but not natural law? Examples?
- Where do the following types of law come from: (1) Constitutional law; (2) statutory law; (3) case law; and (4) administrative law?
- How did common law shape American criminal law?
- Contrast *substantive* and *procedural* criminal law.
- What are the main purposes of the law?
- What do you think is the most important purpose of the criminal law?
- Describe the typical lawmaker in the United States. How does he or she differ from the average American?
- Describe the typical voter in the United States. How does he or she differ from the average American?
- Provide an example of how money shapes the law.
- Do you think the law represents the interests of Americans? Why or why not?
- Which is more accurate in explaining the interests served by the law—the *consensus* model of lawmaking or the *conflict* model of lawmaking? Why?
- Is downsizing in American business good or bad for America? Explain your answer.

CHAPTER THREE

CRIME: WHICH IS WORSE, CRIME ON THE STREETS OR CRIME IN THE SUITES?

KEY CONCEPTS

- **What is a crime?**
- **Types of crimes in the United States**
- **Sources of crime information: Do we really know how much crime is out there?**
- **Issue in Depth: Tobacco—The Greatest Crime in World History?**

INTRODUCTION

Close your eyes and picture a crime. What do you see? What does the offender look like? What about the victim? The image that you probably see is likely consistent with those vigorously pursued by American criminal justice agencies and portrayed in the American mass media. But what is a crime? Why are some crimes considered more serious than others? How do we know how much crime there is in the United States? Is the crime problem getting worse or is it getting better? This chapter answers these questions. I will argue that crime in the United States is probably not as bad as you think it is, and that our criminal justice system is focused almost exclusively on street crimes committed by a small segment of our population. Implications for justice are discussed.

WHAT IS A CRIME?

When you think of the word *crime*, you probably have a good idea of what it means. Although there is a straightforward legal definition of *crime*, most of us think of crimes as any behaviors that are done intentionally and cause physical or financial harm to another person. For example, if you were standing on a street corner minding your own business, and someone came up and poked a pencil into your eye, causing a loss of vision, you would probably feel that you had been victimized by crime. Even if it was not against the law, you would probably think it should be. If a corporation manufactured a toaster that shot sparks into your eyes, you might also feel like a victim of crime, even if it was not specifically a violation of the criminal law to manufacture such a toaster. Whether or not any act violates the law, you may feel like a crime victim when you are harmed by another. Crime as a "natural" concept, then, is any act that is seen as "fundamentally wrong, strongly disapproved, and deserving of punishment," regardless of whether it is legal or not (Gottfredson, 1999: 47). Recall the discussion of natural law in Chapter Two. Some argue that behaviors that violate natural law should be considered crimes.

> Crime as a "natural" concept is any act that is seen as "fundamentally wrong, strongly disapproved, and deserving of punishment," regardless of whether it is legal or not (Gottfredson, 1999: 47).

Legalistic Definition of Crime

This natural view of crime, which appeals to our common sense, is very similar to the "legalistic" definition of crime, with one significant exception. Legally, a crime occurs only when an act violates the criminal law. As you saw in Chapter Two, there is no crime without law. Clearly, there are scores of behaviors that kill and injure us and take our property; many of them are committed intentionally but are not against the criminal law. Such acts are *not* legally considered crimes, even if we all think the act is wrong, immoral, deviant, or bad. What makes the act a crime is that it is written down as a crime by the government.

This means that crime is made up—invented—by people. Quinney (1970: 15) makes this point clear in his book *The Social Reality of Crime* when he writes:

> Crime is a definition of behavior that is conferred on some persons by others. Agents of the law, representing segments of a politically organized society, are responsible for formulating and administering criminal laws. Persons and behaviors, therefore, become criminal because of the formulation and application of criminal definitions. Thus, crime is created.

Crime does not exist in nature. It is something that human beings have invented and continue to invent every day.

> Crime is made up—invented—by people.

This is not to say that there is no harmful behavior in nature. Many behaviors in nature kill and produce harms. For example, on the plains of Africa, lions and hyenas fight for the right to kill zebras and other animals. This is part of Darwin's concept of "survival of the fittest." When lions and hyenas kill zebras or even one another in order to eat, defend their territory, or gain mating advantages, the zebra police are not called out to round up the killers in the interests of justice. Why not? I hope the answer is obvious—because zebras do not call such killings crimes. It is not illegal for lions or hyenas to kill zebras. Human beings are the only species to legislate killing as a crime (and only under certain circumstances, because there are plenty of ways to kill people, even intentionally, without committing a crime).

Since crime is invented, then no behavior is inherently criminal, and any behavior can be defined as a crime. These commonsense points are important to remember when thinking about crime. If you can remember these points, it will be much easier for you to understand this book. For example, in Chapter Six I will explore drug legalization as an alternative to the war on drugs. In that chapter, you will see that many "drug crimes" are not really all that harmful. They are illegal only because human beings have made them illegal. Drugs that are illegal can also be made legal. Whether they should be is discussed in Chapter Six.

Because crime is a human invention, there is some disagreement among those who study crime for a living about what behaviors should constitute crime. Most criminologists and criminal justice scholars tend to limit their studies to behaviors that violate the criminal law, and a very large share of those study only street crimes such as homicide, forcible rape, aggravated assault, robbery, theft, burglary, motor vehicle theft, and arson. These acts are defined in the following box. I'll discuss the reasons for focusing on these acts later in this chapter.

American street crimes

- *Criminal homicide:* Includes murder and nonnegligent manslaughter: the willful (nonnegligent) killing of one human being by another. Deaths caused by negligence, attempts to kill, suicides, and accidental deaths are excluded. Justifiable homicides are classified separately, and traffic fatalities are excluded.
- *Forcible rape:* The carnal knowledge of a female forcibly and against her will. Rapes by force and attempts or assaults with the intent to rape, regardless of the age of the victim, are included. Statutory offenses (where no force is used but the victim is under the legal age of consent) are excluded.
- *Robbery:* Taking or attempting to take anything of value from the care, custody, or control of a person or persons by force or threat of force or violence and/or by putting the victim in fear.
- *Aggravated assault:* An unlawful attack by one person on another for the purpose of inflicting severe or aggravated bodily injury, which usually is accompanied by the use of a weapon or by means likely to produce death or great bodily harm. Simple assaults are excluded.
- *Burglary:* The unlawful entering of a structure to commit a felony or a theft. Attempted forcible entry is included.
- *Larceny-theft:* The unlawful taking, carrying, leading, or riding away of property from the possession or constructive possession of another. Examples are thefts of bicycles or automobile accessories, shoplifting, pocket-picking, or the stealing of any property or article that is not taken by force and violence or by fraud. Attempted thefts are included. Embezzlement, confidence games, forgery, worthless checks, and so on are excluded.
- *Motor vehicle theft:* The theft or attempted theft of a motor vehicle, defined as a vehicle that is self-propelled and runs on the surface and not

> on rails. Motorboats, construction equipment, airplanes, and farming equipment are specifically excluded from this category.
> - *Arson:* Any willful or malicious burning or attempt to burn, with or without intent to defraud, a dwelling house, public building, motor vehicle or aircraft, or personal property of another.

Legally, a crime occurs when a person either acts, fails to act, attempts to act, or agrees to act in a way that is in violation of the criminal law, and without defense or justification. This legal definition of crime is made up of several elements. The first element, *acts*, includes any behaviors that are actually carried out, such as intentionally taking the life of another (murder) or taking someone's wallet from his or her back pocket (theft). *Attempts* are acts that are not successfully carried out, such as unsuccessfully trying to break into someone's home through a locked front door (attempted burglary). *Agreeing* to act is called a *conspiracy*. An example would be verbally agreeing with a friend to kill the president of the United States even if you did not ever attempt to do so. Examples of *failures* to act include not paying your taxes or not paying child support. The most important element of the definition of crime is the criminal law, which is made up of federal or state statutes that specify what behaviors are in violation of the criminal law. As noted, without the law, there is no crime.

---

*L*egally, a crime occurs when a person either acts, fails to act, attempts to act, or agrees to act in a way that violates the criminal law, and without defense or justification.

The final element of this definition is "without defense or justification." This is an important element, for a person may commit an act *(actus reus)* that is against the law, and even may do so with intent *(mens rea)*, yet may not be a criminal if he or she has a valid reason for committing the act (Schmalleger, 1999). Examples of valid defenses might include self-defense, necessity, coercion, immaturity, involuntary intoxication, entrapment, or insanity. Definitions of each term with examples are provided in the following box.

Valid defenses to criminal charges

- *Duress:* If you are coerced or forced to commit a crime by another—for example, if someone shoves a gun in your face and demands that you help him or her rob a bank—you may plead not guilty because of duress.
- *Self-defense:* If you are afraid for your life and act to protect it (and sometimes to protect your property)—for example, if you attack someone who breaks into your house—you may plead not guilty because of self-defense.
- *Necessity:* If you are personally at risk of dying or becoming ill unless you commit a crime—for example, if you find yourself in danger of freezing to death unless you break into someone's cabin in the middle of the woods—you may plead not guilty because of necessity.

- *Entrapment:* If a government agent such as a police officer approaches you and offers you the opportunity to commit a crime, and the offense did not originate in your own mind—for example, if you buy drugs from an undercover officer who has come to your door while you are at home enjoying a dinner with your family—you may plead not guilty because of entrapment.
- *Immaturity:* If you are too young to understand right from wrong—for example, if you are five years old and you playfully aim a gun at a playmate and pull the trigger—you may plead not guilty because of immaturity.
- *Insanity:* If you are unable to understand the difference between right and wrong or are unable to adjust your behavior accordingly—for example, if you have been diagnosed with a severe mental illness that impairs your thought processes—you may plead not guilty because of insanity.
- *Involuntary intoxication:* If you become impaired by the action of another—for example, if someone slips a drug into your drink and you violently attack another person—you may plead not guilty because of involuntary intoxication.

Additionally, for an act to be legally considered a crime, it must be committed with culpability (or responsibility). This includes acts that are committed under any of the following circumstances:

- *Intentionally:* Committed with a guilty mind on purpose
- *Negligently:* Committed as a result of a failure to meet normal or recognized expectations
- *Recklessly:* Committed without due caution for human life or property
- *Knowingly:* Committed with knowledge

Generally, acts committed with intent are considered more serious than those committed negligently, recklessly, or knowingly. Considering that a person who is killed negligently, recklessly, or knowingly is just as dead as one killed intentionally, you may question the logic of such distinctions.

> *C*ulpability for criminal behavior includes acts committed intentionally, negligently, recklessly, and knowingly.

TYPES OF CRIME IN THE UNITED STATES

Serious/Street Crime

Remember what I asked you to do at the beginning of this chapter? Close your eyes and picture a crime. What do you see? What does the offender look like? What is he or she doing? What about the victim?

Chances are, if you do this, you will see a particular type of crime committed by a particular type of person against another particular type of person. To avoid biasing your images, I will not tell you what you probably saw when you closed your eyes and pictured a crime, a criminal, and a victim—not yet, anyway.

In all likelihood, you saw a crime that is consistent with what our government perceives as "serious" crime, that which is visible to us as ordinary U.S. citizens. What does "serious" mean?

You may consider something serious that is important to you, perhaps something you fear or are worried about. You might consider crimes serious if they cause or threaten great danger and harm (either physical or financial).

The term *serious* also might be related to the frequency of a behavior. For example, a behavior may be very harmful but may occur so rarely that it does not create fear or worry in citizens. Would this type of act be considered serious?

The U.S. government has an answer to these questions. The Uniform Crime Reporting Program (UCR), to be discussed later in this chapter, is a source of crime information compiled by the Federal Bureau of Investigation (FBI) each year. This source of data was created because of a need to gather and disseminate national crime statistics. In the 1920s, the International Association of Chiefs of Police (IACP) formed a committee to create a uniform system for recording police statistics. Crimes were originally evaluated on the basis of the following criteria:

- Harmfulness
- Frequency of occurrence
- Pervasiveness in all geographic areas of the country
- Likelihood of being reported to the police

After a preliminary compilation in 1929 of a list of crimes that met these criteria, the committee completed their plan for developing the UCR. Statistics on these crimes were collected beginning in the 1930s.

As noted within each year's UCR publication: "Seven offenses were chosen to serve as an Index for gauging the overall volume and rate of crime." These offenses, known as "Part I Index Offenses," included the violent crimes of murder and nonnegligent manslaughter, forcible rape, robbery, and aggravated assault and the property crimes of burglary, theft, and motor vehicle theft. In 1979, arson was added to the UCR list, for a total of eight "serious" crimes.

> *P*art I offenses of the UCR are more serious than Part II offenses, supposedly because of their relative harmfulness, frequency of occurrence, pervasiveness in all geographic areas of the country, and likelihood of being reported to the police.

Given their own discussion of what constitutes a serious offense, you might expect that the street crimes listed in the box would be the ones that cause the greatest harm (either physical or financial), occur with great frequency, are pervasive throughout the country, and are likely to be reported to the police. Since the majority of crimes overall are not reported to the police, you may wonder why some crimes are included (e.g., theft) that are highly unlikely to be reported to the police.

In discussing the eight types of serious crime in each annual UCR report, it is claimed that "These are serious crimes by nature and/or volume." That is, these crimes supposedly cause the most harm, occur with the greatest frequency, and are the most widespread.

Other types of crimes, known as Type II offenses of the UCR, are literally considered "less serious." Presumably, it is because they either cause less harm, occur with less frequency, or are not as pervasive throughout the country. This list of Type II offenses is provided in the following box. As a justification for their inclusion in this list, the FBI explains:

> Not all crimes, such as Embezzlement, are readily brought to the attention of the police. Also, some serious crimes, such as Kidnapping, occur infrequently. Therefore, for practical purposes, the reporting of offenses known is limited to the selected crime classifications because they are the crimes most likely to be reported and most likely to occur with sufficient frequency to provide an adequate basis for comparison.

No explanation is offered for their exclusion from the list of Part I or "serious" offenses based on the degree of relative harm they cause, how frequently they occur, and/or how pervasive they are through the country.

Type II Offenses of the UCR

- *Simple assaults:* Assaults and attempted assaults in which no weapon is used and which do not results in serious or aggravated injury to the victim.
- *Forgery and counterfeiting:* Making, altering, uttering, or possessing, with intent to defraud, anything false in the semblance of that which is true. Attempts are included.
- *Fraud:* Fraudulent conversion and obtaining money or property by false pretenses. Confidence games and bad checks, except forgeries and counterfeiting, are included.
- *Embezzlement:* Misappropriation or misapplication of money or property entrusted to one's care, custody, or control.
- *Buying, receiving, or possessing stolen property:* Buying, receiving, and possessing stolen property, including attempts.
- *Vandalism:* Willful or malicious destruction, injury, disfigurement, or defacement of any public or private property, real or personal, without consent of the owner or persons having custody or control. Attempts are included.
- *Prostitution and commercialized vice:* Sex offenses of a commercialized nature, such as prostitution, keeping a bawdy house, procuring, or transporting women for immoral purposes. Attempts are included.
- *Sex offenses:* Statutory rape and offenses against chastity, common decency, morals, and the like. Attempts are included.
- *Drug abuse violations:* State and/or local offenses relating to the unlawful possession, sale, use, growing, and manufacturing of narcotic drugs.
- *Gambling:* Promoting, permitting, or engaging in illegal gambling.
- *Offenses against the family and children:* Nonsupport, neglect, desertion, or abuse of family and children. Attempts are included.
- *Driving under the influence:* Driving or operating any vehicle or common carrier while drunk or under the influence of liquor or narcotics.
- *Liquor law violations:* State and/or local liquor law violations except drunkenness and driving under the influence. Federal violations are excluded.

- *Drunkenness:* Offenses relating to drunkenness or intoxication. Driving under the influence is excluded.
- *Disorderly conduct:* Breach of the peace.
- *Vagrancy:* Begging, loitering, and the like. Includes prosecutions under the charge of suspicious person.
- *Curfew violations and loitering:* Offenses relating to violations of local curfew or loitering ordinances where such laws exist.
- *Running away:* Limited to juveniles taken into protective custody under provisions of local statutes.

Why are such acts considered less serious? We'll return to that issue later in this chapter when we compare harms caused by serious crimes with harms caused by other types of behaviors. I will illustrate that the acts we focus on least actually cause more harm, both physically and financially, and occur with greater frequency than the crimes we consider the most serious. You might correctly wonder, then, whether legal definitions of crime are appropriately limited. If not, why not? Recall the examination of who makes the law in Chapter Two. Why would legislators, who are predominantly older and wealthy Caucasian males, define acts committed by people like themselves as crimes?

Other Conceptions of Crime: White-Collar Deviance

As noted at the onset of this chapter, you may feel like a "crime victim" when you are victimized by an act that is committed against you on purpose. But if this act was not legally defined as a "crime" at the time it was committed against you, then legally, you were not a crime victim.

Does that mean you were not victimized? Of course not. You may be victimized by acts outside the scope of the criminal justice system. For example, "white-collar deviance" is a term put forth by Simon and Hagan (1999: 3–4) in their book of the same name. It includes not only criminal acts but also unethical acts, civil and regulatory violations, and other harmful acts committed intentionally, recklessly, negligently, or knowingly. *White-collar deviance* is a term that encompasses "white-collar" crimes (Sutherland, 1977a, 1977b), "elite deviance" (Simon and Eitzen, 1993), "corporate violence" (Frank and Lynch, 1992), and those "crimes by any other name" (Reiman, 1998) committed by our "trusted criminals" (Friedrichs, 1999). These are acts that cause tremendous physical, financial, and moral harms to Americans.

> *W*hite-collar deviance includes not only criminal acts but also unethical acts, civil and regulatory violations, and other harmful acts committed intentionally, recklessly, negligently, or knowingly.

Here's one example of white-collar deviance: many Americans criticize "big government" for wasting tax money on social programs. Yet, when money is wasted on national defense, Americans seem less concerned (this is not to say that national defense spending itself is a waste of money). Sherrill (1997) describes many defense-spending scandals. According to Sherrill, $13 billion paid to weapons contractors between 1985 and 1995 was simply "lost," and another $15 billion remains unaccounted for. Simon and Hagan (1999: 33) claim that military waste and fraud cost taxpayers $172 billion per year. Is losing money intended for national defense a crime? No. Is anyone held criminally accountable for such losses? No.

Another example of white-collar deviance is what Sennott (2000) calls "corporate welfare," which he claims costs Americans at least $150 billion per year. Essentially, businesses are subsidized by taxpayers in the form of trade missions, funding for support services, tax breaks, and state offices that guide corporations in their business affairs. Frivolous spending by the government also might be considered white-collar deviance. For example, members of Congress enjoy $78 million in free mailing privileges each year (about $120,000 each). They also pay no sales tax on items bought in Washington, D.C., and pay no income taxes there. On top of that, all members of Congress are allowed an extra $3,000 income tax deduction and can have their tax returns prepared free of charge by professionals. They are also accorded free transportation in chauffeured limousines. Most shocking, given that more than 40 million Americans do not have *any* medical insurance, is that members of Congress have free medical and life insurance as well as very generous retirement plans (Simon and Hagan, 1999: 43–44). None of this is criminal, even though many acts of white-collar deviance produce victims.

Currently, the criminal justice system seldom views people as victims unless an individual person becomes a victim (suffers financial or physical harm) specifically as a result of a criminal act. Rush (2000: 353) writes that victimization is "the harming of any *single victim* in a *criminal* incident" (emphasis added). Champion (1997: 128) defines victimization as a "specific *criminal* act affecting a *specific victim*" (emphasis added). The UCR definition of homicide also illustrates how crimes are typically perceived as being committed against one person by another. Murder is the "willful . . . killing of *one human being by another*" (emphasis added).

Notice the common elements in these definitions:

- A single victim
- Suffering harm
- From a criminal act

According to these definitions, victimization occurs when one person suffers some harm from a behavior that violates the criminal law. Yet, people obviously are victimized by behaviors that do not meet these conditions. Table 3.1 sets forth a typology of victimization that illustrates four basic types of victimization:

- Harmful acts committed by an individual person against another individual person (Cell 1)
- Harmful acts committed by an individual person against an entity (e.g., a group of people or a corporation) (Cell 2)
- Harmful acts committed by an entity (e.g., a group of people or a corporation) against an individual person (Cell 3)
- Harmful acts committed by an entity (e.g., a group of people or a corporation) against another entity (e.g., a group of people or a corporation) (Cell 4)

Table 3.1 also provides examples of specific types of behaviors that would fall into each cell. I have provided one example of an act that causes financial harm to victims and one that causes physical harm. Examples in Table 3.1 of harmful acts committed by an individual against another individual include theft (e.g., taking property from another without consent and without the use of force or the threat of force) and battery (e.g., physically striking or beating another person with force). Examples of harmful acts committed by an individual against a group of people or a

TABLE 3.1
A Typology of Victimization

| | | OFFENDER | |
		Individual	Group/Corporation
	Individual	**Cell 1**	**Cell 3**
		Theft	Fraud
VICTIM		Battery	Defective product
	Group/Corporation	**Cell 2**	**Cell 4**
		Forgery	Price fixing
		Terrorist act	Dangerous working conditions

corporation include forgery (e.g., signing another person's name to a check that is not yours in order to cash it) and terrorist acts (e.g., planting and detonating explosives at a building occupied by other people). Examples of harmful acts committed by a group of people or a corporation against an individual person include fraud (e.g., making false or deceptive claims about a product in order to trick the buyer into purchasing it) and manufacturing and selling defective products (e.g., making a car that explodes in a low-impact crash because of a faulty part). Finally, examples of harmful acts committed by a group of people or a corporation against another group of people or corporation include price fixing (e.g., when two corporations keep prices artificially high by agreeing to set a specific price on their products and simultaneously exclude smaller competitors that cannot lower prices to compete for buyers' business) and forcing or allowing employees to work in hazardous conditions (e.g., not complying with federally required safety regulations or ignoring warnings of potential problems).

Although these four types of victimizations are mutually exclusive, the examples provided in Table 3.1 are not. That is, some of the examples provided could also fit well into another category of victimization. For example, acts of fraud can also be committed by an individual against another individual (as when someone sells a fake fur coat to someone after claiming it is "a genuine mink coat") or by a group of people or a corporation against an individual person (as when a corporation sells a product guaranteed to "make you younger!"). Likewise, theft can be committed by individuals against other individuals or against groups and corporations. The examples simply serve to help illustrate the four different types of victimizations defined above.

The significant point is that victimization encompasses many more types of behaviors than can be adequately understood according to the most common definition in criminology. As noted by Karmen (1996: 2), the term *victim* most accurately "refers to all those people who experience injury, loss, or hardship due to *any cause*" (emphasis added). In other words, a broader definition of victimization would be:

> people who experience any harmful behavior, such as "accident victims, cancer victims, flood victims, and victims of discrimination and similar injustices" and people who have been "physically injured, economically hurt, robbed of self-respect, emotionally traumatized, socially stigmatized, politically oppressed, collectively exploited, personally alienated, manipulated, co-opted, neglected, ignored, blamed, defamed, demeaned, or vilified." (Karmen, 1996: 2)

> $\mathcal{V}$ictimization encompasses many more types of behaviors than can be adequately understood according to the most adhered-to definition in criminology.

Although this definition is too broad, legal conceptions of crime and victimization are too restrictive to encompass the wide range of purposive behaviors that create victims, particularly given the fact that "crime" is a label applied by persons with power to have their will enacted into law while simultaneously creating a criminal law not focused on their own harmful and deviant acts (see Chapter Two). A compromise between the traditional definition of victim and the broader one proposed here would be a recognition of a specific set of harmful behaviors that more accurately captures the range of culpable behaviors that cause harm to their victims. As has been discussed, the key word pertaining to criminal justice is *culpability*, which indicates some degree of blameworthiness or responsibility for a resulting action. Because culpability encompasses more than intentionality, acts causing harm can lead to findings of responsibility even when they were not committed intentionally.

> $\mathcal{L}$egal conceptions of crime and victimization do not encompass the wide range of purposive behaviors that create victims, particularly given the fact that *crime* is a label applied by persons capable of having their will enacted into law while simultaneously creating a criminal law not focused on their own harmful and deviant acts.

I have suggested that the concept of victimization be broadened to include *any act that produces financial or physical harm and is committed intentionally, negligently, recklessly, or knowingly* (Robinson, 2002). Following this logic, a new understanding of the term *victim* is in order, one that consists of *individual persons, groups of people, or corporations who are victimized by acts committed intentionally, negligently, recklessly, or knowingly.* Scholars such as Friedrichs (1983), Phipps (1986), and McShane and Williams (1992) have also been critical of the traditional conception of victims, for at least the following reasons:

- Current images of victims reinforce a focus on the state rather than the actual person(s) who suffered physical or financial harm. This "is a logical extension of a legal system which defines crimes as offenses against the state" (Zehr and Umbreit, 1982: 64).
- Current images of the state as victim reinforce a "conservative crime control agenda" or ideology "and have increased the power of the state in criminal proceedings" (McShane and Williams, 1992: 258).
- Criminal justice is focused on street crimes of the poor rather than on white-collar crimes and deviance, which allows white-collar offenders to escape relatively unscathed and unpunished despite their culpability (e.g., see Simon and Hagan, 1999).

Such criticisms have led scholars to call for a widening of the scope of criminal justice beyond street crimes committed by individuals against other individuals.

This is not to say that street crime is not tremendously harmful; it is just not as harmful as other acts that are either not against the law or not vigorously pursued by agencies of social control. Even violent crime, which Americans fear the most, is unlikely to result in actual harm to its victims. For example, fewer than 1 in 10 victims of violent crime will seek treatment for injuries at an emergency room (Donziger, 1996). In fact, the most common violent street crimes, simple assault and aggravated assault, do not even require any injury to be counted in the UCR. An attempt to injure is all that is required. As Kappeler et al. (2000: 122) explain: "all the violent crime, all the property crime, all the crime that we concentrate our energy and resources on combating is less of a threat to society than the crime committed by corporations." Yet, even criminology and criminal justice professors tend to ignore it. At a recent American Society of Criminology meeting in Washington, D.C., of the 503 sessions in which papers were presented by professional criminologists, fewer than 10 dealt with white-collar or corporate crime (Mokhiber and Weissman, 1999: 9).

The label of "crime" is *not* a function of what is most harmful to society.

A Comparison of Harms Associated with Crimes and "Noncrimes"

The label of "crime" is *not* a function of what is most harmful to society. If you believe that you are more likely to be victimized by street crime than by acts of white-collar deviance committed by wealthy individuals or corporations, you are wrong. The belief that white-collar deviance is less harmful than street crime is a myth (Kappeler et al., 2000).

There is considerable evidence that white-collar deviance causes more physical and property damage than all eight serious crimes combined. Kappeler et al. (2000) estimate that economic losses from corporate crime alone cost somewhere between 17 and 31 times as much as street crime. And this says nothing about lives lost by corporate crime. One example proves this point: tobacco use kills more people annually (approximately 420,000) than murder (approximately 20,000) and causes more financial loss ($50 billion in direct health care costs) than all street crime combined ($20 billion) (Robinson, 1998). Whereas murder by definition is intentional, manufacturing and promoting the use of tobacco to kill people is not intentional. Yet, the facts have spoken as lawsuits against the tobacco industry have shown that the tobacco industry's recklessness and negligence have produced hundreds of thousands of deaths each year. Thus, some scholars claim that the law should criminalize any act that causes harm to others, as long as the act is done intentionally, negligently, recklessly, or knowingly, as discussed earlier (and see the Issue in Depth at the end of this chapter).

There is considerable evidence that white-collar deviance causes more physical and property damage than all eight serious crimes combined.

Can a corporation be held responsible for a crime? According to Podgor and Israel (1997: 16):

> The initial common law view was that a corporation could not be held criminally liable, although the individual members of the corporation could. Lacking a mind, the corporation could not form the mens rea necessary for criminality. Not having physical attributes, there was no actus reus. Additionally, even if convicted of an offense, the corporation could not be imprisoned for the crime.

Currently, however, corporations can be held liable for their harmful acts. For example, Section 2.07 of the Model Penal Code suggests that corporate agents can be held responsible for harms inflicted in the course of their work, including harms resulting from a failure to act, and for actions authorized, performed, or recklessly tolerated by the board of directors. The problem is that corporations are rarely held criminally responsible for the harms they inflict on Americans. Why not? Because the "most powerful organization in our society is the corporation. Corporations have become more powerful than governments, or religious institutions, or labor unions" (Mokhiber and Weissman, 1999: 96). Other harms associated with legal acts and/or "crimes" that are not considered serious or worthy of criminal justice and media attention demonstrate that the label of "crime" is not reserved for the most harmful acts in society. For example, Frank and Lynch (1992: 1–11) document the costs of physical damage to individuals and society by means of deadly pollutants, preventable work-related "accidents" (as they are called), occupational diseases and deaths, and faulty consumer products. Simon and Eitzen (1993: 49–73, 113–114, 121–156) discuss individual cases of fraud by companies in the United States and trace harms to the savings and loan (S&L) scandals and tax breaks given exclusively to the rich. They also document the dangers associated with unsafe working conditions and unsafe products, including food products. Friedrichs (1995: 70–88) shows the harms associated with corporate violence against the public, consumers, and workers, and illustrates harms resulting from fraud, tax evasion, price fixing, price gouging, false advertising, and so forth. Weisburd and Schlegel (1992: 22–38) document the nature and extent of antitrust violations, multiple types of fraud, bribery, tax violations, and embezzlement. Rosoff, Pontell, and Tillman (1998) discuss numerous examples of white-collar crimes, including medical crime and computer crime, which demonstrate the cold, calculated acts of individuals and corporations that result in mind-boggling financial and physical harms.

Reiman (1998: 113) estimates the costs of white-collar crimes to be at least $208 billion annually, far more than all street crimes combined. Only one estimate of street crime costs has exceeded this estimate: A 1996 Justice Department report estimated that street crimes led to $450 billion per year in losses, but most of this was due to "quality of life costs" (Miller, Cohen, and Wiersma, 1997). The S&L scandals of the 1980s alone will cost Americans $500 billion over the next 40 years. Yet, the "average prison term for savings and loan offenders sentenced between 1988 and 1992 was 36 months, compared to 56 months for burglars and 38 months for those convicted of motor vehicle theft," even though the average loss in an S&L case was $500,000 (*Criminal Justice Newsletter,* December 5, 1994, p. 5, reported in Reiman, 1998) while the loss in an average property crime is $1,251 (Reiman, 1998: 128).

Reiman, using both official and unofficial sources of data, shows that far more people are killed and injured by preventable occupational diseases and hazards than by crime every year. He convincingly argues that the majority of these—totaling nearly 35,000 deaths and 3.5 million injuries—are as much beyond the control of the workers as being murdered is beyond the control of the murder victim (pp. 74–75). The fact that many of these deaths and injuries result from the negligence or recklessness of people who work for corporations demands our attention. McCaghy, Capron, and Jamieson (2000) suggest that as many as 100,000 workers each year die because of hazardous working conditions. Another 30,000 people die from unsafe and defective merchandise (Coleman, 1998).

The negligent and reckless acts that produce such harms are undeniably disproportionately committed by wealthier Caucasians. Whereas African Americans are rounded up for street crimes, particularly drug crimes (see Chapter Six), white-collar and corporate criminals typically walk away unscathed or with a slap on the wrist. Studies show that prosecution of white-collar criminals represents the "road not taken" (Shapiro, 1995) and that most white-collar criminals are repeat offenders who are nonetheless punished only with administrative sanctions or simple warnings (Weisburd, Chayet, and Waring, 1990). Reiman (1998: 110) writes that when we are talking about

> the kinds of crimes poor people almost never have the opportunity to commit, such as antitrust violations, industrial safety violations, embezzlement, and serious tax evasion, the criminal justice system shows an increasingly benign and merciful face. The more likely that a crime is the type committed by middle- and upper-class people, the less likely it will be treated as a criminal offense. When it comes to crime in the streets, where the perpetrator is apt to be poor, he or she is even more likely to be arrested and formally charged. When it comes to crime in the suites, where the offender is apt to be affluent, the system is most likely to deal with the crime noncriminally, that is, by civil litigation or informal settlement.

Reiman even compares arrest data for street crimes that result in the loss of property with the crime of embezzlement (a property crime whereby property is misappropriated—that is, stolen from its rightful owner after being left in the care or trust of another). He finds that the number of arrests for property crimes is 140 times greater than for embezzlement and that there is "one arrest for every $7,000 stolen [versus] one arrest for every $742,000 'misappropriated'" (p. 115). Arrests of white-collar offenders are made unlikely by deregulation efforts of politicians. Deregulation occurs when a government passes laws to limit its own control over an industry. In the 1980s, budgets of the Consumer Product Safety Commission, Occupational Safety and Health Administration, and Federal Trade Commission were slashed, and requirements relating to pharmaceutical and automotive safety were lifted or softened (Kappeler et al., 2000: 135). Most of these changes in policy were attached as "riders" to large bills in Congress.

In fact, the history of government regulation has been one of businesses regulating themselves for their own benefit and gain. Many regulators are former corporate executives or go to work for corporations after their regulating days are over (Hagan, 1998). Thus, there is a double standard of justice in the United States. While we spend billions each year fighting street crimes that produce *relatively* minor harms, we allow businesses to police themselves, and we give "little effort to enforce the law against [white-collar] criminals. When we do catch them at their nefarious deeds, we tap them on the wrist, make them say they are sorry, and send them about their criminal business" (Kappeler et al., 2000: 134).

Why do white-collar and corporate offenders rarely receive "justice"? In their book *Corporate Predators,* Mokhiber and Weissman (1999: 9) claim it is because of their power to shape the definition of the law and to influence prosecutors not to bring criminal charges. To these, I would also add that they can afford the best defense that money can buy.

In Chapter Two, I showed how this owes itself to the criminal law, which does not usually label such acts as "crimes"; when it does, they are not considered "serious." In defining what is bad, evil, wrong, harmful, and criminal, the criminal law thus creates myths of crime that cause people to view certain acts as most serious and harmful even though they are not, and produces fear of certain actions and people instead of others that pose even greater threats.

The government basically views victims of white-collar deviance as deserving their own victimizations. The phrase "let the buyer beware" is a prime example: "American business has followed 'caveat emptor' (let the buyer beware) and 'laissez faire' economics (the doctrine of government noninterference in business)" (Simon and Hagan, 1999: 158). The former doctrine suggests that if you get ripped off by fraudulent salespeople it is your own fault; you should have known better. The latter doctrine suggests that the government has no legitimate role in regulating business. Of course, if your house is burglarized because you left the windows unlocked, it is not your fault; you are seen as a victim of a "serious" crime, and the government has a legitimate role intervening in this type of activity.

Why does our own government fail to define the acts that are most dangerous to us as the most serious crimes? Kappeler et al. (2000) state:

> The government has a vested interest in maintaining the existing social definition of crime and extending this definition to groups and behaviors that are perceived to be a threat to the existing social order. . . . Similarly, the government has an interest in seeing that the existing criminal justice system's response to crime is not significantly altered in purpose or function.

According to these authors, the government's interests are served by promoting myths about crime and criminal justice. These myths are not only false but dangerous—dangerous because they allow harmful acts to be committed against innocent people by others with virtual impunity, even when done so intentionally. And they are promoted by the mass media, which are owned by powerful U.S. corporations (see Chapter Four). In essence, the definition of crime is a threat to justice in the United States, because people who intentionally, recklessly, negligently, and knowingly kill and injure Americans do so with virtual impunity.

The government's interests are served by promoting myths about crime and criminal justice that are not only false but dangerous, because they allow some people to commit harmful acts against innocent people with virtual impunity.

SOURCES OF CRIME INFORMATION: DO WE REALLY KNOW HOW MUCH CRIME IS OUT THERE?

Now that you have a better understanding of what crime is (and perhaps what it should be), how much of it is out there? To answer this question, you first need to understand where we get our information about crime. Most people get their crime information from media outlets such as television and newspapers, as well as from popular forms of entertainment such as movies, books, and the Internet (see Chapter Four).

The government also collects information about crime. Government sources tend to be more representative of what street crime really is than media sources of crime information. I will use these government sources to illustrate the nature of crime in the United States.

We get our information about street crime from two main sources produced by the U.S. government. One may be better than the other, depending on what you want to learn. Major sources of crime data in the United States include the Uniform Crime Reports, the National Crime Victimization Survey, and self-report studies. Each of these, as well as sources of data on other forms of harmful behaviors, are discussed next.

Major sources of crime data in the United States include the Uniform Crime Reports (UCR), the National Crime Victimization Survey (NCVS), and self-report studies.

Uniform Crime Reports

The Uniform Crime Reports (UCR) is perhaps the most commonly cited source of crime data in the United States. The UCR is a city, county, and state law enforcement program that provides a national source of crime data based on the submission of crime statistics by law enforcement agencies across the country (*UCR Handbook*, 1999). More than 17,000 city, county, and state law enforcement agencies, employing more than 700,000 officers and representing roughly 260 million inhabitants of the United States (96% of the U.S. population) voluntarily send their crime statistics either directly to the Federal Bureau of Investigation or to their own state's bureau of investigation or department of law enforcement for inclusion in the UCR.

> The Uniform Crime Reports (UCR) is perhaps the most commonly cited source of crime data in the United States. The UCR is a city, county, and state law enforcement program providing a national clearinghouse for crime data and crime statistics submitted by law enforcement agencies across the country.

The UCR collects data primarily on a group of Index Offenses, including both violent crimes and property crimes. Of the many limitations of the UCR (see Gove, Hughes, and Geerken, 1985), the most troubling in terms of both crime frequencies and crime trends is that the UCR measures only crimes known to the police. Most crimes are not known to the police, so the measure does not reflect actual crime frequencies accurately. Crimes not known to the police, commonly referred to as the "dark figure of crime," are not addressed by the UCR. Statistics from the Bureau of Justice Statistics (BJS) suggest that victims report only about one out of every three property crimes and that victims are most likely to report their victimizations to the police when they are violent in nature, when an injury results, when lost items are valued at $250 or more, or when forcible entry has occurred (Bureau of Justice Statistics, 1997).

> The most troubling limitation of the UCR, in terms of both crime frequencies and crime trends, is that it measures only crimes known to the police, and thus the measure is not an accurate account of actual crime frequencies. Crimes not known to the police are commonly referred to as the "dark figure of crime."

Additionally, because factors that affect the UCR figures fluctuate from one year to the next, it is not clear how valid the measure is of crime rates over time, known as *crime trends*. For example, rates of forcible rape may appear to be increasing according to the UCR when in fact they may be decreasing or remaining steady over time. For example, if police across the United States get better at detecting rape or if citizens report more rapes to the police, the UCR will show an increase in rape rates even though the actual rate may not have changed at all. One of the most striking limitations of the UCR as a source of valid crime data is that evidence is now available suggesting that police downgrade or upgrade serious crimes to less serious or more serious ones for political purposes (McCleary, Nienstedt, and Erven, 1982; Seidman and Couzens, 1974). Gaines et al. (2000: 43) discuss evidence showing that police departments in Atlanta, New York, and Philadelphia seriously manipulated their crime data.

Despite these weaknesses, and keeping in mind that these figures represent only crimes known to the police, the UCR does teach some interesting facts about crime. The most common crime according to the UCR is theft, making up nearly 60% of all crimes known to the police. The least common type of crime in the United States is murder, which makes up only 0.1% of all crimes known to the police. Figure 3.1 illustrates the percentage of each type of crime known to the police. Most crimes known to the police (about 88%), including theft, burglary, and motor vehicle theft, are committed against property. If you include robbery, which is committed against individuals but is done for property gain, then property crimes make up more than 90% of all crimes known to the police. Given that property crimes are less likely to be reported than violent crimes, it is safe to assume that the true distribution of street crime in the United States would be more like 99% property crimes and 1% violent crimes.

> *The* most common crime, according to the UCR, is theft, making up nearly 60% of all crimes known to the police. The least common type of crime in the United States is murder, which makes up only 0.1% of all crimes known to the police.

Figure 3.2 depicts some alarming statistics from the UCR. This "crime clock" suggests that an Index offense (a serious crime) occurs on average every 3 seconds in the United States, including a violent crime every 22 seconds and a property crime every 3 seconds. There is on average 1 murder every 34 minutes and a theft every 4 seconds! These time estimates are based on the total number of crimes known to the police per year. They do not imply regularity of crime occurrences. Table 3.2 shows how many actual offenses of each type were known to the police in 1999.

FIGURE 3.1
Percentage of Crimes Known to the Police (1999)

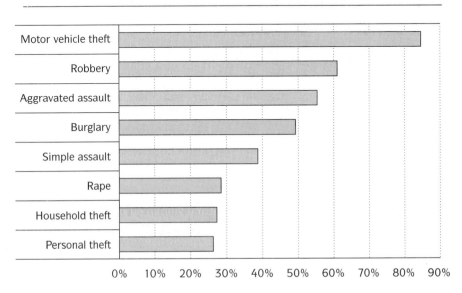

SOURCE: Comparisons of UCR and NCVS crime data.

FIGURE 3.2

The Crime Clock

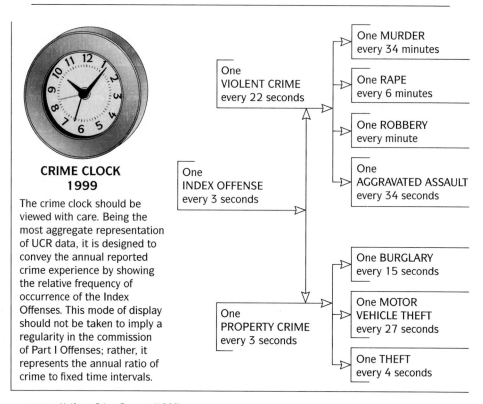

CRIME CLOCK 1999

The crime clock should be viewed with care. Being the most aggregate representation of UCR data, it is designed to convey the annual reported crime experience by showing the relative frequency of occurrence of the Index Offenses. This mode of display should not be taken to imply a regularity in the commission of Part I Offenses; rather, it represents the annual ratio of crime to fixed time intervals.

One INDEX OFFENSE every 3 seconds

One VIOLENT CRIME every 22 seconds

One PROPERTY CRIME every 3 seconds

One MURDER every 34 minutes

One RAPE every 6 minutes

One ROBBERY every minute

One AGGRAVATED ASSAULT every 34 seconds

One BURGLARY every 15 seconds

One MOTOR VEHICLE THEFT every 27 seconds

One THEFT every 4 seconds

SOURCE: Uniform Crime Reports (1999).

From these numbers, you might conclude that the United States is plagued by unusually high crime rates. In fact, this is not the case, with the exception of murder, which many attribute to our violent culture, economic and racial inequality, and the availability of guns in the United States (Beckett and Sasson, 2000: 8). This has led some to claim that "crime is not the problem"—that, instead, lethal violence is (Zimring and Hawkins, 1997).

National Crime Victimization Survey

In part to uncover some of the dark figure of crime—to assess some of the crimes not being reported to the police—the U.S. Department of Justice, Bureau of Justice Statistics designed the National Crime Victimization Survey (NCVS), originally known as the National Crime Survey

> *I*n part to uncover some of the dark figure of crime—that is, to assess some of the crimes not being reported to the police—the National Crime Victimization Survey (NCVS) was designed.

TABLE 3.2

Total Crimes Known to the Police (1999)

Murder	15,533
Rape	89,107
Robbery	409,670
Aggravated assault	916,383
Motor vehicle theft	1,147,305
Burglary	2,099,739
Theft	6,957,412
Total	**11,635,149**

SOURCE: Data from Uniform Crime Reports (1999).

(NCS). The survey was redesigned in the late 1980s, in part to improve survey techniques in order to increase people's ability to recall events, including previously undetected victimizations, and the first annual results for the redesigned survey were published for the year 1993.

The NCVS is a survey of roughly 100,000 people age 12 years and older in approximately 50,000 households. The survey explores the experiences with criminal victimizations of a sample of respondents made up of a nationally representative group of individuals living in U.S. households. Demographic variables such as age, sex, race, and income are used to compare rates of victimizations for different subgroups within the population. The NCVS collects crime data on both personal crimes and household crimes, as noted in the following box. These crimes are very similar to those contained in the UCR, with the notable exception of homicide; the NCVS does not include statistics on homicide simply because it is impossible to ask a homicide victim how many times he or she has been murdered in the past 12 months! Neither the UCR nor the NCVS measures victimizations resulting from white-collar deviance.

> Neither the UCR nor the NCVS measures victimization from white-collar deviance.

Crimes measured by the UCR and NCVS

UCR	NCVS
Homicide	———
Aggravated assault	Aggravated assault
Robbery	Robbery
Forcible rape	Rape and sexual assault
Burglary	Burglary
Theft	Theft
Motor vehicle theft	Motor vehicle theft
Arson	———

Twice each year, citizens are asked about their experiences of victimization from the offenses in the box on page 85. Because the NCVS includes both crimes that citizens report to the police and those they do not report, it is a more valid measure of actual street crime rates than the UCR. This is why the NCVS always indicates higher rates of crime than the UCR. Table 3.3 shows how many actually offenses of each type were reported to NCVS researchers in 1999.

> *B*ecause the NCVS includes both crimes officially reported and those unreported by citizens, it is a more valid measure of actual street crime rates than the UCR. This is why the NCVS always indicates higher crime levels than the UCR.

As you can see, the vast majority of street crime is property crime, and the most common crime is theft. The most common violent crime is aggravated assault, but relatively little crime in the United States is violent, although, as noted, the United States is plagued by an alarmingly high murder rate.

> *A*ccording to the NCVS, most street crime is property crime, and the most common crime is theft. Relatively little crime in the United States is violent crime. The most common violent crime is aggravated assault.

Other than this, the U.S. crime rate is comparable to those of other industrialized countries. Findings from the International Crime Survey, first administered by the Dutch Ministry of Justice in 1988, suggested that crime rates are high in the United States but not much higher than in many other countries (Beckett and Sasson, 2000). The 1996 survey showed that the United States lagged behind six other industrialized countries in crime rates and even was slightly below average overall (Mayhew and Van Dijk, 1997).

> *T*he United States has an alarmingly high murder rate. Otherwise, the U.S. crime rate is comparable to those of other industrialized countries.

TABLE 3.3

Total Crimes Indicated in the NCVS (1999)

Rape	383,000
Robbery	810,000
Aggravated assault	1,503,000
Motor vehicle theft	1,068,000
Burglary	3,064,000
Theft	16,172,000
Total	**23,000,000**

SOURCE: Data from National Crime Victimization Survey (1999).

Why, then, does the United States incarcerate more people than any other country? The answer—that we are tougher on crime than any other country—probably goes against all you have heard from "get tough" politicians attacking their "soft on crime" opponents. In fact, the notion that the U.S. criminal justice system is lenient is a myth, say Kappeler et al. (2000: 257), who write: "we lock up more people, for longer sentences, for more offenses than any nation on the face of the earth." Walker (1998: 146) writes that "the alleged 'loophole' of being soft on dangerous offenders does not exist." In fact, the opposite is true with regard to street crime. The United States is highly punitive against violent street criminals (see Chapter Ten). It is only our response to white-collar crime that is "soft."

The NCVS is also considered a better measure of crime trends than the UCR because the factors that affect victim recall and reporting to researchers are more constant than the factors affecting UCR crime trends. "The victimization surveys are clearly superior to UCR data in that they measure both reported and unreported crime, and they are unaffected by technological changes in police record keeping, levels of reporting by victims and the police, and other factors which call into question the validity of UCR data" (Kappeler et al., 2000: 35). According to the NCVS, street crime rates are at their lowest rates since the inception of the survey and have almost consistently declined since 1973. The next section examines these street crime trends.

> *The* NCVS is thought to be a better measure of crime trends since the factors that affect victim recall and reporting to researchers are more constant than those that affect the UCR crime trends.

American crime trends, according to the UCR and NCVS

The Crime Drop in America is a relatively new book that sums up what is happening with crime in the United States (Blumstein and Wallman, 2000). This book offers evidence that less than 25% of the decline in crime in the 1990s can be attributed to higher rates of imprisonment. More significant are factors such as the ebbing of the crack cocaine epidemic (see Chapter Six) and improvements in the U.S. economy since the 1980s.

Kappeler et al. (2000: 36) write: "Let us be very clear about this. The only reliable, scientific data we have on crime in the United States tells us that crime is decreasing." These authors are referring to the NCVS, which indicates that street crime has decreased consistently since the 1970s.

> *According* to the NCVS, street crime is decreasing. Yet, fear of crime remains very high today.

Believe it or not, you are safer today from street crime than at any time in recent U.S. history. Although fear of crime remains high, the belief that crime is increasing is nothing more than a myth (Kappeler et al., 2000; Walker, 1998). Gallup polls taken every year show that public concern about crime is not a function of fluctuations in actual crime rates. Figure 3.3, for example, compares crime rate fluctuations as measured in the UCR and NCVS with Gallup polls in the 1990s. Note how the percentage of people who ranked crime as the nation's number one problem increased dramatically in the early 1990s even though crime rates were actually going down. In

FIGURE 3.3

American Crime Trends and Concern about Crime, 1982–1995

(a)
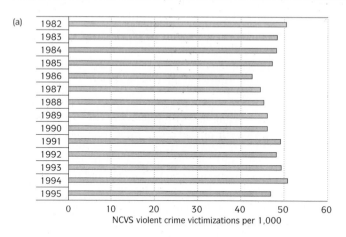

NCVS violent crime victimizations per 1,000

(b)
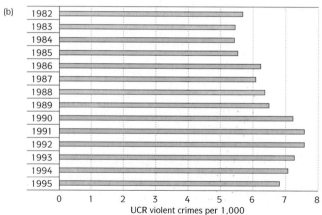

UCR violent crimes per 1,000

(c)
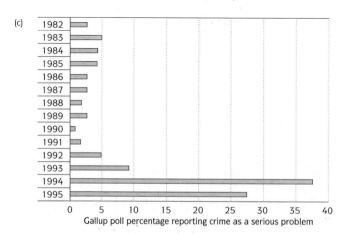

Gallup poll percentage reporting crime as a serious problem

SOURCES:
(a) National Crime Victimization Surveys, 1982–1995;
(b) Uniform Crime Reports, 1982–1995;
(c) Gallup polls, 1982–1995.
Online:
www.albany.edu/sourcebook.

Chapter Four, I attribute these increases to the politicization of crime and resulting media coverage. Walker (1998: 14) writes:

> Crime plagues our daily lives like a plague, affecting the way we think, the way we act, the way we respond to one another. Fear of crime has a corrosive effect on interpersonal relations, making us wary of small acts of friendliness toward strangers. It distorts the political process, with politicians offering quick-fix solutions that offer no realistic hope of reducing crime. Fear and frustration about crime produce irrational thinking.

Even though street crime rates are very low compared with other times in U.S. history, Americans are afraid. Although crime rates in the United States are no higher for most categories than in other industrialized countries, Americans report feeling less safe walking in their own neighborhoods after dark than citizens of other countries with higher crime rates (e.g., see Mayhew and Van Dijk, 1997).

Why are Americans so concerned about street crime even though it has decreased consistently since the 1970s? Is it that we see so much of it in the news and in television shows and movies? Kappeler et al. (2000: 14–15) suggest that our own government must exaggerate the harms associated with street crime in order to justify intervening in it. Think about the massive criminal justice expansion detailed in Chapter One. Does it make sense that we are spending more now than at any time in U.S. history to fight crime even though street crime rates are at their lowest rates in many years?

These authors argue that myths about crime and criminal justice are portrayed in ways that ensure that Americans will spend their tax dollars to expand the criminal justice system. They claim that this portrayal involves several steps:

- A distinct population is identified as "deviant" or "different" and then targeted.
- The harms associated with this population pose a threat to American norms, lifestyles, and traditions.
- Victims are portrayed as "innocent" or "helpless."
- Those who take on the dangerous class of offenders are portrayed as "virtuous" and "brave."

Is this how you see crime and criminal justice? While politicians and the media overemphasize street crime, more harmful acts of white-collar deviance are ignored. This is not consistent with either of the criminal justice system's goals of reducing crime and doing justice.

Self-Report Studies

Another way that criminologists have learned about crime is by studying actual offenders through *self-report studies,* including discussions with both incarcerated offenders and active offenders.

In general, these studies suggest that virtually all people have committed crimes during the course of their lives, including crimes for which they could have been incarcerated for at least

---

*Self-report studies include discussions with incarcerated offenders and active offenders. In general, these studies suggest that virtually all people have committed crimes during the course of their lives, including crimes for which they could have been incarcerated for at least one year in prison.

one year. Even recent self-report studies measuring serious criminality and delinquency show that most people admit to committing harmful acts that are prohibited by law. Robinson and Zaitzow (1999a) even found that the nation's crime experts—members of the American Society of Criminology—admit to illegal, deviant, and unethical behaviors.

The main problems associated with self-report studies revolve around reliability and validity issues. In self-report research, *reliability* refers to the likelihood that offenders will give the same answers to questions if the researcher asks the same question more than once over time. *Validity* means the likelihood that the offender is giving an honest, accurate answer. One thing we have learned about human behavior is that people misrepresent, exaggerate, and sometimes forget the truth. This makes self-report studies somewhat questionable. As stated by Nettler (1984), "Never bet on an animal that talks" (quoted in Jeffery, 1990).

What we have learned about offenders from self-report studies is still considered valuable by most criminologists. For example, we know that almost all offenders admit to having committed a crime for which they could have been incarcerated for at least one year. Self-report studies also indicate that much of what we do to fight crime in the United States will not work. Offenders tell us that they are not highly concerned about getting caught or punished for their criminal acts. Instead, they are motivated by potential gains from their crimes, and they know from experience that the criminal justice system is highly ineffective at even detecting crimes (e.g., see Cromwell, 1995).

---

*S*elf-report studies indicate that most current steps to fight crime in the United States will not work! Offenders say that they are not highly concerned about getting caught or punished for their criminal acts. Instead, they are motivated by potential gains from their crimes and know from experience that the criminal justice system is highly ineffective.

The following box contains some key truths about crime in the United States, taken from NCVS data. How do these trends compare to what you have been led to believe about street crime in your life?

Key truths about crime

- There is no crime wave in the United States. Victimizations from street crime have been steadily declining since the 1970s.
- The overwhelming majority of street crimes are minor, causing neither serious bodily damage nor major economic losses.
- Most acts of violence on the streets are committed by people whom the victim knows.
- In most street crimes, especially acts of violence, the victim and the perpetrator are of the same race.

SOURCE: Adapted from V. Kappeler, M. Blumberg, and G. Potter, *The Mythology of Crime and Criminal Justice,* 3rd ed. (Prospect Heights, IL: Waveland Press, 2000).

Sources of Data on White-Collar Deviance

According to leading consumer advocate Ralph Nader, also the Green party presidential candidate in 2000:

> Our country does not collect statistics on corporate crime the way that it does on street crime. For to do so would begin to highlight a little-attended agenda for law enforcement and other corporate reforms. Neither the Congress nor the White House and its Justice Department have made any moves over the years to assemble from around the country the abuses of corporations in quantifiable format so as to drive policy. (Introduction to Mokhiber and Weissman, 1999)

In fact, there are no national sources of data on white-collar deviance as there are on street crime: "no private or public institution—not the FBI, not the U.S. Department of Commerce—keeps up-to-date statistics on the cost of white collar crime. . . . The last public record was issued by the Department of Commerce in its 1974 *Handbook on White-Collar Crime*" (Kappeler et al., 2000: 123). This fact alone is proof that the U.S. government is less concerned with white-collar deviance than with street crime:

> Every year, the Federal Bureau of Investigation (FBI) issues its *Crime in the United States* report which documents murder, assault, burglary, and other street crimes. . . . The FBI does not issue a yearly *Corporate Crime in the United States* report, despite strong evidence indicating that corporate crime and violence inflicts far more damage on society than all street crime combined. (Mokhiber and Weissman, 1999: 8–9)

There are no national sources of data on white-collar deviance as there are on street crime.

How do we learn about harms associated with acts of white-collar deviance? Most of the evidence comes from studies of wealthy people, governments, corporations, and institutions, conducted by a handful of social scientists. These studies clearly demonstrate that the U.S. criminal justice system is failing to pursue the acts that most threaten us.

CONCLUSION

Clearly, the label of "crime" is applied to only a small portion of acts that are harmful to Americans. The label of "serious" crime is reserved for those acts that the government perceives to be committed primarily by the poor. This explains the focus in the United States on street crime rather than on white-collar deviance, even though the latter is far more dangerous. The sources we rely on for understanding how much crime there is in the United States reflect this bias—we rely on the error-prone Uniform Crime Reports more than we do on more valid measures such as the National Crime Victimization Survey. Yet, both sources show that street crime has declined significantly in the 1990s, in spite of criminal justice policy. Meanwhile, sources of data on white-collar deviance in the government are almost nonexistent, forcing us to rely on individual studies of corporations and wealthy citizens to learn about the harms caused by white-collar deviance. If we know that white-collar deviance is far more dangerous and costly than street crime, why do we, as a nation, fear street crime more? The next chapter examines the role of the mass media in promoting fear of street crime and myths about crime and criminal justice.

ISSUE IN DEPTH
Tobacco—The Greatest Crime in World History?

According to the Centers for Disease Control and Prevention (CDC), in 1994 there were 48 million smokers over the age of 18, accounting for approximately 26% of the U.S. population, plus an additional 3 million smokers under the age of 18 (CDC, 1996a). Given that one-third of smokers will die of smoking-related illnesses, we expect 16 million smoking-related deaths among current smokers over the age of 18 years (CDC, 1996b). Through illnesses such as cancer, heart disease, and stroke, smoking kills approximately 420,000 people each year and also leads to tens of thousands of miscarriages (CDC, 1993).

In order to maintain demand for their product, generate profit, and fulfill their obligation to shareholders, the tobacco industry must constantly replace those who die from continued use of their products. The best source of new recruits are those who are too young to understand the dangers fully, who wrongly believe they are immune to these harms and also wrongly believe they can quit at any time. In 1991, about 82% of smokers had begun smoking before they turned 18—before the age of legal accountability (CDC, 1994c). The tobacco industry exploits this market through advertising and merchandise offers, so 3,000 new young people start smoking every day, adding up to one million new smokers every year (Pierce, Fiore, and Novotny, 1989). Responding to clever, targeted marketing efforts, children choose the three most heavily advertised brands of cigarettes more often than adults (CDC, 1994a, 1994b).

Smoking now kills about 20 times as many people each year in the United States as murder. Currently, three million people worldwide die each year from tobacco use. Smoking also costs Americans $50 billion in direct health care costs per year (CDC, 1996a), more than all street crimes combined. Despite all the government-produced information about the harmful effects of smoking, the manufacture and use of cigarettes are still not criminal even though the link between cigarettes and cancer has been known since 1964, the same year that the American Medical Association (AMA) officially called smoking "a serious health hazard" (CDC, 1996c). Evidence from internal tobacco industry documents shows that tobacco companies knew this even before the federal government revealed it (Glantz et al., 1996). Undoubtedly, much more awaits our discovery when millions of pages of tobacco industry documents become accessible via court orders.

Labels indicating the health hazards of cigarettes first appeared in 1966. In 1970, the World Health Organization (WHO) took a public position against cigarette smoking. Secondhand smoke was officially recognized by the U.S. surgeon general as a health risk in 1972, but it was not until 1993 that the Environmental Protection Agency (EPA) designated secondhand smoke as a Group A carcinogen. Cigarettes were not eliminated from rations to U.S. soldiers and sailors until 1975. In 1981, the surgeon general said that no consumption of cigarettes was safe. In the 1990s, the Food and Drug Administration (FDA) called cigarettes a delivery system for an addictive drug, similar to heroin, cocaine, and alcohol (Anthony, Warner, and Kessler, 1994; CDC, 1994c).

Thousands of pages of internal documents from tobacco companies have already been leaked and published in five articles in the *Journal of the American Medical Association (JAMA)* (1995) and in a book entitled *The Cigarette Papers* (Glantz et al., 1996). These documents, as well as those released by court order as a result of lawsuits across the country, show that tobacco companies have known of the addictive nature of nicotine and the harmful effects of smoking since at least the mid-1960s, although they continued to deny this knowledge publicly through the 1990s. CEOs of major tobacco companies stated before Congress that they believed nicotine was not addictive. The editors of *JAMA*, the usually conservative mouthpiece of the medical profession, stated:

> In summary, the evidence is unequivocal that the US public has been duped by the tobacco industry. No right-thinking individual can ignore the evidence. We should all be outraged, and we should force the removal of this scourge from our nation and by so doing set an example for the world. We recognize the serious consequences of this ambition, but the health of our nation is more important than the profits of any single industry. (1995: 258)

One relatively small company, the first to admit that cigarettes are addictive and harmful, now labels its cigarette packets to indicate that smoking is addictive; this was one factor that caused the "big boys" in the tobacco industry to admit that smoking meets some accepted definitions of addiction. We know that cigarettes contain 43 carcinogens (CDC, 1996a), and smoking may serve as a gateway drug to alcohol, marijuana, and cocaine (CDC, 1994c).

Certainly, if tobacco were invented now, it would quickly be declared illegal and become a part of the war on drugs. But even in light of overwhelming evidence, neither the production of cigarettes nor their use is considered criminal. Instead, the Partnership for a Drug-Free America accepts large contributions from the tobacco industry, and no one is arrested or convicted just for smoking (except for minors in some places). Additionally, no cigarette company executives will be held criminally accountable, despite their actions, which include heavily advertising a deadly product, using cartoon characters to market to children, targeting specific populations such as minorities and women, hiding the truth about cigarettes from society, and even deliberately producing inaccurate results from inadequate and biased scientific studies. Tobacco companies funded diversionary studies via the Tobacco Institute to raise questions about the independently authored scientific evidence.

In 1994, cigarette companies spent $5 billion per year on advertising, which amounts to $13 million per day (Federal Trade Commission, 1996). This makes them the second most advertised product, after automobiles. All this advertising is directed at creating a demand for products few tobacco executives use themselves. When former "Winston Man" David Goerlitz asked an RJ Reynolds executive if he smoked, the response was: "Are you kidding? We reserve that right for the poor, the young, the black, and the stupid" (in Herbert, 1993: 11).

The liability of cigarette companies has been debated in Congress and in numerous civil lawsuits. A case in Florida recently held that tobacco companies were responsible for negligent and reckless conduct resulting in the deaths of former smokers. At the very least, cigarette companies have knowledge of the harm done by their products and have lied to cover up the truth. Theoretically, negligent, reckless, and knowing behaviors that produce harms can be called criminal behavior, but the behavior of cigarette manufacturers appears to be perfectly legal in criminal terms. Representing almost every state, Congress settled with the tobacco industry to the tune of more than $200 billion to be paid over the next 25 years. Cigarette prices have subsequently gone up. Thus, tobacco companies are forcing their own customers to pay for their wrongdoing! The U.S. government generally does not settle with other drug dealers, but because tobacco is a legal industry, very few people seem concerned about the settlement with nicotine dealers.

Discussion Questions

- Compare and contrast the terms *natural crime* and *legal crime*.
- List and define the eight "serious" crimes of the Uniform Crime Reports (UCR).
- What does the term *serious* mean?
- List and define the main elements of a crime.
- Is it possible to show that a person committed an act with intent? Why or why not?
- Outline some defenses that can be used when charged with a crime.
- List and define the main types of culpability, including intentionality, recklessness, negligence, and knowingness.
- In your opinion, are there any less serious crimes (Part II offenses of the UCR) that should be considered "serious" crimes (Part I offenses of the UCR)? Why or why not?
- What is *victimization*?
- Discuss how the definition of criminal victimization is too limited.
- Define *white-collar deviance* and provide a few examples.
- Which is more harmful to Americans, street crime or white-collar deviance?

- What interest does the U.S. government have in maintaining the current image of crime and criminals?
- Identify and discuss the main sources of crime data in the United States, including the UCR, the NCVS, and self-report studies.
- What is meant by the "dark figure of crime"?
- What does the crime clock show us about crime in the United States?
- Does the United States have more crime than other countries? Why or why not?
- Why do you think that the American criminal justice system does not collect national statistics on white-collar deviance?
- Do you think that sales of tobacco should be criminalized? Why or why not?

CHAPTER FOUR

"CRIME IS OUT OF CONTROL!"
MEDIA PORTRAYALS OF CRIME

INTRODUCTION

This chapter introduces you to "the media," a term that includes a wide range of sources of news-related information. I examine what the media do and do not do and then turn to how much people are exposed to the media in the United States. In discussing how the U.S. media cover crime and criminal justice, I show what the media cover, what they ignore, and why the media are so inaccurate when portraying crime and criminal justice. Implications for justice of media inaccuracy are discussed.

AN INTRODUCTION TO THE MEDIA

Many of society's problems are blamed on the media. We hear, for example, that the prevalence of violence in the United States is "because of the media." When school shootings rocked communities across the country in the late 1990s, parents and community leaders called for tougher standards for showing violent content in "the media" because of their suspicion that the media are responsible for copycat crimes.

> *The* media" is an umbrella term for a wide range of sources of news-related information.

But what are "the media"? Surette (1992: 10) defines the mass media as: "media that are easily, inexpensively, and simultaneously accessible to large segments of a population." These sources include newspapers, magazines, books, television, radio, film, and recordings.

Media sources are organized within a hierarchy of controlling institutions. Hess (1981) describes the media as having an inner ring, a middle ring, and an outer ring. The inner ring includes the major television networks such as ABC, NBC, CBS, and CNN; major news magazines such as *Time, Newsweek,* and *U.S. News & World Report;* national newspapers such as the *New York Times,* the *Washington Post, USA Today,* and the *Wall Street Journal;* and the Associated Press wire service.

---

*M*edia sources are organized within a hierarchy of controlling institutions. Hess (1981) described the media as having an inner ring, a middle ring, and an outer ring. The inner ring consists of the major news media outlets such as ABC, NBC, CBS, and CNN; major news magazines such as *Time, Newsweek,* and *U.S. News & World Report;* national newspapers such as the *New York Times,* the *Washington Post, USA Today,* and the *Wall Street Journal;* and the Associated Press (AP) wire service.

These inner-ring sources are the main sources of information for Americans about many issues (Lewis, 1981; Marion, 1995). Crime, as a major issue for society, is usually news (Merlo and Benekos, 2000). The Center for Media and Public Affairs, for example, found that almost 30% of local news is devoted to crime and criminal justice (Center for Media and Public Affairs, 2000).

The media are our main source for news about crime and criminal justice policy. As noted by Krajicek (1998: 139): "The press provides our window on public problems, on the government's strategies to solve them, and on how well those strategies succeed (or fail)." The media sources in the inner ring have greater influence than other sources. According to Harrigan (2000: 120), "The organization at the top of the media hierarchy decides what counts as news." This is true because most journalists consult these sources for their own news (Weaver and Wilhoit, 1986). Reporters of crime news commonly "copy" what other media reporters are doing. When reputable sources cover crime problems in the media, other reporters take their lead and follow with very similar stories.

---

*T*he media are our main source of crime and criminal justice policy news.

As one example, virtually all of the 1,700 newspapers in the United States subscribe to the Associated Press (AP), the largest news organization in the world. The AP is a nonprofit cooperative that serves more than 6,000 television and U.S. radio stations and more than 8,500 media outlets throughout the world through AP online. The AP compiles thousands of stories each day, of which only a couple of dozen are sent to the local, regional, national, and international wires for inclusion in various media outlets (Krajicek, 1998). Historically, crime has been considered newsworthy by the media. Because newsworthy events are determined by media outlets that are owned by large corporations (see the following box), the public's image of crime is at least partially defined by the wealthy and powerful.

The Media and Business

The major news media are owned and thus controlled by major corporations: "By the late 1980s, eight corporations controlled eight of the inner-ring media and a host of middle- and outer-ring media, including 40 television stations, over 200 cable television systems, more than 60 radio stations, 59 magazines, and 41 book publishers" (Parenti, 1993: 26). Half of the nation's newspapers are controlled by just ten large chains, and only about 2% of cities have competing newspapers (Graber, 1996). In fact, about 24 corporations control most of the U.S. culture industry (Herman and Chomsky, 1988).

According to Kappeler et al. (2000: 5): "Fewer than 15 corporations control most of the newspaper circulation in the United States, and Time, Inc. controls about 40% of all magazine sales. The Walt Disney Corporation includes ABC and ESPN. Viacom is the parent company of Paramount Pictures, MTV, Nickelodeon, Nick at Nite, Comedy Central, Showtime, The Movie Channel, All News Channel, UPN, Blockbuster, and CBS." Book publishing, too, is dominated by a few multinational corporations, including Bertelsmann, Time Warner, and Pearson PLC.

Ben Bagdikian's book *The Media Monopoly* (2000), chronicles the ever-growing stranglehold that major corporations have on news in the United States. Although the Federal Communications Commission (FCC) prohibits a corporation or individual from owning both a local television station and a newspaper in the same area to prevent a monopoly on news, many viewers are unaware that the crime news they see on TV and in the newspapers is the version that large corporations choose to air. Would it be logical to expect these corporations to focus on their own acts of deviance and harmful behaviors? As will be discussed later in this chapter, there is substantial evidence that the media tend to ignore corporate crimes.

Perhaps this is why street crime is more likely to be the focus of news than the more harmful behaviors of white-collar deviance discussed in Chapter Three. The disproportionate focus on street crime is a form of labeling whereby certain segments of the society are identified as bad, deviant, or immoral (Gans, 1995). In this process, evil is dramatized, and the notion of "us" versus "them" is reinforced, because we tend to think of criminals as being different from us. This "dualistic fallacy" is troubling because media coverage of crime is more reflective of crime myths than of realities (Kappeler et al., 2000). As images of crime tend to depict certain groups of society as bad, deviant, and immoral, they reinforce stereotypes created by U.S. criminal law.

At the same time, the media do not enlighten the public about other occurrences, such as "a $40 million misleading advertising campaign by the tobacco industry in its successful bid to defeat a 1998 tobacco bill that would have forced tobacco companies to absorb some of the public health costs of dealing with tobacco addiction" (Harrigan, 2000: 122). The tobacco industry characterized the tobacco bill as an $800 billion tax increase that would be passed on to U.S. citizens. Why didn't the media discuss tobacco harms and depict the negligence and recklessness of tobacco companies that perpetuate such harms?

This example demonstrates that U.S. corporations, through the inner ring of media outlets they own and control, define problems, identify crises, and thereby determine "what issues will be brought to the attention of political leaders" and U.S. citizens (Harrigan, 2000:124), while other issues and problems are ignored.

Simon and Hagan (1999: 12) place the media among the nation's group of elite individuals, corporations, and institutions. They suggest that the media have a direct impact on policies, including criminal justice system activity, "because they set limits on the breadth of ideological views that enter the policy-making debate in the United States. The media also choose which stories to emphasize and which to ignore. . . . Finally, the media are merely a group of corporations that are owned by other corporations and financial institutions."

FIGURE 4.1
The Growth of a Crime Problem

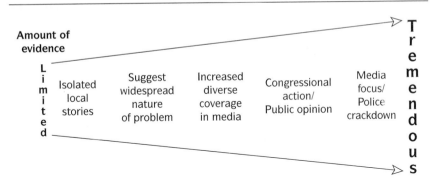

Figure 4.1 illustrates how the media can transform a minor problem into a major one. Try to imagine how crime and criminal justice realities are misconstrued in media coverage. Are the media more likely to cover certain types of crimes than others?

What the Media Do and Do Not Do

Because people do not simply absorb ideological propaganda (Potter and Kappeler, 1998: 19), the media do not tell the public what to think, but they may tell the public what to think about (Bennett, 1980; Iyengar and Kinder, 1987; McCombs and Shaw, 1972). Whatever is covered in the media is perceived to be important and worthy of viewer attention. Whether the attention is actually warranted on the basis of the nature and severity of the issue being covered is debatable.

> *The* media do not tell the public what to think, but they may tell the public what to think about. Thus, whatever is covered in the media is perceived to be important and worthy of viewer attention.

Without question, the news media, in their broadcasts and editorials, alert and even alarm the public and lawmakers about important events and issues (Hollinger and Lanza-Kaduce, 1988). Given that people are "passive consumers" of most forms of the media (such as television), it is not surprising that media coverage shapes a person's conception of reality: "people use knowledge they obtain from the media to construct a picture of the world, an image of reality on which they base their actions" (Surette, 1992: 2).

As explained by Potter and Kappeler (1998: 7), "Media coverage directs people's attention to specific crimes and helps to shape those crimes as social problems." The main problem with media coverage of crime, as you will see, is that it is dangerously inaccurate. Marion (1995) argues that the media alter the perceptions people have of the criminal justice system (Van Horn, Baumer, and Gormley, 1992) and distort the facts about crime.

Marion explains that the "early steps in the [criminal justice] process (law enforcement, investigation and arrest) are emphasized, and the other steps are almost invisible, especially informal procedures such as plea bargaining. Lawyers are often shown as actively investigating crimes, which rarely occurs" (Potter and Kappeler, 1998: 108). This is especially true in the everyday cases of poor people represented by publicly assigned counsel (see Chapter Eight).

In fact, most criminal justice cases receive no coverage from the media (Haltom, 1998: 157). Those rare cases that are covered tend to be atypical. As a result, false conceptions of what is "ordinary" are gained from these extraordinary cases. The O. J. Simpson trial wrongly showed Americans that the criminal justice system works too slowly and is more focused on defendants' rights than on victims' rights. For wealthy clients in highly publicized cases, the process of justice will be slow and deliberate. Yet, most court clients are poor and do not receive a trial; instead, they are convicted through the informal process of plea bargaining (see Chapter Eight). Violent crimes are overrepresented in the media (Surette, 1992), especially the "most terrifying crimes" and those committed by strangers (Scheingold, 1984: 55), whereas corporate crime and white-collar deviance are downplayed or ignored (Parenti, 1993: 10; Steel and Steger, 1988: 77).

> *M*ost criminal justice cases receive no coverage from the media. Those rare cases that are covered are the most atypical cases.

According to Haltom (1998: 157) media coverage of crimes in U.S. courts "tends to emphasize 'Crime Control' values" such as assuring "security from wrongdoers, just deserts, and punishment" while simultaneously devaluing due process concerns such as Constitutional protections of the accused. Haltom maintains that only in celebrated cases do the media highlight due process values. From his analysis, it is clear that media coverage of criminal justice in the courts is partly responsible for the United States' shift to a crime control model of criminal justice.

> *G*iven that reporters rely on insiders for information, it is logical that media coverage of courts will support crime control values.

Given that reporters rely on insiders for information, it is logical that media coverage of courts will support crime control values. The result is that reporters will be encouraged to "cover some aspects of the news more than others" (Haltom, 1998: 158). It is a symbiotic relationship in which the reporters get information and court personnel ensure the type of coverage that is favorable to their daily activities (Schlesinger and Tumber, 1994). Haltom suggests that "court sources 'feed' court reporters, and thus the news is largely what the reporters have 'eaten.'"

There are several reasons why crime control values will be emphasized over due process values. As noted earlier, the main reason is that members of the U.S. crime control bureaucracy are more likely to interact with the media than advocates of due process. Another reason that media slant their coverage of criminal justice in a manner more consistent with a crime control model is that it is simply

> easier to understand for reporters, their editors, and their audiences. Struggles between cops and robbers, good guys and bad guys, protectors and perpetrators are easy to write, to source, and to read or to view. Arcane rules and technicalities elude readers and viewers, many of whom have no idea what the rules are or what they mean. (Haltom, 1998: 165)

One reason that it is easier is that reporters often rely on prosecutors' offices for their stories. Dreschel (1983) suggests that prosecutors are more helpful to reporters than defense attorneys in terms of clarifying facts and offering tips about stories. Because prosecutors are more concerned with crime control than with due process, logically their biases are reflected in any subsequent media coverage.

Of course, the media are not the only source of information from which a person constructs his or her own reality. According to Surette (1992: 4), four primary sources are used, including personal experiences, significant others (peers, family, friends), other social groups and institutions (schools, churches, government agencies), and the mass media (Altheide, 1984; Quinney, 1970; Tuchman, 1978): "knowledge from all of these sources is mixed together, and from this mix, each individual constructs the 'world.'" Logically, the influence of the mass media likely increases as the influence of the other sources declines (Cohen and Young, 1981; Lichter, 1988).

> $\mathcal{P}$eople construct their own perception of reality from four primary sources: personal experiences; significant others (peers, family, friends); other social groups and institutions (schools, churches, government agencies); and the mass media.

Given that 90% of Americans will not be victimized by crime (Barkan, 1997; Kappeler et al., 2000) and that most people do not know anyone who chooses to talk about personal experience of criminal victimization, the media are a prime source of information about crime (Potter and Kappeler, 1998). Other scholars make the same argument, that the U.S. media are basic sources about crime and criminal justice (Barak, 1994; Ericson, Baranek, and Chan, 1989; Graber, 1980).

> $\mathcal{G}$iven that 90% of Americans will not be victimized by crime and that most people do not know anyone who chooses to share his or her own knowledge of criminal victimization, the media are a prime source of information about crime.

An alarming realization is that the media tend to cover the same crime repeatedly as it processes through the criminal justice system. With any recent development in a case, the details of the original crime are rehashed, fostering an impression that the crime occurred more than once. When the case goes to trial or is plea bargained, when a sentence is passed down, and so on, the viewer learns these details from the media once more. The effect is a general feeling that there is much more crime out there than there really is.

To the extent that media coverage of crime is repetitive and pervasive, it is more likely that it will affect people's attitudes about crime (Surette, 1992: 86–87). This is true in terms of not only what the media cover, but also what they fail to cover: "by emphasizing or ignoring topics, [the media] may influence the list of issues that are important to the public" (p. 87). As noted previously, corporate crimes are virtually ignored by the media; thus most people, even criminology and criminal justice students, do not perceive such acts as threatening to their own personal safety (Robinson, 1999).

In this chapter, I will examine how and why media coverage of crime is inaccurate and dangerous. This chapter will compare the realities of crime examined in the previous chapter with the way crime is portrayed on television, in the newspapers, and in popular entertainment. First, I examine the degree to which people actually are exposed to media sources.

DOES IT MATTER? ARE PEOPLE EXPOSED TO THE MEDIA?

Selective media coverage might be less problematic if viewers did not expose themselves to it. A study by the Pew Research Center for the People and the Press (1996) shows that only one in four Americans follows national news closely. Yet, the nature of crime news is that it does not have to be

> *A* study by the Pew Research Center for the People and the Press (1996) shows that only one in four Americans follows national news closely. Yet, the nature of crime news is that it does not have to be followed closely, particularly at the national level.

followed closely, particularly at the national level. As will be illustrated later, crime news is prevalent at all levels of news coverage, even the local level. It should not be surprising, then, that the media are the people's main source of information about crime (Beckett and Sasson, 2000). Tunnell (1992: 295) cites a National Crime Survey that found that 96% of Americans reported they relied on the media for information about crime. Research shows most people responding to Gallup polls have reported that they think the media are accurate in their crime reporting, even though, in all forms of media, crime and criminality are shown out of proportion to actual crime.

> *T*unnell (1992: 295) cites a National Crime Survey that found that 96% of Americans reported they relied on the media for information about crime. Fields and Jerin (1999: 94) cite research that shows most people in Gallup polls have reported that they think the media are accurate in their crime reporting even though in all forms of media, crime and criminality are shown out of proportion to actual crime.

Televison is a more significant source of news than newspapers: 60% of Americans rely on TV for news information (Angolabahere, Behr, and Iyengar, 1993). According to Klain (1989), the average American spends more than four hours per day—roughly one-third of his or her recreational time—watching TV (Stossel, 1997). The average American child watches television between three and four hours per day (American Academy of Pediatrics, 2000; Center for Media Education, 2000). People are less exposed to other sources of news information, such as newspapers, because television is more easily consumed; it can be taken in passively and does not require the ability to read in order to watch (Surette, 1992).

Without question, TV media coverage inaccurately portrays the U.S. criminal justice system. For example, despite all the controversial issues regarding TV in the courts (e.g., see Surette, 1992), the most troubling aspect of the TV camera in the courtroom is the fact that what people see is not representative of the typical court case. While people see trials in their entirety on *Court TV* and in part on shows such as *Dateline NBC*, the reality is that more than 90% of cases do not lead to trial but are handled informally through plea bargaining (see Chapter Eight). People think that trials are the rule when, in fact, they are the "exceptional case" (Cole and Smith, 2000). The media thus "emphasize the rare-in-reality adversarial criminal trial" which leads the viewer to believe that the typical court case in the United States is "a high-stakes, complicated, arcane contest practiced by expert professionals and beyond the understanding of everyday citizens" (Surette, 1992: 40), even though the reality is the assembly-line justice of plea bargaining. In other words, people think we are following a due process model of criminal justice when in fact we are using a crime control model. At the same time, corrections is the least shown aspect of criminal justice, so that the further one moves into the system, the worse the image becomes of American criminal justice (p. 41).

MEDIA COVERAGE OF CRIME AND CRIMINAL JUSTICE

Perhaps the most fascinating research on the media and crime is found in *Scooped!*, written by a former crime reporter, David Krajicek (1998). The subtitle of this inside look at media coverage of crime reflects its author's informed opinion: *Media Miss Real Story on Crime While Chasing Sex, Sleaze, and Celebrities.* Krajicek's main claim about the media is this: "Take a predisposition toward simplicity and anecdote, add unsophisticated reporting, a degenerating peer culture, an overworked news staff, the rapture of sex and celebrities, and—poof!—you've got today's crime journalism" (p. 180).

Disgusted with this type of crime reporting, Krajicek quit his job as a reporter. Why? In his words, he explains:

> While we [reporters] were sitting in vans counting arrests, we missed the most important story on the crime beat: the collapse of the U.S. criminal justice system as an effective means of fighting crime, maintaining order, ensuring public safety, and meting out equitable justice. . . .
> I came to conclude that the media had been scooped by myopia, sleazy story distractions, and an unhealthy devotion to the official police agenda. (p. 111)

Krajicek argues that the media misrepresent reality, much the same as what Reiman (1998) points out about the image of crime in U.S. society. As you may recall from Chapter One, Reiman described the American conception of crime as a problem of the poor as distorted, much like a reflection in a carnival mirror. In Krajicek's words: "Today, reading a newspaper or watching a news telecast can be like looking at the country's reflection in a fun-house mirror. The society we see presented in the news is a warped place, often morbid and alarming" (p. 4). It should be no surprise to you that for a lot of people, "the term crime evokes an image of a young African American male who is armed with a handgun and commits a robbery, rape, or murder. In the minds of many Americans, crime is synonymous with black crime." Why? Because those "crimes that receive the most attention—from the media, from politicians, and from criminal justice policy makers—are 'street crimes' such as murder, robbery, and rape" (Walker, Spohn, and Delone, 2000).

As explained by Krajicek (1998: 5–6), the media provide crime-anxious Americans with excited accounts of horrible crimes; present tenuous evidence that the crimes, however anomalous, could happen to each of us; seek out the accountable individuals (judges and probation officers); devise snappy slogans to package the problem neatly; and serve up images of scowling politicians thumping their lecterns about the latest legislation that surely would stop such atrocities: "We're finally getting tough on crime. We're no longer coddling criminals. We're making America's streets safe again."

Whether crime news is based on fact and is representative of the truth is irrelevant—"the politicians wanted expedient answers, not information"—"efficacy means nothing; image is everything" (Krajicek, 1998: 5, 17). I will return to the issue of how politics is involved in the "framing" of crime and criminal justice later in this chapter.

Focus of Media Reporting on Crime: What the Media Cover and Ignore

As explained before, media portrayals of crime are "selectively determine[d]" by media outlets (Merlo and Benekos, 2000: 5). Generally, decisions are made to feature "the most sensational, emotional, significant, and universally appealing aspects" of crime for public viewing (Sacco, 1995). As Krajicek (1998: 95) said about his own work, crime reports focus on the miserable, the deviant, the strange, and the "particularly cruel." The common saying, "if it bleeds, it leads," accurately characterizes the philosophy of the media in the United States. Platt (1999) calls nightly news "Armageddon—Live at 6 (P.M.)!" Sabato (1993), in his book *Feeding Frenzy*, claims that American media coverage of politics is comparable to an attack of sharks on a helpless victim. Although his research focuses on politics generally, his arguments apply to media coverage of crime and criminal justice as well. Metaphorically speaking, if there is blood in the water, the media will likely cover a story about crime.

> *G*enerally, the media feature "the most sensational, emotional, significant, and universally appealing aspects" of crime for public viewing (Sacco, 1995).

Research clearly demonstrates that crime news is focused on the most violent types of crime (Potter and Kappeler, 1998), at least those that occur at the street level (e.g., see Chiricos, 1995; Kooistra, Mahoney, and Westervelt, 1999). Of particular interest to the media are the rarest and "most egregious examples" of crime. For example, between 1992 and 1993, major network evening news coverage of homicide tripled even as homicide rates remained unchanged, and from 1993 to 1996, major network news increased coverage of homicide 721% (National Center on Institutions and Alternatives, 1999).

Television news generally shows violence at a rate much higher than its incidence in society would seem to justify (Newman, 1990). As noted by Krajicek (1998: 4): "Murder and sexual offenses are the marquee offenses . . . and certain cases, generally based upon nubility or celebrity, are anointed for extravagant coverage." A study cited in Surette (1992: 68) showed that 26% of news stories were focused on murder, even though murder regularly accounts for only 0.1% to 0.2% of all crimes known to the police. Although murder may be the most heinous of all crimes, this disproportionate focus does not seem justified by its prevalence in the United States. At the same time, even though about half of the crimes that are reported to the police are nonviolent, they made up only 4% of the stories in the same study. Additionally, it is the most heinous and bizarre of all murders that tend to be most widely discussed in the media (e.g., see Paulsen, 2000).

> *T*elevision news generally shows violence at a rate much higher than its incidence in society would seem to justify.

Marsh (1991) conducted a review of similar studies and found that for every two stories of property crimes, there were eight stories of violent crimes. Newspapers in the mid-1980s covered the violent crimes of murder, rape, robbery, and assault four times more than they did the property crimes of theft, burglary, and motor vehicle theft, even though property crimes make up at least 90% of street crimes in any given year (recall the crime pie chart discussed in Chapter Three).

By focusing on certain types of crimes over others, the media are thus involved in "constructing" the typical view of crime, even when they are only reporting "extreme, dramatic cases: the public is more likely to think they are representative because of the emphasis by the media" (Chermak, 1994: 580). Potter and Kappeler (1998: 7) explain: "Media coverage directs people's attention to specific crimes and helps to shape those crimes as social problems." This means Americans are much more concerned with violent crimes such as murder, even though they are much more likely to be victimized by property crimes such as theft and burglary.

The media are also preoccupied with random crime (Merlo and Benekos, 2000). Not surprisingly, one type of crime that has received a tremendous amount of coverage in recent years is school violence. After the tragic mass murder of a dozen students and a teacher at Columbine High School in Littleton, Colorado, the national news on each of the three major network news stations (ABC, NBC, CBS) devoted no less than half of each night's newscasts to this subject for approximately a month after the murders. But despite a commonsense impression to the contrary, in fact school violence has not increased recently. Figure 4.2 illustrates trends of violence in U.S. schools. Are these trends consistent with the overwhelming coverage of recent school shootings? The Issue in Depth at the end of this chapter concludes that they are not.

Even though the media give much attention to crime, they typically ignore harmful acts committed by the wealthy, such as white-collar crime (Potter and Kappeler, 1998; Surette, 1992) and corporate crime (Evans and Lundman, 1987; Randell, 1995). This is troubling precisely because the harms associated with such acts clearly dwarf those resulting from all street crimes combined in any given year, as discussed in Chapter Three. Neglect of this topic stems from the risk of libel suits; interrelationships between the media and business; the pro-business orientation of the media; and difficulties associated with investigating white-collar crime (Potter and Kappeler, 1998: 15, citing Mintz, 1992). The media focus almost exclusively on street crimes, so that

FIGURE 4.2
Trends of Violence in American Schools

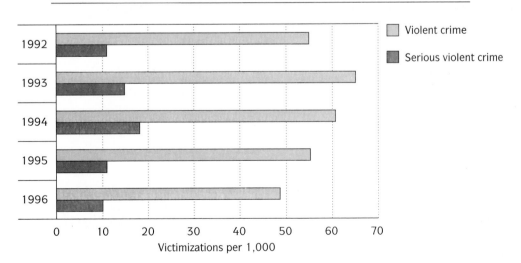

SOURCE: U.S. Department of Justice, National Crime Victimization Survey, 1992–1996.

three classes of people are depicted—the upper class, the middle class, and the "criminal class" (Barak, 1994).

> *E*ven though we can say with confidence that the media give much attention to crime, the media typically ignore harmful acts committed by the wealthy, such as white-collar crime.

When ABC's *Prime Time Live* investigated allegations and uncovered actual examples of food contamination at a Food Lion grocery store in 1996, for example, ABC was successfully sued by Food Lion for using deceptive media techniques to investigate claims of contaminated food products. The fact that Food Lion had intentionally sold unsafe food products to consumers was lost in the resulting coverage. This type of coverage is rare, however, and is limited to news magazine shows such as *Prime Time Live*. This is one result of the intimate relationship between the media and corporate America.

The media also have historically not paid much attention to costly and misguided criminal justice policies. Krajicek writes: "Collectively, journalists were scooped on the biggest crime story of the last quarter of this century by neglecting to adequately inform a puzzled public that our system of law enforcement and punishment, cobbled together with razor wire and prison bars, has been an expensive folly" (1998: 5).

> *T*he media also have historically not given much attention to costly and misguided criminal justice policies.

The media typically do not challenge the legal institution when it needs to be challenged. Although the media may question a particular enforcement (e.g., the vicious beating of Rodney King by Los Angeles police officers, captured on videotape), they rarely challenge the legal institution as a whole (Reiman, 1998). What about police corruption and police brutality as a regular, everyday occurrence for some Americans? What about the way police discretion in the United States permits and perhaps even encourages such actions? The media rarely discuss such issues. As a result, media reporting reinforces the validity of law and the myths inherent in the law: "crime news . . . tends to be ideological insofar as it represents a worldview of state managers" (Welch, Fenwick, and Roberts, 1998: 220).

Some specific events (e.g., Willie Horton's crimes, committed after he was released early on a prison furlough) have been used by politicians, through the media, to reinforce a need for new laws that crack down even harder on street crimes and poor minorities. In these cases, the media act as dupes for sound-bite politicians.

Crime Trends

Even when crime is going down, stories about declines in crime are like "a dinghy bobbing in a rolling sea" of stories about individual, thoughtless, and salacious crime reports (Krajicek, 1998: 12). Individual stories erroneously suggest that crime is increasing (Beckett and Sasson, 2000). This is one example of how media activity reinforces myths about crime: people believe that crime is increasing even when it is not (Kappeler et al., 2000). The media achieve this by provid-

> *I*ndividual stories suggest that crime is increasing, even though it is not.

ing "a steady diet of the growing and omnipotent danger of interpersonal crime" (Barak, 1995: 133).

For example, in the mid-1990s, when violent crime was decreasing to its lowest levels in twenty years, crime coverage on television and in the newspapers increased in one city by more than 400% (Chiricos, Eschholtz, and Gertz, 1997). In 1993, the three major news networks ran 1,632 crime stories on their evening newscasts, up from 785 in 1992 and 571 in 1991. This occurred even though victimization rates of the NCVS and crime rates of the UCR were down during this time (Potter and Kappeler, 1998: 3). Not surprisingly, 88% of Americans in 1994 thought crime was at an all-time high (Barkan, 1997; Jackson, 1994).

Figure 4.3 compares violent crime rates known to the police versus media coverage of violent crime on television and in the newspapers, and shows clearly that amount of coverage is not directly related to actual trends of violence. Generally, the same pattern is found elsewhere: 20% of local television news relates to crime, as does 13% of national news and 25% of newspaper space (Ericson et al., 1989; Surette, 1998). The main problem with this overreporting is that news stories about crime are not rational and tempered. They are not in-depth, critical, informative accounts. Instead, they amount to numerous "raw dispatches about the crime of the moment, the frightening—and often false—trend of the week, the prurient murder of the month, the sensational trial of the year" (Krajicek, 1998: 4).

FIGURE 4.3
Actual Crime Rates and Media Coverage of Violence

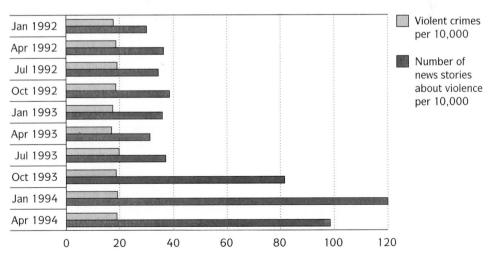

SOURCE: Adapted from T. Chiricos, S. Eschholtz, and M. Gertz, "Crime, News, and Fear of Crime: Toward an Identification of Audience Effects," *Social Problems* 44 (1997): 342–357.

Lack of Critical Coverage: Where's the Context?

Critical coverage about crime and criminal justice is typically lacking in American news. In terms of criminal justice policy, the media simply "cover" what politicians pledge and promise about getting tough on crime because the media are caught up in the same "moral panic" about crime, because they have become so caught up in the chase that they have forgotten to expose the public to intelligent crime reporting, and because crime news is inexpensive and attracts viewers (Krajicek, 1998: 6–7).

> *C*ritical coverage about crime and criminal justice coverage is typically lacking in American news. In terms of criminal justice policy, the media simply "cover" what politicians promise about getting tough on crime because the media are caught up in the same "moral panic" about crime.

A moral panic occurs when

> A condition, episode, person or group of persons emerges to become defined as a threat to societal values and interests; its nature is presented in a stylized and stereotypical fashion by the mass media; the moral barricades are manned by editors, bishops, politicians, and other right-thinking people; socially accredited experts pronounce their diagnoses and solutions. (Cohen, 1972: 9)

Escholtz (1997: 48) adds that because moral panics "typically involve an exaggeration of a social phenomenon, the public response also is often exaggerated and can create its own long lasting repercussions for society in terms of drastic changes in laws and social policy."

One example of a recent moral panic is the crack hype of the 1980s (Reinarman and Levine, 1989) (see Chapter Six). If you are old enough to remember special hour-long media specials such as "48 Hours on Crack Street" (by CBS) from the 1980s, you may recall how alarming such reports about crack cocaine were. Americans were led to believe that crack was the "new fad," the new "dangerous drug," and that crack use was increasing. This, in fact, was not true.

So, why do the media create moral panics about real problems such as crack cocaine by blowing them out of proportion? Harrigan (2000: 130) claims that the media are biased in favor of "visually dramatic or sensational events that will attract a wide viewing audience." Shows such as "48 Hours on Crack Street" certainly fit this profile.

Such media depictions of crime problems are inherently inaccurate—they have to be. The alternative is to tell the truth, which is virtually guaranteed to be more mundane and therefore will not attract as many viewers. Furthermore, such stories do not provide much real information about crime problems. Krajicek (1998) claims that media coverage of crime almost never attempts to answer the most important question of all: "So what?" Instead, the majority of crime coverage can be depicted as "drive-by journalism—a ton of anecdote and graphic detail about individual cases . . . but not an ounce of leavening context to help frame and explain crime" (Krajicek, 1998: 7). Zuckerman (1994: 64) writes: "Television, in particular, is so focused on pictures and so limited by time that in the normal run of reporting it cannot begin to provide the context that gives meaning and perspective." Think of news reporters you have seen on the news, standing live at the scene of a crime that happened hours ago. The fact that there is nothing going on there now is apparently irrelevant. Because the reporter is there live, the illusion of importance is maintained.

Lack of context in the news does not serve Americans well because it misinforms them. It is beneficial for politicians who want to put forth brief and simplistic stances on crime,

---

*L*ack of context in the news does not serve Americans well because it misinforms them.

---

most commonly depicted as the 10- or 15-second "sound bites" heard in any election year (Harrigan, 2000).

One night in 1994, while I was a graduate student, the local television news program reported a series of crime-related stories. The news began with an alarmed-looking news reporter who came on with a "video box" above his left shoulder that announced a "CRIME EXPLOSION!" This video image stayed above his left shoulder as he reported on a local rape, another crime that had occurred elsewhere in the state, and still another heinous act that had been committed somewhere in the United States. After he finished reporting on these stories, the reporter said, in a hushed voice, "Actually, crime statewide is down according to official statistics." The reporter did not elaborate on this statement, did not explain what he meant by "official statistics," and did not provide any insight into how there could be a crime explosion in the midst of declining crime rates. In other words, he failed to place the individual crime stories in the overall context of declining crime rates.

Is this atypical? Is it unique to the recent past? McGucken (1987) suggests that the media may have always, at least during the twentieth century, been focused disproportionately on crime. Her analysis of stories featured in the *New York Times* during the first half of the twentieth century showed that crime was covered by anecdote and that little attention was given to contextual criminal justice policy discussions. As noted by McGucken, the *New York Times* coverage was consistently brief, superficial, and purely descriptive.

This is troubling not just because readers of the *New York Times* are exposed to simplistic crime discussions, but also because the *New York Times* is a primary source of information for other media outlets. Another study (Lichter, Lichter, and Rothman, 1994) compared violent crimes on television with real-world violent crime rates from the mid-1950s through the mid-1980s. The authors found that homicide was represented on prime-time television shows at 1,000 times its actual rate over this time period.

One of the most popular types of television programs since the 1950s has been the police drama: 20% to 40% of prime-time television programs are police-related (Surette, 1992). Because the most effective law enforcers in the media are those who do whatever it takes to beat crime, including using excessive force, engaging in vigilantism, and ignoring due process procedures (Culver and Knight, 1979; Dominick, 1978), viewers may view the courts as "handcuffing the police" and as favoring the "rights of criminals" (Beckett and Sasson, 2000; Merlo and Benekos, 2000). This type of biased coverage would logically promote crime control values over due process values, perhaps explaining in part why American criminal justice has moved in this direction, as discussed in Chapter One.

Media and Fear of Crime

One claim about media coverage of crime that has been confirmed recently is that it is related to level of fear of crime (Livingston, 1996). In particular, so-called crime-time news leads to increased fear among its viewers (Cohen and Solomon, 1994). Kappeler et al. (2000: 42) write: "The Center for Media and Public Affairs found that crime has been the most prominently featured topic on the evening news since 1993, with 7,448 stories, or about 1 in 7 evening news stories." And 1 in 20 stories since 1993 has been about murder (Center for Media and Public Affairs, 1997).

Krajicek (1998: 7) calls the result a "tattooing of the national psyche." The National Criminal Justice Commission demonstrates how the media have created the illusion that all Americans have a realistic chance of being murdered by strangers, even though murder is the rarest of all crimes and is most likely committed by people known to the victims (Donziger, 1996: 9). Once *USA Today* published a headline that claimed: "Random Killings Hit a High." The subtitle claimed "All have 'realistic chance' of being victim, says FBI" (Davis and Meddis, 1994). This was absolutely false. According to Kappeler et al. (2000: 39), the chance that any U.S. resident over the age of 11 years will be murdered was was only 1 in 14,286 in 1996.

Generally, the more viewers are exposed to television, the more likely they are to see the world as a "mean and scary place" and the more likely they are distrust others, feel insecure and vulnerable, and view crime as a serious problem (Gerbner et al. 1980; Morgan and Signorielli, 1990; Signorielli, 1990). Heavy TV exposure also leads to an increased fear of crime, an overestimation of the likelihood of becoming a victim of violence, beliefs that one's neighborhood is unsafe, assumptions that crime rates are increasing, and increased support for punitive anticrime measures (Gerbner, 1994). Another result of TV viewing is that it can "dull the critical-thinking ability" of Americans and lead to apathy (Harrigan, 2000: 131), thereby making simplistic solutions to complex problems more appealing and making Americans less interested in important issues.

> *G*enerally, the more viewers are exposed to television, the more likely they are to see the world as a "mean and scary place" and the more likely they are to distrust others, feel insecure and vulnerable, and view crime as a serious problem.

An analysis of crime news and fear of crime by Chiricos et al. (1997) found that frequency of exposure to television news and radio news were related to fear of crime. Yet, reading newspapers was not found to be related to fear of crime, even though most newspaper crime coverage is violent or sensational in nature (Marsh, 1991). According to their analysis, the effects of television viewing depend on who is doing the viewing (also see Heath and Gilbert, 1996). In their research, television viewing and fear of crime were related only in Caucasian females between the ages of 30 and 54 years. Chiricos and his colleagues suggest that this finding can be attributed to the fact that the most likely depicted crime victims on television are middle-aged or older Caucasian women.

Thus, for some, "the media have the ability, indirectly at least, to manipulate the fear of crime" (Tunnell, 1992: 300). Eschholtz (1997: 50) summarizes the research by claiming that

> for newspaper consumption the character of the message is important: local, random, and sensational stories evoke the most fear, whereas, distant, specific, and less sensational stories may have a calming effect on individuals. For television, the quantity of television viewed in general, violent programming in particular, and certain audience characteristics are generally associated with higher levels of fear.

Few go as far as to suggest that the media intentionally create fear in viewers. But the fear that is created reinforces mythology about crime and criminal justice (Kappeler et al., 2000), causing citizens to avoid, and police to apprehend, people who are perceived as posing the greatest threats to our well-being (e.g., see Culverson, 1998; Rome, 1998). As argued in Chapter Three, these people tend to be darker in skin color and lacking in wealth as compared to the average American.

FIGURE 4.4

Fear of Crime in America

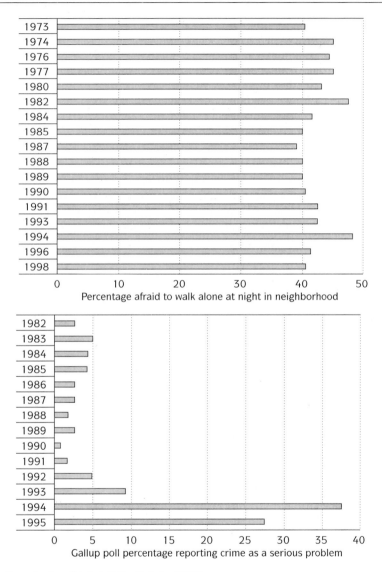

SOURCE: Sourcebook on Criminal Justice Statistics (1998).

Given all this coverage of crime in the United States, for many citizens "the United States must seem to be a hopelessly savage place that stands teetering on the lip of the Apocalypse" (Krajicek, 1998:4). Figure 4.4 shows results from a series of Gallup polls conducted throughout the 1980s and 1990s. Even during a time when crime was actually decreasing, people were more likely to call it the number one problem facing the nation. Additionally, the percentage of people who fear walking alone at night, also shown in Figure 4.4, has been highly variable over the years despite relatively consistent declines in crime since the early 1970s. In March 1994, the Times Mirror Center for the People and the Press reported a poll showing that 50% of the respondents feared they would be victims of crime. Another 30% said that crime was the nation's number one problem. Compare this with the Gallup polls shown in Figure 4.4. Perhaps it is not surprising to learn that coverage of crime on the three major networks peaked a year earlier, in 1993.

Is this attributable to media coverage of crime? It is due at least in part to the "moral panic" about crime that is suggested in headlines from news sources during this time period, as shown in the following box.

Some headlines from major news sources about crime

- *Newsweek* (July 19, 1993): "TEEN VIOLENCE: WILD IN THE STREETS"
- *Newsweek* (September 27, 1993): "IN A STATE OF TERROR"
- *Business Week* (December 13, 1993): "THE ECONOMICS OF CRIME: RAMPANT CRIME IS COSTING AMERICA $425 MILLION A YEAR. WHAT CAN BE DONE? PLENTY"
- *Newsweek* (January 10, 1994): "GROWING UP SCARED: HOW OUR KIDS ARE ROBBED OF THEIR CHILDHOOD"
- *U.S. News & World Report* (January 17, 1994): "VIOLENCE IN AMERICA." First sentence: "A scary orgy of violent crime is fueling another public call to action."
- *U.S. News & World Report* (January 17, 1994): "THE TRUTH ABOUT VIOLENT CRIME: WHAT YOU REALLY HAVE TO FEAR"
- *Time* (February 7, 1994): "LOCK 'EM UP AND THROW AWAY THE KEY: OUTRAGE OVER CRIME HAS AMERICA TALKING TOUGH" (Krajicek, 1998: 22)

Such headlines were surrounded by bloody images and photos of guns and bullets, suggesting that crime is typically violent in nature, even though most crime is committed against property and is relatively mundane. Logic dictates that far more people are exposed to such headlines and magazine covers than to the fine print of the stories, which most likely contains what little context is provided. Perhaps it is not coincidental that so-called crime waves "coincide with election years and demands by law enforcement officials to increase their budgets" (Donziger, 1996: 64–65).

Other research links fear not only to media coverage but also to the extent to which politicians highlight crime as a major concern (Lichter, Lichter, and Rothman, 1994). Perhaps this is why public concern about crime peaked at 52% in the same month in which President Clinton signed the 1994 federal crime bill into law.

Beckett and Sasson (2000) claim that media coverage of crime is also related to the likelihood that viewers will support a "retributive justice perspective" (Roberts, 1992), one that will promote more punitive types of responses to crime and a crime control model rather than a due process model. Fear of crime also may be related to crime entertainment (Donovan, 1998), as will be discussed later in this chapter.

EXPLANATIONS OF MEDIA INACCURACY

According to Cohen and Young (1981), there are two competing explanations for the news media's inaccuracy in covering crime. According to one explanation (the "market" model), crime is considered newsworthy because of the public interest in it, and thus it is covered. According to the other explanation (the "manipulative" model), crime is of interest to the owners of the media and is purposefully distorted to shape public interests in line with those of the owners of the media. Surette (1992: 57) describes both models as simplistic and inadequate, and puts forth an alternative explanation (the "organizational model"), which posits that crime is inherently subjective and thus distorted, but also allows owners to generate profit from using crime.

This is a good starting point. In examining the literature in this area, however, there are other reasons that the media focus on crime and tend to be inaccurate in their coverage of it. Each of these reasons is discussed next.

Lack of Criminal Justice Education

According to the former crime reporter cited throughout this chapter, one of the main explanations for the media's fixation on crime, particularly its mischaracterization of crime, is that reporters and others in the news business are not educated about crime and criminal justice. As Krajicek (1998) puts it, they do not know the difference between a VCR and the UCR. If media owners, reporters, and editors do not understand basic facts of crime and criminal justice, they will merely report what they are told by official sources. For example, you have likely seen headlines and stories about rising and falling *crime* rates that base their arguments on rising or falling *arrest* rates. Arrest rates are not valid measures of crime rates, but it is doubtful that many in the media understand the difference.

> *O*ne of the main explanations for the media's fixation on crime, particularly its mischaracterization, is that reporters and others in the news business are not educated about crime and criminal justice.

The journalist writes crime stories to get on the front page much as the academic criminologist or criminal justice professor writes articles to get published in the best journals. The goal of each is not necessarily to make an actual difference in criminal justice policy but, rather, to play the game successfully within the rules laid out by the discipline. Ultimately, personal and even financial reward may be gained by each, as well as by their respective employers.

While academics practice "real criminology" and have been highly critical of recent criminal justice policy, their findings do not seem to inform criminal justice policy. Politicians practice "kindergarten criminology" (Krajicek, 1998: 5), and reporters have not held politicians or criminal justice policy makers accountable for it.

Peer Culture

Additionally, the "peer culture among journalists is as intense as that at any junior high school. Reporters and editors look to one another—both colleagues and competitors—to determine what is appropriate. If everyone else is doing it, that deserves an affirmation" (Krajicek, 1998: 35). Consistent with social learning theories of crime, the media imitate what others in the business are doing and are likely to continue to cover it when the coverage is positively reinforced (Akers, 1998).

> $\mathscr{C}$onsistent with social learning theories of crime, the media imitate what others in the business are doing and are likely to continue to cover it when the coverage is positively reinforced.

As noted by Fishman (1978), simple imitation also plays a role. Once a news agency picks up on a crime story or theme, other news organizations are likely to pick it up as well. When the theme runs throughout the media industry as a whole or through the mainstream media discussed earlier, it can lead to a "media crime wave" or "moral panic" like that described earlier with regard to crack cocaine and violent crime.

Organizational Factors: Entertainment for Profit

Of course, reporters do not deserve all or even most of the blame. Most are simply following orders of their superiors. Instead, blame resides in "the moguls, stockholders, owners, and publishers" as well as the "editors, reporters, and photographers" (Krajicek, 1998: 5). Those who set the agenda for the media are the most to blame for inaccuracies about crime and criminal justice in the media.

> $\mathscr{T}$hose who set the agenda for the media are the most to blame for inaccuracies about crime and criminal justice in the media.

Given the finite resources of reporters and news space, the fact that crime is so prominent in the news means that other issues are not adequately addressed. Is this intentional? According to Krajicek (1998: 13), "The process of journalism—collecting, organizing, and disseminating information—happens in a series of priority-setting decisions about how to use . . . resources." Those that prioritize crime over other vexing social problems are the most accountable.

Who decides, then, what will be newsworthy? Beckett and Sasson (2000: 81) claim that news is simply defined as what is out of the ordinary (Ericson et al., 1989). Thus, television news comes to be seen as a form of entertainment, whereby the media are highly selective in what they broadcast. Violence is more "sellable" than the mundane aspects of theft and other forms of property crime. This explains what Surette (1992: 14) calls the recent blurring of news and entertainment in media outlets.

However, according to Surette (1992: 22, 32), crime has been the "single most popular story element in the forty year history of U.S. commercial television, with crime-related shows regularly accounting for one-fourth to one-third of all the three major networks' prime time shows" from the 1960s to the 1990s. Why is this so? Since the media are businesses, economic factors are inherently involved in selecting content. The content of the media is shaped in line with the economic interests of the organization that owns the media outlet (Potter and Kappeler, 1998: 19).

According to Stevens and Garcia (1980), TV programming is aimed at attracting and keeping large audiences because the "larger the audience, the more that sponsors are willing to spend for advertising and the greater the profits" (Surette, 1992: 31). Given the organizational needs of the media, including profit-generating news (Beckett and Sasson, 2000; Marion, 1995), crime is valuable because it attracts viewers and because it is relatively easy to write about given the abundance of official sources of information in law enforcement personnel and politicians (Fishman, 1978; Sherizen, 1978). These officials are considered legitimate, authoritative, reliable, and consistently available (Beckett, 1997; Gans, 1979; Schlesinger and Tumber, 1994; Sigal, 1973).

> *C*rime is valuable to the media because it attracts viewers and because it is relatively easy to write about given the abundance of official sources of information in law enforcement and politics.

Beckett and Sasson (2000: 118) conclude that crime entertainment narratives promote three related messages:

- Most offenders are professional criminals.
- Community safety is threatened by judges and defense attorneys who are too much concerned with offenders' rights.
- Criminal justice personnel are out there every day, fighting the war on crime.

These messages have the potential to be highly misleading to the general public. Therein lies the danger to doing justice, as well as to more honest crime control efforts. They also shift support toward a crime control model of criminal justice.

Boundary Reinforcement

Extraordinary events are also used by media outlets to reinforce moral boundaries of the community, or at least those that have been codified in the criminal law. They achieve this by depicting unacceptable acts of evil (Garland, 1990). As noted by Surette (1992: 32): "The popular mass entertainment media . . . have thus become a significant social factor, conveying thematic messages and lessons about whom to emulate and fear in society."

> *E*xtraordinary events are also used by media outlets to reinforce moral boundaries of the community, or at least those that have been codified in the criminal law.

If we examine what passes for television entertainment, we can see whom we should fear. Some of the most popular television entertainment shows on television recently have included *Homicide, Murder She Wrote, Matlock, Law and Order,* and *The Practice.* Such shows almost always involve homicides or other violent crimes, as if these were the typical crimes that people are likely to suffer in the United States.

There were seven national "crime-time" entertainment shows on TV by 1993: *America's Most Wanted, Top Cops, American Detective, Unsolved Mysteries, Rescue 911, Inside Edition,* and *Hard Copy* (Potter and Kappeler, 1998: 3). In addition to these shows, most, if not all, of the popular news magazine shows usually broadcast crime stories. Today there are new crime shows on virtually every network, including *CSI (Crime Scene Investigation); Walker, Texas Ranger;* and *Arrest and Trial.*

Perhaps this explains why ten network and cable channels in 1992 depicted a total of 1,846 violent crimes each day (Barkan, 1997; Lichter and Edmundson, 1992). Crime has been the leading television news topic in the 1990s (Beckett and Sasson, 2000). Approximately 70% of prime-time programs depict violence (Gerbner, 1994).

All of this calls attention to certain groups in the United States more than others. Unfortunately, the groups that are depicted in crime entertainment shows tend to be poor, minority males, who actually pose a much less significant threat to society than we have been led to believe (Robinson, 2000). Even leading criminology and criminal justice texts and journals reinforce crime myths about whom and what to fear by providing scant coverage of anything other than street crime. Most introductory criminal justice texts, for example, give virtually no attention to white-collar deviance. Not surprisingly, even criminology and criminal justice students fail to characterize accurately the relative harms associated with various criminal and noncriminal behaviors (Robinson, 1999).

> *The* groups that are depicted in such crime entertainment shows tend to be poor, minority males, who pose a much less significant threat to society than we have been led to believe.

The irony of today's television content, the main source of entertainment media, is that "Whatever the media show is the opposite of what is true" (Surette, 1992: 42). Television shows highlight the types of crimes that are least likely to occur in real life, they overemphasize acts of violence, and typical criminal and typical victim are not representative of reality. The reality is that crime news takes the rare and turns it into the common crime image (Surette, 1992: 63).

The Role of Politics in the "Framing" of Crime

Ironically, the media, by reporting what such official sources report, create perceptions of the crime problem in viewers, thereby also creating support for particular crime control policies (Roberts and Edwards, 1992; Roberts and Doob, 1990). Because government sources are typically cited in crime reports, it is not surprising that Americans support "more police, more arrests, longer sentences, more prisons, and more executions" (Potter and Kappeler, 1998: 3). State managers cited in media reports about crime also tend to emphasize crime control perspectives over a due process model of criminal justice (Welch, Fenwick, and Roberts, 1998).

Logically, as news becomes routinized—as it follows similar formats to what has proved acceptable to owners of the media and news consumers and to what has evolved in line with needs of advertisers (Potter and Kappeler, 1998: 19)—sources that have been relied on in the past are relied on regularly. This makes getting the news relatively easy. Government sources can be also be cited as "official" and thus reliable (Surette, 1992).

Given that the media are dominant institutions in society, they share similar characteristics with other dominant institutions, such as the state and corporations (Potter and Kappeler, 1998: 17). They reproduce the status quo, which is beneficial to them (Alvarado and Boyd-Barrett, 1992; Gurevitch et al., 1982; Lapley and Westlake, 1988; McQuail, 1994; Stevenson, 1995; Strinati, 1995). An example can be characterized as a form of media inbreeding. Given that "media professionals are trained, educated, and socialized in a way as to internalize the values and norms of the dominant, mainstream culture . . . [they will] interpret or mediate news, information, and complex issues in a way that is usually consistent with the dominant culture and with the interests of powerful groups" (Potter and Kappeler, 1998: 18).

The media will also amplify viewpoints of the powerful, especially when these views are already shared by members of society because they appeal to our "common sense." Anything offensive to consumers, advertisers, or owners will be discouraged (Potter and Kappeler, 1998: 18). News stories about crime also often include "commentary from public officials" (Merlo and Benekos, 2000: 2) or "state managers" (Welch et al., 1998), which supposedly provide expert opinion about crime-related problems. Thus, politicians attempt to "capitalize on the news to further support their political agendas and to gain support of voters" (Merlo and Benekos, 2000: 2).

The best of these politicians—the most effective claims-makers about crime—have their views of crime turned into media coverage; thus, they determine the focus of crime coverage of the media (Edelman, 1988; Gusfield, 1967; Hilgartner and Bosk, 1988; Kitsuse and Spector, 1973). Strangely enough, politicians then see media coverage of crime problems as heightened public concern over crime (Beckett and Sasson, 2000). Yet, most scholars posit that political action occurs before public concern and that public concern stems from actions of politicians, rather than the other way around.

> *The* best politicians—the most effective claims-makers about crime—have their views of crime turned into media coverage; thus, they determine the focus of crime coverage of the media.

For example, Gans (1995) outlines the labeling process of the "underclass" in the United States. The process he discusses is similar to the process whereby politicians create images of crime which are then picked up by media outlets. As discussed in Chapter Two, legislators apply labels to people by defining their acts as criminal. Then media outlets serve to alarm others about who should be feared. Finally, the media rely on official sources of information about crime (called "counters" by Gans, 1995) in order to prove that their claims-making activities are valid.

In the media, the most common way in which crime is framed is as a failure of the criminal justice system (Beckett and Sasson, 2000). For example, misleading and misinforming media coverage of crime highlights the failures of the criminal justice system and characterizes the justice system as inefficient and soft on crime (Roberts, 1992; Roberts and Doob, 1990). This is one of the paradoxes of news coverage of the criminal justice system. Although the media depict the criminal justice system as ineffective, "the cumulative effect of these portraits appears to be increased support for more police, more prisons, and more money for the criminal justice system" (Surette, 1992: 14).

> *In* the media, the most common way in which crime is framed is as a failure of the criminal justice system.

In other words, media coverage of criminal justice advances the status quo of big government when it comes to fighting crime (Fishman, 1978; Graber, 1980). That is, discourse on crime control is limited to present policies (Potter and Kappeler, 1998: 7). Given that the media focus disproportionately on law enforcement crime-fighting activities, the end result is increased support for a crime control model rather than a due process model (Surette, 1992).

As if due process rights were the cause of crime in the United States, politicians have made us all less free in an effort to fight a crime problem that is actually less problematic today than it has been in a long, long time. This attack on due process is consistent with social control theories of crime, which hold that criminality is normal and should be expected in the absence of meaningful societal controls on individual behavior (Hirschi, 1969).

> *A*s if due process rights were the cause of crime in the United States, politicians have made us all less free in an effort to fight a crime problem that is actually less problematic today than it has been in a long, long time.

Even as the United States has been cast by "get tough" politicians as "a victim of its own liberty"—that "U.S. society is too free for its own good and insufficiently fearful of authority" (Krajicek, 1998: 16)—the media have not alerted citizens to how their Constitutional protections have been eroded in the move toward a crime control model of criminal justice. As explained by Krajicek (1998: 139), "the media have uncritically reproduced official, conservative, 'law-and-order' perspectives with little fundamental analysis of their success or failure."

Crime is politically constructed as a function of a breakdown of law and order, two-parent families, and family values. Do you remember vice-presidential candidate Dan Quayle's public ranting in 1992 about the television show *Murphy Brown*, which depicted a working mother choosing to raise a child on her own? Quayle insisted that the character was "mocking the importance of fathers" and that this sent a bad message to Americans, who ought to be raising children only when they could provide two-parent, heterosexual, married households. Eventually, the media insisted, as Barbara Dafoe Whitehead claimed in the April 1993 issue of the *Atlantic Monthly*, that "Dan Quayle Was Right."

> *C*rime is politically constructed as a function of a breakdown of law and order, two-parent families, and family values.

Hence, the media tend to amplify the claims of politicians about crime (Beckett and Sasson, 2000). Sasson (1995: 13) states it this way: "People do crimes because they know they can get away with them. The police are handcuffed by liberal judges. The prisons, bursting at their seams, have revolving doors for serious offenders." Thus, the way to reduce crime is to reduce "loopholes and technicalities that impede the apprehension and imprisonment of offenders" and increase the "swiftness, certainty and severity of punishment"—in other words, to erode due process protections that interfere with the crime-fighting capacity of our criminal justice system (Surette, 1992: 14).

CONCLUSION

Clearly, the media shape our world view about crime and criminal justice. Once the law has defined certain acts as crimes, the media tend to cover those acts that are the most unusual, bizarre, and violent. Because the inner ring of the American media is controlled by large corporations, which are concerned first and foremost with ensuring profits, the media sell crime to Americans—"if it bleeds, it leads." The media's coverage of criminal justice is biased in favor of "get tough" approaches to reducing crime. All of this creates injustice in the United States. Using the media as their mouthpieces, politicians have become like Chicken Little, trying to incite the public about impending doom in the form of crime in this country. They claim we need a "war" to stop crime. When politicians and the media use terms like *war,* it suggests to the public that crime must be "fought" rather than "prevented." The costs to Americans include the failure either to do justice or to reduce crime.

ISSUE IN DEPTH
School Shootings in the Media

There is a perception, measured by increased fear of crime at school, increased media coverage of school crime, and the 1998 mass murder at Columbine High School in Colorado, that crime in U.S. schools is increasing. This perception is simply false. Crimes at school are no more prevalent at the turn of the twenty-first century than they were at any time in the twentieth century. In fact, schools were safer in 1998, the year of the mass murder at Columbine High School, than they were at any other time in the 1990s.

Because of the intensive media coverage of a few highly publicized cases of school violence in the United States, particularly the mass murder at Columbine, students report being more afraid of school violence and more likely to avoid certain places at schools. Yet, schools are relatively safe places. Moreover, as measured by the incidence of serious violent crimes at our nation's schools, they are safer today than they used to be. The rate of violent acts at schools and away from schools per 1,000 people has slightly declined over time.

The perception of violent crime at schools was stated succinctly in a report titled *Early Warning, Timely Response: A Guide to Safe Schools.* The report states: "Violence can happen at any time, anywhere." This statement is not very reassuring for parents, to say the least, particularly since it comes from the U.S. Department of Education and U.S. Department of Justice report based on the work of an independent panel of experts in the fields of education, law enforcement, and mental health.

The realities of school crime in the United States include these facts (U.S. Department of Education, 1998):

- The most common type of school crime is a physical attack or fight without a weapon.
- The least common type of school crime is a murder.
- One's chance of dying at school is roughly one in a million.
- Fewer than 1% of killings of juveniles occur at schools.

Additionally, in the most recent survey of U.S. schools, only 10% of schools reported that they had experienced at least one serious violent crime (National

Center for Education Statistics, 1999). Almost half of schools in the United States (43%) report that they experienced no incidents of serious crime.

Some statistics suggest a more alarming problem. Consider these, for example:

- 900 teachers are threatened per hour in the United States.
- 20% of high school seniors report being threatened with violence every year.
- 2,000 students are actually attacked per hour.
- 40 teachers are attacked per hour (National Education Association, 1999).
- 100,000 guns are brought to school every day (*USA Today*, 1999).
- The ratio of students to counselors in elementary and secondary schools is 513 : 1 (American Counseling Association, 1999).

When one considers how many students and teachers are in U.S. schools, it is easier to get a proper perspective on the problem. There are more than 51 million students and approximately 3 million teachers in American schools. In 1996, there were approximately 380,000 violent victimizations at school against these roughly 54 million people. This means the rate of violent victimization at U.S. schools is about 704 per 100,000 people. Stated differently, about 0.7% of people can expect to become victims of serious violent crimes at schools.

Research shows that the most likely victims are students in the upper grades (9–12), especially for serious violent crimes. Victims are more likely to come from racial and ethnic minority groups (the highest rate is for African Americans). Victims of violent crime tend to be standouts from large, public, city schools. Violence is more common in high schools and middle schools, with bullying reaching a peak in sixth grade. As for teachers, the most likely victims of violence are male teachers in urban middle schools (*Annual Report on School Safety*, 1998). The *American Teacher* (1993) claims that strict teachers with high standards are also more likely to be victimized.

The most likely perpetrators, according to statistics, are students in the middle to upper grades (6–10), especially for serious violent crimes. They tend to be Caucasian males in large, public, urban schools (*Annual Report on School Safety*, 1998; *American Teacher*, 1993). The most likely locations of serious violent crimes at schools are common areas such as hallways, cafeterias, libraries, unattended classrooms, and gyms and locker areas (*American Teacher*, 1993). Serious violent crimes are more commonly reported at schools where there are street gangs and higher levels of drug use (*Annual Report on School Safety*, 1998).

It is clear that violence at school is less common than portrayed in the media. When a child brings a gun to school and ends up using it, the results can be highly tragic and disturbing. Yet, the fact remains that this occurrence is very rare. Perhaps this rarity is what makes the incidents newsworthy. The significant question for this analysis is whether citizens are becoming more concerned about the problem of school violence, particularly school shootings, than they should, given the extremely small likelihood that such an incident will ever affect them or their children. Data such as those reported here suggest that results of increased media coverage of school violence and school shootings include increased fear of crime and perceptions of crime risk at schools.

School shootings are, in fact, incredibly rare. Yet, school administrators report feeling pressure to do something about them, even though it is highly unlikely that any particular school will witness a school shooting. A national survey of school officials found that the most common reasons administrators decided to review and/or update their security plans were because of publicity about violence in the news (56%), responses to school boards or other officials (14%), and responses to concerns raised by parents or students (4%). Only 6% were in response to actual violent acts or threats of violence at school (Agron and Anderson, 2000).

Now, the Federal Bureau of Investigation (FBI) and the Secret Service have produced a report aimed at identifying those children most likely to bring guns to schools and to commit violent crimes at schools. On average, since 1992, 26 students are killed at school with guns each year. Although it is terrible that even one such killing occurs, consider that more than 10,000 children are killed with guns every year *outside* of school! Will the FBI and Secret Service produce reports on how to prevent these killings? Not likely. As long as our attention is focused on school shootings, that is what we will talk about. And the result is that we will not see the big picture.

Discussion Questions

- What is meant by the term *media*?
- Discuss how the "inner ring" of the media has more control over the stream of information than less well known media outlets.
- What are the main types of media that cover crime and criminal justice stories?
- Explain how the media help shape our world view.
- Why do you think the media are so heavily relied on for information about crime and criminal justice?
- Why do the media tend to ignore white-collar deviance even though it causes so much harm?
- What components of the criminal justice system do the media focus on most? Why?
- Why do you think the media focus so much more on violent crimes than on property crimes?
- Provide a few examples of how the media fail to provide the proper context when reporting about crime and criminal justice.

- Do the media promote fear of crime? Why or why not?
- Which reasons discussed in the chapter do you think best explain why the media are so inaccurate when reporting about crime and criminal justice?
- On the basis of the research discussed in the chapter, do you the think the media are biased against any particular group in society? Why or why not?
- What are some likely effects of media coverage of school violence on students and their parents?

CHAPTER FIVE

THE WAR ON CRIME:
INNOCENT BIAS AGAINST THE POOR,
PEOPLE OF COLOR, AND WOMEN

KEY CONCEPTS

- Is the war on crime a war on the poor?
- What about race and ethnicity?
- Gender and criminal justice
- Issue in Depth: Political Crimes

INTRODUCTION

Consider the following facts established in previous chapters:

- The law is made by a group who are not representative of the general public.
- Lawmakers are voted for by a group who are not representative of the general public.
- Most people do not vote.
- Lawmaking is influenced by special interests.
- Crime is not a label used to identify the most serious threats to our lives and property.

Given these facts, is it possible that the criminal justice system is biased against particular groups in society, such as the poor, people of color, and women? In this chapter, I examine the evidence that the criminal justice system as a whole is biased against these groups. In subsequent chapters I will review evidence of bias by the individual components of the criminal justice system—the police, courts, and corrections. The primary purpose of this chapter is to assess the evidence that the criminal justice system as whole is biased and therefore unjust.

IS THE WAR ON CRIME A WAR ON THE POOR?

Jeffrey Reiman (1998) argues that the criminal justice system is biased against the poor at every step of the process, beginning with the law. Reiman, in his book *The Rich Get Richer and the Poor Get Prison,* demonstrates that the criminal law essentially ignores harmful acts committed by the powerful, such as those committed in white-collar jobs and by corporations. As discussed in Chapter Three, these acts are either not illegal (such as the manufacture and sale of tobacco) or are against the law, but are not seen as "serious" and thus not widely pursued by law enforcement agencies (e.g., manufacturing and selling defective products).

> *J*effrey Reiman (1998) argues that the criminal justice system is biased against the poor at every step of the process, beginning with the law.

The label of criminality is almost always reserved for the poor, even though criminality is not a function of social class. According to Tittle and Meier (1990: 292), "Research published since 1978, using both official and self-reported data suggests . . . that there is no pervasive relationship between [social class] and delinquency." Jensen and Thompson (1990: 1021) similarly conclude that "class, no matter how defined, contributes little to explaining variation in self-reports of common delinquency." Yet, we are filling up our prisons with poor street criminals and building more prisons to accommodate the growing number of convicted street criminals. So, is the war on crime a war on the poor?

> *T*he label of criminality is almost always reserved for the poor, even though criminality is not a function of social class.

In a convincing and moving analysis of antipoverty policies in the United States, Herbert Gans (1995) outlines the main components of what he calls *The War against the Poor* throughout American history. Gans analyzes U.S. government policy generally, but his analysis speaks volumes to how the criminal justice system in the United States operates. Keep in mind that politics and criminal justice cannot be separated. Thus, some government attempts to reduce poverty may have implications for criminal justice, and vice versa.

Gans uses the term *underclass* to refer to a segment of the poor who supposedly refuse to "behave in the 'mainstream' ways of the numerically or culturally dominant middle class" (p. 2). William Julius Wilson (1987) used the term *underclass* to explain how a small segment of the United States has become socially isolated and "truly disadvantaged," although he has subsequently replaced this term with *ghetto poor.* Wilson writes that the poor become socially isolated when they are detached from middle-class role models who successfully moved out of poor areas. Singh (1991: 509) concurs, claiming: "Unemployment and growing isolation from the mainstream economy have led to unwed parenting, dependency, lawlessness, joblessness, and school failure."

Gans argues that the label of *underclass* is a term used to describe a culture supposedly unique to poor people. This historical view of the poor suggests that the underclass are to blame for their own problems because of their questionable morality and deteriorating values: "The labeling of the poor as moral inferiors . . . blames them falsely for the ills of the American society and economy, reinforces their mistreatment, increases their misery, and further discourages their moving out of poverty" (p. 1). In essence, application of the underclass label amounts to an accusation against people who are seen as undeserving of assistance because of their bad values and moral deficiencies. Lauer and Lauer (2000: xi) call such depictions of the poor as flawed individuals "simplistic." Simplistic understandings of complex problems—rooted in individuals' own assumptions about human nature and general perspectives about the world rather than in empirical evidence or scientific facts—lead to simplistic and ineffective solutions to social problems such as poverty and crime.

Numerous mainstream explanations of crime are at least based on cultural assumptions about the poor (Bohm, 2001; Vold, Bernard, and Snipes, 1998). Many actually state cultural assumptions explicitly. I would even suggest that conditions of poverty and criminality have traditionally been treated synonymously in criminological theory. Miller's (1958) theory of focal concerns, for example, posits that the lower class has its own unique value system. It is an allegiance to the lower class focal concerns of trouble, toughness, fate, smartness, excitement, and autonomy, Miller contends, that accounts for their higher involvement in street-level criminality. Virtually all American theories of crime have their roots in the Chicago School of Criminology, which studied "delinquency areas" in Chicago, inhabited by waves of immigrants. Scholars such as Shaw and McKay explained criminality as a function of conditions of social disorganization, where citizens in the inner city were not equipped to mobilize community resources to fight criminogenic influences unique to certain areas of the city, typically inhabited by immigrant cultures (Bohm, 2001; Vold et al., 1998).

> *N*umerous mainstream explanations of crime are based on cultural assumptions about the poor, and many actually state cultural assumptions explicitly. I would go as far as to suggest that conditions of poverty and criminality have traditionally been treated synonymously within criminological theory.

Interestingly, this is one of the ways in which Gans claims that the label of the underclass is reified. He writes that "extreme poverty areas" of the U.S. Bureau of the Census and "underclass areas" of other researchers are chosen for stigmatization and a disproportionate withdrawal of poverty-ameliorating facilities and services (p. 64). These are the same areas in which police are disproportionately located because of the assumed higher criminality within these areas (Robinson, 2000).

Gans explores how the United States has always been involved in a war against the poor, which, he argues, has worsened since the 1980s. Incidentally, this is the same time when the country's entrenchment with the crime control model of criminal justice became so evident, as discussed in Chapter One. Given the increasingly punitive nature of U.S. criminal justice policy since the 1980s directed at street criminals, it becomes easy to see the war on crime as really a war on poor crime. Gans argues that this is the result of how Americans have come to see the poor as "deserving" of their poverty and suffering, and "undeserving" of assistance.

Gans (pp. 6–7) lays out four aspects of the "undeserving" nature of the poor (and thus the criminal). He argues:

- If poor people do not behave according to the rules set by mainstream society, they must be undeserving . . . because they believe in and therefore practice bad values, suggesting that they do not want to be part of mainstream America culturally or socially. As a result of bad values and practices, undeservingness has become a major cause of contemporary poverty. If poor people gave up these values, their poverty would decline automatically, and mainstream Americans would be ready to help them, as they help other, "deserving" poor people;

- The men among the undeserving poor are lazy or unable to learn the cultural importance of work and its requirements; in some cases, their bad values turn them into street criminals. If they really wanted to work, jobs would be available for them, and they would be able to earn their own income like other Americans;

- The women among the undeserving poor have an unhealthy and immoral taste for early sexual activity and for having babies as adolescents. If they would wait until they were older, sufficiently mature, and ready to find work as well as husbands who wanted to work, they and their children would not need to be poor, and poverty might even end with the current generation; and

- If the deserving poor do not alter their values and practices voluntarily, they must be forced to do so, for example by ending welfare payments, placing illegitimate children into foster care or orphanages, and by other forms of punishment.

The deserved forms of punishment include criminal sanctions such as imprisonment. Of course, as you saw in Chapter Two, criminal sanctions are specified by the criminal law, which is not made by or informed by poor people.

This is particularly true given that the umbrella label of *underclass* encompasses other labels such as *criminal*. I illustrate this in Figure 5.1. This visual is meant to depict that our war against the poor encompasses many forms, the most significant of which may be our war against crime. As will be discussed in Chapter Six, the so-called war on drugs is a major component of our war on crime. These wars on the poor, the criminal, and those involved in the drug trade lead to massive increases in incarceration, in addition to scores of other destructive outcomes for the underclass. Americans seem to be unconcerned with these outcomes, perhaps because they perceive criminal justice as something that only affects "them"—the poor.

The American view of the poor suggests they are different from the rest of us. This is similar to the conception of criminals versus noncriminals: they deserve what they get, including punish-

FIGURE 5.1
The War on the Poor

> *W*ars on the poor, the criminal, and those involved in the drug trade lead to massive increases in incarceration, in addition to scores of other destructive outcomes for the underclass.

ment, for their wrongdoings. The American notion of "just deserts" or vengeance for punishment is rooted in the assumption that criminals choose to commit crimes and, therefore, deserve whatever punishment they get (see Chapter Nine). When criminals are poor, our view of the poor is reinforced: "See, they are so lazy and immoral they would rather commit crimes than work!" Given that most people who are processed through the criminal justice system are poor, crime is seen as a problem of the poor. Both "underclass" and "criminality" are seen as deserved labels, oftentimes applied to the same people.

> *T*he American view of the poor suggests they are different from the rest of us. Note how this is similar to the conception of criminals versus noncriminals. They deserve what they get, including punishment, for their wrongdoings.

This is not to say that only the poor are "bad apples"; in fact, bad apples exist at all levels. As noted by Gans (1995: 4): "As one moves up the socioeconomic ladder, however, the bad apples and their questionable behavior become less visible." In Chapter Three, you saw that the crimes considered serious by the federal government are those that are committed primarily by the poor; in Chapter Four you saw that these are the same acts covered disproportionately in the media. As a result, these are the most visible crimes to Americans, meaning that we fear them the most and support measures that deal with these acts through any and all means possible.

As noted in Figure 5.1, one means of dealing with these people is through incarceration, often even for relatively minor offenses (see Chapter Nine). This raises the question: Does incarceration serve the function of population control, as suggested in Chapter One? Gans writes: "In an economy in which there may no longer be enough decent jobs for all who want to work, the people who are labeled as undeserving can be forced out of the economy so as to preserve the jobs of the deserving citizens" (p. 8). If the underclass cannot find decent work, they may commit property and drug crimes for income. In these cases, the corresponding views of the poor as undeserving of government assistance and the criminal as deserving of punishment make criminal justice intervention certain.

But is all of this intended? As noted in Chapter One, not necessarily. Functions of a war against the poor or the criminal may not be intended. Rather, they may be so beneficial to those in positions of power that there may exist little incentive to change the system so that it does not serve functions detrimental to a small segment of U.S. society or the United States as a whole. Gans outlines the functions served by the war on the poor. In the box on page 128, I have applied these same functions to the war on crime.

> *F*unctions of a war against the poor or the criminal may not be intended. Rather, they may be so beneficial to those in positions of power that there may exist little incentive to change the system so that it does not serve functions detrimental to a small segment of U.S. society or the United States as a whole.

Functions served by the war on crime

- *Reducing risk:* If we can identify those who are dangerous and deserving of intervention, we can minimize the likelihood that we will have contact with them. In particular, if we lock them up in prison, we do not even have to think about them.
- *Supplying objects of revenge and repulsion:* By identifying them as wrongdoers, we gain the right to punish them, even in a system of justice in which victims play little role in the criminal justice process. In essence, victims regain the right to be involved in the punishment of the guilty, even if their involvement is limited to an emotional one.
- *Creating jobs for the better-off population:* The behaviors of the lower class must be modified so they will act in socially approved ways. This means they must be policed and processed through the system. In Chapter One, you saw how many jobs are provided by the existence of crime.
- *Staffing the reserve army of labor:* In the case of criminal justice, the government obtains a means of very cheap labor in offenders who work when they are locked away from society.
- *Forcing the poor out of the labor force:* What better way to lower the unemployment rate than to take a large portion of the unemployable off of the streets?
- *Value reinforcement:* How would we know what was wrong if people didn't show us by pushing the limits of acceptable behavior? Crime serves the function of demonstrating what is not acceptable behavior.
- *Legitimating values:* The same laws that determine what is illegal also define what is law-abiding. Numerous forms of harmful behaviors are either not considered criminal, or are against the law, but are not considered serious (see Chapter Three). This undeniably serves the interests of dangerous upper-class citizens and corporations.
- *Creating popular cultural villains:* The poor as undeserving and criminals in general are depicted as the enemy in the wars against the poor and against crime. Those who fight these wars are seen as important and even heroic.
- *Scapegoating institutions:* Focusing on the shortcomings of certain groups in society all but guarantees that no attention will be paid to the real problems of poverty and criminality, which are more complex in nature than depicted.
- *Reproducing stigma and the stigmatized:* As we fight our wars against poverty and crime, we virtually guarantee that we will continue to see an enemy to target. In the current era of U.S. crime control and drug reduction policies, for example, more resources have gone toward reactive law enforcement and corrections approaches than to preventive approaches, thereby ensuring failure and guaranteeing that a future segment of the population will commit crime and use drugs.
- *Shifting power to conservatives:* By focusing on crime and poverty through a law-and-order approach, conservative crime control economic campaigns can be launched and strengthened by public support. The result is a shift to a crime control model of justice and a diminishing of due process rights for all Americans.

To the degree that these functions are actually served by U.S. criminal justice processes, the criminal justice system is failing to do justice. How can it be, in the "land of the free and the home the brave," that the criminal justice system is biased against those who are least able to protect themselves? To understand this, it is important to recall an important lesson from Chapter One.

Recall that politics is about who gets what economic benefits in society, when they get them, and how they get them (Lasswell, 1936), and is concerned with deciding who gets to keep most of the income generated in the United States, and how that income will be used (Harrigan, 2000). Similarly, Parenti (1983: 4) defines politics as:

> the process of struggle over conflicting interests carried out in the public arena; it may also involve the process of muting and suppressing conflicting interests. Politics involves activation and mediation of conflict, the setting of public priorities, and goals and the denials of others . . . the bulk of public policy is concerned with economic matters.

Since the 1980s, the effects of politics on poor people and on U.S. crime control policy have been particularly startling. Harrigan (2000) demonstrates how the past twenty years have produced higher incomes for the top 40% of wage earners in the United States, while the bottom 60% actually earn a smaller share of the total national income today. Since 1974, the wealthy have captured more of the national income, while the rest of us have received less. In fact, the top 1% of the wealthy now own an astounding 40% of the nation's wealth. According to a study cited in *U.S. News & World Report* (February 21, 2000), since 1970, average living space has doubled to more than 800 square feet per person, over 60% of households own 2 or more automobiles, and air travel has increased by over 400%. These averages are skewed by those at the top of the economic ladder. The result is "income inequality," whereby 40% of the population gets 70% of the national income and the other 60% gets 30% of the income. Now, the ratio of top 5% of wage earners to bottom 20% of wage earners is nearly 20:1, the largest gap in the United States' recorded history.

> *The* past twenty years have produced higher incomes for the top 40% of wage earners in the United States, while the bottom 60% actually earn a smaller share of the total national income today.

Alan Greenspan, the Federal Reserve Board chairman, claims that this type of income inequality could pose a "major threat to national security" (*U.S. News & World Report*, 2000: 43). As the nation's poor are more and more likely to live together in conditions of "social isolation" (as discussed by Wilson, 1987), they are more likely to be aware of their oppression and logically be less happy about it. They are also disproportionately exposed to increased rates of depression and other forms of mental illnesses, asthma, heart disease, and cancer, as well as joblessness, family disruption, and community instability (Pearson, 2000). The nation's poorest are minorities, who also are exposed to more pollution and toxic waste, what Maher (2000: 147) calls "environmental racism" (also see Boer, Pastor, and Sadd, 1997). Krahn, Hartnagel, and Gartrell (1986) suggest that countries with higher levels of inequality also have higher rates of murder (also see Land, McCall, and Cohen, 1990; Messner and Tardiff, 1986; Sampson, 1987). This is one source of the incredibly high U.S. murder rate.

In general, people living in conditions of extreme and concentrated poverty are exposed to more violence. In fact, about half of all murders in the United States occur in large cities that are inhabited

> $\mathcal{P}$eople who live in poverty are disproportionately exposed to increased rates of depression and other forms of mental illnesses, asthma, heart disease, and cancer, as well as joblessness, family disruption, and community instability.

by less than one-fifth of the population. Within cities, rates of homicide are 20 times the national average in areas where poverty is highly concentrated (Sherman et al., 1997). Politicians are either unaware of these concentrated criminal victimizations or unable to understand their implications. Because of their lack of action, politicians appear unconcerned and unwilling to prevent them. This is one indication that the criminal justice system fails to reduce crime and do justice adequately.

One possible source of income inequality is corporate downsizing, discussed in Chapter Two's Issue in Depth. Ranney (1999) illustrates how efforts such as downsizing aimed at cheapening labor have had the most devastating effects on those with the least political power. For example, in part because of downsizing, income distribution has shifted in favor of corporate executive officers (CEOs). In 1974, the average CEO of the 200 largest U.S. companies earned 35 times as much as its average worker; by 1990, the average CEO earned 150 times as much (Frank, 1994). According to Mokhiber and Weissman (1999: 167), CEO salaries average $5.8 million. Their pay rose 54% between 1995 and 1996, and almost 500% since 1980. Meanwhile, average hourly earnings for working people have dropped since 1980, from $12.70 in 1980 (in 1996 dollars) to $11.81 in 1996. Corporations claim that downsizing is good for business because it allows them to maximize profits (which is good for the U.S. economy). Of course, it is not usually good for the downsized employee.

Levy (1988) documents the upward shift of income and suggests that the middle class is falling behind the well off and that the poor are falling even further behind. This supports at least part of Reiman's (1998) contention that "the rich get richer . . ." as discussed in Chapter One. Harrigan (2000: 215) explains growing income inequality as a function of tax policies passed by Congress that benefit the wealthy, along with cuts in domestic programs that traditionally have benefited poorer people. Taxation has also shifted from corporations to individual citizens. In the 1940s, for example, corporations paid one-third of all taxes; today they pay only about 15%. Simon (1999) illustrates that about 90,000 U.S. corporations pay no taxes each year! At the same time, the poorest of the poor have been left "surrounded by other poor people . . . physically removed from the suburban areas of dynamic job growth, and . . . out of personal contact for the most part with middle-class America." Hence, they "lack the skills, knowledge, and behavioral habits with which to improve their situations" (Harrigan, 2000: 16). Yes, the poor are getting poorer and thus are more likely to end up in prison, supporting the other part of Reiman's argument.

Harrigan, in his book, *Empty Dreams, Empty Pockets: Class and Bias in American Politics*, analyzes American political institutions and argues that the "main institutions of politics today have a significant bias against the economic interests of lower-status people" (p. xii). Harrigan argues that: "American government and politics are not neutral. When government acts, or does not act, some groups of people get most of the benefits, while other groups get most of the costs" (p. 1). Although there are more jobs for the poor and the middle class, especially in the low-paying service sector, "there are still millions of people without health insurance, without secure jobs, and just as economically desperate today as they were at the beginning of the decade before the boom began" (p. xiii). At the same time, the move toward conservative politics and greater crime control efforts has diluted the influence of the nonwealthy. Is any of this consistent with the United States' supposed devotion to justice?

Political and criminal justice policy and practice can be biased and thus unjust both by what they do and by what they do not do. Currently, there are at least 40 million Americans without health insurance (U.S. Census, 1998), meaning that 15% of Americans are not insured. The burden falls, not surprisingly, on the poor and people of color. Harrigan illustrates, for example, that one-third of families who earned more than twice the poverty level in 1991 had no medical insurance, whereas only 6% of those with incomes four times the poverty level lacked health insurance. Because the poor are disproportionately African American and Hispanic, it is not surprising to see that they also suffer from high rates of noncoverage. Simultaneously, politicians enjoy excellent health care benefits. And efforts to guarantee all Americans high-quality, affordable health care, spearheaded in the early 1990s by President Clinton and First Lady Hillary Clinton, were defeated after the health care industry lobbied Congress to vote against it and created the illusion through advertising that a national health care plan would not allow citizens to choose their own doctors. In other words, the efforts were defeated by politics (Hagan, 1998). It is ironic that government policies that harm the poor and people of color simultaneously make it more likely that these groups will live in conditions conducive to criminal activity and thus in need of intervention by the criminal justice system.

> *The* most ironic thing about government policies that harm the poor and people of color is that they simultaneously make it more likely that these groups will live in conditions conducive to criminal activity and thus be in need of intervention by the criminal justice system.

WHAT ABOUT RACE AND ETHNICITY?

With all this focus on the poor, what is the role of race and ethnicity in criminal justice processes? In the next few sections of this chapter, I will address this issue generally. In later chapters, I will review the evidence of specific types of biases against minorities in the war on drugs (Chapter Six), policing (Chapter Seven), courts (Chapter Eight), sentencing (Chapter Nine), incarceration (Chapter Ten), and the death penalty (Chapter Eleven). Again, the purpose of this chapter is to evaluate the evidence that the system as a whole is biased against particular groups in society.

Key Terms

I will begin by defining the key terms. According to Walker, Spohn, and Delone (2000: 5), race has historically been considered the "major biological divisions of mankind," defined as Caucasian, Negroid, and Mongoloid. Yet, it is difficult, if not impossible, to differentiate races of people based on biological characteristics related to behavior (Yinger, 1994). In fact, race is really a social construct (Jeffery, 1990) determined by politically and culturally dominant groups in society (Walker et al., 2000: 5).

> *Race* has historically been considered the "major biological division of mankind," including Caucasian, Negroid, and Mongoloid (Walker et al., 2000: 5).

This means the "White race" is really a myth—there is no race of people who can be considered "White" to the total exclusion of other racial groups. Likewise, "Black" is an inaccurate term for a group of people whose skin color is varies widely even within their own "race." Ethnicity means "differences between groups of people based on cultural customs, such as language, religion, foodways, family patterns, and other characteristics" (Walker et al., 2000: 9). Within the "White race," for example, there are Italian Americans, Irish Americans, German Americans, Jewish Americans, Hispanic Americans, and so on. Hispanic Americans are the fastest growing ethnic group in the United States, and this group is expected to include one of every four Americans by the year 2050 (U.S. Census, 1997). From 1980 to 1993, Hispanics were also the fastest growing minority group in prison (Donziger, 1996: 104).

---

*E*thnicity means "differences between groups of people based on cultural customs, such as language, religion, foodways, family patterns, and other characteristics" (Walker et al., 2000: 5).

In this book, I will refer to racial and ethnic minorities as "people of color," following the lead of Walker et al. (2000: 10). When I refer to Blacks, I will use the term *African American*. When I refer to people of Hispanic descent, I will use the term *Hispanic*. And when referring to Whites, I will use the term *Caucasian* (except in quoting directly from writers who have used other terms).

Is the Criminal Justice System Biased against People of Color?

Numerous scholars claim that the criminal justice system is in essence racist because of its built-in biases against people of color (Mann, 1993). Consistent with this view is the claim by Gans (1995: 16) that: "Although most labels for the poor are literally neutral with respect to ethnicity and race, they have actually been meant mainly for immigrants and dark-skinned people in the United States." Figure 5.2 illustrates one's relative risk, based on race and class, for becoming involved in the criminal justice system.

As you can see, poor people and people of color are at the greatest risk for criminal justice involvement. The highest risk is for poor men of color. The criminal justice system disproportion-

FIGURE 5.2

Risk for Criminal Justice Involvement by Race and Class

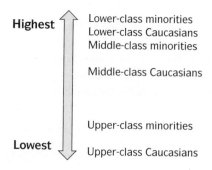

FIGURE 5.3
Degrees of Discrimination

- **Systematic:** Discrimination at all stages of the criminal justice system, at all times, and in all places.
- **Institutionalized:** Racial and ethnic disparities in outcomes that are the result of the application of racially neutral factors such as prior criminal record, employment status, and demeanor.
- **Contextual:** Discrimination found in particular contexts or circumstances.
- **Individual:** Discrimination that results from the acts of particular individuals but is not characteristic of entire agencies or the criminal justice system as a whole.
- **Pure justice:** No racial or ethnic discrimination at all.

SOURCE: Based on S. Walker, C. Spohn, and M. Delone, *The Color of Justice: Race, Ethnicity and Crime in America,* 2nd ed. (Belmont, CA: Wadsworth).

ately arrests, convicts, and punishes poor people and people of color. But does this mean that the criminal justice system is biased against these groups?

> The greatest risks for criminal justice involvement are for poor people and people of color. The highest risk is for poor men of color.

Walker et al. (2000), in their book *The Color of Justice,* conclude that the U.S. criminal justice system is characterized by what they refer to as "contextual discrimination," defined in Figure 5.3. These authors write:

> We believe that the criminal justice system is characterized by obvious disparities based on race and ethnicity. It is impossible to ignore the disproportionate number of minorities arrested, imprisoned, and on death row. Some of the decisions that produce these results involve discrimination. . . . After considering all of the evidence, we conclude that the U.S. criminal justice system is characterized by *contextual discrimination.* (2000: 287; emphasis in original)

Contextual discrimination implies that there is discrimination based on race and/or ethnicity at some places and at some times under certain circumstances in the United States. Walker et al. explain that contextual discrimination is different from *systematic* discrimination, which they define as "Discrimination at all stages of the criminal justice system, at all times, and all places" or *institutional* discrimination, defined as "Racial and ethnic disparities in outcomes that are the result of the

> Contextual discrimination implies that there is discrimination based on race and/or ethnicity at some places and at some times under certain circumstances in the United States.

application of racially neutral factors such as prior criminal record, employment status, demeanor, etc." (p. 16). Note that the presence of contextual discrimination suggests that the problem is more complicated than discrimination resulting from behaviors of particular individuals, and that pure justice does not exist in the United States. The authors argue that the "salience of race and ethnicity varies from jurisdiction to jurisdiction" in part because "the major racial and ethnic minority groups are not evenly distributed across the country" (p. 14). The important point for this book is that since race and ethnicity play *some* role in the criminal justice process across the United States, the criminal justice system by definition is failing to achieve its ideal goal of doing justice (which assumes that race and ethnicity play *no* role).

The U.S. system of justice consistently catches, punishes, and convicts people who are both poor and of color, so it is difficult to establish whether social class or race and ethnicity is driving

> *The U.S. system of justice consistently catches, punishes, and convicts people who are both poor and of color, so it is difficult to establish whether social class or race and ethnicity is driving criminal justice activity.*

criminal justice activity (Weitzer, 1996). Walker et al. (2000: 60) claim that both "[r]ace discrimination and social and economic inequality have a direct impact on crime and criminal justice, accounting for many of the racial disparities in the criminal justice system."

Walker et al. also attribute some racial and ethnic disparities to legal factors such as offense seriousness and offender prior record. This implies that African Americans and Hispanics commit more than their share of criminality. I will examine this assertion later in this chapter. But, even assuming that legal factors explain some racial and ethnic disparities in the criminal justice system, some disparities are explained by extralegal factors based on race, ethnicity, social class, and so forth. In other words, even if it were true that people of color committed disproportionately more crime than we might expect given their percentage in the population, their proportion in prison and on death row cannot be explained by their criminality alone.

Numerous scholars have reviewed the evidence and reached dissimilar conclusions (e.g., see Blumstein et al., 1983; Crutchfield, Bridges, and Pitchford, 1994). This makes reaching a firm conclusion difficult. Yet, a careful analysis of statistics relating to race, ethnicity, and social class and their relationships with crime and criminal justice may lead to some answers. I will start by outlining the relationship between race, ethnicity, and social class.

Race, Ethnicity, and Social Class

There is an intimate relationship between race, ethnicity, and social class in the United States. Specifically, racial and ethnic minorities are disproportionately likely to be poor and to be exposed to harmful environmental conditions. For example, in American slums, where there is far greater despair and deterioration than in the suburbs and rural areas, nearly 7 out of every 8

> *There is an intimate relationship between race, ethnicity, and social class in the United States. Specifically, racial and ethnic minorities are disproportionately likely to be poor and to be exposed to harmful environmental conditions.*

people are minorities (Beckett and Sasson, 2000: 37). Walker et al. (2000: 62–65) explain the differences in social class standing between racial and ethnic groups on the basis of income, wealth, employment, and poverty rates. Income—how much money a family earns in a year—for African

Americans and Hispanics is about 60% of that of Caucasians. Wealth—a measure of all assets accumulated—is nearly 11 times lower for African Americans than for Caucasians and 8 times lower for Hispanics. Meanwhile, the unemployment rate is more than twice as high for African Americans and almost twice as high for Hispanics than for Caucasians. Poverty rates are also higher for African Americans and Hispanics than for Caucasians. Finally, child poverty rates are almost three times higher for African Americans and Hispanics than for Caucasians.

Others discuss the role of "underemployment," which is also higher for people of color than for Caucasians (Bluestone and Rose, 2000). The so-called "poverty wage" (Jennings, 1999: 25) is a major source of poverty. Earning a minimal amount of money for a full-time job leaves people poor and is thus a form of "inclusive exclusion"; that is, these workers are included in the workforce but excluded from enjoying the benefits of full-time, well-paying jobs (George, 1999: 202). According to Kim (1999: 307), "the working poor constitute one of the fastest growing segments of the impoverished population." These "forgotten Americans" cannot make more money, cannot work more hours, and hence are still poor because of factors beyond their own control (Quan, 2000). Such disparities in employment are greatest for young, male minorities, that segment of the population most likely to have encounters with the police (see Chapter Seven). Regular wages are also lower for minorities and women than for Caucasians and men (Weinberger, 2000).

Why do Caucasians have higher average household incomes and higher levels of net worth than people of color (Beckett and Sasson, 2000: 34)? Although Caucasians made up 46% of all people living in poverty in 1997, African Americans made up almost 26% and Hispanics made up 22% (U.S. Census, 1999). Thus, although there are more poor Caucasians than other groups in the United States, the rate of poverty is higher for minorities, particularly African Americans, who account for only 13% of the general population. Why? In 1997 there were 9.1 million poor African Americans (a 27% poverty rate), 8.3 million poor Hispanics (also a 27% poverty rate) and 24.4 million poor Caucasians (an 11% poverty rate). Meanwhile, 24% of African American families live in poverty, as do 25% of Hispanic families, versus only 8% of Caucasian families. Why? The median income for African American families in 1997 was $25,050, $26,628 for Hispanics, and $38,972 for Caucasians. The per capita income for African Americans was $12,351, for Hispanics $10,773, and $20,425 for Caucasians (U.S. Census, 1999). Why?

> $\mathcal{A}$lthough there are thus more poor Caucasians in the United States, the rate of poverty is higher for minorities, particularly African Americans, who account for only 13% of the general population.

Why are African Americans and Hispanics more likely to suffer from poverty than Caucasians? There are two competing explanations. According to Smith (1995: 107), *cultural* perspectives "emphasize the values, beliefs, attitudes, and lifestyles" of the poor, whereas *structural* perspectives "emphasize enduring features of the economic and social systems." The cultural view "sees" the problem as coming from within the poor people themselves; the structural view "sees" the problem as originating outside the poor people. Murray and Herrnstein (1994), supporters of the cultural perspective, posit that the United States will be "dumbed down" as a result of illegitimate children being born to those with lower IQs.

Even if there is a culture unique to people of color or the poor, it may emerge from the U.S. capitalist economy. Such is the claim if Marxist and conflict criminologists, who hold that crime is a reaction by those at the bottom of the capitalist economy to oppression and domination (e.g., see

Greenberg, 1993; Lynch, 1997). Unemployment is a key factor in accounting for this culture or way of life, which has always been higher for African Americans and Hispanics than for Caucasians. Unemployment is associated with murder, suicide, mental illness, divorce, separation, child abuse, and drug abuse (Smith, 1995: 131–132).

The cultural explanation of poverty ignores poverty's structural correlates. Kushnick and Jennings (1999: 1) explain that poverty is produced by structural factors such as the "increasing imbalance in the distribution of wealth, with the rich continually becoming richer; the unbridled mobility of capital, both in finance and in production; and the prevalence of low wages coupled with levels of relatively high unemployment of certain groups." When "national policies . . . allow corporate leaders to pursue profits without consideration of the social costs incurred by their strategies," things only get worse.

Poverty is usually framed in politics as a "lack of work ethic" or a "failure of personal responsibility" among poor people. The media then "racialize" poverty by depicting poverty as a "minority thing," which then diverts attention from the real problems associated with the U.S. economic system. The role of the wealthy and the state in creating and reinforcing inequality is thus virtually ignored (Dill, Zinn, and Patton, 1999: 263). Given the corporate ownership of the media (see Chapter Four), this is not surprising. One example is that African American criminals are depicted as "thoughtless, sadistic, and callous" individuals who commit random crimes (Franklin, 1999: 128). Additionally, in the 1990s, the media "saturated the public with stories and pictures about African American teenager birth rates, African American illegitimate birth rates, and African American female AIDS rates (Franklin, 1999: 130, citing Jackson, 1988). Typically, these images and stories feature members of the poor "African American underclass," who represent less than 1% of the population and who live in the nation's largest urban areas.

> $\mathcal{P}$overty is usually framed in politics as a "lack of work ethic" or a "failure of personal responsibility" among poor people. The media then "racialize" poverty by depicting poverty as a "minority thing," which diverts attention from the real problems associated with the U.S. economic system.

The media also "socialize the entire population, mainstream and minority, young and old, by the way they depict and discuss minorities" (Chaffee and German, 1998: 311; also see Reed, 1993). "The kind of coverage, positive or negative, may also impact the nature of treatment, beneficial or negative, accorded to minorities in the political system" (Chaffee and German, 1998: 312). Overall, positive views of minorities are lacking in media portrayals, and African Americans receive most minority-related news coverage. This is detrimental to African Americans given the biases against minorities in newspaper reports of crime (e.g., see DeLouth and Woods, 1996).

Given the biases of official sources against the poor and minorities, it is not surprising that images of crime are dominated by the poor and minorities (Beckett and Sasson, 2000). The role of the media in promoting crime myths cannot be understated (Kappeler et al., 2000). Beckett and Sasson state it this way: "Crime myths focus on unpopular, minority, and deviant groups in society" (p. 12). Crime is also framed by the media as a problem of poverty, which, of course, is not true given that most crime is not street crime

American politicians go on to depict poor individuals as being born with a unique "ethos" that reflects immorality, a lack of hard work, and low levels of intelligence (Banfield, 1973), as well as being psychologically and programmatically dependent (Murray, 1984). Since the 1980s, politicians have talked about a "lack of family values" as responsible for the "significant decline in living standards for African Americans" in the 1980s (George, 1999: 198). High unemployment rates are thus blamed on lazy people.

Katz (1999: 63) argues that one reason African Americans in particular experience such tremendous poverty is that they historically have lacked an *ethnic niche* in employment: "Every time African Americans gained a modest presence in a promising trade, discrimination undercut their efforts, and whites replaced them." Strain theorists would claim that African Americans thus have been forced either into "retreat" (unemployment and drug use) or into "innovation" (selling African American market goods, including drugs). Innovation involving illegitimate activity is a means to overcome strain (Merton, 1938b) and differential opportunity (Cloward and Ohlin, 1961). When African Americans turn to illegal activity to tilt the scales back in their favor, they become more likely to have run-ins with the law.

Another option for the poor is to seek government assistance in the form of welfare. Although the U.S. government has been willing to assist its own poor to varying degrees throughout its history, antipoverty programs have become anti–poor people efforts since the early 1970s. People who are in trouble are characterized as "people who make trouble" (Beckett and Sasson, 2000: 155). Recently, the U.S. government passed laws that limit the total time period a person can be on welfare over the course of his or her life to five years. This attack on welfare rights during the 1980s and 1990s "has served the interests of corporate capital and its political and media allies" (Kushnick, 1999: 147). As the attack against the poor was stepped up, the code words for welfare dependency became "big government," and right-wing political leaders such as Ronald Reagan, Pat Buchanan, and Newt Gingrich began to call for "smaller government." In reality, the majority of Americans did not vote for the Congress that passed this type of reform: "The majority of Americans either voted for candidates who lost or, even more telling, did not bother to vote at all." Nevertheless, some of the harshest social policies we have seen in generations are being carried out in the name of the American people (Ransby, 1999: 327). Ironically, these same leaders share responsibility for increasing the size and strength of criminal justice agencies in the United States, all of which are funded and operated by the government. That is, these self-styled opponents of big government are responsible for creating big government in the form of the U.S. criminal justice system.

Meanwhile, according to the Children's Defense Fund report, *Poverty Matters: The Cost of Child Poverty in America* (1998), 14.5 million American children live in poverty: "Their lifetime contribution to the economy will decline by an estimated $130 billion because poor children grow up to be less educated, less productive workers." This means that 1 in 5 American children live in poverty. Poor children have worse nutrition, are at a heightened risk of stunted growth, receive less education, and will earn lower incomes. Poor children are also disproportionately minorities and living in single-parent households. Obviously, criminal justice officials are not equipped to address these social facts. What is clear is that every dollar invested by the U.S. government in criminal justice is a dollar not invested in social programs that can assist in alleviating childhood poverty rates in the United States.

---

*O*ne in five American children live in poverty, and poor children have worse nutrition, are at a heightened risk of stunted growth, receive less education, and will earn lower incomes. Such poor children are also disproportionately minorities and living in single-parent households.

Even though most poor, single, childbearing women are *not* African American (Sidel, 1996), "family breakdown is often a thinly veiled attack on the African American urban underclass" and "single mother" is often used as a code word to mean "African American single mother" (Dill et al., 1999: 269). Given that 1996 welfare reform law all but eroded the notion that Americans are "entitled" to assistance from their own government, it is easy to imagine how Americans have come to see African Americans as unentitled, even though "they live in one of the richest countries in the world" and most of them have paid taxes to the federal government (Ransby, 1999: 332).

Meanwhile, "corporate perks are growing. Even Bill Clinton's former secretary of labor, Robert Reich, has spoken critically of the undue benefits enjoyed by corporate elites as a result of government policy" (Ransby, 1999: 324). For example, corporate taxes accounted for about one-third of federal revenues in the 1950s, but only about 10% in the 1990s. In essence, taxation became more of a burden on individual Americans and their families, while corporations pay virtually no taxes today. Corporate profits have increased as a result, but this has not stopped companies from downsizing and even moving overseas or south of the border for cheaper labor costs.

During this same time, prison construction has boomed. It is booming because of the perception created by politicians and the media that crime is exploding all around us as lazy people have taken advantage of the welfare system. Ransby (1999: 324) claims that "it seems clear where most politicians and bureaucrats plan to deposit the excess workforce." Although unemployment rates are very low in the United States today, imprisonment rates are at an all-time high. The majority of prisoners are African American males; given that most states deny convicted felons the right to vote (see Chapter Ten), American criminal justice has created another means of disenfranchising poor African Americans.

As explained by Beckett (1997: 7): "crime discourse that attributes criminal behaviors of the 'underclass' to the expansion of welfare programs is one way of acknowledging the 'common sense' connections between poverty and street crime and [it] simultaneously provides working persons with an explanation for their increasing tax burden." The fact that individual tax burdens have increased as corporate tax burdens have declined escapes the public dialogue. Instead, the public and the media focus on things such as drugs and random violence. Chapter Four showed how media activity tends to create, promote, and reinforce deeply held myths of crime and criminal justice that serve to allow and encourage injustice in the United States.

Race, Ethnicity, Government Policy, and Criminal Justice

From the previous review of the relationship between race, ethnicity, and social class, it is apparent that many of the criminal justice biases against minorities in the United States are at least partly attributable to social class. Of course, one's social class standing is affected by many other factors, including race, ethnicity, and historical and contemporary discrimination against people of color.

Walker et al. (2000: 61) note three important facts that implicate economic factors as major sources of criminal justice bias against people of color: an economic gap between the rich and the poor, regardless of race or ethnicity; an economic gap between Caucasian Americans and people of color; and a growing segment of the population that is very poor. In addition to these factors, widespread patterns of residential segregation still exist. Those residents stuck in our nation's inner cities "find it extremely difficult both to learn about job opportunities and to travel to and from work. Public transportation systems are either weak or nonexistent in most cities" (Walker et al., 2000: 69). Inner-city residents are also less likely to have the necessary contacts to attain jobs. In case you think that anyone who wants to can move away from the inner cities, keep in mind that real estate agents and banking personnel play major roles in maintaining residential segregation by discriminating against poor people and people of color.

> *T*hree important facts that implicate economic factors as major sources of criminal justice bias against people of color are the economic gap between the rich and the poor, regardless of race or ethnicity; an economic gap between Caucasian Americans and people of color; and the growing segment of the population that is very poor.

Criminologists and sociologists claim that being socially isolated in inner cities leads to an increased risk of criminality because these residents have less contact with good role models and less ability to participate in controlling institutions (Skogan, 1990; Wilson, 1987). Increased crime in inner-city neighborhoods lowers the quality of life, as well. Thus, many government policies in the United States promote criminality among the nation's poor and people of color.

> *C*riminologists and sociologists claim that being socially isolated in inner cities leads to an increased risk of criminality because of less contact with proper role models and less ability to participate in controlling institutions.

Simultaneously, race and ethnicity play significant roles in government policy and the criminal justice process. The result is discrimination in numerous government policies and overwhelming disparities throughout the criminal justice system. Mann (1993) calls this "Unequal Justice." The result for young minority males has been "Lock 'Em Up and Throw Away the Key" (Mauer, 1998) because of what some call a "search and destroy" mission by the criminal justice system (Miller, 1996). Although racial disparity does not necessarily imply racial discrimination (Walker et al., 2000), if the disparity is harmful, the intent is really not important, especially if we know about it but do nothing to stop it (Kennedy, 1997).

Some studies do not find evidence of racial bias in the criminal justice system. For example, most studies examining sentencing severity find that length of sentence is typically determined by legal factors such as seriousness of offense and prior record (see Chapter Nine). However, if the law is biased against certain acts, then seriousness of offense is a function of the bias in the law rather than bias in the courts. An offender's prior record would also be affected by criminal justice factors such as presence of police in one's neighborhood. This means that discrimination in the system cannot be dismissed even in the face of findings that legal variables account for offenders' sentences. Other studies that do not appear at first glance to show evidence of bias may also show bias on closer examination. For example, Petersilia (1983) found that African American defendants were actually more likely to have their cases dismissed by prosecutors than Caucasians. Some may use such a study to show that the system is clearly *not* biased against African Americans, but such findings also may suggest that police are more likely to arrest African Americans on weaker evidence, so that the case is ultimately dropped by the prosecutor.

Racism today is less overt—no more fire hoses and police dogs being used to suppress minorities, as was common during the civil rights movement—and is intertwined with legitimate government activity. The following box discusses how things have improved for African Americans since the civil rights movement. For example, crime control is a legitimate state goal, yet "law and order" and "tough on crime" are phrases that are used to conjure up images of dangerous people of color. They are thus "code words," words that refer indirectly to minorities but appear not to revolve around racial themes (Omi and Winant, 1986). Do not be fooled, however. Punitiveness is partially "a manifestation of hostility toward African Americans" (Beckett and Sasson, 2000: 135). Is it a coincidence that most American punitiveness is directed at minorities, particularly African Americans? At the very least, because African Americans are disproportionately poor and are socially isolated in poor communities, they become more susceptible to criminal justice focus. In essence, they live where the police are most likely to patrol, making it more likely that they will be arrested and become involved with the criminal justice system.

---

*R*acism is less overt today—no more fire hoses and police dogs being used to suppress minorities, as was common during the civil rights movement. Today it is intertwined with legitimate government activity.

Race and criminal justice in history

Clearly, the significance of race for criminal justice has declined (e.g., Sakamoto and Tzeng, 1999; Thomas, 1993). The careful analysis by Walker et al. (2000) of bias in the American criminal justice process suggests that racism is not as prevalent as it once was. For example, consider these facts:

- Most police in the early American South were charged with catching runaway slaves.
- Until the 1960s, most police departments in the South refused to hire African American officers. Those African American officers who were hired usually were not permitted to arrest Caucasians.
- Northern police departments that hired African Americans would not assign these officers to patrol Caucasian neighborhoods.
- Calls for service by minorities were historically ignored by the police.
- African Americans were not permitted to serve on juries because they were not entitled to vote.
- African Americans were more likely to be arrested, detained in jail until trial, and tried by all-Caucasian juries, and were more likely to be convicted and sentenced to more severe sentences than Caucasians.

According to Charles Silberman (1978: 117–118):

> For most of their history in this country . . . African Americans were victims, not initiators, of violence. In the Old South, violence against African Americans was omnipresent—sanctioned both by customs and the law. Whites were free to use any method, up to and including murder, to control 'their Negroes.' . . . There was little African Americans could do to protect themselves. To strike back at whites, or merely to display anger or insufficient def-

erence, was not just to risk one's own neck, but to place the whole community in danger. It was equally dangerous, or at best pointless, to appeal to the law.

You may have heard of recent cases in which people of color have experienced similar victimization, but this is not the norm for most people of color today.

In 1968, the same year that the Reverend Dr. Martin Luther King, Jr., was assassinated, the Kerner Commission wrote that "our Nation is moving toward two societies, one African American, one white—separate and unequal" (p. 1). Today, the United States is indeed highly segregated. Civil rights have allowed many African Americans to "make it"; yet, many, if not most, African Americans lag behind Caucasians in economic indicators of success and are vastly more likely to have run-ins with the criminal justice system. And although many middle-class African Americans enjoy successes similar to those of members of the Caucasian middle class, things are the worst for the poorest African Americans (Jaynes and Williams, 1989; Thernstrom and Thernstrom, 1997).

Most scholars agree that our nation has made great strides to become less biased since the civil rights movement of the 1960s. For example, Walker et al. (2000) demonstrate that American schools are less segregated today than they were in the 1960s, that more voters and elected officials are minorities, and that minorities are more likely to work in the criminal justice system and serve on juries. These authors write: "The civil rights movement eliminated *de jure* segregation and other blatant forms of discrimination, but pervasive discrimination in society and the criminal justice system continues" (p. 77; italics in original). The evidence supports this statement. Changes in the law and in attitudes of individuals within the criminal justice system have made systematic discrimination against African Americans much less likely. Yet, even though the civil rights movement led to rapid changes for people of color, economic inequality of racial and ethnic groups has not been widely addressed.

Robert Smith, in *Racism in the Post–Civil Rights Era: Now You See It, Now You Don't*, convincingly argues that institutional racism is alive and well in the United States. Smith, citing Carmichael and Hamilton (1969), defines institutional racism as "the predication of decisions and policies on considerations of race for purpose of *subordinating* a racial group and maintaining control over that group" (p. 2; emphasis in original). Smith provides evidence of racism in several American institutions, including employment, education, housing, health, and consumer services. Disparities in such institutions produce injustice in the United States, and may explain the greater criminal justice involvement of African Americans. Ironically, we don't see higher street crime rates in minority neighborhoods as a product of racial and ethnic discrimination, but as indicators that the residents of those neighborhoods are simply different from (and inferior to) us.

> *T*here is evidence of racism in several U.S. institutions, including employment, education, housing, health, and consumer services. Disparities in such institutions produce injustice in the United States, and may explain higher criminal justice involvement of African Americans.

Smith does not claim that institutional racism is necessarily intentional; rather, he suggests that "whenever one observes policies that have the intent or effect of subordinating a racial group, that phenomenon is properly identified as racism" (p. 29). Institutional racism occurs when the "normal, accepted, routine patterns and practices of society's institutions have the *effect or consequence* of subordinating an individual or group . . ." (p. 33; emphasis in original). Because African Americans are disproportionately affected by criminal justice processes, Smith might claim that the U.S. criminal justice system is involved in institutional racism.

Smith does not address this issue directly, although he does briefly mention the war on drugs as an example of racist U.S. policy (I consider this issue in Chapter Six). Rather, he examines how institutional racism has evolved from individual racism and become entrenched in the contemporary United States. Beckett and Sasson (2000: 39) claim that racial segregation of housing, for example, is a product of racial discrimination. Massey and Gross (1990) calls housing discrimination a form of "American apartheid" that undoubtedly leaves African Americans living in ghettos where jobs and legitimate opportunities for success are scarce. Criminological theories such as social disorganization, strain, and social bonding have historically attributed such environmental conditions to increased risks for criminality (Bohm, 2001; Vold et al., 1998).

When people are not working and may be committing crimes, it becomes easy to characterize them as lazy, inferior, and bad, even though the real villain may be downsizing in corporations and the restructuring of the American workforce from manufacturing to service jobs. The myth of a free economy creates the illusion of equal opportunity for all Americans, which appears to prove that people who do not make it are to blame. Smith documents the historical notion of "black inferiority" among Americans, which has been used to justify both slavery and colonization of other countries. One need only look around to find "official" evidence of African American inferiority—in unemployment rates, relative housing conditions, and educational attainment of various groups, and in rates of family dissolution, out-of-wedlock births, alcohol abuse, and crime. The fact that African Americans are disproportionately likely to be unemployed, live in poor housing conditions, lack formal education, be single parents, abuse some drugs, and commit street crime is used as proof of African Americans' inferiority to Caucasians.

Although Caucasians are less likely now to express openly beliefs in African American inferiority, public opinion polls such as the General Social Survey (GSS) still illustrate high levels of negative views of African Americans. Almost half of Americans believe that African Americans tend

> *A*lthough Caucasians are less likely now to express their beliefs in African American inferiority openly, public opinion polls such as the General Social Survey still illustrate high levels of negative views of African Americans.

to be lazy. More than half think African Americans are violence-prone, and nearly one-third think African Americans are unintelligent (Smith, 1995: 39). The GSS regularly asks questions such as:

> On the average (Negroes/Blacks/African-Americans) have worse jobs, income, and housing than white people. Do you think these differences are . . . A. Mainly due to discrimination? B. Because most have less in-born ability to learn? C. Because most don't have the chance for education that it takes to rise out of poverty? D. Because most just don't have the motivation or will power to pull themselves up out of poverty?

The most recent survey results suggest that Americans are only slightly more likely to answer "yes" than "no" for the question dealing with discrimination. Similarly, just over half of respondents answer that most African Americans don't have the chance for education that it takes to rise out of poverty. And Americans are almost 8 times as likely to answer "no" than "yes" to the question about African Americans having less inborn ability. These answers suggest that negative views of African Americans are not as widely held as they once were. Or perhaps these views are just more hidden. For example, slightly more than half claim that most African Americans just don't have the motivation or will power to pull themselves up out of poverty.

According to Beckett (1997: 84), beliefs about crime and punishment are "highly correlated with race and racial attitudes." For example, those who most strongly believe in a law-and-order approach to crime fighting tend to be more racist and not to support equal rights for minorities. They believe African Americans are inferior to Caucasians and thus are deserving of punitive sanctions when they violate the law. Further, people who have hostilities toward African Americans are more likely to support the death penalty (see Chapter Eleven).

In reality, African Americans cannot be inferior to Caucasians simply because of their skin color or ethnicity, because race is a societal-level variable rather than an individual-level variable. Race cannot be used, for example, as evidence of inborn differences between Americans of African and European descent in terms of intelligence or will power. Genetic variation is higher within the races than between them (Bohm, 2001). Smith claims that anti–African American stereotypes are worse in the 1990s than in the 1970s (at least as reflected in the GSS data). Smith blames this, as well as increased racist violence in the 1980s, on the political dogma generated by Presidents Reagan and Bush, particularly with regard to crime control issues—for example, the use of the Willie Horton incident to make early prison release a campaign issue, as discussed in Chapter One. Smith writes: "The use by the 1988 Bush campaign of the now infamous Willie Horton ad was an indirect, subtle appeal to this racist stereotype" of the libidinous, dangerous African American male. "For twenty-eight days during the 1988 fall campaign an ad [showed] a picture of Horton, a person very dark in skin color and in a photograph that he himself said pictured him as 'depraved and maniacal' and as the 'devil incarnate' (Horton says at the time the photograph was taken he had not been permitted a shave or haircut for six months or more)" (p. 21).

The fact that Horton was accused of raping a Caucasian woman allowed politicians to tap into deeply held fears that characterize African American males as sexually aggressive and dangerous. In reality, most rapists are Caucasian males, and most people out on temporary prison release do not commit crimes, although these facts are not reflected in public opinion polls (Anderson, 1995).

But then, Willie Horton was also poor. Whether the ad campaign was intended to create fear of African Americans or of poor criminals is not entirely clear and perhaps not actually important. As noted, untangling the effects of race and social class is very difficult. As explained by Smith (1995: 34), "any policy having an adverse impact on blacks should not be conceptualized as institutionalized racism because of the intersection of race and class in the United States. African Americans in the United States are disproportionately lower class, and in any class-stratified society most institutional arrangements have an adverse impact on the poor and dispossessed whatever their race." So, "much of what may appear to be institutional racism is simply the effects of routine class bias in a market economy" (p. 53).

An example of negative consequences suffered disproportionately by African Americans is poor health, which has "substantially deteriorated" in the post–civil rights era. Smith (1995) demonstrates that infant mortality rates are nearly twice as high for African Americans as for Caucasians, and that life expectancy is shorter. He writes: "much of the data suggest that the vast differentials in African American and white health are to be explained on the basis of social class and public policy; in terms of the latter, primarily because of the absence of a comprehensive national health insurance program" (p. 69).

FIGURE 5.4
Forms of Institutional Discrimination

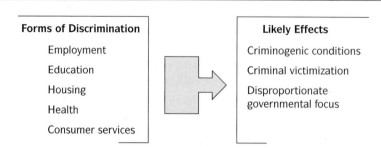

Forms of Discrimination	Likely Effects
Employment	Criminogenic conditions
Education	Criminal victimization
Housing	Disproportionate governmental focus
Health	
Consumer services	

Nevertheless, Smith believes that class-related disparities in health have likely resulted from hundreds of years of individual racism and the institutions created by racists; thus, he includes them as a form of institutional racism. Figure 5.4 depicts five forms of institutional discrimination facing the poor and racial minorities, as well as the likely outcomes, in the areas of: (1) employment, (2) education, (3) housing, (4) health, and (5) consumer services. This results in an increased likelihood of exposure by African Americans to criminogenic conditions such as unemployment, underemployment, lack of formal education, poverty, environmental pollution, and violence. Such conditions lead not only to increased physical and financial harms, but also to lower levels of self-esteem among African Americans living in conditions of severe poverty, expressed through the American polity, church, media, schools, and popular culture.

Smith argues that, because of the negative meanings of the word *black*—which has been "associated with discouragement, despair, depression, coldness, the unknown, the haunting shadow and nightmare" (Anderson and Cromwell, 1977: 76)—some African Americans see themselves as violent, dependent on government assistance, and to a lesser degree, as lazy and unintelligent. He writes that "a significant minority of African Americans (ranging from 10 to 25 percent depending on the survey and the question) continue to tell survey researchers that they hold negative images of the race" (p. 95). It is not surprising that the militant "Black Power" movement of the mid- to late 1960s became the focus of criminal justice agencies. In essence, when African Americans began to rise up in an effort to assert their rights and be recognized as good people—reflected in the slogan "black is beautiful," for example—their actions were criminalized by the dominant Caucasian power structures in southern criminal justice agencies. If they were not jailed and/or threatened with bodily violence, they were beaten during riots initiated by the police, even though they are no more criminal than other groups in society. For example, the Issue in Depth at the end of this chapter discusses "political crimes." How many poor people of color have you heard of who commit these acts?

Race, Ethnicity, and Criminality

Despite all the evidence cited in this chapter, some still believe that the notion of a racist criminal justice system is a myth (Wilbanks, 1987) and/or that skin color is declining in importance when it comes to criminal justice activity (DeLisi and Regoli, 1999). For example, some claim that the criminal justice system is not focused on race, ethnicity, or class, but that it processes the poor and people of color disproportionately because of their higher levels of involvement in criminality (DeLisi and Regoli, 1999; Wilbanks, 1987). Evidence related to this claim is assessed next.

As discussed in Chapter Three, sources of crime data include the Uniform Crime Reports (UCR), National Criminal Victimization Survey (NCVS), and self-report studies. Remember that the UCR is a measure of crimes known to the police, crimes cleared by arrests, and arrests. UCR data do not contain detailed information about ethnicity and crime, and "therefore do not tell us anything about rates of offending" (Walker et al., 2000: 13).

Official rates of offending based on the UCR are in fact higher in poor, minority communities and for African Americans generally (Kennedy, 1997; Tonry, 1995). Yet, relying on the UCR and other such official statistics for discovering offender characteristics is flawed and can create misconceptions about who is dangerous and who should be feared. There is evidence, for example, that violent crime victims are more likely to report their victimizations to the police when the offenders were African Americans (Hindelang, 1978).

> *O*fficial rates of offending from the UCR are in fact higher in poor, minority communities and for African Americans generally.

Miller (1997: 29) writes: "Relying on 'experience' emanating from the justice system is dicey even in the best of circumstances. Its rituals and procedures distort social realities and feed stereotypes at virtually every step." The UCR is a more valid measure of police experience than of crime because it measures the behavior of police rather than that of criminal offenders; therefore, it is not surprising that over 40% of every 100 individuals who are arrested for felonies are never prosecuted, or have their cases dismissed at first appearance (Miller, 1997).

UCR arrest statistics tend to create myths about who is dangerous and who is guilty. If we relied on arrest statistics to develop composites of "dangerous classes," we would not get an accurate picture of those who most threaten us (see Chapter Seven for a lengthier discussion of arrest rates and their meaning). Walker et al. (2000: 37) comment: "the picture of the typical offender that emerges from official arrest statistics may be racially distorted. If police target enforcement efforts in minority communities or concentrate on crime committed by racial minorities, then obviously racial minorities will be overrepresented in arrest statistics."

> *U*CR arrest statistics tend to create myths about who is dangerous and guilty. If we relied on arrest statistics to develop composites of "dangerous classes," we would not get an accurate picture of those who most threaten us.

The following box contains a discussion about Russell's *criminalblackman*, a term for the stereotypical criminal in the United States. Given the many different types of crime in this country (see Chapter Three), why do you think most people "see" street crime when they envision crime generally? Does this explain why the stereotypical criminal is a minority male?

The criminalblackman

Russell (1998: 114) characterizes the stereotypical criminal as the *criminalblackman*. Consider the following quote from the Reverend Jesse Jackson, a long-time civil rights activist who also happens to be an African American: "There is nothing more painful for me at this stage in my life than to walk down the street and hear footsteps and start to think about robbery and then to look around and see if it's somebody white and feel relieved" (Kennedy, 1997: 15). The truth is, people fear African Americans and other minorities and perceive them to pose significant threats to their personal safety (e.g., see Hurwitz and Peffley, 1997; Miethe, 1995; Peffley and Hurwitz, 1997; Skogan, 1995; St. John and Heald-Moore, 1996).

"Blackness," in particular, is treated as a sign of increased risk of criminality (Kennedy, 1997: 387). As illustrated by the Jesse Jackson example, this is a normal phenomenon, which results not from individual racism or bias but, rather, from deep-seated myths about race and crime that are created and reinforced by official sources of crime data such as the UCR.

Recall that the NCVS is a measure of self-reported victimizations, including both crimes reported to the police and those not reported to the police. The NCVS, generally thought to be a more valid measure of criminal behavior than the UCR, shows that households headed by African Americans and Hispanics have higher rates of victimization than Caucasian households. Also, African Americans and Hispanics are more likely than Caucasians to suffer from personal criminal victimization. Finally, one's lifetime risk of being victimized by certain violent street crimes is highly correlated with one's race. According to the Bureau of Justice Statistics (1987), African Americans have an 87% chance of being victimized by any violent street crime, versus 82% for Caucasians. This difference is small, but when it comes to the crime of robbery, the African American risk is 51%, whereas the Caucasian risk is only 27%. And 50% of U.S. homicides in 1997 were African Americans, even though they make up only 13% of the U.S. population. For African American males, the risk of homicide is 8 times the risk for Caucasian males. For young males, the risk is 10 times higher for African Americans than for Caucasians. African American males, who make up only 6% of the population, account for 18% of the nation's homicide victims (Walker et al. 2000: 33). Because most street crimes are intraracial in nature, logic would dictate that African American and Hispanic people are disproportionately committing street crimes against their own households and persons. Yet, higher victimization rates are partially a function of social class, also, because household victimization rates are highest in inner cities (Bureau of Justice Statistics, 1996).

For the purpose of this examination, I assume that people of color commit more *street crime* (but not more crime, generally) than one would logically expect given their proportion of the population. For example, the NCVS also shows that victims report a higher percentage of victimizations at the hands of African Americans than one would expect given their percentage of the population (Kennedy, 1997: 23): "African Americans are overrepresented as offenders for all of the offenses" of the NCVS (Walker et al., 2000: 42). Assuming that NCVS data are valid in this regard is questionable, because NCVS researchers must rely on victims' perceptions of their offenders. Whatever the case, the real question for the issue of whether disparities in the criminal justice system stem from higher involvement in criminality by minorities is whether the very small differences in offending suggested by the NCVS can account for the observed disparities in official arrest, conviction, and incarceration statistics. Virtually no one thinks they can (e.g., see Akers, 1996).

> *The* real issue surrounding disparities in the criminal justice system and whether they stem from higher involvement in criminality by minorities is whether very small differences in offending suggested by the NCVS can account for the observed disparities in official arrest, conviction, and incarceration statistics. Virtually no one thinks they can.

Why are African American males more likely to be incarcerated for crimes than other groups? According to the NCVS, the proportion of violent street crimes committed by African American males has remained steady since the 1980s, yet the disproportionate use of imprisonment has worsened since then (Tonry, 1995: 4). Steffensmeir, Ulmer, and Kramer (1998: 789) call this the "high cost of being black, young, and male." Spohn and Hollerman (2000: 281) suggest that convicted criminals who happen to be young, male, and African American will pay an added "incarceration penalty" on top of the sentence given to other groups in America.

If African American males are no more violent than other groups, why are we more likely to incarcerate them for the same crimes? It is because policymakers have decided to get tougher on violent street criminals. To argue that African Americans are more violent today, however, would be erroneous, because government statistics do not include measures of violent white-collar deviance.

In support of the notion that observed disparities in official arrest, conviction, and incarceration statistics cannot be explained by differences in offending behaviors, Reiman (1998: 103) compares criminal victimization statistics of the NCVS and arrest statistics of the UCR. He concludes that "police are arresting blacks from 30 to 50 percent more frequently than the occurrence of their perceived criminality. Because arrest determines the pool from which charged, convicted, and imprisoned individuals are selected, this suggests that deep bias persists throughout the criminal justice system." This is why Kappeler et al. (2000: 223) write: "Comparisons of UCR and NCVS statistics offer clear evidence of racism." A similar conclusion is reached by Walker et al. (2000: 42): "African Americans are represented in arrest figures in much higher proportions than the perception of offenders from victim interviews suggest."

Tonry (1995) argues that African American males are more involved in crimes that are punishable by imprisonment. To prove this, Tonry examines various sources of data (UCR arrest data, NCVS victim identification records, self-report studies) and concludes that arrests by police and sentences by prosecutors are not discriminatory or biased. For example, Tonry shows that crime victims are only slightly less likely to identify African Americans as their assailants in robbery and aggravated assault cases than one might expect given trends in black arrests for these crimes.

Unfortunately for Tonry's argument, he does not even address the question of whether the law is biased. If the law has disproportionately criminalized what poor people do and if African Americans tend to be poor, then the law is where one needs to look to see bias against African Americans. An example is seen in the case of robbery, a crime committed by the poor. NCVS data show that African Americans are perceived to be offenders in 51% of robberies but in no more than 30% of any other violent offense. African Americans make up about 60% of people arrested for robbery crimes (Bureau of Justice Statistics, 1996). Both data sets suggest that African Americans are disproportionately involved in robberies. Given that monetary gain is the primary motive for robbery, it is not a stretch to conclude that it is the offenders' social class that explains their involvement in the crime of robbery. Rich people do not have to stick a gun in your face to get your money, nor do they have to rob a bank to steal money from a bank. Instead, they can and do steal money through fraud and embezzlement, as in the case of the savings and loan (S&L) scandals, which produced more financial losses than all the bank robberies in the history of the United States. Yet, such crimes have not been treated as "serious" throughout our country's history. Even now when fraud and embezzlement are treated roughly as seriously as theft, law enforcement resources are not adequate to fight fraud and embezzlement. In fact, most American police officers, who work for city and county governments, are not involved in investigating and apprehending acts of white-collar deviance (see Chapter Seven). Instead, they are on the streets, fighting the types of thefts committed primarily by the poor, such as robbery.

You might argue that robbery is more serious than white-collar crime because, technically, it is viewed as violent (that is, it implies that some force or weapon was used to achieve the theft). But robbery is clearly aimed at property gain, just like fraud and embezzlement. The primary difference is that rich people do not have to resort to robbery to acquire wealth illegally—they have the luxury of illegitimate opportunities to engage in other, less risky forms of theft.

So, although Tonry suggests that African Americans actually commit proportionally more felonies than Caucasians, he does acknowledge a potential bias when he writes: "Whatever their race, most felony defendants are poor, badly educated, un- or underemployed, and not part of a stable household" (p. 101). These are America's war enemies.

Self-report studies provide some unique insight into criminal behavior by assessing the degree to which respondents admit to engaging in criminal behaviors. Self-report studies question the disparities found in official criminal justice statistics such as the UCR (e.g., see Pope, 1979). Whereas the UCR may suggest that African Americans commit a disproportionate amount of crime because they are more likely to get arrested by the police, self-report studies do not show such patterns. Instead, self-report studies show that rates of offending in middle-class minority communities are equivalent to those in the general population. Earlier self-report studies showed little or no differences in self-reported delinquent and criminal behavior between different groups.

Unlike early studies, which typically assessed minor acts of delinquency, more recent studies assess more serious criminal behaviors. According to Tittle and Meier (1990) studies assessing relationships between social class and crime show "mixed results"; according to Akers (1996: 127): "Self-report studies find class and race variations in criminal and delinquent behavior, but they are not as great as class and race differences in officially arrested, convicted, and/or imprisoned populations." So, when unemployed citizens are disproportionately found in incarcerated populations (Chiricos, 1991), it is not likely due to their increased involvement with criminal behavior, nor can the overrepresentation of African Americans in the criminal justice system be explained by their higher involvement in criminal behavior. There is some evidence that African Americans tend to underreport their involvement in criminality (e.g., see Hindelang et al., 1981; O'Brien, 1993), but no one knows for sure whether this is true.

It should also be reiterated that self-report studies typically assess involvement in street crimes. If studies examined racial, ethnic, and class differences in people who commit other harmful acts (including legal acts), huge differences would be found—the vast majority of offenders would *not* be African American, Hispanic, or poor. This fact seems to escape those who argue that people of color commit "more crime." The people we end up viewing as criminals depends on what is called crime, and that is a function of who makes the law. As pointed out in Chapter Two, "criminal" is a label generally reserved for people who look very different from lawmakers and voters.

If self-report studies examined racial, ethnic, and class differences in people who commit other harmful acts (including legal acts), huge differences would be found—the vast majority of offenders would *not* be African American, Hispanic, or poor.

GENDER AND CRIMINAL JUSTICE

Gender bias is also prevalent in the U.S. criminal justice system (Boritch, 1992). Gottfredson and Jarjoura (1996: 49) state it this way: "Extreme racial (and gender) disproportionalities have existed in America's prison and jail populations for at least 175 years." Gender bias includes decisions that favor or harm individuals on the basis of gender. Overall, the criminal justice system seems to be less punitive toward women. We can call this a bias against men, who are responsible for a much larger portion of street crime and violence in general than women (Jeffery, 1990). This may be due to what Belknap (1996: 69–70) calls the chivalry or paternalism hypothesis. The state of Texas, for example, has executed only one woman since the Civil War, even though women in Texas commit about 10% of the murders there.

> *O*verall, the criminal justice system seems to be less punitive toward women. Call this a bias against men, who are responsible for a much larger portion of street crime and violence in general than women.

According to the Bureau of Justice Statistics (1994), women convicted of felonies in state courts are sentenced to less time than men for all offenses, including murder, rape, robbery, aggravated assault, burglary, theft, drug possession, drug trafficking, and weapons offenses. Most of this discrepancy is due to the fact that female felons generally have had less involvement in criminal activity, so that their prior records are not as extensive as those of male felons.

There is also some evidence of what Belknap calls the "evil woman hypothesis," which posits that women will be treated more harshly for similar crimes than men. Morgan-Sharp (1999: 384) suggests that the criminal justice system is tougher on women when they "do not adhere to prescribed gender roles."

> *T*here is some evidence of what Belknap (1996: 69–70) calls the "evil woman hypothesis," which posits that women will be treated more harshly for similar crimes than men. Morgan-Sharp (1999: 384) suggests that the criminal justice system is tougher on women when they "do not adhere to prescribed gender roles."

According to the National Criminal Justice Commission, even though the vast majority of people punished in the United States are men, "women are the fastest-growing category of prisoners nationwide" (Donziger, 1996: 146). For example, in the 1980s the rate of female incarcerations increased more than the rate of male incarcerations in every year except one. The commission attributes this fact to changes in sentencing policy that have overcome traditionally lenient sentences for women compared to men (Daly, 1994; Steffensmeir et al., 1998) and to the war on drugs, which I discuss in depth in Chapter Six. From 1990 to 1996, the number of female prisoners per 100,000 people in Florida increased by 65%; for male inmates, the increase was only 45% (Crawford, 2000: 263). Crawford writes: "Although the Florida system is extremely reluctant to classify women as habitual offenders, there is a notable and disturbing exception based on offenders' race and drug-related crimes" (p. 277). Crawford (2000) found evidence of a sentencing bias against minority women in Florida. His research suggests that the state's habitual offender statute was disproportionately being used against African

American women, even after controlling for legal factors such as prior criminal record and crime seriousness.

American sentencing practices and the war on drugs have most dramatically affected women of color (Crawford, 2000). In 1990, for example, the Sentencing Project found that only 1 in 100 Caucasian women ages 18 to 29 years was under some from of criminal justice supervision, versus 1 in 56 Hispanic women and 1 in 37 African American women in this age group (Mauer, 1990: 3). As you will see in Chapter Six, the war on drugs tends to net low-level drug offenders, many of whom are women with little to offer to prosecutors in exchange for lesser sentences.

> *A*merican sentencing practices and the war on drugs have most dramatically affected women of color.

Our criminal justice system's increasingly punitive response to female offenders does not owe itself to a female crime wave. Instead, women are simply more likely to be sent to prison for offenses that typically did not receive imprisonment in the past. According to Bureau of Justice Statistics figures cited by the National Criminal Justice Commission, increases in female arrests and incarcerations were mostly due to relatively minor, nonviolent charges such as shoplifting, check forgery, welfare fraud, and drug crimes (Donziger, 1996: 149). Some female incarcerations for drug offenses stemmed from mandatory sentences, which give judges no discretion in setting punishment. Thus, judges cannot consider factors such as the subordinate role women may have played in criminal offenses, the fact that women are less likely to commit more crimes after release, or women's child care needs (Raeder, 1993). For these reasons, women are hurt more than men by mandatory sentencing.

> *O*ur criminal justice system's increasingly punitive nature toward female offenders does not owe itself to a female crime wave. Instead, women are simply more likely to be sent to prison for offenses that typically did not receive imprisonment at other times in our history.

Most women in prison, like their male counterparts, can be considered "truly disadvantaged." For example: "Two-thirds of women in prison are minorities, about half ran away from home as youths, a quarter had attempted suicide, and a sizable number had serious drug problems. Over half had been victimized by physical abuse and over a third reported sexual abuse. Most had never earned more than $6.50 an hour" (Donziger, 1996: 150). Perhaps the saddest aspect of female incarceration is that three out of every four female inmates are mothers (Bureau of Justice Statistics, 1994).

When the criminal justice system punishes mothers for relatively minor crimes, it increases the harms associated with the mothers' criminality. Children of incarcerated mothers are more likely to be incarcerated later in their lives (Dressel and Porterfield, 1998). These children suffer from "traumatic stress, loneliness, developmental regression, loss of self-confidence, aggression, withdrawal, depression, interpersonal violence, substance abuse, and teenage pregnancy" (Donziger, 1996: 153). The vast majority of incarcerated mothers are not permitted to see their children. Three out of four of the children end up living with relatives other than the natural father, or even in foster care (Bureau of Justice Statistics, 1994). All of this may be considered punishment for the mothers, but it is also harmful to the children. Why would Americans want to separate mothers from their children and increase the likelihood that the children also will come under the supervision of the criminal justice system in the future?

Simultaneously, women are not protected by the criminal justice system from the crimes that most threaten them—domestic violence and sexual assault. According to the Centers for Disease Control and Prevention, more women seek hospital treatment from domestic violence incidents than from all muggings, car accidents, and rapes combined (Donziger, 1996: 146). No one knows how many women are abused in their own homes at the hands of domestic or "intimate" violence, but it is estimated that somewhere between 2 and 27 million women are beaten every year (Donziger, 1996: 156). In fact, in 1992, the U.S. surgeon general ranked abuse by intimates as the leading cause of injuries to women ages 15 to 44 years (Feder, 2000; Gosselin, 2000; Miller, 2000). The National

> *The* criminal justice system does not protect women from the crimes that most threaten them— domestic violence and sexual assault.

Criminal Justice Commission claims: "All things considered, women in this country are nine times more likely to be a victim of crime in the home than out on the streets" (Donziger, 1996: 156).

The criminal justice system does very little to assist women with leaving their abusive husbands and partners, even though women are more likely to be murdered when attempting to leave than at any other time (Browne, 1993). And it does very little to prevent domestic violence even though reducing crime is one of its ideal goals. Given that domestic violence occurs in a cycle— since rationalization for and techniques of behavior are learned—when we fail to prevent it in one generation, we are guaranteeing that it will occur again in the next. Children from violent homes are more likely to become violent and abusive, to commit crimes, and to commit suicide than children from nonabusive homes (Bureau of Justice Statistics, 1992).

In terms of sexual assault, there is evidence that law enforcement officers and prosecutors are less likely to pursue cases where the victim knows the attacker and where the victim has had an active sex life or was dressed in a way thought to provoke the attack. Additionally, judges may set lower bail for alleged rapes where the offender is known to the victim.

These are a few ways in which the American criminal justice system operates based on gender. It is evident that most of the "clients" of the U.S. criminal justice system are men, even above and beyond their representation in the criminal population, Yet, with the war on drugs and the advent of mandatory sentences for some types of drug offenders, more and more women, who are usually poor and of color, are being processed through the criminal justice system. It is the war on drugs that I visit in the next chapter.

CONCLUSION

In this chapter, I demonstrated how the criminal justice system is biased against the poor and people of color, as well as against women to a lesser degree. It is difficult to say why discrimination against people of color persists in the United States, but one thing is certain: it does persist. The findings of this chapter suggest that the U.S. criminal justice system is failing to meet its goal of doing justice, because it is inherently unfair in its treatment of some groups. Thus, the reality of justice in the United States is that it is not blind, as it is ideally thought to be. Although it is not clear that the criminal justice system is intentionally biased against any group, it is obvious that various functions are served for people in positions of power by the fact that the criminal justice system fails to live up to its ideal goal of being just.

ISSUE IN DEPTH
Political Crimes

WHAT IS POLITICAL CRIME?

Political crime refers to illegal acts committed by government, for government, or against government to achieve ideological purposes. Although many acts can be interpreted as political crimes because they are politically motivated (e.g., the World Trade Center bombing and the Oklahoma City bombing), their perpetrators are typically prosecuted by the government for street crimes, such as murder.

In a sense, all crimes can be viewed as political in nature, since behaviors are legislated as criminal through a political process whereby the interests and beliefs of certain groups are protected (Vold, 1958). Generally, political crimes can be differentiated from other types of crimes in that they attack an entire value system of a government rather than a small part of it. According to Rush (2000), such acts represent a direct threat to the established political power, with the criminal acting on behalf of a conflicting system.

TYPES OF POLITICAL CRIME

Political crimes include acts of treason, sedition, and espionage. As defined in the U.S. Constitution: "Treason against the United States shall consist in levying war against them, or in adhering to their enemies, giving them aid and comfort." Sedition includes "issuing any false, scandalous, and malicious statement against the government, the president, or Congress with the intent to defame, disrupt, encourage contempt, or excite hatred of citizens for the U.S. Laws against sedition, however, may not violate First Amendment guarantees." Espionage involves obtaining military information on behalf of foreign governments.

In authoritarian states, criticizing the government is viewed as a political crime. In China, for example, when citizens protested human rights violations in Tienanmen Square in 1989, protestors were immediately rounded up by the government and executed or incarcerated for engaging in political crimes. Many protestors are still behind bars for offenses against the government. In the United States and other democracies, political crime prosecutions are rare and are typically reserved for acts such as espionage and treason.

Other crimes characterized as political include defrauding the government (a form of theft whereby trickery or deceit is used to obtain property or something of value) and embezzling taxpayer money (a form of theft involving misappropriation of property or something of value occurs). Fraud and embezzlement can be considered political crimes only if they are committed to achieve ideological purposes, to attack an entire value system of a government, or as a direct threat to the established political power, as noted. Given that fraud and embezzlement often conflict with rules of fair play implicit in capitalist societies, many such acts would be considered political crimes. For example, antitrust laws, which are aimed at ensuring equal opportunity and consumer protection, forbid businesses from monopolizing a market or restraining free trade (Lyon, 1933). Breaking antitrust laws through fraudulent activity can be considered a political crime because it violates American ideals concerning equal opportunity, thereby threatening an important value of the U.S. government.

Political crimes are best understood as acts committed with political gain in mind. Therefore, other types of behaviors committed to gain unfair advantages could also be considered political crimes. These would include malfeasance, corruption, bribery, extortion, and blackmail. *Malfeasance* is a general term meaning any violation of a moral code or contract; as a political crime, it generally involves misconduct engaged in by public officials. *Corruption* includes all unethical techniques used to gain political advantages in elections, including accepting or offering bribes, ballot-stuffing, tampering with voting machines, and interfering with the voting process. Corrupt practices also can include violations of campaign finance rules. *Bribery* includes offering, giving, or receiving anything of value in order to influence public officials or people in positions of trust to discharge their duty in a manner that benefits the giver. Bribes can include money, property, favors, or positions, and can be made to persons such as court officers, jurors, witnesses, and lawmakers. Bribery is a form of extortion, but *extortion* specifically requires either a threat of physical harm to a person or to a person's property or reputation; that is, a person commits extortion if he or she unlawfully obtains anything of value by threatening eventual physical injury or other harm to compel another person to surrender the property. *Blackmail* is the term for a form of extortion that involves threats to reveal some potentially harmful piece of information or secret (Rush, 2000).

These types of behaviors can be committed by private citizens against other private citizens, with no political or ideological motive. When such acts are engaged in by and against citizens for other motives, such as financial gain, they are not considered political crimes. They are political crimes only if they are committed in order to achieve ideological purposes, to attack an entire value system of a government, or to be a direct threat to the established political power.

HISTORICAL OVERVIEW

Many seemingly normal acts of dissent, rebellion, or challenges to the status quo have been considered political crimes at different times in history. These include protests against wars, the civil rights movement, and the women's movement (Friedrichs, 1996; Rosoff, Pontell, and Tillman, 1998; Simon and Hagan, 1999).

For example, the Reverend Martin Luther King, Jr., as a civil rights leader in the 1960s, was considered the most dangerous man in the United States by the Federal Bureau of Investigation (FBI) because his ideologies posed a threat to racial stratification. The Black Panther party and other components of the New Left were infiltrated by government agencies in order to assess and disrupt potential threats against the U.S. government. Such groups were perceived as vulnerable to communist infiltration and thus as potential political criminals and enemies of the state (Vankin and Whalen, 1999).

Treason

One infamous example of treason is that of Benedict Arnold. Arnold, an American patriot during the Revolutionary War, led numerous military victories against the British. However, Arnold schemed to hand over to the British the American fort at West Point, New York, in 1780. His goal was to gain financial riches from Britain and to ensure his personal and professional stature. His promise to British commander Sir Henry Clinton to surrender West Point and its 3,000 American inhabitants for 20,000 sterling (approximately $1 million today) failed when Major John Andre was captured with incriminating evidence against Arnold. Although Andre was promptly executed as a spy, Arnold received 6,000 sterling from the British government and an appointment as a brigadier general. He then led successful attacks against American forces in the service of King George III and went on to live out his life in England (Henretta et al., 1997). Today, the term "Benedict Arnold" is synonymous with being a traitor.

Sedition and Espionage

The United States has experienced major acts of sedition throughout its history. Illegal acts of sedition include attacks against government employees and property. At the end of the eighteenth century, the Federalists accused the Democratic-Republicans of seditious conspiracies as they disagreed over the right of citizens to engage in public criticism of their own government. The Federalists, who favored a strong federal government, passed the four-part Alien and Sedition Acts of 1798, intended to quell any political opposition from the Republicans. The first of the laws was the Naturalization Act, which required that aliens be residents for 14 years instead of 5 years before they became eligible for U.S. citizenship. The second law was the Alien Act, which authorized the president to deport aliens "dangerous to the peace and safety of the United States" during peacetime. The third law, the Alien Enemies Act, allowed the wartime arrest, imprisonment, and deportation of any alien subject to an enemy power. The Sedition Act, the fourth law, declared that any treasonable activity, including the publication of "any false, scandalous and malicious writing," was a high misdemeanor, punishable by fine and imprisonment. As a result of these laws, 25 men, most of them editors of Republican newspapers, were arrested and their newspapers shut down (*Early America Review*, 1999).

Such acts were quickly repealed under the new president, Thomas Jefferson, who inspired the belief that the rights of individual citizens were more important than those of government. Usually in times of war, charges of sedition are utilized by government powers to deter would-be protests. For example, as the United States entered World War I, the Espionage Act of 1917 prohibited opposing the military draft or being disloyal to the government. This law allowed violators to be imprisoned for up to 20 years. The Sedition Act of 1918 permitted government intervention in cases where writings were thought to promote citizen dissent. The Smith Act of 1940 made it a crime to call for the forcible or violent overthrow of the government. States across the United States passed similar laws, and nearly 2,000 cases of espionage and sedition were tried. Similar activity occurred to allow the government to quell antiwar demonstrations during World War II and the Vietnam War (Bush, 1998).

Malfeasance

As *malfeasance* is a general term for any type of misconduct by public officials, both historical and more recent impeachment charges against politicians serve as good examples of malfeasance. Since 1797, the U.S. House of Representatives has impeached 16 federal officials, including 2 presidents, a cabinet member, a senator, a justice of the Supreme Court, and 11 federal judges, although not all of these men were accused of political crimes. Seven of these men were actually removed by the U.S. Senate, and many more resigned. The first official impeached was Senator William Blount (Tennessee) for his involvement in a plot to assist the British takeover of Louisiana and Florida from Spain. Judge John Pickering (New Hampshire), accused of drunkenness and unlawful rulings, was the first impeached official actually convicted. Supreme Court Associate Justice Samuel Chase (1741–1811) was impeached in 1804 for malfeasance in presiding over two sedition trials. Chase had served in the Maryland General Assembly and the Continental Congress and was a signer of the American Declaration of Independence. Because Chase was charged with being an anti-Federalist, he was acquitted by the U.S. Senate, which held that judges should not be removed from office purely on political grounds. Other officials have been impeached for political crimes such as bribery and treason (Longley, 1998).

Impeachment of U.S. presidents is rare. Usually impeachment proceedings are launched for political reasons, but not because of political crimes. For example, President Andrew Johnson was impeached for his support of post–Civil War Reconstruction and his attempt to oust the secretary of war, in violation of the Tenure Office Act of 1867 (which was later held to be unconstitutional), but Johnson was acquitted in 1868 by the Senate by a one-vote margin (Ross, 1964). Allegations of political crimes committed by Republican President Richard Nixon led Congress to debate his impeachment. Nixon had ordered a burglary of the Democratic party headquarters at Watergate in 1972 and had subsequently tried to hide his involvement. Nixon resigned in 1974 in the face of three impeachment charges and an indictment for illegal wiretapping, misuse of the CIA, perjury, bribery, obstruction of justice, and other abuses (Fremon, 1998; Sussman, 1992).

These acts are political crimes because they were committed against the interests of the U.S. government for limited political interests and gain. In the case of Nixon, his involvement in burglary, wiretapping, violations of campaign finance laws, sabotage, and the use of government agencies such as the FBI and CIA to harm political opponents was aimed at assisting his 1972 reelection campaign. Most recently, in 1999, President Bill Clinton was impeached by the U.S. House on grand jury perjury and obstruction of justice charges, but was not convicted by the U.S. Senate. Although charges against Clinton had originated with his alleged involvement in a failed land deal in Arkansas twenty years earlier, the actions leading to his impeachment were committed while Clinton was president. When a government officer lies to a grand jury and obstructs justice, his or her actions are political crimes if they are committed for ideological purposes—to attack an entire value system of a government—or represent a direct threat to the established political power.

Corruption

Corruption has been commonplace in the United States since the Civil War. In New York City in 1865, for example, William Marcy "Boss" Tweed, head of the Cities Commission of Public Works, awarded contracts to supporters of his regime and received financial kickbacks in violation of criminal law. All were later imprisoned. In 1896, rumors of bribery and illegal campaign contributions during the presidential campaigns of William McKinley and William Jennings Bryan made Americans distrustful of the political process. In 1907, the Tillman Act prohibited direct political contributions from business officials because they were viewed as threatening to the American ideal of democracy. In 1910, Congress passed the Federal Corrupt Practices Act, which required all House candidates to disclose their spending and financial contributions. Federal corruption acts also were passed in 1925 (later revised in 1972) in response to the Teapot Dome scandal of 1922. The Teapot Dome scandal took its name from the Teapot Dome oil reserve in Wyoming, which, along with two other major naval oil reserves, was leased to Harry Sinclair's Mammoth Oil Company and Edward Doheny's Pan-American Petroleum and Transport Company. Senator Albert Fall (New York) authorized the leases while serving as secretary of the interior by persuading President Harding to transfer control of the oil reserves without competitive bidding. He received nearly $400,000 in cash, livestock, and bonds. In 1923 Hall resigned and went into business in the oil industry, but he was convicted in 1929 and sentenced to prison for accepting a bribe. Harry Sinclair was acquitted of fraud but imprisoned for contempt during the Senate investigation (Harris, 1961; Stratton, 1998).

These federal anticorruption acts are intended to deter campaign and election abuses by capping spending. Other laws, such as the Hatch Act of 1939, which limited contributions to congressional candidates to $5,000 per year, and the

Smith-Connally Act of 1943, which prohibited labor unions from making contributions to political campaigns, were aimed at reducing threats to a free democracy. The 1971 Federal Election Campaign Act required full and timely disclosure of individual contributions to political committees and set limits on political advertisements. Ironically, this law was put into effect by President Richard Nixon, who would later resign in the wake of the aforementioned charges above, including allegations of undisclosed financing in his reelection campaign.

In 1974, the Federal Election Commission (FEC) was created to regulate election spending and to limit individual campaign contributions to $1,000 per candidate and $25,000 per election. In 1976, however, the U.S. Supreme Court ruled in *Buckley v. Valeo* that campaign finance laws are unconstitutional because they violate free speech rights. In 1979, the Federal Election Act was altered so that unlimited "soft money" could be legally donated to political parties rather than to individual candidates. In 1996, the Supreme Court decided in *Colorado Republican Federal Campaign Committee v. FEC* that political parties could make unlimited contributions to any individual candidate provided the donations did not result from coordinated efforts with that individual's campaign.

Other recent corruption cases include the "Keating Five" scandal, Operation Greylord, and ABSCAM. The Keating Five were Senators Alan Cranston (California), Dennis DeConcini (Arizona), Donald Riegle (Michigan), John Glenn (Ohio), and John McCain (Arizona), who were accused of interfering with the federal investigation of a failed savings and loan (S&L) at the request of the man who was largely responsible for its failure, Charles Keating, who also had donated more than $1 million to these senators' campaigns. Although it was concluded that Glenn and McCain were not extensively involved, the Senate Ethics Committee cited four of the men for questionable conduct and censured Senator Cranston for reprehensible conduct.

Operation Greylord was a four-year-long undercover investigation by the FBI in the 1970s into the Cook County, Illinois, court system. Approximately 30 persons, including 6 judges, were indicted for corrupt practices, and many of them were also convicted and sentenced to prison for various illegal activities such as accepting illegal fees from attorneys to settle cases in ways favorable to their interests. ABSCAM is the name of a 1978 scam resulting from an FBI-created front company (Abdul Enterprises, Ltd.), whereby FBI agents posing as associates of an Arab sheik offered public officials money in exchange for special favors. One senator and four congressmen were convicted on charges including bribery and conspiracy (Simon and Hagan, 1999). These types of acts are political crimes because they threaten the integrity of the U.S. political and legal systems.

POLITICAL CRIME TODAY: IRAN-CONTRA AND WHITEWATER

More current examples of political crime include the Iran-Contra affair of the 1980s and the Whitewater land scheme associated with President Bill Clinton. In the Iran-Contra affair, which occurred during the presidency of Ronald Reagan, arms were sold to Iran in exchange for hostages. The millions of dollars obtained in the deal were used to assist a rebel force fighting a war against the Marxist Sandinistas in Nicaragua. The arms sales and the assistance to the *contra* rebels violated U.S. policy, including the Boland Amendment passed by Congress in 1984. Government officials indicted and/or convicted for their involvement included Marine Lieutenant Colonel Oliver North of the White House National Security Council, National Security Advisor John Poindexter, retired Air Force Major General Richard Secord, and Secretary of Defense Caspar Weinberger (Foley, 1989; Kornbluh and Byrne, 1993).

"Whitewater" refers to a small real estate deal in 1978 whereby then–Arkansas Attorney General Bill Clinton, his wife Hillary, and James and Susan McDougal entered into an agreement to buy 220 acres of riverfront land in the Ozark Mountains in Arkansas under the name of Whitewater Development Corporation. At the heart of the efforts was a real estate deal known as Castle Grande, a conversion of 1,000 acres of land into a working-class community. James McDougal, who owned the Madison S&L, and Arkansas Governor Jim Guy Tucker were convicted on numerous counts of fraud related to this deal; Susan McDougal was convicted of fraudulently obtaining a loan of $300,000 for this real estate. Two federal agencies concluded that Castle Grande involved insider trading, fictitious sales, and land flips.

These acts are considered here as political crimes because of the alleged involvement of at least one politician in order to benefit limited financial interests unfairly at the expense of U.S. taxpayers. Through questionable activities, the Castle Grande property had been illegally purchased with Madison S&L money through a pyramid scheme that would ultimately be paid for by taxpayers. The S&L was later shut down by federal agents and cost taxpayers over $60 million to bail out.

Seth Ward, who was to receive payments for his role in the real estate deal, had his agreement drafted by Madison's Rose Law Firm, where Hillary Rodham Clinton worked for the Madison S&L. The S&L had been criticized by federal regulators for years because of shady financial practices. Clinton clearly pored over legal documents in the Castle Grande deal, as paperwork would later show. Curiously, this paperwork could not be located when subpoenaed by federal investigators, but it eventually showed up in Bill Clinton's White House two years later. Witnesses claimed that Hillary Clinton had ordered Madison S&L land contract files to be destroyed. Bill Clinton denied any illegal involvement in the deal under oath, but local judge David Hale testified that Clinton pressured him to make the fraudulent loan to Susan McDougal. Webb Hubbell, a friend of Clinton's who served as deputy attorney general for the Justice Department, was convicted of fraud and income tax evasion because of his involvement. Hubbell received $700,000 from friends and political advisors of President Clinton and the Democratic Party just as Hubbell and Hillary Clinton were being scrutinized by Whitewater investigators, leading to allegations that the White House wanted to buy Hubbell's silence (Froomkin, 1998; Young, 1998).

Discussion Questions

- Who are the *underclass*?
- In what ways is the war on crime a war on the poor?
- What functions are served for U.S. society by the war on crime?
- List some major sources of income inequality in the United States.
- How do you think income inequality produces crime?
- Do you think it is "right" that more than 40 million Americans do not have health insurance? Why or why not?
- What is the difference between *race* and *ethnicity*?
- Which groups in the United States have the greatest risks of involvement with the criminal justice system? Why do you think this is true?
- Define *contextual discrimination*.
- Discuss the apparent relationships between race, ethnicity, and social class.
- Identify some possible reasons that people of color are more likely to be poor.
- How have minorities made progress since the civil rights movement?
- In what ways do you think the criminal justice system is biased against people of color?
- Do people of color commit more crime than Caucasians? Why or why not?
- Should the crime of robbery (a Part I offense of the UCR) be considered more serious than crimes such as fraud and embezzlement (Part II offenses of the UCR)? Why or why not?
- How are the responses of the criminal justice system affected by gender?
- Discuss the chivalry or paternalism hypothesis.
- Discuss the "evil woman" hypothesis.
- What groups of people are most likely involved in political crimes? Explain.

CHAPTER SIX

FOCUSING ON THE WRONG THING? THE "WAR ON DRUGS"

INTRODUCTION

This chapter introduces you to the U.S. war on drugs. The drug war is a prime example of a war on crime that serves limited interests and is used to control certain segments of the U.S. population, notably the poor and people of color. This chapter shows who is most affected by the nation's drug war and how ineffective the war is for reducing illicit drug use. In this chapter, you will learn what a drug is, how prevalent drug use is in the United States, and harms associated with various drugs. An interesting issue arises: Why are the most harmful drugs legal while some relatively less harmful drugs are criminalized? I conclude the chapter with an assessment of legalization and decriminalization as strategies for American criminal justice.

THE WAR ON DRUGS

The "war on drugs" is the phrase used to describe the American approach to reducing drug use and abuse in the United States. Unless you've been asleep for the last twenty years, you must have heard something about it. President George Bush declared in a nationally televised message that drug abuse was "our nation's most serious domestic problem" (Beckett, 1997: 6). Earlier, President Reagan had diverted more than $700 million from education, treatment, and research to law enforcement programs. Reagan also gave more money to prisons and to the Drug Enforcement Administration, the federal agency responsible for preventing illicit drug use (Kraska, 1990: 117).

> *The* "war on drugs" is a term used to describe a national approach to reducing drug use and abuse in the United States.

The goals of the war on drugs are summarized by Gaines, Kaune, and Miller (2000: 611):

- To reduce the gang violence associated with the illegal drug trade
- To control the street crimes committed by illegal drug dealers
- To improve the quality of life in communities plagued by illegal drug use
- To deter minors from using illegal drugs
- To improve the physical, social, and economic well-being of illegal drug users

Given these goals, has America's drug war succeeded? Most people say no. Take, for example, this statement from Glaser (1997: 116):

> Narcotics are the bane of our criminal justice system, and control efforts have been much more extensive than for any vice except possibly alcohol use during Prohibition. Attempts to diminish the use of drugs by punishment have been tremendously costly, but usually seem to have no effect on the prevalence of drug abusers and their predations.

The main elements of the war on drugs include three policies: crop eradication efforts, interdiction efforts, and street-level drug enforcement (Kappeler, Blumberg, and Potter, 2000: 159). Best (1999: 144) explains the value of the war metaphor:

> Declarations of war on social problems are dramatic events: they call for society to rally behind a single policy, against a common foe. Typically, the initial pronouncements receive favorable attention in the mass media; the press details the nature of the problem and outlines the efforts designed to wage war against it. Usually, the enemy . . . has no one speaking on its behalf. There is the sense that society is united behind the war effort. Declaring war seizes the moral high ground.

> *The* principal elements of the U.S. drug war include three main policies: crop eradication efforts, interdiction efforts, and street-level drug enforcement.

The National Institute on Drug Abuse (NIDA) clams that we spent $59 billion on drug law enforcement and incarceration in 1998. As a nation, we have spent about $300 billion on the war on drugs since 1980 (Merlo and Benekos, 2000: 19). The cost of the drug war increased sixfold between 1986 and 1996, and most of this money went to domestic law enforcement at the local and state levels of (Gaines et al., 2000: 610). Meanwhile, domestic social programs have been cut dramatically to pay for the war on drugs (Goetz, 1996).

> $\mathscr{A}$s a nation, we have spent about $300 billion on the war on drugs since 1980.

Consider this irony: police departments in the United States have begun to profit from drug seizures and asset forfeitures of drug dealers. American police can seize assets accumulated as a result of illicit drug trafficking and keep a share of the proceeds to fund training and equipment (Gaines et al., 2000). If the police have come to need these funds for their own operating budgets, what would happen if they completely eliminated illicit drugs from our society?

The drug war is aimed at stopping *drug-related* crimes (e.g., acts of violence caused either by the pharmacological effects of drugs on people or by the need to obtain money to buy drugs), and crimes *associated with a drug-using lifestyle* (e.g., drug use itself) (Walker, 1998). In similar terms, Beckett and Sasson (2000: 40), discuss types of drug-related homicides, including "psychopharmacological" homicides caused directly by effects of drugs on the brain. Ironically, the war on drugs also creates *drug-defined* crimes, such as possession and sale of drugs, which obviously would not be "crimes" if drugs were not illegal (Office of National Drug Control Policy, 1994).

Despite the common image of a drug-crazed criminal, most crimes committed by people involved with drugs are not caused by the pharmacological effects of the drugs on behavior. Some criminal justice statistics promote these myths about the overall harmfulness of drugs. For example, research by the National Center on Addiction and Substance Abuse at Columbia University (1998) found that 80% "of prisoners in the United States were involved with alcohol or other drugs at the time of their crimes." This sounds like clear proof of the link between drug use and crime. But consider what this research actually means: "that is to say, 80 percent were either under the direct influence of alcohol or other drugs while committing the crime, had a history of drug abuse, committed the crime to support a drug habit, or were arrested for violating drug or alcohol laws" (Gaines et al., 2000: 51). Considering all that being "involved with drugs" includes, it is hard to imagine *any* prisoner who is *not* "involved with" alcohol or other drugs at the time of their crimes.

> $\mathscr{M}$ost crimes committed by people involved in drugs are not caused by the pharmacological effects of the drugs on behavior.

Drug-related crimes include what Beckett and Sasson (2000) call "economic compulsive" homicides—murders motivated by the need to obtain money to buy high-priced drugs. Others are "systemic" homicides, such as turf war killings aimed at protecting illicit drug markets. In essence, the illegal status of drugs creates criminal subcultures, such as gangs, that develop their own norms: being tough, getting respect, and making money through illicit activity. Reiman (1998) calls such crimes "secondary crimes," which could be virtually eliminated if drugs were not illegal.

Although the United States has always engaged in wars against drugs, as will be examined later in this chapter, the current drug war really started in the 1970s under President Richard Nixon.

In 1973, Nixon created the Drug Enforcement Agency (DEA) within the Department of Justice as the federal government's lead agency for suppressing drugs in the United States (Lyman and Potter, 1998). Since that time, drug use has been blamed for "the dramatic rise in the murder rate in the 1980s [and] gang violence." The resulting focus on drugs by U.S. criminal justice agencies, however, has produced something perhaps more disastrous—"the soaring prison population, the worsening crisis in race relations, and the steady erosion of individual rights in the Supreme Court" (Walker, 1998: 243).

Walker links these results directly to U.S. drug policy, which he calls "nonsensical." Sensible discussion about drugs, Walker claims, does not occur because of the public hysteria accompanying our war against drugs. The national outcries over "reefer madness" in the 1930s and "crack babies" in the 1980s, to be discussed later in this chapter, are prime examples of hysterias that led politicians to promote myths about drug use and crime and to talk tough about how to reduce use of drugs by Americans. The result has been our war on drugs.

Why, then, have Americans supported the addition of police and prisons in efforts to stop drug use, which is mostly "casual and recreational and does not lead to either addiction of criminal activity" (Walker, 1998: 247)? Why has the war on drugs become such a powerful force in the United States? Gaines and Kraska (1997: 4) claim:

> Most people do not question the political/media cries to do something about our "drug problem"; to wage wars on "drugs"; or that "drug use" destroys a person's, or even an entire community's well-being. Drug war ideology lulls us into assuming a number of properties about *drugs*. We refer to certain drugs . . . as if they were little demons committing crimes. Waging war on drugs—as if the drugs themselves constitute our "drug problem"—allows us to overlook the underlying reasons why people abuse these substances. . . . The language of ideology fools us into thinking that we're waging war against drugs themselves, not real people. . . .

These authors describe our war on drugs as "hypocritical, exploitative, and dangerously misleading" (p. 5).

According to Jensen and Gerber (1998: ix), misguided drug policies result from at least three factors: political opportunism; media profit maximization; and desire among criminal justice professionals to increase their spheres of influence. Politicians create concern about drug use in order to gain personally from such claims; they achieve this largely by using the media as their own mouthpiece. I will return to the specific role that the media have played in creating public concern about drugs later in this chapter.

Jensen and Gerber suggest that concern over drugs typically occurs in a cycle whereby some government entity claims the "existence of an undesirable condition" and then legitimizes the concern, garnering public support through the media by using "constructors" (similar to what Gans has called "counters") who provide evidence of the problem. Claims-makers "typify" the drug problem by characterizing its nature (Best, 1989). For example, drugs are typified as "harmful" even if they are being used recreationally. They are characterized as bad regardless of the context in which they are being used. Any drug use is wrong even if it is not abuse (Jensen and Gerber, 1998: 5).

Several myths about drugs exemplify this typification. For example, the "dope fiend mythology" promulgated by the U.S. government in the early 1900s contained these elements: "the drug addict is a violent criminal, the addict is a moral degenerate (e.g., a liar, thief, etc.), drug peddlers and addicts want to convert others into addicts, and the addict takes drugs because of an abnormal personality (Lindesmith, 1940)" (p. 8). Another example typified the use of marijuana, as indicated in a pamphlet circulated by the Bureau of Narcotics in the 1930s:

Prolonged use of Marihuana frequently develops a delirious rage which sometimes leads to high crimes, such as assault and murder. Hence Marihuana has been called the "killer drug." The habitual use of this narcotic poison always causes a marked deterioration and sometimes produces insanity. . . .

While the Marihuana habit leads to physical wreckage and mental decay, its effects upon character and morality are even more devastating. The victim frequently undergoes such moral degeneracy that he will lie and steal without scruple. (Quoted in Bonnie and Whitebread, 1974: 109)

The propaganda circulated by the Bureau of Narcotics included the story of a "murder of Florida family and their pet dog by a wayward son who had taken one toke of marijuana" (Kappeler et al., 2000: 9). Evidence about the relative harmlessness of marijuana was ignored.

The main effects of the war on drugs have included pressure on police to arrest drug violators, the use of drug assets for police benefits (what Jensen and Gerber call "policing for profit"), and increased militarization of police departments (Kraska and Kappeler, 1997). As the soldiers in the war on drugs, police departments have been encouraged by policies first instituted by President Reagan in the 1980s to pursue drug offenders; as a reward, they are allowed to confiscate and keep some drug-related assets (Gray, 1998). Again, think of the irony of law enforcement officials coming to rely on drug assets to purchase equipment and conduct training so that police can exterminate drug use (Rasmussen and Benson, 1994). It may be startling to realize that the majority of law enforcement agencies in the United States have such asset forfeiture programs in place (Jensen and Gerber, 1998; McAnamy, 1992).

According to Webb and Brown (1998), such "wars" on drugs as inanimate objects "tend to be concerned less with the drugs they purportedly target than with those who are perceived to be the primary users of the drugs (Morgan and Signorielli, 1990)" (p. 45). For example, the war on opium in the late 1800s and early 1900s was focused on Chinese laborers who represented unwanted labor competition. Thus, the Harrison Act of 1914, which forbade importation and manufacture of opium by Chinese, excluded the "Chinese living in the United States from fully participating in the labor market" (p. 46). The war on marijuana in the 1930s was grounded in racism against Mexican immigrants, who were characterized as "drug-crazed criminals" taking jobs away from Americans during the Great Depression (Sandor, 1995: 48). Finally, "the use of crack by the urban poor provided political leaders (in the 1980s) with a convenient scapegoat for both diverting attention from pressing social and economic problems and blaming a specific powerless group for social disaster" (Belenko, 1993: 9).

Other effects of wars on drugs include overloaded court systems, increased punitiveness in the form of stiff mandatory sentences for drug offenses, exploding prison populations, and ultimately a worsening of racial disparities in criminal justice (Jensen and Gerber, 1998: 1–2). This chapter examines the American war on drugs in an effort to determine if such effects are justified.

I begin by examining what a drug is, followed by a discussion of types of drugs. I will explore the extent of drug use in the United States and document harms associated with each type of drug. Next, I will consider the question of why some drugs are legal while others are targeted by the criminal justice system. I will attempt to answer the question: Why are the most harmful drugs legal while some relatively harmless drugs are illegal? The chapter concludes with a discussion of how drug decriminalization may serve to make the criminal justice system more just (see the Issue in Depth at the end of this chapter).

WHAT IS A DRUG?

What do you think of when you hear the word *drug*? The meaning of the word really depends on who is asked. To a doctor or pharmacist, for example, a drug is something very different than it is to homeless person living on the street (Liska, 2000).

The term *drug* does have a clear definition. Lyman and Potter (1998: 59–60) begin their examination of drugs in American society with a discussion of the dictionary definition of the term. The tenth edition of *Merriam-Webster's Collegiate Dictionary* (1998) defines a drug as "a substance intended for use in the diagnosis, cure, mitigation, treatment, or prevention of disease." Liska (2000: 3–4), expanding on this, writes that drugs are used to: fight infection; reverse a disease process; relieve symptoms of illness; restore normal functioning of human organs; aid in diagnosing sickness; inhibit normal body processes; and maintain health. This is the relatively positive view of drugs.

Have we as a nation declared a war on substances that help fight disease and maintain health? Clearly not. Obviously, there must be another meaning of drugs. Lyman and Potter (1998: 60) define a drug as "any substance that causes or creates significant psychological and/or physiological changes in the body." Liska (2000: 4) defines a drug as "any absorbed substance that changes or enhances any physical or psychological function in the body." But these definitions of a drug would include coffee, tea, and cigarettes—in fact, virtually any substance. Have we declared war on these substances? Obviously not.

Webster's includes as its last acceptable definition "something and often an illegal substance that causes addiction, habituation, or a marked change in consciousness." Is this the focus of our war on drugs? Clearly, it is. Our American "war on drugs" is being waged against *illegal* forms of drug use and the activities that permit it (manufacturing, distribution, sales, possession, etc.).

> *T*he definition of a drug in *Merriam-Webster's Collegiate Dictionary*, 10th ed., includes as its last acceptable definition, "something and often an illegal substance that causes addiction, habituation, or a marked change in consciousness."

All drugs, whether legal or illegal, affect the brain by interacting with naturally occurring brain chemicals known as neurotransmitters (such as dopamine): "The major drugs of abuse—e.g., narcotics like heroin or stimulants like cocaine—mimic the structure of neurotransmitters, the

> *A*ll drugs, whether legal or illegal, affect the brain by interacting with naturally occurring brain chemicals known as neurotransmitters.

most powerful mind-altering drugs the human body creates" (Lyman and Potter, 1998: 60–61). By altering the brain's chemistry, drugs alter people's behavior. When their effects are dangerous or simply unintended, such as interfering with a person's family, work, or social relations, drugs

> *B*y altering the brain's chemistry, drugs alter people's behavior. When effects are dangerous or simply unintended, such as interfering with a person's family, work, or social relations, drugs can be harmful to the user.

can be harmful to the user (Lyman and Potter, 1998: 60). In fact, every drug—from legal drugs such as aspirin to illegal drugs such as cocaine—is potentially harmful.

The effects of any drug depend on numerous factors, including the type of drug, its potency and quantity, the method in which it is ingested, the setting in which it is ingested, the frequency of use, the mood of the user, and the user's biological and psychological makeup (Gaines and Kraska, 1997; Lyman and Potter, 1998). Effects of particular types of drugs will be discussed below.

> *The* effects of any drug depend on numerous factors, including the type of drug used, its potency and quantity, the method and setting in which the drug was ingested, the frequency of use, the mood of the user, and the user's biological and psychological makeup.

Keep in mind the clear distinction between drug *use* and drug *abuse*. Drug use is generally understood as any consumption of a drug, including recreational or occasional use. Remember President Bill Clinton explaining, as a candidate in 1992, that he had tried marijuana in college, didn't inhale it, and didn't like it? That's drug use, as is the alleged cocaine use of President George W. Bush (son of former president George Bush).

> *Drug* use is generally understood as any consumption of a drug, such as recreational or occasional use. Drug abuse implies a higher degree of drug consumption, suggestive of some problem level of use, or overuse.

Drug abuse implies a problematic level of use, or overuse, of drugs. Lyman and Potter (1998: 60) define drug abuse as "illicit drug use that results in social, economic, psychological or legal problems for the drug user." They also note that the Bureau of Justice Statistics defines drug abuse as "the use of prescription-type psychotherapeutic drugs for nonmedical purposes or the use of illegal drugs."

Drug use, even of illegal substances, is not the same as drug abuse. It is possible to use illegal drugs without abusing them, although this is a lesson that seems to be lost on the U.S. criminal justice system, which has treated drug use as a crime rather than a recreational habit and has not recognized that most people who use drugs do not abuse them. In fact, most drug-related arrests are for simple possession, not for manufacturing, distributing, or selling drugs (Beckett and Sasson, 2000: 172).

Drug abuse varies by individual: "Abuse occurs when the use of the drug—whether aspirin, beer, caffeine, cigarettes, marijuana, diet pills, or heroin—becomes a psychological, social, or physical problem for the user" (Gaines and Kraska, 1997: 6). Only a small portion of drug users, somewhere between 7% and 20% depending on the type of drug in question, actually become drug abusers (Kraska, 1990). In fact, depending on one's definition of a drug, we all use drugs as part of our everyday lives: "some form of drug use is an everyday part of living for most Americans" (Lyman and Potter, 1998: 11).

Drugs are useful because they can alter our moods, create feelings of pleasure, stimulate brain activity, or aid in sedation or enhanced physical and psychological performance (Lyman and Potter, 1998). Some suggest that drug use is innate or natural, as much as the need for food or sex. Weil (1998: 4) writes: "The use of drugs to alter consciousness is nothing new. It has been a feature of human life in all places on the earth and in all ages of history." Hamid (1998: vii) suggests that "the human use of psychoactive drugs is both primordial and nearly universal. In almost every human culture in every age of history, the use of one or more psychoactive drugs was featured prominently in the contexts of religion, ritual, health care, divination, celebration (including the arts, music, and theater), recreation, and cuisine." People use drugs in certain rituals in groups, such as during "Happy Hour" or at parties with friends. People may use drugs to relieve boredom (Glassner and Loughlin, 1987), to alter their moods, to inspire creativity, and sometimes for medicinal and religious purposes.

For numerous reasons, then, people use drugs without experiencing significant problems associated with drug abuse. This does not mean that drug use should be promoted or supported by government, but it does raise the question of why we spend so many physical and financial resources fighting something that is considered normal by most people at some point in their lives, is relatively harmless, and is not likely to be stopped through criminal justice mechanisms. I would argue that *drug abuse* (which is only a small portion of all drug use) should be of concern to our government because of its possible outcomes.

> *F*or numerous reasons, people use drugs and do not e. perience significant problems associated with drug abuse.

Lyman and Potter (1998: 62) list several outcomes of drug abuse:

- *Physical dependence:* The user becomes increasingly tolerant of a drug's effects, so that increased amounts of the drug are needed in order to prevent withdrawal symptoms.
- *Psychological dependence:* The user develops a craving for or compulsive need to use drugs because they provide him or her with a feeling of well-being and satisfaction.
- *Tolerance:* The user who continues regular use of a drug must administer progressively larger doses to attain the desired effect, thereby reinforcing the compulsive behavior known as drug dependence.
- *Withdrawal:* The user experiences a physical reaction when deprived of an addictive drug, characterized by increased excitability of the bodily functions that have been depressed by the drug's habitual use.

> *O*utcomes of drug abuse include physical and psychological dependence, tolerance, and withdrawal.

These outcomes suggest that drug abuse is maladaptive and thus potentially dangerous. Still, whether the U.S. government should wage a war on drug abuse is debatable, given that drug abuse is more likely to respond to medical treatment. It is clear, however, that our investment in stopping simple drug use is costing us far more than it is returning. Kappeler et al. (2000: 150) conclude that illicit drug-related deaths are infrequent and that they are actually more likely to occur because of the effects of drug laws.

TYPES OF DRUGS

Drugs can be categorized according to their principal effects on brain function and hence on human behavior. The major general categories of drugs include stimulants, depressants, hallucinogens, and narcotics/opiates (Inciardi and McElrath, 1998; Liska, 2000). Lyman and Potter (1998) also add inhalants (drugs that are drawn into the body by breathing in) as a separate category because of their use among young people in particular. Inciardi and McElrath (1998) add analgesics (painkillers), sedatives (which produce calm and relaxation), and hypnotics (depressants that produce sleep).

> $\mathcal{T}$he major types of drugs can be categorized according to their major effects on brain function and hence human behavior. General categories of drugs include stimulants, depressants, hallucinogens, and narcotics/opiates.

As defined by Inciardi and McElrath (1998: xii–xiii), these substances are:

- *Stimulants:* Drugs that stimulate the central nervous system (CNS) and increase the activity of the brain and spinal cord
- *Depressants:* Drugs that act to lessen the activity of the CNS, diminishing or stopping vital functions
- *Hallucinogens:* Drugs that act on the CNS to produce mood and perceptual changes varying from sensory illusions to hallucinations

Narcotics are a category of illegal drugs including opium and opium derivatives, as well as their synthetic versions (Lyman and Potter, 1998).

The following box gives some examples of drugs that fall into each category. Note that some of the substances within each category are legal, others illegal. Thus, the nature of the drug does not determine its legal status.

Examples of major drugs

- *Stimulants:* Caffeine, nicotine, cocaine, amphetamines
- *Depressants:* Alcohol, barbiturates, narcotics, heroin
- *Hallucinogens:* Marijuana, lysergic acid diethylamide (LSD), phencyclidine (PCP), psilocybin mushrooms, peyote cactus, ecstasy

As you might guess, stimulants stimulate brain activity. The most common stimulants in the United States are legal—caffeine (in coffee) and nicotine (in cigarettes). These drugs make people feel stronger, alert, decisive, and even exhilarated. Depressants, as you also might guess,

> $\mathcal{S}$timulants stimulate brain activity. The most common stimulants in the United States are legal, such as caffeine (in coffee) and nicotine (in cigarettes). These types of drugs make people feel stronger, more alert, decisive, and even exhilarated.

depress brain activity. Users become sluggish, have impaired judgment and slurred speech, and suffer from loss of motor coordination. Hallucinogens distort perceptions of reality through the auditory (hearing), tactile (touch), and visual (sight) systems. Narcotics, which produce feelings

> *D*epressants depress brain activity. Users become sluggish, have impaired judgment and slurred speech, and suffer from loss of motor coordination.

of euphoria in users, can be accompanied by undesirable effects including nausea, vomiting, drowsiness, apathy, respiratory depression, loss of motor coordination, and slurred speech.

> *H*allucinogens distort perceptions of reality, including auditory (hearing), tactile (touch), and visual (sight) systems.

Another way of categorizing drugs is by the government classification system. The Controlled Substances Act (CSA), Title II of the Comprehensive Drug Abuse Prevention and Control Act of 1970, consolidated many laws regulating the manufacture and distribution of narcotics, stimulants, depressants, hallucinogens, steroids, and chemicals used in the illicit production of controlled substances. This law classified drugs into five categories:

- *Schedule I:* These drugs or other substances have a high potential for abuse and have no currently accepted medical use in treatment in the United States. There is a lack of acceptance for use of the drug or other substance under medical supervision. Examples include heroin, LSD, marijuana, and methaqualone.
- *Schedule II:* The drug or other substance has a high potential for abuse but has a currently accepted medical use in treatment in the United States or a currently accepted medical use with severe restrictions. Abuse of the drug or other substance may lead to severe psychological or physical dependence. Examples include morphine, PCP, cocaine, methadone, and methamphetamine.
- *Schedule III:* The drug has less potential for abuse than the substances in Schedules I and II and has a currently accepted medical use in treatment in the United States. Abuse of the drug or other substance may lead to moderate or low physical dependence or high psychological dependence. Examples include anabolic steroids, codeine and hydrocodone with aspirin or Tylenol, and some barbiturates.
- *Schedule IV:* The drug has a lower potential for abuse than the substances in Schedule III and has a currently accepted medical use in treatment in the United States. Abuse of the drug or other substance may lead to limited physical dependence or psychological dependence relative to the drugs or other substances in Schedule III. Examples include Darvon, Talwin, Equanil, Valium, and Xanax.
- *Schedule V:* The drug or other substance has a low potential for abuse relative to the drugs or other substances in Schedule IV and has a currently accepted medical use in treatment in the United States. Abuse of the drug or other substances may lead to limited physical dependence or psychological dependence relative to the drugs or other substances in Schedule IV. Over-the-counter cough medicines with codeine are classified in Schedule V.

This classification system is useful for reference later in the chapter when we examine which drugs the criminal justice system targets. As you will see, the higher the level of a drug (nearer to Schedule I), the more vigorously it is pursued, regardless of whether it is being used for recreational purposes or is being abused.

EXTENT OF DRUG USE IN THE UNITED STATES

Figure 6.1 lists several popular drugs in the United States and shows how many people use each type of drug and how the drug works to produce the "high" that your friends may have described to you. Figure 6.1 also illustrates the major effects of these drugs. The most commonly used drugs are legal substances such as caffeine, nicotine, and alcohol. According to the National Coffee Association (1998), 130 million Americans use caffeine (in the form of coffee), and 64 million

> *The* most commonly used drugs are those that are legal, such as caffeine, nicotine, and alcohol: 130 million Americans use caffeine through coffee, and 64 million use nicotine through smoking cigarettes.

use nicotine (through smoking cigarettes). The 1997 survey by the National Institutes of Health (NIH) and the National Institute on Drug Abuse found that nearly 14 million Americans 12 years of age or older had used an illegal drug within the past month. The most commonly used illegal drug is marijuana: 11 million used it within the last month. Fewer people use cocaine (1.5 million users), heroin (325,000), and other illegal drugs. Are legal drugs more widely used by Americans because they are less harmful than those that are currently illegal, such as marijuana, cocaine, and heroin? Actually, no. I'll return to this issue later in this chapter.

> *The* 1997 survey by the National Institutes of Health and the National Institute on Drug Abuse found that nearly 14 million Americans 12 years of age or older had used an illegal drug within the past month. The most commonly used illegal drug is marijuana, as 11 million used it within the last month. Fewer people use cocaine (1.5 million users), heroin (325,000), and other illegal drugs.

FIGURE 6.1
Drug Use in the United States

Caffeine (coffee)	130 million
Nicotine (cigarettes)	64 million
(Effects: alertness, decisiveness, exhilaration)	
Alcohol	11 million
(Effects: sluggishness, impaired judgment, slurred speech, loss of motor coordination, decreased social inhibitions)	
Any illegal drug	14 million
Marijuana	10 million
(Effects: sluggishness, impaired judgment, loss of motor coordination, decreased social inhibitions)	
Cocaine	1.5 million
Heroin	325,000
(Effects: distorted perceptions of reality, inense high or euphoria)	

SOURCE: Adapted from M. Lyman and G. Potter, *Drugs in Society* (Cincinnati, OH: Anderson, 1998).

HARMS ASSOCIATED WITH DRUGS

Every drug, legal or illegal, is at least potentially harmful. In the section that follows, I will examine the relative harms of nicotine (found in tobacco) and tetrahydrocannabinol or THC (found in marijuana), two drugs that are consumed through smoking. I'll start with the effects of nicotine. The following box contains the U.S. government's "official line" on the dangers of marijuana versus those of cigarettes. Which sounds worse to you?

---

*ℰvery drug, legal and illegal, is at the very least potentially harmful.

Marijuana versus cigarettes

Short-term effects of using marijuana

- Sleepiness
- Difficulty keeping track of time, impaired or reduced short-term memory
- Reduced ability to perform tasks requiring concentration and coordination, such as driving a car
- Increased heart rate
- Potential cardiac dangers for those with preexisting heart disease
- Bloodshot eyes
- Dry mouth and throat
- Decreased social inhibitions
- Paranoia, hallucinations

Long-term effects of using marijuana

- Enhanced cancer risk
- Decrease in testosterone levels for men; also lower sperm counts and difficulty having children
- Increase in testosterone levels for women; also increased risk of infertility
- Diminished or extinguished sexual pleasure
- Psychological dependence, requiring more of the drug to get the same effect

Risks associated with smoking cigarettes

- Diminished or extinguished sense of smell and taste
- Frequent colds
- Smoker's cough
- Gastric ulcers
- Chronic bronchitis
- Increase in heart rate and blood pressure
- Premature and more abundant face wrinkles
- Emphysema
- Heart disease
- Stroke

- Cancer of the mouth, larynx, pharynx, esophagus, lungs, pancreas, cervix, uterus, and bladder
- Cigarette smoking is perhaps the most devastating preventable cause of disease and premature death.
- Smoking is particularly dangerous for teens because their bodies are still developing and changing and the 4,000 chemicals (including 200 known poisons) in cigarette smoke can adversely affect this process.

SOURCE: Substance Abuse and Mental Health Services Administration, an agency of the U.S. Department of Health and Human Services, 2000.

Nicotine is a drug. It is the substance in tobacco that keeps smokers smoking. Since nearly one-fourth of all Americans smoke, nicotine is the most prevalent psychoactive drug—that is, affecting the mind and mental processes—used in the United States. Nicotine is the second most abused drug in the United States, behind alcohol. This is attributable to many factors, including the legal status of the drug, the numerous social contexts in which smoking nicotine is acceptable and even expected, and the advertising campaigns of the tobacco industry. Given the highly addictive nature of nicotine, tobacco use is thus considered a legal form of substance abuse. According to the Boston University Medical Center, each cigarette delivers about 6 to 8 milligrams of nicotine.

The most likely future nicotine addicts are teens targeted by tobacco industry advertisers. As indicated in Issue in Depth 3 at the end of Chapter Three, children are more than twice as likely as adults to smoke the three most advertised brands. Nicotine addiction occurs when a person has a compulsive need for nicotine, as discussed earlier. Smokers thus feel a persistent craving for a cigarette, which is, in essence, what the Food and Drug Administration calls "a delivery system for an addictive drug" (Centers for Disease Control and Prevention, 1994).

The large majority of smokers begin smoking before the age of 18 (Robinson, 1998). Every day, 3,000 new young people begin to smoke. Teenagers see smoking as "cool" or "sexy," images created by the tobacco industry and reinforced by peers in social situations. The amount of nicotine used and the frequency of use start small but increase over time as the user becomes addicted to nicotine. People continue to use nicotine even after they learn of the health risks associated with smoking. Smokers claim they cannot quit because they experience irritability, lowered concentration, weight gain, cravings for nicotine, and even tremors. These effects suggest nicotine is being used to avoid physical withdrawal symptoms (Boston University Medical Center, 2000).

Nicotine is smoked because it is most rapidly absorbed into the body in this way. About 90% is absorbed into the lungs, oral cavity, and gastrointestinal system. Nicotine particles act on every cell and thus on every organ of a user's body, including the heart, kidneys, skin, and brain. According to the Boston University Medical Center, nicotine increases salivation, stomach acid and motility, heart rate, and blood pressure, and reduces circulation in the blood. It also can lead to impotence in as little as ten years of prolonged use.

Nicotine can be used more safely through alternative methods of ingestion, for example through an inhaler. Tobacco companies developed such a mechanism, similar to that used by asthmatics, but ultimately rejected it because it was inconsistent with their portrayals of cigarettes as harmless and nonaddictive products (Glantz et al., 1996).

When inhaled by smoking, nicotine becomes a very dangerous drug. For example, cigarettes contain 43 known carcinogens as well as thousands of other harmful chemicals such as carbon monoxide, carbon dioxide, formaldehyde, and ammonia (Robinson, 1998). Cigarettes include various amounts of metals such as aluminum, copper, lead, mercury, and zinc. Not surprisingly, then, smoking kills more than twenty times as many people as murder each year, through lung diseases such as cancer, emphysema, chronic mucus secretion and air flow blocks, bronchitis, and respiratory and bacterial infections. It also causes heart disease because of cholesterol buildup, which restricts blood flow (the same thing that causes impotence). Smoking causes stiffness in the artery walls, high blood pressure, blood clots, and oxygen demand in muscles (Boston University Medical Center, 2000).

Lung cancer is not the only type of cancer caused by smoking, which is also a major cause of cancer of the lips, tongue, salivary glands, mouth, larynx, esophagus, stomach, bladder, renal pelvis, uterine cervix, and pancreas. Secondhand smoke also kills thousands (Robinson, 1998), mainly because it contains dozens of dangerous chemicals (Centers for Disease Control and Prevention, 1997). Thus, nonsmokers (such as children of smokers) suffer chronic ear infections, coughing because of phlegm buildup, and acute respiratory illnesses such as bronchitis and pneumonia.

What about marijuana? Does this illegal substance cause the same problems as tobacco, which is legal? Virtually every expert who has studied this issue answers a resounding "no."

Let us start by dispelling some myths about marijuana, which come from Zimmer and Morgan's *Marijuana Myths, Marijuana Facts:*

- Marijuana is relatively harmless. The British medical journal *Lancet* concluded in 1995 that "the smoking of cannabis, even long term, is not harmful to health."
- Most people who smoke marijuana do not smoke it regularly. Only about 1% of users smoke the drug daily.
- Marijuana does not lead to physical dependence or addiction.
- Smoking marijuana does not lead to use of hard drugs (the so-called gateway drug hypothesis). Because marijuana is the most popular illegal drug in the United States, the majority of people who use other drugs have also used marijuana at one time. Most marijuana users, however, never use another illicit drug, and, in fact, virtually every illicit drug user started with tobacco and alcohol.
- Marijuana offenders are not dangerous. The effects of marijuana use are relatively mild. Over 80% of those arrested for marijuana in any given year are arrested for mere possession of the drug, not for growing or selling it.

In 1988, Francis Young, a judge affiliated with the DEA, reached the following conclusions about marijuana (in Kappeler et al., 2000: 152):

- There has never been a single documented cannabis-related death.
- Among the 70 million Americans who have used marijuana, there has never been a reported overdose.
- Marijuana in its natural form is one of the safest therapeutically active substances known to humans.
- In strict medical terms, marijuana is far safer than many foods we commonly consume.

Still, the THC in marijuana is a drug. It is the substance in marijuana that is addictive. The use of marijuana as a psychoactive drug is far less prevalent than nicotine use, for many reasons: marijuana is illegal; there are fewer social contexts in which smoking marijuana is acceptable than smoking cigarettes, and it is not advertised by any corporate industry.

Smoking marijuana is typically a behavior associated with young people. Whereas smoking tobacco increases over time as the user becomes addicted to nicotine, smoking marijuana is consistently limited to relatively small amounts. Effects of marijuana begin immediately upon ingesting the substance into the body, so there is no need to smoke greater and greater amounts over time. As explained by the National Institutes of Health (NIH) (1997):

> THC is quite potent when compared to most other psychoactive drugs. An intravenous (IV) dose of only a milligram or two can produce profound mental and phsyiologic effects (Agurell et al., 1984, 1986; Fehr and Kalant, 1983; Jones, 1987). Large doses of THC delivered by marijuana or administered in the pure form can produce mental and perceptual effects similar to drugs usually termed hallucinogens. . . . *However, the way marijuana is used in the United States does not commonly lead to such profound mental effects.* (emphasis added)

THC is smoked because it is more rapidly absorbed into the body in this way, much like nicotine. THC particles are absorbed within seconds and delivered to the human brain immediately, and they also act on every cell and thus on every organ of a user's body, including the heart, kidneys, skin, and brain.

Marijuana contains over 400 chemicals, including THC and other cannabinoids, which are the psychoactive chemicals in the plant. Yet, it has "remarkably low lethal toxicity" (NIH, 1997). Whereas one in three smokers of cigarettes will die from a smoking-related illness, there has never been a recorded human death associated with marijuana use. The effects of marijuana on the user are numerous, including the following:

> [A] sense of well-being (often termed euphoria or high); feelings of relaxation; altered perception of time and distance; intensified sensory experiences; laughter; talkativeness; and increased sociability when taken in a social setting; impaired memory for recent events; difficulty concentrating; dreamlike states; impaired motor coordination; impaired driving and other psychomotor skills; slowed reaction time; impaired goal-directed mental activity; and altered peripheral vision are common associated effects. (Adams and Martin, 1996; Fehr and Kalant, 1983; Hollister, 1988; Institute of Medicine, 1982; Tart, 1971; cited in National Institutes of Health, 1997)

Other adverse effects can include anxiety, panic, depression, delusions, and hallucinations (Adams and Martin, 1996; Fehr and Kalant, 1983; Hollister, 1988). Such effects usually present themselves rapidly and last only two to three hours. Although marijuana use can heighten the effects of mental illnesses such as schizophrenia and bipolar affective disorder, it is not a significant cause of these illnesses, which are thought to be biologically based (Raine, 1993). Use of the drug can, however, lead to temporary lessening of motivation and impaired educational performance (Pope and Yurgelun-Todd, 1996).

The physical effects of smoking marijuana include temporary increases in heart rate and blood pressure, as well as lowered body temperature, which has not "presented any health problems for healthy and relatively young users" (NIH, 1997). However, chronic use can lead to bronchitis, pharyngitis, and increased frequency of pulmonary and respiratory illnesses because of suppressed antibody formation and resistance to infection from bacterial and viral infections. Still, "[c]onclusive evidence for increased malignancy, or enhanced acquisition of HIV, or the development of AIDS, has not been associated with marijuana use" (NIH, 1997).

From this comparison, we can confidently conclude the following:

- Cigarettes contain nicotine, a physically addictive drug that produces dependence and withdrawal symptoms when ceased.
- Smoking cigarettes is a highly deadly form of drug use.
- Marijuana contains THC and other cannabinoids, which are psychologically addictive drugs that do not cause dependence or physical withdrawal symptoms when ceased.
- Smoking marijuana is a potentially harmful form of drug use.
- Smoking cigarettes is far more dangerous than smoking marijuana.

Nevertheless, smoking cigarettes is generally legal, while smoking marijuana is generally illegal. Even though there are only one-sixth as many marijuana users as nicotine users, smoking kills more than 400,000 people each year, and marijuana kills none. The death rate for tobacco users is around 650 per 100,000 people in the United States, versus a rate of 0 per 100,000 for marijuana users.

---

*E*ven though there are only one-sixth as many marijuana users as there are nicotine users, smoking kills more than 400,000 people each year, and marijuana kills none. This equates to a death rate of around 650 per 100,000 people in the United States for tobacco users, versus zero per 100,000 for marijuana users.

Government-funded studies in the 1970s, as summarized by Hamid (1998: 47–51), were far more pessimistic and alarmist in their conclusions with regard to marijuana. These studies found evidence of what Hamid calls amotivational syndrome, cannabis psychosis, mental and physical deterioration, brain damage, and escalation to harder drugs. Evidence from more recent studies shows that these effects were, at best, grossly overstated.

Use and abuse of other illicit drugs include adverse health consequences (Jensen and Gerber, 1998; Liska, 2000). In 1993, for example, 123,000 people visited emergency rooms for treatment of cocaine overdoses and unexpected reactions to cocaine use. Another 63,000 sought emergency medical assistance for heroin- and morphine-related problems (Maguire and Pastore, 1995). Long-term health consequences of opiates include hypotension, allergies, and insomnia; overdose can cause fatal convulsions and seizures. Cocaine's adverse effects include death via seizures and strokes (Fishbein and Pease, 1996). Most deaths from cocaine are caused by smoking the drug in the form of crack (Goode, 1999); these deaths are not attributable to the dangers of cocaine itself but, rather, to the fact that there are fewer quality controls on street-level crack than on powder cocaine.

Even *relatively* harmless drugs, such as marijuana, produce smoke that is carcinogenic, and chronic smokers of marijuana suffer from "toxic effects on several organs, including the brain, heart [and] lungs" (Fishbein and Pease, 1996: 310). Of course, these outcomes are not as severe as those suffered by users of legal drugs such as tobacco and alcohol. Using the harmfulness of illegal drugs to justify their illegal status while simultaneously ignoring the harms of these legal drugs is hypocritical at best.

Glaser (1997: 117) describes the hypocrisy of the nation's drug war when he writes: "The law prohibits marijuana, cocaine, and the opiates but allows our intake of items that can be equally disabling, including whiskey, wine, and beer, as well as tranquilizers, sedatives, analgesics, stimulants, and antidepressants sold in drug stores, some without prescription." At the same time: "Relatively affluent users (and abusers) of illicit drugs are able to engage in their habits with impunity. They are likely to be able to insulate themselves from the criminal justice system. If they are in need of medical assistance, they are likely to arrange for private care and are likely to have health insurance that covers such treatment." By contrast, poor people who live in urban areas are the most likely to suffer from the horrible side effects of illegal drugs, are most likely to be discovered because of their limited access to medical care, and are most likely to suffer whatever violent crime does result from drug use and abuse (p. 199).

LEGAL STATUS OF EACH DRUG: WHY ARE THE MOST HARMFUL DRUGS LEGAL WHILE SOME RELATIVELY HARMLESS DRUGS ARE ILLEGAL?

Given that illegal drugs (such as marijuana) are typically less dangerous than legal drugs (such as tobacco), why are these drugs illegal? One primary reason is the fear that illegal drug use is associated with an increased risk for criminality.

According to Nuro, Kinlock, and Hanlon (1998: 221): "Evidence of criminal activity among narcotics users is longstanding and abundant; however, it is apparent that relationships among the important variables involved are much more complex than were initially believed." These authors suggest that prevalence and diversity of criminality among narcotics users are high, but that most crime committed by drug users is for the purpose of supporting drug use. Higher levels of drug use, then, tend to be associated with higher involvement in criminality. For heavy users of drugs and persistent criminals, initiation into both criminality and drug use begins at early ages (p. 225).

> *T*he prevalence and diversity of criminality among narcotics users are high, but most crime committed by drug users is to support their drug use.

The smallest portion of criminality among drug users is violent crime (p. 227), and most crime is petty, nonviolent crime (Goldstein, 1998: 246), but amounts and types of crimes vary by individual (Nuro et al., 1998: 229). Drug research thus supports the claims of legalization proponents that legalizing drugs would reduce overall criminality in the United States (see the Issue in Depth at the end of this chapter).

> *T*he smallest portion of criminality among drug users is violent crime; most is petty, nonviolent crime.

The drugs most relevant for a psychopharmacological violence effect are alcohol, stimulants, barbiturates, and PCP (e.g., see Asnis and Smith, 1978; d'Orban, 1976; Ellingswood, 1971; Feldman, Agar, and Beschner, 1979; Gerson and Preston, 1979; Glaser, 1974; Tinklenberg, 1973; Virkunnen, 1974). The suspected and sometimes asserted link between opiates and marijuana and violence has been discredited (e.g., see Finestone, 1967; Greenberg and Adler, 1974; Inciardi and Chambers, 1972; Kozel, Dupont, and Brown, 1972; Kramer, 1976; Schatzman, 1975). In fact, these drugs may actually "ameliorate violent tendencies. In such cases, persons who are prone to acting violently may engage in self-medication, in order to control their violent tendencies" (Goldstein, 1998: 245). Heroin users will refrain from committing violent crimes to acquire money to buy their drug if alternatives exist (e.g., see Cushman, 1974; Goldman and Duchaine, 1980; Goldstein, 1979; Gould, 1974; Johnson et al., 1985; Preble and Casey, 1969; Swezey, 1973).

> *T*he drugs most associated with a psychopharmacological violence effect are alcohol, stimulants, barbiturates, and PCP.

There is obviously violence in the drug business, so what causes it? According to Reuter (1998: 315): "The violence, overdoses, and massive illegal incomes that are such a prominent part of our current concerns with psychoactive drugs are not consequences of the nature of the drugs themselves, but rather of the conditions of use that society has created." In other words, violence typically does not stem from drug use per se but, rather, from the fact that drug use is illegal and violence is required to protect business interests of drug dealers.

> *V*iolence typically does not stem from drug use per se, but rather from the fact that drug use is illegal and therefore violence is required to protect business interests of drug dealers.

In numerous drug scares throughout U.S. history, this fact has escaped the public. Each drug scare has centered on some type of illicit drug use. Beckett (1997: 45–46) briefly outlines several of these, including the antiopium movement in California in the late 1870s, the temperance (antialcohol) movement of the Women's Christian Temperance Union (WCTU) in the 1890s, the cocaine scare of the post-Reconstruction South, the "killer weed" antimarijuana movement in the southwestern United States in the 1930s, and the crack cocaine scare of the 1980s. Each of these drug scares blamed all sorts of societal evils on "outsiders" (Becker, 1963) or on poor minority groups, from Chinese immigrants (opium smoking in the 1870s) to Mexicans (marijuana in the 1930s) to African Americans (cocaine and crack). As explained by Beckett and Sasson (1998: 37), crime and drug problems were typified as "'underclass' problems resulting from insufficient social control."

Traditionally, drug use becomes characterized as problematic only when it involves particular groups of people (Jensen and Gerber, 1998: 3). In essence, this serves as a form of "institutional racism" (p. 21). Drug use by targeted groups is characterized as a source of other societal problems (Reinarman, 1994) while institutional sources of poverty and crime are ignored. The nation's drug war meets the definition of institutional discrimination proposed by Walker et al. (2000), because race and class are not explicitly stated as valid factors for utilizing the criminal justice system selectively against drug offenders, yet, as discussed in Chapter Five, racial and ethnic disparities appear in criminal justice outcomes that result from the application of racially neutral factors. In the drug war, the racially neutral factor is the fallacious notion that "their drugs" are more harmful than "our drugs." In the case of crack versus powder cocaine, this spurious belief is built directly into the written criminal law.

Because such drug scares are focused on relatively powerless groups such as minorities, immigrants, and lower-class people, you may be wondering whether the drug scares are actually aimed at lowering drug use and abuse rates or whether their legislative intent is aimed at other outcomes. Recall from Chapter One the difference between intended goals and functions served by particular criminal justice policies (policies can serve functions without being intentional). By examining the role of the media in portraying drug scares, you may get a sense of the functions they serve for powerful members of society.

The Role of the Media in Drug Scares

As discussed in Chapter Four, the media, in what they portray and in what they choose not to portray, reinforce moral boundaries in society. At various times, the media have created "moral panics" focused on drug use. The crack cocaine scare is the most recent of those discussed earlier. As Potter and Kappeler write, "The media—particularly news magazines, televison, and newspapers—and the state engaged in a frenzied attempt to create a moral panic in the form of a drug scare as a means of continuing and extending the 'War on Drugs' begun in the Reagan administration" (1998: 9). As noted by Merlo and Benekos (2000: 16), images and stories in the media (especially about crack cocaine) spread fear that drug use was a major source of the nation's problems, especially crime.

Claims by field sources from the Community Epidemiology Work Group (CEWG), established by the National Institute on Drug Abuse to provide community-level surveillance of drug abuse in 20 metropolitan areas, show the concern about crack cocaine in American inner cities. The following box contains some quotes from field sources in the early 1980s.

CEWG field quotes about crack cocaine

- *Boston:* "Cocaine is a massive problem."
- *Miami:* "Cocaine is more available than ever before."
- *Newark:* "Cocaine is gaining rapid popularity."
- *New Orleans:* "Cocaine appears to be dominating the drug scene."
- *Philadelphia:* "There is a significant increase in availability and use."
- *Phoenix:* "Large quantities are available through Miami; prices have dropped."
- *Seattle:* "Cocaine is the county's most important problem."
- *Buffalo:* "There has been a marked increase in cocaine use."
- *Chicago:* "Cocaine is the only drug to have shown consistently increasing patterns of abuse."
- *Denver:* "It's the major drug of abuse in the state."
- *Detroit:* "Cocaine use continues to increase."
- *Los Angeles:* "Cocaine use has reached epidemic levels."
- *New York City:* "Cocaine activity continues to increase."
- *St. Louis:* "Cocaine is readily available throughout the metropolitan area."
- *Washington, D.C.:* "Cocaine use continued to rise."

- *Dallas:* "Pushers were selling cocaine in capsules in African American lower income communities. Cuban cocaine traffickers were arrested."
- *Newark:* "African Americans were dealing large amounts of cocaine."

These quotes from field sources suggest that crack cocaine was becoming a significant problem for American cities. As a result, a war was launched to stop crack cocaine.

Public demand did not create this "war on drugs." Beckett (1997: 55, 58) reports that in 1981 more Americans believed that reducing unemployment would be more effective in curbing drug use than cutting the drug supply. Only about 2% of Americans at that time felt that drug abuse was the nation's most important problem (also see Roberts, 1992). In fact, public concern over drugs increased only after President George Bush made the nationally televised speech mentioned at the beginning of this chapter. After Bush said on national television, "All of us agree that the gravest domestic threat facing our nation today is drugs" (Bertram et al., 1996: 113–114), media coverage of problematic drug use increased, as did concern about drugs among Americans. Thus, public concern did not start the drug war.

The drug war has been aimed at disrupting, dismantling, and destroying the illegal market for drugs (Brownstein, 1996: 45). Of course, a war can be conducted only against people, as noted, not against an abstract target such as "drugs." A "declaration of war suggests an imminently threatening national crisis or open conflict requiring the use of extraordinary power and authority, and the mobilization of massive resources to curb the threat and vanquish the enemy" (Merlo and Benekos, 2000: 17). The real enemy in this war has unquestionably been poor minorities, as indicated by the prison populations in the United States today (see Chapter Ten). In fact, 90% of recent prison admissions for drug offenses were African Americans and Hispanics (Donziger, 1996), largely because of the focus of law enforcement in minority communities (Tonry, 1995). Not surprisingly, the majority of people convicted and sentenced for crack cocaine offenses are African American (Robinson, 2000). Figure 6.2 illustrates that even though Caucasians account for a higher percentage of drug users and people arrested for drugs, minorities account for the majority of inmates convicted of drug offenses.

Imagine if Presidents Nixon, Reagan, Bush, and Clinton had declared war directly against poor people or minorities? Such a thing would have alarmed the media and would have been rejected by Americans as unacceptable, intolerant, and downright bigoted, especially after the struggles of the civil rights movement. A more indirect war against the same people, however, apparently is acceptable.

Imagine also a president suggesting that we take away individual Constitutional rights of all Americans in order to stop some from using drugs. The media would have featured such a story on the front page of every magazine and newspaper in the United States. Americans of all political persuasions—from armed militia members and members of the American Civil Liberties Union (ACLU) alike—would join forces to fight such a move. Yet, the declared war on drugs in the 1980s has led to increased use of law enforcement actions that infringe upon Fourth, Fifth, and Sixth Amendment rights. "Taking away rights of criminals" is how such infringements are sold to Americans, even though all of us enjoy less freedom today. Apparently, we see such sacrifices as necessary to stop drug abuse (Treaster, 1990).

FIGURE 6.2

Race and Drugs

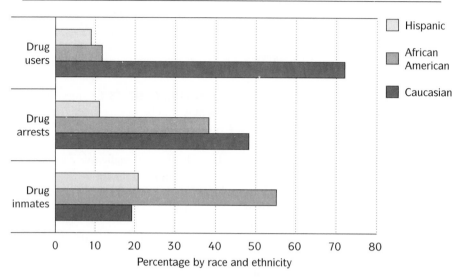

SOURCE: Adapted from K. Beckett and T. Sasson, *The Politics of Injustice: Crime and Punishment in America* (Thousand Oaks, CA: Pine Forge Press, 2000), p. 179.

What if the media reported that the U.S. government wanted to spend $18 billion this year to fight a war against drugs that it could not possibly win? According to a report by the Network of Reform Groups, this is how much the U.S. government spent on the drug war in 1999. Two out of every three dollars went to law enforcement to catch people who used, possessed, manufactured, distributed, or sold drugs. Since 1981, when the drug scare began to take hold, the United States has spent about $300 billion fighting the war on drugs (Frankel, 1997). The majority of American drug war spending is thus reactive rather than proactive or preventive, as shown in Figure 6.3.

Reinarman and Levine (1989a) outline this 1980s drug scare, in which all sorts of societal problems were blamed on crack cocaine. These authors argue that media portrayals of crack cocaine were highly inaccurate. The scare began in 1986, as *Time* and *Newsweek* magazines ran five cover stories each on crack cocaine. *Newsweek* and *Time* called crack the largest issue of the year (Beckett, 1997). In the second half of 1986, NBC News featured 400 stories on the drug. In July 1986 alone, the three major networks ran 74 drug stories on their nightly newscasts (Potter and Kappeler, 1998). Drug-related stories in the *New York Times* increased from 43 in the second half of 1985 to 92 and 220 in the first and second halves of 1986 (Beckett, 1997), and thousands of stories about crack appeared in magazines and newspapers (Reinarman, 1995).

As media coverage of drugs increased, people were paying attention. Consumers of media information are more likely to recognize issues as the "most important problems" when they receive a lot of notable attention in the national news (Bennett, 1980; Iyengar and Kinder, 1987; Leff, Protess, and Brooks, 1986; McCombs and Shaw, 1972). Drug coverage in the media was more extensive in the 1980s than at other times. As one example, the CBS program "48 Hours on Crack Street" obtained the highest rating of any news show of this type in the early 1980s (Reinarman and Levine, 1989a: 541–542). The most startling thing about all of this news coverage is that it did

FIGURE 6.3
Spending on the Drug War

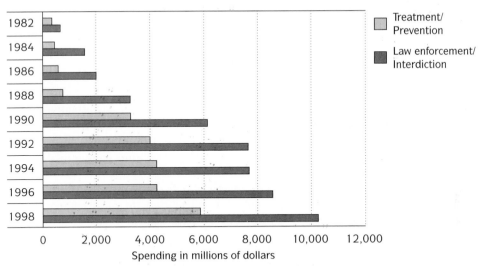

SOURCE: Adapted from K. Beckett and T. Sasson, *The Politics of Injustice: Crime and Punishment in America* (Thousand Oaks, CA: Pine Forge Press, 2000), p. 65.

not reflect reality, as crack cocaine use was actually quite rare during this period (Beckett, 1994; Orcutt and Turner, 1993; Walker, 1998) and, according to research from NIDA, was in fact declining at this time. According to NIDA, most drug use peaks occurred between 1979 and 1982, except for cocaine which peaked between 1982 and 1985 (Jensen and Gerber, 1998: 14).

Media coverage of cocaine use increased in the late 1980s even after drug use had already begun to decline. Jensen and Gerber (1998: 17) suggest that President Reagan's declaration of war against drugs in August 1986 created an "orgy" of media coverage of crack cocaine. Public opinion about the seriousness of the "drug problem" changed as a result. According to Clymer (1986), in mid-August drugs became the most important problem facing the nation in public opinion polls. By late August, 86% of Americans said "fighting the drug problem" was "extremely important" (*U.S. News & World Report*, 1986).

> *M*edia coverage of cocaine use increased in the late 1980s even after its use began to decline.

This coverage of drugs in the media typified social problems as stemming from the pharmacological properties of drugs such as crack cocaine, when in reality most of the associated violence stemmed from volatile crack cocaine markets (Beckett and Sasson, 2000: 28). News stories were also generally inaccurate and/or misleading in the way they characterized addiction to crack cocaine as "instantaneous," as if everyone who tried crack would become addicted immediately (Reinarman, 1995). As a teenager in the 1980s, I recall, adults warned me that one-time use of crack cocaine would lead to inevitable addiction. Without personal experience to rely on, these adults were likely relying on information supplied by the media. In fact, NIDA estimates that very few people of the 22 million people who use cocaine will become addicted: fewer than 3% of users will ever become problem users (Kappeler et al., 2000). Cocaine does not produce physical dependence, as, say, tobacco does, and thus is not considered a physically addictive drug.

> *C*overage of drugs in the media typified social problems as stemming from the pharmacological properties of drugs such as crack cocaine, when in reality most violence stemmed from volatile crack cocaine markets.

The addictive nature of nicotine in tobacco received relatively little if any attention in the 1980s (Reeves and Campbell, 1994), although, for every cocaine-related death in that decade, there were 300 tobacco-related deaths and 100 alcohol-related deaths (Potter and Kappeler, 1998), facts that escaped widespread media coverage. Although there is much more media focus on tobacco these days, the negligent and reckless actions of tobacco companies were not discussed widely until the mid- and late 1990s.

Finally, the coverage of crack in the news did not accurately portray the racial composition of people involved in drugs. For example, even though half of all television news stories about drugs show African Americans using or selling drugs (Reed, 1991), the majority of drug users (70%) are white; only 14% are African American (Walker, 1998). This does not imply that the media are racist in their coverage of drug issues but, rather, that the media, like most Americans, were duped by the focus of the criminal justice system on particular types of drugs and drug users. Harrigan (2000: 137–138) suggests that most Americans

> lead lives that are far removed from the pictures of their lives portrayed on television. They go to work regularly, pay most of their taxes, try to raise their children as best they can, are faithful to their spouses for years on end, do not steal from their employers, have no connection with drug traffickers or organized crime, and live from paycheck to paycheck without margin for economic setbacks.

Because these facts do not make for "news," they are ignored. The stereotypical image of the poor person or the African American person as lazy or criminal results from such ignorance.

Beckett (1997) reviewed media depictions of drug-fighting strategies and found that two types of "frames" for drug issues were most often used. She calls these the "Get the Traffickers" and "Zero Tolerance" frames. Criminal justice policies aimed at reducing drug use do not necessarily have to reflect a "law and order" perspective (see the Issue in Depth at the end of this chapter). Yet, according to Beckett, stories that depict drug raids and tough sentences for drug runners dominate the media. These depictions create and reinforce public support for get-tough measures and hence a "war on drugs," despite the tremendous harms that result.

The influence of drug policies on people's perceptions of drugs, crime, and the proper role of government in intervening in lives of drug users is an example of how "[p]olicy-making is a form of reality construction" (Brownstein, 1996: 59). Although criminal justice policy perhaps should be the primary source of information for policymakers (Barak, 1988; Brownstein, 1991; Burnstein and Goldstein, 1990), criminal justice policy today is neither rational nor orderly. Instead, it is driven by "competition and collaboration of claimsmakers as they strive to advise and influence policymakers [where] . . . lobbyists, political constituents, and anyone else with a vested interest argues in this arena for their own favored position" (Brownstein, 1996: 61).

Even when research clearly shows that crack-related homicides are mostly systemic (because they are related to volatile, illicit crack markets) rather than due to the pharmacological effects of the drug, laws tend to get tough on crack users for fear they will become violent (Brownstein, 1996: 65). And even when disparities in sentencing for crack versus powder cocaine were demonstrated to Congress to be unjustified, given that crack cocaine is no more addictive or dangerous than powder cocaine (Lockwood, Pottieger, and Inciardi, 1996; Moore, 1995), lawmakers voted to reduce the disparities but nevertheless to maintain them. The National Criminal Justice Commission claims that "evidence of meaningful pharmacological differences between crack and powder cocaine is exceedingly thin" and that "violence associated with crack stems more from turf battles between police and crack dealers, and among crack dealers battling between themselves to control lucrative markets, than from the narcotic effect of crack itself" (Donziger, 1996: 119). Perhaps this is why many judges in the United States do not agree with sentencing disparities between crack and powder cocaine.

ON LEGALIZATION

This chapter concludes with an examination of the relative merits of drug legalization as a policy alternative to America's drug war. Before I begin discussing legalization, consider the range of possible outcomes of the drug war.

When law enforcement agencies invade a neighborhood or community in order to interfere with drug activity, any combination of three outcomes may result. These outcomes are depicted in the three models shown in Figure 6.4. These models are ideals and are not necessarily mutually exclusive.

Model 1, which I call the *subterfuge model,* characterizes all neighborhoods where drug-related activity exists. Because selling drugs is illegal, drug dealers must hide their activity from the police. Police are at a distinct disadvantage in the war on drugs because they must identify, locate, and apprehend drug offenders who are typically very good at concealing and disguising their activities. For example, street-level crack cocaine dealers utilize numerous strategies to avoid detection by the police. Two strategies involve moving transactions from street corners to apartment buildings and frisking potential buyers for wires (Gaines et al., 2000: 611). In the subterfuge model, when police efforts are directed at a particular neighborhood, drug dealers utilize lookouts to warn them of police presence. This makes preventing or controlling drug sales very difficult.

It is illogical to assume that police agencies can ever stem the flow of the tide of illicit drug dealing in the United States. There are currently only 2.7 police officers per 1,000 U.S. citizens. Given the amount of illicit drug use among these 1,000 people, it would be impossible for the police ever to be able to stop enough of it to make much of a difference. Additionally, given that drugs can be grown virtually anywhere, and given that growers of drugs "camouflage and protect" their operations from detection efforts (Nadelmann, 1991: 22–23), national and international efforts to stem the production of drugs in the United States and the flow of drugs into the United States are doomed to fail. Consider these facts:

- Thirteen truckloads per year can satisfy the entire national demand for cocaine.
- The United States has 88,633 miles of shoreline, 7,500 miles of international borders with Canada and Mexico, and 300 ports of entry (Frankel, 1997).

FIGURE 6.4
Possible Outcomes of Police Intervention

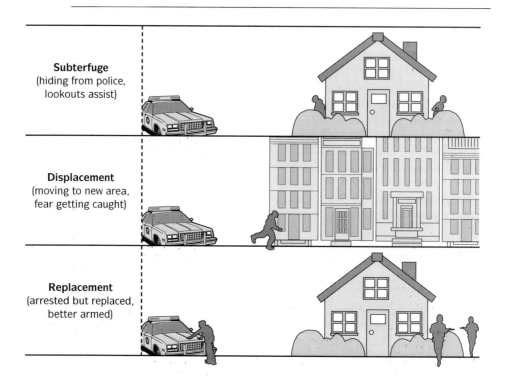

Subterfuge
(hiding from police,
lookouts assist)

Displacement
(moving to new area,
fear getting caught)

Replacement
(arrested but replaced,
better armed)

- Most arrests for drug offenses are for small-time offenders such as people who simply possess drugs (Page, 1999).

Nadelmann (1991: 22) makes an argument consistent with the evidence from the study of street-level crack dealers mentioned above. He writes: "In the final analysis, the principal accomplishment of most domestic drug-enforcement efforts is not to reduce the supply or availability of illegal drugs, or even to raise their price; it is to punish the drug dealers who are apprehended, and cause *minor* disruptions in established drug markets (emphasis added).

In Model 2, the *displacement model*, drug dealers are literally scared away by the police into other neighborhoods and communities. In the presence of so-called zero-tolerance laws, police intervene in even the most minor of criminal infractions and attempt to eliminate "social incivilities" such as the presence of homeless and mentally ill people on the streets. Street sweeps of the homeless and mentally ill are merely means of "sweeping such problems under the rug," so to speak, rather than dealing with them more effectively and, some would say, more humanely. Likewise, efforts to capture and arrest street-level drug dealers, under the umbrella of zero-tolerance laws, is a very ineffective method of attempting to eliminate drug use and abuse in the United States.

Zero-tolerance laws are based on the following assumptions:

- That if there were no drug abusers there would be no drug problem
- That the market for drugs is created not only by availability, but also by demand
- That drug abuse starts with a willful act
- That drug users are not powerless to act against the influences of drug availability and peer pressure
- That most illegal drug users can choose to stop their drug-taking behaviors and should be held accountable if they do not
- That individual freedom does not include the right to self-destruction and societal destruction
- That public tolerance for drug abuse must be reduced to zero (Inciardi, 1991: 11)

With zero-tolerance laws, drug dealers are theoretically deterred from engaging in drug-related crimes in the presence of police. But rather than giving up their illegal and immensely profitable livelihoods, drug offenders simply move their criminal operations elsewhere.

In model 3, the *replacement model,* law enforcement efforts are temporarily successful. In neighborhoods and communities where police efforts result in numerous arrests of drug offenders, drug dealers are temporarily put out of business. Yet, as suggested by the title of this model, when drug dealers are taken off of the street, others simply take their place in the illegal drug market. This is because of the "push-down/pop-up" nature of urban drug markets (Nadelmann, 1991: 23)—when one market is shut down, another simply "pops up" in its place. Glaser (1997: 119) claims: "Arrest of any individual involved in drug production usually impairs the drug supply only briefly, because the trade consists of many independent entrepreneurs in diverse roles, in all types of illegal drug distribution, and most getting the highest income from it. Others hurry to replace anyone removed from the industry by arrest."

Because the new drug dealers will be aware of the increased risks of apprehension, they will be better prepared to avoid detection and arrest. They may also be better armed and more ruthless than the previous drug dealers so that they can better battle the police. Skolnick (1997: 412) calls this the "Darwinian trafficker dilemma" whereby only the "fittest" drug dealers survive.

So we are left with this result: When drug dealers are taken off the street, others simply step in and take their place. We are left with the same number of drug dealers on our streets, but more inmates in our prisons. We're no safer but we're spending more of our money. The National Criminal Justice Commission puts it this way:

> Somebody else almost always steps in to take the place of the dealer when he or she goes to prison. Incarcerating the second drug dealer costs just as much as incarcerating the first. By the time the criminal justice system has passed through several generations of drug dealers, billions of dollars have been spent and the corner is still scattered with empty vials of crack cocaine. (Donziger, 1996: 61)

As noted, these models represent ideals, so any neighborhood or community with any amount of drug-related problems and any level of law enforcement presence will experience some of each outcome. That is, to some degree, subterfuge, displacement, and replacement will occur as police attempt to prevent and control illicit drugs. This means that the likely results of the American drug war are arrests, convictions, and punishment of *some* but *not most* drug dealers, the entrenchment of new drug dealers to replace those who are removed from the market, and displacement of drug offending to areas where law enforcement presence is not as great. Do you consider this a success?

> *A*ny neighborhood or community with any amount of drug-related problems and any level of law enforcement presence will experience subterfuge, displacement, and replacement as police attempt to prevent and control illicit drugs.

For these reasons, success in the war on drugs is not likely. In fact, I argue that because of the effects of subterfuge, displacement, and replacement, it is impossible to win the war on drugs. This is why American drug control efforts, though they may be well intended, are futile at best. Whether this provides a valid rationale for legalizing drugs is debatable, but it does suggest that the United States should abandon its war on drugs—unless, of course, you believe that the war really is successful at something else entirely (see the following box).

> *B*ecause of the effects of subterfuge, displacement, and replacement, it is impossible to win the war on drugs. This is why U.S. drug control efforts, however well intended, are futile at best.

How America's drug war is a success

Failure in the war on drugs may actually amount to success if, as pointed out in Chapter One, the goal is really not to succeed. Erickson and Butters (1998: 177) assert that if we look at the war on drugs as a policy aimed at reducing harm, then prohibition is a failure. Yet, if we look at it as an ideology (an orientation that characterizes the thinking of a group), then it is "one of the great success stories of the twentieth century." That is, as a means to shift control to the political right and lock people up for political gain, the war on drugs is working. It is pretty clear who benefits from the failing drug war and who is most harmed by it. While the incarceration boom may be beneficial for those with vested financial interests, it dispropor-tionately affects poor people and minorities. Given the resulting disparities based on race and class, by definition the drug war is not just. This is why the war on drugs provides evidence that the American system of criminal justice is not blind. Instead, the system seems to have poor people of color clearly in its sight. Tonry (1995: 105) writes: "Urban African-Americans have borne the brunt of the War on Drugs. They have been arrested, prosecuted, convicted, and imprisoned at increasing rates since the early 1980s, and grossly out of proportion to their numbers in the general population or among drug users." Now that we know this to be fact, how can we allow it to continue?

Results of the war on drugs have included "enormous profits for drug dealers and traffickers, overcrowded jails, police and other government corruption, a distorted foreign policy, predatory street crime carried on by users in search of the funds necessary to purchase African American market drugs, and urban areas harassed by street-level drug dealers and terrorized by violent drug gangs." Astonishingly, efforts to prevent drugs from coming into the country stop only about

10% of illicit drugs such as marijuana and cocaine from entering the United states (Inciardi, 1991: 12). Inciardi, a staunch opponent of drug legalization, nonetheless admits that interdiction efforts aimed at reducing the passage of drugs into the United States have failed and that more drug abuse treatment is needed (p. 75). Finally, the nation's drug war is a major source of police and criminal justice system corruption (Lyman and Potter, 1998). This led Kappeler et al. (2000: 166) to call the drug war a "government-sponsored subsidy to organized crime."

Given these startling revelations, an alternative to the American drug war may be justified. One alternative is drug decriminalization, whereby currently illicit substances would be made legal for recreational use. See the Issue in Depth at the end of this chapter, which presents a rational justification for drug decriminalization in the United States. Another alternative includes outright legalization of all drugs, although, considering all the possible negative outcomes, I do not personally support this approach.

> *U*nder drug decriminalization, illicit substances would be made legal for recreational use.

Whereas legalization calls for eliminating drug offenses from the criminal statutes and thus could lead to a complete government withdrawal from drug-related issues, decriminalization does not take the government out of drug prevention efforts. Instead, decriminalization involves limiting the use of drugs and taxing and limiting their production, promotion, sales, and use. Further, profits from drug use would be used to treat those who are involved in harmful drug abuse (Kleiman, 1997). Harm reduction approaches are not necessarily aimed at reducing drug use. Based on the realization that some drug use is inevitable, harm reduction strategies are simply aimed at reducing harms associated with recreational drug use.

> *W*hile legalization calls for eliminating drug offenses from the criminal statutes, and thus may lead to a complete government withdrawal from drug-related issues, decriminalization does not take the government out of drug prevention efforts. Instead, decriminalization involves limiting the use of drugs, taxing their production, sales, and use, and limiting their promotion, sales, and use.

Will Americans embrace alternatives to the drug war? Americans do seem well aware that the drug war is not working. For example, 94% of respondents in a survey by the Harvard School of Public Health reported their belief that drug use was not under control, and 58% thought that drug use would get worse with time (Blendon and Young, 1998). Despite the implications of these findings, Gallup polls still show that Americans want more of the same to stop drug use—more severe criminal penalties, more money for police, and increased military involvement in intervention efforts (Gaines et al., 2000). In other words, Americans may think the war on drugs is failing, but they still want more of it.

CONCLUSION

American history is dotted with wars on drugs. In these wars, which we seem to conduct every so often against drugs perceived to be used by problematic populations, we generally ignore the lessons of the past. The criminal justice system remains blind to its own illogical drug war. Even though actual harms attributed to use of illicit drugs pale in comparison to the harms caused by legal drugs, we seem content to use law enforcement and military efforts to try to solve problems associated with the medical problem of drug abuse. Although our recent efforts have had no appreciable effect on drug use or abuse in the United States, our nation's prisons and jails are filling up with poor street criminals, many of whom are people of color, who have committed very minor drug crimes. The media continue to fall prey to politicians' efforts to wage war against the poor and people of color in the name of the war on drugs rather than independently asserting how the nation's drug war is a massive failure. More violence is attributable to the nation's drug war than to the actual use of drugs. Thus, decriminalization seems to be a legitimate alternative worth pursuing.

ISSUE IN DEPTH
Decriminalize It!

The first important point to consider when discussing drug legalization is the distinction between *legalization* and *decriminalization*. The main difference between the two options is that legalization would simply permit the use of drugs, while decriminalization would not go so far as to legalize such substances. Decriminalization implies less criminal justice emphasis on drug offenses. That is, technically they would still be illegal, but instead of criminal justice sanctions for drug users, decriminalization would allow for alternatives such as confiscation and the establishment of other limitations on use.

There are, of course, a multitude of arguments both for and against both of these types of drug legalization (e.g., see Inciardi, 1991). I will not attempt to review all of the arguments in the drug legalization debate, mostly because a number of questions remain to be answered when considering the debate. James Inciardi (1991: 47–49), editor of *The Drug Legalization Debate*, lays out some of these key questions:

- What drugs should be legalized?
- What potency level of drugs should be allowed?
- Should there be age limits and other restrictions on drug use?
- How much drug use should be allowed?
- Where should drugs be sold?
- Who should manufacture drugs?
- What economic restrictions would be placed on the legal drug market, including rules for advertising and the like?
- Where will people be allowed to use drugs?
- Which government agency or agencies will be charged with regulating drug use?

Although answers to these questions must be developed before we allow legal drug use, I will not attempt to answer them directly here. This should be left to people with experience in policymaking (for an example of one model legalization proposal, see Karel, 1991). Instead, I hope to lay out the main argument in favor of *some level of drug decriminalization*.

The main argument in favor of decriminalization is that the drug war fails so miserably in controlling drug use (which is mostly recreational in nature) and drug abuse (which is in essence a medical problem). The main argument against decriminalization is that drug use and abuse will increase and cause unimaginable harms. Most Americans may think that any form of legalization of drugs is "an invitation to drug infested anarchy" (Nadelmann, 1991: 18), but this does not have to be the case. Even the staunchest drug legalization advocates acknowledge that use of certain substances might increase if they were legalized, not only because they would be more readily available but also because the deterrent effect of the criminal sanction would no longer apply. No one will argue that more drug use would actually be a good thing, but it may not be as bad a thing as you might imagine. The harms associated with increased use would depend on the specific drug legalization proposal. For example, if the government decided to legalize all drugs and then regulated their quality and availability and also restricted their use to competent, mature adults, increased recreational drug use might actually be a cost-effective alternative to the American drug war.

No, decriminalization is not sure to be a success (e.g., see Wilson, 1998), for "No one knows for certain the extent to which it would increase the number of addicts. . . . Few would deny . . . that the greater availability of, and easier access to, drugs would increase drug use (and addiction) beyond current levels" (Nuro, Kinlock, and Hanlon, 1998: 230). This seems a logical and fair conclusion.

Nadelmann (1998) does suggest that drug legalization would increase the availability of drugs, lower their prices, and remove whatever deterrent effect the law has currently, which might suggest increased drug use. Price is a function of supply and demand (Reuter, 1998): when demand for drugs is high, prices are low, and when prices are low, demand may be high. As long as drugs are illegal, sellers can artificially inflate the price to whatever levels they see fit—whatever price warrants the inherent risks associated with being in the illicit drug business.

Could we at least consider decriminalization of illicit drugs as a policy possibility, especially given that current interdiction efforts "have shown little success in stemming the flow of cocaine and heroin into the United States" (Nadelmann, 1998: 289–290)? Law enforcement cannot ever possibly "go to the root of the problem" (Reuter, 1998: 315). Making some drugs illegal "has proven highly costly and counterproductive in much the same way that the national prohibition of alcohol did" (Nadelmann, 1998: 290).

Nadelmann writes that legalization is not a "get out of jail free card" for drug dealers. Rather, it is a way to put them out of the drug business and to remove much of the criminality surrounding drugs, as well. It is also not an excuse for irresponsible use or abuse of drugs. What I propose, echoing the sentiments of Nadelmann, is that the government make currently illicit substances legally available to adults, while simultaneously regulating their production, distribution, and sale. In conjunction with these efforts, the government must provide drug-related education about the true harms associated with *all* drug use, including the use of currently legal drugs such as tobacco and alcohol (Jonas, 1991: 172). It must also offer drug treatment programs for people who are addicted to or abuse any drugs.

I believe the criminal justice system should get out of the drug business for a number of reasons:

- The drug war fails to reduce illicit drug use and abuse.
- Drug control efforts are highly costly, both financially and socially.
- The war on drugs is rooted in politics and anecdotal evidence rather than sound theory and empirical evidence.
- Drug abuse would not likely increase if illicit drugs were decriminalized.
- Drug abuse is a medical problem, not a criminal justice problem.
- The drug war is hypocritical given the harms associated with legal drugs such as tobacco and alcohol.
- The criminalization of drugs creates crime through an illegal black market, which actually encourages people to get into the illicit drug business.
- U.S. drug reduction efforts have led to an erosion of Constitutional protections.
- Because drugs are illegal, there are no quality controls in place to ensure safe use.

The evidence supporting the first three reasons was discussed earlier in this chapter. I demonstrated that drug use trends fluctuate along with factors not related to the drug war and that the United States wastes billions of dollars fighting a drug war that can never be won through law enforcement and criminal justice responses. According to Nadelmann (1998: 299), legalizing drugs would save billions of dollars each year. Freidman (1998) estimates that we could save $75 billion each year by legalizing drugs. Why? Between 1985 and 1995, when the drug war was at its height, 85% of the increase in the federal prison population was the result of drug offenses. According to the Federal Bureau of Prisons (1996), the average sentence for drug offenders sentenced to federal prison terms was 82.4 months, versus 66.9 months for sexual abuse, 26.8 months for manslaughter, and 20 months for auto theft. Decriminalization would reverse such nonsensical sanctioning patterns. The other justifications for decriminalizing drugs are discussed next.

DRUG ABUSE WOULD NOT LIKELY INCREASE IF DRUGS WERE DECRIMINALIZED.

As noted earlier in this chapter, most drug use in the United States is recreational. It is intimately linked to American culture as a whole and to particular subcultures within the larger society, and it is typically limited to certain social situations and social groups. Because most drug users do not become drug abusers, any increase in drug use resulting from decriminalization would not likely lead to very large levels of drug abuse. Experimentation with relatively minor drugs such as marijuana would also not likely lead to the use of "harder" drugs such as cocaine and heroin, as proponents of the "gateway hypothesis" suggest. In fact, most people who use marijuana recreationally do not use or abuse harder drugs; the gateway to illicit drugs is found in legal drugs such as tobacco and alcohol (Casement, 1987; Schoenborn and Cohen, 1986; Trebach, 1987).

As predispositions to drug abuse continue to be discovered, it is likely that we soon will be able to identify those individuals most susceptible to drug addiction and dependence and be able to focus our drug use education programs and drug abuse prevention programs directly at these individuals. Perhaps drug use would become more socially acceptable if all drugs were not criminalized. This could be counteracted with effective education programs that make drug use socially undesirable except in very specific circumstances.

Another reason to doubt that drug abuse would increase is that drugs are already widely available to most people (Inciardi, 1991: 56). Legalization might make it easier to obtain drugs for use, but Americans can already easily obtain illicit substances as they wish. Inciardi cautions that once illicit drugs become legal, the market economy will take over or at least become heavily involved in maintaining drug use. This may be true, given corporate involvement in the U.S. alcohol and tobacco industries. But again, nothing mandates that the government has to permit this.

Interestingly, legalization opponents such as Inciardi argue against all forms of legalization, in part because they hold that drug legalization would be a "program of social management and control that would serve to legitimate the chemical destruction of an urban generation and culture" (Inciardi, 1991: 65). Why? Because disenfranchised segments of the population might end up using more drugs, Inciardi posits that drug legalization would be a racist and elitist policy. I conclude the opposite: that the war on drugs currently results in alarming criminal justice disparities based on race and class, and that these disparities would be lessened if drug offenses were decriminalized. This would make the justice system more just and thus more in line with its ideal goals.

Wisotsky (1991: 108–109) concludes that the American drug war "makes a net negative contribution to the safety, well-being, and national security interests of the American people." If this is true, as I believe it is, then the criminal justice system, by waging a war against drugs, is not only failing to meet its goal of reducing crime but may in fact be exposing U.S. citizens to greater threats to their personal safety.

DRUG ABUSE IS A MEDICAL PROBLEM RATHER THAN A CRIMINAL JUSTICE PROBLEM.

Decriminalization would also deemphasize the use of criminal justice resources to deal with the medical problem of drug abuse (Nadelmann, 1998). Our money might be better spent dealing with tobacco and alcohol use and abuse, as well as serious violent crimes. As Nadelmann (1998: 294) points out, "the standard refrain regarding the immorality of drug use (such as that in Nancy Reagan's 'Just Say No' campaign) crumbles in the face of most Americans' tolerance for alcohol and tobacco use."

The war on drugs has allowed American policing to get bigger and meaner, resulting in numerous tragic abuses of human rights. Growing use of undercover operations and electronic surveillance may infringe upon our freedoms, and the growing use of informants flies in the face of crime control goals. Says Nadelmann (1998: 195):

> Overzealous enforcement of the drug laws risks undermining (the ethic of tolerance toward those who are different but do no harm to others) and propagating in its place a society of informants. Indeed, enforcement of the drug laws makes a mockery of an essential principle of a free society, that those who do no harm to others should not be harmed by others, and particularly not by the state.

Decriminalization would allow people to engage in drug using behaviors that are relatively harmless while simultaneously leading to the development of possible mechanisms to identify and treat drug abusers medically. Criminal justice responses to drug use and abuse do not allow for this.

THE DRUG WAR IS HYPOCRITICAL.

Without doubt, one primary purpose of the criminal law is to promote morality (see Chapter Two). Thus, a primary function of the government is "the promotion of moral behavior and good health practices among its citizens" (Rouse and Johnson, 1991: 185). To focus on some drugs and characterize them as immoral, while virtually ignoring others that cause more harm, seems illogical at best.

As discussed earlier in this chapter, far more harms are associated with legal drugs like tobacco and alcohol than with illicit drugs such as marijuana, cocaine, and heroin. Even relative to their levels of use in the United States, some legal drugs are far more deadly and dangerous than many illicit drugs (Jonas, 1991). So, Nadelmann (1991: 25) concludes:

> There is little question that we could reduce the health costs associated with use and abuse of alcohol and tobacco if we were to criminalize their production, sale, and possession. *But no one believes that we could eliminate their use and abuse, that we could create an "alcohol-free" or "tobacco-free" country. Nor do most Americans believe that criminalizing the alcohol and tobacco markets would be a good idea.* (emphasis added)

As explained by Nadelmann, criminalizing legal drugs is a bad idea because of two primary beliefs of Americans: "that adult Americans have the right to choose what substances they will consume and what risks they will take; and that the costs of trying to coerce so many Americans to abstain from those substances would be enormous."

Still, we have identified and isolated some drugs that, even when used recreationally or when merely possessed, are criminalized on the basis of their likelihood of causing harm. This focus seems hypocritical, given that a shift from casual alcohol use to the recreational use of marijuana would likely lead to a decrease in violence in the United States (Nadelmann, 1991: 31). Yet, Americans overwhelmingly support the drug war and draw a "moral line in the sand" between unlawful and lawful substances. However, just because "the American people simply do not want it" (Inciardi, 1991: 66), that does not mean that legalization of drugs is wrong. To the degree that Americans base their opinions about crime and justice on media information and public stances of politicians (see Chapter Four), it is not surprising that they tend to oppose decriminalization.

THE CRIMINALIZATION OF DRUGS CREATES CRIME AND AN ILLEGAL, AFRICAN AMERICAN MARKET.

If drugs were decriminalized, systemic violence related to the illegal drug trade would all but be wiped out. These acts include (Goldstein, 1998: 246):

- Disputes over territory
- Violence committed within organized hierarchies to establish and reinforce normative expectations for behavior
- Elimination of informers
- Punishment for selling fake drugs
- Punishment for failing to pay back debts
- Disputes over drugs and paraphernalia

Some drug users also commit crimes to support their habits. Hamid (1998: 106) claims: "The greater the police presence on the streets, the greater the resort to risky behaviors on the part of users." These risky behaviors include stealing, selling sex for money, breaking and entering, robbery, and even murder. Vigorous drug enforcement by police may actually lead to more rather than less "organized, professional and enduring forms of criminality" (p. 109, citing Dorn and Smith, 1992). In short, legalizing drugs would "take the crime out of the drug business" (Nadelmann, 1998: 288).

Currently, "Because [drug] criminal entrepreneurs operate outside of the law in their drug transactions, they are not bound by business etiquette in their competition with each other. . . . Terror, violence, extortion, bribery, or any other expedient strategy is relied upon by these criminals" (Goldstein, 1998: 249, citing Glaser, 1974). Decriminalization would also lessen the disproportionate amount of suffering the poor and minorities experience at the hands of the criminal justice system. According to Hamid (1998: 122), "minority persons who have been arrested for drug offenses and other crimes far outnumber European Americans." The penalties they receive are frequently harsh and unfair.

There is a positive relationship between a drug's perceived seriousness by government and the price at which it sells. That is, as a drug is made illegal and especially as it is labeled a serious threat to the community, it becomes more expensive to buy, even though production costs for most illicit drugs are comparable to those for many legal drugs. As noted by Nadelmann (1991: 29), "most of the price paid for illicit substances is in effect a value-added tax created by their criminalization which is enforced and supplemented by the law-enforcement establishment, but collected by the drug traffickers." This amounts to a subsidy by the government (i.e., taxpayers) paid to the black market drug offenders. Herbert Packer (1968) called it a "crime tariff" paid to those individuals and groups who must be willing to take tremendous risks to succeed in the drug business. Essentially, as the risks associated with drug offenses increase, so too will the rewards that drug offenders will expect. The American drug war, aimed at deterrence through increased risk, seems simultaneously to achieve higher rewards for those willing to engage in the drug trade.

Wisotsky (1991: 107) claims that the war on drugs has made things worse by spinning a "spider's web of black market pathologies," including homicides and other street crimes and widespread governmental corruption. Wisotsky claims that these pathologies were foreseeable because of the laws of supply and demand inherent in the market for an illicit substance that is in high demand. The crime tariff is the result. It is "what the seller must charge the buyer to monetize the risk he takes in breaking the law, in short, a premium for taking risks" (p. 107).

THE DRUG WAR ERODES CONSTITUTIONAL PROTECTIONS.

As explained by Wisotsky (1991: 108), the U.S. drug war has led to greater levels of pretrial detention resulting from a statutory bias in favor of such detention for those facing certain drug offense charges. Second, within the political framework of the war on drugs, the Supreme Court has eroded defendants' rights *not* to have illegally seized evidence used against them in a court of law. Wisotsky (1991: 109) outlines some of these erosions, which I summarize here:

- Establishing the authority of police officers to stop, detain, and question people who fit the "profile" of drug couriers in airports, even without probable cause
- Permitting travelers' luggage to be sniffed by dogs without probable cause
- Making searches of automobiles without a warrant
- Searching ships in inland waterways without probable cause
- Obtaining warrants based on informants' tips
- Establishing the "good-faith exception" for police who use flawed warrants
- Permitting warrantless searches of open fields and barns adjacent to residences
- Enlarging the authority of police to stop motorists on the road without probable cause
- Permitting warrantless aerial searches over private residences and of motor homes used as residences
- Allowing warrantless searches of public high school students' purses

Police also can claim exigent circumstances to justify gathering and using unlawful evidence, including evidence that was in their plain view or within reach.

THERE ARE NO QUALITY CONTROLS FOR ILLICIT DRUGS.

The Food and Drug Administration (FDA) does not have the jurisdiction to regulate illicit drugs (or to regulate nicotine in tobacco, according to the Supreme Court in 2000). This means the levels of active ingredients in drugs are typically not known and certainly not intentionally managed as is alcohol content. "Imagine that Americans could not tell whether a bottle of wine contained 6%, 30%, or 90% alcohol, or whether an aspirin tablet contained 5 grams or 500 grams of aspirin" (Nadelmann, 1991: 33). Also imagine if manufacturers of legal drugs like alcohol were permitted to add far more dangerous substances to their products, as in the case of cocaine and heroin. The drug war makes even relatively harmless recreational drug use much more dangerous than it would be if drugs were legal and regulated for quality control.

According to Nadelmann (1998: 299), legalization of drugs would accomplish the following:

- Shift control of drug manufacturing and distribution to the government
- Afford consumers opportunities to make more informed decisions about drug use
- Lessen the degree of harms associated with impure substances
- Correct the hypocritical and dangerous message that legal drugs are harmless
- Allow government to shape drug consumption patterns

The bottom line is that the U.S. war on drugs creates far more harm than it stops. An alternative to waging war on drugs would be a policy of harm reduction, which "is the emphasis on the reduction of adverse consequences rather than the elimination of drug use":

> Harm reduction is a *framework* from which policy and program strategies are conceptualized, developed, and implemented with the outcome goal being the reduction or minimization of harm (without requiring user abstinence or less consumption). (p. 179)

It is aimed at reducing adverse physical, social, and economic consequences of drug use.

A more effective antidrug strategy would thus be characterized by the following (Jensen and Gerber, 1998):

- A focus on harm reduction
- No mention of war or war-related rhetoric, which create enemies
- Less criminal justice spending
- Honesty and research-informed policy

For such an approach to be effective, it must be "accompanied by the view of users as mainstream or potentially functional members of society rather than marginal deviant misfits." Also, truths about drug use must emerge, meaning myths of drug use must be overcome (p. 189). One example is that most of the population of virtually every nation *never* tries cocaine. Of those who do, most do not become addicted. In fact, only 5% to 10% of cocaine users use the drug frequently (Erickson, 1993). Imagine politicians and the media trying to sell the war against cocaine to Americans in the face of these facts.

Let me conclude by echoing the sentiment of Kappeler et al. (2000: 167), who I think speak for most within the disciplines of criminology and criminal justice when they write: "Drug control policy has not failed for lack of resources, funding, legal powers, or adequate personnel. It has failed because the problem is not amenable to a criminal justice solution." We know this. Failing to correct it produces outcomes inconsistent with the ideal goals of the U.S. criminal justice system.

Discussion Questions

- What is the war on drugs?
- Identify and discuss the main elements of the drug war in the United States.
- Can a war really be fought against inanimate objects like drugs? Why or why not?
- What are the main goals of our nation's drug wars?
- Do you think we need a war on drugs? Why or why not?
- Identify examples of how wars on drugs have been declared on powerless groups in the United States.
- What is a drug?
- Contrast drug use with drug abuse.
- Discuss some of the potential outcomes of drug abuse.
- Make a list of the major categories of drugs and discuss the effects they have on those who use them.
- Differentiate the five schedules of drugs.
- Do you think drug use would increase if drugs were not illegal? Why or why not?
- Why do you think more people smoke cigarettes than marijuana?
- According to the evidence discussed in the chapter, which is more harmful to smoke, cigarettes or marijuana? Why?
- Is there a link between drugs and crime? If so, what are some of the relationships?
- Discuss the role of the media in promoting drug scares.
- Outline and compare the main arguments for and against legalization of drugs.
- Identify and discuss three possible outcomes of drug intervention, including subterfuge, displacement, and replacement.
- Do you think zero-tolerance laws are a logical approach to fighting drugs? Why or why not?
- Identify the main arguments in favor of decriminalization.

CHAPTER SEVEN

LAW ENFORCEMENT:

INNOCENT BIAS IN AMERICA

KEY CONCEPTS

- Basic roles and responsibilities of police officers: What police do and how they do it
- How police serve crime victims
- The move to community policing
- Innocent bias: How policing is organized in the United States
- American stop rates and arrest rates
- Use of force
- Differential views of the police
- Corruption in American policing
- Issue in Depth: Corruption in the Criminal Justice System

INTRODUCTION

What do images of police from television and movies suggest to you about American policing? What lessons does Hollywood teach you about what police do? This chapter will show you how police are mischaracterized in the United States. In fact, police spend very little time fighting crime, one significant reason that the criminal justice system is very ineffective at reducing crime. At the same time, because police are responsible for enforcing the criminal law, any biases in the criminal law will also be found in the activities of law enforcement. In this chapter, I also outline the main ways in which innocent bias against the poor and people of color arises.

BASIC ROLES AND RESPONSIBILITIES OF POLICE OFFICERS: WHAT POLICE DO AND HOW THEY DO IT

Because Americans are exposed to a stereotypical view of policing from television entertainment shows and daily crime news (see Chapter Four), one surprising reality of policing in the United States is that police spend most of their time actually *not* dealing with crime. This fact runs counter to the image of high-speed car chases and "good guys versus bad guys" depicted in the media.

In fact, most of what American police do on a daily basis is mundane and routine. According to Wrobleski and Hess (2000), police officers in the United States serve five basic roles:

- *Enforcing laws:* This includes investigating reported crimes, collecting and protecting evidence from crime scenes, apprehending suspects, and assisting the prosecution in obtaining convictions.
- *Preserving the peace:* This includes intervening in noncriminal conduct in public places that could escalate into criminal activity if left unchecked.
- *Preventing crime:* This includes activities designed to stop crime before it occurs, such as education campaigns, preventive patrols, and community policing.
- *Providing services:* This includes performing functions normally served by other social service agencies, such as counseling, referring citizens for social services, assisting people with various needs, and keeping traffic moving.
- *Upholding rights:* This includes respecting all persons' rights regardless of race, ethnicity, class, gender, and other factors, and respecting individual Constitutional protections.

> *P*olice officers in the United States serve five basic roles: enforcing laws, preserving the peace, preventing crime, providing services, and upholding rights.

Of these five roles, the "typical police officer" spends most of his or her time each day *not fighting crime* (Fyfe et al., 1997). So how do police spend their time? According to Wrobleski and Hess (2000: 128), "approximately 90% of a police officer's time is spent in the social service function." Services provided by police include checking buildings for security violations, regulating traffic, investigating accidents, providing information to citizens, finding lost children, providing first aid, handling animal calls, mediating disputes, and negotiating settlements between citizens (Cox and Wade, 1998: 99, 103). As noted by Manning (1997: 93), "Of the police functions or activities most central to accumulated police obligations, none is more salient than supplying the range of public services required in complex, pluralistic, urban societies." So, although "law enforcer" or "crime fighter" is the stereotypical image of the police officer, the typical city patrol officer or county sheriff in the United States spends the smallest amount of his or her day dealing with crime.

> *A*lthough stereotyped as a law enforcer or crime fighter, the typical police officer in the United States—for example, the city patrol officer or county sheriff—spends the smallest amount of his or her day dealing with crime.

Others, such as Bayley (1994) claim that police spend about 75% of their time on routine patrol or administrative tasks. Whatever the case, police spend only about 5% to 10% of their total time handling criminal matters (Cox and Wade, 1998: 99). An examination of activities of police officers at various levels of government illustrates this point equally well. Table 7.1 shows the main functions served by U.S. police officers by level of government in 1996. Most officers have primary responsibility for answering calls for service (64%), followed by investigative duties (15%), administrative/technical/training duties (10%), jail-related duties (8%), and court-related duties (3%). Of

TABLE 7.1
Functions of American Police

	LEVEL OF GOVERNMENT (1996)	
	Local/State	Federal
Calls for service	64%	16%
Investigative duties	15%	56%[a]
Administrative/technical/training	10%	0%
Jail-related duties	8%	21%
Court-related duties	3%	4%
Security/protection	0%	3%
Total	100%	100%

[a]Of federal officers involved in investigation, 43% were involved in criminal investigation and enforcement, and 13% were involved in noncriminal investigation and enforcement.

SOURCE: Data from U.S. Department of Justice, *Sourcebook of Criminal Justice Statistics* (Washington, DC: U.S. Government Printing Office, 1998).

the sworn officers serving local police agencies, 70% were involved in patrol and responding to calls for service, 16% in investigative duties, 12% in administrative/technical/training duties, and 2% in jail and court duties (U.S. Department of Justice, 1998). County sheriff officers had similar duties, including 42% involved in patrol and responding to calls for service, 30% with jail duties, 12% with investigative duties, 11% with court duties, and 5% with administrative/technical/training duties (U.S. Department of Justice, 1998). The main difference between local police and county sheriffs' officers is that county sheriffs' officers are more heavily involved in jail and court duties.

> *P*olice spend only about 5% to 10% of their total time handling criminal matters.

At the state and federal levels, the picture is very similar. State officers were most frequently assigned to responding to calls for service (69%), followed by investigative duties (15%), administrative/technical/training duties (14%), and court-related duties (2%). At the federal level, 56% of federal officers have primary responsibility for investigations and enforcement (43% for criminal matters), followed by 21% for corrections-related duties, 16% for police services, 4% for court operations, and 3% for security and protection. The majority of federal officers (58%) work for the Immigration and Naturalization Service (INS) (12,403), Bureau of Prisons (11,329), Federal Bureau of Investigation (FBI) (10,389), and U.S. Customs Service (9,749) (U.S. Department of Justice, 1997). Whereas most INS workers are border patrol agents, FBI officers have broad investigative responsibilities for more than 250 federal crimes, including bank fraud, embezzlement, and kidnaping.

The 1994 crime bill, discussed in Chapter One, aims to put 100,000 more police on the streets. Do you find it ironic that politicians have emphasized how important it is to put more police on the streets, even though they spend so little time actually fighting crime? Given that less than one in two crimes is even known to the police (and this only counts street crimes), and only one in five of these leads to an arrest, it is not surprising that police have some free time on their hands. How could this time be better spent? I will discuss this issue in Chapter Twelve. Politicians offer more of the same—more police—even though the evidence suggests that what we need is not more but better policing (Sherman et al., 1997).

These moves—to hire more police, better arm police, and allow increasingly tough and intrusive policing to crack down on relatively minor offenders—all interfere with one responsibility of police: to safeguard citizens' Constitutional protections. A significant problem with "get tough,"

> *The* move to hire more police, better arm them, and allow increasingly tough and intrusive tactics against relatively minor offenders, all interfere with one responsibility of police—to uphold Constitutional protections of citizens.

"law and order" approaches to reducing crime is that they interfere with citizens' Constitutional rights. For example, the exclusionary rule, established by *Mapp v. Ohio* (1961), requires that if evidence is obtained illegally it cannot be used against the accused in court. This rule grew out of the Fourth Amendment, which reads: "The right of the people to be secure in their persons, houses, papers, and effects, against unreasonable searches and seizures shall not be violated, and no Warrants shall issue, but upon probable cause, supported by Oath or Affirmation, and particularly describing the place to be searched, and the persons to be seized." Any evidence obtained without a valid warrant thus would not be admissible in court.

> *The* exclusionary rule does not make it harder for the police to gather and use meaningful evidence against suspected criminals.

Yet, as we have become more and more entrenched in a crime control model of criminal justice, numerous exceptions have been created that allow police to get around the exclusionary rule. Each is discussed in the following box.

Exceptions to the exclusionary rule

- *Searches incident to lawful arrests:* Police may search the area within the immediate control of the suspect upon arresting him or her.
- *Searches with consent:* Police may search any area that is voluntarily consented to by citizens.
- *The plain view doctrine:* Evidence in plain view of the police may be seized without a warrant.
- *The plain touch doctrine:* Evidence that is felt by the police while they are legally searching a person or place may be seized without a warrant.
- *The good faith exception:* If it can be determined that the police officer was acting in good faith that a warrant was valid even though it is not, then seized evidence can still be used against the accused.
- *Inevitable discovery:* Police can use illegally seized evidence against a suspect if they can demonstrate that the evidence would have ultimately been discovered by lawful means.
- *Exigent circumstances:* During emergencies, police may find evidence that can ultimately be used against a citizen.

These exceptions seem logical enough, but are they necessary? Fyfe (1983) has demonstrated that the exclusionary rule really does not make it harder for the police to gather and use meaningful evidence against guilty criminals. As explained by Walker (1998: 87): "[T]he police solve crimes when they immediately obtain a good lead about a suspect, from either the victim or a witness. Physical evidence, independent of some other kind of identification of the suspect, is rarely the primary factor in making an arrest and convicting the offender." This means that even fewer cases will be dismissed because of evidence that is thrown out as a result of the exclusionary rule. Fyfe described such a likelihood as "minuscule" and "infinitesimal." Ask yourself: Does such a small likelihood that a guilty person will go free justify allowing courts to use illegally seized evidence against accused criminals?

Walker concludes that the exclusionary rule is valuable and in fact is supported by most police administrators. For example, former FBI Director William Sessions stated that "protections that are afforded by the exclusionary rule are extremely important to fair play and the proper carrying out of the law enforcement responsibility" (cited in Walker, 1998: 89). In essence, the exclusionary rule results in better police work and lowers the possibility that citizens will be wrongfully convicted by overzealous agents of government.

> *T*he exclusionary rule is valuable and is supported by most police administrators.

HOW POLICE SERVE CRIME VICTIMS

Although police officers spend most of their time *not* dealing with crime, they do provide valuable services to victims of crime. Generally, as police "are the first representatives of the criminal justice system that victims encounter in the immediate aftermath of crimes," they serve victims in the following ways (Karmen, 1996: 166):

- Responding quickly to calls for help
- Launching thorough investigations into alleged crimes
- Preserving and collecting evidence
- Solving crimes by capturing suspected offenders
- Assisting with criminal prosecutions of criminal suspects

> *P*olice serve crime victims by responding quickly to calls for help, launching thorough investigations into alleged crimes, preserving and collecting evidence, solving crimes by capturing suspected offenders, and assisting with criminal prosecutions of criminal suspects.

Technically, all crime-related police work is in service to victims—recording crimes, investigating crimes, collecting and preserving evidence, apprehending and arresting suspects, interviewing witnesses and victims, interrogating and booking suspects, testifying in court, and so forth (Cox and Wade, 1998: 99). Such services are crucial to achieving justice as an outcome for victims of crime. The main problem with American policing is that it is structured to be reactive to crime and incident-driven rather than proactive and problem-oriented.

Because street crime is "the product of social and economic disadvantage, much of it traceable to racial bias and discrimination" (Tonry, 1995: 3), police have little effect on crime rates. Such factors are beyond the reach of the criminal justice system. Police themselves know this. For example, Klockars (1991: 250) writes:

> All of the major factors influencing how much crime there is or is not are factors over which police have no control whatsoever. Police can do nothing about the age, sex, racial, or ethnic distribution of the population. They cannot control economic conditions; poverty; inequality; occupational opportunity; moral, religious, family, or secular education; or dramatic social, cultural, or political change. These are the "big ticket" items in determining the amount and distribution of crime. Compared to them what police do or do not do matters very little.

This, in part, explains why American policing has shifted toward the community policing ideal. Wrobleski and Hess (2000: 161) explain that community policing is more proactive and problem-oriented—a "customer service" approach to law enforcement.

THE MOVE TO COMMUNITY POLICING

The main buzz word in policing today is "community policing," which refers to a crime prevention partnership between the police and the community (Wrobleski and Hess, 2000). Although the term has no clearly defined set of characteristics in practice, in philosophy it is aimed at solving problems before they become crimes rather than merely reacting to crimes after they occur. That is, it is an approach aimed at identifying problems with the community before they lead to crime (Goldstein, 1990).

"*C*ommunity policing" can roughly be understood as a crime prevention partnership between the police and the community.

Community policing is rooted in a problem-solving approach and is sometimes referred to as problem-oriented policing. Problem-oriented policing is based on the following principles, as described by the Bureau of Justice Assistance (1993: 5):

- A problem is something that concerns the community.
- A problem will likely indicate a pattern of related incidents that will require unique police interventions.
- Problem solving is a long-term strategy requiring increased police creativity and initiative.

Community policing in its current forms began to take hold in the United States during the 1970s. It grew out of the recognition that professional policing was unsuccessful at reducing crime, as well as unpopular with certain segments of the public. From roughly 1920 to 1970, American policing was more professional in nature; that is, it placed a high value on efficiency and crime fighting while being separate and distinct from public influence. Community policing places more emphasis on providing services to the community and developing police–community relations (Gaines et al., 2000: 178).

*C*ommunity policing in its current forms began to take hold in the United States in the 1970s. It grew out of the recognition that professional policing was unsuccessful at reducing crime, as well as unpopular with certain segments of the public.

Research demonstrates that the success of formal social control depends, at least in part, on informal social controls in a community. Police know that they need the help of communities to fight crime. Social control can be understood as "attempting to persuade persons or groups to conform to group expectations" (Cox and Wade, 1998: 94). Formal social control achieves that conformity through the use of official or governmental means, such as law enforcement, whereas informal social control is achieved through families, peers, teachers, and others. Coercing people to abide by the law (formal social control) depends to a great degree on a criminal justice system that can efficiently detect crime and apprehend criminals. Clearly, American criminal justice is highly inefficient. In part, this is because many Americans avoid getting involved in the process— for example, by not calling the police when they witness crimes. Given that there are only 2.7 police officers per 1,000 citizens in the United States, it is highly unlikely that formal social control mechanisms will effectively deter would-be lawbreakers. This "should be enough to convince us that the likelihood of detection and apprehension for those who violate laws is quite low if we rely totally on the police for such detection and apprehension" (Cox and Wade, 1998: 94).

Community policing is also theoretically based on sound crime analysis, so that police resources and personnel are assigned to geographic areas where and when they are most needed. This goes back to a notion of Sir Robert Peel, who in 1829 founded the London Metropolitan Police Department in England. The following box illustrates the core ideas of Sir Robert Peel and discusses how and why they are still important for American policing. Compare this with the realities of policing discussed in this chapter.

Key ideas of Sir Robert Peel

American policing evolved from English policing traditions. As the early colonists brought over their customs and traditions to this new country, they also brought over their law enforcement customs and traditions. In 1829, Home Secretary Sir Robert Peel established the London Metropolitan Police Department (LMPD) in England. The officers became known as "bobbies" after their founder. Peel put forth certain principles that he believed police should follow for law enforcement to be successful. As consistent as they are with today's version of community policing in the United States, keep in mind that he actually posited these ideas over 170 years ago!

Peel insisted that the police be chosen from the people so that they would be familiar with and essentially the same as the people whom they policed. He insisted that police be uniformed and be unarmed except for a small truncheon beneath their coats. Peel clearly laid out his vision of the personality of the ideal police officer. Police, he said, should be highly trained, stable, quiet yet determined, and in control of their tempers. Peel also thought officers should keep up a good appearance in order to gain respect.

Peel insisted that the police force be under government control and organized in military fashion to maximize accountability and ensure cohesiveness. He also held that officers should be required to keep records of all of their interactions with citizens, also for accountability purposes. Keeping records of all interactions would also allow the police to track incidents by time and place. Thus, Peel believed in what we now call *crime analysis,* which would allow police to deployed to those areas and at those times when they were needed most. This would also permit the police department to distribute crime news for the benefit of the public (as is done in today's police newsletters).

Peel envisioned a police force whose officers would be hired on a probationary basis (much like today's probationary patrol officer, fresh out of the police academy). This would permit police officers to be adequately trained while on the street and would reduce the possibility of hiring negligent personnel. Unlike the current situation, in which law enforcement success has been measured in terms of more and more arrests, Peel believed that police efficiency could be demonstrated by the absence of crime—that is, by crime prevention.

In the 1850s, Peel's law enforcement ideas spread across England, and England's police force became the largest and most organized in the world. Eventually, legislators from New York actually visited the LMPD to copy their ideas and to build a similar foundation for American police forces.

Has American policing become detached from its roots? Have we lost our way? Or is community policing a means to return to Robert Peel's core ideals?

According to the National Criminal Justice Commission, community policing is based on the notion that police "should *serve* residents in a neighborhood rather than simply *police* them" (Donziger, 1996; emphasis in original). Yet, one significant problem with community policing is that many minority communities "feel both *overpoliced and underprotected*—overpoliced because the drug trade flourishes with the same vitality as before [as discussed in Chapter Six], and because police are often slow to respond to 911 calls from minority neighborhoods" (p. 160; emphasis in original).

Legislators have voted to place more police in these neighborhoods on the basis of the belief that there is more crime there and that the presence of more police will reduce crime. The evidence from studies such as the now famous Kansas City Patrol Study (Kelling et al., 1974) and its replications (Police Foundation, 1981) suggests that more police will not reduce crime. These studies found no evidence that patrol activities of police, whether proactive, reactive, or even absent, had any effects on crime rates. This is why the National Criminal Justice Commission concludes that "we need to learn how to police *better* before we add new police" (Donziger, 1996: 160, emphasis added).

Walker (1998: 79) explains why adding more police will have no effect on crime rates. He argues that patrol will always be spread thin in a geographic area, so that its crime-preventive benefits will be minimal. He also suggests that many crimes are not suppressible by patrol because they happen in private areas between people who know one another. Thus, it is past time to recognize that adding more police will not reduce crime.

Even if we add more police, policing will be ineffective in reducing crime because police still will not spend a substantial amount of time fighting crime. Of crime calls, which make up only a small minority of calls for service, "almost all calls come when it is too late to catch the perpetrator" (Donziger, 1996: 162). These are known as cold crimes. The fact that about 75% of offenders are not caught at the scene of the offense is what makes arrest the weakest stage of the criminal justice process. Such facts have led even police chiefs to make statements such as: "Adding more police may be good politics, but it will do little to reduce crime and violence in America" (Moran, 1994; quoted in Krajicek, 1998).

Alternatively, *better* policing may reduce crime. Fewer than 5% of officers nationwide are assigned to crime prevention efforts (Bayley, 1994). If we want to prioritize community policing, we must invest more resources in problem-solving approaches that are proactive rather than reactive.

INNOCENT BIAS: HOW POLICING IS ORGANIZED IN THE UNITED STATES

If individual police officers are biased against certain groups of people, we may conclude that they are involved in unjust activity, what Walker et al. (2000) called individual discrimination. Yet, bias in policing does not necessarily mean "bad cops." Biased law enforcement only requires bad law, which can lead to so-called innocent bias on the part of individual police officers. In Chapter Two, it was shown that the criminal law is biased against poor people and people of color. Given this fact, enforcement of this law (through policing) will logically reinforce the bias within the law.

This means that even if every individual police officer was *not biased, prejudiced,* or *bigoted,* American law enforcement would still be biased because it simply reflects the biases of the law. This is what I call "innocent bias." The following box discusses how American police engaged in more overt forms of bias against some groups of Americans.

> *E*ven if every individual police officer was *not biased, prejudiced,* or *bigoted,* U.S. law enforcement would still be biased since it simply reflects the biases of the law. This is "innocent bias."

Police as oppressors in the United States

Gotham (2000) provides shocking evidence of how law enforcement agencies used their investigative powers to monitor and invade social groups aimed at reforming the political system. Agencies such as the FBI used counterintelligence methods to subvert and divide legal groups aimed at promoting social change in the areas of warfare and civil rights.

Not surprisingly, then, government agencies have placed the blame on the police for their role in promoting race riots in the 1960s. For example, the National Advisory Commission on Civil Disorders (1973) identified police treatment of minorities in U.S. inner cities as a significant factor leading to acts of violence and destruction of property across the country. It has also cited the "deep hostility" between police and the African American community as a major cause of inner-city unrest (National Advisory Commission on Civil Disorders, 1973: 157).

The Black Panther party and other components of the New Left of the 1960s were infiltrated by government agencies in order to assess and disrupt potential threats against the U.S. government. Such groups were perceived as vulnerable to communist infiltration and thus were viewed as potential political criminals and enemies of the state (Vankin and Whalen, 1999).

Today, people of color have lower views of police than Caucasians do. What do you think explains this?

Innocent bias can come in several forms. Next, I trace how innocent bias in policing comes from the following factors:

- The use of police discretion
- The particular focus of police on certain types of crimes
- Policing of the "war on drugs"
- The use of "police profiling"
- The location of police on the streets of the United states

"*Innocent bias*" comes from the use of police discretion, the particular focus of police on certain types of crimes, policing the "war on drugs," the use of "police profiling," and the location of police on the streets of the United States.

Before I discuss each of these issues individually, take a look at the following box, which contains "The Law Enforcement Code of Conduct" passed by the International Association of Chiefs of Police. Consider this the ideal of American policing, and compare it with the reality of policing as reflected in the sections that follow.

The Law Enforcement Code of Conduct

All law enforcement officers must be fully aware of the ethical responsibilities of their position and must strive constantly to live up to the highest possible standards of professional policing.

The International Association of Chiefs of Police believes it important that police officers have clear advice and counsel available to assist them in performing their duties consistent with these standards, and has adopted the following ethical mandates as guidelines to meet these ends.

Primary Responsibilities of a Police Officer

A police officer acts as an official representative of government who is required and trusted to work within the law. The officer's powers and duties are conferred by statute. The fundamental duties of a police officer include serving the community, safeguarding lives and property, protecting the innocent, keeping the peace and ensuring the rights of all to liberty, equality and justice.

Performance of the Duties of a Police Officer

A police officer shall perform all duties impartially, without favor or affection or ill will and without regard to status, sex, race, religion, political belief or aspiration. All citizens will be treated equally with courtesy, consideration and dignity.

Officers will never allow personal feelings, animosities or friendships to influence official conduct. Laws will be enforced appropriately and courteously and, in carrying out their responsibilities, officers will strive to obtain maximum cooperation from the public. They will conduct themselves in appearance and deportment in such a manner as to inspire confidence and respect for the position of public trust they hold.

Discretion

A police officer will use responsibly the discretion vested in his position and exercise it within the law. The principle of reasonableness will guide the officer's determinations, and the officer will consider all surrounding circumstances in determining whether any legal action shall be taken.

Consistent and wise use of discretion, based on professional policing competence, will do much to preserve good relationships and retain the confidence of the public. There can be difficulty in choosing between conflicting courses of action. It is important to remember that a timely word of advice rather than arrest—which may be correct in appropriate circumstances—can be a more effective means of achieving a desired end.

Use of Force

A police officer will never employ unnecessary force or violence and will use only such force in the discharge of duty as is reasonable in all circumstances.

The use of force should be used only with the greatest restraint and only after discussion, negotiation and persuasion have been found to be inappropriate or ineffective. While the use of force is occasionally unavoidable, every police officer will refrain from unnecessary infliction of pain or suffering and will never engage in cruel, degrading or inhuman treatment of any person.

Confidentiality

Whatever a police officer sees, hears or learns of that is of a confidential nature will be kept secret unless the performance of duty or legal provision requires otherwise.

Members of the public have a right to security and privacy, and information obtained about them must not be improperly divulged.

Integrity

A police officer will not engage in acts of corruption or bribery, nor will an officer condone such acts by other police officers. The public demands that the integrity of police officers be above reproach. Police officers must, therefore, avoid any conduct that might compromise integrity and thus undercut the public confidence in a law enforcement agency. Officers will refuse to accept any gifts, presents, subscriptions, favors, gratuities or promises that could be interpreted as seeking to cause the officer to refrain from performing official responsibilities honestly and within the law. Police officers must not receive private or special advantage from their official status. Respect from the public cannot be bought; it can only be earned and cultivated.

Cooperation with Other Police Officers and Agencies

Police officers will cooperate with all legally authorized agencies and their representatives in the pursuit of justice.

An officer or agency may be one among many organizations that may provide law enforcement services to a jurisdiction. It is imperative that a police officer assist colleagues fully and completely with respect and consideration at all times.

Personal-Professional Capabilities

Police officers will be responsible for their own standard of professional performance and will take every reasonable opportunity to enhance and improve their level of knowledge and competence.

> Through study and experience, a police officer can acquire the high level of knowledge and competence that is essential for the efficient and effective performance of duty. The acquisition of knowledge is a never-ending process of personal and professional development that should be pursued constantly.
>
> ### Private Life
>
> Police officers will behave in a manner that does not bring discredit to their agencies or themselves.
>
> A police officer's character and conduct while off duty must always be exemplary, thus maintaining a position of respect in the community in which he or she lives and serves. The officer's personal behavior must be beyond reproach.

The Use of Police Discretion

Discretion is the ability of an agent to act according to his or her own professional judgment rather than some preset rules or procedures. Even though all criminal justice decision making must occur within limits imposed by the U.S. Constitution, state constitutions, state laws, and precedents set forth by previous courts, many actors within the criminal justice system have wide discretion. The very nature of policing, whereby officers are entitled to use their own unchecked discretion to make decisions (e.g., see National Association of Criminal Defense Lawyers, 1996), allows racial stereotypes and myths of crime to infiltrate police work, resulting in racial disparities in stops, arrests, and police use of force (Cole, 1999).

> *D*iscretion is the ability of an agent to act according to his or her own professional judgment rather than some preset rules or procedures.

Pratt (1992: 99–100) argues that police officers are given discretion to act or not to act on the basis of their own judgment because we assume they are honest and trustworthy. In addition, extensive inservice training leaves police officers uniquely qualified to judge which behaviors pose significant threats to society. Finally, police must be allowed to use discretion for their own protection.

> *P*olice officers are given discretion to act or not to act on the basis of their own judgment because we assume they are honest and trustworthy.

According to Bittner (1970: 107), police officers have "a greater degree of discretionary freedom in proceedings against offenders than any other public official." After all, if the police do not take people into custody, make arrests, and issue citations, the criminal justice system has no clients and thus cannot operate. This is why Gottfredson (1999: 30) writes about police: "To a great extent, they exercise discretion in deciding whether to invoke the criminal justice system."

When police are given discretion over criminal matters, the potential for abuse is clearly there. The National Criminal Justice Commission writes that American police have the power to decide how to apply the law and determine the crime-fighting agenda of a community:

> They have wide discretion to decide who will be stopped and searched, which homes will be entered into, and which businesses will be inspected. *If misused,* that power can cause everything from a minor inconvenience to the destruction of life and property. *If used properly,* it can save lives and help make neighborhoods safer. (Donziger, 1996: 161; emphasis added)

Corruption in police departments and discrimination by the police were factors that led to the move by police away from the community and toward neutral, professional models of policing in the early twentieth century (Fyfe et al., 1997).

Discretion seems vital to the success of American policing; the problem is determining how to ensure that it will not be misused. It seems more likely that police will misuse their discretion when the political climate of their communities, states, and country is so focused on fighting poor street criminals that they lose sight of what should be the real goals of law enforcement: to serve citizens and reduce harmful behaviors while simultaneously upholding Constitutional protections.

It seems more likely that police will misuse their discretion when the political climate of their communities, states, and country are so focused on fighting street criminals that they lose sight of what should be the real goals of law enforcement: to serve citizens and reduce harmful behaviors while simultaneously upholding Constitutional protections.

A prime example of misused discretion is seen in the enforcement of speeding laws. The police cannot possibly enforce laws regulating speeding on all roads at all times, so they selectively choose roads and times to patrol for speeding and even target individual cars. Cox and Wade (1998: 98) write: "While an officer is writing a citation to one speeder, several other speeders may escape his or her attention." The threat of a speeding ticket may deter some drivers from intentionally speeding at some times, but it is evident that most drivers exceed the speed limit at times, sometimes even intentionally. Robinson and Zaitzow (1999b) found that more than 90% of American criminologists admitted to speeding intentionally. There are times when one must speed in order to stay out of the way of other drivers or to keep up with the flow of traffic. This may explain why many speeders get upset with police officers for selecting them out of the dozens of surrounding vehicles on the roads.

The point is not that speeding should be legalized, that speed limits should be lifted, or people should be free to drive as fast as they want. Rather, I want to demonstrate what can happen if police are looking for particular types of cars, or even types of people, to pull over for speeding. Because police have a wide range of discretion in deciding whom to pull over, very little can stop them from abusing this discretion and applying the law differentially to different types of people.

Racial, cultural, or gender differences may lead officers to stop and arrest individuals from some groups of people more than others. African Americans may be more fearful and thus may run from or refuse to cooperate with the police (Black, 1980). Hispanics may not make direct eye contact with officers, and this may be misinterpreted as a lack of respect (Zatz, 1985). If police are not trained to recognize such group differences, their discretion may be biased against groups who are unlike the officers.

At the arrest stage, the police officer "possesses considerably discretionary power . . . [where] there is no one physically present to supervise the officer's actions, and he or she may respond to a variety of cues . . . [such as] the age, gender, race, dress, prior history, or location of a suspect" in deciding to arrest or not (Cox and Wade, 1998: 101). Granting police this awesome power is asking for trouble if police are dishonest, partial, bigoted, or unethical.

Cox and Wade (1998: 101) claim:

> It is the existence of discretion by individual police officers in thousands of police–citizen encounters everyday that helps shape public attitudes toward the police. . . . If an officer arrests one person for a particular offense but allows another who has committed the same offense to go free, the arrested party . . . can hardly be expected to feel that the criminal justice network is just.

Neither are everyday citizens who become aware of such discrepancies likely to think the system is just. Decisions about whom to stop, pull over, and suspect of criminal activity are informed by images of crime created by the criminal law and broadcast in the news media. Therefore, what is known as police *profiling* begins with the biases built into the law and the news media.

The Particular Focus of Police on Certain Types of Crimes

Local policing in the United States focuses on street crime, the eight "most serious" Part I Index Offenses of the Uniform Crime Report (UCR), as pointed out in Chapter Three: theft, burglary, motor vehicle theft, arson, homicide, aggravated assault, forcible rape, and robbery. These acts are generally perceived by society and government agencies alike to be the behaviors that cause

---

Local policing in the United States focuses on street crime, the eight "most serious" Part I Index Offenses of the Uniform Crime Report (UCR).

---

the most physical and financial harm and occur with the greatest frequency. As pointed out by Wrobleski and Hess (2000:132): "Usually [police] departments concentrate law enforcement activities on serious crimes—those that pose the greatest threat to public safety and/or cause the greatest economic losses." The main conclusion is that the general focus of law enforcement in the United States is on a very small number of criminal acts, and an even smaller number of culpable harmful acts. The majority of types of victimizations, even those that stem from harmful, culpable behaviors, are virtually ignored by law enforcement in the United States.

The general focus of law enforcement in the United States is on a very small number of criminal acts, and an even smaller number of culpable harmful acts. This means that the majority of victimization types, even those that stem from harmful, culpable behaviors, are virtually ignored by law enforcement in the United States.

Figure 7.1 illustrates the way in which law enforcement in the United States is most focused on criminal victimizations of individuals caused by acts of individual persons. The shaded region in Figure 7.1 indicates the main focus of police when it comes to victimizations. Law enforcement is much less concerned with victimizations against individuals that are committed by entities such

FIGURE 7.1
American Police Focus

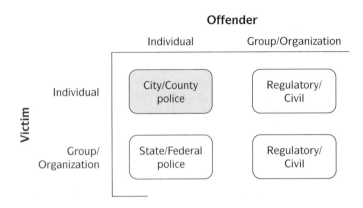

as groups or corporations (these are usually under the jurisdiction of state or federal law enforcement). Victimizations against individuals or entities such as groups and corporations committed by other entities are *generally not handled* by the criminal justice system and hence do not fall within the primary domain of law enforcement. Instead, harms and victimizations resulting from such acts are handled through civil law (as in the case of major lawsuits against large tobacco corporations) or regulatory agencies (as in the case of outbreaks of bacterial contamination in food products). Other harmful culpable behaviors, especially those that do not violate any law, are completely ignored.

These facts indicate that people can be victimized by acts that result in death, physical injury, and/or loss of property, with virtual impunity from the U.S. criminal justice system. Given that "justice" implies that the guilty will be punished for their actions, the fact that our justice system ignores harmful acts committed with culpability means that the criminal justice system does not achieve justice as an outcome. It also means that our system of justice is ineffective at reducing these types of crimes.

> *People* can perpetrate acts that result in death, physical injury, and/or loss of property with virtual impunity from U.S. criminal justice.

Policing the War on Drugs

One main focus of policing in the contemporary United States seems to be on drug offenses. As discussed in Chapter Six, our prisons and jails are filling up with drug offenders at unprecedented rates. In fact, police in 1997 made nearly 1.6 million arrests for drug offenses. One outcome of the police focus on drug offenses is that police forces have become increasingly militarized, with more paramilitary units and better technology and weaponry (Kraska and Kappeler, 1997). In spite of this, the war on drugs is generally focused on low-level offenders engaged in illegal activity related to certain types of drugs. For example, of all 1997 arrests for drug offenses, an amazing

80% were for possession rather than for sale and/or manufacturing of illicit substances. The highest percentage of drug arrests (44%) were for marijuana offenses (38% for possession, 6% for sale and/or manufacturing), followed by cocaine or heroin (25% for possession, 10% for sale and/or manufacturing). This means the largest share of drug arrests in any given year in the United States is for simple possession of marijuana, which, as discussed in Chapter Six, is much less harmful than legal substances such as alcohol and tobacco. Is this a wise use of police resources?

> *The* war on drugs is generally focused on low-level offenders engaged in illegal activity related to some types of drugs. For example, of all 1997 arrests for drug offenses, an amazing 80% were for possession rather than for sale and/or manufacture of illicit substances.

Given that the war on drugs is generally focused on low-level offenders engaged in illegal activity related to marijuana, cocaine, and heroin, enforcement of drug laws also reflects these same biases. One indicator of "innocent" police bias thus would be racial disparities in arrests. In 1997, approximately 37% of arrests for drug offenses in 1997 were of African Americans, who account for only 13% of the U.S. population. Another indicator would be drug seizures. In 1998, federal drug seizures accounted for approximately 2 million pounds of illegal substances, 1.7 million pounds of which were marijuana. Of all the seizures made by the U.S. Customs Service in 1998, most (15,545) were of marijuana, accounting for nearly 1 million pounds. The Drug Enforcement Administration (DEA) alone removed more than 500,000 pounds of marijuana from the domestic market. Yet, of the 135 million marijuana plants eradicated and seized by the DEA, 132 million were of the ditchweed variety—plants that grow wild. DEA officers alone made 13,603 arrests for marijuana violations.

> *In* 1997, approximately 37% of arrests for drug offenses were of African Americans, even though they only account for 13% of the U.S. population.

The U.S. government has chosen to take a reactive approach to drug use rather than a proactive approach. This means American law enforcement spends more money attempting to reduce the supply of drugs coming into the United States than it spends on efforts to reduce the demand for drugs. According to an investigation into police corruption related to the war on drugs by the General Accounting Office (GAO) in 1998, police officers have become frustrated with their inability to stop drug use in their communities, despite their best efforts. This, along with general cynicism and dissatisfaction, leads to police corruption. Add to this the tremendous potential for profits to be had from stealing money and drugs from dealers, selling drugs, and so on, and it is easy to understand how some good cops turn bad (Merlo and Benekos, 2000: 37). The Issue in Depth at the end of this chapter discusses corruption in the criminal justice system.

With the U.S. war on drugs, police officers on our streets have been using more and more aggressive techniques. I believe our nation's law enforcement leaders are ignoring lessons from the past. In 1968, the National Advisory Commission on Civil Disorders, commonly referred to as the Kerner Commission, published a report that found a direct relationship between aggressive police patrols and tensions between police and minority communities. The type of intrusive law enforcement that is occurring in the United States' inner cities is aggravating racial tensions between citizens and the police in particular and worsening racial relations in the United States generally.

> *W*ith the U.S. war on drugs, police officers on our streets have been using more and more aggressive techniques.

Police profiling is also particularly pronounced in the American "war on drugs." In the section that follows, I will examine the issue of police profiling as a form of innocent bias in policing.

The Use of Police Profiling

American police focus on particular types of people because of their own personal experience or that of their institution and profession, which suggests that certain people are more likely than others to violate the law. This practice, known as *police profiling*, results in startling disparities in police behavior (Harris, 1999; Roberts, 1993; Son, Davis, and Rome, 1998). For example, one study found that although African Americans make up about 17% of drivers and only 17.5% of traffic violators, they made up nearly 73% of those pulled over and searched by the police (Gaines et al., 2000: 645–646). When police use race as a proxy for risk, being young, African American, and male equals probable cause (Gaynes, 1993), a phenomenon that is even supported by courts as legitimate when race is used in conjunction with other factors. Police profiling may explain why police target minority communities—"where drug dealing is more visible and where it is thus easier to make arrests"—more than other areas (Walker et al., 2000: 265).

> *A*merican police focus on particular types of people because of their own personal experience or that of their institution and profession, which suggests that certain people are more likely to violate the law. This practice, known as "police profiling," results in startling disparities in police behavior.

Part of this perceived "social threat" to communities (Jackson, 1997) results from an honest, unintentional exaggeration of risk on the part of police, but it creates significant disparities nevertheless. "Race dependent policing erodes the difficult-to-maintain habit of individualizing persons and strengthens the reflex of lumping people together according to gross racial categories" (D. Kennedy, 1997: 157).

Other outcomes of police profiling of particular offenders include "a climate of alienation, hostility, social unrest, and violence in the nation's inner cities" and a basic distrust and resentment of the police. Not surprisingly, several studies reflect a lower view or approval of law enforcement and government among African Americans than among whites (e.g., see Donziger, 1996). In areas where it is the worst, such as Washington, D.C., courses are available to teach citizens how to handle themselves if stopped by the police (R. Miller, 1997: 26). Some studies show that police may overcharge arrestees with crimes they did not commit in order to make some charges stick (e.g., see Smith, 1990). Some of these arrests and overcharging practices have been found to be racially motivated (e.g., see Nazario, 1993). Therefore, jury nullification on the part of African Americans who refuse to convict other African Americans charged even with violent crimes may suggest that, for this targeted group, outrage against violent criminals may be dwarfed by apathy or hostility toward the justice system (J. Miller, 1997).

Profiling may be part of what Eddings (2000: 197) calls "stealth racism" in the United States. The term *stealth racism* suggests that racism is not gone but, rather, has become harder to see. It is more subtle because it is less likely to be admitted or is passed off as part of a legitimate function, such as maintaining order. Eddings suggests several examples of stealth racism—taxis that do not stop for minorities, shoppers who are identified as suspicious on the basis of their race, customers who receive unequal service because of race. Chapter Five explained how discrimination based on race persists in the United States even today.

The Location of Police on the Streets of the United States

Police are disproportionately located in some areas of our country while being nearly absent from others. Specifically, more police are allocated to the nation's inner cities. Why? First, there is more demand for police services in these areas. Benjamin and Miller (1991: 21) explain (with regard to drug crimes) that "the inner city is an expedient locale for police to rack up impressive arrest numbers, with little fear for consequences if mistakes are made." Of course, the nation's inner cities are characterized by very high poverty rates. The average poverty rate in central cities was 18.8 in 1997, versus 9.0 for suburbs (U.S. Census, 1999). This may explain why there are more police patrols directed at these areas.

> *P*olice are disproportionately concentrated in some areas of our country while being nearly absent from others. Specifically, more police are allocated to the nation's inner cities.

The allocation of police officers to various government levels (i.e., city, county, state, federal governments) in the United States will also have major effects on what police do. Policing at different levels of government is focused on different forms of behaviors. An examination of the levels of government at which the police work in the United States provides a good picture of the types of behaviors to which U.S. police *generally* dedicate their efforts. Table 7.2 demonstrates that most law enforcement activity occurs at the local level (i.e., city or county government). More than half (56%) of sworn officers are city police officers, followed by 21% who are county sheriff officers. This means that 77% of sworn officers are local law enforcement officers. Another 13% are state-level officers, and 10% are federal officers. This law enforcement focus results in a rate differential of 2.7 local and state police officers per 1,000 citizens versus only 0.28 federal officers per 1,000 persons (U.S. Department of Justice, 1998).

> *M*ost law enforcement activity occurs at the local level (that is, city or county government). More than half (56%) of sworn officers are city police officers, followed by county sheriff officers (21%). This means that 77% of sworn officers are local law enforcement officers.

Table 7.3 shows that most U.S. police departments are local-level agencies (13,758), followed by county sheriffs' departments (3,088) and specialized police departments (1,316). There are currently only 27 federal law enforcement agencies with an employment of at least 100 agents. Overall, local and state agencies employed 921,978 people on a full-time basis in 1996, including

TABLE 7.2
Police Officers by Level of Government (1996)

	LEVEL OF GOVERNMENT				
	Local		State	Federal	Total
	City	County			
Number of officers	410,956	152,922	99,657	74,493	738,028
Percentage of total	56%	21%	13%	10%	100%

SOURCE: Data from U.S. Department of Justice, *Sourcebook of Criminal Justice Statistics* (Washington, DC: U.S. Government Printing Office, 1998).

663,535 full-time sworn officers with general arrest powers (72%) and 258,443 nonsworn officers or civilians (28%) (U.S. Department of Justice, 1998). As noted by the U.S. Department of Justice (1998: 3), "general purpose local police departments were the largest employer with 521,985 full-time employees as of June 1996."

> *M*ost U.S. police departments are local level agencies (13,758), followed by county sheriffs' departments (3,088), and specialized police departments (1,316). There are currently only 27 federal law enforcement agencies with an employment of at least 100 agents.

AMERICAN STOP RATES AND ARREST RATES

Technically, anyone suspected of committing a criminal act can be arrested. An arrest occurs when a person is legally detained to answer to criminal charges (Rush, 2000: 20). *Black's Law Dictionary* (1991: 72) defines *arrest* as follows: "To deprive a person of his liberty by legal authority. Taking, under real or assumed authority, custody of another for the purpose of holding or detaining him to answer a criminal charge . . ." Wrobleski and Hess (2000: 344) elaborate on this definition by demonstrating that arrest includes four main elements: (1) the officer must have intent to make an arrest, (2) the officer must have authority to make an arrest, (3) the person must be seized or restrained, and (4) the person must understand that he or she is being arrested.

TABLE 7.3
Police Agencies by Level of Government (1996)

Local	13,578
Sheriff	3,088
Special	1,316
Constables	738[a]
Primary state	49
Federal	27[b]
Total	18,796

SOURCE: Data from U.S. Department of Justice, *Sourcebook of Criminal Justice Statistics* (Washington, DC: U.S. Government Printing Office, 1998).

[a]State of Texas.
[b]Includes agencies employing more than 100 agents.

Typically, a warrant is required to make an arrest, but officers do not need warrants when crimes are committed in their presence or when they are responding to the scene of a crime and an offender is at the scene (Wrobleski and Hess, 2000).

> *A*n arrest occurs when a person has been legally detained to answer for criminal charges.

The Supreme Court has explained that an *arrest* is not the same thing as a *stop*. A stop must only be justified by reasonable suspicion that some wrongdoing has occurred or is likely to occur (*Terry v. Ohio*, 1968). An arrest requires probable cause, meaning that all the facts and circumstances known to the officer would suggest to a person of reasonable caution that a crime has been committed or is likely to be committed (*Draper v. United States*, 1959).

> *A* stop must be justified by reasonable suspicion that some wrongdoing has occurred or is likely to occur. An arrest requires probable cause, all the facts and circumstances known to the officer that would suggest to a person of reasonable caution that a crime has been committed or is likely to be committed.

Essentially, a stop will occur if police officers come upon a person they reasonably feel looks suspicious or is acting suspiciously. For their own protection, police officers are justified in conducting a frisk or pat-down search of the suspect if they feel the suspect is armed (Hess and Wrobleski, 1997: 122). The Supreme Court ruled in *United States v. Cortez* that reasonable suspicion should be based on the totality of circumstances, including the officer's inferences and deductions. A police officer who is carrying around a mental stereotype of the "typical criminal" may be more likely to stop some types of people than others.

If you can imagine that police might stop some people more than others, then consider the following scenario: a police officer sees a dark-skinned man (race unclear to the officer) lurking outside a store late at night and feels that the man looks suspicious. The man looks suspicious in part because the store is getting ready to close and because the neighborhood is mostly inhabited by Caucasians. The police officer approaches the man, stops him, and conducts a pat-down search of the man's outer clothing. In doing so, the officer feels something hard in the man's jacket pocket and then reaches inside to find a knife. If, by being in possession of the knife, the man has violated state law, the police officer would be justified in making an arrest of the man. This type of stop would likely be considered legal given that the officer is allowed to use his or her discretion to justify the stop and frisk, regardless of the man's intent. This man would likely have committed a crime against his state law. But what if the man was simply waiting for his girlfriend to get off of work and was carrying the knife for his own protection? This probably would not matter to the police officer or to the court.

Now, what if the man outside the store was a Caucasian? Would the officer think that a Caucasian man hanging around a store at closing time in a Caucasian neighborhood was suspicious? Justifying a stop on the basis of the totality of the circumstances allows officers to use their own discretion to determine who looks dangerous and who does not. This may allow police profiles of the "typical offender," created by the criminal law and reinforced by media coverage of crime and criminal justice, to come into play.

If every group in the United States committed equal amounts of crime and if police did not discriminate against any group, we would expect to see relatively equal stop rates and arrest rates for all groups. Any diversion from this expectation would suggest either that some groups commit more crime, that the police discriminate against some groups, or both.

> *If* every group in the United States committed crimes in equal numbers and if police did not discriminate against any one group, we would expect to see relatively equal stop rates and arrest rates for all groups. Any deviation from this expectation would suggest either that some groups commit more crime than others, that the police discriminate against some groups, or both.

Evidence suggests that Hispanics, African Americans, and other people of color are more likely to have run-ins with police (Bureau of Justice Statistics, 1997). Friedman and Hott (1995) found in a survey of high school students that people of color were more likely to report that they had been stopped by the police and treated in a disrespectful manner. Chicago police were found to be using an unconstitutionally vague loitering statute to stop and question people of color (Roberts, 1993). This pattern has also been found in other big cities, such as Los Angeles and New York. Clearly, race is used as a cue for potential trouble-making activity on the part of citizens. In essence, police allow their personally held stereotypes to invade their professional work (Skolnick, 1994).

> *Evidence* suggests that Hispanics, African Americans, and other people of color are more likely to have run-ins with police.

The significance of being stopped by the police cannot be understated. Logically, being stopped would increase a person's risk of being arrested or of having force used against him or her, especially to the degree that the person does not cooperate with the police. Beyond this, being stopped can be bothersome and even intimidating if the police have bad attitudes or if a person is constantly harassed for no valid reason. Disproportionate arrest rates are accompanied by disproportionate harassment by the police (Chambliss, 2000).

The typical arrestee in the United States is a young, urban, poor, African American male: "This is the Typical Criminal feared by most law-abiding Americans. Poor, young, urban, [disproportionately] African American males make up the core of the enemy forces in the war against crime" (Reiman, 1998: 55). Kappeler et al. (2000: 221) concur: "The vast majority of people arrested and processed through the criminal justice system are poor, unemployed, and undereducated."

> *The* typical arrestee in the United States is a young, urban, poor, African American male.

Given that police focus on crimes of the poor, because the law defines their acts as criminal more often than those acts of the wealthy, the police target particular populations they perceive to be threatening, especially within inner cities. This calls into serious question official statistics suggesting that African Americans commit more than their "fair share" of criminal behavior. As noted

> *Given* that police focus on crimes of the poor, because the law defines their acts as criminal more often than those acts of the wealthy, the police target particular populations they perceive to be threatening, especially within inner cities.

by Kappeler et al (2000: 222): "Research on the police clearly shows that suspects from lower socioeconomic groups and suspects who are members of minority groups are arrested more frequently, on weaker evidence, and for more crime than their white, affluent counterpoints."

The fact that police typically arrest urban street criminals should not be surprising. Arrest rates from the UCR consistently are four to five times higher for African Americans over age 18 than for whites over 18 and two to three times higher for African Americans under age 18 than for whites under 18. It is alarming that African Americans make up roughly one-third of arrests in any given year even though they account for only 13% of the U.S. population. The percentage of African American arrests is also higher in cities (33% African American) than in suburban communities (23% African American) and rural areas (16% African American), as expected given their relative residential concentration in inner cities (U.S. Department of Justice, 1998). Walker et al. (2000) claim that the arrest rate for African Americans is two and one half times higher than it would be if simply predicted by their proportion of the population.

> *A*rrest rates from the UCR are consistently four to five times higher for African Americans over age 18 than for whites over age 18, and two to three times higher for African Americans under age 18 than for whites under age 18.

American police officers in 1997 made an astounding 15.3 million arrests, the majority of which *were not* for "serious" street crimes. R. Miller (1997: 484) is thus correct when he asserts: "Most of the frenetic law enforcement in the black community has nothing to do with violent or serious crime." In fact, only 2.7 million arrests were for Index Offenses of the Uniform Crime

> *I*n 1997, U.S. police officers made an astounding 15.3 million arrests, the majority of which *were not* for "serious" street crimes.

Reports, including 2 million arrests for property crimes and just over 700,000 arrests for violent crimes. Of arrests in 1997, 31% were of African Americans, who, as noted, account for only 13% of the U.S. population. African Americans are overrepresented in every category of arrests, with the exceptions of driving under the influence (DUI) and liquor law violations. They made up 41% of arrests for serious violent crimes and 32% of arrests for serious property crimes.

> *I*n fact, only 2.7 million arrests were for Index Offenses of the Uniform Crime Reports, including 2 million arrests for property crimes and just over 700,000 arrests for violent crimes.

In Chapter Three, it was demonstrated that African Americans are generally no more "criminal" than other groups of people. Even when evidence does show that African Americans account for a disproportionate amount of some "serious" crimes, *serious* is a term defined by lawmakers. As you learned in Chapter Two, legislators are less likely to be African American and not at all likely to be poor. Thus, if you learn that African Americans made up 57% of all arrests for robbery and 56% of all arrests for murder, perhaps you should ask yourself, but what is "robbery" and what is "murder"? No one would argue that these crimes are *not serious* or *not harmful*. But there are many ways to take someone's money by force or to kill a person that are not currently considered robbery or murder, respectively. The fact that these acts are not legislated as criminal or treated as serious is a function of who makes the law, as discussed in Chapter Two. The disproportionate focus of law enforcement on poor, minority communities, though rooted to a degree in the criminal law, is nevertheless extremely detrimental to minority communities. As Miller writes, "a major contributor to breakdown in the inner cities is the criminal justice system itself."

Black (1980) found that race of suspects played little or no role in officers' decisions to arrest. According to Walker et al. (2000: 99), officers are more likely to arrest a suspect when there is strong evidence that he or she is guilty, when the crime is of a serious nature, when a victim requests that an arrest be made, when the alleged offender is a stranger rather than a person known to the victim, and when the suspect is disrespectful to the officer. The bulk of the evidence counters the Black study and suggests that race does matter when it comes to arrest because police are more likely to arrest alleged offenders when the victim is a Caucasian and the suspect is a member of a minority group (Smith, Visher, and Davidson, 1984).

USE OF FORCE

Limits have been placed on police use of force to protect citizens and police officers alike. Ideally, use of force by the police is determined by the behaviors of citizens with whom police come into contact. Police use of force can range from verbal commands to deadly force whereby a citizen is

> *L*imits have been placed on police use of force in order to protect citizens and police alike. Ideally, use of force by the police is determined by the behaviors of citizens that police have contact with.

actually killed. Figure 7.2 shows a continuum of options for the use of force available to police based on the behavior of citizens. As the figure illustrates, the more resistant a citizen is to the police, the more force can be legally used against him or her.

> *P*olice use of force can range from verbal commands that convince someone to comply, to deadly force whereby a citizen is actually killed by the police.

FIGURE 7.2
Options for Police Use of Force

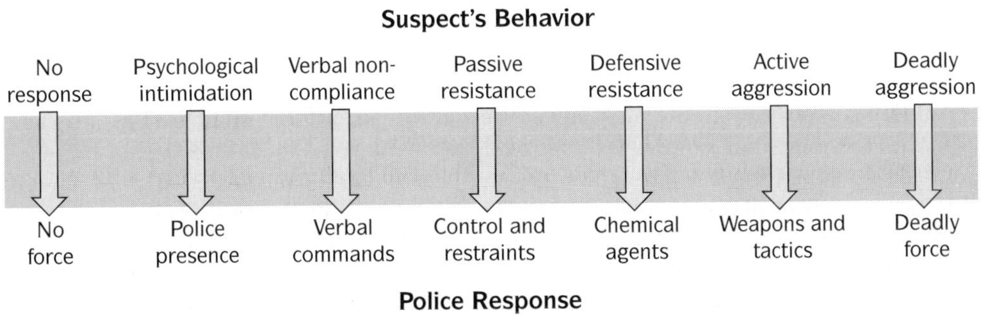

Suspect's Behavior

No response	Psychological intimidation	Verbal non-compliance	Passive resistance	Defensive resistance	Active aggression	Deadly aggression

No force	Police presence	Verbal commands	Control and restraints	Chemical agents	Weapons and tactics	Deadly force

Police Response

A report by the U.S. Department of Justice entitled "National Data Collection on Police Use of Force" (1996) summarizes this issue very well:

> The feature distinguishing police from all other groups in society is their authority to apply coercive force when circumstances call for it. Police may be called on to use force when making an arrest, breaking up an altercation, dispersing an unruly crowd, or performing a myriad of other official activities during their daily routines. The force may range from pushing a person to get his attention to using a firearm. Between those extremes are several other types of force, including firm grips on an arm, use of debilitating chemical agents, and blows with a baton. Whatever method is used, police are expected to apply only the force necessary to resolve a given situation.

The necessary degree of force to be used against a citizen is determined in the officer's own judgment (i.e., his or her discretion), based on the behaviors of the citizen. It is also constrained by the U.S. Constitution (Hall, 1992). McEwen and Leahy (1994) place force techniques along a

---

The degree of necessary force to be used against a citizen is determined in the officer's own judgment (i.e., his or her discretion), based on the behaviors of the citizen.

---

continuum from no force to verbalization techniques to deadly force, with several nonlethal mechanisms somewhere in the middle, including the following:

- Impact weapons (e.g., batons and flashlights)
- Chemical weapons (e.g., pepper spray)
- Electrical weapons (e.g., electronic stun guns)
- Other less-than-lethal weapons (e.g., projectile launchers)

Luckily for both citizens and the police, use of police force is relatively rare. Force is used in only about 1% of all citizen encounters (Bureau of Justice Statistics, 1996). In 1996, for example, American police officers questioned almost 4.5 million people as suspects in crimes, and in less than 2% of cases was force used or threatened (Bureau of Justice Statistics, 1997). A large majority of instances of the uses of force are deemed justified. Table 7.4, from a national study of police use of force by Pate and Fridell (1994), found what one might expect about police use of force: less serious types of force are used more frequently than more serious types. Their study also found that citizen complaints for excessive force were rarely filed. Nationally, the rate for city police departments was 11.3 complaints per 100,000 people.

Use of police force is relatively rare, as it is used in only about one percent (1%) of all citizen encounters.

We cannot know for certain the prevalence of excessive use of force by police. We do know, however, that it is minority men who are most likely to be subjected to it (Ross, 1999). In a 1991 Gallup poll, respondents were asked, "Have you ever been physically mistreated or abused by the police?" Five percent of all respondents said they had been physically mistreated or abused by the police. Nine percent of non-Caucasians answered in the affirmative to the question of physical mistreatment or abuse by the police. And 20% of respondents said they knew someone who had been physically mistreated or abused by the police (U.S. Department of Justice, 1996). A study in

TABLE 7.4
Actual Incidence of Police Use of Force

TYPE OF FORCE	RATE PER 1,000 SWORN OFFICERS
Handcuff/leg restraint	490.4
Bodily force	272.2
Come-alongs	226.8
Unholstering weapons	129.9
Swarm	126.7
Twist locks/wrist locks	80.9
Firm grip	57.7
Chemical agents	36.2
Batons	36.0
Flashlights	21.7
Dogs	6.5
Electrical devices	5.4
Shots at civilians (missed)	3.0
Other impact devices	2.4
Neck restraints	1.4
Vehicle rammings	1.0
Shots at civilians (killed)	0.9
Shots at civilians (injured)	0.2

SOURCE: Data from T. Pate and L. Fridell, "Police Use of Force: Official Reports, Citizen Complaints, and Legal Consequences, 1991–1992" (Ann Arbor, MI: Interuniversity Consortium for Political and Social Research, 1994).

Cincinnati, Ohio, found that African Americans were more than four times as likely as Caucasians to indicate that they had been hassled by the police (Browning et al., 1994). According to the American Civil Liberties Union, polls conducted decades earlier showed similar results:

- A 1965 Gallup poll showed that 35% of African American men believed there was police brutality in their areas, compared with only 7% of white men.
- A 1966 survey conducted for a U.S. Senate subcommittee found that 60% of African American residents of the Watts neighborhood in Los Angeles who were between the ages of 15 and 19 years believed there was some police brutality; 50% said they had witnessed such conduct.
- A 1967 Urban League study of the Detroit riot area found that 82% believed there was some form of police brutality.

Apparently, fear of police hostility persists among people of color. Things have improved much since the 1960s. We can also tell that minorities suffer from higher levels of police use of force and harassment because they file a disproportionate number of citizen complaints against the police. Walker et al. (2000: 289) claim:

> Pervasive evidence indicates that racial minorities suffer discrimination at the hands of the police. They are more likely than whites to be shot and killed, arrested, and victimized by excessive physical force. In addition, there is evidence of police misconduct directed at racial minorities, as well as evidence that police departments fail to discipline officers found guilty of misconduct.

Studies show that minorities in the United States are more likely to have force used against them by the police (Geller and Toch, 1995). African Americans are most likely to be shot and killed by the police, followed by Hispanics and then Caucasians (Geller and Scott, 1992). Disparities in police involvement in shootings have lessened since the Supreme Court abolished the fleeing felon rule in the 1985 case *Tennessee v. Garner*. Walker et al. (2000) suggest that since this case, police officers are less able to justify shooting a fleeing felon on the basis of his or her race alone as a sign of dangerousness. Thus, the law has made it more difficult for police to use their own stereotypes to inform split-second decisions about whether or not to kill a suspect.

> *S*tudies show that minorities in the United States are more likely to have force used against them by the police. African Americans are most likely to be shot and killed by the police, followed by Hispanics, and then Caucasians.

The 1999 and 2000 shootings by New York city police of Amadou Diallo and Malcolm Ferguson, two unarmed African American men, show that unjustified police shootings still persist. These two men were shot only two blocks away from each other by the New York City Police Department's Street Narcotics Enforcement Unit. Given that both men were unarmed, the police have been accused of using excessive force. Although the four officers in the first case, who shot a combined 41 rounds at the fleeing Diallo, were acquitted of criminal charges because they shot Diallo as he reached for his wallet (which the officers claimed they thought was a gun), many Americans are not satisfied with the verdicts, and a march on New York City and Washington, D.C., was organized in protest of these shootings.

The report by the U.S. Department of Justice (1996) states that: "When police go beyond reasonable force to use excessive force during an arrest or in precipitous response, as during the decades of protest demonstrations involving labor, civil rights, or other controversial issues, citizens become victims of police, and the public's confidence in a police force can plummet." I now turn to the issue of how citizens view the police.

DIFFERENTIAL VIEWS OF THE POLICE

An outcome of even innocent bias in policing is that those who are most subjected to police activity will likely view the police differently than those who are not generally targeted by the police (Weitzer and Tuch, 1999). Even in the wake of all of the recent stories about police corruption and excessive of use of force by the police, you may be surprised to learn that most Americans generally have a positive view of the police. Even 40% of African Americans would support having more police on the streets, according to a 1993 Gallup poll.

> *M*ost Americans generally have a positive view of the police.

Data published in the *Sourcebook of Criminal Justice Statistics* show that when asked how they would rate the honesty and ethical standards of people in various professions, Americans rank police near the top. Table 7.5 shows that 49% of Americans rank police as very high or high, 40% rank them as average, and only 10% rank them as low or very low. This puts police behind

TABLE 7.5
Public Opinion of the Police

Honesty and ethical standards	
Very high or high	49%
Average	40%
Low or very low	10%
Rating of the police in your community	
Responding to calls/*not* using excessive force	68% excellent/good
Preventing crime/treating people fairly	65% excellent/good
Solving crime	60% excellent/god
Confidence in the police	
A great deal/a lot	57%
Some	33%
Very little	10%

SOURCE: U.S. Department of Justice, *Sourcebook on Criminal Justice Statistics*, (Washington, DC: U.S. Government Printing Office, 2000).

only druggists and pharmacists, members of the clergy, medical doctors, college teachers, and dentists, but ahead of nearly two dozen other professions. Additionally, Table 7.5 illustrates that Americans seem satisfied with police performance in their own communities. In response to the question, "How would you rate the police in your community?," 68% reported either excellent or good to police responding to calls, police *not* using excessive force, and police being helpful/friendly. Sixty-five percent reported either excellent or good to police treating people fairly and to preventing crime. Finally, 60% reported either excellent or good to police solving crime.

Table 7.5 illustrates the degree of confidence Americans express in the police. As shown in the table, 57% of Americans report they have a great deal or quite a lot of confidence in the police; 33% have some; and only 10% have very little confidence in the police. Because most police activity involves providing services to citizens, we may conclude from these data that citizens are generally satisfied with the level of services police have provided to them.

Despite this good news for police, there seems to be variation in views of police by race and other demographic characteristics. For example, whereas 59% of Caucasians report having a great deal or quite a lot of confidence in the police, only 40% of African Americans report that they do. At the same time, only 8% of Caucasians have very little confidence in the police, versus 26% of African Americans. Similarly, although 85% of Americans in 12 U.S. cities report that they are satisfied with police in their neighborhoods, racial variation is also present. That is, 90% of Caucasians report that they are satisfied with police in their neighborhood, versus 76% of African Americans. Thus, there appear to be at least two contrasting opinions about police in the United States.

To the question, "Do you think the police in your community treat all races fairly?," 59% of Americans answer yes, but the difference between the races is startling: 67% of Caucasians report that they think the police treat all races fairly, versus 48% of Hispanics and only 30% of African Americans. Age variation also is evident in the percentage who say yes. The groups most likely to answer yes to the question are Americans aged 65 and older (76%); the least likely are Americans 18 to 24 years old (35%).

To the question, "Are there any situations you can imagine in which you would approve of a policeman striking an adult male citizen?" 66% of Americans answer yes. The percentage of Caucasians who answer yes (71%) is higher than for African Americans (47%). It is also higher for those who earn more money each year than for those who make less. For example, of those who make $50,000 or more per year, 73% say that they can imagine approving of a policeman striking an adult male citizen, versus 55% of those who make less than $20,000 per year.

When asked, "Would you approve of a policeman striking a citizen who was attacking a policeman with his fists?," 90% of Americans say yes (92% of Caucasians and 83% of African Americans). The percentage who answer yes falls to 68% (73% of Caucasians and 50% of African Americans) when the question addresses a citizen merely attempting to escape from custody. The significant point is that African Americans and poor people seem less likely to approve of police force than Caucasians and wealthier citizens.

What accounts for these different views of police in the United States? Could it reflect differential treatment at the hands of police? As I have shown, there is evidence that people of color are disproportionately likely to suffer at the hands of the police. Extensive human rights abuses by police against poor minorities (such as immigrants) have been documented and reported by various agencies such as Amnesty International (e.g., see *The Economist*, 1998b; Federal Bureau of Investigation, 1994). Although Constitutional constraints are placed on the use of force by law enforcement officers (e.g., see Hall, 1992), the abuse of police discretion and the existence of racial bias in policing may subvert such restraints.

According to Ross (1999), Caucasian officers are most likely to be resisted, and the average person who resists police authority is a 22-year-old male. African Americans are disproportionately likely to resist the police, as they make up only 13% of the population but 43% of suspects who resist. It is unclear why African Americans are more likely to resist than Caucasians, but it is not inconceivable that African Americans may fear police more than Caucasians do, given both the deep-seated historical roots of police oppression and brutality against minorities and the recent stories of widespread police corruption in major American cities.

African Americans and poorer Americans do report being more afraid that they will be stopped and arrested by the police under circumstances in which they are completely innocent. Whereas 22% of all Americans are afraid of this, 43% of African Americans are afraid, versus only 16% of Caucasians. Approximately one-fourth (26%) of Americans who earn annual salaries of $15,000 or less report that they are afraid that they will be stopped and arrested by the police even when they are completely innocent, versus only 15% of those who earn over $75,000 per year. Younger Americans also seem to be more afraid of this: just over one-third (34%) of citizens between the ages of 18 and 24 say yes, versus only 10% of Americans 65 or older.

> *A*frican Americans and poorer Americans do report being more afraid that they will be stopped and arrested by the police under circumstances where they are completely innocent.

People are probably more likely to view crime as more problematic or bothersome when they have had more experiences with it. In fact, African Americans and the poor are more likely than Caucasians and the wealthy to experience street crime. For example, 1 in 24 African Americans was victimized by violent crime in 1998, versus 1 in 28 Caucasians. Amazingly, African Americans made up 47% of murder victims. Also, persons with household incomes of less than $35,000 per year were significantly more likely to become victims of violent street crime. Urban dwellers and property renters were also disproportionately likely to be victimized by street-level property crimes (Bureau of Justice Statistics, 1998).

African Americans, central-city residents, renters, and multiunit dwellers are likely to answer yes to crime when asked, "Is there anything in your neighborhood that bothers you?" In 1995, the data showed that 14% of African Americans, versus only 6% of Caucasians, said crime was bothersome in their neighborhoods. Additionally, 15% of central-city residents reported that crime was bothersome in the neighborhood, versus only 5% and 2% of suburban and rural residents, respectively. Renters were nearly three times as likely as home owners to identify crime as bothersome (12% versus 5%, respectively), as were multiunit residents versus single-unit residents (14% versus 5%, respectively).

Given these data, it may not surprise you to learn that non-Caucasians and the poor are more likely to answer that the nation is spending too little money fighting crime in the United States. For example, 70% of non-Caucasians say this is true, versus 59% of Caucasians. Nearly two-thirds (64%) of those who earn less than $20,000 annually say this is true, versus 55% of those who make $50,000 or more per year. Less well educated and poorer Americans are also more likely to report that they believe there is more crime in the United States this year than last year. For example, 60% of those with no college experience report they believe there is more crime, versus just over one-third (34%) of those with graduate school experience. Additionally, 63% of those who earn less than $20,000 annually say they believe there is more crime this year, versus 39% of those who earn $75,000 or more. These same patterns show up when respondents are asked about the level of crime in their own neighborhoods.

CORRUPTION IN AMERICAN POLICING

Earlier you saw that different groups in society have different views of the police. As noted, this may be attributable in part to their own experiences at the hands of police. Corruption, a perversion of policing stemming from a lack of integrity or honesty, is widespread and highly likely to affect poor people and people of color. Goldstein (1975: 3) defines *corruption* as a misuse of police authority "in a manner designed to produce personal gain." That is, corruption results in some benefit to the officer, even if the benefit is only emotional.

---

*C*orruption, a perversion of policing stemming from a lack of integrity or honesty, is widespread and most likely to affect poor people and people of color.

One recent example shocked even those who had a negative view of police to begin with. In the summer of 1997, a Haitian immigrant, Abner Louima, was attacked by four police officers. Two officers used the baton of one of the officers to sodomize Louima and then shoved the baton into his mouth, knocking out several of his teeth, as if they hated him personally. These officers were fired and convicted on criminal charges. Is this type of police attack common?

In fact, we do not know how extensive and prevalent police corruption in the United States is because problems such as citizen mistreatment and falsification of records and evidence have never been subjected to a national study (Donziger, 1996: 163). However, there are numerous well-known examples, particularly within larger American cities, of alarming corruption in American police departments (see the Issue in Depth at the end of this chapter). For example, the Mollen Commission in New York found evidence of police involvement in theft, drug trafficking, drug use, falsification of police reports, lying in court, and police brutality (Mollen Commission, 1994). Shockingly, the most common form of corruption in New York was not police brutality (although the city has lost over $100 million in lawsuits recently for brutality); rather, it was for falsifying police records and testimony at criminal trials, a practice known as "testilying," whereby officers often made up testimony in order to ensure criminal convictions. They would invent stories to justify their illegal and unethical police techniques, which violated suspects' Constitutional rights.

There can be no greater threat to justice—including the presumption of innocence and equality before the law—than such police misconduct. Imagine yourself, an innocent citizen, facing arrest, charges, and the threat of criminal prosecution for crimes you did not commit. Because you happened to be in the wrong place at the wrong time (e.g., in an inner-city neighborhood where police were patrolling), and because a police officer has lied in his reports and is willing to lie at trial, you know you are likely to be convicted. What would you do? Would you consider accepting a lesser sentence through a plea bargain? I'll return to the issue of how plea bargaining interferes with justice in Chapter Eight.

Other large police departments have witnessed major corruption scandals, as well. In Washington, D.C., partly as a result of a massive hiring of unqualified officers, some of whom even had criminal records, more than 200 police officers since 1989 have been arrested and charged with crimes, including 79 officers in 1993 (Harriston and Flaherty, 1994). Departments that were faced with losing millions of dollars in federal funding if they did not hire more officers are the same ones that ended up hiring some very bad people.

In Philadelphia, officers confessed in 1995 to planting evidence, personally profiting from the illegal drug trade, and making false arrests. This led to the reexamination of 2,000 criminal cases that may have led to wrongful conviction because of bad policing. Additionally, nearly 200 police officers in New Orleans were disciplined for their questionable activities, and 4 were charged with murder related to their involvement in drug offenses (Cromwell, 1995). The Christopher Commission in Los Angeles found "a significant number of LAPD officers who repeatedly misuse[d] force and persistently ignore[d] the written policies and guidelines of the Department regarding force" (Christopher, 1991).

More recently, Bernard Parks, chief of police for Los Angeles, issued the report of the Rampart Area Corruption Incident. This involved police officers being involved in a bank robbery, false imprisonment and beating of a handcuffed arrestee at a police substation, and the theft of 3 kilograms of cocaine from a police evidence room (see the Issue in Depth at the end of this chapter).

Amazingly, the National Criminal Justice Commission reports that in several of these incidents, superiors were to some degree aware of the police corruption, yet decided not to intervene because of their fear of bad press (Donziger, 1996). Meanwhile, citizens were learning about corruption firsthand from the actions of the officers on the streets. Daily activities are far more important to the way police are perceived by citizens than public relations campaigns or bumper stickers aimed at promoting partnerships between citizens and the police (Wrobleski and Hess, 2000).

Unfortunately, several aspects of police corruption differentially affect the poor and citizens of color, which may explain the differential view of police by people of color and the poor. Police use of force is a significant problem in our inner cities where the poor and African Americans are more likely to reside. Not surprisingly then, in the 1990s, a majority of adults believed that the police were more likely to beat minorities than Caucasians (NAACP, 1993). This is why the authors of the NAACP report claimed that African Americans were more likely to be shot by police and bitten by police dogs, and thus concluded that the "risk of abuse, mistreatment or even death" accompanied any minority interaction with the police (p. vi).

> *S*everal aspects of police corruption differentially affect the poor and citizens of color, which may explain their differential view of police.

Current law enforcement strategies revolving around so-called zero-tolerance approaches exacerbate such problems. For example, the National Criminal Justice Commission discusses an antigang sweep of streets called Operation Sunrise in Los Angeles, which led to 63 arrests. Of those arrested, only 1% were charged with a violent felony. Such efforts were characterized as part of the "squeegee strategy," named after the street dwellers who, uninvited, wash the windows of cars that stop at red lights on city streets (Donziger, 1996: 169).

Zero-tolerance policing runs counter to community policing and logical crime prevention efforts. To whatever degree street sweeps are viewed by citizens as brutal, suspect, militaristic, or the biased efforts of "outsiders," citizens will be discouraged from taking active roles in community-building activities and crime prevention initiatives in conjunction with the police. Perhaps this is why the communities that most need neighborhood watch programs are least likely to be populated by residents who take active roles in them (Sherman et al., 1997). Zero-tolerance policing will fail because its practice destroys several important requisites for successful community policing, namely police accountability, openness to the public, and community cooperation (Cox and Wade, 1998: 106).

> *T*o whatever degree street sweeps are viewed by citizens as brutal, suspect, militaristic, or the biased efforts of "outsiders," citizens will be discouraged from taking active roles in community-building activities and crime prevention initiatives in conjunction with the police.

Some link these types of police corruption to the unique nature of policing, particularly the police subculture that "exalts loyalty over integrity" and "a hostility and alienation between the police and the community in certain precincts which breeds an 'Us versus Them' mentality" (Mollen Commission, 1994). Walker (1998: 15) argues that this allows police officers to treat suspects as if they did not have the same Constitutional rights as the rest of us. This police subculture results in part from the nature of police work, but also from how citizens interact with police.

A *subculture* is a group of people in a larger society with its own way of life, norms, beliefs, attitudes, and values. The existence of a police subculture suggests that in some very real way, police are different from "civilians." These differences are attributable in part to the work environment

> *A* subculture is a group of people in a larger society with its own way of life, norms, beliefs, attitudes, and values. The existence of a police subculture suggests that in some very real way, police are different than "civilians."

of policing. According to Cole and Smith (2000), the main elements of the police subculture include the following:

- *Working personality of the officer:* The personality of the officer changes over time as he or she is exposed to the threat of danger and is forced to exert his or her authority over citizens who do not automatically defer to the authority of the officer.
- *Social isolation:* Police officers separate themselves from civilians professionally and personally because of the nature of their jobs. In part, this is because they are expected to live exemplary lives and are always on duty. Police officers use technical jargon to discuss their work and often literally speak in codes.
- *Stress:* Police officers face numerous sources of stress and thus suffer high rates of suicide, divorce, heart disease, alcohol and other drug abuse.

Other research suggests that the police officer personality can be described as authoritarian and cynical in nature (Skolnick, 1966). Officers can also become suspicious, insecure, hostile, and prejudiced, in addition to several other characteristics (Schmalleger, 2001).

Cox and Wade (1998: 98) claim: "Many segments of the public are uncooperative with the police and some openly hostile a good deal of the time. Other segments criticize the police for being unable to do anything about the crime problem or appear largely apathetic regardless of police action or inaction." Thus, the police become "equally critical of and hostile toward some segments of the population." Others link police corruption to a lack of understanding on the part of the police of the people they are policing. Consistent with this are the findings that the largest police departments show more indications of police corruption and also tend to be the least diverse in terms of race and ethnicity (Donziger, 1996).

CONCLUSION

Police, the first component of the criminal justice system, are responsible for enforcing the criminal law. Law enforcement in the United States results in innocent biases against the poor and people of color. This innocent bias owes itself to the use of police discretion, the particular focus of police on street crimes rather than acts of white-collar deviance, the role of police in the "war on drugs," the use of "police profiling," and the location of police on the streets of this nation. Not only does policing create innocent bias, which in turn results in injustice, but it also is highly ineffective at reducing crime. Police behavior, as well intentioned as it certainly is, is inconsistent with the goals of the U.S. criminal justice system.

ISSUE IN DEPTH
Corruption in the Criminal Justice System

Recall the discussion in Chapter One about the role of politics in criminal justice. The American criminal justice system was created by and is currently maintained by people with tremendous power. For example, legislators are the only people in the country who can define your behavior as a crime, even if it is relatively harmless or harms only you. Police officers are the only people in the country who can legally use force against you—in some cases, lethal force—if you violate the law. The U.S. criminal justice process can thus be viewed as a system of oppressive power: "Criminal justice is, literally, state power. It is police, guns, prisons, the electric chair" (Friedman, 1993: 462). The problem with power is that it "corrupts; and power also has an itch to suppress."

With corruption comes wrongdoing and, potentially, criminal acts on the part of criminal justice officials. These crimes of the criminal justice system itself are virtually ignored, but, according to Henderson and Simon (1994: xi), "there is clearly evidence that deviance, corruption, and immorality exist in the system." Crimes within the criminal justice system are "remarkably frequent" and "constant throughout the system" (Henderson and Simon, 1994: iii). They include corruption, abuse of authority, jury tampering, bribe taking and payoffs, brutality, sexual exploitation of prisoners, and formal approval of such acts by administrators. Such acts cause physical, financial, and moral harm.

Because power corrupts, "politicians probably represent the single most corrupt group involved with the criminal justice system" (Henderson and Simon, 1994: 61). Yet, because of the long history of corruption in American policing, it is the component of the system most often identified with corruption (e.g., see Fyfe and Skolnick, 1993).

Research into police corruption has "consistently unearthed substantial and wide-ranging forms of police bribery" (e.g., see Coleman, 1990), including about a hundred drug-related cases that are heard by courts each year (Henderson and Simon, 1994). Drug law enforcement may present the most significant opportunity for police bribery (Kellner, 1988). Police corruption also includes violation of search-and-seizure laws, evidence tampering (Douglas and Johnson, 1977), and perjured testimony (Kittel, 1986). Abuse of authority in corrections also has been described as a "nationwide problem" (Henderson and Simon, 1994: 47).

The most recent example of a highly publicized corruption case in criminal justice is the Rampart Scandal in Los Angeles, California. According to the "Board of Inquiry into the Rampart Corruption Incident, Executive Summary":

a. In late 1997 and early 1998, three incidents occurred in which Los Angeles Police Officers were identified as suspects in serious criminal activity. The incidents began on November 6, 1997, when three suspects robbed a Los Angeles Bank of America. The investigation into that robbery led to the arrest of Officer David Mack, who was assigned to West Los Angeles Area at the time, and his girlfriend, an employee of the bank. The second incident occurred on February 26, 1998, and involved the false imprisonment and beating of a handcuffed arrestee at the Rampart Substation. The officer who beat the suspect was Rampart CRASH Officer Brian Hewitt. Two other CRASH officers, one of whom was Ethan Cohan, were present and acquiesced to the beating. The third incident involved the March 2, 1998, theft of three kilograms of cocaine from the Department's Property Division. The investigation into that theft led to the arrest of Officer Rafael Perez, who was assigned to Rampart CRASH.

b. The investigations into these incidents disclosed that the suspect officers were closely associated, either as working partners or close friends, and all but one of them were assigned to Rampart Area. The only exception, David Mack, had previously been assigned to Rampart and was a close friend of Rafael Perez. Due to the seriousness of the criminal activity, commonality among the officers and potential for involvement of more Department employees, Chief of Police Bernard C. Parks formed a special criminal Task Force in May 1998, to investigate these incidents.

c. Hewitt and Cohan were terminated following their Board of Rights hearings, but the third officer was found not guilty by his board. (In Los Angeles, a three-member Board of Rights, composed of two staff or command officers and one community member, hears allegations of major misconduct. Each accused officer may select a separate Board and the Chief of Police can impose no greater penalty than the Board recommends.) The case against Hewitt has been presented to the District Attorney on two occasions, but was rejected both times for a lack of sufficient evidence. The District Attorney's Office is now reconsidering the case. The case has also been presented to the State Attorney General's Office, which declined to take further action on the matter. David Mack was convicted in federal court of bank robbery and resigned from the Department in lieu of termination. He has been sentenced to 14 years and 3 months in prison. The $722,000 stolen in the robbery has not been recovered and his two accomplices have not been identified.

d. Rafael Perez' first trial resulted in a jury deadlock, eight to four in favor of a guilty verdict. The Department's investigative efforts during and after the first trial produced additional evidence that Perez was responsible for three additional cocaine thefts. He was also identified as being closely associated with known narcotics dealers, one of whom accompanied Perez, Mack, and a third officer on a trip to Las Vegas immediately after Mack committed the bank robbery.

e. As the evidence against Perez mounted, Perez offered to plead guilty to the charges and cooperate with the LAPD Task Force detectives in exchange for a reduced prison sentence. Perez indicated that he could provide information on other Rampart officers who were involved in serious criminal activity and misconduct. Just prior to the second trial in September 1999, an agreement was reached for a reduced prison sentence in return for Perez' guilty plea and cooperation in providing information on corruption activities within the Department. Subsequent interviews of Perez have indicated that much deeper corruption was occurring at Rampart than was originally suspected. The Task Force, in conjunction with the Los Angeles District Attorney's Office and Office of the United States Attorney General, is pursuing that investigation. On September 21, 1999, Chief Parks convened a Board of Inquiry (BOI) to assess the totality of the Rampart corruption incident without infringing on the work of the Task Force.

The final report was organized around more than one hundred recommendations for positive change within the Los Angeles Police Department, in the following areas:

*   Testing and screening of police officer candidates
*   Personnel practices
*   Personnel investigations and management of risk

- Corruption investigations
- Operational controls
- Anticorruption inspections and audits
- Ethics and integrity training
- Job-specific training

Amazingly, despite the scores of breakdowns within the LAPD that led to this corruption scandal, the final report recommended that no outside investigation by the FBI take place.

According to news reports, LAPD Rampart officers routinely and unnecessarily punched, kicked, and choked suspects in an effort to intimidate them. The officers then fabricated stories in police reports to account for their victims' injuries. The corruption probe uncovered information about unjustified shootings, evidence planting, and even false arrests of innocent people. More than 50 convictions have been overturned, and more than 20 officers have been relieved of duty or fired, or have quit because of the scandal.

At a 1999 press conference, District Attorney Gil Garcetti expressed his concern about one very troubling aspect of the Rampart scandal—the fact that innocent people were coerced into confessing for crimes that they did not commit. Garcetti said: "It raises the specter, obviously, that they pleaded guilty to something [even though] they were telling their lawyer, 'I'm not guilty, I'm innocent.' That raises a question for everyone in the criminal justice system."

Because crimes of the criminal justice system are not widely studied, we do not know precisely why they occur, but here are some likely reasons: there is only a small chance of such acts leading to punishment; criminal justice personnel become jaded over time in their fight against crime; and these crimes are supported to some degree by institutional factors (Henderson and Simon, 1994).

This book does not directly address the issue of criminality within the criminal justice system. Instead, I argue that even with completely "noncriminal" criminal justice personnel—that is, even in the absence of corruption—the criminal justice system fails to do justice or reduce crime effectively. At the same time, the criminal justice system tends to focus its attention on acts that, though harmful, are not the most harmful behaviors in the United States. All of this amounts to what I consider a "crime"—not in the legal sense, of course, but in the sense that it is not right or just.

Discussion Questions

- Identify the main roles of police officers in the United States, and provide a few examples of behaviors that fit into each role.
- To which role do police officers devote most of their time? Why?
- Compare the main functions of local police versus state and federal police.

- Do you think more police on the streets will reduce crime in the United States? Why or why not?
- What is the exclusionary rule? How does it protect you?
- List some exceptions to the exclusionary rule. Do you think these exceptions are reasonable? Why or why not?
- In what ways do police serve crime victims?
- What is community policing?
- Contrast the community police officer with the stereotypical view of the police officer.
- Discuss the main tenets of Sir Robert Peel.
- What does the term *innocent bias* mean?
- What factors produce innocent bias in policing?
- What do you think are the most important elements of the Law Enforcement Code of Conduct? Explain.
- Why is it so important that police have discretion in deciding whom to stop, detain, arrest, and so on?
- On which types of crimes are American police most focused? Why?
- Do you think there is a valid rationale for police profiling? Explain.
- Why do more police officers work for local governments (e.g., cities, counties) than for states or the federal government?
- Explain the difference between a *stop* and an *arrest*.
- Explain why people of color are disproportionately more likely to be stopped by and arrested by the police.
- In your opinion, when has excessive force been used by police against a citizen?
- Why do you think Americans rate the police so highly in public opinion polls?
- How does zero-tolerance policing run counter to the notion of community policing?
- Identify and discuss the main elements of the police subculture.
- What produces corruption in the criminal justice system?

CHAPTER EIGHT

RIGHT TO TRIAL?
INJUSTICE IN PRETRIAL
AND TRIAL PROCEDURES

KEY CONCEPTS

- The U.S. court structure
- What courts do
- The courtroom workgroup: An imbalance of power in the court
- Pretrial procedures and justice
- The unequal right to a defense in the United States: Public versus private attorneys
- The "exceptional case" of trial
- Issue in Depth: Wrongful Convictions

INTRODUCTION

This chapter continues the assessment of the criminal justice process by examining the operation of American courts. I begin with a brief examination of the U.S. court structure and then go on to discuss what courts actually do. Because of an imbalance in the courts in favor of the government, criminal proceedings are inherently biased against individual defendants. Additionally, because most defendants are indigent and therefore are appointed defense attorneys, biases against the poor and people of color continue in the courts. The institutions of bail, plea bargaining, and trials often do not promote the ideal goals of the criminal justice system.

THE U.S. COURT STRUCTURE

Because of the separation of powers clause of the U.S. Constitution, the United States has a "dual court" system; that is, federal and state governments each have their own distinct court systems,

> $\mathscr{B}$ecause of the U.S. Constitution's separation of powers clause, the United States has a "dual court" system, meaning that federal and state governments each have their own distinct court systems, operating independently of each other.

and the two systems operate independently of each other (Marion, 1995). State and federal courts can be differentiated by their *jurisdictions*—that is, where they have "the authority or power to hear a case" (Cox and Wade, 1998: 130). Where a case is heard depends on what type of law is violated. Crimes against states are typically handled in state courts, whereas crimes against the federal government are held in federal courts. And yes, cases can be heard in both courts without violating suspects' Fifth Amendment rights to freedom from double jeopardy. If both federal and state laws are violated, both courts can and often do hold trials.

> $\mathscr{S}$tate and federal courts can be differentiated by their jurisdictions, or the authority or power to hear a case. Where a case is heard depends on what type of law is violated.

Courts with general jurisdiction can hear most types of cases, whether they be criminal or civil matters, whereas courts of specific or limited jurisdiction can only hear cases within their specific expertise (e.g., juvenile courts hear only juvenile cases). Courts with original jurisdiction are typically trial courts, because their jurisdiction grants them the power to hear facts of cases initially. Appellate courts, or courts of appeals, do not decide matters of fact but, rather, decide matters of law. They hear cases that were first heard by courts with original jurisdiction and then appealed.

> $\mathscr{A}$ppellate courts, or courts of appeals, do not decide matters of fact but, rather, decide matters of law. They hear cases that have already been heard by courts with original jurisdiction and then appealed.

The power of appeals courts lies in their ability to set precedents. Once a decision is made, a precedent is created that, under the principle of *stare decisis* (let the decision stand), must be followed by all other courts within the same jurisdiction.

> $\mathscr{T}$he power of appeals courts is in their setting of precedents. Once a decision is handed down, a precedent is made that, under the principle of *stare decisis* (let the decision stand), must be followed by all other courts within the same jurisdiction.

There is no stereotypical court in the United States because the system is decentralized. Instead, there are a variety of types of courts, each with their own distinct names, purposes, and functions served (Cole and Smith, 2000; Schmalleger, 2001). Federal courts in the United States include 94 trial courts (called district courts) and 12 appeals courts (called circuit courts). Of course, the United States also has an appeals "court of last resort," the U.S. Supreme Court, made up of nine justices. State courts include trial courts of original jurisdiction, intermediate courts of appeals in about half of the states, and appellate courts of last resort (state supreme courts). As indicated earlier, not all states have intermediate courts of appeals, but states with larger populations tend to have them in order to relieve the burden on the state supreme courts

(Chapper and Hanson, 1990). State courts are very diverse; Cox and Wade (1998: 132) write that the term that best describes state courts is *variation* because "there is no one state that adequately depicts the other fifty systems."

> *There* is no stereotypical court in the United States because our system is decentralized. Instead, there are a variety of types of courts, each with their own distinct names, purposes, and functions.

Types of crimes handled by federal and state courts are often very different. Table 8.1 shows the types of felonies leading to convictions in each court in 1996. Federal courts convicted a total of 60,958 adults, 43% of them for drug crimes, 23% for property crimes, and the rest for immigration or weapons offenses. State courts convicted a total of 997,000 adults, 35% of them for drug crimes, 22% for property crimes, and 17% for violent crimes. Thus, the majority of people convicted of felonies in each court were not convicted for violent crimes. Compare this with media coverage of crime in Chapter Four.

Most criminal justice scholars also differentiate between lower courts (e.g., courts that hear traffic cases or misdemeanors) and higher level courts (e.g., courts that hear felony cases). They are differentiated on the basis of how they ideally process defendants. Lower courts tend to emphasize speed and routinization of cases, so that large numbers of cases are disposed of quickly through fines, community service, and other such sanctions. Higher level courts are ideally less characterized by "assembly-line justice" and more accurately described as adversarial. The reality of even higher level trial courts for most defendants, as you will see later in this chapter, is that trials are the rare exception to the assembly-line nature of plea bargaining.

Not surprisingly, in light of our examination of American police, court defendants are disproportionately poor. For example, indigents, people who cannot afford their own attorneys, make up about 80% of people charged with felonies in the United States (Gaines et al., 2000). Charac-

> *Court* defendants are disproportionately poor. For example, indigents (people who cannot afford their own attorneys) make up about 80% of people charged with felonies in the United States.

teristics of both federal and state court defendants demonstrate who our system pursues. African Americans make up roughly 1 out of every 4 of U.S. district court cases (federal courts) in any given year and nearly 1 out of 2 of those convicted for felonies in state courts. African Americans

TABLE 8.1
Types of Crime Handled in America's Courts

CRIME TYPE	FEDERAL COURTS	STATE COURTS
Drug crimes	43%	35%
Property crimes	23%	22%
Immigration/weapons offenses	34%	
Violent crimes		17%
	60,958 adults	997,000 adults

SOURCE: Bureau of Justice Statistics. Online: www.ojp.usdoj.gov/bjs.

are more likely to have pretrial detention hearings than Caucasians (49% versus 32%, respectively) and are slightly more likely to be held in pretrial detention than Caucasians (64% versus 58%, respectively), perhaps because African Americans are less able to afford even modest bail (Miller, 1997) and also because they are more likely to be represented by public defenders. African Americans make up 31% of those convicted in federal courts and are slightly more likely to be incarcerated than Caucasians (82% versus 77%, respectively). Also, African Americans are disproportionately likely to be sentenced under federal sentencing guidelines (Free, 2000). The most pronounced disparity in federal sentencing occurs with drug offenses (U.S. Department of Justice, 1997), as will be illustrated in Chapter Nine. Many factors explain such disparities, but social class and plea bargaining play significant roles. I will examine these factors later in this chapter.

WHAT COURTS DO

When citizens are arrested by police, they become clients for the courts. What do courts do? The following statement answers this question:

> Simply stated, a court is a place where arguments are settled. The argument may be between the federal government and a corporation accused of violating environmental regulations, between business partners, between a criminal and the state, or any other number of parties. The court provides an environment in which the basis of the argument can be settled through the application of the law. (Gaines et al., 2000: 270)

In deciding arguments, the primary function of American courts is to determine the legal guilt of the accused—that is, to determine if a person is guilty beyond a reasonable doubt of committing a crime (Peoples, 2000; Stuckey, Robertson, and Wallace, 2001). The National Criminal Justice Commission writes of the courts: "Their responsibility is to be fair to all citizens charged with a crime and to impose a just punishment on those found guilty" (Donziger, 1996: 181). These are the key functions served by American courts.

The primary function of U.S. courts is to determine the legal guilt or innocence of the accused—that is, to determine if a person is guilty beyond a reasonable doubt of committing a crime.

But courts do much more than determine guilt or innocence. They also are "responsible for determining bail, conducting preliminary hearings (or grand juries), ruling on the admissibility of evidence, and determining the appropriate sentence when a finding of guilty has been reached" (Cox and Wade, 1998: 130).

Essentially, courts take over where the police leave off. As I will show in this chapter, the U.S. courts are demonstrably biased against poor people and people of color. Pretrial procedures such as bail and plea bargaining, as well as trial procedures, are biased against relatively powerless groups. This bias begins with an imbalance in the courts.

THE COURTROOM WORKGROUP: AN IMBALANCE OF POWER IN THE COURT

To ensure justice, the court is supposed to be impartial. Ideally, this means that neutral actors are involved in objectively determining the relevant facts of each case in order to ensure that the guilty are convicted and the innocent are not. The importance of this is explained by Gaines et al. (2000: 271): "In theory, each party in a courtroom dispute must have an equal chance to present its case and must be secure in the belief that no outside factors are going to influence the decision rendered by the court."

> *In* order to ensure justice, the court is supposed to be impartial. Ideally, neutral actors are involved in objectively determining the relevant facts of each case in order to guarantee that the guilty get convicted and the innocent do not.

Keep in mind as you read this chapter that the people who work in the courts are very different from the people who are typically processed through the courts. Minorities and women are underrepresented in American courtroom workgroups (Bonsignore et al., 1998; Spire, 1990). Graham (2000) demonstrates how African Americans are underrepresented as attorneys and judges. Thus, much as legislators are not representative of Americans (see Chapter Two), those who work to convict or acquit suspected criminals also are not representative of Americans. Whether this is sufficient to explain injustice in the courts is unclear, but an unrepresentative courtroom workgroup is probably less likely to produce an outcome of justice than a representative workgroup.

> *M*inorities and women are under-represented in U.S. courtroom workgroups.

Formal rules of procedure also are supposed to assist with objectivity. For example, "there are limitations as to how evidence may be introduced, what types of evidence may be admitted, and what types of questions may be asked" (Cox and Wade, 1998: 130). Later in this chapter I will return to whether the American criminal courts really act in an objective manner. First, I examine who works in the courts.

The *courtroom workgroup* is a term used to describe the main actors in this process within the criminal courts—the prosecutor, the defense attorney, and the judge (Cole and Smith, 2000; Cox and Wade, 1998; Schmalleger, 2001; Walker, 1998). A *workgroup* can be understood as a collective of individuals who interact, share goals, follow court norms, and develop interpersonal relationships (Fleming, Nardulli, and Eisenstein, 1992). This concept is important because it helps us understand why the workgroup's overriding concern is speeding up the process and getting rid of cases as efficiently as possible rather than "doing justice."

> *The* courtroom workgroup is a term used to describe the main actors in this process within the criminal courts: the prosecutor, the defense attorney, and the judge. A workgroup can be understood as a collective of individuals who interact, share goals, follow court norms, and develop interpersonal relationships.

Ideally, each member of the courtroom workgroup plays its own roles and has its own goals. In reality, each member's main job is not to rock the boat in the daily operations of American courts, which are described as follows:

> Every day, the same group of courthouse regulars assembles in the same courtroom, sits or stands in the same places, and performs the same tasks as the day before. The types of defendants and the nature of the crimes they are accused of committing also remain constant. Only the names of the victim, witnesses, and defendants are different. (Neubauer, 1998: 41)

The prosecutor, as a representative of the court, fights for the "people" in an effort to "get justice" (as an outcome) for the crime victim and the community. His or her main job is to decide whether or not to press charges on the basis of the amount of quality evidence available to obtain a conviction. If the prosecution decides to press criminal charges, the next decision is to decide which charges to press. This decision will ultimately have a great effect on the resulting criminal sentence, as you will see in Chapter Nine.

The prosecutor, as a representative of the court, fights for the people in an effort to get justice (as an outcome) for the crime victim and the community. His or her main job is to decide whether to press charges on the basis of the amount of quality evidence available to obtain a conviction.

Criminal charges come in the form of an *indictment* (if the state uses a grand jury system) or an *information* (in cases of a preliminary hearing). The primary difference between grand juries and preliminary hearings is that grand juries are one-sided presentations by the prosecution, whereas preliminary hearings are adversarial in nature. Some have called the grand jury a "rubber stamp" for the prosecutor because grand juries almost never fail to return an indictment. Both grand juries and preliminary hearings result in a determination of whether there is enough evidence to pursue the case further (e.g., to a criminal trial).

A prosecutor must consider numerous factors when deciding either to accept a case for prosecution or to reject the case. Most cases that come before prosecutors' offices do not lead to a prosecution. In fact, just under half of arrests lead to prosecution. Despite what you may have heard about "legal technicalities," most cases are in fact dropped because of a lack of high-quality evidence. Of course, decisions to prosecute do not emanate from formal rules but from informal relationships with people such as the police, victims, and other community members. This is another reason that it is imperative that positive relationships be established and maintained among citizens, police, and other criminal justice officials.

Walker (1998: 46) reviews the evidence of factors that influence prosecutors' decisions to accept cases for prosecution and concludes that the largest share of cases that are not prosecuted are dropped because of evidence problems—not enough high-quality evidence to obtain a conviction at trial. He claims that "due process problems—illegal searches or confessions—are not a major cause of rejections or dismissals." Thus, those who argue that "legal technicalities" should be disallowed may be off the mark. Pizzi (1999), in his book *Trials without Truth*, claims that trials are too focused on winning and losing rather than on truth. One reform he advocates is eliminating the exclusionary rule as a means of convicting more guilty criminals. His reforms are aimed at achieving justice as an outcome rather than ensuring justice as a process. On the basis of the review of evidence in Chapter Seven, do you agree that the exclusionary rule should be abolished?

The prosecutor also serves as "trial counsel for police" (fighting crime) and "house counsel for police" (giving legal advice) (Cole and Smith, 2000). Examples of the role of trial counsel for the police include zealously prosecuting suspected criminals and pursuing community crime control interests to achieve justice as an outcome. Examples of the role of house counsel for the police include "providing legal advice to [the police], providing training for police on criminal law and legal processes, preparing drafts of search warrants and wiretapping applications, participating in decisions regarding court administration, and engaging in a wide variety of public information and community relations programs" (Holten and Jones, 1982: 185). In both cases, the prosecutor can be accurately understood as a partner with the police.

As a representative of the court, the prosecutor also must be concerned with justice as a process. A prosecutor is "obliged to protect the rights of the defendant" (Cox and Wade, 1998: 148), just as a police officer is obligated to uphold the Constitutional rights of a suspect (Wrobleski and Hess, 2000). There is evidence, however, that many prosecutors ignore possible indications of innocence of defendants simply in order to gain convictions and clear cases.

Prosecutors have tremendous power in the criminal justice process. This power imbalances the court in favor of the state rather than the defendant. "Ideally, this power is balanced by a duty of fairness and a recognition that the prosecutor's ultimate goal is not to win cases, but to see that justice is done" (Gaines et al., 2000: 302). The American Bar Association (1993, 1997), for example, expects that prosecutors will "seek justice, not merely convict" criminals because they have the "responsibility of a minister of justice." Justice Sutherland wrote, in *Berger v. United States* (1935), that the prosecutor "may prosecute with earnestness and vigor—indeed he should do so. But, while he may strike hard blows, he is not at liberty to strike foul ones."

Prosecutors have tremendous power in the criminal justice process. This power prejudices the court in favor of the state rather than the defendant.

Yet, most prosecutors are also elected officials, meaning that they will at times be concerned with what they perceive their community wants, as well as with the underlying philosophy of the voters (DeFrances and Steadman, 1998; Merlo and Benekos, 2000). Gershman (2000: 286) demonstrates that the typical jury is biased toward the prosecution, meaning that jurors will be more tolerant of misconduct by prosecutors than by defense attorneys, including promises made about evidence in opening statements of a trial but not delivered during the trial and purposeful mention of inadmissable evidence. Ensuring high conviction rates sends a signal to the community that the prosecutor is tough on crime. The desire to be tough on crime while simultaneously being fair and making sure that innocent people are not convicted seem to conflict.

Are prosecutors biased against any particular group of people? That is, is there any evidence that they are more likely to press charges against some groups of people? The *Harvard Law Review* (1988) suggested that prosecutors may abuse their discretion by upgrading charges against minorities and downgrading them against Caucasians.

The defense attorney represents the "defendant" and has the main duty of being an advocate for the defendant. This is the main actor in the criminal justice process who is responsible for ensuring that Constitutional protections of the accused are upheld and protected. Defense attorneys are the actors in the court process responsible for upholding the due process function of the court, protecting "individuals from the unfair advantages that the government—with its immense

> *The* defense attorney represents the defendant and has the main duty of being an advocate for the defendant. This is the main actor in the criminal justice process who is responsible for ensuring that Constitutional protections of the accused are upheld and protected.

resources—automatically enjoys in legal battles" (Gaines et al., 2000: 271). Standard 4–1.2(b) of the American Bar Association's *Standards for Criminal Justice* (1991) states that the basic duty of the defense attorney is "to serve as the accused's counselor and advocate with courage and devotion, and render effective, quality representation." The ideal functions of defense attorneys include the following (Siegel, 1998: 487–488):

- Investigating the facts of the case against his or her client
- Preparing his or her client's case for trial
- Submitting motions in favor of his or her client's case
- Representing the defendant at trial
- Negotiating sentence with the prosecutor if the client is convicted
- Appealing convictions

The reality is that these functions may be carried out by some defense attorneys but not by others. It all depends on what type of defense attorney a person can afford.

Defense attorneys include nationally known attorneys, other private attorneys, and "courthouse regulars" (e.g., public defenders) (Cole and Smith, 2000). There are generally three types of systems available to defend those who cannot hire their own attorneys, including public defender systems (a salaried staff of government attorneys paid for by taxpayers), assigned counsel programs (private attorneys assigned to particular cases by courts), and contracting attorney programs (private attorneys hired to defend a group of defendants for a specified period of time) (Bureau of Justice Statistics, 1998). These systems are necessary primarily because the majority of defendants in criminal cases are indigents, or people who cannot afford their own attorney. The Supreme Court, in *Gideon v. Wainwright* (1963), held that the right to fair trial was jeopardized if state court defendants were not granted assistance by defense. In *Mempa v. Rhay* (1967), the Supreme Court extended the right of indigents beyond trial to other critical stages of the criminal justice process, including arraignment, preliminary hearing, entering of the plea, sentencing, and first appeal.

The typical defendant is not a wealthy person out to beat the system: "The average defendant in a criminal proceeding is indigent and not capable of hiring the 'best attorney money can buy." Instead, he or she is assigned a courthouse regular, who is usually paid a very low salary, works in a depressing environment, and has very few support services available (Merlo and Benekos, 2000: 57). The result is the inconsistent procedural justice discussed in Chapter One. Harrigan (2000: 319) writes that "the quality of state-provided representation seldom equals the representation you would obtain if you could afford to hire your own criminal layer." This is in part because they are "often so overloaded with cases they find it impossible to devote much of their time or effort to any specific case." Also, "because assigned lawyers get paid on a per-case basis rather than on an hourly basis, they have a great incentive to speed up the cases as much as possible." This led Blumberg (1967) to call many defense attorneys "double agents" and "cons" often working against the interests of their clients (Uphoff, 2000). Others assert that public defenders do as well at defending their clients as private attorneys do (Hansom and Ostrom, 1993).

The judge, as leader of the courtroom workgroup, has the goal of ensuring that proper legal procedures are followed as a case is processed through the courts. The roles of judges include adjudicator (passes sentence), negotiator (referee between parties), and administrator (keeps up the docket). Judges decide if arrests are based on probable cause, inform charged suspects of their rights, determine if bail will be granted to defendants, rule on motions filed by the prosecution and the defense, officiate trials to make sure they are fair, and impose sentences on the legally guilty.

The judge, as the leader of a courtroom workgroup, has the goal of ensuring that proper legal procedures are followed as a case is processed through the courts. The roles of judges include adjudicator (passes sentence), negotiator (acts as referee between parties), and administrator (keeps up the docket).

Ideally, judges embody justice and ensure due process, but in reality, judges spend most of their time in the administrative role, which would include such activities as preparing budgets, scheduling cases, supervising employees, and maintaining court records (Cole and Smith, 2000; Cox and Wade, 1998). Because of the number of cases they must handle, and because of the amount of time courthouse employees spend together, the group may generally share the overriding goal of disposing of cases as quickly as possible more often than they may fight for justice. As more and more citizens have "run-ins with the law"—that is, as more police are put on the street and as American police make more arrests—the courts suffer the consequences. Today, the courts are forced to handle too many cases. As a result, many cases are simply dismissed before they are even considered (Donziger, 1996). Walker (1998: 13) writes: "The justice system can only handle so much business. It does not 'collapse' like a building. It keeps on going, but only through adjustments that are often undesirable."

The intimate nature of the daily operations of American courts makes the courtroom workgroup a "community" (Nardulli et al., 1988) because the members develop shared understandings of what cases should be worth and "reach a general consensus about how different kinds of cases should be handled" (Walker, 1998: 51). This means that even though prosecutors and defense attorneys are supposed to be *adversaries*, they rarely act this way.

By examining the reality of courtroom interactions today, you can learn a great deal about American priorities. For example, it is clear that prosecutors have much more power in the criminal justice process than judges or defense attorneys. Power is the ability to influence actions of others. The judge is theoretically the most powerful member of the court, in that he or she can decide matters of law that affect courtroom operations and in that he or she presides over trials: "Since they are deciding benefits, judges are political actors with power" (Marion, 1995). Yet, since the "final decision about whether an alleged offender will be brought to court rests with the prosecutor" exclusively, the prosecutor has an enormous amount of discretion and is clearly the most powerful member of the court. Cox and Wade (1998: 147) state: "The decision not to prosecute (*nollee prosequi*), in addition to the discretion in determining the number and severity of charges, renders the prosecutor a very powerful figure in the court process." Stated plainly, if the prosecutor decides not to prosecute a case, the defense attorney and judge will in essence have no say in the outcome of that case. It is the discretion of the prosecutor to act or not to act that gives him or her so much power (Albonetti, 1987).

A former U.S. attorney general once claimed: "The prosecutor has more control over life, liberty, and reputation than any other person in America" (in Cox and Wade, 1998: 147). This becomes even more true as larger numbers of cases are sent from the police to courts. As American courts have become bogged down with more cases, judges have lost significant power, because they are even more reliant on prosecutors to determine which cases merit charges, trials, and justice (Marion, 1995). The power of judges also has been significantly reduced by new sentencing rules, which I will examine in Chapter Nine. Milovanovich (2000: 516) claims that the power of the prosecutor in the United States is essentially unchallenged.

Because of this imbalance of power in the court, justice is severely threatened. Ideally, if Americans value justice, due process, "innocent until proven guilty," Constitutional protections, and equality before the law, it seems that defense attorneys would have more power and a greater share of resources to ensure that their clients are processed fairly through the system. Because most criminal defense attorneys work for the government (e.g., as public defenders), they have heavy caseloads, limited resources to investigate the facts of a case, and little or no financial incentive to take a case to trial (Casper, 1972; Cole and Smith, 2000). This may result in unequal justice for the rich and the poor: "The general suspicion is that equal justice is not available to rich and poor alike . . . indigents receive a lower quality of legal service, which results in their being more likely to suffer harsher penal sanctions than similarly situated defendants who can afford to buy good legal talent" (Sterling, 1983: 166). Despite this suspicion, others assert that because public defenders are members of the courtroom workgroup, they have the advantage of assuring a reasonable sentence from prosecutors with whom they interact on a daily basis (Skolnick, 1967; Wice, 1985).

> *I*deally, if Americans value justice, due process, the concept of "innocent until proven guilty," Constitutional protections, and equality before the law, it seems that defense attorneys would have more power and a greater share of resources to ensure that their clients are processed fairly through the system. Because most criminal defense attorneys work for the government (e.g., as public defenders), they have heavy caseloads, limited resources to investigate the facts of a case, and little or no financial incentive to take a case to trial. This may result in unequal justice for the rich and the poor.

PRETRIAL PROCEDURES AND JUSTICE

Everything that goes on in the criminal justice process between arrest, booking, and the criminal trial is called the pretrial phase (Peoples, 2000; Stuckey et al., 2001). The term can be misleading

> *E*verything that goes on in the criminal justice process between arrest, booking, and the criminal trial is called the pretrial phase.

in that it is called "pretrial" whether or not a trial actually results. The pretrial phase contains two major decisions that must be made before a case can proceed to trial (or be disposed of through some other means). These two decisions concern the issuing of bail and whether or not a case gets plea bargained. Next, I will examine each of these two processes and demonstrate how each severely threatens justice.

> *T*he pretrial phase contains two major decisions that must be made before a case can proceed to trial (or be disposed of through some other means): the issuing of bail and whether or not a case is plea bargained.

Bail As an Injustice

First, there is the decision about bail. After a suspect is arrested and brought to court to make an initial appearance (where the suspect is notified of the charges against him or her and is advised of his or her rights), the suspect may be released from the supervision of the court through the process of bail. *Bail* is a specified sum of money paid to the court for a suspect's release, to be paid back to the suspect if he or she returns for his or her court date. That is, bail is not the same thing as a fine, because it is not meant to be a form of punishment. It is important to point out that people are not supposed to be punished unless they commit a crime (under the policy of *nulla poena sine crimine*). Instead, bail is meant to ensure the presence of the defendant at trial. The logic is that if someone pays a sum of money to the court, he or she will come back in order to have the money returned.

> *B*ail is a specified sum of money paid to the court for a suspect's release, to be paid back to the suspect if he or she returns for his or her court date.

Types of bail are highlighted in the following box:

Types of bail

- *Percentage bail:* The defendant must pay only a percentage of the bail amount set by the judge up front, with the rest due if the defendant does not show up for his or her next trial date.
- *Fully secured bail:* The defendant must pay the entire bail amount set by the judge up front.
- *Unsecured bail:* The defendant must not pay any of the bail amount set by the judge up front, but must pay the full amount if the defendant does not show up for his or her next trial date.

Bail is based on the premise that no one—since everyone is supposedly innocent in the eyes of the law at this point—should be unduly burdened by being held against his or her will until the

> *B*ail is based on the premise that no one—since everyone is considered innocent in the eyes of the law at this point—should be unduly burdened by being held against his or her will until the trial date.

trial date. Because many crimes are relatively minor, holding many offenders would be a waste of taxpayer money. It would not be fair to interrupt a person's life—to separate him or her from his or her family and force him or her to stop working and lose important wages—just to ensure that the state has its right to prosecute someone who is accused of a criminal offense.

There are, however, cases in which bail is not granted to suspected offenders. In some cases, people are detained in jail until their trial dates. For example, ex–football star O. J. Simpson spent two of his birthdays in jail while awaiting trial and during his trial. He was detained because it was feared that if he was let out, he would abscond (jump bail) and not return for his court date. It was also feared that he might be dangerous to the community, given that he was accused of two heinous murders. The fact that Simpson was later acquitted (found not guilty) led some to question whether he was entitled to any compensation for his time served.

The answer is no. According to the Bail Reform Act of 1984, accused criminals can be held in jail in "preventive detention" for two primary purposes: to prevent them from fleeing the state's jurisdiction, and to protect the community. Thus, judges may deny bail when there is either a flight risk or some potential danger to the community. The Constitutionality of this practice was upheld by the Supreme Court in *U.S. v. Salerno* (1987).

> *A*ccording to the Bail Reform Act of 1984, accused criminals can be held in jail in "preventive detention" for two primary purposes: to prevent them from fleeing the state's jurisdiction and to protect the community. Thus, judges may deny bail when there is either a risk of flight or some potential danger to the community.

Bail, however, cannot be "excessive," according to the Eighth Amendment to the U.S. Constitution, although there is no clear understanding of what *excessive* really means. Instead, prosecutors may ask for a certain amount of bail, defense attorneys may ask for a reduction, and judges ultimately decide what the acceptable bail amount will be. Ideally, defense attorneys ensure that bail is not excessive for their clients; in reality, however, they rarely challenge the amount (Gaines et al., 2000: 312). A "going rate" for particular crimes seems to develop over time so that a person charged with a particular crime may have a rough idea of what he or she will have to come up with to be granted bail. The nature of the charges; the defendant's prior record (if any); and extralegal factors such as employment status, ties to the community, and status in the community are also considered when bail is being determined (Eisenstein et al., 1988).

The application of bail has several major problems. First, it is biased against certain groups in the United States. Erving and Houston (1991) found evidence of judges using excessive bonds against minorities. Spohn and Delone (2000) found that pretrial detention was disproportionately used against African Americans and Hispanics in two cities and against African Americans in another. Other studies show biases against the poor and minorities (Ayers and Waldfogel, 1994;

> *T*he application of bail has several major problems.

Harmsworth, 1996). Such findings suggest that the bail decision can be biased against certain Americans. Kappeler et al. (2000: 226) claim that "[b]ail itself is inherently discriminatory." Logically, people who cannot afford bail are less likely to come up with the money or property to make bail and thus are forced to sit in jail awaiting trial. This may explain why jails are considered the poorhouses of the twentieth and twenty-first centuries (Cole and Smith, 2000): they are filled with poor criminals and accused criminals who could not afford bail.

Second, bail flies in the face of "innocent until proven guilty"—how can a person be detained if he or she has not been found guilty by a jury of his or her peers for any criminal act? In reality, more than half of the people in jail in any given year are awaiting trial and thus have not been convicted of any criminal offense; yet they are living away from their families, in the company of convicted criminals, mentally ill citizens, and homeless people detained for minor crimes.

Third, courtroom workgroups inflate bail amounts for those they want to detain, meaning that two people charged with the same crime or same type of crime may see drastically different bail amounts. This practice is contradictory to equal justice under the law. Fourth, bail may encourage guilty pleas. After all, if accused of relatively minor crimes, many would likely take a guilty plea and receive probation or a fine rather than being forced to sit in jail awaiting trial.

Fifth, preventive detention may increase the likelihood that a defendant will be convicted and sentenced to prison. Walker (1998: 118) reports findings from the National Pretrial Reporting Program illustrating that defendants held in preventive detention were more likely to be convicted of both felonies and misdemeanors. Whether this is because detained citizens appear in court wearing "jail garb" and thus "look guilty," while freed clients appear wearing normal clothes, is unknown. Logically, it would seem that seeing a person wearing jail clothing and perhaps in handcuffs or shackles would suggest to the normal citizen that "this person must be guilty if he or she is in jail." Another possible explanation of why detained suspects are more likely to be convicted is that when a suspect is in jail, he or she is far less able to gather evidence in his or her defense. If the defense attorney is a public defender, the defendant will not receive quality efforts from the attorney, as will be illustrated later in this chapter. In their study, Spohn and Delone (2001) found that those offenders held in pretrial detention were somewhat more likely to be sentenced to incarceration. Of course, it is possible that pretrial detainees are more often convicted and sentenced to prison because they are actually guilty and perhaps committed more serious crimes.

Finally, preventive detention may not *generally* be necessary, because most people who are let out on bail do not commit another crime while awaiting trial (Walker, 1998: 121–122). The bottom line is that it is impossible to predict who might be dangerous if let out: "there are no reliable methods for either measuring or predicting future offense rates" (Greenwood and Turner, 1987, in Walker, 1998: 126). As stated by Fagan and Guggenheim (1996: 445), "the accuracy of prediction of dangerousness during the pretrial period remains questionable." Some crime control model advocates might conclude that we should therefore keep all people in jail until trial in order to protect our communities from those few who might become dangerous. The other extreme is advocated by Fagan and Guggenheim, who conclude that "preventive detention appears to be unjustified" (p. 448).

Given these limitations, there are also alternatives available to judges, as outlined in the following box.

Bail alternatives

- *Release on own recognizance:* The defendant is released on the basis of his or her promise to appear.
- *Release into third-party custody:* The defendant is released into the custody of another person (e.g., a parent), who agrees to ensure that the defendant will show up for his or her next court date.
- *Conditional release:* The defendant is released on the basis of his or her promise to follow certain rules while free.

Plea Bargaining As an Injustice

The ideal of American justice is an "adversarial" process whereby prosecutors and defense attorneys fight for the truth and justice in a contest at trial. Yet, "the reality is that an *administrative* system is in effect, with a high degree of consensus and cooperation" (Walker, 1998: 51–52). Most cases are handled informally in hallways and offices rather than in courtrooms, as in a crime control model rather than a due process model. Instead of criminal trials in which prosecutors and defense attorneys clash in an effort to determine the truth and do justice for all concerned parties, prosecutors, defense attorneys, and sometimes judges "shop" for "supermarket" justice through plea bargaining (Feeley, 1979).

Shockingly, more than 90% of felony cases in the United States in any given year are disposed of via plea bargaining. This led Cole and Smith (2000) to call trials the "exceptional case" and Cox and Wade (1998) to call trials a "great American myth." Criminal trials are a formalized means of determining the legal guilt of your fellow citizens. Meanwhile, plea bargaining is an informal pro-

> *M*ore than 90% of felony cases in the United States in any given year are disposed of via plea bargaining.

cess whereby defendants plead guilty to lesser charges in exchange for not taking up the court's valuable time or spending the state's money on trials. Clients give up their Constitutional rights to cross-examine witnesses, to present a defense, to not incriminate themselves, to testify on their own behalf, and to appeal their convictions, all in exchange for a dismissal or reduction in charges, and/or a lesser sentence (Blumberg, 1967; Casper, 1972). Gaines et al. (2000: 294) write that this type of assembly-line justice, consistent with a crime control model, "implies injustice. The term suggests that defendants are being hurried through the process, losing the safeguards built into our criminal justice system in the blur."

> *P*lea bargaining is an informal process whereby defendants plead guilty to lesser charges in exchange for not taking up the court's valuable time and spending the state's money on trials. Clients give up their Constitutional rights to cross-examine witnesses, to present a defense, not to incriminate themselves, to testify on their own behalf, and to appeal their convictions, all in exchange for a dismissal or reduction in charges, and/or a lesser sentence.

There are three basic types of plea bargaining: horizontal, vertical, and charge bargaining. In horizontal bargaining, additional charges or counts are not filed against the accused in exchange for a guilty plea. Vertical bargaining involves reducing the severity of charges—for example, being charged with manslaughter instead of murder. Finally, charge bargaining suggests that some provable charges simply will not be pressed against the defendant on the basis of his or her guilty plea (Milovanovich, 2000).

Walker (1998: 157) claims that: "[v]irtually all of the studies of plea bargaining have found a high degree of regularity and predictability in the disposition of cases," meaning that the resulting sentence can be reliably predicted on the basis of the nature of the charges and the defendant's prior record (e.g., see Nardulli et al., 1988). Thus, a "going rate" is established for particular types of crimes committed by particular types of people, one that becomes established over time and is learned by each member of the courtroom workgroup. Plea bargains typically closely parallel this going rate, and defendants charged with particular crimes can easily learn what sentence they likely face if they plead guilty.

Plea bargaining is a process driven by large numbers of caseloads, understaffed courts, and the renewed emphasis on using law enforcement to solve drug use and public order offenses. Not

> $\mathcal{P}$lea bargaining is a process driven by heavy caseloads, understaffed courts, and the renewed emphasis on using law enforcement to solve the problems of drug use and public order offenses.

surprisingly, plea bargaining results in a bias against poor clients, who are typically minorities, as well as the uneducated, who may not even know what is being done to them in the criminal justice process (Gorr, 2000; Kaminer, 1999; Palermo, White, and Wasserman, 1998). Stephen Bright, director of Atlanta's Southern Center for Human Rights, says it this way: "If you're the average poor person, you are going to be herded through the criminal justice system about like an animal is herded through the stockyards" (in Herbert, 1998: 15).

> $\mathcal{P}$lea bargaining results in a bias against poor clients, who are typically minorities and often undereducated; these clients may not even know what is happening to them during the criminal justice process.

Some may argue that no one would enter a guilty plea for a crime he or she did not commit, but a person living in conditions of poverty who is charged with a minor crime and refuses to plead guilty will only guarantee himself or herself a longer stay in jail awaiting a hearing—often longer than the likely sentence to be imposed upon conviction through a guilty plea (R. Miller, 1997). If a public defender is representing the case, chances are the defendant will not have much of a chance to win at trial even if he or she is actually innocent, because: "In many jurisdictions, public defenders and state appointed attorneys are grossly underpaid, poorly trained, or simply lack the resources and time to prepare for a case—a pattern documented in cases ranging from the most minor to the most consequential, capital crimes" (Weitzer, 1996: 113).

The U.S. Supreme Court has granted the defendant the right to a defense attorney during the plea-bargaining process (*Brady v. United States*, 1969). It is also required that the defendant voluntarily give his or her guilty plea (*Boykin v. Alabama*, 1969). When a prosecutor offers a particular sentence in exchange for a guilty plea, the prosecutor must keep his or her promise related to the sentence (*Santabella v. New York*, 1971). Finally, when a defendant enters a guilty plea, he or she is asked numerous questions by the judge in order to ensure that the defendant understands that he or she is giving up many Constitutional rights and that the guilty plea was not coerced.

Coercion is not clearly defined for the defendant in this process. Pleas might be understood as coerced if one considers the quality of defense provided by public defenders. Oftentimes, defendants plead guilty because of the threat of losing at trial and receiving a much more severe sentence. Langbein (2000: 27) claims that "the plea bargaining system operates by threat." In the face of threats by the prosecution, defense attorneys essentially may tell their clients: "So you want your Constitutional right to jury trial? By all means, be our guest. But beware. If you claim this right and are convicted, we will punish you twice, once for the offense, and once again for having displayed the temerity to exercise your Constitutional right to jury trial." In other words, the goal of the public defender is to coerce his or her clients into surrendering their rights by threatening them with the possibility of greater sanctions.

The work environment of public defenders, who are responsible for defending the indigent (those who cannot afford their own attorneys), is typically depressing. Public defenders have large caseloads and limited resources relative to the prosecution, they work long hours, and they receive low pay (Cole and Smith, 2000). The indigent defendant must know that the likelihood of winning is remote. The result should not be surprising: "Some public defenders seem to have little interest in using every possible strategy to defend their clients. On numerous occasions, legal errors are made by prosecutors and judges to which the public defender raises no objection. In addition, appeals are sometimes not initiated by public defenders even when chances of successful appeal seem to be good" (Cox and Wade, 1998: 149).

> *The* work environment of public defenders responsible for defending the indigent (those who cannot afford their own attorneys) is depressing. Public defenders have large caseloads and limited resources relative to the prosecution, work long hours, and receive low pay.

Note that the U.S. Constitution does not guarantee a competent attorney. In *Strickland v. Washington* (1984), the Supreme Court set forth the standard for competence. In essence, a defendant must be able to prove that his or her sentence was directly affected by the conduct of the defense attorney—an impossible standard to prove.

> *The* U.S. Constitution does not guarantee a competent attorney. In *Strickland v. Washington* (1984), the Supreme Court set forth the standard for competence. In essence, a defendant must be able to prove that his or her sentence was directly affected by the conduct of the defense attorney.

Factual guilt is not determined in plea bargaining as it would be at a criminal trial. Guilt is assumed rather than established. Langbein (2000: 31) calls plea bargaining "condemnation without adjudication"—that is, sentencing without an establishment of guilt. Little investigation of the case against the defendant is conducted. Witnesses and victims are not present to see or approve of justice being meted out to the guilty. The question addressed by plea bargaining is not whether the defendant is actually guilty of the charges but, rather, what to do with the defendant. And one more thing—when guilty people plea bargain, they receive relatively lighter sentences than those convicted at trial for all crimes (Smith, 1986). This means people convicted at trial for murder, rape, robbery, aggravated assault, burglary, drug possession, and drug trafficking get longer sentences than people convicted through plea bargains (Bureau of Justice Statistics, 1998). And victims of crime have no say in the matter.

> *F*actual guilt is never determined in plea bargaining as it would be at a criminal trial. Guilt is assumed rather than established.

For all of these reasons, everyone seems to be against plea bargaining. It is surprising, then, that it happens so often:

> Conservatives believe it is a major loophole through which criminals beat the system and avoid punishment. Liberals, meanwhile, believe that it is a source of grave injustices: prosecutors deliberately "overcharge"; defense attorneys make deals rather than fight for their clients; defendants are coerced into waiving their right to a trial; some defendants get much better deals than others. (Walker, 1998: 153)

Cox and Wade (1998: 139) write: "Victims, the public, and the police are frequently unhappy about this practice, but if it were to be discontinued, the delays would be unconscionable." Thus, the large number of cases before today's courts seem to be driving the American plea-bargaining binge. Bradley (2000: 507) writes that the original approval of plea bargaining by the Supreme Court in *Santobello v. New York* (1971) "was based largely on the pragmatic concern that the criminal justice system could not afford to accord every defendant his constitutional rights, rather than on a claim that such a practice was inherently desirable."

When we shine a light on the outcome of justice in the United States, we see that the reality of plea bargaining is not consistent with the American ideal of the criminal trial, which is mentioned in the Declaration of Independence, three amendments to the U.S. Constitution, and scores of Supreme Court cases. Remember the two conceptions of justice discussed in Chapter One. Then ask yourself: Does plea bargaining achieve either of these forms of justice? Donziger (1996: 182) answers that plea bargaining bestows "lenient treatment on the guilty" and "coercive treatment on the innocent." Either way, it is unjust.

> *T*he reality of plea bargaining is not consistent with the American ideal of the criminal trial, which is mentioned in the Declaration of Independence, three amendments to the U.S. Constitution, and scores of Supreme Court cases.

THE UNEQUAL RIGHT TO A DEFENSE IN THE UNITED STATES: PUBLIC VERSUS PRIVATE ATTORNEYS

Think about the so-called dream team that O. J. Simpson employed during his double murder trial in 1995. Not only did Simpson enjoy the talents of one of the best attorneys in the world, he also enjoyed the talents of many of the best attorneys in the world, as well as some of the top expert witnesses. Yet, the "overwhelming majority of people accused of crimes" cannot afford even one attorney, and certainly not even one expert witness. In such cases, a defendant is granted *one attorney,* who will have few resources and thus little ability to subject the evidence against his or her client to any scrutiny. This explains how, in the face of evidence against their clients, public defenders see their clients as guilty anyway and thus not worthy of a trial (Cole and Smith, 2000), especially since they carry 350 cases or more at a time and they receive less than 5% of all criminal justice expenditures in any given year (Donziger, 1996: 188, 189).

> *P*ublic defenders carry 350 cases or more at a time and receive less than 5% of all criminal justice expenditures in any given year.

The American Bar Association calls the underfunding of defense attorneys for the indigent a "crisis of extraordinary proportions" (Tuohy, 1995). As explained by the National Criminal Justice Commission, " [t]he Constitutional right to an attorney is meaningful only to the extent that resources are available to adequately prepare a defense," which "includes access to investigators, expert witnesses, paralegals, and support staff, as well as time to research the law and prepare the legal motions" (Donziger, 1996: 189).

Everyone in the United States does have the right to counsel, as granted by the Sixth Amendment to the U.S. Constitution. And the U.S. Supreme Court granted indigents the right to a defense in felony cases in the case of *Gideon v. Wainwright* (1962). But although the poor thus have an *equal* right to counsel, they clearly do not have the right to *equal* counsel (Cole, 1999; Reiman, 1998). The average courthouse regular who is assigned by the court to indigent defendants has more than 1,000 cases a year to handle (Cole and Smith, 2000); he or she has no time to investigate the facts of a case and put on an appropriate and thorough defense. Compare this with prosecutors "who can draw on big police departments, teams of investigators and lawyers to prepare their cases." It's no wonder many prosecutors enjoy conviction rates of more than 90%. Even the "typical murder defendant has little money and is represented by an underpaid, overworked public defender" (Streisand, 1994: 63). Adding to the built-in bias against the typical criminal defendant in the United States is the fact that criminal defense attorneys are usually from "less prestigious law schools, have less training, and come from lower socioeconomic backgrounds" (Kappeler et al., 2000, citing Ladinsky, 1984).

> *E*veryone in the United States does have the right to counsel, as granted by the Sixth Amendment to the U.S. Constitution.

Why would a public defender, who is ideally responsible for upholding the Constitutional right to due process of law for the most vulnerable of all citizens—poor defendants faced with the incredible power of the government—take part in plea bargaining? Reiman (1998: 118) answers: "Because the public defender works in day-to-day contact with the prosecutor and the judge, the pressures on him or her to negotiate a plea as quickly as possible, instead of rocking the boat by threatening to go to trial, are even greater than those that work on court-assigned counsel."

Supreme Court rulings also permit and even encourage judges to treat inadequate defense attorneys as effective even when they fail to investigate the facts of the case or to cross-examine crucial witnesses, fall asleep during testimony, or even come to court drunk (Cole, 1999). Perhaps it is easy to understand the claim of Kappeler et al. (2000: 225) that public defenders are generally less likely than private attorneys to get cases against their clients dropped or to achieve an

> *S*upreme Court rulings permit and even encourage judges to treat inadequate defense attorneys as effective counsel even when these attorneys fail to investigate the facts of the case, do not cross-examine crucial witnesses, fall asleep during testimony, or even come to court drunk.

acquittal: "In essence, justice is correlated with the ability to pay by the hour."

People of color are also more likely than Caucasians to be represented by public defenders (Walker et al., 2000). Public defenders, although they are indeed "experts" in criminal practice, are still "among the most inexperienced" lawyers, often recent law school graduates in "positions . . . typically characterized by low salaries and limited support services" (Merlo and Benekos, 2000: 57).

THE "EXCEPTIONAL CASE" OF TRIAL

Cases that are not dismissed by the prosecutor and are not plea-bargained end up going to trial. That is, a trial results only when other forms of case disposition are either not sought or not obtained (Schmalleger, 2001). As noted earlier, trials are the exception to the rule of plea bargaining. They are very rare.

There are significant problems with the American trial process, most notably how rarely trials occur. Aside from that, several stages of the criminal trial process seem to result in biases against the poor and people of color. Before I move on to those stages and outline the main problems associated with bias, I want to point out that Americans charged with crimes are "innocent until proven guilty" of their crimes at trials. Americans ideally enjoy this presumption of innocence before and during trials. Former U.S. Supreme Court Justice Thurgood Marshall once said that American "principles of justice declare that the defendant is as innocent on the day before his

> *S*everal stages of the criminal trial process seem to result in biases against the poor and people of color.

trial as he is on the morning after his acquittal" (in Gaines et al., 2000: 338). This is the ideal, but do all Americans equally enjoy this presumption?

Stages of the Criminal Trial

Stages of the typical American trial include voir dire, opening statements, the presentation of the prosecution's case, the presentation of the defense's case, the calling of rebuttal witnesses, closing arguments by the prosecution, closing arguments by the defense, and jury instructions by the judge. After these stages, the jury is given the case by the judge and the deliberations begin.

> *S*tages of the typical U.S. trial include voir dire, opening statements, the presentation of the prosecution's case, the presentation of the defense's case, the calling of rebuttal witnesses, closing arguments by the prosecution, closing arguments by the defense, and jury instructions by the judge. After these stages end, the jury is given the case by the judge and the deliberations begin. Finally, the jury issues its verdict and, if the defendant is found guilty, the sentence is subsequently handed down by the judge.

Finally, the jury issues its verdict and, if the defendant is found guilty, the sentence is subsequently handed down by the judge (Peoples, 2000; Stuckey et al., 2001).

Voir dire

Voir dire, meaning "to speak the truth" (Gaines et al., 2000: 343), is an examination of potential jurors to ensure a fair trial for the defendant. Its ideal purpose is to gain a cross-section of the community so that the defendant can have a jury of his or her "peers." Potential jurors must answer questions verbally and/or in writing about their potential biases. Ideally, voir dire will result in an impartial jury for the trial of the accused. We want juries "to have no axes to grind, no prejudgments about the people or issues they confront. We also want them to have the ability to empathize with others, to evaluate credibility, to know what is fair" (Minow, 2000: 365). Thus, an unlimited number of jurors can be eliminated through "challenges for cause," if a potential bias is identified. A limited number also may be eliminated through "peremptory challenges," where no cause needs to be identified.

> *V*oir dire is a term that means "to speak the truth" (Gaines et al., 2000: 343). Voir dire is an examination of potential jurors to ensure a fair trial for the defendant. Its ideal purpose is to gain a cross-section of the community so that the defendant can have a jury of his or her peers.

There are at least three significant problems with the first stage of the criminal trial. First, some groups are underrepresented in jury pools. Second, peremptory challenges can be used against certain groups without explanation. Third, jury consultants can be used to help select sympathetic juries. Each of these problems results in a bias in favor of people with greater resources. I discuss these problems next.

Juries in the United States are drawn from voting lists and thus are less representative of poor people, people of color, the young, and the uneducated, because these members of society are less likely to vote. As a result, poor people, people of color, and young people are less likely to be represented by juries who are like them. If this affects the outcomes of cases, it would likely do so in a manner biased against these groups.

> *J*uries in the United States are drawn from voting lists and thus are less representative of poor people, people of color, the young, and the uneducated because these members of society vote less than other groups. Given this fact, poor people, people of color, and young people are less likely to be represented by juries who are like them.

Prosecutors and defense attorneys can use peremptory challenges to eliminate potential jurors without any explanation. Thus, lawyers can reject people for jury service on the basis of their style of dress or their demeanor without giving any valid reason. Bradley (2000: 508) claims that "peremptory challenges are largely a matter of wild guesses about how jurors will decide the case based upon their answers to one or two questions in the voir dire." Even if this is true, peremptory challenges allow a very troublesome practice. As in the use of drug courier profiles by police, these challenges allow attorneys to eliminate people who they feel "look wrong" (*The Economist*, 1998; Kadish, 1997). Additionally, racial minorities can be, and often are, denied the opportunity to serve on juries, even though rejecting potential jurors on the basis of race is specifically illegal based on the Supreme Court case of *Batson v. Kentucky* (1986) (Crook, 1995; Johnson, 1993; Reuben, 1996; Siebert, 1999). Lawyers use race as a proxy to develop peremptory challenges, in part because of racial myths and stereotypes, in part because courts allow subjective qualifications for jury service, and in part because it simply benefits their cases (Kennedy, 1997). Minorities are simultaneously inhibited from jury service for a variety of other reasons, many intimately related to their social class, social status, and past run-ins with the law (e.g., see Fukurai et al., 1993).

> $\mathscr{P}$rosecutors and defense attorneys can use peremptory challenges to eliminate potential jurors without any explanation.

The reality of jury selection, very different from the ideal, is that neither the defense nor the prosecution actually seeks an impartial jury. Barber (1994) explains that each side seeks out a jury that is likely to be partial to their side of the story. The problem with this for justice is that poor people and people of color are less able to hire professional jury consultants to analyze potential jurors so that they can select a jury more likely to sympathize with the defendant (Smith, 1993; Varinsky, 1993). Wealthy individuals, such as O. J. Simpson, can afford to hire the best jury consultants that money can buy and, in essence, have a much greater chance that a jury sympathetic with the defendant will find reasonable doubt and thus vote to acquit (McElhaney, 1998; Smith, 1993; Varinsky, 1993). The jury in the O. J. Simpson case was hand-picked with the help of a millionaire jury consultant who surveyed thousands of people prior to voir dire in order to pick a sympathetic jury. The defense was able to isolate eight questions from an 85-page questionnaire that would identify jurors sympathetic to the defense's argument (Miller, 1995). The final O. J. Simpson jury was made up entirely of people who did not regularly read the newspaper, 75% of whom thought that Simpson was not likely to have committed the murders because he excelled at football, and 42% of whom thought that it was acceptable to use force on a family member (Davis and Davis, 1995). Clearly, everything about the O. J. Simpson case was unusual. Yet, it serves as an excellent example of how jury consultants can be used to create a jury that will find reasonable doubt.

> $\mathscr{T}$he reality of jury selection, much different from its ideal, is that neither the defense nor the prosecution actually seeks an impartial jury.

The National Criminal Justice Commission outlines many other problems with the American jury system. Jurors are exposed to endless waiting, must put up with insensitive questioning, are sometimes sequestered from their families, may lose substantial income, and can be eliminated without just cause through peremptory challenge (Donziger, 1996: 184).

Opening statements

After a jury is impaneled, both sides of the case (the prosecution and the defense) make opening statements in order to lay the foundation of their cases. Opening statements are not allowed to be argumentative and cannot be considered as evidence by the jury. Opening statements are road maps laying out where each side intends to take its case.

Prosecution presents its case

Because the prosecution has the burden of proving its case beyond a reasonable doubt, it presents its case first. Its goal is to present relevant facts to the jury that prove that the named defendant(s) committed the named crime(s). Ingraham (1994) explains that because defendants are innocent in the eyes of the law, they do not have to present a case unless they feel the prosecution can prove its case that they are guilty of crimes beyond a reasonable doubt. Rush (2000: 113) defines reasonable doubt as "[t]he state of mind of jurors in which, after the comparison and consideration of all the evidence, they cannot say that they feel an abiding conviction, a moral certainty, of the truth of a criminal charge against a defendant." Essentially, if another theory of the crime for which the defendant is accused is reasonably likely to be true, jurors are required by law to find the defendant not guilty of the crime, even if they think the person is actually guilty of the act(s). Why do we have such a high standard of proof to establish legal guilt at criminal trials? "This high standard of proof in criminal cases reflects a fundamental social value—the belief that it is worse to convict an innocent individual than to let a guilty one go free." At least, that is the ideal (Rush, 2000: 113).

The reality of the prosecution is that it is generally much more powerful and better equipped to present its case than the defense. Most accused criminals, who are indigent and thus cannot hire private attorneys, do not have the resources to subject the state's evidence to meaningful scrutiny. This means little or no investigation of the charges against the defendant, no expert witnesses to rebut or refute the prosecution's case, and very short trials. The presumption of innocence may be a myth for most criminal defendants in the United States.

> *The* reality of the prosecution is that it is generally much more powerful and better equipped to present its case than the defense. Most accused criminals, who are indigent and thus cannot hire private attorneys, do not have the resources needed to subject the state's evidence to meaningful scrutiny.

Defense presents its case

If the defense attorney feels the defense must answer the charges of the prosecution, the defense will present its own case. It is not required that the defense present a case. If the defense feels that the prosecution's case is weak, it can ask that the charges be dropped against the defendant through a directed verdict. If the defense puts on its case, it will either provide contrary evidence to the prosecution, offer an alibi (e.g., that the accused was somewhere else at the time of the crime), or present an affirmative defense (which admits that the defendant committed the act or acts of which he or she is charged but that the defendant is nevertheless not guilty of a "crime"). The purpose of the defense presentation is to raise reasonable doubt so that the defendant will not be convicted. Once again, wealthier clients who can afford better attorneys are more likely to ensure that reasonable doubt will be found because they are more likely to subject the evidence to independent examinations, to construct alternative theories of the crime, and to hire expert witnesses in their defense.

Rebuttal witnesses

After each side has presented its primary case, both sides have the option of calling rebuttal witnesses to discredit the testimony of previous witnesses for the other side. Clearly, poor clients and people of color are generally at a disadvantage here because of their lack of resources and the quality of their attorneys.

Closing arguments

At the end of each side's case, prosecutors and defense attorneys are permitted to make an argument to the jury that presents the facts in a manner that is most favorable to their side. Prosecutors might choose to ignore evidence pointing to the innocence of the defendant, and defense attorneys might choose to point out alternative theories of who committed the crime(s). Truth is irrelevant here; what counts are the strong points of each side's case. Obviously, attorneys with some incentive to argue vehemently for the benefit of their clients will make better closing arguments on their clients' behalf.

Jury instructions

After closing arguments, the judge instructs the jury as to how the law bears on their decisions. At a minimum, the jury instructions will include a definition of "reasonable doubt" and will explain what elements of the crime or crimes must be established to show guilt of the defendant. Both sides will meet with the judge and hammer out the specific content and wording of the instructions. Because of the importance of jury instructions, "one would expect jury instructions to be carefully drafted to maximize juror comprehension, but they are not" (Steele and Thornburg, 2000: 118). Some research shows that jurors may not even understand jury instructions given to them, a frightening thought given that the jurors are expected to follow these instructions carefully when deliberating about the guilt or innocence of the accused (Dattu, 1998; Steele and Thornburg, 1991). Once again, private attorneys of powerful and wealthy citizens have a significant advantage here, as they can assure that the instructions are most favorable for their clients.

Jury deliberations

Once juries are given the case by the judge, they may consider only the evidence entered into the trial to determine whether the person(s) charged with the crime(s) is/are legally guilty beyond a reasonable doubt. In almost every state, the verdict must be unanimous, or else the result is a hung jury and a mistrial. It is hard to know whether juries follow the law in making decisions because of the secrecy afforded to jury deliberations. Much research into jury deliberations (mainly from mock trials) shows that jurors consider a lot of what they are not supposed to consider, including the defendant's appearance, his or her past record, and other facts not admitted to trial but learned about from other sources (Devine, 1988). Postinterview verdicts with jury members, mock juries, a few televised jury deliberations, and even transcripts of jury deliberations on the Internet show that juries frequently consider evidence they should not consider (MacCoun, 1990; Kassin, 2000). This is why some argue that jury deliberations should be open to judicial review, in order to make sure that justice is being done according to the law (e.g., see Ruprecht, 1997). Gershman (2000) maintains that jurors consider strong opening statements (which may include promises of evidence to be presented even when such evidence is not delivered during trial) and purposefully mentioned inadmissible evidence, which is not supposed to be considered by the jury.

> *O*nce juries are given the case by the judge, they may consider only the evidence entered into the trial to determine whether the person(s) charged with the crime(s) is/are legally guilty beyond a reasonable doubt.

CONCLUSION

Scholars have argued that no trial system is deserving of public respect if it cannot be trusted to acquit the innocent and convict the guilty, if it fails to treat those who come into contact with the system with respect, and if does not appropriate judicial resources wisely. The American court system, highly consistent with a crime control model of criminal justice, handles cases in an administrative manner rather than an adversarial manner. More resources are given to prosecutors than to defense attorneys, adding to the immense power of American prosecutors. The clear evidence of bias in plea bargaining and the use of bail and preventive detention, as well as the low quality of defense afforded to those most in need, provides further evidence that the criminal justice system fails to do justice as expected. In essence, the courts have been left to do the best they can with increasing numbers of cases and relatively less resources than police and corrections.

ISSUE IN DEPTH
Wrongful Convictions

It is impossible to know how many innocent people are convicted of crimes they did not commit each year. Huff, Rattner, and Sagarin (1996: 53), in their book, *Convicted but Innocent: Wrongful Conviction and Public Policy*, write: "Quite clearly, there is no accurate, scientific way to determine how many innocent people are convicted, or put another way, how many of those convicted of crimes are innocent." Unfortunately, we also do not know how many innocent people *are executed* for crimes they did not commit. One study found that 343 persons were wrongfully convicted of capital crimes since 1900, including 23 who were actually executed and 22 others who came within 72 hours of being executed (Bedau and Radelet, 1987). I will revisit the issue of wrongful convictions in capital cases in Chapter Eleven. What follows here is a brief discussion of some actual cases in which people have been wrongfully convicted of crimes, as well as the factors that produce wrongful convictions in the United States.

Of most importance for the main argument of this book is that wrongful convictions are obviously a direct threat to justice—to justice as an outcome (because the factually guilty are not punished for their wrongdoings and because innocent people do not deserve to be punished) and to justice as a process (because wrongful convictions suggest that the criminal justice system is not fair and unbiased). In the Foreword to Huff et al.'s book, Dinitz (1996: xii–xiii) states it this way:

> Wrongful convictions, however infrequent, are anathema to the American due process system and to all who believe in the fairness of our law enforcement and judicial systems and the constitutional protections guaranteed individual citizens. Not only do such wrongful convictions violate trust in our system, but . . . such convictions undermine public safety by leaving the "true" positives—the guilty—in the community to commit future grave offenses.

So, a lot is at stake when wrongful convictions occur. First, the "conviction of the innocent leaves the guilty free to commit more crimes, thus threatening public safety" and "each instance of the conviction of an innocent enhances the possibility that there will be more not-guilty verdicts against the truly guilty" (Huff et al., 1996: 12) because of a distrust in the government resulting from wrongful convictions.

As I have stated, no one can know for sure how often errors are made, but a statement by Huff et al. (1996: xxii) suggests the significance of the problem. They write: "the American criminal justice system is so large and has so many arrests each year that even if the system were 99.5% accurate, it would still generate more than 10,000 wrongful convictions a year for the eight serious index crimes alone" and even more for relatively less serious crimes. Huff et al. mailed a survey to various actors in the Ohio criminal justice system in order to estimate how frequently wrongful convictions occur; they make what they call "a conservative prevalence estimation made by a largely conservative sample," mostly because the people they surveyed would have reasons to deny the wrongful conviction of the innocent (p. 55). After throwing out cases where there were serious and reasonable doubts about the innocence of the convicted parties, along with cases in which people were punished and subsequently released but their innocence was not clearly established, they were left with individual cases where actual innocence is known. Some of these cases are discussed in this section. The first of these would not be included by Huff et al., for there is still some doubt about the convicted man's guilt; yet, I include it because it points out the absurdity of how our system sometimes operates.

- James Hicks was a 31-year-old man who had served 7 years of a 10-year sentence for the murder of his wife after she disappeared in Maine. He denied on the stand that he had killed his wife and also admitted to having been living for about 5 years with another woman, with whom he had fathered two children. After being sentenced to prison, he attempted to marry his girlfriend but was denied a marriage license because there was no death certificate for his presumed dead wife. Huff et al. (1996: 7) write: "So, although he was convicted of murdering his wife on the basis of evidence that convinced 12 men and women beyond a reasonable doubt, the authorities entertained some doubt that his wife was dead."

In the remaining cases, we know the wrong people were actually convicted and/or punished for crimes they did not commit:

- David Fedderson is a Caucasian man convicted of raping a woman he did not know in Dubuque, Iowa. The victim identified Fedderson as her attacker as he walked in a crowd of people after her attack. Fedderson was walking along a street he normally walked along, and he had no history of violent behavior; but he also had no alibi for his whereabouts at the time of the crime. Only one person, the victim, saw the attacker, so her eyewitness testimony alone led to his conviction for rape. When Fedderson rose to speak on his behalf after his conviction, he did not express remorse for his actions or sympathy for the victim, for he *knew* he was actually innocent of the crime. Fedderson spent two years in prison before he was finally able to convince all parties that he was in fact innocent. The same judge who convicted him now set him free and stated that the fact that an innocent man could be convicted "is scary."

- Nathaniel Carter was sentenced to life imprisonment after being convicted of the stabbing death of Clarice Herndon. His conviction was based almost solely on the testimony of the actual killer, his ex-wife, who was found by police at the scene with blood on her hands (they assumed she, too, had been attacked). After Carter had spent two years in prison, his ex-wife came forward, after being promised immunity from being prosecuted, and testified that she had committed the murder.

- Johnny Binder is an African American man convicted in Houston, Texas, for a robbery committed by a group of African Americans driving a yellow Cadillac similar to Binder's car. Binder lived in Houston but was in Dallas at the time of the crime. Binder had no criminal record and knew he was innocent of the crime, but after hearing about the make and color of the car involved in the crime, he voluntarily went to the police to tell them that he was not involved in the crime. Binder was arrested and convicted by an all-white jury, despite the fact that several eyewitnesses claimed that he was not involved. After Binder had spent four years in prison, the real criminals were discovered, and Binder was taken back to court where, however, he could not be set free or given a new trial by the judge. Binder was returned to his cell. An appeal for a writ of habeas corpus was denied because "it was not the appropriate route to be taken when there is a claim for a new trial based on newly discovered evidence" (Huff et al., 1996: 18). Binder was eventually set free by the judge, even though she did not have the authority to do so, and the state granted him a special pardon, which did not contain anything about Binder's actual innocence.

- Todd Neely was a young man in Florida convicted of raping one of his neighbors. A woman in Neely's apartment complex had been raped by a boy she described as no older than 16 who wore braces on his teeth. Neely was 18 years old, did not have braces, and was 11 miles away having dinner with his parents at the time of the rape. The victim picked out a photograph of Neely from a photo line-up, but the photograph was several years old and showed Neely at an age more similar to that of the attacker. It turned out that the real rapist was a 14-

year-old boy who also lived in the complex and who had a history of exhibition-ism and voyeurism in the neighborhood (he also had told friends that he was the one who committed the rape). Neely was eventually freed, after spending 92 days in jail, mostly because his family spent $300,000 of their own money inves-tigating the case. This case shows what can happen when the police and prose-cution zero in on a suspect and ignore obvious evidence of his or her innocence.

Given all of these shocking cases, you may wonder why such wrongful convic-tions occur. According to Huff et al., the most common cause, responsible for more than half of wrongful convictions, is eyewitness identification—that is, victims and witnesses who pick out the wrong person even though they may truly believe that the people they have identified are the real criminals. Also of significance is

> *police and prosecutorial overzealousness:* the anxiety to solve a case; the ease with which one having such anxiety is willing to believe, on the slightest evidence of the most negligible nature, that the culprit is in hand; the willingness to use improper, unethical, and illegal means to obtain a conviction when one believes that the per-son at the bar is guilty. (Huff et al., 1996: 64, emphasis in original)

EYEWITNESS TESTIMONY

Consider the case of Jeffrey Streeter, convicted and sentenced to a year in jail for the assault of an elderly man. Streeter, who was uninvolved in the case, had been sitting outside the courtroom when the defense attorney asked him to come in and sit in the defendant's usual place. Although the defendant was also in the courtroom, three eyewitnesses to the assault picked Streeter as the man who had committed the crime, as if, because Streeter was sitting where the defendant normally sits, he must be guilty. Streeter spent one night in jail before the error was realized. As this defense atorney had set out to demon-strate, eyewitness testimony is patently unreliable. Yet, many consider it to be undeniable proof of guilt, and cases lacking eyewitness identification are often dismissed as "purely circumstantial" and thus inherently weaker.

Research clearly demonstrates that human brains (of witnesses and victims of crimes, for example) store information from environmental experiences in chem-ical bits and pieces. When attempting to recall events, our brains actually recon-struct these events from the fragments stored in our brains. During the stages of acquisition, retention, and retrieval, falsehoods are pulled into our memories so that we "remember" things that really did not happen (Loftus, 1979). As one example, a victim of crime may retrieve pieces of information gleaned from dis-cussions with friends and families, news clippings, and other sources, and may wrongly attribute these recollections to the criminal event. Buckhout (1974: 23) explains why eyewitness identification is inherently unreliable:

> Research and courtroom experience provide ample evidence that an eyewitness to a crime is being asked to be something and do something that a normal human being was not created to be or do. Human perception is sloppy and uneven, albeit

remarkably effective in serving our need to create structure out of experience. In an investigation or in court, however, a witness is often asked to play the role of a kind of tape recorder on whose tape the events of the crime have left an impression. . . . Both sides, and usually the witness, too, succumb to the fallacy that everything was recorded and can be played back through questioning.

The criminal justice process serves to reinforce the likelihood that innocent people will be wrongly convicted. For example, witnesses and victims may see a photo lineup or actual physical lineup of real people and then choose one as the offender. From that point on, the face of the person picked will be the offender, even if it is not the actual offender. When asked to pick out the offender at court, witnesses and victims will point to that person as the offender because his or her identity matches that of the person picked out from the lineup. The memory of the face from the crime may be replaced with the memory of the face from the lineup. That this may be the wrong face is not considered by the person who is convinced he or she has chosen the right person (e.g., see Brown, Defenbacher, and Sturgill, 1977).

As a college student, I was one of two witnesses to a failed burglary attempt. Ironically, I had just watched a video in one of my criminology classes about the unreliability of eyewitness identification. In the video, a college professor set up an experiment whereby a stranger walked into the classroom, took the professor's bag from the desk, and then ran away. After the offender had left, the professor said, "All I recall is that the man had a large nose." Many of the subjects noted to the police that they recalled the man having a distinctive nose (even though he did not). Other witnesses (who were wearing hats) said they remembered the man wearing a hat (even though he did not). Most of the students could not pick out the actual offender from a photo lineup when the offender's photo was included. When the actual offender's photo was not included, many of the student witnesses picked out an innocent person.

So, when I witnessed the burglary attempt, I made sure I was prepared to provide a perfect description to the police. Here's what happened: Late one night I was up sick, unable to sleep. I heard someone hanging around outside, checking the doors and window screens. After listening for a while, I heard someone trying to force his way into my next door neighbor's bedroom window. I went outside to see what was going on, as did a neighbor on the other side of the apartment, and we scared the offender away. He ran right by me, so I got a great look at him. I followed him down the stairs and proceeded to watch him climb a fence in order to get away. As I watched him run away, I took mental notes about the offender's appearance.

When the police arrived, they asked me what he looked like. My description was very precise and included details about the offender's height, weight, hair color and style, approximate age, clothing, shoes—even shoelaces! About two hours later (around 4:00 A.M.), the police came back to my apartment to ask me to accompany them to the rear of an abandoned house, where they had apprehended someone who resembled the offender. Upon arriving, the police shone a bright spotlight on the man and asked me if this was the offender. This man had been tracked by police dogs from the scene of the attempted burglary (when he climbed the fence to get away, his watch, along with his scent, got stuck at the top of the fence). The apprehended man was *exactly* like the man I described, with one significant exception—he was slightly shorter and heavier than I remembered. The police asked me if I could be sure that this was the man (I could not ethically say that I was 100% sure it was he, even though it had to be based on the dogs tracking his scent). He was too stocky to be the offender I saw.

As we waited in a police squad car, I asked the other witness what he had told the police, and he said that he thought the offender was taller and thinner than the man they had apprehended. This made me very uncomfortable—how could it be that we both had been so wrong about what we thought the offender looked like, given that the man the police apprehended was wearing the same outfit, including the same shoes and even shoelaces, had the same hair color and braids as I had described, and was also a Hispanic male? As I have thought about that experience over the years, I realized that my run-in with the burglar was not unlike the experiences of most crime victims and witnesses: I saw the man very briefly, it was late at night, I was tired when I witnessed the crime; and so on. Why shouldn't I expect to be wrong about some details? More important, how can the criminal justice system be so dependent on eyewitness identifications such as this one when they are so unreliable? Yet, prosecutors are more willing to press charges and pursue convictions in court when eyewitnesses are part of the case, and jurors are more likely to convict given eyewitness testimony, even given results like those in the cases described here.

OVERZEALOUSNESS

As for overzealousness by police and prosecutors, I restrict my comments to the following main point: we must expect our police and prosecutors to pursue arrests and convictions zealously (in the pursuit of justice as an outcome); it is the current "tough on crime" environment that makes overzealousness more likely. Huff et al. (1996: 71) write that such overzealousness

> might come from a desire to add points to a scorecard, to enhance a reputation as a tough and successful prosecutor because of an impending election, or to receive commendation and promotion in the police department for having nabbed a vicious criminal and solved a difficult case . . . may sometimes derive from the inability, unwillingness, or lack of funds and personnel available to police to make true and proper investigations . . . [and] might also conceal bigotry and racism, or sometimes greed.

Other sources of overzealousness may be "the inability, unwillingness, or lack of funds and personnel available to police to make true and proper investigations."

Partly because of the overzealousness of the police and prosecution, as well as because of the presumption of guilt that accompanies an arrest and the immense power of the prosecution relative to the typical defense attorney, many innocent people will plead guilty (and some even confess to the police) to crimes they did not commit. Many of these plea bargains result in immediate freedom for the accused, through either release for time served or a probation sentence. Remember—a plea of guilty is not necessarily an admission of guilt. It can be as much a strategy for avoiding punishment as a not guilty plea is by a factually guilty suspect.

Consider this case involving presumption of guilt: Willie Jones, a 33-year-old African American man with a criminal record involving many minor criminal acts, was arrested for using Connecticut subway tokens on the New York City subway system. Jones was remanded to jail awaiting his arraignment, referred to a public defender, and thereafter confronted with a long rap sheet of serious crimes and an outstanding warrant for jumping bail on another charge. Jones correctly pointed out that the rap sheet was not his, that it must belong to another Willie Jones. The other Jones had a file with no photo and no fingerprints, so the police and his own attorney did not believe that he was *really* "innocent." He spent three months in jail awaiting trial because he refused to plead guilty to the serious charge for which the other Jones was accused. On his trial date three months later, the mistake was realized, and Jones was released. So much for "innocent until proven guilty."

I will concede that many of those wrongfully convicted, like Willie Jones, do in fact have criminal records. Some may assert that this gives the police reason to suspect them of future criminal activity. I want to point out the irony of this expectation: society gets upset when criminals continue to offend after their punishment, even though we simultaneously seem to expect them to commit more crimes.

At the extreme end of overzealousness are false confessions. Police may occasionally resort to any and all tactics necessary to gain convictions of people they truly believe to be guilty so that the end—a conviction, or justice as an outcome—in their minds justifies the means, violating justice as a process. In fact, some early texts on criminal interrogations and confessions encourage trickery by police to encourage confessions, which is actually allowed by courts (e.g., see Inbau and Reid, 1967). Cases of false confessions abound in the United States.

The case of James Richardson, a poor African American farm worker with an IQ of only 77, stands out. Richardson confessed to poisoning seven of his own children and stepchildren and was imprisoned and sentenced to death in 1968. Richardson served 22 years before being freed for this crime, which he did not commit. The prosecution, suggesting that Richardson laced his children's lunches with poison and planned their deaths in advance, showed evidence that Richardson had sought life insurance policies for his children right before their deaths (in fact, a door-to-door insurance salesman had visited the day before and simply left his card). The children's babysitter, who was ultimately admitted to medical care for Alzheimer's disease, admitted more than one hundred times that she had killed the children. Richardson said he had been beaten into confessing his crime. The sheriff's deputy who allegedly coerced the confession out of Richardson probably believed that Richardson was guilty, but his unjust means resulted in an unjust outcome.

Such cases serve as the ugliest incidents uncovered by the research of Huff et al. (1996), cases that "involved outright lying, the fabrication and alteration of evidence, the intimidation and coaching of witnesses, and perjury and the suborning of perjury" (p. 143). As I stated earlier, my assertion is that these tactics, and thus wrongful convictions, are more likely in the current get-tough attitude promoted by politicians and emphasized in media coverage of crime and criminal justice. The research shows that wrongful convictions often start with a presumption of guilt on the part of criminal justice actors (characteristic of a crime control model of justice) and are made more likely because of numerous system breakdowns (which occur more often in the assembly-line process of American criminal justice).

Discussion Questions

- Why is the U.S. court system called a *dual court system*?
- Define the term *jurisdiction*.
- Contrast trial courts with appellate courts.
- List and discuss the key functions of U.S. courts.
- Identify the main actors in the courtroom workgroup and discuss the main roles of each member.
- What factors affect whether prosecutors decide to press charges against accused criminals?
- What important decisions are made during the pretrial phase of courts?
- What is bail?
- What is meant by saying that bail is not intended to be punishment?
- Identify the main types of bail and discuss alternatives to bail.
- How is preventive detention justified?
- What are some of the main problems associated with the administration of bail?
- What is plea bargaining?
- Explain how plea bargaining is inconsistent with the ideal of justice as a process.
- Do you think that guilty pleas are ever coerced? Why or why not?

- Is there a difference in the quality of the defense offered by private versus public defense attorneys? Why or why not?
- Given how rare trials are in the United States, does the typical defendant have a reasonable expectation of trial?
- Identify and discuss the main stages of the criminal trial.
- What are some problems with the voir dire process?
- What factors produce wrongful convictions?

CHAPTER NINE

PUNISHMENT: DOES IT WORK

AND IS IT FAIR?

KEY CONCEPTS

- An introduction to sentencing
- Why do we punish?
- Methods of punishment
- Is punishment effective?
- Bias in the sentencing process
- Issue in Depth: What Works, What Doesn't

INTRODUCTION

This chapter examines the posttrial phase of the criminal courts—sentencing of the guilty by the courts to some form of punishment. I illustrate types of sentences available to sentencing judges and methods of punishment in the United States, including probation, imprisonment, and intermediate sanctions. A detailed discussion of why we punish provides insight into what's wrong with the American approach to punishment. I also show what we have learned about the effectiveness of various types of punishment. The chapter concludes with an examination of bias in the sentencing process. Again, clear evidence of sentencing bias is illustrated, lending support to the notion that the criminal justice system fails to do justice.

AN INTRODUCTION TO SENTENCING

What Is Sentencing?

A *sentence* is a penalty or sanction imposed on a person by a court upon conviction for a criminal offense (Rush, 2000: 295). For example, when a person is convicted of murder, he or she may be sentenced to the death penalty, life in prison, some other term of imprisonment, or, in rare cases, a long term of probation and/or house arrest.

> $\mathcal{A}$ sentence is the penalty or sanction imposed by the court upon a person's conviction for a criminal offense.

A sentence, then, is any criminal sanction or punishment. Herbert Packer, in his book *The Limits of the Criminal Sanction* (1968), defines *punishment* as inflicting pain or unpleasant circumstances for an offense against legal rules on an offender or alleged offender for his or her offense, intentionally administered by human beings within a legal system that grants authority to do so. He argued that the only valid justifications for punishment were deterrence and retribution on an offender whose moral responsibility had been established beyond a reasonable doubt. I will define deterrence and retribution later in this chapter. Similarly, Hart (1968: 4) defined punishment as the infliction of pain for offenses against legal rules, applied to the actual offender, that is intentionally administered by a legal authority (cited in Jeffery, 1990).

Types of Sentences

The three primary forms of sentences are determinate sentences, indeterminate sentences, and mandatory sentences. Determinate sentences set forth a specified criminal sanction for a particular type of crime. Based on the severity of the offense, determinate sentences are generally the same for each person convicted of a particular type of crime. Although determinate or fixed sentences are generally set by law, judges have limited discretion when it comes to passing each sentence, based on certain aggravating and mitigating factors. As defined by Rush (2000: 8), *aggravating factors* are "circumstances relating to the commission of a crime which cause its gravity to be greater than that of the average instance of the given type of offense." For example, any crime committed with a weapon is considered more serious than one without a weapon, so the presence of a weapon would be an aggravating factor at sentencing. Thus, a rape committed at gunpoint may lead to a greater sentence than a rape without a weapon. *Mitigating factors* reduce the perceived seriousness of crimes (Rush, 2000: 216). Any motives of the offender that may make crimes more understandable to the court may be considered as mitigating factors. For example, a bank robber who is unarmed, does not pretend to have a weapon, and is truly motivated by the hunger of his children may receive a less severe sentence than a ruthless, armed bank robber motivated only by monetary gain.

> $\mathcal{S}$entences come in three primary forms: determinate, indeterminate, and mandatory.

Indeterminate sentences are not fixed on the basis of the crime but are a function of characteristics unique to each offender. Thus, indeterminate sentences establish a range within which each individual offender may be sanctioned, somewhere between the minimum and maximum

> $\mathcal{D}$eterminate sentences set forth a specified criminal sanction for a particular type of crime. Based on the severity of the offense, determinate sentences are generally the same for each person convicted of a particular type of crime.

allowable sentences allowed in the law. Indeterminate sentences give judges more discretion in establishing what any given offender may receive for his or her crimes. The advantage of indeterminate sentences is that they allow judges to take into account both aggravating and mitigating factors. One murder may be either more or less serious than other murders; indeterminate sentences allow judges to reflect this in the sentences they hand down. The main drawback of indeterminate sentences is that they allow judges to abuse their discretion. That is, there is at least the potential that longer sentences will be passed down against particular groups of people who are convicted of the same offenses as other groups. For example, judges may consciously or subconsciously treat African Americans more harshly than Caucasians for identical offenses, especially given that African Americans are not well represented in courtroom workgroups.

> *I*ndeterminate sentences are not fixed on the basis of the crime; rather, they are a function of characteristics unique to each offender. Indeterminate sentences establish a range of minimum and maximum allowable sentences within which each individual offender may be sanctioned.

To address such concerns, many states and the federal government have passed sentencing guidelines that minimize the amount of discretion to which judges are entitled when considering sentences for convicted offenders. Judges weigh various factors in determining the most appropriate sentence. Generally, the most important factors include the seriousness of the offense and the offender's prior record; the more serious the offense and the longer the prior record, the more severe the sentence will be. This allows for biases in the criminal law and policing to affect sentences.

Mandatory sentences simply establish a minimum sanction that must be served upon conviction for a criminal offense. Thus, everyone who is convicted of a crime that calls for a mandatory sentence will serve that amount of time. As explained by Walker (1998: 130): "Mandatory sentencing usually means two things: mandatory imprisonment for a certain crime and/or a mandatory minimum prison term." Judges have no discretion in mandatory sentencing because, by definition, the sentence is mandatory. A specified imprisonment term must be given to the convicted offender by law. As I showed in Chapter Six, the war on drugs is responsible for a large share of mandatory sentences. Consider, for example, 20-year-old Nicole Richardson of Mobile, Alabama, who was dating a drug dealer. When approached by an undercover officer about where to buy some drugs, Nicole said to talk to her boyfriend. Her sentence was 10 years in prison with no possibility of parole; her boyfriend, who cooperated with authorities, received a 5-year imprisonment sentence (Donziger, 1996: 25). Sentencing judges, with no discretion in mandatory sentencing, are generally opposed to it: Sileo (1993) reports that 90% of federal judges and 75% of state judges do not support mandatory sentences.

> *M*andatory sentences simply establish a minimum sanction that must be served upon conviction of a criminal offense. Everyone convicted of a crime that calls for a mandatory sentence will serve that amount of time.

Good examples of mandatory sentences are the so-called three-strikes-and-you're-out laws that have been passed by more than half the states in the United States. These laws usually require that upon conviction for a third felony, the offender will be sentenced to a period of imprisonment for the remainder of his or her natural life: "Neither the particular circumstances, nor the seriousness of the crimes charged, nor the duration of time that has elapsed between crimes is given consideration" in three-strikes laws (Beckett and Sasson, 2000: 180). These laws also mandate that judges must "ignore mitigating factors in the background of offenders, as well as their ties to community, employment status, potential for rehabilitation, and obligations to children." Tonry (1995) argues that mandatory sentences are unwise because they do not allow judges to consider mitigating factors such as economic deprivation.

I will discuss whether three-strikes laws make any sense at all later in this chapter. The following box highlights some important facts about these laws.

Facts about "three strikes" laws

- According to a 1997 National Institute of Justice (NIJ) report, between 1993 and 1995 alone, 24 states and the federal government passed three-strikes laws. In 20 of these states, the law requires three strikes for a mandatory sentence. In many of these states, at least one strike must be a violent felony. And in 12 of these states, the mandatory term of punishment is life without the possibility of parole. California's law, which has been the most scrutinized, only requires that two of the offenses be serious felonies, whereas the last strike can be for any crime. This explains why one person was sentenced as a three-strikes offender for stealing four chocolate chip cookies from a restaurant (Elikann, 1996).
- The logic of three-strikes laws is to increase penalties for second offenses and to require life imprisonment without possibility of parole for third offenses.
- Many states, such as California, passed laws that were intended primarily for violent offenders but that failed to specify this intent. Many nonviolent offenders are being incarcerated under this law. Perhaps this is why California's law will cost about $5 billion or more each year—five times more than originally expected (Greenwood et al., 1994). The NIJ (1997: 1) report states: "The vast majority of California 'strike' inmates have been sentenced under the two-strikes provision and for nonviolent crimes."
- Three-strikes laws are based on a false premise that "an increasingly larger portion of serious crimes are committed by recidivating felons" (Welsh and Harris, 1999: xii).
- Experts estimate that every single dollar of new money in the state will have to be used to pay for this effort.
- Three-strikes inmates in California are about 13 times as likely to be African Americans as Caucasians—43% of them in one study (Greenwood et al., 1994) were African American, even though they make up only 7% of the state's population and 20% of the state's felony arrests.
- One "three-striker" is Michael Garcia, who stole a $5.62 package of chuck steak from a grocery store after his mother's social security check

failed to arrive on time (Schiraldi, Sussman, and Hyland, 1994). His previous strikes also were nonviolent offenses.

- The California three-strikes law is about four times as likely to be used against a person for marijuana possession than for murder, rape, and kidnaping combined. Specifically, 85% of California's sentenced inmates were for nonviolent offenses, including 192 for marijuana possession (versus 40 murderers, 25 rapists, and 24 kidnappers).

- Most Americans support three-strikes laws. According to Lacayo (1994), 81% of Americans support life imprisonment for persons convicted of three serious crimes. One Gallup poll found that 78% of respondents believed that their local courts did not deal harshly enough with criminals (Maguire and Flanagan, 1997).

Truth-in-sentencing laws are also examples of mandatory sentences. These laws, which have been passed by as many as 40 states, require that before offenders can be released, they must serve a certain percentage of their sentence, usually 85% (Gaines, Kaune, and Miller, 2000: 381). Although truth-in-sentencing laws may sound logical, what they do is eliminate reductions in sentencing for good behavior and mandate that correctional facilities keep inmates in prison for longer periods of time than they would normally serve. In some states, these longer sentences have created an extraordinary burden because of the added expense to correctional budgets and the growth of overcrowding problems.

Another example of mandatory sentencing is seen in the federal sentencing guidelines put into effect in 1987. The range of possible sentences was reduced, meaning that judge discretion was minimized, and discretionary early release from prison was abolished. Generally speaking, prison terms increased as a result of such mandatory sentencing revisions. A fundamental problem with these federal sentencing guidelines is that those criminal offenders who have information on other crimes may get lesser sentences than those without. This is because of Section 5K1.1 of the guidelines, which in essence allows prosecutors to use their discretion in charging to give breaks to cooperative defendants (Walker, 1998: 136). Given the definitions of justice in Chapter One, such practices can be considered unjust, as small-time offenders who have no information to give to prosecutors may get more severe sentences than big-time offenders who simply know more.

Walker (1998: 136) concludes that mandatory sentences are responsible in part for the shift of power in the courts to prosecutors, as well as for "unduly harsh" punishments for some crimes. Tonry (1992: 243) states it very clearly: "Mandatory penalties do not work." The American Bar Association has concluded that no mandatory sentencing should be in effect for any category of offenses.

> The longest sentence actually imposed by a court was 10,000 years! The sentence was imposed in Tuscaloosa, Alabama, on Dudley Wayne Kyzer, age 40, for a triple murder in 1981.

Although the longest time a person can actually serve is the term of his or her natural life, as in the case of mandatory life sentences, the longest sentence actually imposed by a court was 10,000 years! The sentence was imposed in Tuscaloosa, Alabama, on Dudley Wayne Kyzer, age 40, for a triple murder in 1981. Obviously, no one can ever serve such a sentence—they are handed down by judges who want to make political or moral statements. In fact, the longest sentence ever served for a crime was by Paul Geidel, convicted of second-degree murder in 1911 as a 17-year-old in New York City, who served 68 years, 8 months, and 2 days (Rush, 2000: 295).

> *The* longest sentence ever served for a crime was by Paul Geidel, convicted of second-degree murder in 1911 as a 17-year-old in New York City. He served 68 years, 8 months, and 2 days.

Sentencing Facts

According to the Bureau of Justice Statistics, 1996 was the first time in U.S. history that more than one million adults were convicted of felonies in state and federal courts. This includes consistent 5% increases throughout the 1990s. Nearly 7 in 10 (69%) convicted felons are sentenced to some term of incarceration, either in jail (38%) or in prison (31%). This is not surprising, given that felonies are generally perceived as more serious in nature than misdemeanors.

The average sentence to state prison in 1996 was 38 months for all crimes (62 months for prisoners, 6 months for jail inmates). Average sentences were longer for violent crimes (78 months) than for property crimes (30 months), weapons violations (29 months), drug offenses (28 months), or other offenses (24 months). Figure 9.1 illustrates the types of crimes that typically receive the longest sentences.

FIGURE 9.1
Sentences for Various Crimes

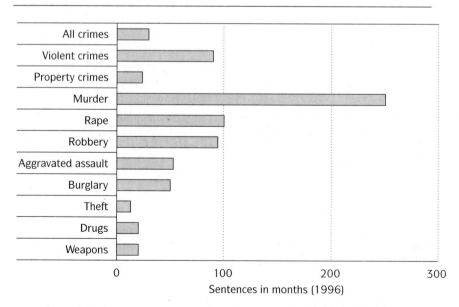

SOURCE: U.S. Department of Justice, *Sourcebook of Criminal Justice Statistics* (Washington, DC: U.S. Government Printing Office, 1998).

Offenders with prior records were more likely to be sentenced to prison for a felony conviction (58%) than were those with no prior felony convictions (21%). From these facts, we can conclude that more severe punishments are generally handed down for violent offenders and repeat offenders. Although judges ultimately hand down sentences to convicted offenders, the law is the instrument that sets forth minimum and maximum sentences. This gives legislators tremendous power in determining the direction of U.S. sentencing practices: "If lawmakers feel that the other two bodies—judges and officials of the executive branch—are being too lenient in their sentencing decisions, they can pass truth-in-sentencing laws that require convicts to serve the amount of time indicated in criminal codes" (Gaines et al., 2000: 382).

We can also conclude, by comparing punishment in the United States with that of other countries, that the U.S. is very "tough" on crime. In fact, the United States sentences convicted murderers and robbers roughly to the same length of incarceration as Canada and England (and we have the death penalty!). For relatively petty offenses, we sentence offenders to much longer terms of incarceration than these countries (Beckett and Sasson, 2000: 29). Thus, the notion that the U.S. criminal justice system is lenient on criminals is simply a myth (Kappeler, Blumberg, and Potter, 2000). Part of the rush to be tough on even low-level, nonviolent drug dealers is that punishment in the United States is in some ways counterintuitive. For example, according to Keve (1995), mandatory sentencing laws that have been used primarily for drug offenders have prompted the release from prison of violent offenders who were not sentenced under these mandatory sentencing laws. To some degree, then, the criminal justice system has prioritized drug criminals over violent criminals.

> The United States is very tough on crime. The United States sentences convicted murderers and robbers to roughly the same length of incarceration as Canada and Great Britain (and we have the death penalty!). However, for relatively petty offenses, we sentence offenders to much longer terms of incarceration than these countries.

WHY DO WE PUNISH?

Punishment is natural: "Parents punish children by taking away privileges. The punishment is often characterized as 'teaching a lesson.' Teachers discipline students who don't follow the rule; managers penalize unproductive employees" (Kappeler et al., 2000: 234). Given that punishment is natural, it is unlikely that we can ever put a complete end to the use of punishment as a means to control crime. Yet, many criminal justice scholars do believe that the United States is overrelying on punishment generally and on certain forms of punishment in particular. The Issue in Depth at the end of this chapter discusses what works and does not work to reduce crime.

Here I assess why American criminal justice administers punishment to offenders. John Stuart Mill (1859) argued that we should punish people only to prevent harms to others. Sir James Stephen (1883) disagreed with this position and stated that the purpose of punishment is to enforce the morality of the community—to allow the community to hate the criminal and to get revenge against him or her. Similarly, Immanuel Kant saw punishment as virtuous because the guilty deserve to suffer. However, Kant did not believe that punishment should be used to deter others who had not yet done anything wrong, nor did he believe in rehabilitation (cited in Jeffery, 1990: 63). The great legal scholar Oliver Wendell Holmes did not support vengeance; he believed the only justifications for punishment were deterrence and reform.

Lord Patrick Devlin (1959) attacked Mill's position and supported Stephen's view that punishment should be used to enforce morality. H. L. A. Hart (1968: 231) defended Mill and argued that the law could not successfully be used to enforce morality. Hart thought the only justification for punishment was the prevention of harm. Hart did support retribution, as well, and claimed that "the justification for punishing men (who have committed wickedness) is that the return of suffering for moral evil voluntarily done, is itself just or morally good."

Whatever your own personal beliefs, most criminal justice scholars agree that there are four primary justifications for criminal punishment:

- Retribution
- Incapacitation
- Deterrence
- Rehabilitation

Each of these justifications for punishment is discussed next.

> *T*he four primary justifications for criminal punishment are retribution, incapacitation, deterrence, and rehabilitation.

Retribution

Retribution implies "an eye for an eye, a tooth for a tooth." That is, when a criminal harms a victim, he or she deserves to suffer a similar if not identical harm. In Western societies, the notion of retribution has evolved out of religious convictions found in the Old Testament.

> *R*etribution has two related meanings. The first deals with the natural human emotion of vengeance, or the desire to get even—to give the offender his or her "just deserts." The second deals with a more rational approach to justice. It assumes that when an offender commits a harmful act against a victim, he or she has gained an unfair advantage to which he or she is not entitled under the law. Punishment must be administered to rebalance the scales of justice. In essence, when rules are broken, rule breakers must be punished.

Retribution has two related meanings. The first deals with the natural human emotion of vengeance—the desire to give the offender his or her "just deserts." At various times in U.S. history, notable people have attempted to achieve such literal retribution. For example, Thomas Jefferson proposed to the legislature that for the crime of murder by poisoning, poisoning be the just penalty. For the crime of rape, he proposed castration of the rapist as retributive justice. For treason, he suggested that the offender be buried alive (Gottfredson, 1999: 3).

The second meaning of retribution deals with a more rational approach to justice. It assumes that when an offender commits a harm against a victim, the offender gains an unfair advantage to which he or she is not entitled under the law. To balance the scales of justice, punishment must be administered to counteract the advantage gained through crime. In essence, when rules are broken, rule breakers must be punished.

With regard to the first meaning of retribution, Beckett and Sasson (2000: 164) claim that "those [victims of crime] who believe that revenge will bring them relief often discover that it does not" (e.g., see Prejean, 1993; Shapiro, 1997). When you or a loved one becomes a crime victim, the desire to get even with the offender is natural and easy to understand. Yet, this does not mean that getting even will make you feel a sense of justice or relief. Given the long delays in the administration of justice, the fact that victims are not highly involved in this process, and the fact that punishment is so detached from the victim, it is just as logical to assert that the criminal justice system cannot effectively make victims feel better.

It is tough to argue against the logic of the second meaning of retribution. If people freely choose to commit crime, they deserve some form of punishment for the harms they have inflicted on society. After all, one conception of justice, discussed in Chapter One, requires that the guilty be held accountable for their crimes in order that justice be achieved as an outcome. Yet, as I have attempted to demonstrate throughout this book, we should not let our goal of punishing the guilty so interfere with our goal of being fair and impartial in the criminal justice process that humans become generally less free, especially when this burden is imposed on some groups in society more than on others.

One clear benefit of retribution administered by the criminal justice system is that it limits the likelihood that escalation will occur (Glaser, 1997). That is, if victims were allowed to get "justice" for themselves, without the assistance of their government, the desire for vengeance would not be limited by the law. Thus, a single murder might lead to two more deaths—the death of the guilty offender and perhaps also the death of someone standing next to the offender when the victim's family opens fire. This in turn could lead to a desire for vengeance on the part of the offender's family and the family of the innocent bystander. Without state-controlled retribution, where would the cycle of vengeance and escalation end?

Incapacitation

Incapacitation involves restricting the freedom of the offender so that he or she cannot offend again. The logic of incapacitation is summed up by Friedman (1993: 237) as follows: "[A] burglar in jail can hardly break into your house. This effect is called 'incapacitation.' . . . If all the crooks are behind bars, they cannot rape and loot and pillage." Most people think of prisons and jails when they think of incapacitation, because they envision the offender being removed from society, but in fact the most typical form of incapacitation is not incarceration; probation is more commonly used to restrict the freedom of offenders, as will be discussed.

> *I*ncapacitation involves restricting the freedom of the offender so that he or she cannot offend again.

Unless you believe in reincarnation, the ultimate form of incapacitation is death. When an offender is killed, he or she can no longer offend against society. Thus, incapacitation becomes a justification for the death penalty, which is discussed in more detail in Chapter Eleven. Aside from death, however, we cannot be assured that offenders who are locked up behind bars will not continue to offend against society, and there is overwhelming evidence of crimes committed within prisons and jails against other inmates and correctional personnel. Because such crimes are not widely discussed or broadcast in the news, society can easily ignore them, but this does not make them any less real or harmful. It also does not deny that offenders who are locked away with other criminals will ultimately learn to be better offenders. These issues will be discussed further in Chapter Ten.

One thing we can conclude is that the United States is currently on an incarceration binge that is unprecedented in the history of the world. Yet, Americans seem generally unconcerned with the long-term social and economic implications of this trend for the United States. Incapacitation, whether it be achieved through incarceration or through the death penalty, suggests an "I give up" attitude toward crime and criminals. If we are unwilling to treat those who are sick, unwilling to change those environments that are conducive to street crime, and unwilling to invest in long-term approaches to crime prevention, then the easiest alternative is simply to lock people away from society (or kill them) so that we do not have to think about them.

> *The* United States is currently on an incarceration binge that is unprecedented in world history.

Incapacitation takes two main forms—general and selective (Walker, 1998). General or collective incapacitation occurs when society uses incarceration and other forms of incapacitation as a general punitive strategy for many forms of criminality. It is based on the belief that incarceration and other forms of incapacitation are effective means of controlling crimes. Selective incapacitation occurs when these punishment mechanisms are reserved for the most dangerous offenders, those in most need of incapacitation because of their likelihood of repeating their criminality. Selective incapacitation is based on scientific research demonstrating that a small percentage of offenders commit a very large portion of all crimes (e.g., see Wolfgang, Figlio, and Sellin, 1972).

> *Incapacitation* takes two major forms—general and selective. In general or collective incapacitation, society makes an effort to utilize incarceration and other forms of incapacitation as a general punitive strategy for many forms of criminality. In selective incapacitation, these punishment mechanisms are reserved for the most dangerous offenders, who require incapacitation because they are likely to repeat their criminality.

The main problem with general or collective incapacitation is that not every offender deserves or warrants it, especially given the enormous costs associated with incarcerating and executing offenders. Collective incarceration may make us feel safer, but incarcerating more people has a "limited capacity to actually make us safer" (Gottfredson, 1999: 431). As for selective incapacitation, the main problem is known as the "prediction problem" (Gottfredson and Gottfredson, 1994). Because we simply are unable to predict accurately which offenders pose the greatest risk of repeating their crimes, it is difficult to use selective incapacitation accurately. We do know that the most minor offenders are the ones who are most likely to reoffend. For example, thieves are more likely to commit more thefts after release than murderers are to commit more murders. Yet, the costs of incarceration do not seem to be warranted for these minor offenders on the basis of the minor harms they are likely to inflict on society. Keeping thieves in jail or prison because of the likelihood that they will reoffend is not good criminal justice policy.

Deterrence

Deterrence is based on the logical notion that being punished for criminal activity will create fear in people so that they will not want to commit crime. There are two types of deterrence, special or specific deterrence and general deterrence. The former means punishing an offender with the specific intent of instilling fear in that offender so that he or she will not commit crimes in the future. The latter involves punishing offenders in order to instill fear in society generally so that the rest of us will not want to commit crimes. Special or specific deterrence is aimed at stopping a known criminal offender from committing future crimes, whereas general deterrence is aimed at teaching the rest of us a lesson about what might happen to us if we were to commit crimes. Deterrence is evident in all that we do in the United States to fight crime, as discussed in the following box.

---

*D*eterrence is based on the logical notion that being punished for criminal activity will make people fearful so that they will not want to commit crimes. There are two types of deterrence—special or specific deterrence and general deterrence. The former punishes an offender with the specific intent of instilling fear in that individual so that he or she will not commit future crimes. The latter punishment attempts to instill fear in society generally so that the rest of us will not want to commit crimes.

Deterrence in American punishment

- *Probation:* Offenders on probation are "hassled" by their probation officer and must follow many rules that they would not have to follow even in prison. Thus, they should be deterred from committing future crimes for fear that they might be put on probation again.
- *Incarceration:* Prisons and jails are horribly violent and repressive places. Any criminal who goes to prison ought to be afraid to go back. Additionally, all of society should fear suffering the pains of imprisonment. Thus, crime will be specially and generally deterred.
- *Boot camps:* Juvenile offenders sentenced to boot camps are forced to go to classes, work, and train through various physical fitness activities. It is hoped that these juveniles will fear being forced to experience such conditions again in the future, so that boot camps will deter juvenile delinquency.
- *Chain gangs:* Forcing inmates to work on the side of the road doing hard labor will not only instill fear in those inmates, but also show others what can happen if they commit crimes. Thus, crime is both specially and generally deterred.
- *Death penalty:* Not only does the death penalty incapacitate the offender, it sends a message to all of society that anyone who commits murder can be executed for his or her offense.

The logic of deterrence is summarized in the following statements:

- "Stiffen the backbone of the system, make it more certain that criminals pay for their crimes, and pay hard; surely crime will dwindle as a consequence. Deterrence—that is the key" (Friedman, 1993: 456).

- "The public wants criminals to be dealt with in a way that not only controls their behaviors but symbolizes society's anger and desire to exclude, hurt, or eliminate law violators" (Crouch et al., 1999: 98).

Deterrence as a justification for punishment is based on several assumptions:

- Offenders are hedonistic or pleasure-seeking (e.g., crime provides various pleasures).
- Offenders seek to minimize costs or pains associated with crimes (i.e., they do not want to get caught and be punished).
- Offenders are rational (i.e., they choose to commit crime after weighing the potential costs or punishments and benefits or rewards).

Such assumptions are beyond direct empirical observation, so we do not actually know if humankind fits these criteria. Many criminologists believe that we do (Bohm, 2001). Yet, numerous human behaviors seem quite irrational. For example, the other day I witnessed six young women riding in a Jeep. As they passed through an intersection, each (including the driver) was smoking a cigarette and waving her arms around while listening to the radio, which was playing very loudly. The car was clearly traveling faster than the speed limit, and no one (including the driver) was wearing a seatbelt. Is any of this rational? In fact, much behavior, as in this example, is not motivated by rationality but instead is impulsive and shortsighted. Similarly, many types of crimes, are committed with only short-term gain in mind and with little or no thought of likely outcomes. This is not consistent with the view of the rational criminal.

To deter would-be offenders effectively, punishment must be certain (or at least likely), swift (or at least not delayed by months or years), and severe enough to outweigh the pleasures associated with crimes. Of these requirements, the most important is certainty. The more likely that punishment is to follow a criminal act, the less likely the criminal act will occur. Think of this example: if a lightning bolt were guaranteed to strike an offender who stole property, how many thefts do you think we would have each year? Probably not many. If it was absolutely certain that some higher being would strike you dead upon stealing someone else's property, then everyone would know this and would refrain from committing theft in order to remain alive.

> *For* punishment to deter would-be offenders, it must be certain (or at least likely), swift (or at least not delayed by months or years), and severe enough to outweigh the pleasures associated with crimes.

Such punishment would be certain, swift, and severe. But this example is misleading. For deterrence to be effective, it must be certain and somewhat swift, but it has to be only severe enough to outweigh the pleasure gained by committing the offense. For most crimes, certain death by lightning strike is not required! The noted Italian criminologist Cesare Beccaria wrote, in *An Essay on Crime and Punishments* (1776), that:

> The certainty of punishment, even though it be moderate, will always make a stronger impression than the fear of one more severe if it is accompanied by the hope that one may escape that punishment, because men are more frightened by an evil which is inevitable even though minor in nature. Further, if the punishment be too severe for a crime, men will be led to com-

mit further crimes in order to escape punishment for the crime. . . . It is essential that it be public, prompt, necessary, minimal in severity as possible under given circumstances, proportional to the crime, and prescribed by the laws.

Contemporary research supports Beccaria's original statement. For example, Blumstein (1995: 408–409) writes: "Research on deterrence has consistently supported the position that sentence 'severity' (that is, the time served) has less of a deterrent effect than sentence 'certainty' (the probability of going to prison). Thus, from the deterrence consideration, there is clear preference for increasing certainty, even if it becomes necessary to do so at the expense of severity."

What do you think? Is American criminal justice doing a good job of providing certain, swift punishments that outweigh the potential benefits of committing crimes? The evidence says no.

For every 100 serious street crimes (as measured in the National Crime Victimization Survey), only about 40 are known to the police (as measured in the Uniform Crime Reports). Of these 40, only about 10 will lead to an arrest. Of those arrested, some will not be prosecuted, and some will be prosecuted but not convicted. Only about 3 of the original 100 crimes will lead to an incarceration. Punishment is anything but certain in the United States. Offenders know this. They tell criminologists that they know from personal experiences and from the experiences of fellow criminals that their risks of being apprehended by the police and convicted in court are very low (Cromwell, 1995). Because there are only 2.7 police officers in the United States for every 1,000 citizens (see Chapter Seven), is this surprising?

What many offenders do tell us, and what is evident from their offending patterns, is that the great bulk of criminal behavior seems to be motivated by the desire to obtain short-term, immediate pleasures and gains. Long-term concern about potential punishment seems not to enter the minds of most offenders. If they thought there was a good chance of getting caught, after all, offenders would not likely engage in their criminal behaviors, especially if they are as rational as criminologists tell us.

The main problem with deterrence as a justification for punishment is that it is impossible to demonstrate empirically that deterrence works. How can one prove *the absence* of criminal activity as a result of some criminal justice policy or program? This is why many criminal justice scholars argue that there is no empirical evidence supporting deterrence (Bohm, 2001).

Even if the threat of punishment does deter some would-be offenders from committing crimes, our common experiences also suggest that deterrence is a myth. For example, do you ever intentionally exceed the speed limit while driving? If so, what makes you slow down? A police officer in his or her car on the side of the road? If this scares you temporarily, why do you speed up again once the officer is out of sight? And why do people buy radar detectors so that they can get away with speeding?

Rehabilitation

Rehabilitation, probably the least popular of all justifications for punishing people today, is justified to the degree that something within offenders or their environments causes them to commit crime. Rehabilitation is aimed at eliminating the causes of crime by making the offender "better"—restoring him or her to a healthy condition—or altering conditions in his or her "sick" environment. Rehabilitation would also include what Glaser (1997: 36) calls "anticriminal enculturation" ("[c]lassifying and separating inmates, promoting good staff–inmate relations, encouraging noncriminal visitors, providing law-abiding role models"), "retraining" ("[p]roviding academic and vocational instruction and employment during confinement, providing postrelease aid and personal counseling") and "reintegrative shaming" ("[c]ondemning the offense but accepting the offender's apology, and granting public respect").

> *R*ehabilitation is aimed at eliminating the causes of crime by making the offender "better"—restoring him or her to a healthy condition—or altering conditions in his or her "sick" environment.

There is very little rehabilitation in American punishment today, mostly because of the widespread but false belief that we do not know what works or how best to use it. A major report by Martinson (2000: 23), a criminologist, stated that "with few and isolated exceptions, the rehabilitative efforts that have been reported so far have had not appreciable effect on rehabilitation." Such reports led to the decline of the rehabilitative ideal in the 1970s.

> *T*here is very little rehabilitation in American punishment today, mostly because of the false belief that we do not know what works or how best to use it.

There is very little going on in the world of corrections today that we can call rehabilitation (Gottfredson, 1999: 420). This can be attributed, in part, to the use of crime as an election issue by politicians seeking to get elected and maintain power through law-and-order, get-tough-on-crime rhetoric. The shift from rehabilitative to law-and-order approaches coincided with the use of crime for national political gain, as discussed in Chapter One. Beckett and Sasson (2000: 55) explain how the rehabilitative ideal collapsed in the United States

> in the context of a growing chorus of criticism, from scholars and activists across the political spectrum, of "rehabilitation" as a primary justification for punishment. Conservatives opposed rehabilitation on the grounds that punishment must be harsh and painful if it is to deter crime. Liberals also criticized policies associated with rehabilitation, arguing that the open-ended ("indeterminate") sentences designed to facilitate "correction" created the potential for the intrusive, discriminatory, and arbitrary exercise of power.

Dozens of reviews of the ineffectiveness of rehabilitation were published in the 1960s and 1970s (for multiple citations, see Gottfredson, 1999: 423).

Walker (1998: 203) explains that we must, at least to some degree, still be committed to rehabilitation, because we still call the facilities that punish offenders "corrections" (which suggests that we hope to correct their behavior). Public opinion polls of Americans show that there is widespread support for rehabilitation, treatment, and crime prevention as alternatives to punitiveness (Roberts and Stalans, 2000). In fact, some treatment does work for some people (see multiple citations in Gottfredson, 1999: 434). In Chapter Twelve, I will argue that the future of criminal justice policy must be directed toward programs that are less punitive and more treatment-based.

The following box summarizes each justification for punishment by providing an example. I hope it goes without saying that these goals can be both expensive and conflicting.

How imprisonment is intended to serve the goals of punishment

An example of each of the main justifications for punishment is used by Crouch et al. (1999: 85) when discussing prisons. They write: "[W]e expect prisons to keep honest citizens honest (general deterrence), deter offenders from additional law-breaking behavior (specific deterrence), isolate criminals from the community (incapacitation), inflict a just measure of suffering on them (retribution), and yet somehow 'cure' them of their anti-social attitudes and behavior (rehabilitation)." Is it possible to achieve each of these goals with one form of punishment?

Punishment: A Summary

The bottom line is that punishment should be aimed toward the future, not the past. When we say, "Don't cry over spilled milk," we mean that it does very little good after the milk is spilled to cry about it. The milk should be cleaned up, and precautions should be taken so that no more milk will be spilled in the future. If this requires punishing the offender for being careless, reckless, or even intentionally spilling the milk, so be it. But it would not make much sense to punish the milk-spiller simply to get even with him or her. It would not get the floor clean (unless the punishment included cleaning the floor), it would not increase the likelihood that more milk would not be wasted in the future, and it might even be detrimental or destructive to the future of the milk-spiller, particularly if the punishment far exceeded the act. We wouldn't want to do anything that would make it more likely that the milk- spiller would spill more milk in the future, would we?

I argue that our system of punishment should be future based, aimed at crime prevention, and rooted in utilitarianism. Utilitarianism, based on the writings of John Stuart Mill, for example, holds that actions should be aimed at doing the greatest good for the greatest number of people. Some of what we do may ideally be based on utilitarian goals of crime prevention through deterrence, but most of what we do in the United States to punish criminals is based on retribution, which is backward looking: it aims to get even with the offender for past wrongs. The methods of punishment available to the U.S. system of criminal justice are not being best utilized to achieve the goals set forth in Chapter One.

METHODS OF PUNISHMENT

When you think of punishment, what do you see? Prisons? The electric chair? These are currently considered valid sentencing options for judges who are responsible for meting out punishments in the United States. However, prison and death are two punishments that are relatively infrequently administered. I say "relatively infrequently" not to suggest that their administration is not plagued with problems, but to make the point that, relative to probation, imprisonment and death are rare. In Chapters Ten and Eleven, I will take a close look at incarceration and the death penalty, respectively.

There are four main categories of punishment used in the United States: probation, incarceration, intermediate sanctions, and death.

FIGURE 9.2

Types of Punishment

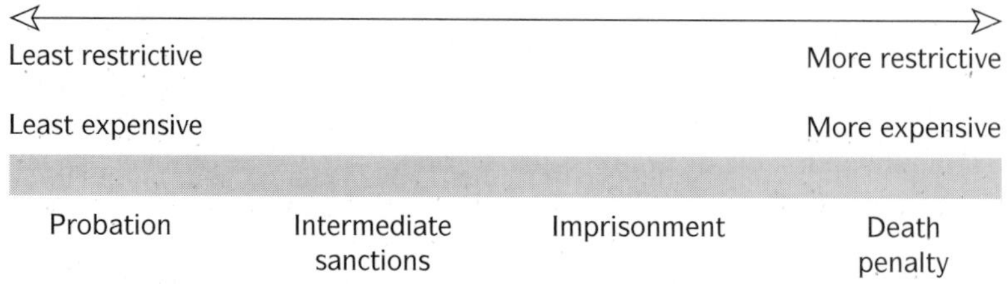

Least restrictive   More restrictive

Least expensive   More expensive

| Probation | Intermediate sanctions | Imprisonment | Death penalty |

Generally speaking, four main categories of punishment are used in the United States—including probation, incarceration, intermediate sanctions, and death. These are depicted along a continuum in Figure 9.2. Punishments (also known as criminal sanctions) on the left of this figure are generally less restrictive and less expensive than those to the right of the continuum.

Probation, the least restrictive of punishments depicted in Figure 9.2, is also the most commonly used criminal sanction in the United States. According to the U.S. Department of Justice, probation is the court-ordered community supervision of convicted offenders by a probation agency, requiring the adherence to specific rules of conduct while living in the community. The following box lists some of these requirements. If violated, probation can be revoked and the offender sent to prison or jail, whatever was stated in the original sentence by the judge.

Typical rules of probation

These are listed in order, from most common to least common.

- Pay supervision fees.
- Pay fines.
- Pay court costs.
- Attend substance abuse treatment.
- Gain and maintain employment.
- Participate in drug testing.
- Pay victim restitution.
- Perform community service.
- Gain education and/or training.
- Have no contact with the victim.
- Remain drug-free.
- Attend counseling.
- Abide by driving restrictions.
- Abide by movement restrictions.

The use of probation tripled from 1980 to 1997, a rate equal to the increase in the use of incarceration (Gaines et al., 2000: 420). You might think that because most convicted criminals do not go to prison, this is proof that the United States is "soft on crime," but in fact the U.S. leads the world in incarceration rates (see Chapter Ten). Probation is not intended for serious, repetitive, violent criminals. Generally, it is not intended for people convicted on multiple charges, for people who were arrested while on probation or parole, for repeat offenders, for drug addicts, or for violent offenders (Petersilia and Turner, 1986). In fact, the offense most likely to lead to a sentence of straight probation or a split sentence between incarceration and probation is simple drug possession, while the least likely is murder, followed by rape. For every type of crime, people sentenced to probation generally receive shorter sentences than those sentenced to prison.

> *P*robation is not intended for serious, repetitive, violent criminals. Generally, it is not intended for people convicted on multiple charges, people who were arrested while on probation or parole, repeat offenders, drug addicts, or violent offenders.

According to the Bureau of Justice Statistics' "Probation and Parole Statistics," on December 31, 1998, approximately 3,417,600 adults were under federal, state, or local jurisdiction on probation, and nearly 705,000 were on parole. Nearly three out of five of all offenders on probation in 1998 were on probation for a felony (57%). Two out of five were on probation for a misdemeanor. Twenty-four percent were on probation for a drug law violation and 17% for driving while intoxicated or under the influence of alcohol. Figure 9.3 illustrates the percentage of criminals on probation who were convicted of various types of crimes.

Walker (1998) claims that we use probation for various reasons. First, as noted, many crimes are relatively minor and thus do not warrant a term of incarceration. Second, there are not enough prison and jail cells for those we have already sentenced to incarceration, which is why U.S. prisons are operating above maximum capacity. Third, probation is much cheaper than prison. Walker estimates that it is costs about $600 per year per offender for probation. He maintains it costs about 37 times as much to incarcerate an offender for a year in prison (plus the fact that you don't have to build a facility to house people on probation). Fourth, probation is no less effective than prison. In fact, probation is actually more successful at reducing recidivism than more severe sanctions.

Incarceration takes many forms, notably being sent to prison or jail. It involves having one's freedoms taken away while one is locked away from society. A *prison* is a state or federal correctional

FIGURE 9.3
Types of Crime Most Likely to Receive Probation

MOST SERIOUS CONVICTION OFFENSE (state and federal probationers)

Property offenses	38%
Other minor offenses	37%
Weapons offenses	31%
Drug offenses	27%
Violent offenses	21%

SOURCE: Bureau of Justice Statistics (1998). Online: www.ojp.usdoj.gov/bjs.

facility used to house those sentenced to more than one year of incarceration. A *jail* is a local correctional facility used to hold persons awaiting trial, awaiting sentencing, serving a sentence of less than one year, or awaiting transfer to another facility.

---

*I*ncarceration takes many forms, most typically being sent to prison or jail. It involves having one's freedoms taken away while being locked away from society.

On June 30, 1999, there were 1,333,561 prisoners under federal or state jurisdiction in prisons, and at midyear 1999, there were 605,943 inmates held in the nation's local jails. Figure 9.4 illustrates the percentage of criminals incarcerated in prisons and jails who were convicted of various types of crimes. As you can see, incarceration is used more for violent criminals than for property criminals. It is a sanction supposedly intended for more severe offenders.

A prison is a state or federal correctional facility used to house those sentenced to more than one year of incarceration.

Unlike those on probation, people who are incarcerated are not allowed to live in the community. They are taken away from their families and loved ones and are subjected to numerous discomforts (see Chapter Ten). Think of being locked away from free society, not being able to come and go as you please, being told what to do, when to do it, and how to do it. Does this sound like soft punishment?

A jail is a local correctional facility used to hold persons awaiting trials, awaiting sentencing, serving a sentence of less than one year, or awaiting transfer to another facility.

Because of the enormous costs of incarceration—approximately $30,000 per year per inmate—and because most offenders do not warrant incarceration, yet probation comes off as a

FIGURE 9.4

Types of Crime Most Likely to Receive Imprisonment

MOST SERIOUS CONVICTION OFFENSE (state and federal prisoners)	
Violent offenses	57%
Weapons offenses	44%
Drug offenses	38%
Property offenses	34%
Other offenses	32%

SOURCE: Bureau of Justice Statistics (1999). Online: www.ojp.usdoj.gov/bjs.

slap on the wrist for many of them, a wide array of intermediate sanctions have become available to sentencing judges. The following box lists several of these.

Some types of intermediate sanctions

- *Boot camps:* Usually intended for juveniles, these facilities are run as paramilitary organizations, attempting to instill discipline in wayward youth through hard work and exercise, and to increase educational and vocational skills.
- *House arrest:* This is intended for less severe offenders, who are required to stay within a certain distance of their actual residence.
- *Electronic monitoring:* This is usually used in conjunction with house arrest. An offender is monitored via an electronic device attached to his or her leg which assures that the offender does not violate the terms of his or her house arrest.
- *Community service:* This is typically used for the least severe offenders, who are required to spend a specified number of hours serving their community by picking up garbage or performing other necessary tasks.
- *Day reporting center:* This is a facility where probationers are sent to attend treatment and counseling sessions each day.

IS PUNISHMENT EFFECTIVE?

There are several sources of information to consider when attempting to determine which types of punishment are effective. One valuable source is offenders themselves. Another is criminal justice research, which sheds some light on the effectiveness of various kinds of punishment. Next, I summarize what these sources suggest about the effectiveness of punishment in the United States.

What We've Learned from Offenders

Many scholars have spent time with known offenders, both incarcerated and free, to discover their motivations and mechanisms for committing crimes. Offenders report that they have learned from personal experience that their likelihood of getting punished is extremely low in the United States. Figure 9.5 illustrates the likelihood of being caught by the police, convicted by the courts, and sentenced to incarceration for various crimes. As you can see, the only crime for which there exists a substantial risk of arrest, conviction, and imprisonment is murder, and the risk is still less than 50%.

> *The* only crime with a substantial risk of arrest, conviction, and imprisonment is murder, and that risk is still less than 50%.

The crime of burglary, committed by rational offenders who carefully choose their targets on the basis of certain environmental characteristics, provides an excellent example of how the

FIGURE 9.5

The Likelihood of Getting Caught, Convicted, and Imprisoned

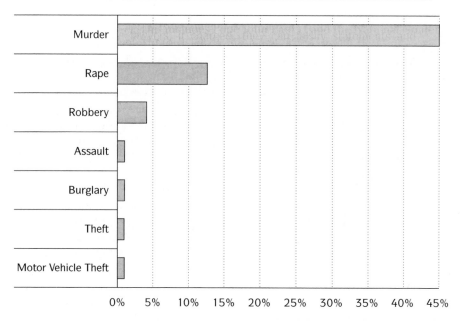

SOURCE: Adapted from M. Robinson and J. Darley, *Justice, Liability, and Blame* (Boulder, CO: Westview Press, 1997)

threat of punishment can never deter would-be offenders (Wright and Decker, 1994). First, consider when burglars choose to commit their offenses. Many burglary studies show that residences are at highest risk for burglary when they are left unoccupied—that is, when no one is home. Burglar interview studies (Cromwell, Olson, and Avary, 1991; Maguire and Bennett, 1982; Walsh, 1980; Wright and Decker, 1994) and analyses of times of burglary (Reppetto, 1974; Waller and Okihiro, 1978; Winchester and Jackson, 1982) have both demonstrated the importance of nonoccupancy in the occurrence of burglary. Scarr (1973) found in a study in Washington, D.C., that residential burglary occurred during the daytime and on weekends, following relatively regular patterns of nonoccupancy. Approximately half of all residential burglaries in Scarr's study occurred during a six-hour period between the hours of 10:00 A.M. and 4:00 P.M. Rengert and Wasilchick (1985) also found that the occurrence of burglary corresponded with occupants' schedules, because burglaries occurred during times when dwellings were left unoccupied.

Offenders tell researchers that they prefer not to enter residences that are occupied (Cromwell, 1995). According to Cromwell et al. (1991: 37), 28 of the 30 burglars in their ethnographic study of breaking and entering indicated they would never intentionally enter an occupied residence. In Wright and Decker's (1994) study of residential burglary, occupancy served as a the major risk factor associated with the decision not to enter a potential target residence. Thus, the major risk to burglars is not law enforcement, courts, and corrections but, instead, the threat of run-ins with residential occupants. Consider also what these offenders tell researchers about their likelihood of being punished by the criminal justice system. They know from experience that this likelihood is very small. As many offenders have stated, "If I thought I was going to get caught, I wouldn't be doing it, now would I?" The data presented in Figure 9.5 confirm this.

What We've Learned from Other Criminal Justice Research

The discussion in the Issue in Depth at the end of this chapter illustrates that, overall, American punishment is highly ineffective at reducing crime. Regardless of the type of punishment, virtually every type of criminal sanction fails to reduce recidivism. Even the most common type of criminal sanction, probation, is relatively unsuccessful. A study by the U.S. Justice Department found that 43% of convicted felons in the 1980s were rearrested for another felony within three years of completing their probation terms (Bureau of Justice Statistics, 1992). Petersilia (1983) reported similar, though less promising, results in a study of California felony probationers. She found that 65% had been rearrested within 40 months. (Remember that being rearrested is not the same thing as being reconvicted.) Yet, even assuming that all those who were rearrested were actually found guilty of another crime, this means that somewhere around 50% of probationers will commit another crime for which they will be caught within a three- to four-year period. Given that offenders spend very little or no time being supervised by probation officers, and that this form of punishment does nothing to change the social conditions that produce criminality, 50% is not a bad success rate, particularly when probation is compared to other forms of punishment such as imprisonment (see Chapter Ten). Petersilia and Turner (1986) estimate that probationers will be about half as likely to be rearrested as people released from prison. If we are going to follow approaches that fail at reducing crime, we might as well invest in programs that are slightly more effective and save money in the long run.

> *O*verall, American punishment is highly ineffective at reducing crime. Regardless of the type of punishment, virtually every type of criminal sanction fails to reduce recidivism.

A couple of important factors explain the failure of probation. First, only about one-tenth of the corrections budget in any given year is allocated to probation, even though two-thirds of people under the supervision of corrections are on probation (Petersilia, 1998). Also, even though probation populations have grown since 1980, funding for probation has remained virtually unchanged (Langan, 1994). Further, individual probation officers have large caseloads, making their jobs difficult if not impossible. Petersilia (1998) estimates that the nation's probation officers average nearly 260 offenders per officer.

BIAS IN THE SENTENCING PROCESS

Recall from Chapter One that for a criminal justice process such as sentencing to be just, it must be fair and "not be affected by extraneous factors, such as race, gender, or socioeconomic status" (Kappeler et al., 2000: 228). Instead, sentences should be based on legal factors such as seriousness of offense and prior criminal record. The use of legal factors to determine appropriate sentence, though obviously less troublesome than sentencing based on extralegal factors, is still problematic. Using prior record and seriousness of offense to determine sentence allows biases of the criminal law and police behavior to come into play.

According to Kappeler et al. (2000: 28): "The empirical research done by criminal justice scholars has demonstrated with remarkable regularity that minority group members (particularly African Americans) and the poor get longer sentences and have less chance of gaining parole or probation, even when the seriousness of the crime and the criminal record of the defendants are held constant." Pratt (1998) illustrates how race continues to play a role in sentencing into the twenty-first century. Such conclusions would lead you to believe that power has a direct influence on justice because relatively less powerful groups in the United States don't receive equal justice. For example, a study of incarceration in Florida found that the people most likely to be imprisoned were unemployed African American males, even when the seriousness of the offense and the prior record of the defendant were held constant (Chiricos and Bales, 1991).

Walker et al. (2000: 218) conclude that sentencing in the 1990s was characterized by contextual discrimination because they found evidence of bias in many court jurisdictions in various areas related to sentencing. They write:

> Judges in some jurisdictions continue to impose harsher sentences on racial minorities who murder or rape whites, and more lenient sentences on racial minorities whose victims are of their own racial or ethnic group. Judges in some jurisdictions continue to impose racially biased sentences in less serious cases; in these "borderline cases" racial minorities get prison, whereas whites get probation. In jurisdictions with sentencing guidelines, judges depart from the presumptive sentence less often when the offender is African American or Hispanic than when the offender is white. Judges, in other words, continue to take race into account, either explicitly or implicitly, when determining the appropriate sentence.

It is in borderline cases, then, the only cases in which discretion *can* come into play, where discretion *does* come into play. In other words, race and class biases affect sentencing when it is possible for them to do so.

---

*I*t is only in borderline cases that discretion *can* and *does* come into play. In other words, race and class biases do affect sentencing when they can.

If one were to look at sentencing nationally without distinguishing between types of offenses, sentencing generally does *not* appear to be biased against any race of people; that is, African Americans and Caucasians appear to receive the same sentences within the same categories of offenses. An earlier review of sentencing and race by the National Academy of Sciences claimed that factors other than racial discrimination in sentencing account for most of the disproportionate representation of blacks in U.S. prisons, although "racial discrimination in sentencing may play a more important role in some regions or jurisdictions, for some crime types, or in the decisions of individual participants" (Blumstein et al., 1983: 13).

---

*S*entencing, generally, does *not* appear to be biased against any race of people.

The average prison sentences imposed on convicted felons by state courts in 1996 are virtually identical for African Americans and Caucasians for violent, property, drug, weapons, and other felonies. Yet, there is evidence of clear sentencing bias against African Americans and Hispanics at the federal level, particularly with regard to drug offenses (Albonetti, 1997).

> *The* average prison sentences imposed on convicted felons for violent, property, drug, weapons, and other felonies by state courts in 1996 were virtually identical for African Americans and Caucasians.

Data from the Bureau of Justice Statistics (1997) do show that African Americans (who make up only 13% of the general population) made up an alarming 44% of felons convicted in state courts in 1996. And data based on convictions for felonies in the nation's 75 largest counties show that African Americans made up 50% of defendants charged with all felony offenses, 53% of drug felonies, 52% for violent felonies, and 48% of property offenses. In the nation's 75 largest counties, African Americans make up 50% of defendants charged with all felony offenses, 53% of drug felonies, 52% of violent felonies, and 48% of property offenses. Such statistics do not imply sentencing bias. Instead, they reflect built-in biases of the criminal law (see Chapter Two) and biases in U.S. law enforcement processes (see Chapter Seven).

> *There* is evidence of clear sentencing bias against African Americans and Hispanics at the federal level, particularly for drug offenses.

African Americans also are no more likely than Caucasians nationally to be sentenced to a term of imprisonment by state courts for violent crimes (25% versus 26%, respectively) and are even less likely to be sentenced to imprisonment for property offenses (24% versus 31%, respectively). African Americans are, however, more likely than Caucasians to be sentenced by state courts to incarceration in prison for drug offenses (40% versus 25%, respectively). The data in Table 9.1 show that African American males receive the longest average sentences for all felony offenses whereby offenders are sentenced to jail time for violent, property, drug, and weapons felonies. Finally, there is evidence of contextual discrimination against people of color, because there are patterns of discrimination in some cities (Walker et al., 2000: 183).

> *African* Americans (who make up only 13% of the general population) accounted for an alarming 44% of felons convicted in state courts in 1996.

TABLE 9.1
Race and Jail Sentences

RACE	PERCENTAGE OF LOCAL JAIL INMATES
African American	41.5
Caucasian	41.3
Hispanic	15.5
Other	1.7

SOURCE: Data from S. Walker, C. Spohn, and M. Delone, *The Color of Justice: Race, Ethnicity, and Crime in America,* 2nd ed. (Belmont, CA: Wadsworth, 2000).

> *A*frican American males receive the longest average sentences for all felony offenses whereby offenders are sentenced to jail time for violent, property, drug, and weapons felonies.

It is unclear why African Americans appear to be discriminated against when sentenced to imprisonment for drug felonies but not for violent and property felonies. It is also not clear why African Americans are sentenced to longer jail terms than Caucasians but not prison terms generally. With regard to drugs, African Americans probably receive longer average sentences than Caucasians because of prior record, which thus reflects a bias—not a court bias, but a policing bias—as African Americans are more likely to be arrested for drug offenses (see Chapter Six). The use of discretion by prosecutors in the charging phase of the criminal justice process probably explains the apparent biases against African Americans in jail terms. In serious felonies that will likely result in substantial prison terms, it would be very difficult for prosecutors to use their discretion in a biased manner. It would, however, be substantially easier for them to be biased in relatively minor felonies, where they have substantially more discretion to charge defendants with more or less severe offenses. The same would be true for judges, whose discretion is limited when sentencing for major felonies but substantially wider in less serious felonies that may lead to jail time rather than imprisonment.

This may be why some studies have found sentencing bias against minorities for crimes where the nature of the crime and the offender's prior record do not point clearly to the appropriate sentence (e.g, see Unnever and Hembroff, 1988). Such findings suggest that in at least some jurisdictions, when prosecutors and judges have discretion, they may be more likely to be biased against minorities than Caucasians. Other studies, in larger states and in areas where income inequality is higher, have found sentencing disparities based on race, even after controlling for legal factors (e.g., see Bridges and Crutchfield, 1988; Myers, 1987; Petersilia, 1985).

There is also evidence of discrimination in sentences to probation. African Americans made up 35% of probationers in 1997 and Hispanics made up another 16% (U.S. Department of Justice, 1998). Caucasians are overrepresented among probationers, leading Walker et al. (2000: 270) to suggest that the less severe sentence of probation is more likely to be reserved for Caucasians, especially in borderline cases where either probation or a short sentence of incarceration are both options.

Some court clients are subjected to sentencing laws that are clearly biased. For example, the "three-strikes-and-you're-out" laws introduced earlier in this chapter are claimed to be "wasting prison resources on non-violent, low-level offenders and reducing resources available to lock up violent offenders" (Harvard Medical School researcher William Brownsberger, in National Center on Institutions and Alternatives, 1999). A study by Clark, Austin, and Henry (1997) of California's three-strikes law found that two years after its implementation that a large majority of offenders sentenced under the law were not convicted of violent felonies.

Walker (1998: 137) writes that three-strikes laws "have been almost universally condemned by criminologists and other experts on sentencing. Franklin Zimring calls it 'the voodoo economics of California crime.' Jerome Skolnick says it represented the values of 'the dark ages.' One book labels it *Vengeance As Public Policy.*"

Researchers confidently conclude that the laws cost billions of dollars, cause lengthy delays in the criminal justice process, and that they are biased against members of the poor and racial minorities. A Rand Corporation study estimates that if California fully carried out its version of the three-strikes law, it would cost more than $5 billion per year (Greenwood et al., 1994). The likely result: a drastic drop in street crime (about 28%, they estimate, mostly in assaults and burglaries), but also a simultaneous pillaging of the state's higher education and social welfare budgets. Three-strikes laws are disinvestments in America's future.

And who is getting caught? The shocking fact is that most offenders sentenced are not repeat violent murderers, rapists, and robbers. More than 80% of convicted "three-strikers" in California have been nonviolent felons. More have been sentenced for the relatively benign offense of marijuana possession than for all violent crimes combined. Consider, for example, some cases discussed by Walker (1998: 139):

- Jerry Williams, who stole a piece of pizza
- A woman who bought $20 worth of cocaine, 14 years after her second conviction
- A robber of a sandwich shop in Washington who stole $151 (his two previous robberies netted $460).

Other similar examples have received similar attention. Consider these offenders sentenced under three-strikes laws:

- A teenager sentenced to life for stealing a cellular phone (Domanick, 1998)
- A man sentenced to 25 years to life for stealing a bottle of vitamins from a grocery store (Gaines et al., 2000: 394)
- A man convicted of stealing a carton of cigarettes from Target, with prior offenses 15 years earlier of burglary and assault
- A woman who gained $5 in a cocaine sale, whose prior offenses included robbery, burglary, and prostitution
- A man convicted of receiving stolen property (a 1985 car), whose prior offenses included burglary, drug possession, and a robbery that involved a pack of cigarettes from another inmate (Dodge and Harris, 2000: 356).

Others charged with third-strike offenses have been relatively minor offenders. Consider these cases (Dodge and Harris, 2000: 355–356):

- A homeless man, whose only possession was a bicycle, charged with stealing a $2 bicycle lock
- A severely retarded 34-year-old woman, who was homeless and living in a park, charged with possession of a $5 rock of cocaine
- A man who allegedly bought a crushed macadamia nut from the police, charged with attempting to possess drugs

Many three-strikers are drug offenders, including those who were convicted and sentenced simply for possessing drugs. Meanwhile, the Rand Corporation claims that mechanisms such as drug treatment, parent training, delinquent supervision, and graduation incentives are up to seven times more effective at reducing recidivism than mandatory prison terms, and are more cost-effective as well (Robinson, 2000).

> *The Rand Corporation claims that mechanisms such as drug treatment, parent training, delinquent supervision, and graduation incentives are up to seven times more effective at reducing recidivism and are also more cost-effective than mandatory prison terms.*

When drug offenses are included in mandatory sentencing, such sentencing laws become a major source of criminal justice bias. For example, although 13% of monthly drug users are African Americans, they account for 25% of arrests for drug possession, 55% of convictions, and 74% of prison sentences (Mauer and Huling, 1995a). Additionally, whereas 39% of crack users are African American, 89% of people sentenced for federal crack crimes are African American. Throughout the United States, convicted drug offenders are disproportionately low-income minorities. And according to the Bureau of Justice Statistics (1998), African Americans are sentenced to prison more than half the time for drug offenses, whereas Caucasians are sentenced to incarceration only about one-third of the time for the same offenses. From 1990 to 1996, the number of African Americans in federal prisons for violent and property crimes decreased by 726 persons, but for drug offenses the number increased by 12,852!

> *Throughout the United States, convicted drug offenders are disproportionately low-income minority group members.*

The impact of sentencing laws on minorities (especially African Americans) is greatest at the federal level. Thus, the number of federal inmates in 1980 who were minorities was 8,085 (33%), but this increased to 65,000 (64%) in 1995 (Coalition for Federal Sentencing Reform, 1999). Such bias counters the myth that the criminal justice system is fair. Some even suggest that the war on drugs amounts to genocide "because African Americans constitute a disproportionate number of those subjected to arrest, prosecution, and incarceration for illicit drug trafficking" (e.g., see Meddis, 1993). Federal sentencing against drug dealers demonstrates clear evidence of bias against people of color. One study, for example, found that African American and Hispanic drug offenders received longer sentences than Caucasian drug offenders, even after controlling for relevant legal factors (Albonetti, 1997), and that Caucasian defendants received more benefit from departures from federal sentencing guidelines. Albonetti concludes that her findings "strongly suggest that the mechanism by which the federal guidelines permit the exercise of discretion operates to the disadvantage of minority defendants" (p. 818).

> *The impact of sentencing laws on minorities, especially African Americans, is greatest at the federal level.*

In the wars against drugs and violence, federal sentencing has become much more complex. From 1987 to 1998, federal sentencing guidelines increased from 325 to 1,194 pages. The federal sentencing grid now contains 258 boxes, and calculations needed to determine the proper sentence occupy a 393-page rule book with 539 pages of appendixes. The prosecutor, who decides what to charge and how many counts to charge (among the thousands of offenses in the federal criminal code), thereby effectively determines the likely sentence. Such concentration of power creates bias in favor of the government and against the client who is supposedly innocent until proved guilty, as I discussed in Chapter Eight. Also, judges have little oversight in the process, and only prosecutors can reward suspects for turning state's evidence against other suspects.

Federal sentencing is also viewed as unfair. For example, 86% of judges want to modify guidelines to increase their sentencing discretion. A 1992 survey of judges found they believed only one in four sentences imposed under guidelines is appropriate (Coalition for Federal Sentencing Reform, 1997). A particularly striking unfair pattern is the 100 : 1 ratio for sentences for crack cocaine and powder cocaine, meaning that to receive a mandatory sentence of five years imprisonment, a person would need 100 times as much powder cocaine as crack (500 grams of powder versus 5 grams of crack). No one can say for sure if this discrepancy is racially motivated, but, as noted before, African Americans account for 39% of crack cocaine users (and for only 13% of the general population) but 89% of those sentenced for federal crack crimes (Coalition for Federal Sentencing Reform, 1999). Media portrayal of crack use reinforces the stereotype or myth that it is an "African American drug" (e.g., see Reeves and Campbell, 1994). Because harms associated with crack cocaine (e.g., "crack babies") were so broadly portrayed and discussed, not even a single African American member of Congress spoke out against the sentencing disparities between crack and powder cocaine at the time that the law was originally proposed and debated (Kennedy, 1997).

Criminal sentencing also appears to be affected by gender. For example, Kappeler et al. (2000: 229) claim: "Judges influence and decide cases based on their stereotyped notions of the roles of women. Courts have consistently demonstrated a gender bias in mediating domestic violence and rape cases." I discussed the evidence in this area in Chapter Five. With regard to sexual assault cases, law enforcement officers are reluctant to arrest; prosecutors are reluctant to prosecute; and juries are reluctant to convict and to sentence in any sexual assault cases where (1) a woman is perceived as precipitating her own rape or assault by her style of dress, her drinking or drug-consuming activity, or her participation in certain activities, such as going to a bar or hitchhiking, or (2) there is a lack of physical evidence of a severe injury proving forced intercourse (e.g., see Estrich, 1987; LaFree, 1989).

Of course, bias in sentencing can be found when we look at crimes committed by the wealthy. As noted by Kappeler et al. (2000: 230), this is where the courts tend to be "kinder and gentler." Compare people in one study who were convicted for grand theft versus those convicted of fraud in the health care industry, for example. This study (Tillman and Pontell, 1992) showed that those who were convicted of fraud were only half as likely as those convicted of grand theft to be sentenced to prison even though the damages they caused were 10 times greater. The average sentence given to offenders in the savings and loan crisis was 36 months, versus 38 months for people who committed auto theft and 56 months for burglars (Pontell, Calavita, and Tillman, 1994). Failing to sentence the guilty simply because of their social class and skin color is as unjust as sentencing a small group of the guilty more harshly because of their social class or skin color. White-collar deviance (see Chapter Three) is one place where justice truly is not blind. Instead, she knowingly shrugs off the harms caused by wealthy Caucasian criminals.

> *The* criminal justice system is very soft on white-collar offenders.

CONCLUSION

Sentencing is the process whereby a person who has been convicted of a crime or crimes is sanctioned for his or her wrongdoings by a court. The American criminal justice system is apparently dedicated to sentencing criminals to punishments that have clearly been proven ineffective, particularly imprisonment. Meanwhile, punishment in the United States is also biased in some ways against poor people, people of color, and women. Although biases in sentencing are not institutional, there is clear evidence of sentencing disparities based on class, race, and gender. These biases serve as further evidence of unjust practices of the U.S. criminal justice system.

ISSUE IN DEPTH
What Works, What Doesn't

Several criminologists (Sherman et al., 1997) published a congressionally mandated evaluation of state and local crime prevention programs funded by the U.S. Department of Justice. The study, titled *Preventing Crime: What Works, What Doesn't, What's Promising*, clearly laid out the few programs we know work to reduce crime, the many more that we know don't work, and the largest share that appear to be promising.

It seems logical to invest in the programs that we know work to reduce crime while simultaneously acknowledging and abandoning the programs that we know to be failures. In the words of the authors (Sherman et al., 1998: 1): "Many crime prevention programs work. Others don't. Most programs have not yet been evaluated with enough scientific evidence to draw conclusions. Enough evidence is available, however, to create provisional lists of what works, what doesn't, and what's promising," as well as what is still unknown.

The authors proceeded from the assumption that crime prevention means "any practice shown to result in less crime than would normally occur without the practice." Programs aimed at crime prevention, including reducing drug abuse and youth violence, were assessed and placed in the "seven local institutional settings in which these practices operated": in communities, in families, in schools, in labor markets, in places, by police, and by courts and corrections (p. 2).

The authors identified the hundreds of programs operated under U.S. Department of Justice funding and then developed the "Maryland Scale of Scientific Methods" so that the effectiveness of each study could be determined. As mentioned before, each individual type of crime prevention program was categorized as either something that works, something that does not work, something that is promising, or something that is unknown. These terms are defined as follows:

- *What works:* Programs that the authors believe are "reasonably certain" to prevent crime or reduce risk factors for crime
- *What doesn't work:* Programs that the authors believe are "reasonably certain" to fail to prevent crime or reduce risk factors for crime
- *What's promising:* Programs for which the level of certainty is too low to make firm conclusions, but for which, on the basis of the limited evidence, there is some reason to expect some successful reduction in crime

- *What's unknown:* Programs that the authors could not classify into one of these categories because of a lack of studies testing the programs' effectiveness

The programs that were characterized as effective, or "what works," depended on the specific nature of the problem being addressed. The study found that no one type of crime prevention approach would work for all types of crime-related problems. There is no magic bullet in crime prevention. The following table shows what programs the authors concluded would work for the specific types of problems listed.

WHAT WORKS?

- *For infants:* Frequent home visits by nurses and other professionals reduce child abuse and injuries to infants.
- *For preschoolers:* Classes with weekly home visits by preschool teachers reduce the risk of later arrest.
- *For delinquent and at-risk preadolescents:* Family therapy and parent training reduce aggression and hyperactivity.
- *For schools:* Organizational development for innovation reduces crime and delinquency; communication and reinforcement of clear, consistent norms reduces crime and delinquency; teaching of social competency skills reduces delinquency and substance abuse; coaching of high-risk youth in thinking skills reduces substance abuse.
- *For older male ex-offenders:* Vocational training reduces repeat offending.
- *For rental housing with drug dealing:* Nuisance abatement action against land-lords reduces drug dealing and crime.
- *For high-crime hot spots:* Extra police patrols reduce crime in those hot spots.
- *For high-risk repeat offenders:* Monitoring by specialized police units reduces the crimes committed by repeat offenders on the streets. Incarceration of high-risk offenders keeps them from committing crime on the streets.
- *For domestic abusers who are employed:* On-scene arrests reduce subsequent domestic assaults.
- *For drug-using offenders in prison:* Therapeutic community resident programs reduce repeat offending after release.

You may have noticed from this table that no community-level programs are included. This is because "there are no community-based crime prevention programs proved to be effective at preventing crime" (p. 6). As you will see later, some community-based efforts are considered promising. Additionally, in terms of places, "there are as yet no place-focused crime prevention programs proved to be ineffective. . . . [R]elative to other areas of crime prevention, few place-focused crime prevention methods have been studied" (p. 9).

The next table summarizes the programs the authors claim do not work. Note that many of these programs are those that are either currently being practiced by the U.S. criminal justice system or being advocated by politicians in the United States.

WHAT DOESN'T WORK?

- Gun buyback programs without geographic limitations.
- Community mobilization against crime in high-poverty areas.
- Police counseling visits to homes of couples days after domestic violence incidents.
- Counseling and peer counseling of students in schools.
- Drug Abuse Resistance Education (the DARE program).
- Drug prevention classes focused on fear and other emotional appeals, including increasing self-esteem.
- School-based leisure-time enrichment programs.
- Summer jobs or subsidized work programs for at-risk youth.
- Short-term, nonresidential training programs for at-risk youth.
- Diversion from court to job training as a condition of case dismissal.
- Neighborhood watch programs organized with police.
- Arrests of juveniles for minor offenses.
- Arrests of unemployed suspects for domestic assault.
- Increased arrests or raids on drug market locations.
- Storefront police offices in high-crime locations.
- Police newsletters with local crime information.
- Correctional boot camps using traditional military basic training.
- "Scared Straight" programs whereby minor juvenile offenders visit adult prisons.
- Shock probation, shock parole, and split sentences adding jail time to probation or parole.
- Home detention with electronic monitoring.
- Intensive supervision on parole or probation.
- Rehabilitation programs using vague, unstructured counseling.
- Residential programs for juvenile offenders using challenging experiences in rural settings.

The final table summarizes those crime prevention programs the authors claim are promising. These are programs that have been demonstrated to be effective by at least one study and thus should continue to be practiced and further evaluated in order to assess their effectiveness.

WHAT'S PROMISING?

- Proactive drunk driving arrests with breath testing may reduce accident deaths.
- Community policing with meetings to set priorities may reduce perceptions of crime.
- Police showing greater respect to arrested offenders may reduce repeat offending.
- Polite field interrogations of suspicious persons may reduce street crime.
- Making arrest warrants to domestic violence suspects who leave the scene before police arrive.
- A higher number of police officers in cities may reduce crime.
- Gang monitoring by community workers and probation and police officers may reduce gang violence.

- Community-based mentoring by Big Brothers/Big Sisters of America may prevent drug abuse.
- Community-based after-school recreation programs may reduce juvenile delinquency.
- Battered women's shelters may reduce repeat domestic violence.
- Schools within schools that group students into smaller units may reduce drug use and delinquency.
- Training or coaching in thinking skills for high-risk youth may prevent crime.
- Building school capacity through organizational development may prevent substance abuse.
- Improved classroom management and instructional techniques may reduce alcohol use.
- Job Corps residential training programs for at-risk youth may reduce felonies.
- Prison-based vocational education programs may be beneficial for adult inmates in federal prisons.
- Moving urban public housing residents to suburban homes may reduce risk factors for crime.
- Enterprise Zones may reduce area unemployment.
- Having two clerks in already-robbed convenience stores may reduce repeat robberies.
- Redesigning the layout of retail stores may reduce shoplifting.
- Improved training and management of bar and tavern staff may reduce violence and driving under the influence of alcohol.
- Metal detectors may reduce skyjacking and the presence of weapons in schools.
- Street closures, barricades, and rerouting traffic may reduce violence and burglary.
- Target hardening may reduce vandalism of parking meters and crimes against phones.
- Problem-solving analyses unique to crime situations at particular locations may reduce the types of crimes problematic in given areas.
- Proactive arrests for carrying concealed weapons may reduce gun crime.
- Drug courts may reduce repeat offending.
- Drug treatment in jails followed by urine testing in the community may reduce subsequent drug use.
- Intensive supervision and aftercare of juvenile offenders may reduce repeat offending.
- Fines may reduce repeat crimes.

Even given these findings, the authors of the study reach only very cautious conclusions:

> The central conclusion of the report is that the current development of scientific evidence is inadequate to the task of policymaking. Many more impact evaluations using stronger scientific methods are needed before even minimally valid conclusions can be reached about the impact on crime of programs costing billions each year. (p. 12)

More money needs to be invested in studying crime and crime prevention. Perhaps our government will soon begin to redirect a greater share of the money we currently spend on ineffective and harmful crime control policies toward crime prevention programs that we know work and evaluation of crime prevention programs that are promising yet understudied. When politicians promote policies they know to be ineffective, it is unjust. When politicians do not know which policies are effective, it is unacceptable. Neither situation can be tolerated.

Doesn't it make sense to invest in programs that we know work and abandon those that do not? In the final chapter, I advocate a crime reduction approach based on planned change rather than unplanned change. Whereas unplanned change is based on little more than opinion or individual philosophies, planned change involves careful analysis of crime problems and planned interventions to reduce them.

Discussion Questions

- What is sentencing?
- Identify and discuss different types of sentences.
- Identify some of the drawbacks to determinate and indeterminate sentences.
- Why do you think judges are generally opposed to mandatory sentences?
- What types of crimes generally receive the longest sentences? Why?
- Identify and discuss the main justifications for punishment.
- Why has the U.S. criminal justice system largely given up on rehabilitation?
- Identify and discuss the main methods of punishment in the United States.
- Which type of punishment is the most used? Which is the least used? Why?
- Why are some people sentenced to probation and others sentenced to terms of incarceration, even though they are convicted for the same crimes?
- Why is the administration of punishment in the United States so ineffective at reducing crime?
- Identify the main sources of bias during the sentencing process.
- How does criminal sentencing reflect biases of the criminal law and policing?
- Identify and discuss the main problems with the so-called three-strikes laws.
- Why do you think the criminal justice system pursues crime prevention strategies that have been proved ineffective?

CHAPTER TEN

IMPRISONMENT: LOCK 'EM UP
AND THROW AWAY YOUR MONEY

INTRODUCTION

The end result of the criminal justice process is our corrections system. The corrections system in the United States is made up of a group of agencies and programs that are responsible for administering punishment to people accused and convicted of criminal offenses. As discussed in the last chapter, forms of punishment include incarceration in prisons and jails, probation in the community, and a wide array of intermediate sanctions. This chapter gives separate attention to incarceration, specifically to imprisonment, because it is one of the most destructive and expensive forms of punishment in the United States. It is also a method that clearly does not meet the ideal goals of the criminal justice system.

AMERICA'S INCARCERATION RATE

Currently, the United States has the highest rate of incarceration in the world, just ahead of Russia and more than five times greater than most industrialized nations (Beckett and Sasson, 2000; Irwin and Austin, 1997). This is due to massive increases in incarceration in the last thirty years (e.g., see Beck, 1999). Just how many people are incarcerated in the United States? If we took all the people who are incarcerated and put them in one place, it would be the sixth largest city in the country.

> *C*urrently, the United States has the highest rate of incarceration in the world, just ahead of Russia and more than five times greater than most industrialized nations.

The U.S. incarceration rate includes inmates in both prisons and jails. Although prisons and jails are both forms of incarceration, they are not the same thing. Prisons are typically run by states and the federal government, whereas jails are typically run by local governments such as counties. Prisons are intended for offenders who have been convicted of crimes that will require more than one year of incarceration. Jails are for offenders who have been convicted of crimes that will require less than one year of incarceration. Jail populations also include people awaiting trial in preventive detention, people awaiting sentencing or transfer to another facility, and mentally ill and homeless citizens being held for relatively minor public order offenses (Clear and Cole, 1994).

It is estimated that roughly one in ten of the nation's prisoners is mentally ill (Weisman, 2000: 105), although some suggest that the figure may be more like 40% (Torrey et al., 1992). The mentally ill are in jail largely because the nation's mentally ill populations were released from state hospitals in the expectation that they would be able to get treatment in their communities. But community treatment programs are not available in many communities; in places where such programs are available, systems are not in place to ensure that people who need them will obtain treatment. Thus, "Jails and prisons have become the de facto providers of mental health services in this country" (Weisman, 2000: 106). In most states, the largest provider is the prison system; the nation's largest provider is the Los Angeles County Jail.

Jail may represent the largest waste of resources on offenders: most people in county jails who were convicted of crimes committed very minor crimes, and the average sentence they will serve is a few days. Prisoners, by contrast, will serve longer sentences because of the perceived severity of their offenses. I focus on prisons in this chapter because of the prolonged stay of their inmates.

The National Criminal Justice Commission writes: "Since 1980, the United States has engaged in the largest and most frenetic correctional buildup of any country in the history of the world" (Donziger, 1996: 31). This is true for incarceration in prisons and jails and also for probation and parole populations, which have grown to over 5 million (The Sentencing Project, 1997). Altogether, more than 6 million people are under some form of criminal justice supervision in the United States.

Think about the irony of this. Professor Todd Clear, an expert on corrections, writes in the foreword to Irwin and Austin's (1997) book *It's About Time: America's Imprisonment Binge*:

> As Americans, we think of ourselves as a free people. And we think that our freedoms are central to what sets us apart from the rest of the world. . . . It is ironic, then, that in America more people are denied these freedoms by law than in any other Western nation: we lock up more citizens per capita than any other nation that has bothered to count its prisoners. (p. xiii)

Without much doubt, the U.S. imprisonment rate alone (which does not include jail populations) stands as a testament to how far our nation's leaders are willing to go to fight crime—or, more accurately, to fight some types of crime committed by some types of people.

Walker (1998) describes recent crime control efforts in the United States as "an imprisonment orgy." Figure 10.1 documents the unprecedented explosion of imprisonment in the United States from the early twentieth century through the 1990s. First, note how the U.S. imprisonment rate has historically been relatively constant. It has fluctuated over the years, but never until the 1970s did it consistently and dramatically increase. In fact, scholars had written about the "stability of

FIGURE 10.1

America's Imprisonment Rate

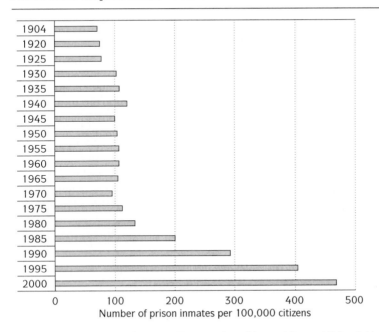

SOURCE: Data from S. Walker, *Sense and Nonsense about Crime and Drugs: A Policy Guide,* 4th ed. (Belmont, CA: Wadsworth, 1998).

punishment" because there was so little fluctuation in the nation's incarceration rate for so long (Blumstein and Cohen, 1973). Second, note how the imprisonment explosion began in the early 1970s. Since that time, there has been approximately a 6.5% increase each year (Blumstein, 2000: 6). Most of this increase has been due to drug convictions (including a 478% increase in drug offenders sentenced to state prisons and a 545% increase in drug offenders sentenced to federal prisons from 1985 to 1996). From 1980 to 1993, the percentage of prisoners in state prisons serving sentences for drug offenses more than tripled; in federal prisons, it more than doubled (Welch, 1999: 52). Meanwhile, drug treatment in prison is insufficiently funded, although it is supported by most Americans (Welch, 1999: 62).

The imprisonment rate in the United States has historically been relatively constant. It has fluctuated over the years, but never until the 1970s did it consistently and dramatically increase.

According to Kappeler, Blumberg, and Potter (2000: 161), the number of sentenced prisoners in both state and federal prisons increased almost 7 times from 1972 to 1998 alone. The United States now has more than twice the number of prisoners per 100,000 citizens as any other democracy, and more than 5 times the rate of democracies such as Canada, England, Germany, and France (The Sentencing Project, 1997). Also, jail, probation, and parole populations in the United States have tripled since 1980.

> *The* number of sentenced prisoners in both state and federal prisons increased almost seven times from 1972 to 1998 alone.

Does sound, scientific evidence suggest that this will work to make us safer? Absolutely not. May (2000: xvi), editor of a series of essays on prison titled *Building Violence,* suggests that "[t]he United States is conducting a social experiment unparalleled in its size and implications" and that "[c]riminological research has not been able to demonstrate convincingly that the incarceration of more people, and longer sentences, ultimately provide more security."

Let me state unequivocally that the dramatic upward shift in the U.S. imprisonment rate is not attributable to increases in street crime. In Chapter Three, you saw that most forms of street crime have decreased since 1973. The murder rate has held relatively constant prior to and after the boom in incarceration. One trend that corresponds with the increased use of imprisonment as a criminal sanction is an upward shift in income, documented nicely by Phillips (1991) in *The Politics of Rich and Poor* and by Barlett and Steele (1992) in *America: What Went Wrong?* These authors demonstrate how, during the 1980s, the wealthiest Americans got richer while most Americans actually lost ground. In an environment of corporate-friendly legislation, including the deregulation efforts and tax breaks of Presidents Reagan and Bush, many more Americans found themselves living in conditions conducive to criminality. For example, from 1977 to 1988, the average after-tax family income for Americans in the bottom 10% declined nearly 11%, while for the upper 10%, it increased almost 25%, and for the top 1% it increased almost 75%. Also, compensation for CEOs of corporations increased more than 100%, and the number of millionaires and billionaires increased by 250%. Do you think that any of these figures are relevant for understanding why the United States is incarcerating so many people?

> *The* dramatic upward shift in the U.S. imprisonment rate is not attributable to increases in street crime.

If you compare these rising imprisonment rates to crime rate declines since the early 1970s (see Chapter Three), you might conclude that incarceration is an effective means of reducing crime. But this conclusion would be wrong. First, there has not been a dramatic drop in crime during this same time period, as you would expect given that incarceration rates are nearly four times what they were twenty years ago (Blumstein, 2000). Second, the modest declines in crime rates are more likely due to changes in demographic characteristics in society and changes in illicit drug markets. One major reason street crime rates have declined in the United States is that Americans have gotten older. Street crime is generally a young male phenomenon, so an older population means less crime. Irwin and Austin (1997: 144) attribute 60% of the decline in U.S. crime rates between 1980 and 1988 to reductions in the size of the population aged 15 to 24 years old. Additionally, as illicit drug markets have become more stable, new markets rarely open up, thus eliminating the unstable situations where people fight it out for the right to provide drugs to users (Beckett and Sasson, 2000: 192). Reductions in violent street crimes, then, are attributable to the stabilization of the drug market, which persists even as the United States fights its war on drugs (see Chapter Six).

*M*odest declines in crime rates are more likely due to changes in demographic characteristics in society and changes in illicit drug markets than to incarceration increases.

Todd Clear, in the foreword to Welch's (1999: ix) *Punishment in America: Social Control and the Ironies of Imprisonment,* claims that the U.S. incarceration rate has little to do with crime rates in the United States: "prison populations continue to grow, despite five consecutive years of falling crime; indeed, since 1975, we have had 10 years of declining crime rates and then 13 years of increasing crime rates—but prison populations have gone up every year regardless." Welch (1999) claims that prison populations are being driven more by economic and market forces than by crime. He claims that

> political leaders, rather than simply treating lawbreakers firmly but fairly, are becoming increasingly intolerant and vindictive. In a sense, the state appears to have crossed the line from "getting tough" to "getting rough" by encouraging institutions and authorities to bully individuals lacking the power to defend themselves adequately against an ambitious and overzealous criminal justice system. (p. xix)

*T*odd Clear, in the foreword to Welch's (1999: ix) *Punishment in America: Social Control and the Ironies of Imprisonment,* claims that the U.S. incarceration rate has little to do with crime rates in the United States: "since 1975, we have had 10 years of declining crime rates and then 13 years of increasing crime rates—but prison populations have gone up every year regardless."

Lynch (1998) also points out that imprisonment has no real effect on crime rates, and Wilkins (1991) suggests that its use is related to unemployment rates rather than crime rates.

The U.S. imprisonment binge is ironic given that numerous scholars and organizations have demonstrated that incarceration is destructive to the United States and that our war on crime "has made things worse: that it has not deterred crime, that it is racially biased, and that it has contributed to the destruction of inner-city communities" (Walker, 1998: 10–11). Currie (1998: 56–57) demonstrates that there is *not* clear evidence showing that states and countries that incarcerate more people have lower crime rates. Irwin and Austin (1997: 146) show that states that incarcerate more people do not necessarily have lower crime rates; in fact, the opposite is true overall, although the differences between states are inconsequential. Within the academic disciplines of criminology and criminal justice, a consensus has emerged against overrelying on incarceration, and yet we continue to lock up more and more people. You will recall from earlier chapters that crime is a political issue that can be "sold" to voters and viewers of the mass media, and that politicians must appear "tough on crime" to get elected and stay in office. Nevertheless, criminal justice policies motivated by politics are not in line with the scientific knowledge generated within the academic disciplines of criminology and criminal justice.

Irwin and Austin (1997: xvii–xviii) discuss the main tenets of the political agenda that justifies more and more prisons, which include the following:

• The War on Poverty, which sought to fight crime through education, job training, and rehabilitation in the 1960s and 1970s, was a total failure.

- Dangerous criminals repeatedly go free because of liberal judges or decisions made by the liberal Supreme Court that help the criminal but not the victim.
- Swift and certain punishment in the form of more and longer prison terms will reduce crime by incapacitating the hardened criminals and making potential lawbreakers think twice before they commit crimes.
- Most inmates are dangerous and cannot be safely placed in the community.
- In the long run, it will be far cheaper for society to increase the use of imprisonment.
- Greater use of imprisonment since the 1980s has in fact reduced crime.

Does any of this sound familiar to you? It is likely that these are the kinds of statements you have heard from politicians of both major political parties in the last several election cycles. For example, on C-SPAN, I recently saw a congressional representative from my home state of Florida who made a simplistic association between falling crime rates in New York and tougher, zero-tolerance law enforcement. His argument was that if we engaged in tougher law enforcement across the nation, crime rates would fall everywhere. In fact, crime rates are already falling everywhere and they have fallen in major cities that have not pursued zero-tolerance policing as much as, if not more than, in New York. Furthermore, crime rates began declining in New York before the implementation of the zero-tolerance law enforcement policies. The member of Congress was either misinformed or dishonest about the issue.

What It Costs

It is difficult to put a price tag on the U.S. corrections system, because the cost of building and maintaining prison cells varies from state to state. Additionally, true costs of building prisons cannot be known unless one considers the added costs of interest over time on loans to build prisons. Irwin and Austin (1997: 139) write that

> when a state builds and finances a typical medium-security prison, it will spend approximately $268,000 per bed for construction alone. . . . [I]n the states that have expanded their prison populations, the cost per additional prisoner will be about $39,000 per year [which] includes the cost of building the new cell amortized 30 years. In other words, the 30-year cost of adding space for one prisoner is more than $1 million.

For every $100 million spent on prison construction, the government will ultimately have to pay $1.6 billion over the next 30 years (Ambrosio and Schiraldi, 1997: 5).

Estimates suggest that incarceration in the United States costs over $20 billion annually, with over 11 million new admissions each year (National Center on Institutions and Alternatives, 1999). Operating the entire criminal justice system costs over $100 billion annually, in part due to the $100,000 it takes to build a new cell, $200,000 over 25 years to pay off debt for construction, and an average of $23,000 per year per cell (National Center on Institutions and Alternatives, 1999). To accommodate new correctional clients, 38 federal prisons were built between 1980 and 1995, compared with only 41 built between 1900 and 1980. More federal prisons are currently under construction. With correctional populations exploding from 24,000 (1980) to 41,000 (1987) to 106,000 (1996) to 118,000 prisoners (1998), and with federal sentencing being more complex, federal appeals increased from 225 to 8,731 between 1988 and 1995. Currently, federal prisons are operating at over 100% of capacity. This is not surprising given the growing number of criminal records in the United States today, which now amounts to about 50 million, with 60% of the

> *E*stimates suggest that incarceration in the United States costs over $20 billion annually, with over 11 million new admissions each year.

increase coming in the last decade (Miller, 1997). States are also embarking on "record-level prison construction programs. Between 1990 and 1994, the bed capacity of the country's prison system increased by nearly 200,000 prison beds" (Irwin and Austin, 1997: 65).

> *O*perating the entire criminal justice system costs over $100 billion annually, in part due to the $100,000 it takes to build a new cell, $200,000 over 25 years to pay off debt for construction, and average $23,000 per year per cell.

For every inmate that is incarcerated at a cost of about $30,000 per year, the cost per inmate is equivalent to the tax burden of four American families (Coalition for Federal Sentencing Reform, 1997). Additional costs come in the form of cuts in educational funding, student loans, libraries, work incentives, opportunity-creating programs, employment programs, and highway repair and construction (J. Miller, 1997). As such programs were being cut, in the 1980s alone, federal, state, and local expenditures for police grew 416%, for courts they increased 585%, for prosecution and legal services they grew by 1,019%, for public defenders they grew 1,255%, and for corrections they increased 986%. Federal justice spending overall increased 668%, county justice spending increased by 711%, and state spending increased 848% (Miller, 1998).

> *F*or every inmate who is incarcerated at a cost of about $30,000 per year, the cost per inmate is equivalent to the tax burden of four American families.

The evidence suggests that the U.S. war on crime is not only costing us dearly now but will continue to do so in the future. For every dollar we spend on fighting crime, for example, we take away from other social services, including education, public health, and the infrastructure of roads and bridges. Ironically, crime funding may actually exacerbate criminogenic factors. For example, the three-strikes laws in California will produce shortfalls in education funding for at least an entire decade (see Chapter Nine). Less money for education means less access to education. Less education can lead to less opportunity for legitimate success, leading in turn to conditions of strain, which historically have been linked to increased risk for criminality (Agnew, 1993; Merton, 1938a). "If education has historically been an investment in the future of society, then the cuts in education to finance prison represent a *dis*investment in the future (Walker, 1998: 13; emphasis in original). According to the National Association of State Budget Officers (1996: 77, 98), the total cost of state-issued bonds to build prisons surpasses the total issued to build colleges.

WHO'S IN PRISON?

Why do we lock up so many more of our citizens than other countries do, even though we have no more crime overall? One primary reason is that criminal justice in the United States is much harsher toward relatively minor criminals than in other countries (Donziger, 1996: 10). In fact, the majority of people in our nation's jails and prisons were convicted of nonviolent offenses. For example, 84% of prison admissions between 1980 and 1993 were for nonviolent offenses (Bureau of Justice Statistics, 1994). These statistics may explain why many prison wardens feel that up to half of the offenders under their supervision could be released without making the country any less safe (Simon, 1994). Perhaps Ingley's (2000: 21) summary of who's in prison says it best:

> Today's corrections reality is such: the fastest growing [prison] populations are those captured from our "war on drugs," the deinstitutionalization of our mental health system, and mandatory minimum sentencing policies. . . . [T]he majority of our prisoners are chronic substance abusers, functionally illiterate, indigent, or possess few, if any, job skills.

The majority of people in our nation's jails and prisons were convicted for nonviolent offenses. For example, 84% of prison admissions between 1980 and 1993 were for nonviolent offenses.

What has happened in the United States has been likened to a bait-and-switch scam, because politicians have talked tough about violent criminals and promised tougher punishment for them, yet most of the people being sent to prison are *not* violent offenders (Donziger, 1996: 18). This works because Americans see "crime" and "violence" as essentially the same thing (Zimring and Hawkins, 1997). Most incarcerated criminals are *not* violent criminals, nor are most incarcerated criminals "career criminals" (Irwin and Austin, 1997). Americans may support imprisonment as punishment for repeat, violent criminals. It is doubtful they would support it for relatively minor offenders. It is, after all, their money that pays for prisons. Yet, mass releases of prisoners will certainly not occur, even with the realization that it may be cost effective and relatively safe to release nonviolent and drug offenders from prison to serve probationary parole sentences (Bureau of Justice Statistics, 1995).

A possible danger of incarcerating relatively minor offenders is that as Americans become aware of this, some may begin to disrespect law generally. Rold (2000: 45) claims: "People are more likely to follow laws when they agree with them and respect the legitimacy of the community and agency administering the laws." Because prisons are used against many relatively harmless offenders, "the fabric of our social order and our view of ourselves as a compassionate nation" are threatened. This is also the argument of Packer, whose crime control and due process models of criminal justice were discussed in Chapter One. Packer suggested that victimless crimes (such as drug use and prostitution) should be decriminalized because their illegal status led to disrespect for the law generally.

Recall from Chapter One the discussion of alternative goals of the criminal justice system. I suggested that the criminal justice system may be serving limited interests by controlling certain segments of the population. According to Alexander (2000: 52), the only *Fortune* 500 company to employ more people than corrections is General Motors. Companies lobby and make hundreds of thousands of dollars in political contributions to maintain a stranglehold on criminal justice.

Additionally, politicians benefit from the incarceration boom by getting elected to office. An irony is that as the nation's economy provides substantially more wealth to the richest of Americans, more of the rest of us support more prisons simply because they provide us with jobs that allow us to enjoy some of the benefits of the good economy.

American prisons and jails are used disproportionately against the nation's "riffraff." Williams (2000: 72) writes that the nation's "lost souls find their only productive social role is as fodder for the ever-growing number" of prisons and jails. Irwin and Austin (1997: 8) write that what explains the U.S. reliance on incarceration as a means to control serious crime is "the American people's strong desire to banish from their midst any population of people who are threatening." Rothman (1971) makes a similar point in *The Discovery of the Asylum* by analyzing the history of American corrections. Rothman shows that the United States has always set aside the poor, mentally retarded, and mentally ill under the guise of corrections. A study by del Carmen and Robinson (2000) shows how both tuberculosis and crime prevention efforts used at the turn of the century in the nation's big cities were aimed primarily at poor immigrants.

> *U*.S. prisons and jails are used disproportionately against the nation's "riffraff."

Although this chapter deals with prisons, jail populations serve as further evidence of whom our system pursues, so I briefly mention them here. Welch (1999: 89) calls the jailing of offensive but nondangerous populations a form of "social sanitation" reserved mostly for the urban underclass or our nation's "rabble" (Irwin, 1985). People in jail are generally "either members of the working poor or permanent members of the underclass," with low educational attainment and "limited means to survive economically" (Welch, 1999: 94).

Do Americans really support these policies? Public opinion research has consistently shown that Americans prefer that inmates in the nation's prisons be granted access to rehabilitation (Roberts and Stalans, 2000). It is doubtful, too, that many Americans truly understand who is in prison. The typical prisoner, as you have seen, is not a repetitive, violent criminal. Rather, he or she (most likely a "he") is typically a property or drug offender. Slightly less than half of Irwin and Austin's (1997: 40) sample of incarcerated prisoners were characterized as "career criminals." Of those who were, about 60% were imprisoned for what Americans view as "petty crimes." Of the 25% of their sample who were serving lengthy sentences, many did not warrant these sentences on the basis of the relative nonseriousness of their offenses.

Thus, Irwin and Austin (1997: 57) write: "Most crimes are much pettier than the popular images promoted by those who sensationalize the crime issue (such as politicians and the media). More than half of the persons sent to prison committed crimes that lacked any of the features the public believes compose a serious crime." Even the high-risk inmates, the career criminals, are typically uneducated, unskilled, and underemployed. From public poll results, Irwin and Austin claim that if Americans knew this, they would not likely support the massive use of incarceration as a means to reduce crime.

Consider an alarming possibility about U.S. prisons, then: one of their functions may be to warehouse a significant portion of the population that is not employable. Consider that most convicted offenders sentenced to a term of imprisonment are poor, uneducated, and underemployed. To the degree that people are targeted, then, one function served by incarceration is a reduced need to provide social services to those people. In fact, virtually everyone in prison is poor. Table 10.1 illustrates that many people in prison were underemployed (i.e., not employed full-time) in the year prior to their incarceration, that most offenders in prison earned less than $10,000 per year, and that the vast majority of offenders in prison did not go to college. These statistics prove that the war on crime disproportionately affects poor people. Americans view street crimes (committed by the poor) as "our problem," when in reality it is mostly "their problem" (because criminal victimization is disproportionately directed at the poor). Our criminal justice reactions, particularly imprisonment, aimed at making it better for "us," actually make it worse for "them." This is another ironic, unintended consequence of U.S. criminal justice practices (Walker, 1998).

---

*M*ost people in prison were underemployed (i.e., not employed full-time) in the year prior to their incarceration, made less than $10,000 per year, and had not gone to college.

As noted throughout this book, incarceration also disproportionately affects people of color. Is this a recent phenomenon? According to Cahalan (1986), we can confidently say that prison populations have been disproportionately made up of African Americans since 1926, the first year that national prison statistics were collected. In that year, African Americans made up 9% of the population but 21% of the prison population. Today, African Americans make up 13% of the population but about half of the prison population. The first time that more African Americans were admitted to U.S. prisons than non-African Americans was in the late 1980s, during the height of the war on drugs. Even worse, only about 10% of those seeking college degrees are African American (Walker, Spohn, and DeLone, 2000: 260). Hispanics now make up more than 18% of

TABLE 10.1
Selected Characteristics of State Prison Inmates

Education	
Some college	12%
High school graduate	22%
High school	46%
No high school	19%
Employment	
Full-time	55%
Part-time	12%
Unemployed	33%
Income	
$25,000 or more	15%
$15,000–$24,999	16%
$10,000–$14,999	17%
$5,000–$9,999	21%
Less than $5,000	32%

SOURCE: Data from U.S. Department of Justice, *Survey of State Prison Inmates.*

the nation's prison inmates (Mumola and Beck, 1997), and their incarceration rate since the mid-1980s has increased twice as much as those of African Americans and Caucasians (Walker et al., 2000: 261). The picture in American jails is very similar, as 41% of jail inmates in 1998 were African American and almost 16% were Hispanic. This means the majority of jail inmates were people of color (Gilliard, 1999). I will return to the issue of bias at the end of this chapter, but first I will dispel some myths about what it is like to be in prison.

---

*P*rison populations have been disproportionately made up of African Americans since 1926, the first year that national prison statistics were collected. In that year, African Americans made up 9% of the general population but 21% of the prison population. Today, African Americans make up 13% of the general population but about half of the prison population.

WHAT HAPPENS IN PRISON? PAINS OF IMPRISONMENT

Most people who are in prison will one day get out (see the section on parole later in the chapter). It may be easy to lock up criminals and believe that we are somehow safer for it. But 9 out of 10 inmates will one day be released. Thus, Americans must realize that their own safety depends on what happens to prisoners while they are incarcerated. And prison, contrary to popular belief, is a horrendous place.

Contrary to the mythical view of the comfortable prison, American prisons are terribly hot, loud, and violent places to live (and work—keep in mind that many people in prison simply work there). The myth of "country club" prisons has led state lawmakers to pass some laughable legislation and make startling threats. The National Criminal Justice Commission reports the following examples:

- A Mississippi law forbidding individual air conditioners, even though no inmate actually had an individual air conditioner
- A Louisiana law forbidding inmates from taking martial arts classes, even though such classes were not currently available
- A complaint by the governor of Connecticut about the landscaping outside a prison, even though the plantings were made at the request of residential neighbors (Donziger, 1996: 45)

---

*C*ontrary to the mythical view of the comfortable prison, U.S. prisons are terribly hot, loud, and violent places to live (and work—keep in mind that many people in any prison simply work there).

Add to these examples efforts by state lawmakers to take away inmates' cigarettes (which contain the addictive drug nicotine and are used as a form of currency within prisons), the resurgence of chain gangs in many southern states, and other efforts to humiliate inmates by making them wear orange, pink, or striped jumpsuits. From all these efforts to make prison less pleasant, you might imagine that prison is a pretty nice place to be. In fact, because of the numerous "pains of imprisonment" (Sykes, 1958), the typical prison is not anything like a country club.

Gresham Sykes (1958), in his groundbreaking work *The Society of Captives*, outlined the major pains of imprisonment:

- Loss of liberty
- Loss of autonomy
- Loss of security
- Deprivation of heterosexual relationships
- Deprivation of goods and services

To these, I add three more:

- Loss of voting rights
- Loss of dignity
- Stigmatization

> *The* major pains of imprisonment include loss of liberty, loss of autonomy, loss of security, deprivation of heterosexual relationships, deprivation of goods and services, loss of voting rights, loss of dignity, and stigmatization.

I will discuss each of these in turn.

Loss of Liberty

First and foremost, prisoners lose their freedom. Many Americans seem to conceive of prisons as comfortable places where offenders watch televison free of charge, eat three square meals per day at no cost, enjoy various extracurricular activities such as weight lifting and basketball, and get a free education. Most of these conceptions are false. The Florida Department of Corrections maintains a web page where myths about its prisons are disputed, as shown in the following box.

Myths of Florida prisons

- *"Inmates don't work."* On June 30, 1999, there were 68,599 inmates in the Florida prison system. Private prisons housed 3,783 inmates; the remaining 64,816 were in Department of Corrections (DOC) facilities. Eighty-one percent of the inmates in DOC institutions and facilities in Florida on the last day of the fiscal year (June 30, 1999) worked, participated in programs such as vocational education or adult education classes, or a combination of work and programs. The remaining 19% either were physically unable to work, were participating in a reception and orientation process, or were in some type of confinement for management purposes, including death row. Inmate labor is used to construct new correctional facilities, and support and maintain the ongoing operation of correctional institutions. Inmates also prepare all meals; help maintain the prison grounds, farm, and garden; participate in sanitation and recycling processes; and work for PRIDE (Prison Rehabilitative

Industries and Diversified Enterprises) and PIE (Prison Industry Enhancement) programs. Additionally, inmates are assigned to Community Work Squads provided by the department. These inmates perform services under agreements with the Department of Transportation, other state agencies such as the Division of Forestry and the Department of Highway Safety, counties, cities, municipalities, and nonprofit organizations. Last fiscal year, the DOC's Community Work Squad Program saved Florida taxpayers more than $30 million through inmate labor.

- *"Inmates have cable television and satellite dishes."* There are no correctional facilities with cable television. The few prisons that have satellite dishes use them for staff training and academic classes for inmates as part of the Corrections Distance Learning Network (CDLN). The CDLN saves money by training staff throughout the state simultaneously and teaching inmates via satellite. The satellites are not used for recreational viewing. Most prisons have televisions available to inmates for use when inmates are not working or attending educational programs. The televisions are located in dormitory dayrooms for group viewing. Most of the department's televisions were paid for by proceeds from sales to inmates from the inmate canteens. However, state law now prohibits the purchase of televisions for recreational purposes.

- *"Why don't inmates grow their own food and save taxpayers some money?"* Inmates do grow some of their own food, and plans are under way to expand the farming areas from a few hundred to several thousand acres. The goal is to increase the number of inmates growing their own food to 10% of the inmate population, or about 6,800 inmates. Last year, the DOC's farm and gardening program operated at 64 facilities, covering 462 acres, producing approximately 3.5 million pounds of produce. The new program would almost double the farmland to 825 acres in fiscal year 1999–2000 and increase the number of inmates farming them by 25% in this fiscal year. Inmates will be responsible for all planting, harvesting, and crop maintenance. Inmates at Avon Park CI in Polk County would also have the opportunity to work in a hen house, where there are 900 hens laying eggs. DOC expects this program to save taxpayers approximately $825,000 during the first year of expansion. The ultimate goal of the self-sufficiency food program is to locate one large farming operation at one prison in each of the DOC's seven statewide service center areas. The Aquaculture Program, now active at 12 institutions, produced 30,000 pounds of fish last year.

- *"The Department of Corrections determines how long inmates serve in prison."* The Department of Corrections does not determine the length of prison sentences or the length of time inmates serve in prison. These decisions are made by judges and juries in accordance with state laws and sentencing guidelines. The department is solely responsible for the care and custody of offenders under its jurisdiction.

- *"Inmates still aren't serving most of their sentences."* For offenses committed on or after October 1, 1995, inmates are required to serve a minimum of 85% of their sentences. Since most of the inmates in prison today committed their crimes before that date, the 85% rule does not apply to them, although the percentage of the sentence they are serving continues to rise. The average percentage of sentence served by inmates released in June 1999 was 77.9%, as compared to 61.6% in June 1995.

- *"Prisons are air-conditioned."* Only 6 of the 53 major state-managed prisons in Florida have air-conditioning in some portion of the facility housing inmates (specialized units such as medical or mental health are air-conditioned), and many of these are located in South Florida.
- *"Inmates who get life sentences don't really stay in prison for life."* Today anyone sentenced to life in prison will serve a life term. Offenders sentenced to life for noncapital crimes committed on or after October 1, 1983, are serving life sentences without any chance of release. Offenders sentenced to life for capital crimes committed on or after October 1, 1983, are parole-eligible after serving 25-year mandatory sentences. However, if an offender committed capital murder on or after May 25, 1994, or capital sexual battery on or after October 1, 1995, then he or she is not eligible for parole.

SOURCE: Florida Department of Corrections. Online: www.dc.state.fl.us/.

Prisons in most states are similar in their conditions. For example, the following box describes a day in the North Carolina Department of Correction Division of Prisons.

Twenty-four hours in the North Carolina Department of Correction Division of Prisons

Type of Facility by Severity

Hour	Minimum	Medium	Close
Morning			
5:00	Sleep	Wake up	Sleep
6:00	Wake up	Breakfast	Wake up
7:00	Breakfast/travel to work site	Travel to work site/work	Breakfast/go to work in prison
8:00–10:00	Work	Work	Work
11:00	30 minutes for lunch	30 minutes for lunch	Work
Afternoon			
12:00	Work	Work	30 minutes for lunch
1:00–2:00	Work	Work	Work
3:00	Work/travel to prison	Travel to prison/off duty	Work day ends/time on prison yard
4:00	Off duty/time on prison yard	Time on prison yard	Return to cell
5:00	30 minutes for supper	30 minutes for supper	30 minutes for supper

Evening

6:00–7:00	Time for religious and specialized programming such as religious services, Narcotics Anonymous, anger management		
8:00	Return to dorm	Return to dorm	Return to cellblock
9:00–10:00	Remain in housing area	Remain in housing area	Remain in housing area
11:00	Lights out	Lights out	Lights out
12:00–4:00	Sleep	Sleep	Sleep

Maximum-security units consist of cells with sliding cell doors that are remotely operated from a secure control station. Maximum-security units are designated by the director of prisons at selected close-security prisons. These units are utilized to confine the most dangerous inmates, those who are a severe threat to public safety, correctional staff, and other inmates. Inmates confined in a maximum-security unit typically are in their cells 23 hours a day. During the other hour, they may be allowed to shower and exercise in the cellblock or an exterior cage. All inmate movement is strictly controlled with the use of physical restraints and correctional officer escort.

Close security prisons typically comprise single cells and are divided into cellblocks, which may be in one building or multiple buildings. Cell doors generally are remotely controlled from a secure control station. Each cell is equipped with its own combination plumbing fixture, which includes a sink and a toilet. The perimeter barrier is designed with a double fence with armed watchtowers or armed roving patrols. Inmate movement is restricted and supervised by correctional staff. Inmates are allowed out of their cells to work or attend corrective programs inside the facility.

Medium-security prisons typically consist of secure dormitories that provide housing for up to 50 inmates each. Each dormitory contains a group toilet and shower area as well as sinks. Inmates sleep in a military-style double bunk and have an adjacent metal locker for storage of uniforms, and other clothing. Each dormitory is locked at night, with a correctional officer providing direct supervision of the inmates and sleeping area. The prison usually has a double-fence perimeter with armed watchtowers or armed roving patrols. There is less supervision and control over the internal movement of inmates than in a close-security prison. Some medium-security prisons may be designed with dry cells as the method of inmate housing. Dry cells contain no toilet fixture. Most inmate work and self-improvement programs are within the prison, although selected medium-custody inmates work outside the prison under armed supervision of trained correctional officers. These inmate work assignments support prison farm operations or highway maintenance for the Department of Transportation. Each medium-security prison typically has a single-cell unit for the punishment of inmates who violate prison rules.

Minimum security prisons consist of nonsecure dormitories, which are routinely patrolled by correctional officers. Like medium-security dorms, they have their own group toilet and shower area adjacent to the sleeping quarters, which contain double bunks and lockers. The prison generally has a single perimeter fence, which is inspected on a regular basis, but no armed watchtowers or roving patrol. There is less supervision and control over inmates in the dormitories and less supervision of inmate movement within the prison than at a medium-security facility. Inmates assigned to minimum-security prisons generally pose the least risk to public safety. Minimum-custody inmates at minimum-security prisons usually participate in community-based work assignments such as the Governor's Community Work Program, road maintenance with Department of Transportation employee supervision, or work release with civilian employers. Also, inmates may participate in prerelease transition programs with Community Volunteers and family sponsors.

SOURCE: North Carolina Department of Correction. Online: www.doc.state.nc.us/.

Although recreation is permitted and even encouraged within most U.S. prisons, it is allowed for the safety of correctional personnel. And funding for educational, vocational training, and treatment programs within prisons has been slashed dramatically. In part, treatment is lacking because of prisoners' protections from government intervention. McLaughlin (2000: 24) states, for example: "Federal regulations for the Protection of Human Subjects . . . are extended to prisoners due to past abuses and the concern that prisoners may be limited in their ability to give truly informed consent." Many, if not all, medical treatments are discouraged because of these strict requirements. In essence, the criminal justice system can stick a needle in a person's arm for punishment, but not for treatment. At the same time; "Behavioral interventions . . . are developed and conducted frequently by people with little or no training in the area, no monitoring or thought as to the potential damage that an intervention may cause, and no informed consent" (McLaughlin, 2000: 24–25). Although somewhere between 70% and 85% of inmates need substance abuse treatment, only about one-tenth actually receive it (National Center on Addiction and Substance Abuse, 1998; Simpson, Knight, and Pevoto, 1996). This is true even though studies have proved how much more effective drug treatment is than expanding the use of prisons in reducing recidivism (Caulkins et al., 1997).

Some Americans might prefer to throw inmates into freshly dug holes in the ground and provide them with nothing but the bare minimum to survive. Others would like to "make 'em break rocks" (McGinnis, 2000: 35). Former Massachusetts governor William Weld publicly stated that life in prison should be "akin to walking through the fires of hell" (in McGinnis, 2000: 35). But these people misconceive the purpose of imprisonment. We send people to prison *as* punishment, not *for* punishment. As explained by Ingley (2000: 20): "The incarceration itself [is] supposed to be the punishment, not an occasion for the state to arbitrarily inflict additional punishment." In other words, the main part of the punishment is losing one's freedom. Individual freedom may be the most cherished part of being American. Prisoners, because they are locked up, away from friends and family, have lost their liberty. This means they are not free to do all the things you and I can do as they see fit. Their activities are decided by others.

Loss of Autonomy

Related to loss of freedom is the loss of autonomy that accompanies being incarcerated. Inmates do not decide for themselves when or where to sleep, wake up, shower, eat, engage in recreation, or live. They are told when and how to do virtually everything they do. Thus, prisoners lose the capacity and, some argue, the ability to govern their own lives and behaviors. What are the implications of this for society? If we want people to be responsible for themselves, their lives, their families, their children, wouldn't it make sense to equip them with the ability to live in the free world? Is our desire to make prisoners suffer more important than protecting us from their future acts of crime and violence?

May (2000: xvii) claims that incarceration can "foster dependency" and, for some, actually "becomes a way of life—even a generational phenomenon." For them, the criminal justice system "becomes their only source of social support, structure, discipline, validation, and even power and respect." These people typically have family and friends who have been processed through the system and live in communities where incarceration is simply an expected part of life.

Loss of Security

Prisoners are subjected to numerous forms of victimization that are much more prevalent in correctional facilities than outside in the free world. Prisoners are subjected to psychological victimization, economic victimization, social victimization, physical victimization, and sexual victimization. May (2000: 134) describes prisons this way:

> Prisons are violent places, and prisons teach violence. Anyone walking into a prison for the first time can feel the tension. The concrete and steel walls and floors serve to echo and intensify the noises of chains, steel doors slamming, yelling, cursing, and beatings. For an inmate who must make the prison his or her home, whether for months, years, or even a lifetime, avoiding a violent attack becomes a daily concern. The need to maintain constant vigilance creates stress, tension, and chronic anxiety. Even in their sleep, they do not feel safe. They almost instinctively react to provocation with violence, as adjustments to this sense of vulnerability.

Page (2000: 138, 141) claims that "[v]iolence is a dominant and defining thread running through the fabric of jail and prison life" and describes facilities of incarceration as "factories of rage and pain."

As explained by the National Criminal Justice Commission: "Inmates learn to strike first and seek strength in gangs often comprised of dangerous offenders. Sexual assaults are frequent and usually go unpunished" (Donziger, 1996: 43). Rather than being a deterrent to future criminality, the commission concludes that "the violent subculture of the correctional facility increasingly acts as a vector for spreading crime in our communities" (Donziger, 1996: 44). Ironically, then, imprisonment escalates the very behavior it is intended to deter (Marx, 1981) because it increases violence instead of decreasing it (Poporino, 1986; Welch, 1999).

American criminals who are imprisoned are locked away in overcrowded warehouses and forced to live in closet-sized rooms (Clark, 1994). Most are subjected to some type of physical abuse and many to sexual abuse (Donaldson, 1995). Violence inflicted for the purpose of causing pain or as punishment is illegal and prohibited by the American Correctional Association (Martin, 2000: 114). Additionally, many of the inmates who become victims in prison were convicted of relatively minor acts—acts that many of us may have committed at one time in our lives. And remember, most of these inmates will one day get out of prison.

Human rights violations are commonplace in prison. As examples, Welch (1999) discusses chain gangs, inhumane prison conditions, and the use of political imprisonment in the United States. He writes: "American prisons are neither *civilized* nor *civilizing*. Simply put, inmates are subjected to a degrading prison environment, then returned to the community" (p. 199; emphasis in original).

Deprivation of Heterosexual Relationships

Although not everyone is heterosexual, most Americans are. Incarceration means being forced to live without sexual encounters with a member of the opposite sex. This is likely worst for married couples who are separated by imprisonment. But, for any heterosexual person, being imprisoned generally means living without sexual contact with a member of the opposite sex. Consequently, heterosexuals may have to abstain completely from sexual encounters, turn to self-gratification, or engage in homosexual encounters. Even if a prisoner chooses to abstain, there is, of course, the risk of being forced to engage in homosexual relations because of the threat of rape in prison. And even though prison administrators know that rapes occur within the walls of American prisons, these attacks generally are not pursued or prevented (Mariner, 2000: 129).

A growing number of American prisoners are being deprived of virtually all relationships, including contact with other people. One reason is that more and more prisons are being built in rural areas, far from the offenders' family members and significant others. Prisons are promoted in rural communities as a blessing—a source of jobs to boost the local economy. Another reason is that the United States has begun incarcerating some of its most dangerous offenders in "super-maximum" or "maxi-maxi" prisons. These facilities restrict inmate contact with other inmates and with correctional personnel. Many inmates are locked in their cells for most of the day, in stark cells with white walls. Cells have completely closed front doors, no windows, and bright lights on at all hours of day and night.

Examples of supermaximum facilities include Marion (Illinois) and Pelican Bay (California). Welch (1999: 200) describes the conditions in these prisons:

> [In Marion] all prisoners are confined to their cells for 23 hours per day, granted 1 hour of exercise outside of their cell, and allowed to shower 2 or 3 days a week. Handcuffs are fastened to inmates while they are transported within the facility . . . [and they are chained] "long-term . . . to their beds";

> [In Pelican Bay] [i]nmates are confined to their 8- by 10-foot cells, where the temperature registers a constant 85 to 90 degrees, for twenty-two and a half hours per day. The unrelenting heat produces headaches, nausea, and dehydration and drains the inmates of their mental and bodily energy.

Human rights violations in supermax facilities, of course, are hidden from the public. When abuses of prisoners in other types of prisons become known, Americans do not become concerned because state-controlled media outlets do not construct these harms as social problems (Welch, 1999: 208). The Pelican Bay facility in California was built at a cost of $278 million for 2,080 maximum security inmates. That's $134,000 per inmate! The organization Human Rights Watch calls these expensive facilities "a clear violation of human rights" and a breach of an international treaty implemented by the United States in 1992 (Weinstein, 2000: 120). Yet, Americans are generally unaware or unconcerned over human rights violations against convicted criminals.

Deprivation of Goods and Services

Another significant loss associated with imprisonment is being deprived of goods and services. Imagine all of your worldly possessions being inaccessible to you, along with virtually every service and product that a free person can enjoy. This would be a major loss associated with having your freedom taken away. More and more, prison life is becoming a boring, uniform routine with what inmates consider to be "chickenshit rules" (Irwin and Austin, 1997: 75). Prisoners become "prisonized" and unable to make it in the real world (Clemmer, 1940).

Loss of Voting Rights

According to Walker et al. (2000: 279), 46 states place restrictions on the voting rights of felons, and 14 states permanently deprive felons of the right to vote. Although you may not consider this an important loss, especially if you do not currently vote, it is inconsistent with the goal of integrating ex-convicts into free society. A member of free society has the right to vote and thus to help shape the direction of his or her life, as well as that of his or her family and community. In a representative democracy, when a person cannot vote, by definition, that person's voice cannot be heard and he or she is not represented. In the United States, the loss of the right to vote is a burden disproportionately imposed on poor people and people of color.

Loss of Dignity

Associated with each of the losses described here is a loss of dignity. Prisoners are not treated as individual human beings, but as numbers. At worst, they lose respect for themselves because of this treatment. They come to be dependent on the government to live their lives. Jeffery (1990), on the basis of psychological theories of behavior, outlined significant reasons that imprisonment does not work. Many of these may help you understand how imprisonment leads to a loss of dignity for the incarcerated person. Professor Jeffery's comments on the futility of punishment, most of which are highly relevant to imprisonment, are summarized in the following box.

Professor C. Ray Jeffery on why punishment does not work

- To be successful, the time lag between the behavior and punishment must be short . . . punishment must be swift. . . . Punishment is anything but swift with long delays between the crime, arrest, conviction, sentencing and imprisonment. Today, it may take years before a criminal is punished.
- To be successful, punishment must be certain. In our system of criminal justice we have many unknown and unreported crimes, which can run as high as five unreported crimes for one reported crime. Of those crimes reported, few arrests are made, few convictions are made, and few criminals are sentenced to prison. . . . For the same crime the sentence can vary in many ways. . . . To be effective, punishment must overcome positive reinforcement. . . . When a reinforcer such as money can be gotten by an illegal response, the person can weigh the risk of punishment versus the monetary gain. Since the risk of punishment is low, the criminal has the odds in his/her favor as he/she commits a crime. The prospect of gaining money immediately outweighs the threat of punishment in the distant future.
- To make punishment effective, we must provide the person with alternative means for reinforcement. If a person is offered an alternative to the punished response, the punished response will be diminished or eliminated. This implies the establishment of crime prevention programs that block the illegal opportunities structure, as well as behavioral programs that create legitimate opportunities.
- Punishment can become a conditioned stimulus for positive reinforcement. If a child is spanked and then given candy, the child will misbehave in order to get candy. If the only time a child is noticed by the parent is when the parent is punishing the child, the child will act in an antisocial manner in order to get attention.

- Punishment creates escape and avoidance behaviors. . . . A person does not learn through punishment to obey the law; rather, he or she learns how to commit crimes and to escape punishment. Criminals can avoid punishment by avoiding detection and arrest; if arrested, they can give an alibi or hire lawyers; if charged, they can falsify statements and attempt to win an acquittal; if found guilty, they can tell the social worker a story that may result in probation; if sentenced, they can try to manipulate the prison community to gain privileges and an early release. The criminal justice system is one huge escape and avoidance conditioning system. Rather than conditioning people to legal behavior, it conditions them to escape and avoid the law.
- Punishment creates aggression in those who are punished. This aggression can be operant—that is, against the aggressor, in order to remove the aggression—or reflexive. Reflexive aggression occurs when pain is administered to a person and the person strikes out against any object or person in the environment. When we put people in prison, we make them more vicious and hateful than before. This is a major failure of our prison system to rehabilitate.
- Any stimulus associated with punishment can become a conditioned stimulus (CS) for punishment. A child who avoids or hates a parent or teacher may run away from home or become a truant from school. Many delinquent careers start with such behavioral problems at home or in school. The use of punishment to control behavior creates major behavioral problems of its own.
- If an animal is conditioned to receive unavoidable shocks, with no possibility of escape or avoidance, the animal will not learn to avoid shock even later, when the shock is avoidable. This is called learned helplessness, and it is also an important aspect of psychological depression. Punishment of prisoners can create learned helplessness. The ability to control one's environment is an important aspect of healthy adaptive behavior; criminal behavior, by contrast, can reflect learned helplessness, a trust in fate, and a loss of control over the environment.
- The punisher (lawyer, parent, teacher, police officer) may be angry or hostile toward the person punished. Aggression rewards those doing the punishing. It allows for a feeling of power over others, it releases feelings of revenge and hatred, and it allows one to be aggressive in a legitimate manner. Aggression can be either lawful or unlawful. The criminal justice system continues to punish and execute criminals not because of the impact of punishment on the criminal but because of the impact of punishment on those doing the punishing, including you and me.
- Punishment, then, is not a successful way to control criminal behavior, because it is so disruptive to other, lawful behaviors.

SOURCE: Adapted from C. Ray Jeffery, *Criminology: An Interdisciplinary Approach* (Belmont, CA: Prentice Hall, 1990), pp. 241–244.

Stigmatization

As I showed earlier in this chapter, most people in U.S. prisons are truly disadvantaged: poor; uneducated; underemployed. Irwin and Austin (1997) illustrate that the typical offender enters prison with a tenth-grade education and leaves with a tenth-grade education plus the stigma of being an "ex-con." Most inmates "leave prison with all their previous disadvantages plus the additional stigma of a felony conviction" (Kappeler et al., 2000: 251). Perhaps this is why estimates suggest that inmates will lose about 70% of the income level they were accustomed to prior to entering a prison (The Sentencing Project, 1998), a level that already was low relative to the national average. Not surprisingly, then, when prisoners are released, the "ex-con" label makes it difficult for them to find places to live and work.

> *The* typical offender enters prison with a tenth-grade education and leaves with a tenth-grade education, plus the stigma of being an "ex-con."

Labeling theory asserts that when people are labeled by the criminal justice system as "criminals," "convicts," or "offenders," the label can affect how these offenders view themselves, thus potentially changing their self-concepts. Once they begin to see themselves as "deviant" or "different," they will continue committing crime in order to live up to the expectations that society has set forth for them (Bohm, 2001). Sampson and Laub (1997) suggest that employers use the ex-con label as a warning against hiring former offenders. According to Bushway (2000: 144), "federal legislation explicitly denies ex-felons employment in *any* job in the financial sector, as well as in other areas such as child care and private investigations. Most states also have legislation mandating screening on the basis of criminal history records for literally hundreds of jobs" (emphasis in original).

Irwin and Austin (1997: 82) summarize the issue this way:

> The disturbing truth is that growing numbers of prisoners are leaving our prisons socially crippled and profoundly alienated. Moreover, they understand that they will be returning to a society that views them as despicable pariahs. They are also aware that they will have major difficulty finding employment than formerly, and consequently their expectations are low.

Shouldn't we be able to expect more out of a system of "corrections"? As May (2000: xvii) correctly points out, the term *corrections* is really a misnomer.

After some period of confinement in a prison, offenders typically are not yet off the hook. Even after their term of imprisonment is reduced (or when they are released early), they typically will still be under some form of criminal justice supervision. In the next section, I address how one such mechanism—parole—can increase the risk of repeat offending.

FORGIVING THE OFFENDER: WHY HARASS PAROLEES?

As noted in Chapter One, parole means conditional release to community supervision, whether by parole board decision or by mandatory conditional release after serving a prison term. On December 31, 1998, approximately 705,000 adults were on parole under federal, state, or local jurisdiction. Most of them were paroled through mandatory release rather than discretionary release. Parolees are subject to being returned to jail or prison for rule violations or other offenses. This is because parole can be revoked when a person either commits another criminal act or violates one of the rules of release.

> *P*arole is conditional release to community supervision, either by parole board decision or by mandatory conditional release after serving a prison term.

If rearrest is a sign of parole failure, then parole is a failure. Irwin and Austin (1997: 113) write: "In general, most inmates are rearrested at least once after being released from prison." This does not mean that they committed new crimes, only that they either were suspected of having committed a new crime or violated some rule of their parole. In some ways, police harassment of parolees makes sense. When a crime is committed in the vicinity of a known offender, especially one that fits his or her M.O., the ex-con becomes a logical suspect. Yet, some feel that once an offender has paid his or her debt to society, police should not automatically assume that an "innocent" person is guilty of a crime.

In fact, most people who fail parole fail *not* because they committed new crimes but because of technical violations. The following box illustrates some typical rules required of parolees by state and federal governments. The Bureau of Justice Statistics (1999) reports that of all adults who left parole in 1998, 45% successfully completed their terms, and 42% were returned to incarceration. Yet, only 13% were returned to prison with a new sentence. This means most did not actually commit another crime. Irwin and Austin (1997: 116, 123) attribute parole failures to increased supervision capacities of parole officers and to an increased focus on the law enforcement function of parole as opposed to its social service function.

Typical rules of parole

Rule	Percentage of jurisdictions that require it
Obey all laws	98
Report to parole officer as directed	96
Refrain from possessing dangerous weapon	92
Remain within jurisdiction	90
Permit the parole officer to visit	82
Obey all rules of the parole office	78
Maintain employment	78
Abstain from association with felons	61
Pay fines or restitution	53
Meet family responsibilities	47
Undergo treatment	45
Pay supervision fees	37
Attend course of study or training	17
Perform community service	14

SOURCE: Adapted from E. Rhine, W. Smith, and R. Jackson, "Parole: Issues and Prospects for the 1990s," *Corrections Today* 51 (1991): 78–83.

> *Most* people who fail parole fail *not* because they committed new crimes but because of technical violations.

Irwin and Austin (1997) lay out the main reason that people who go to prison will likely eventually end up back there upon release. They suggest that, in addition to the pains of imprisonment discussed earlier, and the harassment of parolees by the police, the following reasons make it easy to understand why the prison experience followed by parole fails to reform prisoners:

- Reentering society is literally a shock to offenders who are used to the routine of prison life lived under government-controlled rules and orders.
- Finding a job is next to impossible, given ex-prisoners' lack of employment skills, educational deficits, and criminal record.

In essence, prisons are not really supposed to make people better, they are just supposed to warehouse criminals.

HOW AND WHY CORRECTIONS REFLECTS CRIMINAL JUSTICE BIAS

Recall from Chapter Five the difference between disparity and discrimination. Walker et al. (2000) explain that a disparity is present when one group suffers disproportionately from some social policy. Discrimination implies the intentional singling out of different groups of people for disparate treatment. Clearly, U.S. prisons reflect a significant disparity in punishment in the United States. This led Irwin and Austin (1997: 164) to write: "In effect, we are gradually putting our own apartheid into place."

> *W*alker et al. (2000) explain that a disparity is present when one group suffers disproportionately from some social policy. Discrimination implies the intentional singling out of different groups of people for disparate treatment. Clearly, our prisons reflect a significant disparity in punishment in the United States.

The characteristics of those being caught and punished include the following: 94% are male; about 65% did not complete high school; one-third are unemployed; one-third earn less than $5,000 annually; almost 60% self-report being under the influence of drugs at the time of their offenses; and African American males are incarcerated at a rate four to five times that of Black males in South Africa (Mauer, 1991, 1992, 1994). In federal prisons, 93% are male, 39% are African American, and 30% are Hispanic. Whereas nearly 60% of federal prisoners were sentenced for drug crimes, only 3% were sentenced for violent crimes and 6% for white-collar offenses. From these statistics, it is clear where our criminal justice priorities are.

> *T*he characteristics of those being caught and punished include: 94% are male; about 65% did not complete high school; one-third are unemployed; one-third make less than $5,000 annually; almost 60% self-report being under the influence of drugs at the time of their offenses; and African American males are incarcerated at a rate four to five times that of Black males in South Africa.

The result is that nearly half of incarcerated people in the United States are African Americans, and so a prison industry is being built "on the backs of blacks" (Blakemore, 1998: 4). In fact, there are more African American males incarcerated than enrolled in higher education. While we build and build and build new prisons, 38 states and the District of Columbia witnessed an increase in racial disparity in their rates of incarceration from 1988 to 1994. Thus, in 1997, the imprisonment rate of African American males (3,209 per 100,000) and Hispanic males (1,273 per 100,000) was much greater than for Caucasian males (386 per 100,000) (U.S. Department of Justice, 1998). The same is true for women: the imprisonment rate for African American women (200 per 100,000) and Hispanic women (87 per 100,000) was greater than for Caucasian women (25 per 100,000). Also, 12 states and the District of Columbia incarcerate African Americans at a rate more than 10 times that of whites (Mauer, 1997). In 1970, there were 133,000 African Americans in prisons and jails, but in 2000 it is expected that number will increase to almost 1.1 million, a 780% increase. In 1950, African Americans made up about 35% of state and federal prisoners, but in 2010 it is expected they will account for about 68% (National Center on Institutions and Alternatives, 1999).

The result of such disparities is devastating. For example, 1 in 7 African Americans cannot vote because of felony convictions (Mauer, 1997). Almost 80% of African American males can expect to have been arrested by age 35 (National Center on Institutions and Alternatives, 1999; also see Miller and Holman, 1992; Tillman, 1987). Whereas 1 in 3 African American males is somehow involved in the criminal justice system, only 1 in 15 young Caucasian males and 1 in 8 Hispanic males are (The Sentencing Project, 1997). African Americans make up 3% of California's population, but 40% of its inmates (Miller, 1997a: 28).

---

*W*hile 1 in 3 African American males is somehow involved in the criminal justice system, only 1 in 15 young Caucasian males and 1 in 8 Hispanic males are.

Miller (1997a) claims that contact with the criminal justice system is now a "rite of passage" for young African American men. As a result,

> it is now a sad reality that most of the young African American men can anticipate being at least briefly ushered through a series of hothouses for sociopathy: prisons, jails, detention centers, and reform schools—all of which nurture those very characteristics that can subsequently be labeled as pathological.

Blakemore (1998: 5) calls contact with the criminal justice system a "badge of honor" for some African American males, and claims that punishment thus loses its deterrent effect for them. Also, criminal justice system targeting of minorities exacerbates problems such as single parenthood and unemployment (Blakemore, 1998), which undoubtedly increases the likelihood of criminality.

Other minorities and disenfranchised groups suffer as well. For example, the percentage of Hispanics in state and federal prisons doubled between 1980 and 1993, to over 14% (Mauer and Huling, 1995b). The greatest increase in incarceration between 1989 and 1994 was 78% for African American women (Mauer and Huling, 1995b). From 1986 to 1991, the number of African American women incarcerated for drug offenses in state prisons increased 828% (Mauer and Huling, 1995b). More and more African American women are being incarcerated, partly because they do not have anything to offer the prosecutors who are looking for "bigger fish," and so the "small fish" in the drug markets go to prison (Miller, 1997a).

The United States pays $20 billion per year just for federal criminal justice operations (Coalition for Federal Sentencing Reform, 1997). Yet, in part because of drugs, 94% of federal prisoners sentenced and 77% admitted in 1994 were sentenced for nonviolent crimes. Almost 95% of increases in new court commitments from 1980 were for drug, property, and public order offenses (Mauer, 1994). From 1985 to 1994, drug offenders accounted for 36% of the increases in state prison populations and more than 70% in federal prison populations (Families Against Mandatory Minimums, 1999). From 1988 to 1994, national prison populations increased 52% for violent criminals but 156% for drug offenders (Mauer, 1997). From 1980 to 1993, drug incarcerations increased 510% (Mauer and Huling, 1995b). Between 1980 and 1996, new court commitments to state prisons rose 400% for drug offenses, compared with only 29% for aggravated assaults (Beck, 1999). Do you think Americans would support this if they knew?

From 1986 to 1991, there was a 466% increase in African Americans imprisoned for drug offenses in state prisons (Mauer, 1997), versus a 106% increase for Caucasian males (The Sentencing Project, 1997). In 1992, the federal system had 12,727 nonviolent, low-level drug offenders with no criminal history, serving an average time of 6 years (U.S. Department of Justice, 1994); today, low-level, nonviolent drug offenders make up over 21% of total federal prison populations (National Center on Institutions and Alternatives, 1999). Figure 10.2 shows drug offenders as a percentage of all offenders sentenced to federal prisons. There has been a dramatic increase in drug offender imprisonment, as now drug offenders make up 60% of all federal

FIGURE 10.2

Drug Offenders as Percentage of All Sentenced Offenders—Federal Prisons

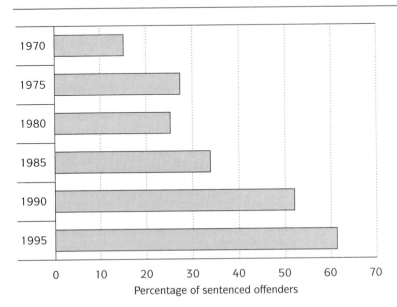

Percentage of sentenced offenders

SOURCE: Federal Bureau of Prisons.

inmates (Federal Bureau of Prisons, 1998). It is largely the same at the state level. As explained earlier, over half of state prison inmates were convicted of crimes that are considered petty by the American public. Drug offenders made up 1 in 11 offenders in 1983, but now make up about 1 in 4 inmates nationally, costing over $6 billion per year, in part because the probability of imprisonment for drug offenses has increased 500% since 1980 (Beck, 1999).

So there is clearly a correlation between punitiveness in the United States generally, the U.S. wars on crime and on drugs in particular, and racial disparities in the criminal justice system. Whether intended or not, our nation's crime control efforts disproportionately affect poor people and people of color. Since these disparities cannot be explained by differences in offending patterns (see Chapter Five), the most valid explanation of these disparities is discrimination in the criminal justice system, beginning with bias in the criminal law, reinforced by the media, and continuing with the police and courts. Discrimination in the criminal justice system makes criminal justice operations incompatible with its ideal goal of being fair, neutral, unbiased, and nondiscriminatory. In other words, correctional populations serve as evidence of an unjust U.S. criminal justice system.

CONCLUSION

This chapter illustrated how the use of imprisonment will ultimately add to the crime problem in the United States, even if it temporarily locks some criminals away from society. Imprisonment, a main component of the unprecedented U.S. incarceration rate, has increased dramatically since the early 1970s. This chapter demonstrated that this increase had little or nothing to do with crime, is incredibly expensive, and is very unlikely to make Americans safer. In fact, given that most people in prisons are *not* repeat, violent offenders, many have claimed that we are wasting too much money on relatively harmless offenders such as drug criminals. This chapter also demonstrated that, contrary to the myth of the comfortable prison, prisons in the United States are rough places to stay and serve as more than sufficient punishments for most crimes. Because of these pains of imprisonment and because we harass parolees after they complete their sentences, it is very difficult for street criminals to "go straight" upon their release. Thus, we are guaranteeing our failure by choosing to imprison so many of our citizens. Most important for the theme of the book, imprisonment serves as a clear example of how the U.S. criminal justice system fails to meet its ideal goal of doing justice. Plainly stated, the use of imprisonment in the United States is biased against the poor and people of color.

ISSUE IN DEPTH
The Failures of Prison

Given the pains of imprisonment described in Chapter Ten, it's no wonder that most prisoners will end up back in prison in the future. As Irwin and Austin (1997: 62) explain: "Because most will be released within two years, we should be deeply concerned about what happens to them during their incarceration." We have to decide, as states and as a nation, what we think is most important—punishing offenders for retribution or preventing their future crime. If we want to make inmates mad at society and want to create a sense of vengeance in them, we should continue doing what we are doing. If we want them to become part of legitimate U.S. society, we must witness a change of direction in punishment. In Chapter Twelve, I will lay out a plan that will make American criminal justice more just and more effective.

For the past several decades, U.S. prisons do little more than warehouse inmates. Irwin and Austin (1997: 62) describe it this way:

> Convicted primarily of property and drug crimes, hundreds of thousands of prisoners are being crowded into human (or inhuman) warehouses where they are increasingly deprived, restricted, isolated, and consequently embittered and alienated from conventional worlds and where less and less is being done to prepare them for their eventual release. As a result, most of them are rendered incapable of returning to even a meager conventional life after prison.

Simultaneously, as indicated earlier, opportunities for education, vocational training, and recreation have substantially decreased in the prevailing punitive environment of American punishment. Irwin and Austin (1997: 80) suggest that fewer than 20% of all prisoners are enrolled in any type of educational program.

Incarceration also hurts more than the criminal. Effects of imprisonment on families can be tremendous. Obviously, imprisonment runs counter to the goal of maintaining a two-parent family. The National Criminal Justice Commission writes:

> For many young women in the inner city, there is a scarcity of available men of marriage age because so many are going in and out of jails and prisons. . . . In some inner-city areas, virtually every resident has a close relative and over 50 percent have a parent who is in prison, on probation, on parole, in jail, or hidden because there is a warrant out for their arrest. (Donziger, 1996: 47)

Whitehead (2000: 87) reports that in a study of inner-city women, some African American females (15 to 19 years old) reflected on this situation in their comments on dating. They were asked, "What recommendations would you have for other young women your age, who have met a new boy with whom they are thinking of entering into a relationship?" Some of their answers included: "make sure the police isn't looking for him" and "make sure he didn't recently get out of jail" (Whitehead, 1997). Think of the irony of politicians speaking of the value of two-parent families while simultaneously promoting policies that split them up. Is it any wonder that about 60% of prisoners have been there before and will end up there again?

Given that prison is such an awful place, does imprisonment reduce crime? That is, is it a deterrent to future criminal activity? I explained earlier that recent declines in crime are not attributable to massive increases in imprisonment. The National Criminal Justice Commission claims: "Academic research has shown little or no correlation between rates of crime and the number of people in prison." In fact, "[m]any experts believe the decline has resulted from a combination of demographic changes . . . more effective law enforcement, and greater stability in the drug trade" (Donziger, 1996: 42, 43). States with higher rates of incarceration do not necessarily have lower crime rates, and states that increase prison admissions do not necessarily see declines in crime rates. These findings do not support politicians' claims that imprisonment is an effective method of reducing crime rates and making people safer. Politicians, in essence, promote a failing means of crime reduction to Americans who have sworn an allegiance to it, even though it does not work. Even if you believe that imprisonment is a special deterrent, a punishment that instills fear in the offender, making it less likely that he or she will commit crimes in the future, consider this possibility: for individuals who see no promising options in the legitimate economy, for whom life in the street is very risky anyway, and who have not been effectively socialized against committing crimes, the prospect of spending time in prison, perhaps with others they know, of being assured meals and a bed (even if far from luxurious), may not deter them from criminal activity. Prison may not be a very attractive option, but its increment of pain is likely to be far less than it is to middle-class populations (Blumstein, 2000: 10).

There is also substantial evidence that prisons serve as "colleges of crime." Think about it: a logical outcome of placing large numbers of convicted criminals together is that they will teach one another new tricks of the trade! Amazingly, although we know that having criminals live in close proximity to one another will ultimately produce more crime, for this reason and others, we still continue to build more and more facilities to house more and more inmates. Politicians who claim that crime is down because of increased use of imprisonment are, at best, misinformed and shortsighted. The long-term effects of mass imprisonment will be disastrous and costly.

Walker (1998: 14) shows how the United States' fight to reduce crime by means such as imprisonment parallels efforts of some overweight people to lose weight: "Just as people go on crash diets, lose weight, put it all back on, and then take up another diet fad a year later, so we tend to 'binge' on crime control fads." Many people fail to recognize that fighting fat through fad diets will never work, and that weight-loss fads result in billions of dollars of profit each year for those who misrepresent even the most bizarre programs and products. It is ironic that people who want to lose weight are most likely to try approaches that actually increase their weight. Similarly, reducing crime cannot be achieved through fad crime control policies that are proposed for purely symbolic reasons by politicians and inadequately designed by criminal justice policymakers. Even though they are enormously profitable for some, prisons do not reduce crime. There is no "miracle cure" for crime. Reducing crime, like losing weight, requires dedication and time. In Chapter Twelve, I will explore some criminal justice options that might work to reduce crime in the United States.

Yet, we continue with our "crime control theology," rooted not in empirical evidence and sound scientific argument but, rather, in belief and common sense. As discussed in Chapter One, the 1994 crime bill essentially puts more police on the streets and allows more people to be sent to prison. Even though incarceration is only a temporary fix, the crime bill was widely supported by the public (Walker, 1998: 75). Irwin and Austin (1997) suggest that imprisonment is rooted in a false image of the typical offender, created by politicians and by media attention to violent crimes (see Chapter Four) and rooted in what they call "voodoo criminology." They write that

> the idea that increased penalties will reduce crime is based on a simplistic and fallacious theory of criminal behavior [that] starts with the idea that every person is an isolated, willful actor who makes completely rational decisions to maximize his or her pleasure and to minimize his or her pain. . . . If penalties for being caught are small or nonexistent, then many persons who are not restrained by other factors . . . will commit crimes . . . a *lot* of crimes. Only by increasing the certainty and severity of punishment, this thinking goes, will people "think twice" and be deterred. (p. 156; emphasis in original)

Based on the research discussed in Chapter Nine, these are fallacious assumptions about the motivations for criminal behavior.

Yet, we use imprisonment even for nonviolent drug offenders. An examination of the drug war by McNeece et al. (1999: 9) found that:

- Incarceration does little to break the cycle of illegal drug use and crime.
- Offenders sentenced to incarceration for substance-related offenses exhibit a high rate of recidivism once they are released.
- Drug abuse treatment has been shown to be demonstrably effective at reducing both drug abuse and drug-related crime.

As I pointed out in Chapter Six, a certain level of drug use is inevitable and relatively harmless. A harm-reduction, restorative approach to reducing drug use and abuse, based on a public health model rather than a criminal justice model, would be much more effective (Bullington, 1998; McNeece et al., 1999) and would free up expensive prison beds for those offenders who really need (and really deserve) them.

Discussion Questions

- Why is the United States' incarceration rate so high compared with rates for other countries?
- Differentiate between *prisons* and *jails*.
- Do you think there is a link between crime rates and incarceration rates? Why or why not?
- Identify the claims of politicians that would justify building more prisons.
- What are some of the costs associated with imprisonment?
- In what ways might imprisonment increase crime?
- Describe the typical prisoner.
- Why do you think politicians have passed laws that have led to a removal of educational, vocational, and drug treatment opportunities within prisons?
- Think back over the course of your life and try to recall any crimes you may have committed that could have led to your own imprisonment. What made you commit those crimes?
- What is parole?
- What are the typical conditions required of parolees?
- Outline the ways in which imprisonment can be considered a failure.

CHAPTER ELEVEN

THE ULTIMATE SANCTION:

DEATH AS JUSTICE?

KEY CONCEPTS

- A brief history of capital punishment
- Death penalty facts
- Public support for capital punishment
- Justifications for capital punishment: Logical or not?
- What's wrong with the death penalty?
- Issue in Depth: A Broken System

INTRODUCTION

The death penalty, also known as capital punishment, is the ultimate punishment imposed by any society. America has had a long and sordid history with this criminal sanction, including both state-sanctioned killings and the murders of African American men through lynchings carried out in the name of "punishment" for alleged wrongdoings. This chapter briefly examines this history, and then turns to the issue of whether the death penalty makes any sense at all. The question of whether capital punishment is moral or immoral, right or wrong, good or bad, necessary or unnecessary, just or unjust, and so forth, has been asked and answered numerous times throughout history. There is no one answer to which all people agree, but most of us have made up our own minds as to what side of the debate we are on. However you feel about the death penalty personally, capital punishment is a highly emotional issue. As you read this chapter, you should attempt to put your personal opinions aside and understand that your personal opinion may not be supported by empirical evidence. In this chapter, I critically analyze the justifications for the death penalty and conclude with a discussion of what's wrong with capital punishment in the United States.

A BRIEF HISTORY OF CAPITAL PUNISHMENT

The earliest recorded execution in America was in 1608, of Captain George Kendall, a member of the Virginia colony. His punishment was for the crime of spying for Spain (Espy and Smykla, 1987). Since that time, about 22,500 people have been executed in America (Espy, personal correspondence reported in Bohm, 1999: 2). Another 10,000 or so were lynched in the nineteenth century (Bedau, 1982). Most of those executed have been men—only 2% were women—and the largest share of those executed were put to death prior to 1866 (Schneider and Smykla, 1991). Originally, death sentences were mandatory for certain crimes, such as murder, but this began to change in 1838 when Tennessee enacted a discretionary death sentence (Acker and Lanier, 1998). Today, mandatory death sentences are considered unconstitutional.

> *The* earliest recorded execution in America was in 1608 of Captain George Kendall, a member of the Virginia colony. His punishment was for the crime of spying for Spain. Since that time, there have been about 22,500 people executed in the United States.

The decade that saw the largest number of executions was the 1930s, when the average number of executions per year was 167 (Schneider and Smykla, 1991). Since 1977, there have only been 499 people executed in the United States, or about 25 per year (see Figure 11.1).

> *The* majority of those executed have been men—only 2% were women—and the largest share of those executed were put to death prior to 1866.

FIGURE 11.1
Executions over Time

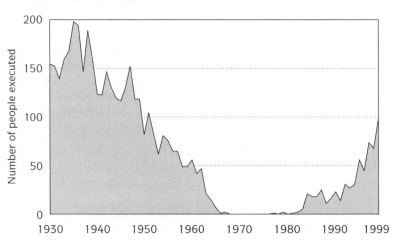

SOURCE: Bureau of Justice Statistics (1999). Online: www.ojp.usdoj.gov/bjs.

> *The* decade that saw the largest number of executions was the 1930s, when the average number of executions per year was 167. Since 1977, there have only been 499 people executed in the United States, or about 25 per year.

According to Costanzo (1997: 13–15), there have been four consistent trends in the application of the death penalty:

1. A dramatic shrinking in the number and types of crimes punishable by death
2. Attempts to lessen the cruelty of executions
3. Attempts to ensure that death sentences are imposed fairly and rationally
4. Efforts to sanitize executions by making them private

As you will see in this chapter, the combined effect of these death penalty trends is a freakish experience with executions in America.

Throughout U.S. history, many states have temporarily abolished the death penalty, and the United States as a whole briefly witnessed a moratorium on the death penalty from 1967 to 1977. Cases heard by the U.S. Supreme Court about racial discrimination in the administration of capital punishment, particularly for cases of alleged rapes of Caucasian women by African American men, led to an "unofficial suspension" of the death penalty after June 1967 (Bohm, 1999: 13). The Supreme Court formally prohibited capital punishment with *Furman v. Georgia* (1972) but later ruled it Constitutional with *Gregg v. Georgia* (1976). I discuss each of these cases later in the chapter.

> *Many* states have temporarily abolished the death penalty at some point in U.S. history, and the United States as a whole briefly witnessed a moratorium on the death penalty from 1967 to 1977.

The first person executed after the death penalty was reinstated was Gary Gilmore, who requested to be killed by the state of Utah (Bohm, 1999: 13). Gilmore insisted that he be put to death by the state. Gilmore's brother now discusses how ironic it is that his brother's last gift to mankind, created by his own push to be executed as rapidly as possible, was a return to capital punishment in the United States.

> *The* U.S. Supreme Court formally prohibited capital punishment with *Furman v. Georgia* (1972) but later ruled it constitutional with *Gregg v. Georgia* (1976).

The U.S. is the only democratic country still practicing the death penalty. Most of our western European allies abolished capital punishment after the horrors of World War II (Zimring and Hawkins, 1986). This may suggest that American respect for life is less than in other countries. In 1961, the law professor Gerald Gottlieb wrote that "the death penalty was unconstitutional under

> *The* United States is the only democratic country still practicing the death penalty, and most of our western European allies abolished capital punishment after the horrors of World War II.

the Eighth Amendment because it violated contemporary moral standards, what the U.S. Supreme Court in *Trop v. Dulles* . . . referred to as 'the evolving standards of decency that mark the progress of a maturing society'" (Bohm, 1999: 11). In the case of *Weems v. United States* (1910), the Supreme Court held that punishments are excessive only if they violate "evolving social conditions." The fact that we administer the death penalty in the United States must mean that the courts do not believe our country has evolved enough socially to warrant a cessation of capital punishment. Public opinion shows widespread support for capital punishment generally.

---

*A*lthough we continue to use the death penalty, its use began to decline in the wake of World War II and the move of our allies to abolish it. For example, 1,289 people were executed in the 1940s, but only 715 were executed in the 1950s. From 1960 through 1976, only 191 were executed.

Although we continue to use the death penalty, its use began to decline after World War II as our allies moved to abolish it. For example, 1,289 people were executed in the 1940s, but only 715 were executed in the 1950s. From 1960 through 1976, only 191 were executed (Bedau, 1982). Recently, the United States has witnessed a rebirth of capital punishment, despite overwhelming evidence that the death penalty is highly discriminatory and erroneously applied. Consider the following (Costanzo, 1997: 1):

- In 1992, Robert Alton Harris was the first person executed in California in a quarter century.
- Presidential candidate Bill Clinton interrupted his 1992 campaigning to fly back to Arkansas to preside over two executions.
- In 1993, Wesley Allan Dodd became the first person executed in Washington in almost thirty years.
- In 1994, Maryland carried out its first execution in more than 30 years, Nebraska killed its first citizen in 35 years, and Idaho began executing citizens again after 36 years.
- In 1995, New York reinstated the death penalty.
- In 1996, Congress passed a law allowing death row inmates only one federal appeal unless new evidence proves clearly and convincingly that the person is innocent. In that same year, Oregon carried out its first execution in 34 years.
- In 1997, Arkansas executed three prisoners in one night.

Figure 11.2 shows that the number of people on death row began to increase in the 1970s as our nation moved more toward a crime control model of criminal justice.

---

*R*ecently, the United States has witnessed capital punishment's resurgence, despite overwhelming evidence that the death penalty is highly discriminatory and erroneously applied.

As I mentioned above, the case of *Furman v. Georgia* (1972) led to a temporary abolition of capital punishment in the United States. William Henry Furman, a 25-year-old African American with an IQ of only 65, was convicted of the murder of Wiliam Micke, Jr., a Coast Guard petty officer in Georgia who was also the father of four children and the stepfather of six others. This case, in which Furman was convicted of killing his victim in a failed burglary attempt, was not the

FIGURE 11.2
Prisoners on Death Row

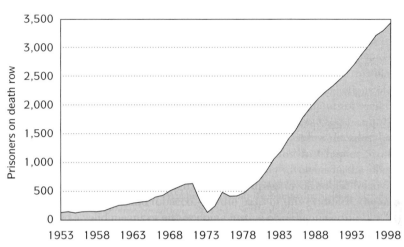

SOURCE: Bureau of Justice Statistics (1999). Online: www.ojp.usdoj.gov/bjs.

stereotypical killing in the United States. Most murders are intraracial—that is, committed against a person of the same race as the murderer—and, historically, most have been committed by persons known to the victims rather than by strangers. Because Furman was an African American and a stranger, and his victim was a Caucasian as well as a family man who served in the military, Furman's chance of *not* receiving the death penalty was slim, especially in a southern state with a history of racial unrest.

Furman's attorneys argued to the Supreme Court that capital punishment in Georgia was unfair because capital trials essentially gave the jury unbridled discretion about whether to impose a death sentence on convicted defendants. The *Furman* case was only one of three heard by the Supreme Court at the same time, all dealing with death sentences imposed against African American men. The other two cases specifically involved rapes of Caucasian women by African American males (Coyne and Entzeroth, 1994), a crime that has been a primary source of discriminatory punishment in American history.

The *Furman* case led to nine separate opinions by each of the justices of the Supreme Court, and the ruling was 5–4 that the death penalty statutes in question were "cruel and unusual" because they violated the Eighth and Fourteenth Amendments of the U.S. Constitution. In essence, the Supreme Court found that capital punishment was being imposed "arbitrarily, infrequently, and often selectively against minorities" (Bohm, 1999: 23). So, it was not the death penalty itself that was at issue, it was how this penalty was being applied arbitrarily and disproportionately to some groups of people.

Bohm (citing Anderson, 1983) writes: "A practical effect of *Furman* was the Supreme Court's voiding of 40 death penalty statutes and the sentences of 629 death row inmates." The Supreme Court, however, did not conclude that the death penalty per se was unconstitutional. It was only unconstitutional to the degree that is was imposed arbitrarily and unfairly. Thus, "36 states proceeded to adopt new death penalty statutes designed to meet the Court's objections" (p. 24).

States, concerned with their image as much as with the public safety of their citizens, quickly passed death penalty laws that would be considered Constitutional by the Supreme Court.

Nearly one-third of states enacted mandatory death sentences for some crimes (Acker and Lanier, 1998), taking the issue of discretion of judges and juries out of the picture. Most states passed "guided discretion" statutes that would give juries and sentencing judges some guidelines to follow when considering death sentences (Bohm, 1999: 25). The mandatory death sentence statutes were rejected by the Supreme Court as unconstitutional, but in the case of *Gregg v. Georgia* (1976), the Court ruled by a 7–2 vote that guided discretion statutes were acceptable in death penalty cases. The Court also upheld the use of bifurcated trials, where guilt or innocence would be decided in the first phase and sentencing decided in the second, as well as automatic appellate review of convictions and sentences, and, finally, proportionality reviews to compare sentences of particular cases against similar cases to ensure just sentencing practices. Thus, suggestions made in 1959 by the American Law Institute's Model Penal Code and aimed at making the death penalty fairer were finally put into place.

At year end 1996, 36 of the 38 states that still practiced the death penalty provided an automatic appeal of all death sentences, whether the defendant wanted it or not (Snell, 1997). The use of appeals supposedly makes it less likely that a death sentence will be inappropriately handed down. Automatic appeals, do not, however, lessen the likelihood that an innocent person will be wrongfully executed, for evidence pointing to the defendant's innocence may arise or be discovered only years later. Contrary to popular belief, many discretionary appeals initiated by defendants are not frivolous. In fact, between January 1, 1973, and April 1, 1998, there have been 1,642 cases in which defendants have either had their convictions overturned or had their sentences reduced by appeals courts (*Death Row, U.S.A.*, 1998). Using these statistics, Bohm (1999: 45) estimates that approximately 21% to 32% of imposed death sentences "have been found faulty" by appeals courts, for reasons such as ineffective counsel, prosecutors referring to defendants' refusal to testify (as if this is a sign of guilt rather than a Constitutional right), denial of an impartial jury, and use of bad evidence such as coerced confessions of guilt (Freedman, 1998). A more recent report shows an even higher incidence of error (see the Issue in Depth at the end of this chapter).

> $\mathcal{A}$t year end 1996, 36 of the 38 U.S. states that still practiced the death penalty provided an automatic appeal of all death sentences whether the defendant wanted it or not.

Despite the implementation of these reforms, little has changed in the outcome of death penalty cases. Steiker and Steiker (1998: 70) claim:

> The Supreme Court's death penalty law, by creating an impression of enormous regulatory effort, while achieving negligible effects, effectively obscures the true nature of our capital sentencing system. The pre-*Furman* world of unreviewable sentencer discretion lives on, with much the same consequences in terms of arbitrary and discriminatory sentencing patterns.

In other words, the death penalty still does not pass Constitutional muster *in practice.*

Yet, the last time the death penalty was seriously challenged, the Court failed to abolish capital punishment once and for all. In *McClesky v. Kemp* (1987), the Supreme Court heard testimony from a sociologist (Dr. Baldus) who showed that the death penalty was applied disproportionately to African Americans in Georgia. The study utilized a multiple regression analysis including 230 variables likely to affect the outcome of death penalty cases in order to test the hypothesis that race of defendant and race of victim played a role in death penalty sentences. This study found that only 1% of Caucasians received the death penalty in homicide cases between 1973 and 1979, whereas 11% of African Americans received the death penalty. Additionally, the study found that 22% of African Americans who killed Caucasians received death sentences, versus only 3% of Caucasians who killed African Americans. The Court recognized the validity of these findings and even acknowledged a general pattern of discrimination in the application of death sentences in Georgia. Yet, the Court held that an individual defendant must demonstrate discrimination in his or her specific case in order for the case to be considered unconstitutional. That is, he or she must be able to demonstrate that the prosecutor acted in a discriminatory fashion in the individual case or that the legislature intended to make discriminatory law. Can this standard ever be met by an individual person?

> *The* death penalty faced a serious judicial challenge in *McClesky v. Kemp* (1987). In that case, the Supreme Court heard testimony from a sociologist (Dr. Baldus) who showed that the death penalty was applied disproportionately to African Americans in Georgia. In the end, however, the Court failed to abolish capital punishment.

The point is this: we know, and the Supreme Court even acknowledged in this case, that the death penalty is disproportionately applied to African Americans who harm Caucasians; yet, the Court failed to use this evidence to overturn the death penalty. A majority of Americans still say that they support the use of capital punishment, as if evidence of injustice is not enough to change their views.

> *At* the end of 1998, those states with the death penalty and the federal government held 3,452 prisoners who had been sentenced to death.

DEATH PENALTY FACTS

At year end 1998, the 27 states with the death penalty and the federal government held 3,452 prisoners who had been sentenced to death. Of these men and women (mostly men) who sit on the nation's death rows, some have been there only months while others have been there for more than twenty years. Although I will discuss the issue of deterrence and the death penalty later in this chapter, it is impossible not to point out this important discrepancy at the outset: Between 1976 and 1998, there have been 462,720 murders and nonnegligent manslaughters in the United States (only counting street crime killings), yet only 3,452 people sit on death row. Another 499 people have been executed since 1977. This means that only 0.0085% of people who have committed murder and nonnegligent homicides have either been executed or are currently on death row.

> *Between* 1976 and 1998, there have been 462,720 murders and nonnegligent manslaughters in the United States (counting only street crime killings). Yet, only 3,452 people sit on death row. Another 499 people have been executed since 1977. This means that only 0.0085% of people who have committed murder and nonnegligent homicides have either been executed or are currently on death row.

> *O*nly some types of killings are eligible for the death penalty—most notably, aggravated murder. Yet, even of aggravated murderers, we sentence only about 1% to 2% to death.

Why do we kill so few of our nation's killers? As you will see later, only some types of killings are eligible for the death penalty—most notably, aggravated murder. Yet, even of aggravated murderers, we sentence only about 1% to 2% to the death penalty (Bohm, 1999: 144). Bohm claims that "not only are the vast majority of capital offenders able to escape execution, but there is no meaningful way to distinguish between the eligible offenders who were executed and those who were not." This is one reason death penalty opponents argue that capital punishment is applied so arbitrarily that it is not fair.

> *S*ince 1990, the United States has executed an average of 42 persons per year, and only 25 per year since 1977.

Since 1990, the United States has executed an average of 42 persons per year, and only 25 per year since 1977. "Even during the peak of executions in the United States in the 1930s, only 20 percent of all death-eligible offenders were executed." How can it be that our nation, supposedly devoted to justice, tolerates a punishment that is, and always has been, so arbitrarily applied? Bowers, Pierce, and McDevitt (1984: 188) calls the application of the death penalty "an occasional product of chance—an unpredictable occurrence." Even after the modifications to the death penalty after the *Furman* ruling, its application is still "rare," "uncommon," and "freakish" (Bohm, 1999: 146).

> *O*f the 1,333,561 inmates in U.S. prisons and the 687,973 inmates in local jails at midyear 1999, only 3,452 were on death row. This means that of the 2,021,534 people in our nation's correctional facilities, the 3,452 death row inmates account for only 0.0017%.

Of the 1,333,561 inmates in the nation's prisons and the 687,973 inmates in local jails at midyear 1999, only 3,452 were on death row. This means that of the 2,021,534 people in our nation's correctional facilities, the 3,452 death row inmates account for only 0.0017% of the nation's inmates. Of death row inmates, most are Caucasians, but minorities are overrepresented (see Figure 11.3). In 1998, there were 1,906 Caucasians (55%), 1,486 African Americans (43%), 29 American Indians (0.8%), 18 Asians (0.5%), and 13 people of some "other" race (0.4%) on death row. The increase in Americans on death row since 1990 has been higher for African Americans (58%) than for Caucasians (38%) and other ethnic groups. The vast majority of inmates on death row, 3,404 of 3,452 (99%), are males; only 48 (1%), are females. The average age of death row inmates at the time of arrest was 28 years. I'll visit the issue of bias in the application of the death penalty in the United States later in this chapter.

> *O*f death row inmates, most are Caucasians but minorities are overrepresented among death row populations. In 1998, there were 1,906 Caucasians (55%), 1,486 African Americans (43%), 29 American Indians (0.8%), 18 Asians (0.5%), and 13 people of some other race (0.4%) on death row.

FIGURE 11.3

Prisoners on Death Row, by Race

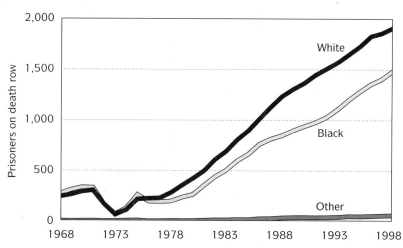

SOURCE: Bureau of Justice Statistics (1999). Online: www.ojp.usdoj.gov/bjs.

In 1998, 68 people were executed in 18 states. The average time on death row for those executed in 1998 was 10 years, 10 months.

In 1998, 68 people were executed in 18 states. The average time on death row for those executed in 1998 was 10 years, 10 months—hardly proof of a swift system. Table 11.1 illustrates which states executed people in 1998. As you can see, Texas leads the nation in executing its killers, proving once again, "Don't Mess with Texas!" Executions are so infrequent in most states (even in Texas) that it is almost laughable to assert that the death penalty deters would-be murders. But, if there should be a deterrent effect anywhere, it should be in Texas! Yet, Texas has one of the highest murder rates in the country.

You might expect that California would have a low murder rate, as well, given that it has more death row inmates than any other state (see Table 11.2, which shows the states with the most death row inmates in 1998). Again, there is Texas, trying to displace California as the nation's leader. Jurisdictions without the death penalty include the District of Columbia, Alaska, Hawaii, Iowa, Maine, Massachusetts, Michigan, Minnesota, North Dakota, Rhode Island, Vermont, West Virginia, and Wisconsin.

---

*J*urisdictions without the death penalty include the District of Columbia, Alaska, Hawaii, Iowa, Maine, Massachusetts, Michigan, Minnesota, North Dakota, Rhode Island, Vermont, West Virginia, and Wisconsin.

TABLE 11.1
Number of Executions (1998)

STATE	NUMBER	PERCENTAGE OF TOTAL
Texas	20	29
Virginia	13	19
South Carolina	7	10
Arizona	4	6
Florida	4	6
Oklahoma	4	6
Missouri	3	4
North Carolina	3	4
Alabama	1	1
Arkansas	1	1
California	1	1
Georgia	1	1
Illinois	1	1
Indiana	1	1
Maryland	1	1
Montana	1	1
Nevada	1	1
Washington	1	1

SOURCE: Data from Bureau of Justice Statistics (2000). Online: www.ojp.usdoj.gov/bjs.

Most people executed today will be killed by lethal injection. Table 11.3 documents the method of execution of the 68 people executed in 1998. There has been a move to make the death penalty as sanitary and "clean" as possible, so that allegations of cruel and unusual punishment will be harder to prove against states that use capital punishment.

> *M*ost inmates executed in the United States today will be killed by lethal injection.

Methods of capital punishment have evolved with evolving standards of decency; that is, as beliefs about what is acceptable punishment have changed, so too have methods of capital punishment. Bohm (1999) notes that hanging has been the most common form of capital punishment in American history, although electrocution was the most commonly used form of the death penalty in the twentieth century. It is likely that the future will see new forms of capital punishment developed; until then, lethal injection is likely to be the most popular from of capital punishment in the United States in the twenty-first century. Currently authorized options for methods of executions include lethal injection (34 states), electrocution (10 states), lethal gas (4 states), hanging (3 states), and firing squad (2 states). The U.S. government and the U.S. military utilize lethal injections, as well (Bohm, 1999).

America has made great strides to make its executions more humane, so that they will not be considered cruel and unusual. Prior to the *Furman* decision, individual methods of punishment

TABLE 11.2
Death Row Inmates (1998)

STATE	NUMBER	PERCENTAGE OF TOTAL
California	512	15
Texas	451	13
Florida	372	11
Pennsylvania	224	6
Ohio	191	5
North Carolina	187	5
Alabama	178	5
Illinois	157	4
Oklahoma	144	4
Arizona	120	3
Georgia	109	3
Tennessee	97	3
Missouri	90	3
Nevada	84	1
Lousiana	75	1
South Carolina	68	1
Mississippi	65	1
Other	328	10

SOURCE: Data from Bureau of Justice Statistics (2000). Online: www.ojp.usdoj.gov/bjs.

were considered cruel and unusual only if they involved torture, unnecessary cruelty, or lingering death due to inhuman and barbarous punishments (Bohm, 1999: 20). Of course, human beings have historically been subjected to executions that today would be considered cruel and unusual. Bedeau (1982: 14) writes about some historical examples of methods of execution, including "flaying and impaling, boiling in oil, crucifixion, pulling asunder . . . burying alive, and sawing in half."

One highly recognized example of a brutal execution is that of Robert-François Damiens, who in 1757 attempted to assassinate King Louis XV of France. His execution is described by Jones (1987a: 26):

> At seven o'clock in the morning of his execution day, Damiens was led to the torture chamber, where his legs were placed in "boots" that were squeezed gradually as wedges were inserted.

TABLE 11.3
Method of Executions (1998)

METHOD	NUMBER	PERCENTAGE OF TOTAL
Lethal injection	60	88
Electrocution	7	10
Lethal gas	1	1

SOURCE: Data from Bureau of Justice Statistics (2000). Online: www.ojp.usdoj.gov/bjs.

A total of eight wedges were inserted, each at fifteen-minute intervals, until the attending physicians warned that an additional wedge could (prematurely) provoke [Damien's death]. Thereupon, Damiens was removed to the place where he would be executed. . . . The condemned man was placed on a scaffold, where a rope was tied to each arm and leg. Then, Damiens' hand was burned with a brazier containing burning sulphur, after which red-hot tongs were used to pinch his arms, thighs, and chest. Molten lead and boiling oil were poured onto his open wounds several times, and after each time the prisoner screamed in agony. Next, four huge horses were whipped by attendants as they pulled the ropes around Damiens' bleeding wounds for an hour. Only after some of the tendons were cut did two legs and one arm separate from Damiens' torso. He remained alive and breathing until the second arm was cut from his body. All parts of Damiens' body were hurled into a nearby fire for burning.

Executions often were public spectacles of excess. Adler, Mueller, and Laufer (1995: 56) write that, at the execution of Damiens, so many people wanted to watch the hour-long killing that window seats overlooking the site were sold at high prices. Criminal defendants in Europe were stretched on their backs, in public, and had large rocks or iron weights placed on their chests until they confessed or died.

Early methods of execution included stoning, "death by a thousand cuts," hanging, being drawn and quartered, being "parbolied" (cooked in salt and cumin seed), being drowned, being beaten to death, beheading, "breaking on the wheel," being pressed to death, and burning at the stake (Costanzo, 1997).

Even in the United States, executions have been carried out in public. Costanzo (1997: 7) describes how public executions in America were similar to those in Europe: "The condemned was forced to take a slow wagon ride to the gallows, often sitting atop the very coffin he or she would soon occupy. The rowdy crowds who witnessed the hangings often numbered in the thousands." Bohm (1999: 4) notes that the first state to "hide executions from the public" was Pennsylvania, in 1834. The last public execution in the United States was in Galena, Missouri, in 1937, before a crowd of nearly 20,000 (Costanzo, 1997: 9). Since this time, executions have occurred in the nation's prisons, in isolated rooms, inaccessible to the general public, late at night, without much attention by the media. This is to prevent or reduce the "public disorder, rioting, and even murder," as well as public knowledge of botched executions and disappointment associated with last-minute reprieves, that accompanied public executions (Bowers, 1984: 8; Denno, 1994: 564).

You may imagine that executions should be public as a deterrent to would-be criminals, but there is no evidence to support this assertion. In fact, when executions were public in Europe just prior to the French Revolution, large crowds of witnesses would attract pickpockets, who would steal from witnesses watching the public spectacle. Yet theft was a crime punishable by death (Adler et al., 1995)! I'll return to the issue of deterrence later in this chapter.

As I have mentioned, most people executed today will be executed after being convicted for aggravated murders. The following box lists specific death penalty offenses at the state level.

Death penalty offenses at the state level

- *Alabama:* Capital murder with a finding of at least 1 of 9 aggravating circumstances (Ala. Code Sec. 13A-5-40 and Sec. 13A-5-49).
- *Arizona:* First-degree murder accompanied by at least 1 of 10 aggravating factors.
- *Arkansas:* Capital murder (Ark. Code Ann. 5-10-101) with a finding of at least 1 of 10 aggravating circumstances; treason.
- *California:* First-degree murder with special circumstances; train wrecking; treason; perjury causing execution.
- *Colorado:* First-degree murder with at least 1 of 13 aggravating factors; treason. Capital sentencing excludes persons determined to be mentally retarded.
- *Connecticut:* Capital felony with 9 categories of aggravated homicide (C.G.S. 53a–54b).
- *Delaware:* First-degree murder with aggravating circumstances.
- *Florida:* First-degree murder; felony murder; capital drug trafficking.
- *Georgia:* Murder; kidnaping with bodily injury or ransom where the victim dies; aircraft hijacking; treason.
- *Idaho:* First-degree murder; aggravated kidnaping.
- *Illinois:* First-degree murder with 1 of 15 aggravating circumstances.
- *Indiana:* Murder with 16 aggravating circumstances (IC 35-50-2-9). Capital sentencing excludes persons determined to be mentally retarded.
- *Kansas:* Capital murder with 7 aggravating circumstances (KSA 21-3439). Capital sentencing excludes persons determined to be mentally retarded.
- *Kentucky:* Murder with aggravating factors; kidnaping with aggravating factors.
- *Louisiana:* First-degree murder; aggravated rape of victim under age 12; treason (La. R.S. 14:30, 14:42, and 14:113).
- *Maryland:* First-degree murder, either premeditated or during the commission of a felony, provided that certain death eligibility requirements are satisfied.
- *Mississippi:* Capital murder (97-3-19(2) MCA); aircraft piracy (97-25-55(1) MCA).
- *Missouri:* First-degree murder (565.020 RSMO).
- *Montana:* Capital murder with 1 of 9 aggravating circumstances (46-18-303 MCA); capital sexual assault (45-5-503 MCA).
- *Nebraska:* First-degree murder with a finding of at least one statutorily defined aggravating circumstance.
- *Nevada:* First-degree murder with 13 aggravating circumstances.
- *New Hampshire:* Six categories of capital murder (RSA 630:1 and RSA 630:5).
- *New Jersey:* Purposeful or knowing murder by one's own conduct; contract murder; solicitation by command or threat in furtherance of a narcotics conspiracy (NJSA 2C:11-3C).
- *New Mexico:* First-degree murder in conjunction with a finding of at least 1 of 7 aggravating circumstances (Section 30-2-1 A, NMSA).

- *New York:* First-degree murder with 1 of 12 aggravating factors. Capital sentencing excludes persons determined to be mentally retarded.
- *North Carolina:* First-degree murder (N.C.G.S. 14–17).
- *Ohio:* Aggravated murder with at least 1 of 8 aggravating circumstances. (O.R.C. secs. 2903.01, 2929.01, and 2929.04).
- *Oklahoma:* First-degree murder in conjunction with a finding of at least 1 of 8 statutorily defined aggravating circumstances.
- *Oregon:* Aggravated murder (ORS 163.095).
- *Pennsylvania:* First-degree murder with18 aggravating circumstances.
- *South Carolina:* Murder with 1 of 10 aggravating circumstances (Section 16-3-20(C)(a)). Mental retardation is a mitigating factor.
- *South Dakota:* First-degree murder with 1 of 10 aggravating circumstances; aggravated kidnaping.
- *Tennessee:* First-degree murder.
- *Texas:* Criminal homicide with 1 of 8 aggravating circumstances (TX Penal Code 19.03).
- *Utah:* Aggravated murder (76-5-202, Utah Code annotated).
- *Virginia:* First-degree murder with 1 of 12 aggravating circumstances (VA Code sec. 18.2-31).
- *Washington:* Aggravated first-degree murder.
- *Wyoming.* First-degree murder.

At the federal level, the situation is much the same. Most crimes punishable by death involve murder. The 1994 crime bill discussed throughout this book specifically increased the number of crimes punishable by death to more than 50, but most of them involve the crime of murder. The following box lists specific death penalty offenses at the federal level.

Death penalty offenses at the federal level

- 8 U.S.C. 1342: Murder related to the smuggling of aliens.
- 18 U.S.C. 32–34: Destruction of aircraft, motor vehicles, or related facilities resulting in death.
- 18 U.S.C. 36: Murder committed during a drug-related drive-by shooting.
- 18 U.S.C. 37: Murder committed at an airport serving international civil aviation.
- 18 U.S.C. 115(b)(3) [by cross-reference to 18 U.S.C. 1111]: Retaliatory murder of a member of the immediate family of law enforcement officials.
- 18 U.S.C. 241, 242, 245, 247: Civil rights offenses resulting in death.
- 18 U.S.C. 351 [by cross-reference to 18 U.S.C. 1111]: Murder of a member of Congress, an important executive official, or a Supreme Court Justice.
- 18 U.S.C. 794: Espionage.
- 18 U.S.C. 844(d), (f), (i): Death resulting from offenses involving transportation of explosives, destruction of government property, or destruction of property related to foreign or interstate commerce.
- 18 U.S.C. 924(i): Murder committed by the use of a firearm during a crime of violence or a drug-trafficking crime.

- 18 U.S.C. 930: Murder committed in a federal government facility.
- 18 U.S.C. 1091: Genocide.
- 18 U.S.C. 1111: First-degree murder.
- 18 U.S.C. 1114: Murder of a federal judge or law enforcement official.
- 18 U.S.C. 1116: Murder of a foreign official.
- 18 U.S.C. 1118: Murder by a federal prisoner.
- 18 U.S.C. 1119: Murder of a U.S. national in a foreign country.
- 18 U.S.C. 1120: Murder by an escaped federal prisoner already sentenced to life imprisonment.
- 18 U.S.C. 1121: Murder of a state or local law enforcement official or other person aiding in a federal investigation; murder of a state correctional officer.
- 18 U.S.C. 1201: Murder during a kidnaping.
- 18 U.S.C. 1203: Murder during a hostage taking.
- 18 U.S.C. 1503: Murder of a court officer or juror.
- 18 U.S.C. 1512: Murder with the intent of preventing testimony by a witness, victim, or informant.
- 18 U.S.C. 1513: Retaliatory murder of a witness, victim, or informant.
- 18 U.S.C. 1716: Mailing of injurious articles with intent to kill or resulting in death.
- 18 U.S.C. 1751 [by cross-reference to 18 U.S.C. 1111]: Assassination or kidnaping resulting in the death of the president or vice president.
- 18 U.S.C. 1958: Murder for hire.
- 18 U.S.C. 1959: Murder involved in a racketeering offense.
- 18 U.S.C. 1992: Willful wrecking of a train resulting in death.
- 18 U.S.C. 2113: Bank-robbery-related murder or kidnaping.
- 18 U.S.C. 2119: Murder related to a carjacking.
- 18 U.S.C. 2245: Murder related to rape or child molestation.
- 18 U.S.C. 2251: Murder related to sexual exploitation of children.
- 18 U.S.C. 2280: Murder committed during an offense against maritime navigation.
- 18 U.S.C. 2281: Murder committed during an offense against a maritime fixed platform.
- 18 U.S.C. 2332: Terrorist murder of a U.S. national in another country.
- 18 U.S.C. 2332a: Murder by the use of a weapon of mass destruction.
- 18 U.S.C. 2340: Murder involving torture.
- 18 U.S.C. 2381: Treason.
- 21 U.S.C. 848(e): Murder related to a continuing criminal enterprise or related murder of a federal, state, or local law enforcement officer.
- 49 U.S.C. 1472–1473: Death resulting from aircraft hijacking.

PUBLIC SUPPORT FOR CAPITAL PUNISHMENT

According to public opinion polls, most people in the United States support the death penalty. In fact, the percentage of Americans who report that they support capital punishment has increased consistently since the 1960s. According to Bohm and Vogel (1994) most people who support the

> $\mathscr{A}$ccording to public opinion polls, most people in the United States support the death penalty.

death penalty are Caucasian and believe that the death penalty achieves revenge against offenders and deters would be murderers. Other research shows that support for the death penalty is associated with stereotyping of people of color and antipathy toward African Americans (Barkan and Cohn, 1994).

> $\mathscr{M}$ost people who support capital punishment are Caucasian and believe that the death penalty exacts revenge against offenders and deters would-be murderers. Other research shows that support for the death penalty is associated with stereotyping of people of color and antipathy toward African Americans.

This apparently clear-cut support for the use of the death penalty becomes more ambiguous when citizens are provided with alternatives; the percentage of Americans who say they support the death penalty for convicted murderers declines when the option of life imprisonment without the possibility of parole is given as a sentencing option. Perhaps if people were better informed about capital punishment facts, they would change their opinions to an anticapital punishment stance. Haas and Alpert (1999: 167) predicts that increased use of capital punishment will reveal its flaws to more people and ultimately lead to its abolition. He writes that they will "become convinced by the weight of the evidence that the death penalty is useless, dangerous, and self-defeating" (p. 186).

> $\mathscr{T}$he apparent clear-cut support for imposing the death penalty becomes more ambiguous when citizens are provided with alternatives such as life in prison without the possibility of parole; the percentage of Americans who say they support the death penalty for convicted murderers declines when this sentencing option is given.

Results from the Harris poll question, "Do you believe in capital punishment, that is, the death penalty, or are you opposed to it?" are shown in Table 11.4. These figures show that although a

TABLE 11.4

"Do you believe in capital punishment, that is, the death penalty, or are you opposed to it?"

	BELIEVE IN IT	OPPOSE IT
1965	38%	47%
1969	48%	38%
1973	59%	31%
1976	67%	25%
1997	75%	22%
1999	71%	21%

SOURCE: Harris poll.

majority of Americans still say they support the death penalty, the percentage who say they do has recently begun to decline. A 1999 Harris poll shows that support is higher among males (75%) than females (66%) and higher among Caucasians (77%) than Hispanics (65%) or African Americans (39%). It is also higher for people aged 50 to 64 years (78%) than for persons under 24 years (59%) and is higher for people with less than a college education (72%) than for people with some graduate school (59%). Generally, people who earn more income are more apt to support the death penalty, as 75% of those earning over $75,000 favor it, compared to 68% of people who earn less than $15,000. Finally, support is higher among Republicans (81%) than Independents (75%) or Democrats (64%).

Gallup polls show that when asked, "What do you think should be the penalty for murder—the death penalty, or life imprisonment with absolutely no possibility of parole?," most Americans favor the death penalty (see Table 11.5). As you can see, support for capital punishment is far from universal. A study by Sandys and McGarrell (1995) found that only about 9% of respondents in their survey of Indiana residents could be categorized as universally supportive of the death penalty. Their findings suggest that many Americans may simply accept capital punishment without actually supporting it.

A Gallup poll conducted in 2000 found that, for persons convicted of murder, 66% favor the death penalty while 28% do not favor it. As in the Harris poll, support is higher among males (73%) than females (60%) and among Caucasians (70%) than non-Whites (49%) and African Americans (43%). It is also higher among people aged 50 to 64 years (78%) than among those under 24 (59%) and is higher among people with less than a college education (70%) than among people with some graduate school (52%). Support is higher among people living in rural areas (72%) than those living in suburban (67%) or urban areas (61%). Finally, support is higher among Republicans (82%) than Independents (63%) or Democrats (57%).

TABLE 11.5

"What do you think should be the penalty for murder— the death penalty, or life imprisonment with absolutely no possibility of parole?"

	DEATH	LIFE
1985	56%	34%
1986	55%	35%
1991	53%	35%
1992	50%	37%
1993	59%	29%
1994	50%	32%
1997	61%	29%
1999	56%	38%
2000	52%	37%

SOURCE: Gallup poll (2000).

TABLE 11.6

Reasons Americans Give for Favoring the Death Penalty

An eye for an eye / they took a life / punishment fits the crime	40%
Save taxpayers money / cost associated with prison	12%
Deterrent for potential crimes / set an example	8%
Depends on type of crime committed	6%
Fair punishment	5%
They will repeat their crime / keeps them from repeating it	4%
Biblical reasons	3%
Serve justice	2%
Don't believe they can be rehabilitated	1%
Other	10%

SOURCE: Gallup poll (2000).

Table 11.6 shows reasons that Americans give for favoring the death penalty. Half (50%) say they support the death penalty because of retribution (an eye for an eye; they took a life; punishment fits the crime; fair punishment; biblical reasons; to serve justice). Another 8% support it for its deterrent value, and 5% support it for incapacitation (they will repeat their crime; keeps them from repeating it; don't believe they can be rehabilitated). Another Harris poll, from 1999, asked, "Do you feel that executing people who commit murder deters others from committing murder, or do you think such executions don't have much effect?" About half (47%) reported that they felt it deterred others, while about half (49%) said it did not have much effect.

Let me now turn to the issue of whether these beliefs of Americans are justified on the basis of either logic or empirical evidence. If you support the death penalty, I think you will be surprised by much of what you will read.

JUSTIFICATIONS FOR CAPITAL PUNISHMENT: LOGICAL OR NOT?

Why do we have a death penalty? There seem to be only three possible justifications: retribution, incapacitation, and deterrence. Retribution is the most commonly cited reason that people support the death penalty; incapacitation is the second most often stated justification for supporting the death penalty. Americans today rarely mention deterrence as a reason for supporting capital punishment, and most criminologists and criminal justice scholars no longer think of it as a valid justification for capital punishment.

> *There seem to be only three justifications for capital punishment: retribution, incapacitation, and deterrence.

Retribution

One major reason we administer capital punishment in the United States is to do to the offender what he or she has done to someone else, to get even with the offender or, stated differently, to give the offender his or her "just deserts." The death penalty as a form of justice is motivated both by the rational desire to rebalance the scales of justice (retribution) and by raw emotion (vengeance).

---

*O*ne major reason we administer capital punishment in the United States is to do to the offender what he or she has done to someone else, or, stated differently, to give the offender his or her "just deserts." The death penalty as a form of justice is motivated both by the rational desire to rebalance the scales of justice (retribution) and by raw emotion (vengeance).

A benefit of state-sanctioned retribution is that it limits the emotional aspects of vengeance, which often prompt retaliation on the part of victims and ultimately lead to escalation rather than resolution of the situation. For example, when a murder has been committed, only the state has the legal authority to seek justice for the harm inflicted. In the absence of this formal system of justice, victims would be left to seek out revenge for their loved ones and would likely end up killing not only the offender, in the name of justice, but whoever happened to be with the offender when the vengeance was carried out. This would ultimately lead to the killing of even more people in the name of justice for the new victims, with little hope of a successful ending to the killing. Jesse Jackson has said that the problem with "an eye for an eye, a tooth for a tooth, a life for a life" is that, eventually, we all end up blind, toothless, and dead.

State-sanctioned vengeance, ideally, does provide the advantage of preventing retaliation and escalation. Without punishment of the guilty, "there [would] exist the typical progression or spiraling process by which each offense [would be] countered by another offense more severe until the complete destruction of one of the parties [would be] achieved. It is the establishment of a social order that attempts to break this cycle of destruction" (Marongiu and Newman, 1987: 4). There is certainly evidence of such escalation in history, which may justify state-sanctioned and state-administered vengeance. In ancient tribes, before the establishment of the Magna Carta in A.D. 1215 and the philosophy on which it was based (*lex talionis*, or an "eye for an eye"), retaliation threatened the social order as a result of "blood feuds." As stated by Jeffery (1990: 61), "tribal law was based on revenge and the blood feud. The offended group carried out revenge against the offending group until some form of restitution was made by the offending group." If one individual offended against another, retaliation ensued, which would lead to escalation, clearly a destructive force. The only solution to this problem, according to Marongiu and Newman (1987: 5) is the development of an acceptable formal means of social control, such as a criminal justice system.

By limiting retaliation to an "eye for an eye," no more than one "eye" could be paid to right a wrong. The process of escalation should effectively be wiped out by punishing a guilty party for his or her acts. As explained by Jeffery (1990: 62):

> Legal systems emerged . . . to control the blood feud and private vengeance. The law said, "You cannot kill another person in retaliation for an injury to you or your tribe." However, the political state proceeded to establish criminal law based on the basis of public vengeance; that is, the state arrested, convicted, and killed the offender through legal procedures. Although the victim or his family is not allowed to kill the offender, the state is. Public vengeance replaced private vengeance.

This is an important point to remember when considering the validity of any punishment. But, why do we have to kill people rather than subject them to some other form of punishment? "An eye for an eye" does not *mandate* plucking an eye from one who plucks an eye from you, it means that this is the *most* you can possibly do to the offender (Johnson, 2000). Similarly, when one person kills another, we do not *have* to kill the offender, we just cannot do *more* to the offender (e.g., torture and kill the offender).

That is, retribution does not *mandate* an eye for an eye (Erez, 1981). The state could easily administer some other punishment to achieve retribution. After all, the state does not rape rapists, burn the property of arsonists, or assault people who assault others (Amsterdam, 1982).

One reason people support the death penalty as a form of retribution is the perception that it is supported by the Bible. In fact, among the earliest justifications for the death penalty in Colonial America were religious passages, quoted in early criminal statutes (Bohm, 1999: 1). Costanzo (1997: 11) writes:

> Early justifications for killing wrongdoers rested on religious authority. Religious leaders insisted that executions were means of carrying out the will of God. According to the laws of Moses, the death penalty was a way to appease God and avert famines, plagues, and other misfortunes that might result from "God's fierce anger" against any community that failed to punish sinners.

A thorough analysis of the Bible by one criminal justice scholar surprisingly shows less support for capital punishment than one might think (Johnson, 2000). Johnson focuses on instances where the Bible either mandates, explicitly acknowledges, or implicitly implies a state-sponsored execution. He writes: "People often cite specific verses of the Bible to justify a particular position on capital punishment, but these passages are frequently acontextual, failing to consider the significance of the passages containing these verses or the Bible as an entire document" (p. 15). Because the Bible is more ambiguous on the death penalty than one might believe, both supporters and opponents can find evidence supporting their arguments in the Bible.

A thorough analysis of the Bible by one criminal justice scholar surprisingly shows less support for capital punishment than one might think.

Consider that "[t]he majority of biblical statements that support capital punishment are found in the Old Testament, more specifically the first five books of the Old Testament . . . the Pentateuch . . . the books of Genesis, Exodus, Leviticus, Numbers, and Deuteronomy." These are the oldest books of the Bible and they "clearly mandate the use of the death penalty for premeditated homicide" (p. 17). They also allow for capital punishment for the crimes of blasphemy and sacrifice to false gods, dishonoring parents, disrespecting priests or elders, adultery, incest, and homosexuality!

The New Testament, a more recent testimony to God, "provides no overt statement in which Jesus or New Testament authors endorse the use of death as a punishment for crimes" and "also fails to reveal any overt rejection of capital punishment," although death was clearly used as a state-sanctioned punishment during this time (p. 23). Yet, the New Testament "also contains many passages that seem to refute the death penalty" (p. 26). For example, the Bible at times argues against taking revenge and seems to advocate forgiveness. Jesus even says:

> You may have heard that it was said, "An eye for an eye and a tooth for a tooth." But I tell you to resist an evil person . . . whoever slaps you on your right cheek, turn the other also. . . . You

have heard that it was said, "You shall love your neighbor and hate your enemy." But I say to you, love your enemies, bless those who curse you, do good to those who hate you, and pray for those who spitefully use you or persecute you . . . (Matthew 5: 38–45).

Perhaps the clearest example of ambiguity about the death penalty in the Bible comes in the form of the outcomes of people who committed murder in the Bible. Johnson (2000: 29) identifies 22 murderers in the Bible, only 4 of whom are executed by the state. I replicate Johnson's table in Table 11.7. As explained by Johnson: "It seems difficult to suggest that the Bible sincerely endorses state sponsored capital punishment, when so few murderers in the Scriptures receive the death penalty" (p. 31).

Considering the lack of a clear mandate for executions in the Bible, Bohm (1999: 182) poses an interesting question: How can people, "particularly people whose lives are governed by the

TABLE 11.7

Murderers in the Bible and Their Dispositions

NAME	VERSE OF CRIME	OUTCOME
Cain	Genesis 4:8	Marked by God
Ehud	Judges 3:21	Liberates Israel from Moabites
Gideon	Judges 8:22	Nothing
Abimelech	Judges 9:5	Killed in military defeat
Rechab and Baanah	2 Samuel 4:6	Executed by King David
David	2 Samuel 11:15	Cursed by God to always have strife
Absalom	2 Samuel 13:29	Killed by Joab
Joab	2 Samuel 3:27	Executed by King Solomon
Baasha	1 Kings 15:28	Cursed by God
Zimri	1 Kings 16:10	Commits suicide
Jezebel	1 Kings 21:8–10	Killed by her eunuchs
Hazael	2 Kings 8:12–15	Becomes King of Aram
Jehu	2 Kings 9:24	Nothing
Athaliah	2 Kings 11:2	Executed by Jehoiada, High Priest
Jozachar and Jehozabad	2 Kings 12:20–21	No further mention
Shallum	2 Kings 15:10	Killed by Menahem
Menahem	2 Kings 15:14	Serves as King of Israel
Pekah	2 Kings 15:25	Killed by Hoshea
Hoshea	2 Kings 15:30	Imprisoned by King of Assyria for later crime
Amon's servants	2 Kings 21:23	Executed by leaders of Judah
Jehoram	2 Chronicles 21:4	Cursed by God
Ishmael	Jeremiah 41:2	Escapes to Ammonites
Herodias	Matthew 14:8–11	No further mention

SOURCE: Data from S. Johnson, "The Bible and the Death Penalty: Implications for Criminal Justice Education," *Journal of Criminal Justice Education,* Vol. 2, No. 1 (2000): 15–33.

Bible . . . endorse revenge, support or oppose capital punishment, and use the Bible as a basis of their support or opposition, when they know the Bible is ambiguous on the subject"?

Even though the Bible may not provide the answer, consider that the "leaders of most organized religions in the United States no longer support the death penalty and actually openly favor its abolition" (Bohm, 1999: 177). This includes Pope John Paul II and the National Conference of Catholic Bishops, who suggested that death by execution is "uncivilized," "inhumane," "barbaric," and assaultive of human life (Gow, 1986: 80).

Since human life is precious, shouldn't we mourn the loss of any human life, including that of the offender? Keep in mind that when a person is executed, his or her family is victimized by the loss of their own loved one. In many ways, the loss of the convicted killer is just as bad as the loss of the innocent victim. Consider these points by Vandiver (1998: 486):

- The families of condemned prisoners know for years that the state intends to kill their relatives and the method that will be used. They experience a prolonged period of anticipatory grieving, complicated by the hope that some court or governor will grant relief.
- Their relatives' deaths will come about as the result of actions of dozens of respected and powerful persons. Their deaths are caused not by a breakdown in social order but by a highly orchestrated and cooperative effort of authority.
- Their relatives are publicly disgraced and shamed; they have been formally cast out by society and judged to be unworthy to live.
- The deaths of their relatives are not mourned and regretted as other violent deaths are; rather, the death is condoned, supported and desired by many people, and actively celebrated by some.

Whatever the case, all acts of retribution and vengeance are motivated by concerns for equality, justice, and reciprocity, as well as the safety of society (Marongiu and Newman, 1987). This means that people who support capital punishment may seek to achieve legitimate and positive goals for society. Even the U.S. Supreme Court, in the case of *Gregg v. Georgia* (1976) recognized that retribution is a legitimate purpose of administering capital punishment; the Court even suggested that executing the guilty serves the purpose of satisfying the feelings and needs of the public for revenge (Bedau, 1987). A significant drawback to their reasoning is that family members who survive murder victims are not well served by the execution of their loved ones' killers. Vandiver (1998) shows that there are many reasons that family members of murder victims do not want the killers executed, including these:

- They do not support capital punishment.
- An execution would diminish the memory of their relative.
- They do not want to be forced to have prolonged contact with the criminal justice system.
- They do not want the condemned killer to have any added public attention for his or her wrongdoing.
- They prefer the finality of a sentence of life imprisonment without the possibility of parole and the obscurity of prisoners over the continued uncertainty and publicity of the death penalty.
- They want the offender to reflect on his or her wrongdoing for life and to feel remorse.
- They may hope to develop, from the offender, a sense of understanding of why he or she committed the act.

As I discussed in Chapter Nine, the desire to get even with those who harm us is a natural human emotion. In fact, it may be the strongest human emotion of all. Marongiu and Newman (1987), in their book *Vengeance,* illustrate the strength of vengeance. Many stories of vengeance appear in the Bible, including some that are graphic in their descriptions of violence. For example, in Psalm 58: 10, 11: "The righteous shall rejoice when he seeth the vengeance: he shall wash his feet in the blood of the wicked. So that a man shall say, Verily there is a reward for the righteous."

Another book suggests in its title that the death penalty is no more than *Just Revenge* (Costanzo, 1997). Vengeance consists of a "vengeful, aggressive act . . . performed in cold blood, after the damage has been done, and . . . is not a defense against immediate danger . . . which is of great intensity, often crude, vicious, and insatiable" (Marongiu and Newman, 1987: 2; citing Erich Fromm). You can see how the death penalty fits this definition of vengeance in that the penalty is administered years after the criminal offense after the damage has been done. The death penalty also is not administered in the face of any immediate danger: once an offender is properly confined in custody, he or she no longer poses a threat to society.

This may be one limitation to retribution as a justification for punishment. As stated by the criminologist Frederic Faust (1995), "no other species will expend the energy to kill the enemy after it is clear that it has already won." Yet, once a person has been arrested and convicted for murder and is thus no longer capable of killing another free member of society, we may still kill the person.

There are many other limits of retribution as a justification for punishment. For example, Jeffery (1990: 64) writes: "Retribution perpetuates the human urge for revenge, and it brutalizes societies and individuals by its use. . . . Although retribution is justified as a moral position, it is an immoral, vulgar, and self-defeating response to human behavior." Such statements are representative of those who feel that getting even to make us feel better is, simply stated, evil.

Others point to the hypocritical assertion that we can teach people that killing people is wrong by killing people who kill people: "[Some may] reap revenge in order to cancel out an offense, yet those same persons are perpetrating the very same behavior that they wish to avenge" (Marongiu and Newman, 1987: 3). As asked on the humorous bumper stickers you might have seen on cars, "Why do we kill people who kill people to show them that killing people is wrong?" The idea that the death penalty is hypocritical was also put forward by the British criminologist Jeremy Bentham, who claimed that the state could no more justly take the life of a person than could an individual person. In essence, the crime and the punishment become indistinguishable.

Obviously, not everyone feels that the death penalty is evil or hypocritical, given Americans' support of capital punishment. Virtually every politician claims to support the death penalty, at least publicly. To be against the death penalty today is virtually to ensure that you will not get elected. Many philosophers, as discussed in Chapter Nine, have claimed that retribution is a valid justification for punishment by positing that offenders who harm others are deserving of punishment. By killing, killers give up their right to life.

Many politicians echo these statements to justify their own support of capital punishment. A prosecutor in Florida said publicly in 1995 that the state should speed up the process of administering the death penalty by using "electric bleachers." Even though he was probably joking, his point was not only that he supported capital punishment, but also that he was fed up with how long it takes to carry out an execution.

Other supporters of the death penalty claim that it is the only form of justice to which individual victims are entitled. For example, Ernest Van den Haag states that punishment is a "collective reaction aimed at the satisfaction of the desire for retaliation by the injured party" (cited in Marongiu and Newman, 1987: 3). Perhaps this is so, but the question remains: Could we more effectively and humanely achieve retribution through some alternative method of punishment?

Incapacitation

Without question, the death penalty achieves the goal of incapacitating the offender. Once an offender has been executed, there is no chance that he or she will commit another crime. The question is, can we achieve incapacitation with a form of punishment other than the death penalty? The answer is yes: incapacitation can be achieved with life imprisonment without the possibility of parole.

> *W*ithout question, the death penalty achieves the goal of incapacitating the offender. Once an offender has been executed, there is no chance that he or she will commit another crime.

Luckily for taxpayers, the costs associated with life imprisonment without the possibility of parole for one offender are actually less than the costs associated with an execution of the same offender. Administering this alternative punishment would also eliminate the possibility of killing innocent people, as we now know has been done.

The alternative I would likely advocate would be life imprisonment without the possibility of parole, plus restitution (LWOP+R)—that is, where people convicted of aggravated murders would spend the rest of their lives behind bars and be required to work to pay for part of their incarceration costs and repay families of victims of their crimes. Costanzo (1997: 163) claims that "detailed surveys of attitudes toward the death penalty show that Americans favor LWOP+R because it reduces the cost of incarceration, provides some form of restitution to victims, and is more likely to teach murderers to accept responsibility for their crimes." Since most jurors are reluctant to impose death sentences (regardless of their general support of capital punishment), because errors are inevitable, and because appeals in death penalty cases are numerous, LWOP+R sentences would be swifter, surer, and more final, and we would never again have to worry about killing an innocent person.

Deterrence

Another supposed reason for administering capital punishment is to deter would-be murderers from committing capital crimes. I should point out from the outset that most people probably no longer really believe that the death penalty is a deterrent to murder. It is currently the least mentioned reason for supporting the death penalty.

Recall from Chapter Nine that there are two types of deterrence—*special* or *specific* deterrence aimed at preventing one offender from committing future crimes, and *general* deterrence aimed at preventing members of society from engaging in criminality by making examples of criminals who already have. Some assert that the death penalty is at the very least a special deterrent, but this is an incorrect statement based on a misunderstanding of the meaning of special deterrence. Special deterrence implies that a convicted offender will fear punishment for future offenses and will thus refrain from committing crimes in the future. Since an execution results in the death of an offender, it is not a special deterrent because it does not create fear in the offender. Instead, it kills the offender, meaning he or she is incapacitated.

So, is the death penalty a general deterrent? That is, when a person is executed, does it create a sense of fear in other Americans so that they will refrain from committing murder? If so, the death penalty would save lives (Costanzo, 1997: 12). Logically, when Americans learn of executions, they should get the clear message: "SEE WHAT CAN HAPPEN TO YOU IF YOU GET CAUGHT COMMITTING SUCH AN OFFENSE!" Recall that much of what we do to punish criminals is based on logic. It appeals to our common sense that the death penalty should deter would-be murders. The problem with common sense is that it is often more "common" than "sense." Common sense would suggest, for example, that the sun revolves around the earth, but we know that the opposite is true (Costanzo, 1997: 95).

A significant problem comes from the assumption about murderers on which the death penalty is based. As explained by Costanzo (1997: 104), when we elect to impose a death sentence on murderers, we assume "that potential killers engage in a dispassionate weighing of the costs and benefits of killing." In other words, we assume that offenders choose to commit murder because the pleasure outweighs the potential pains associated with committing murder; thus, if we can somehow make the potential pains outweigh any benefits gained from committing murder, would-be murderers would not choose to commit murder. Costanzo claims: "This assumption is simply wrong." Most people who kill another do not carefully weigh the pleasures and pains associated with committing a murder; most, instead, act in the heat of the moment, without much thought about getting caught, convicted, and punished for their acts. Most murders in the United States are committed with guns. How long does it take to grab a gun and pull the trigger? Is it likely that these murderers even think of the death penalty in the short time it takes to pull the trigger?

Van den Haag (1982: 326) sums up the logic of deterrence by suggesting that since "our penal system rests on the proposition that more severe penalties are more deterrent than less severe penalties," logic would dictate that "the most severe penalty—the death penalty—would have the greatest deterrent effect." Bohm (1999: 84) responds by saying that this assertion" is based on a debatable assumption and a testable proposition with no scientific evidence to support it." Van den Haag's assumption that the death penalty is more severe than life imprisonment is debatable and has been contested for hundreds of years. Perhaps it is far worse to have to live in prison for the rest of your life than to be executed after spending only ten years on death row. However you feel about this issue personally, the fact remains that: "[t]here is no evidence that capital punishment deters more than an alternative noncapital punishment, such as life imprisonment without opportunity for parole. Instead, statistics indicate that capital punishment makes no discernible difference on homicide or murder rates" (Bohm, 1999: 85).

> *It* does not matter if one compares states with and without the death penalty, nations with and without the death penalty, or if one studies jurisdictions before and after executions—all methods show *no valid empirical evidence* that the death penalty deters murders.

It does not matter if one compares states with and without the death penalty, nations with and without the death penalty, or jurisdictions before and after executions—all methods show *no valid empirical evidence* that the death penalty deters murders. In fact, more studies show a *brutalization* effect of the death penalty—that is, that capital punishment increases the rate of murder rather than decreasing it. Bowers et al. (1984: 90) write:

> The evidence that capital punishment has no deterrent advantage over imprisonment is now stronger and more consistent than when the Court last considered this issue.... Indeed, a comprehensive review of previous studies and recent analyses of refined statistical data both support the contention that the death penalty has a "brutalizing" rather than a deterrent effect—that executions can be expected to stimulate rather than to inhibit homicides.

Why might we expect the death penalty to increase rather than decrease murders? In effect, the would-be murderer sees that killing is an acceptable means of righting a wrong against a person who has offended him or her, so that the lesson of capital punishment may be that lethal vengeance is acceptable.

Perhaps this is one reason that the American Society of Criminologists—the largest association of crime experts in the United States—passed a resolution calling for the abolition of the death penalty in 1989. As pointed out by Bohm (1999: 90–91), "a recent survey of 67 current and past presidents of the top three criminology professional organizations—the American Society of Criminology, the Academy of Criminal Justice Sciences, and the Law and Society Association—found that about 90 percent of them believe that the death penalty 'never has been, is not and never could be a deterrent to homicide over and above life imprisonment.'" Also opposed to the death penalty are medical organizations, the American Bar Association, and the widow of Martin Luther King, Jr. (Costanzo, 1997).

The rarity of the application of the death penalty alone, as I have mentioned, ensures that it can never deter offenders. Recent legislative initiatives have increased the number of offenses punishable by death in an effort to increase its application, presumably to send a message to criminals that "crime does not pay." Yet, the reality is, and always will be, that most murderers are not even charged with capital offenses and therefore do not receive the death penalty.

Even of those who do receive the death penalty, most will not be executed. For example, in 1998, 22 states reported that 80 persons had their sentences overturned or removed. This included 43 vacated sentences, where the convictions were upheld, and 36 where the convictions were overturned. Forty-eight of the 80 were serving a reduced sentence, 15 were awaiting new trials, 10 were awaiting new sentences, 1 was sentenced to time served, and 4 had no further action taken against them. Since 1977, 5,709 people have entered prison under a sentence of death. Of these people, only 500 have been executed, but 2,137 were removed from their death sentence or died of natural causes.

> *S*ince 1977, 5,709 people have entered prison under a sentence of death. Of these people, only 500 have been executed, but 2,137 had their death sentence removed or died of natural causes.

WHAT'S WRONG WITH THE DEATH PENALTY?

There are many reasons that the application of capital punishment is unjust (Nelson and Foster, 2001). Streib, in the Foreword to *Death Watch* (2001) suggests: "We have given capital punishment ample opportunity to prove whether or not it can reduce violent crime. It has made us only more violent and less sensitive to human suffering. We now must put this barbaric practice behind us and confess our shame at having used it for so many centuries before seeing the light."

Do you agree? Think about why or why not, and then consider some of the main problems with capital punishment:

- *Death penalty juries are not representative of the population.*

As you saw in this chapter, most Americans say they are in favor of capital punishment, generally, and for aggravated murderers specifically. When juries are faced with making decisions about whether convicted murderers ought to live the remainder of their natural lives in prison or be executed by the government, these juries are not representative of the general population. First, as I demonstrated in Chapter Eight, the groups least likely to be represented on juries are the ones most likely to be processed through the criminal justice system. This is also true for capital juries.

> $\mathcal{D}$eath penalty juries are not representative of the population.

Equally important, jurors who refuse to consider death as a valid option at sentencing are routinely denied service on capital juries. Bohm (1999) cites research indicating that "death-qualified juries," as they are called, are more conviction prone and more likely to recommend a sentence of death (Dillehay and Sandys, 1996; Ellsworth, 1991; Luginbuhl and Burkhead, 1994; Robinson, 1993). Defendants accused of capital crimes are at a significant disadvantage when the jurors who will determine their fate are more likely to hold crime control values consistent with the goals of the prosecution rather than due process values more in line with the defense. Stated differently, capital juries are more likely to be concerned with justice as an *outcome* (i.e., giving the alleged offender what he or she deserves) rather than justice as a *process* (i.e., making sure that the trial is fair) (see Chapter One).

Similar to the issue of jury instructions discussed in Chapter Eight, research also shows that capital juries rarely understand how jury instructions should structure their deliberations. Although instructions do explain to capital jurors the meaning of aggravating and mitigating factors, juries are typically instructed to "weigh" these factors. Many scholars conclude that this type of setup is confusing to juries, given that judges are "loath to offer any clarification beyond the vague charge of the jury instructions." Therefore, it is likely that jurors will have tremendous difficulty assessing which convicted people deserve death and which do not (Costanzo, 1997: 36).

- *The death penalty discriminates against men, the poor, and people of color.*

Recall from Chapter One that for something to be just, it must be fair. Justice requires that all persons will be treated equally in the eyes of the law. Injustice is present when any group is singled out for differential treatment by the law. Using this definition, the application of the death penalty in the United States is clearly unjust (McAdams, 1998).

> $\mathcal{T}$he death penalty discriminates against men, the poor, and people of color.

According to Nakell and Hardy (1987: 16), discrimination is deliberate, whereas disparities may not be. There is no doubt that capital punishment in the United States is applied in a disparate fashion. The question is, is this disparity intentional? I say that when it comes to deaths intentionally caused by the government, it does not really matter. Injustice does not require intentional discrimination by police, courts, and correctional personnel. As I have argued throughout this book, it can also arise out of innocent biases created in the criminal law and reinforced by media coverage of crime.

When juries must decide a person's fate, it is obvious that stereotypes about dangerous criminals infiltrate their thought processes. This works to the disadvantage of men, the poor, and minorities. Consider these facts:

- Women commit about 15% of murders (as defined by the criminal law) each year, yet account for less than 1% of executions.
- No wealthy person has been executed in America.
- People of color are more likely to receive the death penalty than Caucasians, especially when they are convicted of killing Caucasians (Bohm, 1999: 149–160).

According to Costanzo (1997: 8), the death penalty has always been applied in a discriminatory fashion. Consider North Carolina, for example, where "capital offenses [once] included circulating seditious literature among slaves, inciting slaves to insurrection, slave stealing, and harboring slaves for the purpose of setting them free." Further, "Virginia listed only five capital crimes for whites, but seventy for blacks."

Proof of racism in the administration of capital punishment is harder to demonstrate (Walker et al., 2000). Rather than stemming from overt racism, the problem today lies in abuse of discretion. The entire system of justice is "saturated with discretion" that works to the disadvantage of people of color and the poor (Black, 1974: 90–91). When deciding to arrest or not, police discretion is at issue; when deciding to charge or not, to plea bargain or go to trial, or to seek the death penalty or not, prosecutor discretion is at issue; when conviction or acquittal and sentencing are at hand, discretion of the jury and/or judge is at issue; and so on. The accumulated effects of these discretionary decisions results in the discriminatory application of the death penalty in the United States.

While every American *ideally* has the right to a competent defense attorney, in fact not every American can *really* afford a high-quality defense. Recall from Chapter Eight the distinctions between private and publicly appointed attorneys. Costanzo (1997: 75) claims: "The sad, shameful fact is that money makes the difference between life and death for many defendants." This is true because publicly appointed attorneys are often inexperienced at capital cases and have limits on how much they can spend to prepare their defense. In terms of race, Costanzo (1997: 80) writes

> since the reinstatement of the death penalty in 1977, 39.3 percent of the people killed in the execution chamber have been black, and 86 percent of the executions have been people convicted of killing whites, even though roughly half of all murder victims in the United States are black. . . . There have been more than 16,000 executions in American jurisdictions since 1608, yet only 31 whites have been executed for killing a black person.

The death penalty, because it is applied in a discriminatory fashion, threatens justice. If you look up the word *discrimination* in any dictionary, you will find definitions suggesting that it means "distinguishing" or "differentiating." Human beings, who assign blame and punishment, distinguish and differentiate on the basis of their own perceptions and preferences. This means that all punishments, including the death penalty, will inevitably be applied in a discriminatory fashion. The significant problem with the death penalty is that it is final: once it is administered, it cannot be "taken back" or undone.

When the law is applied in an arbitrary and discriminatory manner, it can lead to a general disrespect for the law. When the law is not respected, one can logically conclude that it will be violated more often. This would suggest that the death penalty might actually increase law violations rather than reduce them. This leads me to the next major point.

- *The death penalty may increase murder rates.*

The *brutalization* hypothesis suggests that the death penalty shows people that killing is an acceptable means to settle disputes; thus, when an execution is held, murders actually increase for a short period of time. At least two studies in the 1990s showed support for brutalization in one state (Bailey, 1998; Cochran, Chamlin, and Seth, 1994). Although effects on homicide tend to be relatively small, the point is that homicides seem to increase in the short term after an execution, rather than decreasing. Even if these findings turn out to be false, there still is absolutely no valid, scientific evidence showing a deterrent effect on homicides. It may be that the death penalty has *no effect,* overall, on murders in the United States (Bohm, 1999).

- *The death penalty kills the innocent, mentally ill, and mentally incompetent.*

Recall the logic of the due process model of criminal justice, discussed in Chapter One. The most important values in this model are liberty, individual freedom, and the protection of Constitutional rights from unnecessary government intervention. Proponents of the due process model would argue that it is far better to let guilty people go free than to punish even one innocent person. The killing of even one innocent individual, especially when it is state-sanctioned and carried out by state officials, is the ultimate evil. It might also be considered unacceptable to kill people who acted because of a biological brain disorder (the mentally ill) or who cannot develop the full mental capacity or intent to be held accountable for their actions (the mentally incompetent).

> *The* death penalty kills the innocent, the mentally ill, and the mentally incompetent.

Let me start with the issue of innocence. The U.S. Supreme Court ruled in *Herrera v. Collins* (1993) that a claim of actual innocence is not relevant for decisions about whether new hearings should be granted in federal courts (Bohm, 1999: 37). Because only issues of law are decided by appeals courts, issues pertaining to factual guilt or innocence are not relevant for these courts. Only when state courts violate Constitutional procedures are federal appeals courts really able to correct wrongful convictions. This leaves the wrongfully convicted with little hope of being set free other than executive clemency, which, for politican reasons, is rarely granted.

How often are the innocent actually executed? With the recent renewal of debate about the death penalty in the United States, many politicians have claimed that there is absolutely no evidence that a single innocent person has been executed in the United States. Yet, Espy (reported in Bohm, 1999: 125) estimates that of the 19,000 executions since 1608, 5% have been of innocent persons: about 950 wrongful executions have been carried out.

The evidence suggests that at least 6 or 7 wrongful convictions in capital cases are discovered each year. And Bohm (1999: 131) claims: "As many as a dozen people (and likely more) may have been executed in error in the United States since 1976 and the implementation of super due process [a term meaning that since the death penalty is different from all other criminal sanctions, extra precautions must be in place to assure that defendants' Constitutional rights are not violated]. That represents nearly three percent of all executions through April 1, 1998." A study conducted by the Columbia Law School found that at least 7% of all death penalty cases appealed between 1973 and 1995 were found to be innocent (see the Issue in Depth at the end of this chapter).

Even if you still doubt that innocent people have been executed, remember that we also know that hundreds of wrongfully convicted Americans have been set free from death row. Consider these two cases:

- In 1996, Rolando Cruz was freed after 11 years on death row. He had been convicted of the rape and murder of a 10-year-old Chicago girl on the basis of phony evidence invented by the police. The real murderer confessed to the crime 8 years prior to Cruz's release, but Cruz was not released until a DNA test proved he had not committed the crime.
- In 1993, Walter McMillan was released from death row in Alabama after the state admitted that it had withheld evidence that an eyewitness had lied. Kirk Bloodworth was also released that year in Alabama after a DNA test proved him to be innocent.

Wrongly convicted Americans typically will have spent about ten years in prison for crimes that they did not actually commit, in isolation from their families and even from other inmates. Bohm (1999: 126) writes that these inmates would have been executed if "not for sheer luck." Politicians who use these cases as evidence that the system works to (eventually) set free the innocent, while simultaneously promoting policies to speed up the system and limit appeals of death row inmates, are hypocritical and a threat to justice in the United States.

Why are innocent people wrongfully convicted of capital crimes, even with all the protections put into place by states to ensure that this does not occur? The answers are straightforward and not surprising. The bottom line is that errors are inevitable. To *not* make mistakes is beyond the capabilities of human beings. Many wrongful convictions stem from errors made by eyewitnesses to crimes (Huff, Rattner, and Sagarin, 1986). Think of the recent execution of Gary Graham in Texas. Graham was convicted on the basis of the eyewitness identification of one person, even though another five people claim that Graham was not the actual offender.

Another major reason that people are wrongfully convicted of capital crimes is the incompetence of their defense attorneys. In the Graham case, two of his attorneys reportedly never made an effort to interview or call to the stand the witnesses who claimed that Graham was not the offender. A 1990 study found that many capital defense attorneys "had never handled a capital trial before, lacked training in life-or-death cases, made little effort to present evidence in support of a life sentence, or had been reprimanded, disciplined, or subsequently disbarred" (Bohm, 1999: 134). The standard for a competent attorney in capital cases is very low and is inconsistent with justice as a process. According to the standard set forth in *Strickland v. Washington* (1984), an individual defendant must show that his or her attorney was deficient in performance and that this deficiency contributed to the outcome of the case. Given that virtually every capital defendant lacks the resources necessary to prove such deficiencies, this is an impossible standard to meet.

Apparently, Americans are not bothered enough by the thought of executing the innocent to diminish their overwhelming support of capital punishment. A recent Gallup poll found that, if they knew for a fact that the death penalty resulted in the wrongful execution of 1% of people subjected to it, three-fourths reported that they would still support the death penalty for people convicted of murder. This serves as evidence that Americans value justice as an outcome rather than justice as a process, and prefer crime control values over due process ones.

As I showed in Chapter Nine, we punish people on the basis of the assumptions that individuals rationally choose to engage in criminal behaviors because they are pleasurable and that we can make them not choose crime if the pains associated with choosing crime outweigh the pleasures resulting from criminal behavior. How, then, do Americans tolerate punishing people with diminished capacity to choose freely to engage in criminal behavior, or, put another way, how can we justify punishing people who have limited ability to utilize self-restraint to stop themselves from engaging in it? According to Bright (1997: 17), only 11 states prevent executing the mentally retarded, and at least 27 mentally retarded defendants have been executed since 1977.

- *The death penalty is very expensive.*

Administering the death penalty to a convicted murderer costs 2.5 to 5 times as many taxpayer dollars as locking up an offender for life without the possibility of parole. When you add the costs of posttrial reviews, executions become about 24 times as expensive as life imprisonment without parole. The death penalty is so much more expensive than life imprisonment because of the high rates of error that occur at each stage and the persistence of high error rates over time and across the nation, which mandate multiple, expensive judicial inspections (Liebman, Fagan, and West, 2000).

> The death penalty is 2.5 to 5 times as expensive as life imprisonment without parole, and when you also figure in the costs of posttrial reviews, executions become about 24 times as expensive as life imprisonment without parole.

Consider these statistics:

- Taxpayers in California could save about $90 million each year if the state abolished the death penalty (Magagnini, 1988).
- California spent more than $1 billion on its death penalty system between 1977 and 1996 but executed only 5 people, one of whom asked to be killed (Costanzo, 1997: 61).
- In Florida, the average cost of an execution is $3.2 million (Von Drehle, 1988).
- Texas capital cases cost about $2.3 million (Hoppe, 1992).
- In North Carolina, capital cases cost taxpayers an additional $2.16 million, added onto the costs of the typical murder case (Cook, Slawson, and Gries, 1993).

The added costs mount simply by maintaining an elaborate system of capital punishment. When they do result, capital trials are more complex and time-consuming, and appeals are costly. Costanzo (1997: 66) reviews these statistics and concludes: "Massive resources are squandered, courts and prisons are strained, just so that, eventually, a few condemned prisoners can be killed." Thus, he concludes that the death penalty is an elaborate, costly charade.

The social costs are harder to identify, but the bottom line is this: the death penalty does not teach Americans that killing is wrong, it teaches them that killing is acceptable under certain circumstances. Humankind says, through its criminal law, that killing is sometimes acceptable; only murder is wrong. Killing to humans is not *always* wrong; but, "no matter if done by a legitimate authority such as the state under the term of 'retribution' or if done by a private citizen in the name of 'vengeance,' the act of killing becomes no more moral, only more legitimate" (Marongiu and Newman, 1987: 6).

The United States stands out as a shining example of injustice, ironic given that this country is supposed to be a beacon of justice and freedom for the rest of the world. In fact, by continuing to administer capital punishment, we place ourselves in the company of other countries such as China, Iraq, Iran, Libya, Nigeria, and Uganda, countries whose civil rights violations we deplore.

CONCLUSION

America's long and sordid history with capital punishment has provided plenty of rationale for abolishing the death penalty, something that many states have in fact done. The United States briefly witnessed a moratorium on the death penalty in the face of overwhelming evidence that it was being applied in an arbitrary and discriminatory fashion, but capital punishment has since been reinstated and is now being increasingly used despite the evident bias and inequity in its application. One exception is the state of Illinois, which recently began a moratorium on executions after realizing that 13 innocent people had been freed from death row since 1977, while only 12 persons had been executed. Public support for capital punishment, though apparently widespread, is not as clear-cut as it may seem from opinion polls, and without doubt is lessening. With knowledge that the death penalty does not achieve its goals of retribution and deterrence, and that incapacitation can be achieved more fairly, humanely, and cheaply through life imprisonment without the possibility of parole, public support for capital punishment will likely dwindle in the years to come.

ISSUE IN DEPTH
A Broken System

An alarming study was recently published by James S. Liebman, Jeffrey Fagan, and Valerie West, titled *A Broken System: Error Rates in Capital Cases, 1973–1995*. These authors undertook "the first statistical study ever undertaken of modern American capital appeals (4,578 of them in state capital cases between 1973 and 1995)" and found that capital trials end up placing people on death row who do not belong there (either because serious errors were made during their cases or because they were innocent of the crimes of which they were charged), and that it takes a long time to carry out sentences of death in the United States because of the numerous errors in the process. According to the findings of this report, "American capital sentences are so persistently and systematically fraught with error" that their reliability is seriously undermined. The authors claim that capital punishment in the United States is "collapsing under its own mistakes . . . a system that is wasteful and broken and needs to be addressed."

Here are some of the key findings of this report:

- Nationally, the overall rate of prejudicial error was 68%—that is, "courts found serious, reversible error in nearly 7 of every 10 of the thousands of capital sentences that were fully reviewed during the period."
- Serious error was "error substantially undermining the reliability of capital verdicts."
- "Capital trials produce so many mistakes that it takes three judicial inspections to catch them—leaving grave doubt whether we *do* catch them all" (emphasis in original). State courts dismissed 47% of death sentences because of errors, and a later federal review dismissed 40% of the remaining cases.
- The most common errors found in the cases were (1) egregiously incompetent defense attorneys who missed evidence of the defendant's innocence or evidence that he or she did not deserve a death sentence and (2) suppression of evidence by police and prosecutors.
- Eighty-two percent of those whose death sentences were overturned by state courts were found to be deserving of less than a death sentence, and 7% were found to be innocent of the crimes for which they were convicted.
- Serious errors have been made in every year since the death penalty was reinstated, and more than half of all cases were found to be seriously flawed in 20 of the 23 study years.
- Serious errors are made in virtually every state that still executes people, and over 90% of these states make errors more than half of the time.
- "In *most* cases, death row inmates wait for years for the lengthy review procedures needed to uncover all this error. Then, their death sentences are *reversed*" (emphasis in original).
- "This much error, and the time needed to cure it, impose terrible costs on taxpayers, victims' families, the judicial system, and the wrongly condemned. And it renders unattainable the finality, retribution and deterrence that are the reasons usually given for having a death penalty."
- The death penalty ranges from 2.5 to 5 times as expensive as life imprisonment without parole. When you add the costs of posttrial reviews, executions become about 24 times as expensive as life imprisonment without parole. The death penalty is so much more expensive than life imprisonment because of the high rates of error that occur at each stage and the persistence of high error rates over time and across the nation, which mandate multiple expensive judicial inspections.
- The death penalty is rarely applied—of the 5,760 state death sentences handed down between 1973 and 1995, only 313 (5.4%) led to an execution during this time. Additionally, since 1984 when post-*Furman* executions began in earnest, we have executed only about 1.3% of our nation's death row inmates each year. This makes "the retributive and deterrent credibility of the death penalty" very low.
- In fact, homicide rates were slightly higher in death sentencing states than in non-death-sentencing states during the study years.

From their findings, the authors conclude that the administration of capital punishment in America is nothing less than irrational. On the basis of their research, capital punishment is also a farce. They note: "Death penalty states sentenced 22 times more defendants per 1,000 homicides than they executed.

And they sentenced 26 times more defendants per 100,000 population than they executed" (p. 45). I would characterize these types of findings as bizarre. Consider this: "there is *no* relationship between death-sentencing and execution rates" (p. 92; emphasis in original). It is as if death sentences really have nothing to do with justice, but more to do with politics.

In fact, the study found a not-so-surprising relationship between politics and the death penalty—that political pressure plays a role in capital punishment. The authors explain:

> In general, the more electoral pressure a state's judges are under, the *higher* the state's death-sentencing rate, but the *lower* the rate at which it carries out its death sentences. [This] suggests that political pressure tends to *impel* judges—or to create an environment in which prosecutors and jurors are impelled—to *impose* death sentences, but then tends to *interfere* with the state's capacity to carry out the death sentences that are imposed . . . a desire to curry favor with voters may lead elected prosecutors and judges to cut corners in an effort to secure that premium—simultaneously causing death-sentencing rates, *and error rates,* to increase. (p. 103; emphasis in original)

On the basis of this research, as well as that reported throughout Chapter Eleven, I agree. I will conclude by saying that the continued administration of the death penalty in the United States is proof that our system of criminal justice fails to achieve justice.

Discussion Questions

- What are the main means of executions in the United States?
- Why do you think more men are executed than women?
- Why do you think so many of our allies have abolished the death penalty?
- Why do you think that executions declined in the United States between the 1930s and the 1970s?
- What are the main factors that lead to legal errors in death penalty cases?
- Why didn't the Supreme Court abolish the death penalty with the case of *McClesky v. Kemp*?
- Why do so few murders lead to executions in the United States?
- Why do the vast majority of executions take place in the southern states?
- Is there any evidence that suggests that public executions would deter murderers?
- Discuss why most Americans say they support the death penalty.
- Identify and discuss the main justifications for capital punishment.
- Is there support for the death penalty in the Bible? Why or why not?
- Does the death penalty deter murders? Why or why not?
- In your opinion, do the errors in American capital punishment warrant a halt in executions? Explain.

CHAPTER TWELVE

SUMMARY, CONCLUSIONS, AND RECOMMENDATIONS FOR THE FUTURE

KEY CONCEPTS

- **Summary: The criminal justice system fails to do justice and reduce crime**
- **Where to go from here: Alternatives to current criminal justice practice**
- **Likelihood of success**
- **Issue in Depth: Toward Social Justice**

INTRODUCTION

This final chapter summarizes the main arguments made throughout the book. I illustrate precisely how the U.S. criminal justice system fails to achieve its goals of doing justice and reducing crime. I then provide recommendations to overcome the factors that produce injustice in American criminal justice. My hope is that the reality of criminal justice in America can mover closer to the ideals of criminal justice in America, if these recommendations are adopted and implemented. I end the chapter with a discussion of how likely it is that the recommendations will be adopted.

SUMMARY: THE CRIMINAL JUSTICE SYSTEM FAILS TO DO JUSTICE AND REDUCE CRIME

In Chapter One, I argued that the U.S. criminal justice system is ideally aimed at doing justice and reducing crime. I also suggested some alternative goals of the system, including controlling certain segments of the population in order to serve limited interests. I illustrated clearly that politicians in the United States have allocated resources and employees disproportionately to law enforcement and corrections, at the expense of American courts. I argued in this chapter that the United States has shifted toward a crime control model of justice since the 1970s at the expense of due process rights of citizens. Ironically, this shift has not made Americans safer from the harms that most threaten them.

Injustice in the criminal justice system most greatly affects poor people and people of color. In recent years, the groups most likely to suffer at the hands of the criminal justice system are poor women of color. Figure 12.1 summarizes criminal justice bias in the United States. The diagram is organized around the areas discussed in the book: the law; the media; the police; courts; and corrections.

All criminal justice activity stems from the law, so bias in the criminal justice process begins with the law. As I showed in Chapter Two, the law in the United States does not represent all Americans. Specifically, legislators at the federal and state levels are not representative of Americans in demographic terms, voters are not representative of Americans in demographic terms, and most people do not vote. Additionally, I illustrated how monied interests assert their influence on lawmakers through lobbying and donations to elections and political parties. These facts lead to the possibility that the criminal law does not label the most dangerous acts as the most serious crimes.

Chapter Three illustrated that crimes do not exist until they are invented by human beings who write down the law. Perhaps because U.S. lawmakers and others are not demographically representative, American criminal law does not define as crimes those acts that are most threatening to the safety and well-being of Americans—acts of white-collar deviance. Instead, it labels as the most serious crimes those acts that are committed primarily by the poor and by people of color. Our criminal justice focus is squarely focused on those acts, while we virtually ignore other acts that are more dangerous and costly. This is not consistent either with doing justice or with reducing crime.

As I showed in Chapter Four, the media promote stereotypes about crime and criminal justice by focusing on the most violent, bizarre, and random types of crime in the United States. The media, which are largely for-profit institutions owned by large corporations, serve the interests of wealthy and powerful members of society by providing inaccurate reports about crime and crimi-

FIGURE 12.1
Justice Bias

LAW	MEDIA	POLICE	COURTS	CORRECTIONS
Legislators not representative	Inaccurate reporting	Discretion	Charging	Incarceration
Voters not representative	Focus on violent, bizarre	Profiling	Bail and preventive detention	Death penalty
Money drives politics through lobbying, soft money	No context provided	Location by place	Plea bargaining	
		Stops and arrests	Voir dire	
		Use of force	Private attorneys	
			Expert witnesses	
			Sentencing	

nal justice that lack critical context. The media also give relatively little attention to acts of white-collar deviance, even though these acts are much more damaging to society as a whole than common street crimes.

Given these facts, I illustrated in Chapter Five that the criminal justice system as a whole is focused almost exclusively on crimes perceived to be the acts of the poor and people of color. Thus, the criminal justice system is characterized by discrimination against these groups. Although this systemwide discrimination is not intentional, the system is nevertheless biased against poor people, people of color, and in some cases women. Most of this bias is "innocent"; that is, it comes from the criminal law rather than from the intentional actions of "bad apples" in the system. But because the biases are functional for powerful segments of society, efforts aimed at overcoming them are typically resisted.

Drug crimes, a major focus of criminal justice focus in the past few decades, have led to major increases in the incarcerated populations in the United States. In Chapter Six, I demonstrated that our criminal justice system punishes people for being involved in the illicit drug trade—mostly for simple possession—even though the illegal drugs involved are relatively less harmful than such legal drugs as alcohol and tobacco. On the basis of this evidence, the nation's drug war cannot be considered a valid means of either doing justice or reducing crime.

The police, as gatekeepers of the criminal justice system and soldiers on the front lines of the American wars on crime and drugs, are biased against poor people and people of color. This is not because of bad police officers (although they clearly exist) but because of what I termed "innocent bias" in Chapter Seven. This innocent bias—a function of enforcing bad law—comes in many forms. Because police are able to use discretion—to act according to their own personal judgments—stereotypes about groups of people are allowed to seep into policing. Police profiling based on fallacious stereotypes of dangerous groups, the concentration of police in the United States' inner cities, and the focus on street crimes all explain why poor people and people of color are disproportionately likely to be stopped, questioned, and arrested by law enforcement officers. They are also more likely to be victims of excessive force by the police. The criminal law and the organization of policing in the United States combine to create unjust outcomes.

Courts are also biased against the poor and against people of color. The bias occurs in all three phases of the court process, including the pretrial, trial, and posttrial phases. Most of the criminal justice bias occurs in the pretrail phase behind closed doors, where decisions about bail and charging are made. The bail process, by definition, is biased against people without money. Poor people and people of color are less likely to be offered bail and thus are more likely to be detained in jail awaiting their trial dates. As I illustrated in Chapter Eight, more than 90% of court cases are disposed of through plea bargaining, so most people charged with crimes do not have a reasonable expectation of a criminal trial. When cases go to trial, poor people and people of color are less likely to receive justice as an outcome because of biases in the voir dire process, such as the use of peremptory challenges to exclude minorities and the use of jury consultants by those with money. Poor people also are less able to afford private attorneys and hire expert witnesses; thus, they receive less competent defenses when charged with crimes.

Sentencing, the subject of Chapter Nine, is biased in some places against poor people, people of color, and women, making it a form of contextual discrimination. Overall, minorities in the United States receive no more severe sanctions than Caucasians for most crimes, but they are disproportionately sentenced to imprisonment for drug felonies. African Americans also are sentenced to longer jail terms than Caucasians. I tied these findings to false conceptions of dangerousness created in the criminal law and media coverage of crime and criminal justice. Examples of biased sentencing practices include mandatory sentences such as the three-strikes laws that are almost universally condemned by criminologists and criminal justice experts. Clearly, American punishment is driven mostly by the desire for retribution (getting even with offenders), incapacitation (warehousing offenders), and deterrence (creating fear in people to prevent future crime). Yet, a majority of Americans report that they support rehabilitation (eliminating the factors that produce crime), which is now largely absent in American criminal justice. Our criminal justice system practices punishments that have been shown by research to be ineffective on the very offenders we try to catch—more evidence that the system fails to meet its ideal goals.

Corrections, the last phase of the criminal justice process, was addressed in Chapter Ten (imprisonment) and Chapter Eleven (the death penalty). The U.S. incarceration rate has exploded since the early 1970s, at a tremendous cost to American taxpayers and to the residents of our inner cities. The incarceration binge did not result from increased crime rates and has not resulted in large declines in crime. Surprisingly, most offenders in our nation's prisons are *not* repeat violent offenders as one might expect given tough talk by politicians and media coverage of crime and criminal justice. In fact, a large share of our nation's prisoners are nonviolent property and drug offenders who are suffering the tremendous pains of imprisonment discussed in Chapter Ten. In essence, we seem intent on making prisoners suffer enormous hardships in hopes that they will be somehow be turned into law-abiding citizens. Yet, most offenders enter prison uneducated, unskilled, and underemployed (and thus poor) and leave prison the same way, yet also with the stigma of being ex-convicts. Offenders return to the same criminogenic environments that produced them, and police and parole officers harass parolees, increasing the likelihood that they will end up back in prison. Indeed, prison is a massive failure; yet, politicians have sworn an allegiance to it. We now spend more money building prisons than on higher education.

In Chapter Eleven, I discussed the use of capital punishment, the rarest of all criminal sanctions. In essence, the death penalty is a punishment that is applied so arbitrarily that it is freakish and clearly unjust. I illustrated how and why the death penalty is disproportionately used against the nation's poor and people of color and why we are *likely* to execute even the innocent, with the apparent acceptance of Americans. Given the irrefutable evidence that the death penalty is biased against particular groups in the United States and that executions do not deter crime, its practice is the clearest proof that the criminal justice system does not meet its ideal goals of doing justice and reducing crime.

WHERE TO GO FROM HERE: ALTERNATIVES TO CURRENT CRIMINAL JUSTICE PRACTICE

This book has shown you that the U.S. criminal justice system fails to achieve its goals of doing justice and reducing crime. Of course, it is easy to criticize people, institutions, and policies without attempting to suggest alternatives. This seems to be the American way: we know how to criticize but are less well equipped to offer alternatives for our own failed policies.

To counter this, in this chapter I provide 50 recommendations for creating positive change within the U.S. criminal justice system. Each recommendation suggests an alternative to the current direction of criminal justice policy in the United States. Because the recommendations stem directly from the literature reviewed in this book, I arrange them in a manner consistent with the overall organization of the book. Thus, I offer recommendations in the following areas: general recommendations about government and informing citizens; recommendations about law and crime; recommendations about the media; recommendations about police; recommendations about the courts and sentencing; and recommendations about corrections.

I firmly believe that we can change the direction of American criminal justice to make it more just and more effective at reducing crime. These recommendations are a step in that direction (for other ideas, see Currie's *Crime and Punishment in America*, 1998).

Before I move to the specific recommendations, I offer a few words about predicting the future. There are many texts that essentially guess at the future of American criminal justice. One, *Visions for Change: Crime and Justice in the Twenty-First Century*, by Muraskin and Roberts (1999), is particularly helpful because of its breadth of scope. In the final chapter, Muraskin (1999: 435) asks: "Can we predict the future with any precision?" She answers: "Probably not." She notes, however—consistent with the great majority of criminologists and criminal justice scholars—that crime problems will be solved "not by the building of bigger and better cells, but through education, alternative programs, and [by] stopping problems before they begin. . . . Violence is a symptom of other problems and we must deal with those problems" (p. 436).

In the next section, I offer suggestions for preventing crime and promoting justice in the United States. I believe our only hope lies in the careful creation of criminal justice policies that strive to move away from the reactive, carelessly constructed criminal justice policies of the late twentieth century. As Muraskin explains: "Policies are needed that attack the root of the problem. 'Band-aid' programs do not work. Without strong policies, the next millennium will see crime as a growing and larger problem than in prior centuries" (1999: 436).

General Recommendations about Government and Informing Citizens

1. Our government should write clear statements reflecting the goals of American criminal justice.

Given the importance of justice as a process, due process values should be emphasized over crime control values. At every step of the criminal justice process, we must ensure that every individual's Constitutional rights are protected and that innocent people are not wrongfully subjected to the criminal justice system. In other words, we must act in ways consistent with the ideal of "innocent until proven guilty."

2. Our government should develop clearly stated policies of government aimed at *not discriminating* on the basis of race, social class, and gender.

If justice is to be blind, and thus fair, we must first state clearly that we will not, under any circumstances, tolerate discrimination based on factors such as race, class, and gender. These values should be codified and exhibited by government for all to see.

3. The government should also make a commitment to evaluate the performance of the criminal justice system at regular periods of time, in order to assess how well we are achieving our stated goals.

How can we know how well we are doing unless we assess our performance carefully? Evaluation can be relatively inexpensive. Given the importance of the goal of providing justice, an evaluation of the criminal justice system's performance on a regular basis is warranted. Criminologists and criminal justice experts should be involved in this regular evaluation.

4. To be more effective at reducing crime, our government must encourage a fundamental shift away from punitiveness toward prevention, treatment, and restoration.

Conditions in communities and society that produce criminality must be eliminated, sick people who commit crimes must be treated, and both victims of crime and criminal offenders must work together toward restoration of each to noncriminal and nonvictim status. For this to happen, we must commit ourselves to forgiveness rather than vengeance. Forgiveness is the only mechanism proven to produce peace for victims of crime.

5. Our government must shift its focus from criminal justice system responses to violence toward medical, public-health models to treat violence as an epidemic in the United States.

As I explained in this book, violence is the main problem in the United States when it comes to crime. Crime rates are not exceedingly high relative to other similar countries. Yet, we suffer from alarmingly high rates of violent victimization, especially murder. We must shift our focus away from criminal justice approaches toward public-health approaches to reducing violence by treating violence as the epidemic that it is.

6. Our government should also stop "shooting itself in the foot" by hurting its own citizens. For example, we need to reinvest in American labor—to stop engaging in practices such as downsizing to increase profits.

Government should regulate businesses by requiring victim impact statements when decisions affecting a company's workers will be made. Politicians who talk about the importance of families should not tolerate the practice of maximizing profits by moving jobs overseas and south of the border at the expense of American workers and families. Sudden unemployment has been related to many adverse consequences, including depression, family instability, and domestic violence. When corporations plan to make decisions that will affect American workers and their families, criminal justice implications should be considered.

7. Other legitimate opportunities must be developed for citizens who find themselves living in conditions of poverty.

On the basis of a review of evidence, street crimes are not the most harmful types of crime committed. Yet, street crime is tremendously harmful and disproportionately affects poor people. Politicians claim that poor people choose to commit criminal acts in order to maximize pleasure, gain rewards, earn money, and so forth. Our response, based on this premise, has been to increase the punishments and other pains associated with choosing crime. An alternative to this futile approach would be to increase the benefits associated with choosing noncriminal acts. That is, the American Dream must be made available to all Americans.

8. Overall, Americans must insist that politics be taken out of crime and criminal justice issues.

Politicians have created cynicism in Americans by using partial facts and distorted truths about crime that have made developing sensible policy impossible. Recall the Willie Horton example from Chapter One. Horton had been out on furlough eight times in Massachusetts without committing any apparent criminal acts. On his ninth release, he committed a rape and aggravated assault. The 1988 presidential candidate, George Bush, used the image of Horton as evidence that his opponent, Michael Dukakis (who was then governor of Massachusetts), was soft on crime. This was, at the least, dishonest of the Bush campaign; at worst, it was deceitful and racist. Politicians promote criminal justice policies that they should know do not and cannot work, and Americans should call them on it.

9. A rational system of planned change should be used to reduce crime in the United States.

Currently, criminal justice policy seems to be made based on subjective decisions, characterized by unreliability, low validity, bias, and variability among decision makers (Gottfredson, 1999: 443). According to Walker (1998: xxi), most American crime control policies simply do not work: "they are nonsense." Walker critically assesses U.S. criminal justice policy, including both conservative "get tough" approaches and liberal efforts at "rehabilitation," and concludes that almost none of them is effective. Neither conservative nor liberal approaches are carefully planned. The conservative approach has traditionally involved more police, more prisons, and swifter, harsher punishment, whereas the liberal approach has focused more on rehabilitation and treatment. As noted in Chapter One, both conservatives and liberals now support more police, more prisons, and the death penalty as effective means of fighting crime.

The following box highlights an alternative approach to reducing crime. Planned change (see Walsh and Harris, 1999) is an alternative to quick-fix, feel-good, short-term approaches to reducing crime in the United States.

Planned change

Planned change is an alternative way to reduce crime. Crime, despite its many functions and the interests it serves, has always been viewed as a problem, and problems require solutions. To be effective, solutions require time, thought, and planning. Criminal justice policy driven by short-term thinking and unplanned change results in inefficiency, wasted resources, and failure.

Planned change is spearheaded by change agents who have specifically thought about a problem and investigated it thoroughly. Unplanned change, by contrast, involves little explicit or proactive planning and "comes about as a reaction to a crisis, a dramatic incident publicized by the media, a political opportunity, a lawsuit against criminal justice officials or an untested set of assumptions about a specific problem" (p. 3).

In today's heated political environment, where U.S. crime problems are typically created and/or used at election time as political issues, criminal justice policy is often shortsighted and poorly planned (and at times reactive and altogether unplanned). Not surprisingly, current criminal justice policy fails to produce significant declines in crime-related problems. Such failure stems from poorly planned criminal justice policy.

To overcome our current path of injustice and ineffectiveness, we must dedicate ourselves to planned change and must insist that our policymakers use strategies of planned change to reduce crime. Planned change can be achieved through policies, programs, and projects.

Policies are a "set of rules or guidelines for how to make a decision" (p. 5); *programs* are a "set of services aimed at achieving specific goals and objectives within specified individuals, groups, organizations or communities"; and *projects* are essentially time-limited programs (p. 6). Policies are more general than programs and projects and often motivate the development of specific programs and projects aimed at reducing some problem.

To solve problems related to crime, a step-by-step approach to problem analysis and criminal justice planning must be utilized. This includes analyzing the problem, setting goals and objectives, designing programs and policies, developing action plans, developing monitoring plans, designing evaluation plans, initiating the program or policy, and then fully evaluating the program or policy so that it can be altered and continued.

The first step in policy or program design is analyzing the problem, including the need for change, the history of the problem, and potential causes of the problem. A systems approach to addressing casual factors based on the belief that crime problems stem from factors at various levels of analysis—individual, group, organizational, community, and social-structural—will likely lead to the most fruitful policy changes. Policy and program designers or "change agents" should look for all causes of a problem and carefully document such causes with scientific evidence. Previous interventions that have been used to change the problem should be examined, and opponents and supporters of change should be identified. Once it is determined what works, what is promising, and what does not work, and once vital supporters are brought on board and opponents are appeased or defeated, effective crime reduction policies can be successful.

The next stage in policy and program development is setting goals and objectives. *Goals* lay out the general aims of the policy or program, and *objectives* more specifically restate the goals in measurable form. Clear goals and objectives are vital to success, for one cannot know if a policy has succeeded or failed unless one clearly specifies what one wants to achieve and sets forth a means of measuring the degree of effectiveness.

Effective action plans, the "blueprint" of policies or programs, must specify "all the necessary materials, supplies and tools required" to achieve successful planned change (p. 135). Action planning involves specifying the entire sequence of activities and completion dates required to carry out the program or policy design.

Monitoring must assess how well a planned policy or program is being implemented (i.e., how well the ideal matches the reality). Evaluation of the policy or program—assessing how well the policy or program achieved its goals and objectives—is also important. Data must be collected to monitor the implementation of the policy or program, to evaluate its degree of success, and to decide how to manage potential problems and confounding factors. How much longer can we afford to continue with our massive and failing American criminal justice experiments?

Nothing less than a dramatic transformation in the formulation of criminal justice policy, from unplanned change to planned change, is necessary if criminal justice in the United States is to turn its direction from one of disastrous failure to one of success.

SOURCE: Adapted from W. Walsh and P. Harris, *Criminal Justice Policy and Planning* (Cincinnati, OH: Anderson, 1999).

10. **The nation's crime experts must strive to educate citizens about injustice in American criminal justice and about their true risks of victimization.**

It is highly unlikely that many Americans are aware of how the criminal law is biased against particular groups of people in the United States. Given our devotion to justice, it is likely that when Americans become aware of injustice, they will revolt against it and demand change, as they did during the civil rights movement. Victims of other forms of culpable harmful acts, such as victims of white-collar deviance, "are often much more confused than are victims of conventional crime about where to turn for help, and a much larger group of such victims are not even conscious about having been victimized" (Friedrichs, 1996: 277). If we truly want to stop victimization, we must make sure people know they are being victimized, and then increase and clarify their options for law enforcement assistance.

Recommendations about Reforming the Law and Crime

11. **As the criminal law currently is not made by people who are representative of the population, it should not be a surprise that the criminal law does not serve the interests of most Americans. Thus, we need to make the law more representative by increasing the representativeness of lawmakers.**

This would entail increasing informed voting behavior by educating citizens about crime and criminal justice, as well as minimizing and equalizing the funding of elections, candidates, and parties by special interests and lobbying groups.

12. **We must shift our focus from criminalization to harm reduction.**

Americans and their leaders apparently think that we can stop people from engaging in harmful behaviors by criminalizing them. In fact, the most effective controls may very well be informal in nature—that is, instilled by families, peers, churches, and schools rather than by police, courts, and corrections. Instead of criminalizing behaviors to reduce harms, we ought to encourage policies of harm reduction, aimed at preventing harms associated with behaviors such as drug use and abuse. Rather than punishing drug users and sellers, for example, treatment options ought to be available for addicts, and alternative means of employment ought to be made available for sellers.

13. **The government must define crimes based on degree of harm caused.**

This entails careful study (much of which has already been done and is discussed in this book), about which behaviors are really most likely to kill, injure, and result in property loss for Americans. Those behaviors that are most harmful ought to be called the most "serious" and should be the focus of law enforcement, courts, and corrections.

14. **"Victimless" crimes such as drug use and possession ought to be decriminalized.**

American police spend a disproportionate amount of time and resources on some "victimless" street crimes, called this not because they are truly harmless but because they are engaged in by consenting adults so that no one involved feels victimized. The best example is the war on drugs. As explained in this book, law enforcement focus on drug crimes and mandatory sentencing laws that call for longer minimum sentences for drug offenders explain the United States' unprecedented overreliance on imprisonment. Many of those we are incarcerating are first-time, low-level drug dealers or people who simply were found in possession of marijuana. Meanwhile, victims of other forms of harms are virtually ignored. Drug use can be a normal behavior that occurs in various recreational contexts, and government can decriminalize drug use while simultaneously discouraging people from using drugs. Criminalizing drug use will not deter our children from experimenting. In fact, the illegal status of drugs is precisely what leads to much drug use, as well as a lot of crime and violence in the United States.

15. Create and administer a national source of data on white-collar deviance.

To discover more accurately how much damage is caused by these types of acts, our government must create a measure to gather valid data on acts of white-collar deviance, much as it does on street crime. If we are to shift our focus toward the acts that cause the most harm in society, we must first commit ourselves to collecting data on the acts.

Recommendations about the Media

16. Educate the media about crime and criminal justice through planned workshops.

The nation's crime experts can no longer afford to sit on the sidelines, watching the media continue to get it wrong. We seem to know how and why the media are misinforming citizens about the true nature of crime and criminal justice in the United States. It is our responsibility to ensure that this misinformation stops, especially given that most Americans get their crime information from media outlets.

17. Insist that the media get it right by reducing consumer demand for sleazy news.

We must encourage citizens to pursue alternative forms of education and news rather than crime shows and sensational news. Research clearly shows that crime entertainment and news promote a "siege mentality" among some viewers, who become more likely to stay inside and to fear the poor and people of color rather than wanting to help them achieve legitimate success. The news media should develop and broadcast clear statements reflecting their intention to cease broadcasting sleazy, sensationalized crime stories.

18. Develop a network of contacts between criminal justice scholars and the media.

Every criminologist and criminal justice expert owes it to the nation to insert himself or herself into the media when stories about crime and criminal justice are discussed. We cannot afford to allow politicians and the police to be the primary sources of information about crime and criminal justice in the United States, given their clear biases in favor of the status quo.

Recommendations about the Police

19. Reorganize police resources (including the numbers of law enforcement officers allocated to each level of government, the types of behaviors they focus on, and the ways in which they use their time) so that victims of all culpable harmful acts, whether legal or illegal, will be served by law enforcement.

Policing in the United States is organized in a manner that mandates that officers focus almost exclusively on street crime victimization. Simultaneously, U.S. police officers spend most of their time doing work not related to crime or victimization. This must change so that police can serve all victims of culpable harms.

To correct this, we must do the following:

20. Reallocate policing resources away from local government to states and, to a lesser degree, to the federal government.

21. Increase training of local, state, and federal police on matters related to white-collar deviance.

22. Reallocate policing resources in order to better assist victims of all culpable, harmful acts.

We must reeducate police officers about forms of victimization other than street crimes because state and federal officers are currently best equipped, given their special training, to provide assistance to victims of other forms of harm. To ensure that victims of such acts receive sufficient attention, police agencies at the state and federal levels must be granted more resources, including both employees and funding, relative to local police. Local police must be educated about forms of culpable harm other than street crime, particularly to the degree that they will likely be called on to assist with victims of such harms. City and county law enforcement assistance would not be possible unless allocation of local police personnel by location and time was systematically changed from urban areas, where street crime is perceived to occur, to areas where other forms of culpable harms occur. That is, for local police to provide their traditional services to a more diverse set of victims, the times and places they patrol would also change. Since police "tend to respond most emphatically to . . . events that they perceive as conforming to legal definitions of serious crimes" (Sacco and Kennedy, 1996: 65), they would be unlikely to sympathize with victims of culpable behaviors other than street crimes, unless such acts were recognized as serious crimes by society and treated as such by the criminal justice system.

Police should devote free time to forms of victimization other than street crimes committed by individuals against individuals. We might also decide as a society to let police exclusively fight victimization, and leave service functions to other agencies. Perhaps we could also redesign our social service agencies to operate on a 24-hour basis, so that police could devote themselves exclusively to fighting victimization and/or crime through their law enforcement function. Given the amount of time police at all levels of government spend on service functions, it is apparent that this time is not being allocated to victim assistance, although it is difficult to ascertain how much police service time is spent on precisely this function. Additionally, many criminal victimizations are never discovered, and virtually all noncriminal victimizations are ignored. From these facts, we can confidently conclude that police are not very effectively serving victims of culpable harms.

The following box illustrates how the criminal justice system generally deals with victims of white-collar deviance. Typically, such victims receive very little justice.

Victims of white-collar deviance and the criminal justice system

Many victims, including those who are physically maimed or injured at work, receive little attention from law enforcement agencies. As noted by Friedrichs (1996: 271), "the proportion of apparent white collar crimes that are officially investigated and lead to enforcement actions is lower than is the case for conventional crime. In the simplest and most colloquial terms, what occurs in the street is more visible and more easily investigated than what occurs 'in the suite,' behind closed doors." Just because it is hidden, however, does this mean its victims are not worthy of both compensation for their suffering and justice for the harms committed against them?

Such victims are typically left to seek assistance from state and federal law enforcement agencies, or from regulatory agencies, because of the "complex, often interjurisdictional character" of the harmful acts that produce the victimizations (Friedrichs, 1996: 272). Law enforcement agencies involved include "over two dozen separate federal agencies" including "the Federal Bureau of Investigation (FBI), the Inspector Generals, the U.S. Postal Inspection Service, the U.S. Secret Service, the U.S. Customs Service, and the Internal Revenue Service Criminal Investigative Division" (Friedrichs, 1996: 273). Recall how few officers work for these agencies relative to city and county police forces in the United States.

Regulatory agencies include the Occupational Safety and Health Administration (OSHA) for negligent workplace injuries and deaths, the Food and Drug Administration (FDA) for adulterated food products, the Consumer Product Safety Commission (CPSC) for unsafe products, and the Environmental Protection Agency (EPA) for acts against the environment. According to Friedrichs (1996: 285), "regulatory agencies are greatly understaffed and underfunded. . . . Public pressure for agency action is small relative to that for conventional crime, and business interests have traditionally lobbied for various limitations on agency powers and budgets." For example, OSHA has only hundreds of inspectors, who must investigate millions of businesses. Although victims of culpable harms committed by entities such as groups of people or corporations can also turn to the civil law for redress, it is clear that their victimizations are not treated as seriously as street crimes. Lynch and Stretesky (1999: 24) add that "administrative agencies rarely use the criminal penalties that some of them can access to control corporate criminality. Many are staffed by people who were once top executives in the industries they police and oppose regulation of corporate activities" (also see Burkholz, 1994; Claybrook, 1984; Glantz et al., 1996). We can easily understand why most policing in the United States is focused exclusively on street crimes instead of other harmful acts committed intentionally, recklessly, negligently, or knowingly. Friedrichs (1996: 271) claims this is due to a lack of jurisdiction, expertise, and resources. To facilitate police involvement in victimizations caused by other culpable harmful acts, changes must be made in police jurisdiction, expertise, and resources.

23. **Increase educational qualifications for American police officers to a minimum of a bachelor's degree.**

The Police Executive Research Forum claims that education benefits the police and the community. Through education, police gain greater maturity and increase their knowledge base about criminal justice and American government, as well as an increased understanding and appreciation of people of different cultures (Carter and Sapp, 1993). These factors, along with high intelligence, flexibility, and honesty, have been shown to be related to better policing.

24. **Increase police officer pay to reduce police corruption.**

It is understandable that some good cops will "go bad" when they are paid very little and see huge amounts of money exchanged regularly in criminal enterprises. To reduce the likelihood that police will steal cash from offenders, we must pay our police officers more and create other mechanisms to show our appreciation for the valuable services they provide to Americans.

25. **Develop mandatory multicultural educational efforts within police academies.**

As evidence shows that police disproportionately hassle ethnic minorities and people of color, police should be exposed to more educational materials about other cultures to increase their understanding of, and appreciation for, people unlike themselves, especially given that most police are Caucasians.

26. **Outlaw the use of police profiling based on race and ethnicity.**

There is no valid justification for this practice. Even if profiling results in more arrests, more seizures of evidence related to criminal activity, and so on, the ends cannot be justified by the means. Recall that justice as a process is what the criminal justice system in America ideally values. Police profiling is an ugly practice that should never be tolerated. We should require police to gather statistics about interactions with citizens and then evaluate each jurisdiction for evidence of racial profiling. When racial profiling is found, departments must be punished accordingly.

27. **Develop police–community partnerships where they are needed most.**

Community policing, the buzzword in policing for the past three decades or so, has not been beneficial to the communities where it is needed most. Inner cities and high-crime areas have witnessed the highest lack of respect for police and the least police involvement in community policing. These are the areas where community policing strategies must be stepped up.

Recommendations about the Courts and about Sentencing

28. **Reallocate criminal justice resources so that they are more equitable, particularly to "courthouse regular" defense attorneys.**

This book has shown that most money spent on criminal justice is allocated to law enforcement and then to corrections. In essence, we spend more money trying to catch criminals and punish them than making sure that we have caught the right ones. Is it any wonder, given the presumption of guilt inherent in plea bargaining, that sometimes we end up punishing the wrong people for crimes they did not commit? If we truly believe in due process and "innocent until proven guilty," we must give defense attorneys the resources necessary to defend their clients adequately. Ideally, each side must be assured of the resources necessary to take cases to trial.

29. Increase representation by racial and ethnic minorities in courtroom workgroups.

As was shown, people of color are underrepresented as members of the courtroom workgroup. Here, the government could assist by providing targeted scholarships to people of color to attend law school, with the stipulation that they will serve a minimum number of years working for the government as officers of the court.

30. Reassign sentencing discretion to judges, instead of prosecutors.

The current move to allow prosecutors to decide sentences through the charging process has resulted in an imbalance in the court. Sentencing discretion must reside in the hands of judges, not prosecutors. Judges tell researchers that they do not support mandatory sentences such as three-strikes laws because of their inability to consider mitigating factors when sentencing some of the nation's truly disadvantaged. Prosecutors, as elected officials, are more likely to be concerned about their image as "tough on crime" and to maintain high conviction rates at virtually any cost. Their discretion must be reduced if we want to ensure that justice is done.

31. Prohibit preventive detention based on the criterion of "to protect the community," and permit it only when a significant flight risk exists.

Stated plainly, there is no justification for locking up people who have yet to be convicted of criminal offenses. Only under rare circumstances, as when officers witness a person in the act of committing violence or when a person is found to be mentally unstable because of a severe brain disorder, can we justify locking up a person who is supposedly "innocent until proven guilty." Yet, approximately half of the people now in our nation's jails have *not* been convicted of any crimes. These people are being punished without conviction.

32. Assess bail outcomes regularly to ensure that bail is not being used to discriminate against any group of persons.

Given the evidence showing biases in bail against the poor and people of color, something must be done to correct bail biases. At regular intervals, bail outcomes should be evaluated to ensure that unreasonably high bail is not being used disproportionately against any group. If bail is found to be differentially applied, mandatory bail amounts should be established by independent assessors of the courts.

33. Create a system of structured bail based on how much the accused can afford to pay.

If bail is simply to be used to ensure the presence of the defendant at trial, and not as punishment, unreasonably high bails for the poor cannot be tolerated. Many poor citizens are forced to sit in jail even for accusations of relatively minor criminality because they cannot afford bail.

34. Prohibit plea bargaining.

The plea bargaining process does not address the guilt or innocence of the accused. Rather, the issue addressed by plea bargaining is what to do about the defendant, who is assumed to be guilty by everyone involved in the criminal justice process. Neither justice as an outcome nor justice as a process is achieved through this process. Decriminalization initiatives would aid in the effort to ensure that court caseloads do not grow to the point where it would be impossible to hold a trial for each criminal case.

35. Insist that indigent clients be given quality counsel by creating incentives to represent poor clients zealously.

Part of this incentive should be financial. Courthouse regulars who make their living defending the poor ought to be able to afford to investigate the charges against their clients thoroughly and to mount an adequate defense.

36. Jurors ought to be selected from sources other than voter lists, for a majority of people in the United States do not vote.

Voters tend to be unrepresentative of the nation's population, so biases will result against those who do not vote. Alternative jury lists must be created from other sources.

37. Prohibit the use of peremptory challenges in jury selection.

There is no valid reason to allow any challenge to a juror without adequate cause being stated to (and supported by) a judge. Because peremptory challenges are used to disqualify people of color and people who "look suspicious," the jury process has been corrupted by the use of these challenges.

38. Encourage citizens to participate in jury duty by providing adequate financial compensation.

Jurors provide a valuable service to the country. They are supposed to be the backbone of the criminal justice system, ensuring that arbitrary and overzealous governments do not unnecessarily interfere in the lives of American citizens. Thus, they should be paid a reasonable amount to compensate for their lost wages and service to the government and people of the United States. Jury duty should not be something Americans dread.

39. Prohibit the use of jury consultants during voir dire.

The use of jury consultants clearly biases the trial phase in favor of those clients who can hire individuals to hand-pick a jury sympathetic to their case. The poor and, often, people of color do not enjoy this privilege.

40. Allow jurors to ask questions and take notes during the trial phase.

Currently, jurors must listen to long trials and complex testimony and other forms of evidence without being able to write anything down or ask questions for clarification. This likely gives more credence to opening and closing arguments than to the actual evidence presented during trial.

41. Make jury instructions understandable.

Research clearly shows that jury instructions cannot be understood by many Americans. They should be written with the lay person in mind, and examples of major terms should be provided to help the jury make just decisions.

42. Require monitoring of jury deliberations.

To be sure that juries are considering only the evidence allowed by judges when making their decisions, jury deliberations should be subjected to judicial review in order to identify and correct unjust jury decisions. This does not mean that jury verdicts should be overturned upon review; it means that when juries use invalid criteria in their decisions, verdicts should be reconsidered by a panel of judges and perhaps adjusted on the basis of legal precedent.

43. Acknowledge that deterrence is a myth and not a likely outcome of criminal sentencing.

Very few criminal sanctions provide a deterrent effect, especially for those most likely to commit street crimes. Those with little legitimate opportunity for success—a "stake in conformity"—are far less likely to be scared into crime-free lifestyles when other means of earning income are so restricted and unavailable to them.

44. Eliminate three-strikes laws unless it is assured that they will be used *only* against repeat violent felons.

We may very well need to lock some criminals away from society for our own protection, but many relatively minor offenders do not warrant such severe sentences. Mandatory sentences are not a cost-effective way to punish these offenders. These sanctions also contribute to the "get tough" approach that permeates much of U.S. society, a major impediment to effective change within the criminal justice system.

Recommendations about Corrections

45. Increase the use of intermediate sanctions as cost-effective alternatives to prison.

These sanctions are not necessarily any more effective than prison, but they are certainly less expensive. Many such sanctions are at least considered promising by criminologists and criminal justice experts, but they are not used widely enough to demonstrate how well they work. For relatively minor offenders likely to end up in prison, these sanctions seem to be a better investment.

46. Humanize prisons—minimize the pains of imprisonment.

Those criminals who simply must be kept away from society for our protection should not be subjected to unnecessary forms of punishment while incarcerated. Instead, they should be humanely incapacitated and treated as human beings, not as wild animals.

47. Insist on educational and vocational skill development in prison as a criterion for release.

Prisoners should be required to demonstrate that they will likely make it in the free world before they are released. This means correctional facilities must do more than simply warehouse offenders. Imprisoned offenders ought to be encouraged, indeed required, to work, study, make decisions for themselves, and be prepared to live in the free world. This may be unpopular with Americans who want to see the guilty suffer, but it likely will be more effective in preventing future crimes than brutal punishment.

48. Shift the role of probation and parole officers to social service functions rather than supervisory, law enforcement functions.

Probationers and parolees are currently sent to prison for violating rules not imposed on free people. This must stop. Those who are charged with supervising the progress of such offenders ought to be rewarded for successes and urged to help offenders make it in the free world by assisting their clients with necessary vocational, educational, and medical rehabilitation.

49. Provide more resources for probation and parole officers.

Currently, it is impossible for probation and parole officers to supervise their large caseloads. A society as wealthy as the United States ought to be able to afford to pay for enough officers to ensure successful integration of offenders into society during and after punishment.

50. Prohibit the death penalty.

The United States is the only Western democracy that still practices capital punishment, a shameful practice that is applied so rarely and arbitrarily that its use is clearly unjust. It is so evidently biased against the poor and minorities that one wonders how it can possibly be legal. There is no valid evidence showing that the death penalty deters crime, and there is some evidence that an opposite effect may occur. Capital punishment should be replaced by an ultimate sanction of life imprisonment without possibility of parole, plus restitution for victims (LWOP+R).

LIKELIHOOD OF SUCCESS

I do not pretend that these reforms will be rapidly accepted and implemented in the United States. In fact, considering past efforts by criminologists and criminal justice scholars to make the criminal justice system more just, it may be unwise to expect many of these reforms to be adopted in the immediate future. Yet, change is possible, and, on the basis of the evidence presented in this book, change is necessary. American criminal justice policy is misconceived and dangerous. We must invest in prevention rather than more prisons (Greenwood, 1998).

Most change is gradual, but gradualism can lull us all to sleep. As Americans, we must insist that the criminal justice system achieve justice as both an outcome and a process. The debate over the death penalty is now raging across the country, so it is possible that capital punishment will soon be stopped (probably through a temporary moratorium, but perhaps through a permanent abolition). Some discussion has occurred with regard to police profiling and abuse of power by criminal justice professionals, but less debate is occurring with regard to many of the other issues addressed in this book. I hope this book serves as a starting point for such debate.

Vila (1997) has pointed out how ironic it is that as knowledge about what works to reduce crime becomes clearer, we live in a time when effective or promising efforts are less likely to be implemented. His research, like that presented here, suggests that the media, politicians, and public impatience will be significant barriers to effective change. I advocate a team approach, based on consensus building between the media, politicians, and the public, to bring about effective change. And you, the reader of this book, have a tremendous opportunity to work from within the system to bring about positive change.

CONCLUSION

This chapter summarized the main findings of *Justice Blind?* and put forth recommendations for overcoming injustice in the United States. Our criminal justice system is supposed to do justice and reduce crime, yet, according to the findings reported in this book, we fail miserably at both. Since the 1970s, we have chosen a crime control model of justice at the expense of due process rights of citizens. Ironically, this shift has not made Americans safer from the harms that most threaten them. As I demonstrated in this book, injustice in the criminal justice system most greatly affects poor people and people of color, and it has begun to affect poor, minority women at a rate higher than that for men. The late Martin Luther King, Jr., would be saddened to know that injustice in America is more prevalent now than at any time during his life. For example, the percentage of African American males in our nation's prisons and jails has increased consistently since King's death. In effect, the war on crime is one of the nation's leading causes of segregation. The Issue in Depth that follows considers an alternative approach to justice, called social justice, that we should pursue if we are ever to realize the goals of Dr. King.

ISSUE IN DEPTH
Toward Social Justice

Is justice blind? The obvious answer is *no*. In this book, I have outlined numerous ways in which police, courts, and corrections fail to produce justice as a process. I hope this troubles you as much as it does me. After all, the United States is supposed to be devoted to the notion of blind justice, based on the U.S. Constitution, the American Declaration of Independence, and the figure of a blindfolded woman holding scales that adorns many of our courthouses and legislative buildings.

Supposedly, Americans will *not* support a criminal justice system that fails to punish those who deserve it. Ideally, they will *not* support a system that wrongfully convicts the innocent or is biased against any group. Why, then, do we tolerate the shortcomings of our criminal justice system?

In this last chapter, I outlined numerous recommendations to make our system of criminal justice more just. I hope that these recommendations are taken into account as criminal justice reforms are debated now and in the future. I want to conclude by drawing your attention to an important point about justice: that injustice in the justice system is a threat to what scholars call "social justice."

Social justice is perhaps the broadest conception of justice. It is bigger than the criminal justice system and exists when all forms of culpable harmful behaviors are abhorred, opposed, denounced, combated, and abolished (Barak and Henry, 1999: 152). It exists when all people are treated equally under the law. The criminal justice system is not necessarily aimed at achieving social justice, nor must it be. According to Arrigo (1999: 9, 253), the goals of the criminal justice system (to do justice and to reduce crime) may be completely separate and distinct from the goal of achieving social justice. In fact, the way the criminal justice system is organized may actually make it harder to achieve social justice (Barak and Henry, 1999).

I believe that one goal of the criminal justice system should be to achieve social justice—that is, "to advance principles of fairness, equity, reasonableness, and so forth, through police, court, and correctional practices" (Arrigo, 1999: 253). In other words, I believe that the criminal justice system not only must seek to achieve justice as an outcome and justice as a process, but also must never be allowed to interfere with the realization of social justice. The criminal justice system must, in its operations, remain anchored in "fairness, equity, proprietorship, due process, and so forth" (Arrigo, 1999: 9). Otherwise, social justice will not be possible.

Many of the impediments to realizing social justice exist outside the criminal justice system. Achieving social justice may not be possible simply by adopting the recommendations made in this chapter. It may require making changes to the basic structure of the United States' governments. One example is suggested by Reiman, who, in *The Rich Get Richer and the Poor Get Prison,* advocates a redistribution of wealth as a means of reducing the conditions of poverty that produce much of the street crime in the United States. He does not suggest handouts to the poor but, rather, writes that our government needs to give the poor more of a helping hand to achieve the so-called American Dream. Reiman does not specifically lay out how this would be achieved, leading many to wonder how this can be achieved without socializing our government.

I do not seriously believe that the fundamental structure of American government will soon, if ever, be changed in such a way. Instead of advocating such structural changes, I advocate an approach that seeks change from within. That is, you, who may one day work within the system of criminal justice in the United States (or, at least, most likely will live in this country as an American), will be called upon to put into practice the changes required to make the criminal justice system more just. It will be up to you to achieve social justice in America.

Crime victims must be involved in achieving the goal of social justice. Consider, for example, SAFES (Survivors Advocating for an Effective System). This organization, located in Oregon but relevant for every state in the United States, is based on this premise:

> Our vision is a safer and more humane Oregon. Oregon's justice system is based on vengeance. We believe it should be based on what works:
>
> - Prevention;
> - Rehabilitation;
> - Restitution.

SAFES was founded by Arwen Bird, who, in February 1993 (at age 18), was hit by a drunken driver in Oregon. Twenty-five-year-old Kevin Nielsen, the drunken driver, had spent the night drinking at a bar and was speeding when he collided with Bird's car from behind, sending the car into an embankment, where it rolled 360 degrees.

Arwen Bird's cervical spine was dislocated, and the accident left her paralyzed below the waist. Her sister, who was also in the car, suffered permanent brain damage. Nielsen, who was uninjured, was convicted of assault and of driving under the influence of alcohol (DUI). Part of his sentence was to pay

$115,000 to Arwen for her medical bills, but she has not received much of that money.

You might think that Arwen Bird, as a crime victim, would favor victims' rights measures aimed at getting tougher on criminals. Instead, Arwen, now 25, has formed an alternative group called Survivors Advocating for an Effective System (SAFES). According to Bird, many so-called victim's rights measures will not benefit crime victims.

Arwen was quoted in a July 4, 1999, article in *The Oregonian*: "I feel [the legislature has] lost sight of what victims' rights are. It reflects a vengeful attitude and an unproductive one." Arwen believes priority should be placed on strengthening victims' assistance programs and restitution collection. Her efforts have included testifying against some "victims' rights" measures being debated by her state legislature.

Arwen, who graduated with a biology degree in 1996 from Lewis & Clark College, now counsels teen mothers for a living. According to Arwen, she has little time to be angry: "It does not serve me well to be angry. That's energy I can use to heal and be productive and go fight the Legislature." Consider the irony of a crime victim having to fight the legislature to stop passing crime bills that were supposedly in her best interests.

According to the SAFES web site, "the legal system may consider us victims, but we're more active than that. We're survivors interested in shaping Oregon's approach toward reducing crime." They envision "a member-driven organization, speaking with a strong voice, advocating for services that will produce an effective criminal justice system."

Of course, Arwen does not speak for all or even most crime victims. But her message is one that cautions us about being too quick to jump on the bandwagon of efforts by politicians to erode Constitutional protections that all Americans, including those accused of committing crimes, enjoy.

A special message from Arwen appears on her organization's web page, located at http://crimevictims.net/SAFES/message.html. It states:

Dear Friends—

My life changed forever on a cold and clear February evening six years ago when my sister and I were hit by a drunk driver. I never could have imagined the philosophic and lifestyle changes that have resulted from my paralysis. I'm grateful for this new perspective, though I could do without the wheelchair.

As we've worked to heal from that fateful day, we've learned something important. Nobody out there truly speaks for survivors of crime who believe as we do. Plenty of "victims rights" groups are vying for attention, but we don't consider ourselves victims. We're survivors.

We've learned something else that's important. Most of the people spouting "get tough on crime" rhetoric claim to speak for us. They don't!

We disagree with the death penalty, mandatory minimum sentences, rampant prison construction and all the other planks of a criminal justice philosophy motivated by revenge and profit.

We favor prevention, rehabilitation and restitution. We favor positive action over emotional and political action.

We founded this organization because the voice of survivors has not yet been heard in Oregon. Some of us have been assaulted or robbed. Some of us have had family members murdered. The events that altered our lives may have differed, but we now share a common goal: to shift the debate in Oregon from what gets people elected (get tough rhetoric) to what works to reduce crime.

We will work wherever we can be most effective. With the media, in the legislature, at the ballot box. Please consider adding your voice to this movement toward a safer and more human Oregon by joining us. Together we can make a difference.

Sincerely, Arwen Bird, SAFES founder

In case you think that Arwen Bird is alone, or that her vision is unusual for a crime victim, consider the growing list of organizations who feel the same way. For example, visit these web sites:

- Murder Victims Families for Reconciliation (www.mvfr.org)
- Crime Victims for a Just Society (www.crimevictims.net)
- Center for Restorative Justice and Peacemaking (http://ssw.che.umn.edu/rjp/)

Compare these sites with the following "official" sites and examine the differences in content. While all of these organizations promote some aspect of justice—either justice as an outcome (justice for victims), justice as a process, and/or social justice—the ones that follow say little about changing the system to make it more just. What do you think the reasons are for this?

- The National Center for Victims of Crime (www.nvc.org)
- Office for Victims of Crime (www.ojp.usdoj.gov/ovc)

This book has demonstrated that the U.S. criminal justice system fails to achieve any of these conceptions of justice. And so we've come full circle, returning back to the first words of the book:

"Injustice anywhere is a threat to justice everywhere."
—Martin Luther King, "A Letter from the Birmingham Jail"

As I wrote in the preface, injustice anywhere in the United States is a threat to all persons living in the United States. And injustice in America is every American's business. Now that you understand the many ways in which the American criminal justice system is unjust, let's get down to the business of making our system more just.

Discussion Questions

- Do you agree with the overall assessment of the U.S. criminal justice system as it was summarized in this chapter? Explain.
- Explain each step of planned change.
- Are the U.S. criminal justice system's efforts to reduce crime consistent with planned change? If so, how? If not, why not?
- Which of the recommendations discussed in this chapter do you think is most likely to be implemented in the near future? Explain.
- What is social justice? How is it related to criminal justice?

REFERENCES AND FURTHER READINGS

Acker, J., and C. Lanier. (1998). Death penalty legislation: Past, present, and future. In J. Acker, R. Bohm, and C. Lanier, eds., *America's experiment with capital punishment: Reflections on the past, present and future of the ultimate penal sanction*. Durham, NC: Carolina Academic Press.

Adams, I., and B. Martin. (1996). Cannabis: pharmacology and toxicology in animals and humans. *Addiction* 91(11): 1585–1614.

Adler, F., G. Mueller, and W. Laufer. (1995). *Criminology*. New York: McGraw-Hill.

Agnew, R. (1993). An empirical test of general strain theory. *Criminology* 30: 475–499.

Agron, J., and L. Anderson. (2000). School security by the numbers. *American School and University* 72(9): 6–11.

Akers, R. (1996). *Criminological theory: Introduction and evaluation*. Los Angeles: Roxbury.

Albonetti, C. (1987). Prosecutorial discretion: The effects of uncertainty. *Law and Society Review* 21: 291–313.

Albonetti, C. (1997). Sentencing under the federal sentencing guidelines: Effects of defendant characteristics, guilty pleas, and departures on sentencing outcomes for drug offenses, 1991–1992. *Law and Society Review* 31: 789–822.

Alexander, E. (2000). The care and feeding of the correctional-industrial complex. In J. May, ed., *Building violence: How America's rush to incarcerate creates more violence*. Thousand Oaks, CA: Sage Publications.

Altheide, D. (1984). TV news and the social construction of justice: Research issues and policy. In R. Surette, ed., *Justice and the media*. Springfield, IL: Charles C Thomas.

Alvarado, M., and O. Boyd-Barrett. (1992). *Media education: An introduction*. London: Milton Keynes.

Ambrosio, T., and V. Schiraldi. (1997). *From classrooms to cell blocks: A national perspective*. Washington, DC: The Justice Policy Institute.

American Academy of Pediatrics. (2000). Online: www.aap.org.

American Bar Association. (1991). Standards for criminal justice. Online: www.abanet.org/crimjust/standards/home.html.

American Bar Association. (1993). Online: www.abanet.org/crimjust/standards/home.html.

American Bar Association. (1997). Online: www.abanet.org/crimjust/standards/home.html.

American Counseling Association. (1999). Online: www.counseling.org.

American Teacher. (1993). *Violence in America's public schools: The Metropolitan Life survey.* New York: Louis Harris and Associates.

Amsterdam, A. (1982). Capital punishment. In H. Bedau, ed., *The death penalty in America.* New York: Oxford University Press.

Anderson, C., and R. Cromwell. (1997). Black is beautiful and the color preferences of Afro-American youth. *Journal of Negro Education* 46: 76.

Anderson, E. (1995). *Streetwise: Race, class and change in an urban community.* Chicago: University of Chicago Press.

Anderson, K. (1983). An eye for an eye. *Time,* January 24: 28–39.

Angolabahere, S., R. Behr, and S. Iyengar. (1993). *The media game: American politics in the television age.* New York: Macmillan.

Annual report on school safety. (1999). U.S. Department of Education and U.S. Department of Justice. Online: www.ed.gov/pubs/edpubs.html.

Anthony, J., L. Warner, and R. Kessler. (1994). Comparative epidemiology of dependence on tobacco, alcohol, controlled substances and inhalants: Basic findings from the National Comorbidity Survey. *Experimental and Clinical Psychopharmacology* 2: 244–268.

Arnst, C. (1994). Out one door and in another: Effects of corporate job-cutting. *Monthly Labor Review* 3459: 41.

Arrigo, B., ed. (1999). *Social justice/criminal justice: The maturation of critical theory in law, crime, and deviance.* Belmont, CA: Wadsworth.

Asnis, S., and R. Smith. (1978). Amphetamine abuse and violence. *Journal of Psychedelic Drugs* 10: 317–377.

Ayers, I., and J. Waldfogel. (1994). A market test for race discrimination in bail setting. *Stanford Law Review* 46 (May): 987.

Bagdikian, B. (2000). *The media monopoly,* 6th ed. Boston: Beacon Press.

Bailey, W. (1998). Deterrence, brutalization, and the death penalty: Another examination of Oklahoma's return to capital punishment. *Criminology* 36, 711–733.

Baker, R., and F. Meyer. (1980). *The criminal justice game: Politics and players.* Lexington, MA: D. C. Heath.

Banfield, E. (1973). *Unheavenly city.* Boston: Little, Brown.

Barak, G. (1988). Newsmaking criminology: Reflections on the media, intellectuals, and crime. *Justice Quarterly* 5: 565–587.

Barak, G. (1994). *Media, process, and the social construction of crime.* New York: Garland.

Barak, G. (1995). Between the waves: Mass-mediated themes of crime and justice. *Social Justice* 21(3): 133–147.

Barak, G., and S. Henry. (1999). An integrative-constitutive theory of crime, law, and social justice. In B. Arrigo, ed., *Social justice/criminal justice: The maturation of critical theory in law, crime, and deviance.* Belmont, CA: Wadsworth.

Barber, J. (1994). The jury is still out. *American Criminal Law Review* 31: 1225–1252.

Barkan, S. (1997). *Criminology: A sociological understanding.* Englewood Cliffs, NJ: Prentice Hall.

Barkan, S., and S. Cohn. (1994). Racial prejudice and support for the death penalty by whites. *Journal of Research in Crime and Delinquency* 31: 202–229.

Barlett, D., and J. Steele. (1992). *America: What went wrong?* Olympia, WA: Democratic Media Services, House of Representatives.

Bayley, D. (1994). *Police for the future.* New York: Oxford University Press.

Beard, C. (1913). *An economic interpretation of the Constitution of the United States.* New York: MacMillan.

Beccaria, C. (1776). *Dei delitti e della pena [An essay on crime and punishments],* 6th ed.

Beck, A. (1998). Trends in United States corrections population. In K. Haus and G. Alpert, eds., *The dilemmas of corrections.* Prospect Heights, IL: Waveland Press.

Becker, H. (1963). *Outsiders.* New York: The Free Press.

Beckett, K. (1994). Setting the public agenda: "Street crime" and drug use in American politics. *Social Problems* 41: 425–447.

Beckett, K. (1997). *Making crime pay: Law and order in contemporary American politics.* New York: Oxford University Press.

Beckett, K., and T. Sasson. (2000). *The politics of injustice: Crime and punishment in America.* Thousand Oaks, CA: Pine Forge Press.

Bedau, H., ed. (1982). *The death penalty in America,* 3rd ed. New York: Oxford University Press.

Bedau, H. (1987). *Death is different: Studies in the morality, law, and politics of capital punishment.* Boston: Northeastern University Press.

Bedau, H., and M. Radelet. (1987). Miscarriages of justice in potentially capital cases. *Stanford Law Review* 40: 21–179.

Belenko, S. (1993). *Crack and the evolution of the anti-drug policy.* Westport, CT: Greenwood Press.

Belknap, J. (1996). *The invisible woman.* Belmont, CA: Wadsworth.

Benjamin, D., and R. Miller. (1991). *Undoing drugs: Beyond legalization.* New York: Basic Books.

Bennett, L. (1980). *Public opinion in American politics.* New York: Harcourt Brace Jovanovich.

Berry, J. (1984). *The interest group society.* Boston: Little, Brown.

Bertram, E., M. Blachman, K. Sharpe, and P. Andreas. (1996). *Drug war politics: The price of denial.* Berkeley: University of California Press.

Best, J., ed. (1989). *Images of issues.* Hawthorne, NY: Aldine de Gruyter.

Best, J. (1999). *Random violence.* Berkeley: University of California Press.

Biskupic, J. (1991). Letter writing and campaigns. *Congressional Quarterly Weekly Report* 49: 171–174.

Bittner, E. (1970). The police and the "war on crime." In *The functions of police in modern society.* Washington DC: U.S. Government Printing Office.

Black, C. (1974). *Capital punishment: The inevitability of caprice and mistake.* New York: Norton.

Black, D. (1980). The production of crime rates. In D. Black, ed., *The manners and customs of the police.* New York: Academic Press.

Black's law dictionary, 6th ed. (1991). St. Paul, MN: West.

Blakemore, E. (1998). The effect of mandatory minimum sentencing on black males and black communities. Online: www.udayton.edu/~race/annotate/s98blake.htm.

Blendon, R. J., and J. T. Young. (1998). The public and the war on illicit drugs. *The Journal of the American Medical Association* 279 (March 18): 827–832.

Blomberg, T. (1996). Review of *Crime and Disrepute. Social Forces* 75(1): 389–392.

Bluestone, B., and S. Rose. (2000). Overworked and underemployed. In R. Lauer and J. Lauer, eds., *Troubled times: Readings in social problems.* Los Angeles: Roxbury.

Blumberg, A. (1967). The practice of law as confidence game: Organizational cooption of a profession. *Law and Society Review* 4: 115–139.

Blumstein, A. (1993). Racial disproportionality of U.S. prison populations revisited. *University of Colorado Law Review* 64: 743–760.

Blumstein, A. (1995). Prisons. In J. Wilson and J. Petersilia, eds., *Crime.* San Francisco: San Francisco Institute for Contemporary Studies.

Blumstein, A. (2000). The connection between crime and incarceration. In J. May, ed., *Building violence: How America's rush to incarcerate creates more violence.* Thousand Oaks, CA: Sage Publications.

Blumstein, A., and J. Cohen. (1973). A theory of the stability of punishment. *Journal of Criminal Law and Criminology* 35(1): 133–175.

Blumstein, A., J. Cohen, S. Martin, and M. Tonry, eds. (1983). *Research on sentencing: The search for reform.* Washington, DC: National Academy Press.

Blumstein, A., and J. Wallman, eds. (2000). *The crime drop in America.* New York: Cambridge University Press.

Boer, J., M. Pastor, and J. Sadd. (1993). Is there environmental racism? The demographics of hazardous waste in Los Angeles County. *Social Science Quarterly* 78(4): 793–810.

Bohm, R. (1999). *Death quest: An introduction to the theory and practice of capital punishment in the United States.* Cincinnati, OH: Anderson.

Bohm, R. (2001). *A primer on crime and delinquency,* 2nd ed. Belmont, CA: Wadsworth.

Bohm, R., and R. Vogel. (1994). A comparison of factors associated with uninformed and informed death penalty opinions. *Journal of Criminal Justice* 22(2): 125–143.

Bonnie, R., and C. Whitebread. (1974). *Marihuana conviction: A history of marihuana prohibition in the United States.* Charlottesville: University of Virginia.

Bonsignore, J., E. Katsh, P. D'Errico, R. Pipkin, S. Arons, and J. Rifkin. (1998). *Before the law: An introduction to the legal process,* 6th ed. Boston: Houghton Mifflin.

Boritch, H. (1992). Gender and criminal court outcome: An historical analysis. *Criminology* 30: 293–325.

Boston University Medical Center. (2000). Online: www.bmc.org.

Bowers, W., G. Pierce, and J. McDevitt. (1984). *Legal homicide.* Boston: Northeastern University Press.

Bradley C. (2000). Reforming the criminal trial. In G. Mays and P. Gregware, eds., *Courts and justice: A reader,* 2nd ed. Prospect Heights, IL: Waveland Press.

Bridges, C., and R. Crutchfield. (1988). Law, social standing, and racial disparity in imprisonment. *Social Forces* 66: 699–724.

Bright, S. (1997). *Capital punishment on the 25th anniversary of* Furman v. Georgia. Atlanta, GA: Southern Center for Human Rights.

Brown, E., K. Defenbacker, and W. Sturgill. (1977). Memory for faces and the circumstance of encounters. *Journal of Applied Psychology* 62: 311–318.

Browne, A. (1993). Family violence and homelessness: The relevance of trauma histories in the lives of homeless women. *American Journal of Orthopsychiatry* 63: 370–384.

Browning, S., F. Cullen, L. Cao, R. Kopache, and T. Stevenson. (1994). Race and getting hassled by the police: A research note. *Police Studies* 17: 1–11.

Brownsberger, W. (1999). In National Center on Institutions and Alternatives, *What every American should know about the criminal justice system.* Online: www.ncianet.org/ncia/facts.html.

Brownstein, H. (1991). The social construction of public policy: A case for participation by researchers. *Sociological Practice Review* 2: 132–140.

Brownstein, H. (1996). *The rise and fall of a violent crime wave: Crack cocaine and the social construction of a crime problem.* Albany, NY: Harrow and Heston.

Brunk, G., and L. Wilson. (1991). Interest groups and criminal behavior. *Journal of Research in Crime and Delinquency* 28: 157–173.

Buckhout, R. (1974). Eyewitness testimony. *Scientific American* 231: 23–31.

Buckley, M., and B. Barovick. (1994). *Urban growth: Development, prospects, and issues.* Washington, DC: Urban Land Institute.

Bullington, B. (1998). America's drug war: Fact or fiction? In R. Coomber, ed., *The control of drug users: Reason or reaction?* Amsterdam: Harwood.

Bureau of Justice Assistance. (1993). Online: www.ojp.usdoj.gov/bja.

Bureau of Justice Statistics. (1992). *Drugs, crime , and the justice system.* Washington DC: U.S. Department of Justice. Bureau of Justice Statistics.

Bureau of Justice Statistics. (1992). Online: www.ojp.usdoj.gov/bjs.

Bureau of Justice Statistics. (1994). Online: www.ojp.usdoj.gov/bjs.

Bureau of Justice Statistics. (1995). Online: www.ojp.usdoj.gov/bjs.

Bureau of Justice Statistics. (1996). Online: www.ojp.usdoj.gov/bjs.

Bureau of Justice Statistics. (1997). Online: www.ojp.usdoj.gov/bjs.

Bureau of Justice Statistics. (1998). Online: www.ojp.usdoj.gov/bjs.

Bureau of Justice Statistics. (1998). *Sourcebook of criminal justice statistics—1997.* Washington DC: U.S. Government Printing Office.

Bureau of Justice Statistics. (1999). Online: www.ojp.usdoj.gov/bjs.

Bureau of Justice Statistics. (2000). Online: www.ojp.usdoj.gov/bjs.

Burkholz, H. (1994). *The FDA follies.* New York: Basic Books.

Burnstein, H., and P. Goldstein. (1990). Research and the development of public policy. *Journal of Applied Psychology* 7: 77–92.

Bush, G. (1998). *The American press and the American presidency.* Washington, DC: National Legal Center for the Public Interest.

Bushway, S. (2000). The stigma of a criminal history record in the labor market. In J. May, ed., *Building violence: How America's rush to incarcerate creates more violence.* Thousand Oaks, CA: Sage Publications.

Butterfield, F. (1995). New prisons cast shadow over higher education. *New York Times,* April 12: A21.

Cahalan, M. (1986). *Historical corrections statistics in the United States, 1850–1984.* Washington, DC: Bureau of Justice Statistics, U.S. Department of Justice.

Capelli, P. (1997). *Change at work.* New York: Oxford University Press.

Carlson, J., and T. Williams. (1993). Perspectives on the seriousness of crimes. *Social Science Research* 22: 190–207.

Carmichael, S., and C. Hamilton. (1969). *Black power.* New York: Vintage Books.

Carter, D., and A. Sapp. (1993). Police response to street people: A survey of perspectives and practices. *FBI Law Enforcement Bulletin* 62: 5–10.

Casement, M. (1987). Alcohol and cocaine. *Alcohol and Health Research World II* 4: 18–25.

Casper, J. (1972). *American criminal justice: The defendant's perspective.* Englewood Cliffs, NJ: Prentice Hall.

Caulkins, J., C. Rydell, W. Schwabe, and J. Chiesa. (1997). *Mandatory minimum drug sentences.* Santa Monica, CA: Rand Corporation.

Center for Media and Public Affairs. (1997). *Media Monitor.* Washington, DC: Center for Media and Public Affairs.

Center for Media and Public Affairs. (2000). Online: www.cmpa.com/factoid/agenda.htm.

Center for Media Education. (2000). Online: www.cme.org.

Centers for Disease Control and Prevention. (1993). *Morbidity and Mortality Weekly Report* 42: 45–49.

Centers for Disease Control and Prevention. (1994a). Changes in brand preference of adolescent smokers in the United States, 1989–1993. *Morbidity and Mortality Weekly Report* 43: 577–581.

Centers for Disease Control and Prevention. (1994b). Cigarette smoking among adults in the United States, 1994. *Morbidity and Mortality Weekly Report* 45: 588–590.

Centers for Disease Control and Prevention. (1994c). *Preventing tobacco use among young people: A report of the surgeon general.* Atlanta, GA: U.S. Department of Health and Human Services.

Centers for Disease Control and Prevention. (1996a). *CDC's tobacco use prevention program: Working toward a healthier future.* Atlanta, GA: U.S. Department of Health and Human Services.

Centers for Disease Control and Prevention. (1996b). Projected smoking-related deaths among youth in the United States. *Morbidity and Mortality Weekly Report* 45: 971–974.

Centers for Disease Control and Prevention. (1996c). *Significant developments related to smoking and health, 1964–1996.* Atlanta, GA: Centers for Disease Control and Prevention.

Centers for Disease Control and Prevention. (1997). *CDC's tobacco use prevention program: Working toward a healthier future.* Atlanta, GA: Centers for Disease Control and Prevention.

Chaffee, R., and D. German. (1998). New frontiers in political socialization research. In K. Hufer and B. Wellie, eds., *Sozialwissenschaftliche und bildungstheoretische Reflexionen: Fachliche und didaktische Perspektiven zur politisch-gesellschaftlichen Aufklarung.* Cambridge, MA: Gaida and Wilch Verlag.

Chairs-Sims, L. (1991). *Long-range planning to minimize the negative effects of downsizing in an organization.* National-Louis University.

Chambliss, W. (2000). *Power, politics, and crime.* Boulder, CO: Westview Press.

Champion, D. (1997). *The Roxbury dictionary of criminal justice.* Los Angeles: Roxbury.

Chapper, J. A., and R. A. Hanson. (1990). *Intermediate appellate courts: Improving case processing.* Williamsburg, VA: National Center for State Courts.

Chermak, S. (1994). Crime in the news media: A refined understanding of how crime becomes news. In G. Barak, ed., *Media, process, and social construction of crime: Studies in news making criminology.* New York: Garland.

Children's Defense Fund. (1992). *The state of America's children.* Washington, DC: Children's Defense Fund.

Children's Defense Fund. (1998). *Poverty matters: The cost of child poverty in America.* Washington, DC: Children's Defense Fund.

Chiricos, T. (1995). The moral panic of the drug war. In M. Lynch, ed., *Race and criminal justice.* Albany, NY: Harrow and Heston.

Chiricos, T., and W. Bales. (1991). Unemployment and punishment: An empirical assessment. *Criminology* 29, 701–724.

Chiricos, T., and M. Delone. (1992). Labor surplus and punishment: A review and assessment of theory and evidence. *Social Problems* 39: 421–446.

Chiricos, T., S. Eschholz, and M. Gertz. (1997). Crime, news and fear of crime: Toward an identification of audience effects. *Social Problems* 44: 342–357.

Christie, N. (1994). *Crime control as an industry.* New York: Routledge.

Christopher, W. (1991). *Report of the Independent Commission on the Los Angeles Police Department.* Los Angeles: The Commission.

Clark, C. (1994). Prison overcrowding. *Congressional Quarterly Researcher* 4 (February): 100.

Clark, J., J. Austin, and D. Henry. (1997). *Three strikes and you're out: A review of state legislation.* U.S. Department of Justice. National Institute of Justice Research in Brief.

Claybrook, J. (1984). *Retreat from health and safety.* New York: Patterson.

Clear, T., and G. Cole. (1994). *American corrections.* Belmont, CA: Wadsworth.

Clemmer, D. (1940). *The prison community.* Boston: Christopher.

Cloward, R., and L. Ohlin. (1961). *Delinquency and opportunity: A theory of delinquent gangs.* London: Routledge.

Clymer, A. (1986). Public found ready to sacrifice in drug fight. *New York Times,* September 2: A1, D16.

Coalition for Federal Sentencing Reform. (1997). Online: www.sentencing.org.

Coalition for Federal Sentencing Reform. (1999). Online: www.sentencing.org.

Cochran, J., M. Chamlin, and M. Seth. (1994). Deterrence or brutalization? An impact assessment of Oklahoma's return to capital punishment. *Criminology* 32, 107–134.

Cohen, M. (1991). Some new evidence on the seriousness of crime. *Criminology* 26: 343–353.

Cohen, S. (1972). *Folk devils and moral panics: The creation of the mods and the rockers.* London: Macgibbon and Kee.

Cohen, S., and S. Solomon. (1995). How *Time* magazine promoted a cyberhoax. *Media Beat.*

Cohen, S., and J. Young, eds. (1981). *The manufacture of news.* Newbury Park, CA: Sage Publications.

Cole, D. (1999). Conditional sentencing: Recent developments. In J. Roberts and D. Cole, eds., *Making sense of sentencing.* Toronto: University of Toronto Press.

Cole, G., and C. Smith. (1998). *The American system of criminal justice,* 8th ed. Belmont, CA: Wadsworth.

Cole, G., and C. Smith. (2000). *The American system of criminal justice,* 9th ed. Belmont, CA: Wadsworth.

Coleman, J. (1990). *The criminal elite,* 2nd ed. New York: St. Martin's Press.

Coleman, J. (1998). *The criminal elite,* 4th ed. New York: St. Martin's Press.

Common Cause. (1999). Online: www.commoncause.org/laundromat/results.html.

Community Epidemiology Work Group. (1999). *Identifying and monitoring emerging drug use problems: A retrospective analysis of drug abuse data/information.* Bethesda, MD: National Institute on Drug Abuse.

Congressional Quarterly. (1999). New Congress is older, more politically seasoned. *Congressional Quarterly,* January 9: 60–63.

Cook, P., D. Slawson, and L. Gries. (1993). *The cost of processing murder cases in North Carolina.* Raleigh: North Carolina Administrative Office of the Courts.

Costanzo, M. (1997). *Just revenge: Costs and consequences of the death penalty.* New York: St. Martin's Press.

Cox, S., and J. Wade. (1998). *The criminal justice network: An introduction.* New York: McGraw-Hill.

Coyne, R., and L. Entzeroth. (1994). *Capital punishment and the judicial process.* Durham, NC: Carolina Academic Press.

Crawford, C. (2000). Gender, race, and habitual offender sentencing in Florida. *Criminology* 38(1): 263–280.

Cromwell, P. (1995). *In their own words.* Los Angeles: Roxbury.

Cromwell, P., J. Olson, and D. Avary. (1991). *Breaking and entering.* London: Sage.

Cronin, F., T. Cronin, and M. Milakovich. (1981). *The U.S. versus crime in the streets.* Bloomington: Indiana University Press.

Crouch, B., A. Alpert, J. Marquart, and K. Haas. (1999). The American prison crisis: Clashing philosophies of punishment and crowded cell blocks. In K. Haas and G. Alpert, eds., *The dilemma of corrections,* 4th ed. Prospect Heights, IL: Waveland Press.

Crutchfield, R., G. Bridges, and S. Pitchford. (1994). Analytical and aggregation biases in analyses of imprisonment: Reconciling discrepancies in studies of racial disparity. *Journal of Research in Crime and Delinquency* 31(2): 166–182.

Cullen, F., B. Link, and L. Travis. (1985). Consensus in crime seriousness: Empirical reality or methodological artifact? *Criminology* 23: 99–118.

Culver, J., and K. Knight. (1979). Evaluative TV impressions of law enforcement roles. In R. Baker and F. Mayer, eds., *Evaluating alternative law enforcement policies.* Lexington, MA: Lexington Books.

Culverson, D. (1998). Stereotyping by politicians: The welfare queen and Willie Horton. In C. Mann and M. Zatz, eds., *Images of color, images of crime.* Los Angeles: Roxbury.

Currie, E. (1998). *Crime and punishment in America.* New York: Holt.

Curtis, D., and J. Resnick. (1987). Images of justice. *Yale Law Journal* 96: 1727–1772.

Cushman, P. (1974). Relationship between narcotic addiction and crime. *Federal Probation* 38: 38–43.

D'Orban, P. (1976). Barbiturate abuse. *Journal of Medical Ethics* 2: 63–67.

Daly, K. (1994). *Gender, crime, and punishment.* New Haven, CT: Yale University Press.

Dattu, F. (1998). Illustrated jury instructions. *Judicature* 82 (September–October): 79.

Davis, J., and T. Smith. (1996). *General Social Surveys, 1972–1996.* Chicago: National Opinion Research Center.

Davis, M., and K. Davis. (1995). Star rising for Simpson jury consultant. *ABA Journal* 81: 14.

Davis, R., and S. Meddis. (1994). Random killing hit a high. *USA Today,* December 5: 1a.

Death Row, U.S.A. (1998). New York: NAACP Legal Defense and Educational Fund, Inc. Address: 99 Hudson, Street, Suite 1600, New York, NY 10013-2897.

DeFrances, C., and G. Steadman. (1998). Prosecutors in state courts, 1996. *Bureau of Justice Statistics Bulletin,* July: 1–10. Washington DC: U.S. Department of Justice.

del Carmen, A., and M. Robinson. (2000). Crime prevention through environmental design and consumption control in the United States. *Howard Journal of Criminal Justice* 39(3): 267–289.

DeLisi, M., and B. Regoli. (1999). Race, conventional crime, and criminal justice: The declining importance of skin color. *Journal of Criminal Justice* 26(6): 549–557.

DeLouth, T., and C. Woods. (1996). Biases against minorities in newspaper reports of crime. *Psychological Reports* 79(2): 545–546.

Denno, D. (1994). Is electrocution an unconstitutional method of execution? The engineering of death over the century. *William and Mary Law Review* 35: 551–692.

Dentzer, S. (1996). The fall-out from dumping workers: Layoffs, effects on economy and morale. *U.S. News & World Report,* March 11.

Devine, F. (1988). Inside the jury room: Deliberations of a mock jury. *Trial* 24: 74–78.

Devlin, P. (1959). *The enforcement of morals.* London: Oxford University Press.

Dill, B., M. Zinn, and S. Patton. (1999). Race, family values, and welfare reform. In L. Kushnick and J. Jennings, eds., *A new introduction to poverty: The role of race, power, and politics.* New York: New York University Press.

Dillehay, R., and M. Sandys. (1996). Life under *Wainwright v. Witt:* Juror dispositions and death qualification. *Law and Human Behavior* 20: 147–165.

Dinitz, S. (1996). Foreword. In R. Huff, A., Rattner, and E. Sagarin, *Convicted but innocent: Wrongful conviction and public policy.* Thousand Oaks, CA: Sage Publications.

Dodge, M., and Harris, J. (2000). Calling a strike a ball: Jury nullification and three strikes cases. In L. May and P. Gregware, eds., *Courts and justice: A reader.* Prospect Heights, IL: Waveland Press.

Domhoff, G. (1998). *Who rules America: Power and politics in the year 2000,* 3rd ed. Mountain View, CA: Mayfield.

Dominick, J. (1978). Crime, law enforcement, and the mass media. In C. Winick, ed., *Deviance and the mass media.* Beverly Hills, CA: Sage Publications.

Dominick, J. (1997). Dumb kid: Petty crimes: A life term? *Los Angeles Times,* July 24: B9.

Donaldson, S. (1995). *Rape of incarcerated prisoners: A preliminary statistical look.* New York: Stop Prison Rape, Inc.

Donovan, P. (1998). Armed with the power of television: Reality crime and programming and the reconstruction of law and order in the United States. In G. Cavender and M. Fishman, eds., *Entertaining crime: Television reality programs.* Hawthorne, NY: Aldine de Gruyter.

Donziger, S., ed. (1996). *The real war on crime: The report of the National Criminal Justice Commission.* New York: HarperPerennial.

Dorn, N., and N. Smith. (1992). *Traffickers.* London: Routledge.

Douglas, J., and J. Johnson. (1977). *Official deviance—Readings in malfeasance, misfeasance, and other forms of corruption.* Philadelphia: Lippincott.

Douglas, S. (1996). Pooh-poohing populist discontent: Mass media and corporate responsibility. *The Progressive* 60(5): 17.

Downs, A. (1995). *Corporate executions: The ugly truth about layoffs—How corporate greed is shattering lives, companies, and communities.* New York: American Management Association.

Dreschel, R. (1983). *News making in the trial court.* New York: Longman.

Dressel, P., and J. Porterfield. (1998). Mothers behind bars: Incarcerating increasing numbers of mothers has serious implications for families and society. *Corrections Today* 60(7): 90–94.

Early America Review. (1999). The Alien and Sedition Acts of 1798. Online: www.animus.net/~earlya/review/index.html.

Easton, D. (1953). *The political system.* New York: Knopf.

The Economist. (1998a). A social profile. *The Economist* 346(8061): 27–28.

The Economist. (1998b). Too poor to be defended. *The Economist,* no. 8063 (April 11): 346.

Eddings, J. (2000). The covert war: Stealth racism in America. In R. Lauer and J. Lauer, eds., *Troubled times: Readings in social problems.* Los Angeles: Roxbury.

Edelman, M. (1988). *Constructing the political spectacle.* Chicago: University of Chicago Press.

Edmondson, G. (1997). A continent at the breaking point: Europeans are rebelling against the demands of global capitalism. *Business Week,* February 24.

Edsall, T., and M. Edsall. (1991). *Chain reaction: The impact of race, rights, and taxes on American politics.* New York: Norton.

Elikann, P. (1996) *The tough on crime myth.* New York: Insight.

Ellingswood, E. (1971). Assault and homicide associated with amphetamine use. *American Journal of Psychiatry* 127: 90–95.

Ellsworth, P. (1991). To tell what we know or wait for Godot? *Law and Human Behavior* 15: 77–90.

Ellsworth, P. C. (1991). Unpleasant facts: The Supreme Court's response to empirical research on the death penalty. In K. Haas and J. Inciardi, eds., *Challenging capital punishment.* Newbury Park, CA: Sage Publications.

Epperlein, T., and B. Nienstedt. (1989). Reexamining the use of seriousness weights in an index of crime. *Journal of Criminal Justice* 17(5): 343–360.

Erez, E. (1981). Thou shalt not execute: Hebrew law perspective on capital punishment. *Criminology* 19: 25–43.

Erickson, P. (1993). Prospects of harm reduction for psychostimulants. In N. Heather, A. Wodak, A. Nadelmann, and P. O'Hare, eds., *Psychoactive drugs and harm reduction.* London: Whurr.

Erickson, P., and J. Butters. (1998). The emerging harm reduction movement: The de-escalation of the war on drugs? In E. Jensen and J. Gerber, eds., *The new war on drugs: Symbolic politics and criminal justice policy.* Cincinnati, OH: Anderson.

Ericson, R., P. Baranek, and J. Chan. (1989). *Negotiating control: A study of news sources.* Toronto: University of Toronto Press.

Erving, J., and B. Houston. (1991). Some judges punish people without benefit of a trial. *Hartford Courant,* June 17: A1.

Eschholz, S. (1997). The media and fear of crime: A survey of the research. *University of Florida Journal of Law and Public Policy* 9(1): 37–59.

Espy, M., and J. Smykla. (1987). *Executions in the United States, 1608–1987: The Espy file.* Machine-readable data file. Ann Arbor, MI: Inter-University Consortium for Political and Social Research.

Estrich, S. (1987). *Real rape.* Cambridge, MA: Harvard University Press.

Evans, D. (1997). Exploring police–probation partnerships. *Corrections Today* 59: 86.

Evans, S., and R. Lundman. (1987). Newspaper coverage of corporate crimes. In M. Erdman and R. Lundman, eds., *Corporate and government deviance: Problems of organizational behavior in contemporary society.* New York: Oxford University Press.

Fagan, J., and M. Guggenheim. (1996). Preventive detention and the judicial prediction of dangerousness for juveniles: A natural experiment. *Journal of Criminal Law and Criminology* 86(2): 415–448.

Families Against Mandatory Minimums. (1999). Online: www.famm.org.

Faust, F. (1995). Personal communication, August 14.

Feder, L. (2000). Likelihood of an arrest decision for domestic and nondomestic assault calls: Do police underenforce the law when responding to domestic violence? In R. Muraskin, ed., *It's a crime: Women and criminal justice,* 2nd ed. Upper Saddle River, NJ: Prentice Hall.

Federal Bureau of Investigation. (1994). Online: www.fbi.gov.

Federal Bureau of Prisons. (1996). Online: www.bop.gov.

Federal Bureau of Prisons. (1998). Online: www.bop.gov.

Federal Trade Commission. (1996). Report to Congress, pursuant to the Federal Cigarette Labeling and Advertising Act.

Fehr, A., and H. Kalant. (1983). Behavioral effects of prolonged administration of delta 9-tetrahydrocannabinol in the rat. *Psychopharmacology* 80(4): 325–330.

Feldman, H., M. Agar, and G. Beschner, eds. (1979). *Angel dust: An ethnographic study of PCP users.* Lexington, MA: Lexington Books.

Finestone, H. (1967). Narcotics and criminality. *Law and Contemporary Problems* 22: 60–85.

Fishbein, D., and S. Pease. (1996). *The dynamics of drug abuse.* Boston: Allyn and Bacon.

Fishman, M. (1978). Crime waves as ideology. *Social Programs* 25: 531–543.

Flemming, R., P. Nardulli, and J. Eisenstein. (1992). *The craft of justice: Politics and work in criminal court community.* Philadelphia: University of Pennsylvania Press.

Florida State Department of Corrections. (2000). Online: www.dc.state.fl.us/.

Foley, M. (1989). *Mumbling across the branches: The Iran-Contra scandal, the Boland amendments and the American foreign policy making process.* Aberystwyth: Department of International Politics, University College of Wales.

Forst, J. (1996). *Job insecurity: The consequences of organizational downsizing and the mediating effects of role ambiguity and role overload.* Texas Christian University.

Frank, N., and M. Lynch. (1992). *Corporate crime, corporate violence.* Albany, NY: Harrow and Heston.

Frank, R. (1994). Talent and the winner-take-all society. *American Prospect* 17: 99.

Frankel, G. (1997). Federal agencies duplicate efforts, wage costly turf battles. *Washington Post*, June 8: A1.

Franklin, R. (1999). White uses of the black underclass. In L. Kushnick and J. Jennings, eds., *A new introduction to poverty: The role of race, power, and politics.* New York: New York University Press.

Free, M. Jr. (2000). The impact of federal sentencing reforms on African Americans. In R. Lauer and J. Lauer, eds., *Troubled times: Readings in social problems.* Los Angeles: Roxbury.

Freedman, E. (1998). Federal habeas corpus in capital cases. In J. Acker and C. Lanier, eds., *America's experiment with capital punishment: Reflections on the past, present and future of the ultimate penal sanction.* Durham, NC: Carolina Academic Press.

Freidman, M. (1998). A quarter-century later, "war on drugs" is still misguided. *Seattle Post-Intelligencer,* January 15: A11.

Fremon, D. (1998). *The Watergate scandal in American history.* Springfield, NJ: Enslow.

Friedman, L. (1993). *Crime and punishment in American history.* New York: Basic Books.

Friedman, W., and M. Hott. (1995). *Young people and the police: Respect, fear and the future of community policing in Chicago.* Chicago: Chicago Alliance for Neighborhood Safety.

Friedrichs, D. (1983). Victimology: A consideration of the radical critique. *Crime and Delinquency* 29(2): 283–294.

Friedrichs, D. (1995). *Trusted criminals: White collar crime in contemporary society.* Belmont, CA: Wadsworth.

Froomkin, D. (1998). Untangling Whitewater: Whitewater special report. *Washington Post.* Online: www.washingtonpost.com.

Fyfe, J. (1983). The NIJ study of the exclusionary rule. *Criminal Law Bulletin* 19: 253–260.

Fyfe, J., and J. Skolnick. (1993). *Above the law: Police and excessive use of force.* New York: The Free Press.

Fyfe, J., J. Greene, W. Walsh, O. Wilson, and R. McLaren. (1997). *Police administration,* 5th ed. New York: McGraw-Hill.

Gaines, L., M. Kaune, and R. Miller. (2000). *Criminal justice in action.* Belmont, CA: Wadsworth.

Gaines, L., and P. Kraska, eds. (1997). *Drugs, crime, and justice.* Prospect Heights, IL: Waveland Press.

Gans, H. (1979). *Deciding what's news.* New York: Vintage Books.

Gans, H. (1995). *The war against the poor.* New York: Basic Books.

Gardner, J. (1995). Worker displacement: A decade of change. *Monthly Labor Review* 118(4): 45.

Garland, D. (1990). *Punishment and modern society: A study in social theory.* Chicago: University of Chicago Press.

Gaynes, E. (1993). The urban criminal justice system: Where young + black + male = probable cause. *Fordham Urban Law Journal* 20: 621.

Gebotys, R., and B. Dasgupta. (1987). Attribution of responsibility and crime seriousness. *Journal of Psychology* 121: 607–613.

Gebotys, R., J. Roberts, and B. Dasgupta. (1988). News media use and public perceptions of crime. *Canadian Journal of Criminology* 30: 3–16.

Geller, W., and M. Scott. (1992). *Deadly force: What we know.* Washington, DC: Police Executive Research Forum.

Geller, W., and H. Toch, eds. (1995). *And justice for all.* Washington, DC: Police Executive Research Forum.

George, H. Jr. (1999). Black America, the underclass, and the subordination process. In L. Kushnick and J. Jennings, eds., *A new introduction to poverty: The role of race, power, and politics.* New York: New York University Press.

Gerbner, G. (1994). Television voice: The art of asking the wrong question. *Currents in Modern Thought,* July: 385–397.

Gerbner, G., et al. (1980). The mainstreaming of America: Violence profile No. 11. *Journal of Communications* 30: 10–29.

Gershman, B. (2000). Why prosecutors misbehave. In G. Mays and P. Gregware, eds., *Courts and justice: A reader,* 2nd ed. Prospect Heights, IL: Waveland Press.

Gerson, L., and D. Preston. (1979). Alcohol consumption and the incidence of violent crime. *Journal of Studies on Alcohol* 40: 307–312.

Gilliard, D. (1999). *Prison and jail inmates at midyear 1998.* Washington, DC: Bureau of Justice Statistics, U.S. Department of Justice.

Gilmer, W. Jr. (1986). *The law dictionary,* 6th ed. Cincinnati, OH: Anderson.

Glantz, S., J. Slade, L. Bero, P. Hanauer, and D. Barnes. (1996). *The cigarette papers.* Berkeley: University of California Press.

Glaser, D. (1974). Interlocking dualities in drug use, drug control, and crime. In J. Inciardi and C. Chambers, eds., *Drugs and the criminal justice system.* Beverly Hills, CA: Sage Publications.

Glaser, D. (1997). *Profitable penalties: How to cut both crime rates and costs.* Thousand Oaks, CA: Pine Forge Press.

Glassner, B., and J. Loughlin. (1987). *Drugs in adolescent worlds: Burnouts to straights.* New York: St. Martin's Press.

Goetz, E. (1996). The U.S. war on drugs as urban policy. *International Journal of Urban and Regional Research* 20: 539–549.

Gold, S. (1990). *The state fiscal agenda for the 1990s.* Denver, CO: National Conference of State Legislatures.

Golden, M. (1997). *Heroic defeats: The politics of job loss.* New York: Cambridge University Press.

Goldstein, H. (1975). *Police corruption: A perspective on its nature and control.* Washington, DC: Police Foundation.

Goldstein, H. (1990). *Problem-oriented policing.* New York: McGraw-Hill.

Goldstein, P. (1979). *Prostitution and drugs.* Lexington, MA: D. C. Heath.

Goldstein, P. (1998). The drugs/violence nexus: A tripartite conceptual framework. In J. Inciardi and K. McElrath, eds., *The American drug scene: An anthology,* 2nd ed. Los Angeles: Roxbury.

Goldstein, P., and N. Duchaine. (1980). Daily criminal activities of street drug users. Paper presented to the annual meeting of the American Society of Criminology.

Good, C. (1995). *Employee downsizing: Analysis and effects.* Southwest Missouri State University.

Goode, E. (1999). *Drugs in American society,* 5th ed. New York: Knopf.

Goode, E., and N. Ben-Yehuda. (1994a). Moral panics: Culture, politics, and social construction. *Annual Review of Sociology* 20: 149–171.

Goode, E., and N. Ben-Yehuda. (1994b). *Moral panics: The social construction of deviance.* Cambridge, MA: Blackwell.

Gordon, D. (1996). *Fat and mean: The corporate squeeze of working Americans and the myth of managerial "downsizing."* New York: Martin Kessler.

Gorr, M. (2000). The morality of plea bargaining. *Social Theory and Practice* 26(1): 129–151.

Gosselin, D. (2000). *Heavy hands: An introduction to the crime of domestic violence.* Upper Saddle River, NJ: Prentice Hall.

Gotham, K. (2000). The FBI and covert repression. In R. Lauer and J. Lauer, eds., *Troubled times: Readings in social problems.* Los Angeles: Roxbury.

Gottfredson, D. (1999). *Exploring criminal justice: An introduction.* Los Angeles: Roxbury.

Gottfredson, S., and D. Gottfredson. (1994). Behavioral prediction and the problem of incapacitation. *Criminology* 32(3): 441–474.

Gottfredson, S., and G. Jarjoura. (1996). Race, gender, and guidelines-based decision making. *Journal of Research in Crime and Delinquency* 33: 49–69.

Gould, L. (1974). Crime and the addict: Beyond common sense. In J. Inciardi and C. Chambers, eds., *Drugs and the criminal justice system.* Beverly Hills, CA: Sage Publications.

Gove, W., M. Hughes, and M. Geerken. (1985). Are uniform crime reports a valid indicator of the index crimes? An affirmative answer with minor qualifications. *Criminology* 23: 451–501.

Gow, H. (1986). Religious views support the death penalty. In B. Szumski, L. Hall, and S. Bursell, eds., *The death penalty: Opposing viewpoints.* St. Paul, MN: Greenhaven.

Graber, D. (1980). *Crime news and the public.* Westport, CT: Praeger.

Graber, D. (1996). The new media and politics: What does the future hold? *Political Science and Politics,* March: 33–36.

Graham, B. (2000). Judicial recruitment and racial diversity on state courts: An overview. In G. Mays and P. Gregware, eds., *Courts and justice: A reader,* 2nd ed. Prospect Heights, IL: Waveland Press.

Gray, Mike. (1998). *Drug crazy.* New York: Random House.

Greenberg, E. (1993). *The American political system: A radical approach,* 5th ed. Glenville, IL: Scott, Foresman.

Greenberg, S., and F. Adler. Crime and addiction: An empirical analysis of the literature, 1920–1973. *Contemporary Drug Problems* 3: 221–270.

Greenwood, P., et al. (1994). *Three strikes and you're out—estimated benefits and costs of California's new mandatory sentencing law.* Santa Monica, CA: Rand Corporation.

Greenwood, P. (1998). *Diverting children from a life of crime: Measuring costs and benefits.* Santa Monica, CA: Rand Corporation.

Greenwood, P., and S. Turner. (1987). *Selective incapacitation revisited: Why the high rate offenders are hard to predict.* Santa Monica, CA: Rand Corporation.

Gurevitch, M., et al. (1982). *Culture, society, and the media.* London: Methuen.

Gusfield, J. (1967). Moral passage: The symbolic process in public designations of deviance. *Social Problems* 15: 175–188.

Haas, K., and G. Alpert, eds. (1999). *The dilemma of corrections,* 4th ed. Prospect Heights, IL: Waveland Press.

Hagan, J. (1989). Why is there so little criminal justice theory? Neglected macro- and micro-level links between organization and power. *Journal of Research on Crime and Delinquency* 26(2): 116–135.

Hagan, J. (1994). *Crime and disrepute.* Thousand Oaks, CA: Pine Forge Press.

Hagan, J. (1998). *Political crime, ideology, and criminality.* Boston: Allyn and Bacon.

Hall, J. (1992). *Deadly force: The common law and the Constitution.* Washington, DC: Federal Bureau of Investigation, U.S. Department of Justice.

Haltom, W. (1998). *Reporting on the courts: How the mass media cover judicial elections.* Chicago: Nelson-Hall.

Hamid, A. (1998). *Drugs in America: Sociology, economics, and politics.* Newbury Park, CA: Sage Publications.

Hammer, M. J., and Champy. (1994). *Reengineering the corporation.* New York: Harper Business.

Hansen, D. (1999). Answer to question about origin of lady of justice. Online: www.commonlaw.com/Justice.html.

Hansom, R., and B. Ostrom. (1993). Litigation and the courts: Myths and misconceptions. *Trial* 29: 40–44.

Harmsworth, E. (1996). Bail and detention: An assessment and critique of the federal and Massachusetts systems. *New England Journal on Criminology and Civil Confinement* 22: 213.

Harrigan, J. (2000). *Empty dreams, empty pockets:Class and bias in American politics.* New York: Addison-Wesley Longman.

Harris, D. (1999). *Driving while black: Racial profiling on our nation's highways.* New York: American Civil Liberties Union.

Harris, W. (1961). Harry F. Sinclair and the Teapot Dome scandal: Appearance and realities. Master's thesis, Indiana University, Bloomington.

Harriston, K., and M. P. Flaherty. (1994). Law and disorder—the District's troubled police. *Washington Post,* August 28–31.

Hart, H. (1968). *Punishment and responsibility.* New York: Oxford University Press.

Harvard Law Review. (1988). Developments in the law—race and the criminal process. *Harvard Law Review* 101: 1496.

Heath, L., and K. Gilbert. (1996). Mass media and fear of crime. *American Behavioral Scientist* 39: 379–386.

Henderson, J., and D. Simon. (1994). *Crimes of the criminal justice system.* Cincinnati, OH: Anderson.

Henretta, J., E. Brownlee, D. Brody, S. Ware, and M. Johnson. (1997). *American history.* New York: Worth.

Herbert, B. (1993). Tobacco dollars. *New York Times,* November 28: D11.

Herbert, B. (1998). Cheap justice. *New York Times,* March 1: 15.

Herman, E., and N. Chomsky. (1988). *Manufacturing consent.* New York: Pantheon.

Hess, S. (1981). *The Washington reporters.* Washington, DC: Brookings Institution.

Hess, K., and H. Wrobleski, H. *Police operations,* 2nd ed. (St. Paul, MN: West).

Hilgartner, S., and C. Bosk. (1988). The rise and fall of social problems: A public arenas model. *American Journal of Sociology* 94: 53–78.

Hindelang, M. (1978). Race and involvement in common law personal crimes. *American Sociological Review* 43: 93–109.

Hindelang, M., T. Hirschi, and J. Weis. (1980). *Measuring delinquency.* Beverly Hills, CA: Sage Publications.

Hirschi, T. (1969). *Causes of delinquency.* Berkeley: University of California Press.

Hollinger, R., and L. Lanza-Kaduce. (1988). The process of criminalization. *Criminology* 26: 101–126.

Hollister, L. (1988). Cannabis—1988. *ACTA Psychiatrica Scandinavica Supplementum* 345: 108–118.

Holten, G., and M. Jones. (1982). *The system of criminal justice,* 2nd ed. Boston: Little, Brown.

Hoppe, C. (1992). Life in jail, or death? Life term is cheaper. *Charlotte Observer,* March 22: 12A.

Huff, C., A. Rattner, and E. Sagarin. (1986). Guilty until proven innocent: Wrongful conviction and public policy. *Crime and Delinquency* 32: 518–544.

Huff, C., A. Rattner, and E. Sagarin. (1996). *Convicted but innocent: Wrongful conviction and public policy.* Thousand Oaks, CA: Sage Publications.

Hurwitz, J., and M. Peffley. (1997). Public perceptions of race and crime: The role of racial stereotypes. *American Journal of Political Science* 41(2): 375–401.

Inbau, F., and J. Reid. (1967). *Criminal interrogation and confessions.* Baltimore, MD: Williams and Wilkins.

Inciardi, J., ed. (1991) *The drug legalization debate: Studies in crime, law, and justice.* Newbury Park, CA: Sage Publications.

Inciardi, J., and C. Chambers. (1972). Unreported criminal involvement of narcotic addicts. *Journal of Drug Issues* 2(2): 57–64.

Inciardi, J., and K. McElrath, eds. (1998). *The American drug scene: An anthology,* 2nd ed. Los Angeles: Roxbury.

Ingley, S. (2000). Corrections without corrections. In J. May, ed., *Building violence: How America's rush to incarcerate creates more violence.* Thousand Oaks, CA: Sage Publications.

Ingraham, B. (1994). The right of silence, the presumption of innocence, the burden of proof, and a modest proposal. *Journal of Criminal Law and Criminology* 85: 59–95.

Irwin, J. (1985). *The jail: Managing the underclass in American society.* Berkeley: University of California Press.

Irwin, J., and J. Austin. (1997). *It's about time: America's imprisonment binge.* Belmont, CA: Wadsworth.

Iyengar, S., and D. Kinder. (1987). *News that matters: Television and American opinion.* Chicago: University of Chicago Press.

Jackson, D. (1994). Politician crime rhetoric. *Boston Globe,* October 21: 15.

Jackson, J. (1988). Aging black women and public policies. *Black Scholar* (May–June): 33.

Jackson, P. (1997). *Minority group threat, crime and policing: Social context and social control.* New York: Praeger.

Jaynes, G., and R. Williams. (1989). *A common destiny: Blacks and American society.* Washington, DC: National Academy Press.

Jeffery, C. (1990). *Criminology: An interdisciplinary approach.* Beverly Hills, CA: Prentice Hall.

Jennings, J. (1999). Persistent poverty in the United States: A review of theories and explanations. In L. Kushnick and J. Jennings, eds., *A new introduction to poverty: The role of race, power, and politics.* New York: New York University Press.

Jensen, E., and J. Gerber, eds. (1998). *The new war on drugs: Symbolic politics and criminal justice policy.* Cincinnati, OH: Anderson.

Jensen, G., and K. Thompson. (1990). What's class got to do with it? A further examination of power-control theory. *American Journal of Sociology* 95: 1009–1023.

Johnson, B., P. Goldstein, E. Preble, J. Schmeidler, D. Lipton, B. Sprunt, and T. Miller. (1985). *Taking care of business: The economics of crime by heroin abusers.* Lexington, MA: Lexington Books.

Johnson, S. (2000). The Bible and the death penalty: Implications for criminal justice education. *Journal of Criminal Justice Education* 11(1): 15–33.

Joint Center for Political and Economic Studies. (1993). *Black elected officials: A national roster.* Washington, DC: Joint Center for Political and Economic Studies.

Jonas, S. (1991). The United States drug problem and the United States drug culture. In J. Inciardi, ed., *The drug legalization debate: Studies in crime, law, and justice.* Newbury Park, CA: Sage Publications.

Jones, D. (1987a). *History of criminology: A philosophical perspective.* New York: Greenwood.

Jones, R. (1987). Behavioral, psychosocial, and academic correlates of marijuana usage in adolescence: A study of a cohort under treatment. *Clinical Pediatrics* 26(5): 264–270.

Kaminer, W. (1999). Games prosecutors play. *American Prospect* 46: 20–26.

Kappeler, V., M. Blumberg, and G. Potter. (1996) *The mythology of crime and criminal justice.* Prospect Heights, IL: Waveland Press.

Kappeler, V., M. Blumberg, and G. Potter. (2000). *The mythology of crime and criminal justice,* 3rd ed. Prospect Heights, IL: Waveland Press.

Karel, R. (1991). A model legalization proposal. In J. Inciardi, ed., *The drug legalization debate: Studies in crime, law, and justice.* Newbury Park, CA: Sage Publications.

Karmen, A. (1996). *Crime victims: An introduction to victimology,* 3rd ed. Belmont, CA: Wadsworth.

Karmen, A. (1999). The situation of crime victims in the early decades of the twenty-first century. In R. Muraskin and A. Roberts, eds., *Visions for change: Crime and justice in the 21st century,* 2nd ed. Upper Saddle River, NJ: Prentice Hall.

Kassin, S. (2000). The American jury: Handicapped in the pursuit of justice. In G. Mays and P. Gregware, *Courts and justice: A reader,* 2nd ed. Prospect Heights, IL: Waveland Press.

Katz, M. (1999). Reframing the underclass debate. In L. Kushnick and J. Jennings, eds., *A new introduction to poverty: The role of race, power, and politics.* New York: New York University Press.

Kelling, G., T. Pate, D. Dieckman, and C. Brown. (1974). *The Kansas City preventive patrol experiment: A summary report.* Washington, DC: The Police Foundation.

Kellner, L. (1988). Narcotics-related corruption. In *Prosecution of public corruption cases* (pp. 39–53). Washington, DC: U.S. Department of Justice.

Kennedy, D. (1997). Pulling levers: Chronic offenders, high crime settings, and a theory of prevention. *Valparaiso University Law Review* 31(2): 449.

Kennedy, R. (1997). *Race, crime and the law.* New York: Vintage.

Keve, P. (1995). *Crime control and justice in America: Searching for facts and answers.* Chicago: American Library Association.

Kim, M. (1999). The working poor: Lousy jobs or lazy workers? In L. Kushnick and J. Jennings, eds., *A new introduction to poverty: The role of race, power, and politics.* New York: New York University Press.

Kitsuse, S., and M. Spector. (1973). Toward a sociology of social problems: Social condition, value judgments, and social problems. *Social Problems* 20: 407–419.

Kittel, N. (1986). Police perjury: Criminal defense attorneys' perspectives. *American Journal of Criminal Justice* 11: 1.

Klain, J. (1989). *International television and video almanac.* New York: Quarterly.

Kleiman, M. (1997). Neither probation nor legalization: Grudging toleration in drug control policy. In M. McShane and F. Williams, eds., *Drug use and drug policy.* New York: Garland.

Klockars, C. (1991). The rhetoric of community policing. In J. Greene and S. Mastrofski, eds., *Community policing: Rhetoric and reality.* New York: Praeger.

Koning, H. (1993). *The conquest of America: How the Indian nations lost their continent.* New York: Monthly Review Press.

Kooistra, P., J. Mahoney, and S. Westervelt. (1999). The world of crime according to "COPS." In G. Cavender and M. Fishman, eds., *Entertaining crime: Television reality programs.* Hawthorne, NY: Aldine de Gruyter.

Kornbluh, P., and M. Byrne. (1993). *The Iran-Contra scandal: The declassified history.* New York: Norton.

Kozel, N., R. Dupont, and B. Brown. (1972). A study of narcotic involvement in an offender population. *International Journal of the Addictions* 7: 443–450.

Krahn, H., T. Hartnagel, and J. Gartnell. (1986). Income inequality and homicide rates: Cross-national data and criminological theories. *Criminology* 24: 269–293.

Krajicek, D. (1998). *Scooped! Media miss real story on crime while chasing sex, sleaze, and celebrities.* New York: Columbia University Press.

Kramer, J. (1976). From demon to ally—How mythology has and may yet alter national drug policy. *Journal of Drug Issues* 6: 390–406.

Kraska, P. B. (1990). The unmentionable alternative: The need for, and the argument against the decriminalization of drug laws. In R. Weisheit, ed., *Drugs, crime, and the criminal justice system.* Cincinnati, OH: Anderson.

Kraska, P., and V. Kappeler. (1997). Militarizing American police: The rise and normalization of paramilitary units. *Social Problems* 44(1): 1–17.

Kreyche, G. (1996). Does the future have a future? *USA Today* 125(2618): 82.

Kushnick, L. (1999). Responding to urban crisis: Functions of white racism. In L. Kushnick and J. Jennings, eds., *A new introduction to poverty: The role of race, power, and politics.* New York: New York University Press.

Kushnick, L., and J. Jennings, eds. (1999). *A new introduction to poverty: The role of race, power, and politics.* New York: New York University Press.

Lacayo, R. (1994). Lock 'em up! *Time,* February 7.

Ladinsky, J. (1984). The impact of social background of lawyers in legal practice and the law. In J. Bonsignore et al., eds., *Before the law.* Boston: Houghton Mifflin.

LaFree, G. (1989). *Rape and criminal justice: The social construction of sexual assault.* Belmont, CA: Wadsworth.

Land, K., P. McCall, and L. Cohen. (1990). Structural co-variates of homicide rates: Are there any invariances across time and space? *American Journal of Sociology* 95: 922–963.

Langan, P. (1994). No racism in the criminal justice system. *Public Interest* 117: 48–51.

Langbein, J. (2000). On the myth of written constitutions: The disappearance of criminal jury trial. In G. Mays and P. Gregware, eds., *Courts and justice: A reader,* 2nd ed. Prospect Heights, IL: Waveland Press.

Lapley, R., and M. Westlake. (1988). *Film theory: An introduction.* Manchester, England: Manchester University Press.

Lasswell, H. (1936). *Politics: Who gets what, when, how.* New York: McGraw-Hill.

Lauer, R., and J. Lauer, eds. (2000). *Troubled times: Readings in social problems.* Los Angeles: Roxbury.

Lazarus, E. (2000). How Miranda really works and why it matters. Online: http://writ.news.findlaw.com/lazarus/20000605.html.

Leana, C., and D. Feldman. (1992). *Coping with job loss: How individuals, organizations, and communities respond to layoffs.* New York: Lexington Books.

Leff, D., D. Protess, and S. Brooks. (1986). Crusading journalism: Changing public attitudes and policy-making agendas. *Public Opinion Quarterly* 50: 300–315.

Leo, R. (1996). Miranda's revenge: Police interrogation as a confidence game. *Law and Society Review* 30(2): 259–288.

Levy, F. (1988). *Dollars and dreams: The changing American income distribution.* New York: Norton.

Lewis, D. (1981). Crime in the media: Introduction. In D. Lewis, ed., *Reactions to crime.* Beverly Hills, CA: Sage Publications.

Lichter, R., and E. Edmundson. (1992). *A day in the life of television violence.* Washington, DC: Center for Media and Public Affairs.

Lichter, S. (1988). Media power: The influence of media on politics and business. *Florida Policy Review* 4: 35–41.

Lichter, S., L. Lichter, and S. Rothman. (1994). *Prime time: How TV portrays American culture.* Washington, DC: Regnery.

Liebman, J., J. Fagan, and V. West. (2000). *A broken system: Error rates in capital cases, 1973–1995.* New York: Columbia University Law School.

Lilly, J., F. Cullen, and R. Ball. (1995). *Criminological theory: Context and consequences.* Thousand Oaks, CA: Sage Publications.

Lilly, J., and P. Knepper. (1993). The corrections-commercial complex. *Crime and Delinquency* 39: 150–166.

Lindesmith, A. (1940). *Opiate addiction.* Bloomington, IN: Principia Press.

Lindsell-Roberts, S. (1994). *Loony laws and silly statutes.* New York: Sterling Publications.

Liska, K. (2000). *Drugs and the human body,* 6th ed. New York: Macmillan.

Livingston, J. (1996). *Crime and criminology,* 2nd ed. Upper Saddle River, NJ: Prentice Hall.

Lockwood, D., A. Pottieger, and J. Inciardi. (1996). Crack use, crime by crack users, and ethnicity. In D. Hawkins, ed., *Ethnicity, race, and crime.* Albany: State University of New York Press.

Loftus, E. F. (1979). *Eyewitness testimony.* Cambridge, MA: Harvard University Press.

Longley, R. (1998). Impeachment: Unthinkable process. Online: www.about.com.

Lowi, T., and B. Ginsburg. (1990). *American government: Freedom and power.* New York: Norton.

Luginbuhl, J., and M. Burkhead. (1994). Sources of bias and arbitrariness in the capital trial. *Journal of Social Issues* 103.

Lyman, M., and G. Potter. (1998). *Drugs in society.* Cincinnati, OH: Anderson.

Lynch, M. (1997). *Radical criminology.* Brookfield, VT: Aldershot.

Lynch, M. (1998). Beating a dead horse: Is there any basic empirical evidence for the deterrent effect of imprisonment? Unpublished manuscript, University of South Florida, Tampa.

Lynch, M., and P. Stretesky. (1999). Marxism and social justice: Thinking about social justice, eclipsing criminal justice. In B. Arrigo, ed., *Social justice, criminal justice.* Belmont, CA: Wadsworth.

Lyon, L. (1933). *What shall we do about the anti-trust laws?* Chicago: University of Chicago Press.

MacCoun, R. (1990). The emergence of extralegal bias during jury deliberation. *Criminal Justice and Behavior* 17: 303–314.

Magagnini, S. (1988). Closing death row would save state $90 million a year. *Sacramento Bee,* March 28: 1.

Maguire, M., and T. Bennett. (1982). *Burglary in a dwelling.* London: Heinemann.

Maguire, K., and T. Flanagan. (1997). *Sourcebook of criminal justice statistics—1996.* Albany, NY: Hindelang Criminal Justice Research Center.

Maguire, K., and A. Pastore. (1995). *Sourcebook of criminal justice statistics, 1994.* Washington, DC: Bureau of Justice Statistics.

Maguire, K., and A. Pastore, eds. (1997). *Sourcebook of criminal justice statistics, 1996.* Washington, DC: U.S. Department of Justice, Bureau of Justice Statistics.

Maguire, K., and A. Pastore, eds. (1999). *Sourcebook of criminal justice statistics, 1998.* Washington, DC: U.S. Department of Justice, Bureau of Justice Statistics.

Maher, T. (2000). Environmental racism. In R. Lauer and J. Lauer, eds., *Troubled times: Readings in social problems.* Los Angeles: Roxbury.

Mann, C. (1993). *Unequal justice.* Bloomington: Indiana University Press.

Manning, P. (1997). *Police work: The social organization of policing,* 2nd ed. Prospect Heights, IL: Waveland Press.

Mariner, J. (2000). Body and soul: The trauma of prison rape. In J. May, ed., *Building violence: How America's rush to incarcerate creates more violence.* Thousand Oaks, CA: Sage Publications.

Marion, N. (1995). *A primer in the politics of criminal justice.* Albany, NY: Harrow and Heston.

Marongiu, P., and G. Newman. (1987). *Vengeance: The fight against injustice.* Totowa, NJ: Rowman and Littlefield.

Marsh, H. (1991). A comparative analysis of crime coverage in newspapers in the United States and other countries from 1960–1989: A review of the literature. *Journal of Criminal Justice* 19: 67–80.

Martin, S. (2000). Sanctioned violence in American prisons. In J. May, ed., *Building violence: How America's rush to incarcerate creates more violence.* Thousand Oaks, CA: Sage Publications.

Martinson, R. (2000). What works? Questions and answers in prison reform. *The Public Interest* 35: 22–55.

Marx, G. (1981). Ironies of social control: Authorities as contributors to deviance through escalation, nonenforcement, and covert facilitation. *Social Problems* 28: 221–246.

Masci, D. (1994a). The modified crime bill. *Congressional Quarterly Weekly Report* 52: 2488–2493.

Masci, D. (1994b). $30 billion anti-crime bill heads to Clinton's desk. *Congressional Quarterly,* August 27: 2488–2493.

Massey, D., and A. Gross. (1990). *A pessimistic interpretation of recent declines in black residential segregation.* Chicago: Ogburn-Stouffer Center.

Mauer, M. (1990). *Young black men and the criminal justice system.* Washington, DC: The Sentencing Project.

Mauer, M. (1991). *Americans behind bars: A comparison of international rates of incarceration.* Washington, DC: The Sentencing Project.

Mauer, M. (1992). *Americans behind bars: One year later.* Washington, DC: The Sentencing Project.

Mauer, M. (1994). *Americans behind bars: The international use of incarceration, 1992–1993.* Washington, DC: The Sentencing Project.

Mauer, M. (1997). *Americans behind bars: United States and the international use of incarceration.* Washington, DC: The Sentencing Project.

Mauer, M. (1998). "Lock 'em up and throw away the key": African Americans and meals and the criminal justice system. In K. Haas and G. Alpert, eds., *The dilemma of corrections.* Prospect Heights, IL: Waveland Press.

Mauer, M., and T. Huling. (1995a). One in three young black men ensnared in justice system. *Overcrowded Times* 6: 1–10.

Mauer, M., and T. Huling. (1995b). *Young black Americans and the criminal justice system: Five years later.* Washington DC: The Sentencing Project.

May, J., ed. (2000). *Building violence: How America's rush to incarcerate creates more violence.* Thousand Oaks, CA: Sage Publications.

Mayhew, P., and J. Van Dijk. (1997). *Criminal victimization in eleven industrialized countries: Key findings from the 1996 International Crime Victims Survey.* The Hague: Dutch Ministry of Justice.

McAdams, J. (1998). Racial disparity and the death penalty. *Law and Contemporary Problems* 61(4): 153–170.

McAnamy, P. (1992). Asset forfeiture as drug control strategy. Paper presented at the annual meetings of the American Society of Criminology, New Orleans, LA, November.

McCaghy, C., T. Capron, and J. Jamieson. (2000). *Deviant behavior*, 5th ed. Boston: Allyn and Bacon.

McCleary, R., B. Nienstedt, and J. Erven. (1982). Uniform crime reports as organizational outcomes: Three time series quasi-experiments. *Social Problems* 29: 361–372.

McCombs, M., and D. Shaw. (1972). The agenda setting function of the mass media. *Public Opinion Quarterly* 36: 176–187.

McElhaney, J. W. (1998). The jury consultant bazaar. *ABA Journal* 84: 78–79.

McEwen, T., and F. Leahy. (1994). *Less than lethal force technologies in law enforcement and correctional agencies*. Alexandria, VA: Institute for Law and Justice.

McGarrell, E. (1993). Institutional theory and the stability of a conflict model of the incarceration rate. *Justice Quarterly* 10(1): 7–28.

McGinnis, K. (2000). Make 'em break rocks. In J. May, ed., *Building violence: How America's rush to incarcerate creates more violence*. Thousand Oaks, CA: Sage Publications.

McGucken, E. (1987). Crime news reporting in the *New York Times*, 1900 to 1950: A content analysis. PhD dissertation, University of Akron.

McLaughlin, C. (2000). Prisoner rehabilitation: Feeling better but getting worse. In J. May, ed., *Building violence: How America's rush to incarcerate creates more violence*. Thousand Oaks, CA: Sage Publications.

McNeece, C., B. Bullington, E. Mayfield, and D. Springer. (1999). The war on drugs: Treatment, research, and substance abuse intervention in the twenty-first century. In R. Muraskin and A. Roberts, eds., *Visions for change: Crime and justice in the twenty-first century*. Upper Saddle River, NJ: Prentice Hall.

McQuail, D. (1994). *Mass communication theory*, 3rd ed. London: Sage.

McShane, M., and F. Williams. (1992). Radical victimology: A critique of victim in traditional victimology. *Crime and Delinquency* 38(2): 258–271.

Meddis, S. (1993). In twin cities, a tale of two standards. *USA Today,* July 26: 6A.

Meddis, S. (1994). Success of expansion of matter of debate. *USA Today,* December 13: 10A.

Meeker, J. (1984). Criminal appeals over the last 100 years: Are the odds of winning increasing? *Criminology* 22: 551–571.

Meier, R., and J. Short. (1985). Crime as hazard: Perceptions of risk and seriousness. *Criminology* 23: 389–399.

Melosi, D. (1989). An introduction: First years later, punishment and social structure in contemporary analysis. *Contemporary Crisis* 13: 311–326.

Merlo, A., and P. Benekos. (2000). *What's wrong with the criminal justice system: Ideology, politics and the media*. Cincinnati, OH: Anderson.

Merriam-Webster's Collegiate Dictionary, 10th ed. (1998). Springfield, MA: Merriam-Webster.

Merton, R. (1938a). *Science, technology and society in seventeenth century England*. Bruges, Belgium: Saint Catherine Press.

Merton, R. (1938b). *Social structure and anomie*. Indianapolis, IN: Bobbs-Merrill.

Messner, S., and K. Tardiff. (1986). Economic inequality and levels of homicide: An analysis of urban neighborhoods. *Criminology* 24: 297–316.

Miethe, T. (1982). Public consensus on crime seriousness: Normative structure or methodological artifact? *Criminology* 20: 515–526.

Miethe, T. D. (1995). Fear and withdrawal from urban life. *Annals of the American Academy of Political and Social Science* 539: 14–27.

Mill, John Stuart. (1859). *On liberty*. Tokyo: Kenkyusha.

Miller, J. (1994). *African American males in the criminal justice system*. Alexandria, VA: National Center on Institutions and Alternatives.

Miller, J. (1997). African American males in the criminal justice system. *Phi Delta Kappan* (June): 22–30.

Miller, J. (1998). *Search and destroy: African-American males in the criminal justice system.* New York: Cambridge University Press.

Miller, M. (1995). The road to Panama City. *Newsweek* 126(18): 84.

Miller, R. (1997). Symposium on coercion: An interdisciplinary examination of coercion, exploitation, and the Law: III. Coerced confinement and treatment: The continuum of coercion: constitutional and clinical considerations in the treatment of mentally disordered persons. *Denver Law Review* 74: 1169–1214.

Miller, S. (2000). Arrest policies for domestic violence and their implications for battered women. In R. Muraskin, ed., *It's a crime: Women and criminal justice,* 2nd ed. Upper Saddle River, NJ: Prentice Hall.

Miller, T., M. Cohen, and B. Wiersma. (1997). *Victim costs and consequences: A new look.* Washington, DC: U.S. Department of Justice, Office of Justice Programs, National Institute of Justice.

Miller, W. (1958). Lower class culture as a generating milieu of gang delinquency. *Journal of Social Issues* 14: 5–19.

Milovanovich, Z. (2000). Prosecutorial discretion: A comparative perspective. In G. Mays and P. Gregware, eds., *Courts and justice: A reader,* 2nd ed. Prospect Heights, IL: Waveland Press.

Minow, M. (2000). Stripped down like a runner or enriched by experience? Bias and impartiality of judges and jurors. In G. Mays and P. Gregware, eds., *Courts and justice: A reader,* 2nd ed. Prospect Heights, IL: Waveland Press.

Mintz, M. (1992). Why the media cover up corporate crime: A reporter looks back in anger. *Trial* 28: 72–77.

Mokhiber, R., and R. Weissman. (1999). *Corporate predators: The hunt for mega-profits and the attack on democracy.* Monroe, ME: Common Courage Press.

The Mollen Commission. (1994). *Police brutality and excessive force in the New York City Police Department.* New York: The Mollen Commission.

Moore, M. (1996). *Downsize this!* New York: Crown.

Moore, W. (1995). Targeting Harlem, not Hollywood. *National Journal,* February 11: 388.

Morgan, M., and N. Signorielli, eds. (1990). *Cultivation analysis: New directions in media effects research.* Newbury Park, CA: Sage Publications.

Morgan-Sharp, E. (1999). The administration of justice based on gender and race. In R. Muraskin and A. Roberts, eds., *Visions for change: Crime and justice in the 21st century,* 2nd ed. Upper Saddle River, NJ: Prentice Hall.

Morris, E. (1988). *The thin blue line* [film]. New York: Miramax Films.

Mumola, C., and A. Beck. (1997). *Prisoners in 1996.* Washington, DC: Bureau of Justice Statistics, U.S. Department of Justice.

Muraskin, R. (1999). The future. In R. Muraskin and A. Roberts, eds., *Visions for change: Crime and justice in the twenty-first century,* 2nd ed. Upper Saddle River, NJ: Prentice Hall.

Muraskin, R., and A. Roberts. (1999). *Visions for change: Crime and justice in the twenty-first century,* 2nd ed. Upper Saddle River, NJ: Prentice Hall.

Murray, C. (1984). *Losing ground—American social policy, 1950–1980.* New York: Basic Books.

Murray, C., and R. Herrnstein. (1994). *The bell curve: Intelligence and class structure in American life.* New York: The Free Press.

Myers, S. (1987). Introduction. Special issue on race and crime. *Review of Black Political Economy* 16: 5–15.

Nadelmann, E. (1991). The case for legalization. In J. Inciardi, ed., *The drug legalization debate: Studies in crime, law, and justice.* Newbury Park, CA: Sage Publications.

Nadelmann, E. (1998). Experimenting with drugs. *Foreign Affairs* 1: 111–126.

Nader, Ralph. (1999). Introduction to R. Mokhiber and R. Weissman, *Corporate predators: The hunt for mega-profits and the attack on democracy.* Monroe, ME: Common Courage Press.

Nakell, B., and K. Hardy. (1987). *The arbitrariness of the death penalty.* Philadelphia: Temple University Press.

Nardulli, P., J. Eisenstein, and R. Flemming. (1988). *The tenor of justice: Criminal courts and the guilty plea process.* Urbana: University of Illinois Press.

National Advisory Commission on Civil Disorders. (1973). *Report of the National Advisory Commission on Civil Disorders: U.S. Kerner Commission.* New York: Anti-Defamation League of B'nai B'rith.

National Association for the Advancement of Colored People (NAACP). (1993). Online: www.naacp.org.

National Association of Criminal Defense Lawyers. (1996). *Racism in the criminal justice system.* Washington, DC: National Association of Criminal Defense Lawyers.

National Association of State Budget Officers. (1996). *Capital budgeting in the states.* Washington DC: National Association of State Budget Officers.

National Center for Education Statistics, U.S. Department of Education. (1999). *1998 public school principal survey on safe, disciplined, and drug-free schools.* Washington, DC: U.S. Department of Education.

National Center on Addiction and Substance Abuse. (1998). *Behind bars: Substance abuse and America's prison population.* New York: National Center on Addiction and Substance Abuse.

National Center on Institutions and Alternatives. (1999). What every American should know about the criminal justice system. Online: www.ncianet.org/ncia/facts.html.

National Coffee Association. (1998). Statistics reported in M. Lyman and G. Potter, eds., *Drugs in society.* Cincinnati, OH: Anderson.

National Education Association. (1999). Safe schools now. Online: www.nea.org/issues/safescho/.

National Institutes of Health. (1997). SAMHSA's National Clearinghouse for Alcohol and Drug Information: A Service of the Substance Abuse and Mental Health Services Administration.

National Institute of Justice. (1997). *A study of homicide in eight U.S cities: An NIJ intramural research project.* Washington, DC: National Institute of Justice, US Department of Justice.

National Institute on Drug Abuse. (1998). *25 years of discovery to advance the health of the public.* Bethesda, MD: National Institute on Drug Abuse.

Nazario, S. (1993). Odds grim for black men in California. *Washington Post,* December 12: A-9.

Nelson, L., and B. Foster. (2001). *Death watch.* Upper Saddle River, NJ: Prentice Hall.

Nettler, G. (1984). *Explaining crime,* 3rd ed. New York: McGraw-Hill.

Neubauer, R. (1998). The future of women in policing. *The Police Chief* 6 (December).

Newman, G. (1990). Popular culture and criminal justice: A preliminary analysis. *Journal of Criminal Justice* 18: 261–274.

New York Times. (1997). Special reports on downsizing.

Nobling, T., C. Spohn, and M. Delone. (1998). A tale of two cities: Unemployment and sentencing severity. *Justice Quarterly* 15: 459–485.

Noer, D. (1993). *Healing the wounds: Overcoming the trauma of layoffs and revitalizing downsized organizations.* San Francisco: Jossey-Bass.

North Carolina Department of Correction. (2000). Online: www.doc.state.nc.us/

Nuro, D., T. Kinlock, and T. Hanlen. (1998). The drugs-crime connection. In J. Inciardi and K. McElrath, eds., *The American drug scene: An anthology,* 2nd ed. Los Angeles: Roxbury.

O'Brien, D. M. (1993). *Storm center.* New York: Norton.

O'Connell, M., and A. Whelan. (1996). Taking wrongs seriously: Public perceptions of crime seriousness. *British Journal of Criminology* 36: 299–318.

Office of National Drug Control Policy. (1994). *The national drug control strategy.* Washington, DC: Office of National Drug Control Policy.

Omi, M. (1987). *We shall overturn: Race and the contemporary American right.* Dissertation, University of California at Santa Cruz.

Omi, M., and H. Winant. (1986). *Racial formation in the United States.* New York: Routledge and Kegan Paul.

Orcutt, J., and J. Turner. (1993). Shocking numbers and graphic accounts: Quantified images of drug problems in the print media. *Social Problems* 6: 217–232.

Packer, H. (1968). *The limits of the criminal sanction.* Palo Alto, CA: Stanford University Press.

Page, C. (1999). Hasta la vista, baby. *Chicago Tribune,* January 13: 17.

Page, J. (2000). Violence and incarceration: A personal observation. In J. May, ed., *Building violence: How America's rush to incarcerate creates more violence.* Thousand Oaks, CA: Sage Publications.

Palermo, G., M. White, and L. Wasserman. Plea bargaining: Injustice for all? *International Journal of Offender Therapy and Comparative Criminology* 42(2): 111–123.

Parenti, M. (1983). *Democracy for the few,* 4th ed. New York: St. Martin's Press.

Parenti, M. (1993). *Inventing reality: The politics of the news media.* New York: St. Martin's Press.

Parton, D., M. Hansel, and J. Stratton. (1991). Measuring crime seriousness: Lessons from the National Survey of Crime Severity. *British Journal of Criminology* 31: 72–85.

Pate, T., and L. Fridell. (1994). *Police use of force: Official reports, citizen complaints, and legal consequences, 1991–1992.* Ann Arbor, MI: Interuniversity Consortium for Political and Social Research

Paulsen, D. (2000). Murder in black and white: The newspaper coverage of homicide in Houston, 1986–1994. PhD dissertation, Sam Houston State University.

Pearson, D. (2000). Minority health. In R. Lauer and J. Lauer, eds., *Troubled times: Readings in social problems.* Los Angeles: Roxbury.

Peffley, M., and J. Hurwitz. (1997). Racial stereotypes and whites' political views of blacks in the context of welfare and crime. *American Journal of Political Science* 41(1): 30–60.

Peoples, E. (2000). *Basic criminal procedures.* Upper Saddle River, NJ: Prentice Hall.

Petersilia, J. (1983). *Racial disparities in the criminal justice system.* Santa Monica, CA: Rand Corporation.

Petersilia, J. (1995). Racial disparities in the criminal justice system: A summary. *Crime and Delinquency* 31: 15–34.

Petersilia, J. (1998). Probation in the United States. *Perspectives* 37.

Petersilia, J., and S. Turner. (1986). *Prison versus p[robation?] in California: Implications for crime and offender recidivism.* Santa Monica, CA: Rand Corporation.

Pew Research Center for the People and the Press. (1998). Online: www.people-press.org.

Phillips, K. (1969). *The emerging Republican majority.* New York: Arlington House.

Phillips, K. (1991). *The politics of rich and poor.* New York: Random House.

Phipps, A. (1986). Radical criminology and criminal victimization: Proposals for the development of theory and intervention. In R. Matthews and J. Young, eds., *Confronting crime.* Beverly Hills, CA: Sage Publications.

Pierce, J., M. Fiore, and T. Novotny. (1989). Trends in cigarette smoking in the United States with projections to the year 2000. *Journal of the American Medical Association* 261: 61–65.

Pizzi, W. (1999). *Trials without truth: Why our system of criminal trials has become an expensive failure and what we need to do to rebuild it.* New York: New York University Press.

Platt, L. (1999). Armageddon—live at 6! In R. Hiebert, ed., *Impact of mass media: Current issues,* 4th ed. New York: Longman.

Podgor, E., and J. Israel. (1997). *White collar crime.* St. Paul, MN: West.

The Police Foundation. (1981). *The Newark foot patrol experiment.* Washington DC: The Police Foundation.

Pontell, H., K. Calavita, and R. Tillman. (1994). *Fraud in the savings and loan industry: White collar crime and government response.* Washington, DC: National Institute of Justice.

Pope, C. (1979). Race and crime revisited. *Crime and Delinquency* 25(3): 347–357.

Pope, H., and D. Yurgelun-Todd. (1996). The residual cognitive effects of heavy marijuana use in college students. *Journal of the American Medical Association* 275: 7.

Poporino, F. (1986). Managing violent individuals in correctional settings. *Journal of Interpersonal Violence* 1: 213–237.

Potter, G., and V. Kappeler. (1998). *Constructing crime: Perspectives on making news and social problems.* Prospect Heights, IL: Waveland Press.

Pound, R. (1912). *The scope and purpose of sociological jurisprudence.* Cambridge, MA: Harvard Law Review Association.

Pratt, C. (1992). Police discretion. *Law and Order* (March): 99–100.

Pratt, T. (1998). Race and sentencing: A meta-analysis of conflicting empirical research results. *Journal of Criminal Justice* 26(6): 513–523.

Preble, E., and J. Casey, Jr. (1969). Taking care of business: The heroin user's life in the streets. *International Journal of Addictions.*

Prejean, H. (1993). *Dead man walking.* New York: Random House.

Quan, S. (2000). A profile of the working poor. In R. Lauer and J. Lauer, eds., *Troubled times: Readings in social problems.* Los Angeles: Roxbury.

Quinney, R. (1970). *The social reality of crime.* New Brunswick, NJ: Transaction Publishers.

Quinney, R. (1977). *Class, state, and crime: On the theory and practice of criminal justice.* New York: D. McKay.

Radelet, M., H. Bedau, and C. Putnam. (1992). *In spite of innocence: The ordeal of 400 Americans wrongly convicted of crimes punishable by death.* Boston: Northeastern University Press.

Raeder, M. (1993). Gender and sentencing: Single moms, battered women, and other sex-based anomalies in the gender-free world of the federal sentencing guidelines. *Pepperdine Law Review* 20: 948.

Raine, A. (1993). *The psychopathology of crime.* New York: Academic Press.

Randell, D. (1995). The portrayal of business malfeasance in the elite and general media. In G. Geis, R. Meier, and L. Salinger, eds., *White-collar crime: Classic and contemporary views.* New York: The Free Press.

Ranney, D. (1999). Class, race, gender, and poverty: A critique of some contemporary theories. In L. Kushnick and J. Jennings, eds., *A new introduction to poverty: The role of race, power, and politics.* New York: New York University Press.

Ransby, B. (1999). The black poor and the politics of expendability. In L. Kushnick and J. Jennings, eds., *A new introduction to poverty: The role of race, power, and politics.* New York: New York University Press.

Rasmussen, D., and B. Benson. (1994). *The economic anatomy of a drug war.* Lanham, MD: Rowman and Littlefield.

Rauma, D. (1991). The context of normative consensus: An expansion of the Rossi/Berk model, with an application to crime seriousness. *Social Science Research* 20: 1–28.

Reed, I. (1991). Tuning out network bias. *New York Times*, April 9: A11.

Reed, I. (1993). It's racist. *American Journalism Review* 15(7): 22–23.

Reeves, J., and R. Campbell. (1994). *Cracked coverage: Television news, the anti-cocaine crusade, and the Reagan legacy.* Durham, NC: Duke University Press.

Reiman, J. (1998). *The rich get richer and the poor get prison: Ideology, class, and criminal justice,* 5th ed. Boston: Allyn and Bacon.

Reinarman, C. (1994). Unanticipated consequences of criminilization: Hypotheses on how drug laws exacerbate drug problems. *Perspectives on Social Problems* 6: 217–232.

Reinarman, C. (1995). Crack attack: America's latest drug scare, 1986–1992. In J. Best, ed., *Images of issues: Typifying contemporary social problems.* New York: Aldine de Gruyter.

Reinarman, C., and H. Levine. (1989a). The crack attack: Politics and media in America's latest drug scare. In J. Best, ed., *Images of issues: Typifying contemporary social problems.* New York: Aldine de Gruyter.

Reinarman, C., and H. Levine. (1989b). Crack in context: Politics and media in the making of a drug scene. *Contemporary Drug Problems* 16: 116–129.

Rengert, G., and J. Wasilchick. (1985). *Suburban burglary: A time and place for everything.* Springfield, IL: Charles C. Thomas.

Reppetto, R. (1974). *Residential crime.* Cambridge, MA: Ballinger.

Reuter, P. (1998). Hawks ascendant: The punitive trend of American drug policy. In J. Inciardi and K. McElrath, eds., *The American drug scene: An anthology,* 2nd ed. Los Angeles: Roxbury.

Rhine, E., W. Smith, and R. Jackson. (1991). Parole: Issues and prospects for the 1990s. *Corrections Today* 51: 78–83.

Roberts, D. (1993). Crime, race and reproduction. *Tulane Law Review* 1945: 1.

Roberts, J. (1992). Public opinion, crime, and criminal justice. In M. Tonry, ed., *Crime and justice: A review of research* (Vol. 16). Chicago: University of Chicago Press.

Roberts, J., and A. Doob. (1990). News media influences on public views of sentencing. *Law and Human Behavior* 14: 451–468.

Roberts, J., and D. Edwards. (1992). Contextual affects in judgements of crime, criminals, and the purpose of sentencing. *Journal of Applied Social Psychology* 19: 902–917.

Roberts, J., and L. Stalans. (2000). *Public opinion, crime, and criminal justice.* Boulder, CO: Westview Press.

Robinson, M. (1998). Tobacco: The greatest crime in world history? *The Critical Criminologist* 8(3): 20–22.

Robinson, M. (1999). The historical development of CPTED: 25 years of responses to C. Ray Jeffery's work. *Advances in Criminological Theory* 8: 427–462.

Robinson, M. (2000). The construction and reinforcement of myths of race and crime. *Journal of Contemporary Criminal Justice* 16(2): 133–156.

Robinson, M. (in press). The case for a "new victimology": Implications for policing. In L. Moriarty, ed., *Police and victims.* Upper Saddle River, NJ: Prentice Hall.

Robinson, M., and B. Zaitzow. (1999a). Criminologists: Are we what we study? A national study of crime experts. *The Criminologist* 24(2): 1, 4, 17–19.

Robinson, M., and B. Zaitzow. (1999b). Like the pot calling the kettle black: Criminologists who engage in criminal, deviant, and unethical behavior. Paper presented to the American Society of Criminology, November.

Robinson, P., and J. Darley. (1997). *Justice, liability, and blame.* Boulder, CO: Westview Press.

Robinson, R. (1993). What does "unwilling" to impose the death penalty mean anyway? *Law and Human Behavior* 17: 471–477.

Rold, W. (2000). Legislating barriers to effective solutions: An indelicate tool for a complex problem. In J. May, ed., *Building violence: How America's rush to incarcerate creates more violence.* Thousand Oaks, CA: Sage Publications.

Rome, D. (1998). Stereotyping by the media: Murderers, rapists, and drug addicts. In C. Mann and M. Zatz, eds., *Images of color, images of crime.* Los Angeles: Roxbury.

Rosch, J. (1985). Crime as an issue in American politics. In E. Fairchild and V. Webb, eds., *The politics of crime and criminal justice.* Beverly Hills, CA: Sage Publications.

Rosenbaum, D., and G. Hanson. (1998). Assessing the effects of school-based drug education: A six-year multilevel analysis of project D.A.R.E. *Journal of Research in Crime and Delinquency* 35(4): 381–412.

Rosenbaum, D., A. Lurigio, and R. Davis. (1998). *The prevention of crime: Social and situational strategies.* Belmont, CA: Wadsworth.

Rosoff, S., H. Pontell, and R. Tillman. (1998). *Profit without honor: White-collar crime and the looting of America.* Upper Saddle River, NJ: Prentice Hall.

Ross, D. (1999). Assessing the patterns of citizen resistance during arrests. *FBI Law Enforcement Bulletin* 68(6): 5–11.

Ross, E. (1964). *History of the impeachment of Andrew Johnson, president of the United States, by the House of Representatives, and his trial by the Senate, for high crimes and misdemeanors in office, 1868.* Santa Fe, NM: New Mexican Printing.

Rothman, D. (1971). *The discovery of the asylum.* Boston: Little, Brown.

Rouse, J., and B. Johnson. (1991). Hidden paradigms of morality in debates about drugs: Historical and policy shifts in British and American drug policies. In J. Inciardi, ed., *The drug legalization debate: Studies in crime, law, and justice.* Newbury Park, CA: Sage Publications.

Ruprecht, C. (1997). Are verdicts, too, like sausages? Lifting the cloak of jury secrecy. *University of Pennsylvania Law Review* 146(1): 217–268.

Rusche, G., and O. Kirchheimer. (1939). *Punishment and social structure.* New York: Columbia University Press.

Rush, G. E. (2000). *The dictionary of criminal justice*, 4th ed. Boston: Dushkin/McGraw-Hill.

Russell, K. (1998). *The color of crime*. New York: New York University Press.

Sabato, L. (1993). *Feeding frenzy*. New York: The Free Press.

Sacco, V. (1995). Media constructions of crime. *Annals of the American Academy of Political and Social Science* 539: 141–154.

Sacco, V., and L. Kennedy. (1996). *The criminal event*, 3rd ed. London: International Thompson Publishers.

Sakamoto, A., and J. Tzeng. (1999). A fifty-year perspective on the declining significance of race in the occupational attainment of white and black men. *Sociological Perspectives* 42(2): 157–179.

Salant, J. (1999). Tobacco giant Philip Morris tops list of political contributors. Online: www.nandonet.com.

Sampson, R. (1987). Urban black violence: The effect of male joblessness and family disruption. *American Journal of Sociology* 93: 348–382.

Sampson R., and J. Laub. (1997). A life-course theory of cumulative disadvantage and the stability of delinquency. In T. Thornberry, ed., *Developmental theories of crime and delinquency*. New Brunswick, NJ: Transaction.

Sandor, R. (1995). Legalizing/decriminalizing drug use. In R. Coombs and D. Ziedonis, eds., *Handbook on drug abuse prevention: A contemporary strategy to prevent the abuse of alcohol and other drugs*. Boston: Allyn and Bacon.

Sandys, M., and E. McGarrell. (1995). Attitudes toward capital punishment: Preferences for the penalty or mere acceptance? *Journal of Research in Crime and Delinquency* 32: 191–213.

Sasson, T. (1995). *Crime talk: How citizens construct a social problem*. New York: Aldine de Gruyter.

Scannell, G. (1996). Top priority? Readers tap training: *Safety and Health* journal's survey. *Safety and Health* 154(6): 7.

Scarr, H. (1973). *Patterns of burglary*. Washington, DC: National Institute of Law Enforcement and Criminal Justice.

Schatzman, M. (1975). Cocaine and the drug problem. *Journal of Psychedelic Drugs* 7(1): 7–17.

Scheingold, S. A. (1984). *The politics of law and order: Street crime and public policy*. New York: Longman.

Schiraldi, V., P. Sussman, and L. Hyland. (1994). *Three strikes: The unintended victims*. San Francisco: Center on Juvenile and Criminal Justice.

Schlesinger, P., and H. Tumber. (1994). *Reporting crime: The media politics of criminal justice*. Oxford: Clarendon.

Schlosser, E. (1998). The prison industrial complex. *Atlantic Monthly* (December): 51–77.

Schmalleger, F. (1999). *Criminal law today*. Upper Saddle River, NJ: Prentice Hall.

Schmalleger, F. (2001). *Criminal justice today*, 6th ed. Upper Saddle River, NJ: Prentice Hall.

Schmidt, A. (1991). Electronic monitors—realistically, what can be expected. *Federal Probation* 55(1), June: 31–33.

Schneider, V., and J. Smykla. (1991). A summary analysis of executions in the United States, 1608–1987: The Espy file. In R. Bohm, ed., *The death penalty in America: Current research*. The Death Penalty in America: Current Research.

Schoenborn, C. A., and B. H. Cohen. (1986). *Trends in smoking, alcohol consumption, and other health practices among U.S. adults, 1977 and 1983*. Hyattsville, MD: National Center for Health Statistics, U.S. Department of Health and Human Services, No. 118: 1–16.

Sebba, L. (1984). Crime seriousness and criminal intent. *Crime and Delinquency* 30: 227–244.

Seidman, D., and M. Couzens. (1974). Getting the crime rate down: Political pressure and crime reporting. *Law and Society Review* 8: 457–493.

Sennott, C. (2000). The $150 billion "welfare" recipients: U.S. corporations. In R. Lauer and J. Lauer, eds., *Troubled times: Readings in social problems*. Los Angeles: Roxbury.

The Sentencing Project. (1997). *Facts about prisons and prisoners*. Washington, DC: The Sentencing Project.

The Sentencing Project. (1998). *Facts about prisons and prisoners*. Washington, DC: The Sentencing Project.

Shapiro, B. (1997). Victims and vengeance: Why the victim's rights amendment is a bad idea. *The Nation* 264: 11–19.

Shapiro, S. (1995). Collaring the crime, not the criminal: Reconsidering the concept of white-collar crime. *American Sociological Review* 55: 346–365.

Sherizen, S. (1978). Social creation of crime news: All the news that's fitted to print. In C. Winick, ed., *Deviance and the mass media.* Beverly Hills, CA: Sage Publications.

Sherman, L., D. Gottfredson, D. MacKenzie, J. Eck, P. Reuter, and S. Bushway. (1997). *Preventing crime: What works, what doesn't, what's promising.* Washington, DC: U.S. Department of Justice, Office of Justice Programs, National Institute of Justice.

Sherman, L., D. Gottfredson, D. MacKenzie, J. Eck, P. Reuter, and S. Bushway. (1998). Research in brief: Preventing crime: What works, what doesn't, what's promising. Washington, DC: U.S. Department of Justice. Online: www.ncjrs.org/pdffiles/171676.pdf.

Sherrill, R. (1997). A year in corporate crime. *The Nation,* April 7.

Sidel, R. (1996). *Keeping women and children last.* New York: Penguin.

Siegel, L. (1998). *Criminology,* 6th ed. Belmont, CA: Wadsworth.

Sigal, L. (1973). *Reporters and officials: The organization and politics of newsmaking.* London: D. C. Heath.

Signorielli, N. (1990). Television's mean and dangerous world: A continuation of the cultural indicators perspective. In M. Morgan and N. Signorielli, eds., *Cultivation analysis: New directions in media effects research.* Newbury Park, CA: Sage Publications.

Silberman, C. (1978). *Criminal violence, criminal justice.* New York: Random House.

Sileo, C. (1993). Sentencing rules that shackle justice. *Insight* 11.

Simon, D., and D. Eitzen. (1993). *Elite deviance,* 4th ed. Boston: Allyn and Bacon.

Simon, D., and F. Hagan. (1999). *White-collar deviance.* Boston: Allyn and Bacon.

Simon, J. (1994). *Poor discipline: Parole and the social control of the underclass, 1890–1990.* Chicago: University of Chicago Press.

Simpson, D., K. Knight, and C. Pevoto. (1996). *Research summary: Focus on drug treatment in criminal justice settings.* Fort Worth: Texas Christian University Institute of Behavioral Research.

Singh, V. (1991). The underclass in the United States: Some correlates of economic change. *Sociological Inquiry* 61: 505–521.

Skogan, W. (1990). *Disorder and decline.* Berkeley: University of California Press.

Skogan, W. (1995). Crime and the racial fears of white Americans. *Annals of the American Academy of Political and Social Science* 539: 59–71.

Skolnick, J. (1966). *Justice without trial: Law enforcement in a democratic society.* New York: Wiley.

Skolnick, J. (1967). Social control in the adversary system. *Journal of Conflict Resolution* 11: 52–70.

Skolnick, J. (1994). Wild pitch. *American Prospect* 17: 31–37.

Skolnick, J. (1997). Rethinking the drug problem. In L. Gaines and P. Kraska, eds., *Drugs, crime, and justice,* 3rd ed. Prospect Heights, IL: Waveland Press.

Smith, D. (1986). The plea bargaining controversy. *Journal of Criminal Law and Criminology* 77: 949.

Smith, D., C. Visher, and L. Davidson. (1984). Equity and discretionary justice: The influence of race on police arrest decisions. *Journal of Criminal Law and Criminology* 75: 234–249.

Smith, P. (1990). *Felony defendants in large urban counties, 1990.* Washington, DC: Bureau of Justice Statistics.

Smith, P. (1993). Private prisons: Profits of crime. *Covert Action Quarterly* 4: 1–6.

Smith, R. (1995). *Racism in the post-civil rights era: Now you see it, now you don't.* Albany: State University of New York Press.

Snell, T. (1997). Capital punishment 1996. *Bureau of Justice Statistics Bulletin* (December). Washington, DC: U.S. Department of Justice.

Snyder, D. (1997). *The cliff walk: A memoir of a job lost and a life found.* Boston: Little, Brown.

Son, I., M. Davis, and D. Rome. (1998). Race and its effect on police officers' perceptions of misconduct. *Journal of Criminal Justice* 26(1): 21–28.

Spire, R. (1990). Breaking up the old boy network. *Trial* 26(2): 57–58.

Spitzer, S. (1975). Toward a Marxian theory of deviance. *Social Problems* 22: 638–651.

Spohn, C., and M. Delone. (2001, in press). When does race matter? An analysis of the conditions under which race affects sentence severity. *Sociology of Crime, Law, and Deviance.*

Spohn, C., and D. Hollerman. (2000). The imprisonment penalty paid by young, unemployed, black and Hispanic male offenders. *Criminology* 38(1): 281–306.

St. John, C., and T. Heald-Moore. (1996). Racial prejudice and fear of criminal victimization by strangers in public settings. *Sociological Inquiry* 66(3): 267–284.

Steel, B. S., and M. Steger. (1988). Crime: Due process liberalism versus law and order conservatism. In R. Tantalovich and B. W. Daynes, eds., *Social regulatory policy.* Boulder, CO: Westview Press.

Steele, W. Jr., and E. Thornburg. (1991). Jury instructions: A persistent failure to communicate. *Judicature* 74: 249–254.

Steele, W. Jr., and E. Thornburg. (2000). Jury instructions: A persistent failure to communicate. In G. Mays and P. Gregware, *Courts and justice: A reader,* 2nd ed. Prospect Heights, IL: Waveland Press.

Steffensmeir, D., J. Ulmer, and J. Kramer. (1998). The interaction of race, gender, and age in criminal sentencing: The cost of being young, black, and male. *Criminology* 36: 763–798.

Steiker, C., and J. Steiker. (1998). Judicial developments in capital punishment law. In J. Acker, and C. Lanier, eds., *America's experiment with capital punishment: Reflections on the past, present, and future of the ultimate penal sanction.* Durham, NC: Carolina Academic Press.

Stephen, J. (1883). *Liberty, equality, fraternity.* New York, H. Holt.

Sterling, J. (1983). Retained counsel versus the public defender: The impact of type of counsel on charge bargaining. In W. McDonald, ed., *The defense counsel.* Beverly Hills, CA: Sage.

Stevens, J., and H. Garcia. (1980). *Communicating history.* Newbury Park, CA.: Sage Publications.

Stevenson, N. (1995). *Understanding media culture: Social theory and mass communication.* London: Sage.

Stossel, S. (1997). The man who counts the killings. *Atlantic Monthly* 279(5): 86–105.

Stratton, D. (1998). *Tempest over Teapot Dome: The story of Albert B. Fall.* Norman: University of Oklahoma Press.

Stratton, S. (1996). *Examining the effects of career derailment, organizational strategy and environmental uncertainty.* University of North Carolina at Charlotte.

Streisand, B. (1994). Can he get a fair trial? *U.S. News & World Report,* October 3: 61–63.

Strinati, D. (1995). *An introduction to theories of popular culture.* London: Routledge.

Stuckey, G., C. Robertson, and H. Wallace. (2001). *Procedures in the justice system,* 6th ed. Upper Saddle River, NJ: Prentice Hall.

Sullivan, T., and R. Nachman. (1984). If it ain't broke don't fix it: Why the grand jury's accusatory function should not be changed. *Journal of Criminal Law and Criminology* 75: 1050.

Surette, R. (1992). *Media, crime, and criminal justice: Images and realities.* Pacific Grove: Brooks/Cole.

Surette, R. (1998). *Media, crime, and criminal justice: Images and realities,* 2nd ed. Belmont, CA: Wadsworth.

Sussman, B. (1992). *The great coverup: Nixon and the scandal of Watergate.* Arlington, VA: Seven Locks Press.

Sutherland, E. (1977a). Is "white-collar crime" crime? In G. Geis and R. Meier, eds., *White-collar crime: Offenses in business, politics, and the professions.* New York: The Free Press.

Sutherland, E. (1977b). White-collar Criminality." In G. Geis and R. Meier, eds., *White-collar crime: Offenses in business, politics, and the professions.* New York: The Free Press.

Swezey, R. (1973). Estimating drug crime relationships. *International Journal of the Addictions* 8: 701–721.

Sykes, G. (1958). *The society of captives: A study of a maximum-security prison.* Princeton, NJ: Princeton University Press.

Taylor, J., and G. Whitney. (1999). Crime and racial profiling by U.S. police: Is there an empirical basis? *Journal of Social, Political and Economic Studies* 24(4): 485–510.

Thernstrom, S., and A. Thernstrom. (1997). *America in black and white: One nation, indivisible.* New York: Simon and Schuster.

Thomas, C. (1993). *Sex discrimination.* St. Paul, MN: West.

Tillman, R. (1987). The size of the "criminal population": The prevalence and incidence of adult arrest. *Criminology* 25: 561–579.

Tillman, R., and H. Pontell. (1992). Is justice "collar-blind"? Punishing Medicaid provider fraud. *Criminology* 30: 547–573.

Tinklenberg, J. R. (1973). Alcohol and violence. In P. G. Bourne, ed., *Alcoholism: Progress in research and treatment.* New York: Academic Press.

Tittle, C., and R. Meier. (1990). Specifying the SES/delinquency relationship. *Criminology* 28: 271–299.

Tonry, M. (1992). Mandatory penalties. In M. Tonry, ed., *Crime and justice: A review of research* (p. 16). Chicago: University of Chicago Press.

Tonry, M. (1995). *Malign neglect: Race, crime and punishment in America.* Oxford: Oxford University Press.

Torrey, E., J. Steiber, J. Ezekiel, S. Wolfe, J. Sharftein, J. Noble, and L. Flynn. (1992). *Criminalizing the seriously mental ill: The abuse of jails as mental hospitals.* Washington, DC: National Alliance for the Mentally Ill and Public Citizens Health Research Group.

Treaster, J. (1990). Is the fight on drugs eroding civil rights? *New York Times,* May 6: A1, 9.

Trebach, A. (1997). *The great drug war.* New York: Macmillan.

Tuchman, G. (1978). *Making news: A study in the social construction of reality.* New York: The Free Press.

Tunnell, K. (1992). Film at eleven: Recent developments in the commodification of crime. *Sociological Spectrum* 12: 293–313.

Tuohy, L. (1995). CCLU suit lays bare a public defense system in crisis. *Hartford Courant,* January 8: A1.

Uchida, C., and T. Bynum. (1991). Search warrants, motions to suppress, and "lost cases": The effects of the exclusionary rule in seven jurisdictions. *Journal of Criminal Law and Criminology* 81: 1034.

UCR Handbook. (1999). Online: www.fbi.gov/ucr.htm.

Unnever, J., and L. Hembroff. (1988). The prediction of racial/ethnic sentencing disparities: An expectation states approach. *Journal of Research in Crime and Delinquency* 25: 53–82.

Uphoff, R. (2000). The criminal defense lawyer: Zealous advocate, double agent, or beleaguered dealer? In G. Mays and P. Gregware, *Courts and justice: A reader,* 2nd ed. Prospect Heights, IL: Waveland Press.

USA Today. (1999). Tragedy in Colorado. Online: www.usatoday.com/news/index/colo/colo000.htm

U.S. Census. (1996). Characteristics of the voting-age population reported having registered or voted: November 1994. Online: www.census.gov/.

U.S. Census. (1997). *Statistical abstract of the United States: 1996.* Washington, DC: U.S. Government Printing Office.

U.S. Census. (1998). *Statistical abstract of the United States: 1998.* Washington, DC: U.S. Government Printing Office.

U.S. Census. (1999). Poverty in the United States: 1997. Online:

U.S. Department of Education. (1998). *Early warning, timely response: A guide to safe schools.* Washington, DC: U.S. Department of Education.

U.S. Department of Education. (1999). *Early warning, timely response: A guide to safe schools.* Washington, DC: U.S. Department of Education.

U.S. Department of Justice. (1994). Online: www.usdoj.gov.

U.S. Department of Justice. (1996). *National data collection on police use of force.* Washington, DC: U.S. Government Printing Office.

U.S. Department of Justice. (1997). Online: www.usdoj.gov.

U.S. Department of Justice. (1997). *Sourcebook of criminal justice statistics.* Washington, DC: U.S. Government Printing Office.

U.S. Department of Justice. (1998). Online: www.usdoj.gov.

U.S. Department of Justice. (1998). *Sourcebook of criminal justice statistics.* Washington, DC: U.S. Government Printing Office.

U.S. News & World Report. (2000). The rich get richer: What happens to American society when the gap in wealth and income grows larger? *U.S. News & World Report,* February 21.

U.S. Sentencing Commission. (1995). *Special report to Congress: Cocaine and federal sentencing policy.* Washington, DC: U.S. Sentencing Commission.

Van den Haag, E. (1982). In defense of the death penalty: A practical and moral analysis. In H. Bedau, ed., *The death penalty in America,* 3rd ed. New York: Oxford University Press.

Vandiver, M. (1998). The impact of the death penalty on the families of homicide victims and of condemned prisoners. In J. Acker, R. Bohm, and C. Lanier, eds., *America's experiment with capital punishment: Reflections on the past, present, and future of the ultimate penal sanction.* Durham, NC: Carolina Academic Press.

Van Horn, C., D. Baumer, and W. Gormley, Jr. (1992). *Politics and public policy.* Washington, DC: CQ Press.

Vankin, J., and J. Whalen. (1999). *The 70 greatest conspiracies of all time.* Secaucus, NJ: Carol Publishing.

Varinsky, H. (1993). Trial consulting: The art and science of selling a case to a jury. *Washington State Bar News* 47: 47–50.

Vila, B. (1997). Motivating and marketing nurturant crime control strategies: Reply to comments. *Politics and the Life Sciences* 16: 48–55.

Virkunnen, M. (1974). Alcohol as a factor precipitating aggression and conflict behavior leading to homicide. *British Journal of the Addictions* 69: 149–154.

Vold, G. (1958). *Theoretical criminology.* New York: Oxford University Press.

Vold, G., T. Bernard, and J. Snipes. (1998). *Theoretical criminology,* 4th ed. Beverly Hills, CA: Sage Publications.

von Brachel, J. (1994). *Corporate reengineering: Strategies for growth.* New York: Conference Board.

Von Drehle, D. (1988). Bottom line: Life in prison one sixth as expensive. *Miami Herald* (July 10): 12A.

Walker, S. (1998). *Sense and nonsense about crime and drugs: A policy guide,* 4th ed. Belmont, CA: West/Wadsworth.

Walker, S., C. Spohn, and M. Delone. (1996). *The color of justice: Race, ethnicity, and crime in America.* Belmont, CA: Wadsworth.

Walker, S., C. Spohn, and M. Delone. (2000). *The color of justice: Race, ethnicity and crime in America,* 2nd ed. Belmont, CA: Wadsworth.

Waller, I., and N. Okihiro. (1978). *Burglary: The victim and the public.* Toronto: Centre of Criminology, University of Toronto.

Walsh, D. (1980). *Break-ins: Burglary from private houses.* London: Constable.

Walsh, W., and P. Harris. (1999). *Criminal justice policy and planning.* Cincinnati, OH: Anderson.

Warr, M. (1991). What is the perceived seriousness of crime? *Criminology* 27: 795–821.

Washington Post. (1983). January 11: C10.

Weaver, D., and G. Wilhoit. (1986). *The American journalist: A portrait of U.S. news people and their work.* Bloomington: Indiana University Press.

Webb, G., and M. Brown. (1998). United States drug laws and institutionalized discrimination. In E. Jensen and J. Gerber, eds., *The new war on drugs: Symbolic politics and criminal justice policy.* Cincinnati, OH: Anderson.

Weil, A. (1998). Why people take drugs. In J. Inciardi and K. McElrath, eds., *The American drug scene: An anthology,* 2nd ed. Los Angeles: Roxbury.

Weinberger, C. (2000). Race and gender wage gaps. In R. Lauer and J. Lauer, eds., *Troubled times: Readings in social problems.* Los Angeles: Roxbury.

Weinstein, C. (2000). Even dogs confined to cages for long periods of time go berserk. In J. May, ed., *Building violence: How America's rush to incarcerate creates more violence.* Thousand Oaks, CA: Sage Publications.

Weisburd, D., E. Chayet, and E. Waring. (1990). White-collar crime and criminal careers: Some preliminary findings. *Crime and Delinquency* 36: 342–355.

Weisburd, D., and K. Schlegel. (1992). Returning to the mainstream: Reflections on past and future white-collar crime study. In K. Schlegel and D. Weisburd, eds., *White-collar crime reconsidered.* Boston: Northeastern University Press.

Weisman, A. (2000). Mental illness behind bars. In J. May, ed., *Building violence: How America's rush to incarcerate creates more violence.* Thousand Oaks, CA: Sage Publications.

Weitzer, R. (1996). Racial discrimination in the criminal justice system: Findings and problems in the literature. *Journal of Criminal Justice,* 24: 313.

Weitzer, R., and S. Tuch. (1999). Race, class, and perceptions of discrimination by the police. *Crime and Delinquency* 45(4): 494–507.

Welch, M., et al. (1998). The state versus its dissenters: A content analysis of competing versions of corrections in the media. Unpublished paper, Rutgers University.

Welch, M. (1999). *Punishment in America: Social control and the ironies of imprisonment.* Thousand Oaks, CA: Sage Publications.

Welch, M., M. Fenwick, and M. Roberts. (1998). State managers, intellectuals, and the media: A content analysis of ideology in experts' quotes in feature newspaper articles on crime. *Justice Quarterly* 15(2): 219–241.

Welsh, W., and P. Harris. (1999). *Criminal justice policy and planning.* Cincinnati, OH: Anderson.

Whitehead, B. D. (1993). Dan Quayle was right. *Atlantic Monthly* (April).

Whitehead, T. (1997). Urban low income African American men, HIV/AIDS, and gender identity. *Medical Anthropologist Quarterly* 11(4): 411–447.

Whitehead, T. (2000). The "epidemic" and "cultural legends" of black male incarceration: The socialization of African American children to a life of incarceration. In J. May, ed., *Building violence: How America's rush to incarcerate creates more violence.* Thousand Oaks, CA: Sage Publications.

Wice, P. (1985). *Chaos in the courthouse: The inner workings of the urban criminal courts.* New York: Praeger.

Wilbanks, W. (1987). *The myth of a racist criminal justice system.* Monterey, CA: Brooks/Cole.

Wilkins, L. (1991). *Punishment, crime, and market forces.* Brookfield, VT: Dartmouth.

Williams, C. (1991). The federal death penalty for drug-related killings. *Criminal Law Bulletin* 27(5): 387–415.

Williams, J. (2000). The politics of jailing. In J. May, ed., *Building violence: How America's rush to incarcerate creates more violence.* Thousand Oaks, CA: Sage Publications.

Wilson, E. (1995). *Effects of corporate downsizing on survivors: An empirical assessment.* University of North Carolina at Charlotte.

Wilson, J. (1975). *Thinking about crime.* New York: Basic Books.

Wilson, J. (1998). Foreword: Never too early. In F. Loeber and D. Farrington, eds., *Serious and violent juvenile offenders.* Thousand Oaks, CA: Sage Publications.

Wilson, W. J. (1987). *The truly disadvantaged: The inner city, the underclass, and public policy.* Chicago: University of Chicago Press.

Winchester, S., and H. Jackson. (1982). *Residential burglary: The limits of prevention.* Home Office Research Study No. 74. London: Her Majesty's Stationary Office.

Wisotsky, S. (1991). Beyond the war on drugs. In J. Inciardi, ed., *The drug legalization debate: Studies in crime, law, and justice.* Newbury Park, CA: Sage Publications.

Wolfgang, M., R. Figlio, and T. Sellin. (1972). *Delinquency in a birth cohort.* Chicago: University of Chicago Press.

Wolman, W and A. Calamosca. (1997). *The Judas economy: The triumph of capital and the betrayal of work.* Reading, MA: Addison-Wesley.

Woo, L. (1994) Today's legislators: Who they are and why they run. *State Legislatures,* April: 28–33.

Wright, R. (1993). A socially sensitive criminal justice system. In J. Murphy and D. Peck, eds., *Open institutions: The hope for democracy.* Westport, CT: Praeger.

Wright, R., and S. Decker. (1994). *Burglars on the job: Streetlife and residential break-ins.* Boston: Northeastern University Press.

Wrobleski, H., and K. Hess. (2000). *An introduction: Law enforcement and criminal justice.* Belmont, CA: Wadsworth.

Yinger, J. (1994). *Ethnicity: Source of strength? Source of conflict.* Albany: State University of New York Press.

Young, R. (1998). The Castle Grande deal: Once upon a time in Arkansas. *Frontline.* Public Broadcasting Corporation. Online: www.pbs.org.

Zatz, M. (1987). Pleas, priors and prison: Racial/ethnic differences in sentencing. *Social Science Research* 14: 169–193.

Zehr, H., and M. Umbreit. (1982). Victim offender reconciliation: An incarceration substitute. *Federal Probation* 46(1): 3–68.

Zimmer, L., and J. Morgan. (1997). *Marijuana myths, marijuana facts: A review of the scientific evidence.* New York: Lindesmith Center.

Zimring, F., and G. Hawkins. (1986). *Capital punishment and the American agenda.* New York: Cambridge University Press.

Zimring, F., and G. Hawkins. (1997). *Crime is not the problem: Lethal violence in America.* New York: Oxford University Press.

Zuckerman, M. (1994). The limits of the TV lens. *U.S. News & World Report,* July 25: 64.

Zweig, P. (1995). Reengineering programs achieve shoddy results: The case against mergers. *Business Week,* October 30.

INDEX